Froude's
Life of Carlyle

THOMAS CARLYLE IN 1835. This approximately life-size head, almost in profile, is quite free from pose and is drawn with delicate precision. It is the first likeness that authentically perpetuates Carlyle's features and look. Its definite character makes it the finest of the early portraits of Carlyle. (Pencil-and-crayon drawing signed "D. Maclise" and dated "1835," courtesy of Mrs. Jane S. Napier.)

Froude's
Life of Carlyle

Abridged and Edited

by John Clubbe

OHIO STATE UNIVERSITY PRESS : COLUMBUS

Copyright © 1979 by the Ohio State University Press
All Rights Reserved

Library of Congress Cataloging in Publication Data

Froude, James Anthony, 1818–1894
  Froude's Life of Carlyle
  Abridgement of the author's Thomas Carlyle, a history of the first forty years
of his life, 1795–1835 and Thomas Carlyle, a history of his life in London, 1834–
1881.
  Includes bibliographical references and index.
  1. Carlyle, Thomas. 1795–1881—Biography.   2. Authors, English—19th cen-
tury—Biography.
I. Clubbe, John. II. Title. III. Title: Life of Carlyle.
PR4433.F742 1978   824'.8[B]   78-19158
ISBN 0-8142-0274-8

3 8471 00168 5154

To Rowland E. Cross

Table of Contents

Froude's Life of Carlyle

CONTENTS

CONTENTS

List of Illustrations

ILLUSTRATIONS

Preface

Like many others who have come upon James Anthony Froude's life of Thomas Carlyle for the first time, I found myself dazzled by its literary artistry, impressed by the psychological acuity of its depiction of both Carlyles, and convinced of Carlyle's importance not only by the evidence presented in the narrative but also by the strength of Froude's belief in it. His biography, published in the 1880s soon after Carlyle's death, has the primary merit of making us believe that the portrait he draws of Carlyle is true. His obvious sincerity, the intensity of his convictions, his insistence upon truth though the heavens fall, can only be seen as virtues in a time such as Victorian England when biography often approached hagiography. When I first went through Froude's four volumes, I had read very little of the scholarship on the Carlyles. In the years that followed I read a good deal of it. I saw Froude criticized and abused. I saw him occasionally in outright error. I threw up my hands in despair at his textual lapses. Yet each time I returned to the biography my original impression was reinforced: no one has had a better understanding of Carlyle than Froude. If his contemporaries attacked him for denigrating Carlyle, we may find ourselves today uneasy before his hero-worshipping belief in the Sage of Chelsea's greatness.

Many potential readers have been daunted by the four long volumes or by the book's controversial reputation. This is unfortunate, for few books have more to teach them about the nineteenth century. Whether interested in biography or in nineteenth-century England or more specifically in Carlyle, readers will find, I think, their estimates both of the Victorian prophet and of Froude's achievement higher than they anticipated. It is in the hope of making Froude's work more accessible that I have prepared this abridgment of a book that I believe to be one of the two or three great literary biographies in English. An abridgment should be useful to that body of readers—and they are probably numerous—who have not the stoicism to plow through the full text. In preparing it I became convinced that it was not merely a question of rescuing a biography of the first order from the obscurity into which it had fallen, but of restoring to English literature a work of great art and one of the classics of its prose. These are large claims, but I believe them justified.

It may seem odd at this late date, given the obloquy that Strachey and others have heaped upon Victorian biography, to resurrect an older life of so well-known a figure as Carlyle. My doing so stems from the belief that Froude's work, submerged from the beginning in controversy, has never had the fair hearing it deserves. Having now thought about both Carlyle and Froude for well over a decade, I have found that my initial opinion of the biography has stood up remarkably well. Froude did make a number of small errors, it is true, but few of major import and amazingly few altogether when one considers the problems facing a biographer attempting so complex a subject as Carlyle. James L. Clifford has summed up well the difficulties inherent for the biographer who attempts a contemporary subject: "His basic choice is clear. No attempts at compromise are ever wholly successful. Either he will keep on good terms with all his subject's friends and relations and disappoint posterity—or he will brave the displeasure of his own day and live in hopes of eventual recognition. Happily for us a few do take the harder way."[1]

Froude is one of the few who took the harder way. "If we owe regard to the memory of the dead," Samuel Johnson wrote in his *Rambler* essay "The dignity and usefulness of biography," "there is yet more respect to be paid to knowledge, to virtue, and to truth." Froude would have agreed. He believed that his biography of Carlyle, "if it is still to be condemned at present, will be of use hereafter. A hundred years hence, the world will better appreciate Carlyle's magnitude." The hundred years are almost upon us, and interest in Carlyle—to judge from the number of studies in recent years—has not been greater in this century. We do not see Carlyle exactly as Froude saw him or believe in him as he did, but we realize that to understand the Victorians it helps first to come to grips with Carlyle.

There is really no good, modern one-volume life of Carlyle; and even if there were, it would not have the same kind of interest as this biography, filled as it is with the sense of intimate association over decades of personal acquaintance, by a friend and disciple. To the extent that biography is a work of literary art created by a writer of human sympathy and psychological acumen, it can be supplemented but never superseded. Such a biography is Boswell's *Johnson,* and such Froude's *Carlyle* is also—not, perhaps, to the same degree as Boswell's, but still very high in the roster of English biography. Although other sources can usefully supplement his work, we return to his narrative for its unequaled power and for its understanding of the personalities and psychology involved. Froude probes more deeply into Carlyle's genius than any succeeding biographer. The reader coming to the *Life* today may be assured that no one knew Carlyle better than Froude or knew better how to make that intricately problematic personality come alive.

In 1884, near the end of his labors, Froude wrote a correspondent: "I am finishing Carlyles Life—which when it comes will take every one by surprise."[2] The biography did take everyone by surprise, the last two volumes as much as the first two, and it continues to take readers by surprise today. Part of its effect then and now is that it bears within itself the tensions under which it was written. These tensions include Froude's awareness of the gap between the public and the private Carlyle, particularly his difficulty in reconciling his idea of Carlyle's spiritual greatness with his obvious deficiencies in day-to-day intercourse. How was he to depict in the same volume, often on the same page, the moral sage who for decades had served as England's conscience *and* the private individual, difficult, domineering, apparently unaware of the needs and desires of others?

He had reluctantly accepted the charge to edit Carlyle's papers and to write his life, and he persevered doggedly to complete both tasks. But he was stunned by the extraordinary outburst of hostile criticism that greeted his publication of Carlyle's *Reminiscences* and the initial two volumes of the biography. Throughout the furor he held to the faith that a distant posterity would vindicate what he had done. On an artistic level Froude was troubled in mind over how to reconcile his belief in the importance of Carlyle's message and his awareness that few paid heed to it at the time he was writing. How was he to balance his sense of Carlyle as a modern hero centrally involved in *and* standing apart from an age that both agreed was in spiritual decline? On a personal level Froude agonized over how to depict two extraordinarily strong personalities, husband and wife, locked in a relationship that meant everything to each yet took an enormous toll on Jane Carlyle. How was he to insinuate that the virile stylist was an impotent husband, that Carlyle's infatuation with Lady Ashburton meant unconscionable neglect of his wife, or even to cope with his own ambivalent attitude toward both figures? His conception of biography, derived from Carlyle, was that it should reveal the inner man; yet clearly there existed a need, at times, to be reticent. By adhering to strict standards of biographical truth, was he not betraying the man he venerated? Such tensions in Froude's *Life* may seem puzzling and on the surface contradictory, but they usually resolve themselves satisfactorily on closer view. They indicate that the biographer meant his narrative to work simultaneously on several levels. A number of things will be going on at the same time beneath the surface of the prose. Froude did not always hold these tensions in equipoise, or solve the problems they gave him, but he did so sufficiently often to give the texture of his narrative an impressive psychological depth. If the problems he faced seemed almost insurmountable when he began and often brought him near despair as he progressed, by and large he did surmount them. They forced him to exert his powers to the utmost. Writing the life both exhausted and exhilarated him: even today we can respond to the passion behind the prose.

PREFACE

In the Introduction I have not thought it necessary to re-
tell the story of the controversy surrounding the publication
of the book or to discuss the reception given Froude's editions of the Carlyles. These include two volumes of Carlyle's *Reminiscences* (1881), three of the *Letters and Memorials of Jane Welsh Carlyle* (1883), and Carlyle's
Reminiscences of My Irish Journey in 1849 (1882). The
interpretation of the biography presented in the Introduction
renders previous arguments about the controversy invalid
to a degree, since neither Froude's defenders nor his detractors quite perceived what he was attempting to do in
his depiction of the Carlyles and through his biographical
method. I do not consider the Froude-Carlyle controversy
irrelevant, but it does not explain why the biography became what it is. Nor have I deemed it necessary to discuss
in detail Froude's relationship with Carlyle, for by far the
most eloquent account is his own in the biography.
Whether or not this generation is in a better position than
Froude's was to understand Carlyle, the biography deserves recognition on its own merits.

The Introduction offers an interpretation of the biography's strengths and weaknesses as a portrait of Carlyle.
It delves into Froude's psychology, his need for hero
worship, and his use of style to achieve an ironic position.
It focuses chiefly on the art and technique of the biography
itself, inasmuch as almost nothing exists in print on these
subjects, and is designed more as a series of related ex-
ploratory essays than as a definitive critical treatment. Desirable as the latter may be, it would be premature at this
time. Whereas Boswell's artistry in his *Johnson* receives
study upon study, work on Froude stagnates in what one
might call a prescientific state, in part because a great deal
in Froude's own life remains unknown and uncharted. As
he seems destined to be the last of the major Victorians to
gain critical attention, it is appropriate that rehabilitation
begin with a new edition of the work that lives as his finest
achievement.

This edition has been a number of years in the planning

and preparation, with a first draft typed as far back as 1968–69. My work over this span of time has greatly benefited from my participation as one of the editors of the ongoing *Collected Letters of Thomas and Jane Welsh Carlyle* being published at Duke University. There Xerox copies of most of the letters by both Carlyles, preserved in files assembled by Professor Charles Richard Sanders, general editor of the project, were kindly made available to me. The other editors of the Carlyle letters—Kenneth J. Fielding and Ian Campbell—have also been free with help, not to mention hospitality, during my visits to Edinburgh. On one of these visits I found in the National Library of Scotland a biography of Carlyle in German by Friedrich Althaus, written in 1866, in which Carlyle had made many important comments on his life and works that Froude used extensively. Before proceeding further with my work on Froude, I decided that the Althaus biography with Carlyle's commentary was of sufficient importance to publish separately, and it appeared in 1974 as part of *Two Reminiscences of Thomas Carlyle*. We observe Froude's indebtedness to the Althaus biography in his portrayal of Carlyle's early career.

Many people have had a share in this book. Scholars and friends, not always directly involved in Victorian studies, have generously answered queries or extended aid whenever possible. These include a number of persons who have read, or have heard me read, my Introduction in its various metamorphoses, among them, Bernard D. Frischer, Jerome Meckier, Charles Richard Sanders, Leo Steinberg, Mary Robbins Summe, G. B. Tennyson, and, especially, David J. DeLaura. I am also deeply grateful to Susan E. Allen for her criticism of the Introduction and for much else. Although I did not actually work on the biography during my tenure as a Guggenheim fellow in 1975–76, the fellowship allowed me the opportunity to spend time in Rome and to give the manuscript much thought. I wish to thank Dr. Gordon N. Ray, president of the foundation, for making possible the leisure that led to the thought. Reference librarians at many institutions have been invariably helpful. I wish to thank especially those of the Duke University Library who have, as always, given munificently of their

time and energy. Emerson Ford, head of Duke's Inter-
library Loan Department, found many obscure books for
me. Leland R. Phelps and Herman Salinger, of Duke's
German Department, and Peter H. Burian and Lawrence
W. Richardson, Jr., of the Classics Department, helped
trace quotations. One person's support, in particular, has
meant a great deal to me over the years: that of Dorothy
Roberts, who not only typed the various drafts with un-
failing care, but who also, by her infectious enthusiasm,
kept my own spirits from flagging under the burden of other
commitments. The completed book owes much to her belief in
it.

For permission to quote unpublished manuscripts and for
various courtesies extended during my visits, I wish to thank
the following institutions and persons: the Bodleian Library,
Oxford University; the British Library, London; the Cambridge University Library; the Carlyle House, Chelsea;
the Duke University Library; the University of Edinburgh
Library; the Free Library of Philadelphia; the Hertfordshire County Council and the Honorable David Lytton Cobbold; the Houghton Library, Harvard University; the Henry
E. Huntington Library; the University of Illinois Library;
the University of Kentucky Library; John Murray VI, his
son John Murray VII, and Virginia Murray; the National
Library of Scotland; Mrs. Jane S. Napier; the Henry W.
and Albert A. Berg Collection of the New York Public
Library; the Tennyson Research Centre, City Library,
Lincoln; the Humanities Research Center, University of
Texas; the Library of Trinity College, Cambridge; and the
Beinecke Library, Yale University. At the Beinecke I found
in an uncatalogued collection—after I had completed my
revisions and the manuscript was again in the hands of the
Press—Froude's own copy of the life. In it he had made a
number of marginal annotations, many of which I have incorporated into the text or included in the notes to this
edition. As these notes indicate, my greatest obligation is
to the National Library of Scotland and its unequaled collection of materials concerning Thomas and Jane Welsh
Carlyle. I thank its trustees for permission to quote generously from their holdings and, more specifically, James

S. Ritchie, for his cordial help during my visits. I am grateful to William C. Dowling for permitting me to quote portions of his article on the Boswellian hero. For providing research and travel funds for a number of years, I wish to acknowledge the support of the Duke University Council on Research; more recently, the Research Council of the University of Kentucky has provided valuable assistance. I am grateful to the Duke University Press for allowing me to pilfer several notes from *The Collected Letters of Thomas and Jane Welsh Carlyle* and my *Two Reminiscences of Thomas Carlyle*. The second and third sections of the Introduction appeared in somewhat different form in a volume I edited, also published by Duke, entitled *Carlyle and His Contemporaries: Essays in Honor of Charles Richard Sanders*.

Weldon A. Kefauver, director of the Ohio State University Press, expressed an interest in my manuscript long before he saw it. I am grateful to him for his belief in the worth of the project, for his editorial counseling, and for allowing me to include so many illustrations. To Richard D. Altick, Regents' Professor of English at Ohio State, I owe much for his interest in, and support of, my work over a number of years, probably on more occasions than I am aware. I am also grateful to the Press's official readers for their probing, yet sympathetic, readings of the manuscript, and for allowing me to incorporate several of their judgments on the biography in my Preface and Introduction. I also wish to thank Carol S. Sykes, assistant editor at the Press, for her careful editing of the manuscript. John Gatton, at the beginning, and Patsy Anderson, at the close, have given valiant help with proofs.

Carlyle believed that portraits guided the reader to an understanding of personality, in that a man's physiognomy indicated something about his character. Anyone who visits his home in Chelsea will discover that he surrounded himself with portraits—and later photographs—of the heroes he admired and the friends and relatives he loved. Therefore, it is appropriate to have a number of them among the illustrations to this biography, including several of contemporaries less known but important within Carlyle's life.

Here I have been fortunate in being able to draw upon the
Carlyle family scrapbooks, seven volumes of photographs
now in the Columbia University Library. The other photographs come from the Carlyle House, Chelsea; the Manuscript Division, Duke University Library; the University of
Edinburgh Library; the Glasgow Art Gallery and Museum;
Mrs. Jane S. Napier; the National Gallery of Scotland and
the Scottish National Portrait Gallery; the National Portrait Gallery, London; the National Trust, London; Charles
Richard Sanders; and Sidney Sussex College, Cambridge.
Many of the photographs of sites associated with Carlyle
were taken in the 1890s—the last decade before motor
vehicles began to invade the countryside—by John Patrick
of Kirkcaldy. The negatives are now in the University of
Edinburgh Library, and I wish to thank its curator of manuscripts, Charles Finlayson, and the editors of the Carlyle
letters for making available to me reproductions of so many
of them. They capture Carlyle's homes and haunts in rural
Scotland as do no other photographs I have seen.

1. James L. Clifford, "How Much Should a Biographer Tell? Some
Eighteenth-Century Views," in *Essays in Eighteenth-Century Biography*,
ed. Philip B. Daghlian (Bloomington: Indiana University Press, 1968),
pp. 94–95.
2. Froude to Mr [name crossed out], 18 January 1884. MS: University of Kentucky.

Abbreviations and Works Frequently Cited

JWC	Jane Welsh Carlyle (1801–66), wife of Thomas Carlyle
JAC	John Aitken Carlyle (1801–79), brother of Thomas Carlyle
MAC	Margaret Aitken Carlyle (1771–1853), mother of Thomas Carlyle
TC	Thomas Carlyle (1795–1881)
JBW	Jane Baillie Welsh (1801–66), maiden name of Jane Welsh Carlyle
Bliss, *TC*	Bliss, Trudy, ed. *Thomas Carlyle: Letters to His Wife*. London: Victor Gollancz, 1953
Boswell, *Life of Johnson*	Boswell, James. *Boswell's Life of Johnson*. Ed. R. W. Chapman. London: Oxford University Press, 1953. Reprinted 1969
A. Carlyle, *CMSB*	Carlyle, Alexander, ed. *Letters of Thomas Carlyle to John Stuart Mill, John Sterling, and Robert Browning*. London: T. Fisher Unwin, 1923
A. Carlyle, *LL*	Carlyle, Alexander, ed. *The Love Letters of Thomas Carlyle and Jane Welsh*. 2 vols. London and New York: John Lane, 1909
A. Carlyle, *NLMJWC*	Carlyle, Alexander, ed. *New Letters and Memorials of Jane Welsh Carlyle*. 2 vols. London and New York: John Lane, 1903

A. Carlyle, *NL*	Carlyle, Alexander, ed. *New Letters of Thomas Carlyle*. 2 vols. London and New York: John Lane, 1904
CL	Carlyle, Thomas. *The Collected Letters of Thomas and Jane Welsh Carlyle: 1812–1834*. Duke-Edinburgh Edition. Ed. Charles Richard Sanders, Kenneth J. Fielding, Ian M. Campbell, John Clubbe, Janetta Taylor (vols. 1–4), and Aileen Christianson (vols. 5–7). 7 vols. to date. Durham, N.C.: Duke University Press, 1970, 1977
Reminiscences	Carlyle, Thomas. *Reminiscences*. Ed. C. E. Norton. 2 vols. London and New York: Macmillan, 1887
Works	Carlyle, Thomas. *Works*. Centenary Edition. Ed. H. D. Traill. 30 vols. London: Chapman & Hall, 1896–99
Clubbe, *Carlyle and His Contemporaries*	Clubbe, John, ed. *Carlyle and His Contemporaries: Essays in Honor of Charles Richard Sanders*. Durham, N.C.: Duke University Press, 1976
Clubbe, *Two Reminiscences*	Clubbe, John, ed. *Two Reminiscences of Thomas Carlyle*. Durham, N.C.: Duke University Press, 1974
Dunn, *F and C*	Dunn, Waldo H. *Froude and Carlyle: A Study of the Froude-Carlyle Controversy*. London, New York, and Toronto: Longmans, Green & Co., 1930
Dunn, *Froude*	Dunn, Waldo H. *James Anthony Froude: A Biography*. 2 vols. Vol. 1: 1818–56. Vol. 2: 1857–94. Oxford: Clarendon Press, 1961, 1963
Froude, *LMJWC*	Froude, J. A. *Letters and Memorials of Jane Welsh Carlyle*. 3 vols. London: Longmans, Green, 1883

ABBREVIATIONS

Froude, *My Relations with Carlyle*	Froude, J. A. *My Relations with Carlyle*. London: Longmans, Green, 1903
Froude, *Nemesis of Faith*	Froude, J. A. *The Nemesis of Faith*. London: George Routledge & Sons, 1903
Froude, *Short Studies*	Froude, J. A. *Short Studies on Great Subjects*. 4 vols. London: Longmans, Green, 1868–1883
Froude, *Carlyle*	Froude, J. A. *Thomas Carlyle: A History of the First Forty Years of His Life, 1795–1835; A History of His Life in London, 1834–1881*. 4 vols. London: Longmans, Green, 1882, 1884
Harrold, *Sartor*	Harrold, Charles Frederick, ed. *Sartor Resartus*. New York: Odyssey Press, 1937
Norton, *GC*	Norton, Charles Eliot, ed. *Correspondence between Goethe and Carlyle*. London and New York: Macmillan, 1887
Norton, *L26–36*	Norton, Charles Eliot, ed. *Letters of Thomas Carlyle, 1826–1836*. London and New York: Macmillan, 1889
Norton, *Two Note Books*	Norton, Charles Eliot, ed. *Two Note Books of Thomas Carlyle*. New York: Grolier Club, 1898
Paul	Paul, Herbert. *The Life of Froude*. New York: Scribner's, 1905
Slater, *CEC*	Slater, Joseph, ed. *The Correspondence of Emerson and Carlyle*. New York and London: Columbia University Press, 1964
Tennyson, *Sartor*	Tennyson, G. B. *Sartor Called Resartus: The Genesis, Structure, and Style of Thomas Carlyle's First Major Work*. Princeton, N.J.: Princeton University Press, 1965

Viljoen

Wilson, *Carlyle*

Viljoen, Helen Gill, ed. *The Froude-Ruskin Friendship*. New York: Pageant Press, 1966

Wilson, David Alec. *Carlyle*. 6 vols. London: Kegan Paul, Trench, Trubner & Co.; New York: E. P. Dutton & Co., 1923–34

Editor's Introduction

When Thomas Carlyle died early in 1881 at the age of eighty-five, it was known that James Anthony Froude had begun work on a life of him. The subject was perhaps the most famous Victorian, his biographer a historian and man of letters in his own right, then in his sixties, with an impressive body of work behind him. "The greatest master of English prose within our generation," Frederic Harrison observed, "entrusted the story of his life to one of the most skilful of living writers."[1] Froude, born in 1818, had the advantage of having known both Carlyles since 1849, intimately since 1861. On ethical questions and on contemporary issues, his opinions often verged so close to Carlyle's as to be indistinguishable; indeed, Carlyle had in large measure formed them. Presumably Froude could have directed questions about the biography to Carlyle himself until his death, and it appears likely that on at least several occasions he did so. Known to be Carlyle's intimate in his later years and his chosen biographer, Froude could also ask Carlyle's friends to let him examine their correspondence with the Sage of Chelsea or to reminisce about him. Little was refused him. It would hardly have mattered if it had been. Froude had more than enough to do with the hoard of personal papers—letters, a private journal, reminiscences about himself and his contemporaries—that Carlyle left at his disposal with virtually complete freedom to use as he wished. Few biographers have ever had so much manuscript material by, or relating to, their subjects;

1

certainly it is difficult to imagine a biographer in a better position than Froude when he began his task. But the situation did not remain unclouded for long.

Three weeks after Carlyle's death on 5 February, Froude published the *Reminiscences*, Carlyle's account of his early years, which included candid assessments of contemporaries, unexpected revelations about his personal life, and frequent expressions of his belief that he was largely responsible for the unhappiness and frustration of his wife, Jane. The clear implication was that he had treated her harshly. The public was stunned. When the first two volumes of Froude's biography appeared the next spring, those looking for further revelations about Carlyle were not disappointed. Frederic Harrison voiced the unease of many:

> The biographies and autobiographies, the unroofing of his home and the unveiling of his hearth, the letters, journals, and recorded sayings are intensely interesting. But they have told us things that we would rather not have heard. Those who loved him and those who loved her have been shocked, amazed, ashamed, in turn. Those who love good men and good women, those who honour great intellects, those who reverence human nature, have been wounded to the heart. Foul odours, as from a charnel-house, have been suddenly opened on us. . . .[2]

By treating his subject as a human being to be understood rather than as an idol to be worshipped, as a human being at times irascible and at times petty, Froude flung himself against the mainstream of Victorian biography, which valued reverence for the departed one more than it did honesty about his failings. Yet if Froude found much to censure in Carlyle's personal life, he recognized that in its moral worth and its dedication to the ideal it was a life worthy of emulation. He sincerely believed that the not always edifying details of the life humanized, rather than abased, the revered sage. "If he was to be known at all," Froude said in his Preface, "he chose to be known as he was, with his angularities, his sharp speeches, his special peculiarities, meritorious or unmeritorious, precisely as they had actually been."[3] Set against the standard of eternal truth, Carlyle would arise not unblemished but greater than ever because fallible and human. "The sharpest scrutiny is the condition of enduring fame," Froude wrote in the biography

(322), and he gave Carlyle the scrutiny in order to ensure the fame.[4] Carlyle, he believed, had less to hide than any other man. No Victorian thought to accuse Froude of hero worship, yet the impression we receive from perusing the biography today is that he wished to represent the life of a hero—"the Hero as Man of Letters"—for his own and later generations.

Opinion split almost immediately regarding the degree of truth in Froude's portraits of the Carlyles. In the early 1880s and for many years afterward, the eminent of the day expressed their opinions. Some contemporaries—Tennyson, W. E. H. Lecky, Mrs. Oliphant, Julia Wedgwood, Richard Garnett, Carlyle's nephew and niece Alexander and Mary Aitken Carlyle—disapproved of Froude's exposing what they felt to be the sanctities of the Carlyles' private life. Others—Ruskin, Edward Fitzgerald, Sir James Stephen, John Skelton, two of Carlyle's three surviving sisters, and his surviving brother—defended Froude,[5] praising the biography for capturing the essential truth of Carlyle's character and of his relationship with his wife. Froude worked on despite the furor, facing, in addition to many hostile comments in the press, the possibility of a lawsuit by Alexander and Mary Carlyle. After he completed the final two volumes of the biography in 1884, he was near exhaustion. "I have had so much work on it, with strain of mind and body," he wrote George Bentley.[6] The next year he told a friend of the effects of his ordeal:

> My long anxious work over Carlyle had done me up and I wanted to have my mind swept clear of the whole thing. It has been hanging like a nightmare over me for eleven years. I am myself satisfied that I have told the whole truth, and yet have left people more affectionately interested in Carlyle than they were, and with an even raised respect for his intellect and character.[7]

In the decade of life left to him, Froude was often reminded that many of his readers came away from the biography upset by the unexpected candor of his portrayal. Not even his death in 1894 stopped the controversy that the biography had spawned; at various times in the subsequent decades, Froude's detractors revived it with increased acrimony. Even today its echoes can still be heard.[8]

Most distinguished Victorians were the subjects after

their deaths of commemorative biographies, biographies that Lytton Strachey called in 1918 "those two fat volumes . . . with their ill-digested masses of material, their slipshod style, their tone of tedious panegyric, their lamentable lack of selection, of detachment, of design."[9] These memorial volumes are now unread by the general public and consulted by scholars only for the documents they contain. Froude's life of Carlyle contravenes in almost every respect Strachey's reprimand. The biographer thoroughly grasped his own times in their cultural, social, and religious dimensions; he interwove in a masterly way the main strands of Carlyle's life with those of contemporary English society; he synthesized brilliantly Carlyle's books, his intellectual development, and the impact that his writings had on successive generations of Victorians; he had an understanding of psychology unusually subtle among nineteenth-century biographers, and he feared less to offend his contemporaries through honesty than any of them; he wrote clearly, yet with force and elegance; and he knew how to select the details of a life that cumulatively form a living portrait.[10] Born twenty-three years later than Carlyle, Froude lived through much of the Victorian era himself and had known personally many of the figures he mentioned. Most of all, he had the gift of endowing with life whatever he touched. The most essential quality in a historian was imagination, he once told Tennyson,[11] and this quality everywhere informs the movement of his narrative. His re-creation of the lives of the Carlyles remains not only the most illuminating book about them but the most vibrant affirmation of Carlyle as a commanding intellectual force in Victorian England.

BIOGRAPHY AS DRAMATIC PORTRAITURE

Froude believed that the most difficult challenge for the biographer was to penetrate the surface of his subject. Asked in 1889 to write a biographical sketch of Disraeli, he told Lady Derby that his "difficulty [was] to find out the real man that lay behind the Sphinx-like affectations."[12] The next year (having written the study) he told Stuart J. Reid, "It is worse than useless to attempt the biography of a man unless you know, or think you know, what his inner nature was."[13] Although at Carlyle's death many Englishmen revered the man as much as they admired the writings, few suspected the complexity of the "real man," the mysteries of his "inner nature." Throughout the biography Froude attempted to tell them why he wrote thus of Carlyle.

"History is the account of the actions of men," Froude wrote in the life; "and in 'actions' are comprehended the thoughts, opinions, motives, impulses of the actors and of the circumstances in which their work was executed. The actions without the motives are nothing, for they may be interpreted in many ways, and can only be understood in their causes" (539). Froude understood "action" in an Aristotelian sense: action expresses the totality of man's involvement, intellectual as well as physical, with his environment. Action thus understood is more than the sum of a man's deeds or the events in which he participates, and constitutes as much the motivations and the mental processes as it does the deeds themselves. For Froude the preeminent historian of humanity was Shakespeare. Shakespeare's plays could teach the modern historian to present his characters—and to let them reveal their inner selves—through action. Froude's insistence that we must seize history through drama may strike us today as an awkward, even false, analogy; yet analyzing the actions of men within a dramatic context enabled him to probe their motivations as much as the events in which they took part. "To say that the characters of men cannot be thus completely known," Froude continues, "that their inner nature is beyond our reach, that the dramatic portraiture of things is only possible to poetry, is to say that history ought not to be written, for the inner nature of the persons of whom it speaks is the essential thing about them." The historian must make a greater effort than the dramatist "to penetrate really into the hearts and souls of men," to capture a man's inner nature, "for all is required which is required of the dramatist, with the obligation to truth of ascertained fact besides" (539–40).

The historian thus becomes a kind of superior dramatist, bound as much to the truths of "ascertained fact" as to the truths of the imagination; but what constitutes historical accuracy was no less a debatable subject then than now. The "facts," Froude claimed, could be arranged to support virtually any position that the historian wished to maintain. For history to come alive, to transcend the facts, the historian must sift, select, arrange, and inevitably transform the material at hand. All history is distortion, to a greater or lesser degree. Yet certain distortions, given the powerful imagination of their creator, are more convincing and real than others. Froude made up his portrait of Carlyle with the details that he thought revealed the man. He did not believe in unimpassioned objectivity in biography; "impartiality," he once said, "is but another name for an unworthy indifference."[14] Nor did he claim to tell all. Although he told much, he did not include in his biography all the information available to him; rather, he chose that which enabled him to form, by selection and analogy, a living resemblance to the Carlyle he had known.

Froude wished to reveal in his biography the sources of Carlyle's greatness and to give his contemporaries a true notion of Carlyle's importance for Victorian England. Yet he did not wish to efface the warts in the portrait that he drew of Carlyle's character and personal life. Thus he wrote a biography designed, as he recognized, more for posterity than for his contemporaries. The light of moral strengths blended with the shadow of personal failings to make a rich, many-hued portrait, frank yet penetrating, but one that was to draw down on Froude the wrath of those unprepared for, and unused to, candor in biography. Yet for all the candor and the many years he had to puzzle over Carlyle's "inner nature," he never seems to have been quite certain that he had seized it. His correspondence with Ruskin, recently published, suggests that doubts remained even after he had completed the biography.

> I preferred *not* to attempt to describe (directly) C's character. I preferred to let it appear in the story and in his own clear letters.— Indeed I do not know that I could have described it. . . . He was not selfish, not consciously or deliberately selfish, not selfish at all in the ordinary sense but he required everything to be sacrificed to his convenience. He was intensely occupied with his work & with "the message" which he had to deliver—He never considered those he lived with in the smaller things of every day

6

life. Where they had worked & slaved for him he was really grateful, but he was too shy—or too *something*, to show it.[15]

In his effort to fathom the elusive *"something"* in Carlyle's being—a being that in its complexity must surely rival Johnson's or Byron's—Froude drew upon all the ability he possessed to write the work that he justly regarded as his most important. He himself recognized that "of all that I have written little has any permanent value, except Carlyle's life."[16]

One of Froude's distinctions is that he wrote perhaps the only nineteenth-century English biography to imply—in Victorian England he could do no more than imply—the importance of sex in marriage. In Froude's view both Carlyle and Jane Carlyle would have been happier not married to each other. He said it boldly and he said it often. To a reader today such an assertion about a relationship between two people may seem harmless enough, but the Victorians did not lightly condone attacks on marriage. "The criticism of the book," wrote Isaac W. Dyer, Carlyle's bibliographer, in 1928, "is much more drastic than failure properly to distribute material or draw a pen portrait satisfactory to Carlyle's friends. Mr. Froude is charged with actual misrepresentation. The main issue between Froude and the Carlyleans is his treatment of the relations between Carlyle and his wife. This is the nub of the Carlyle-Froude controversy."[17] That Froude dared to say what he did, especially in regard to such a well-known couple, scandalized many. A biographer's psychological understanding of his subject can always be challenged; and when we have two beings as enigmatic and contradictory as Thomas and Jane Carlyle, the possibilities for misinterpretation of evidence increase proportionately. Yet Froude presents not only a convincing but also a fundamentally sound interpretation of the Carlyles, their courtship, their marriage, and their existence together. He remains by far the most intelligent biographer that they have had, psychologically the most acute; he also had the inestimable advantage of knowing both of them better than did any other biographer. His interpretation of their lives needs qualification, modification even, but no apology.

7

Froude began his career as a novelist, and critics have observed that his interest in the techniques of fiction and his penchant for dramatic contrasts continued into his histories and biographies. His first important work was an autobiographical novel, *The Nemesis of Faith* (1849). When the young Moncure D. Conway read it in the early 1850s, he thought—as did others at the time—that Froude might be the "coming man" in the area of fiction. "Every work Froude thereafter wrote," Conway concluded, "is suffused with the imaginative genius which bequeathed to us this marvellous *Nemesis of Faith*."[18] Froude's mature work does indeed bear the imprint of his early interest in fiction. Learning from his apprenticeship as a novelist, he was able in the biography to use dramatic techniques and models both to heighten narrative impact, and, more importantly, to make implications regarding the married lives of the Carlyles that he could not make directly. "The facts must be delineated first with the clearness and fulness which we demand in an epic poem or a tragedy," he wrote in the biography. "We must have the real thing before we can have a science of a thing" (541). Epic and tragedy provided, in Froude's view, the best models for the literary artist seeking to represent "the real thing" in biography. In writing of the Carlyles, the works that proved most instructive to him were the *Faerie Queene* and, especially, the Greek tragedies centering upon Oedipus and Iphigenia. Whereas Froude used the *Faerie Queene* solely to simulate the Carlyles' friendship with Lord and Lady Ashburton, Greek tragedy served him to represent the Carlyles themselves.[19]

OEDIPUS AND IPHIGENIA

Greek tragedy played a crucial role in shaping Froude's eventual perspective on the Carlyles. During his childhood he had made an intense, if sporadic, study of the tragedians. Not only were the Greeks his first love, but they remained his favorite reading throughout life. He read the classics habitually, with ease and with pleasure, and he often referred to them in his writings. Conway, in his introduction to *The Nemesis of Faith*, had noted that "the depth and intensity

8

of the Greek drama pervade his work."[20] Froude's knowledge of Greek tragedy finds expression in his biography of Carlyle, I suggest, in at least two ways: first, he introduced the device of the Greek chorus to allow him to comment obliquely on the events he described; second, he consciously drew his portraits of Thomas Carlyle and Jane Welsh after models in Greek drama, Carlyle after Oedipus, Jane Carlyle after Iphigenia.

Several times in his first volume, Froude refers to himself as a chorus commenting on—and to an extent participating in—a fateful series of events. The intertwined lives of the Carlyles he perceived as a personal drama that in its intensity approached Greek tragedy. As their biographer he took upon himself the role of a chorus observing this tragedy. Froude openly introduces himself as the "chorus" in the "long drama" of the courtship (170, 199) after quoting from Carlyle's letter to Jane Welsh of 20 January 1825. This letter he views as the turning point in Carlyle's largely epistolary wooing of Miss Welsh. First, he gives extracts from her letter to Carlyle of 13 January 1825. She had written, "I love you . . . but I am not *in love* with you—that is to say—my love for you is not a passion which overclouds my judgement; . . . it is a simple, honest, serene affection, made up of admiration and sympathy."[21] Carlyle's reply of 20 January carefully refutes all her arguments against marriage. In it he reaffirms his love and asks a "noble being" to consent "to unite . . . her judgement, her patience, prudence, her true affection, to mine."[22] After quoting extensively from these letters, Froude writes: "The functions of a biographer are, like the functions of a Greek chorus, occasionally at the important moments to throw in some moral remarks which seem to fit the situation" (170). The words he thought appropriate to insert at this fateful moment in both their lives are these: "The chorus would remark, perhaps, on the subtle forms of self-deception to which the human heart is liable, of the momentous nature of marriage. . . . Self-sacrifice it might say was a noble thing. But a sacrifice which one person might properly make, the other might have no reasonable right to ask or to allow" (ibid.). In writing this, he obviously has in mind Miss Welsh's answer of nine days later. It reveals that Carlyle's arguments had made

9

an impression upon her, for she confessed: "Not many months ago, I would have said it was impossible I should ever be your wife; at present I consider this the most *probable* destiny for me." A year and a half later she told Carlyle that she had considered herself his "affianced wife" from this time forward.[23] Froude, strongly influenced by Geraldine Jewsbury, had come to the conclusion that Carlyle "was one of those persons who ought not to have married."[24] Yet he could not say why openly. A mask was needed, and the device of the Greek chorus came conveniently to mind.

However seriously Froude intended this analogy of himself to the chorus in Greek tragedy—and he unquestionably intended his readers to take it seriously—he also maintained it on an ironic level. Such allusions Froude regularly introduces tongue in cheek. For example, six months before their marriage, Carlyle informed a startled Jane that in domestic matters *"the Man should bear rule in the house and not the Woman*. This is an eternal axiom, the Law of Nature h[erself w]hich no mortal departs from unpunished" (195). Froude, in his role of detached observer, rumbles, "The Greek chorus would have shaken its head ominously, and uttered its musical cautions, over the temper displayed in this letter" (ibid.). The tonal effect that Froude achieves here is complex, difficult to describe accurately, but important for the reader to be aware of in catching the "ironic" Froude. Why, we ask, does he handle so unquestionably serious a matter as the Carlyles' relationship with one another in such a self-protective manner? Does his doing so imply doubts on his part about Carlyle as a prophet or about his "message"? Hardly, for the evidence is strong that Froude never wavered in his respect for Carlyle's intellectual positions. But his adopting the role of a Greek chorus does suggest something about his sense of his relationship to Carlyle the man, a relationship that never became one of complete ease. Irony implies perspective, and perspective was what he desperately tried to attain on the person who, as he admitted in the biography, had brought him out of the wilderness and whose maxims he never questioned. By adopting an ironic stance that undercut Carlyle, Froude in effect asserted the integrity of his own being. Only through irony could he distance himself from the man he genuinely

10

revered and thus assert a measure of the independence that he never allowed himself during Carlyle's lifetime.

This ironic stance, expressed through the Greek chorus but in other ways as well,[25] also indicates that Froude sensed that his readers in the 1880s might have their doubts about the sage of yesteryear. Carlyle was now dead; times were rapidly changing and, in Froude's view, hurtling toward perdition; and the new generation was less interested in moral heroes, perhaps skeptical of the virtues that Carlyle advocated and exemplified. An altogether straightforward narrative of a life whose major components Froude believed to be of unblemished integrity would have brought smiles to the generation of Oscar Wilde, as such lives did later to that of Strachey.

Carlyle had said in his Journal that no one could write a biography of him because no one could understand the mystery that enveloped his life.[26] But if Carlyle could never be completely understood, his life at least had analogies with figures of the past. Froude sought in these analogies clues that would help him unravel Carlyle's enigmatic personality. In this search he had help from Carlyle, who often spoke of himself as a being set apart from others. Carlyle's favorite image of himself was as a prophet alone in the desert, his spirit unbowed, his message of dire import unheeded or misunderstood by an indifferent world. He refers to himself as "Ishmael . . . cast forth into the Desart, with bow and quiver in his coat of wild skins";[27] and at one point Froude dutifully finds Carlyle "fated to be an Ishmaelite" (328). At other times Carlyle saw himself as Isaiah, as John the Baptist, as Saint John on Patmos, as Saint Anthony, as "the poor Arab," as a "Bedouin," or even as Faust.[28] Froude often returns in his biography to the comparison with a prophet isolated, viewing Carlyle alternatively as Isaiah or Jeremiah, once, elsewhere, as *"Athanasius contra mundum."*[29] At the time of Carlyle's marriage, speaking of his search for spiritual truth, Froude notes ironically that "apostles in St. Paul's opinion were better unwedded" (170). Later he compares him explicitly to the apostle to the gentiles (571). He does not restrict himself, however, to biblical figures: he draws analogies with Prometheus, the medieval "knight errant," Owen Glendower, Dante, Don Quixote, and to personages of classical mythology and Renaissance epic.[30] In an unpublished letter he observes of Carlyle that "Nature meant him for a Norse skald."[31] Elsewhere, he compares him to Socrates and Goethe.[32] A few instances suffice to demonstrate Froude's analogical bent. Speaking of Carlyle's failure to dispel his wife's suspicions concerning his relationship with Lady Ashburton, Froude writes that "Carlyle in such matters had no more skill than the Knight of La Mancha would have had" (449). In *My Relations with Carlyle,* a defense of his procedures in writing the biography that he prepared for possible use after his death, Froude refers to Carlyle's correspondence with Lady Ashburton as "masses of extravagant letters . . . to the great lady as ecstatic as Don Quixote's to Dulcinea."[33] To suggest Carlyle's slavish devotion to her, he draws upon Tasso's *Gerusalemme Liberata* and classical mythology: "Rinaldo in the bower of Armida or Hercules spinning silks for Omphale."[34] Carlyle's character and acts, in Froude's view, might be suggested by any or all of these analogies to figures of the past. He puts Carlyle into a number of roles, none permanently, but none without relevance to the complexity of Carlyle's character. No one role by itself "explained" him, none could encompass the uniqueness of his being, but all helped at one time or another illuminate different aspects of his character.

Yet no analogy left Froude certain that he had really seized the mystery. "There is something *demonic* both in him and her which will never be adequately understood," he says at one point.[35] Before Jane Carlyle's death in 1866, Carlyle had seemed to Froude a man "apart from the rest of the world, with the mask of destiny upon him, to whom one could not feel exactly as towards a brother mortal."[36] His sense of mission put inseparable barriers between himself and other men. But Jane Carlyle's death changed both Carlyle and Froude's relationship to him. He saw Carlyle not only more often but in a different perspective. Carlyle undertook a repentance for what he felt to be his grave failings toward her in life. It was "a repentance so deep and passionate" that it "showed that the real nature was as beautiful as his intellect had been magnificent. He was still liable to his fits of temper. He was scornful and overbearing and wilful; but it had become possible to love him—indeed, impossible not to love him." Equally dramatic and far-reaching was the change in Froude's sense of his relationship to Carlyle. From awe before a revered mentor, he moved to an awareness of Carlyle as a tormented human who felt that he had sinned greatly but who was now conscious of his sin and was prepared to make ample and extended atonement for it. And if "the remorse was needed," Froude observed, the "expiation" was "so frank and so complete that it washed the stain away."

References to the lives of the Carlyles singly or together as participants in a tragedy appear frequently in Froude's writings about them. Not until 1871, however, when Carlyle gave Froude the material that constituted the letters and memorials of Jane Welsh Carlyle and his reminiscences of her life, did the dimensions of the mystery—the "something *demonic*" in both Carlyles—begin to come clearly into focus. He read the documents left him, he wrote in *My Relations with Carlyle*, "and then for the first time I realised what a tragedy the life in Cheyne Row had been—a tragedy as stern and real as the story of Oedipus."[37] In the anguished weeks before he wrote *My Relations with Carlyle*, he voiced the dilemma of his recognition in the privacy of his journal. The description of Carlyle given there applies as much to Oedipus:

> What, in the name of truth, ought I to have done? It was a tragedy, as truly and as terribly as Oedipus; nor was the character altogether unlike. His [Carlyle's] character, when he was himself, was noble and generous; but he had absolutely no control over himself. He was wayward and violent, and perhaps at bottom believed himself a peculiar man who had a dispensation to have things his own way [38]

In his effort to penetrate Carlyle's inner nature, Froude found at its heart a paradox, a paradox whose explanation lay in the mysterious figure of Oedipus. The indefinable "something *demonic*" in Carlyle led Froude to view him as a reincarnation of Sophocles' hero: his character was as complex, irrational, and mysterious as that of the Theban king. Carlyle, like Oedipus before him, exemplified the insoluble riddle of man's nature.

Oedipus the King and *Oedipus at Colonus*, then, provided Froude with his surest clues to understanding Carlyle. This revelation did not come until he had known Carlyle more than two decades. Only in *My Relations with Carlyle* and in his journal (neither intended for publication) does he draw the intriguing parallel between Oedipus and Carlyle; he does not mention Oedipus in the biography. But there, sometimes ironically, sometimes seriously, Froude speaks of the Fates "doing their very worst to Carlyle" (242). Carlyle became for him a man who wrestled with the Fates: only the Greek conception of the doomed tragic hero met the measure of his greatness. Before 1866, his career recently crowned by the publication of the final volumes of *Frederick the Great*, Carlyle looms as the mighty hero of *Oedipus the King*; after 1866, his life broken by Jane Carlyle's death, he becomes the tragic wanderer seeking salvation of *Oedipus at Colonus*.

Why Froude does not mention Oedipus in the biography must remain a mystery. He may have felt that, unless elaborated, the comparison would have confused rather than enlightened, or he may not have been fully conscious of it as he wrote Carlyle's life. Both couplings of Carlyle with Oedipus occur after he had completed the biography, although that in *My Relations with Carlyle* clearly implies that he first perceived Carlyle as an Oedipean figure when he read the reminiscence of Jane Carlyle in the early 1870s. And in the life itself Froude describes Carlyle's recognition of what he had done in language recalling Oedipus's experience: "There broke upon him in his late years, like a flash of lightning from heaven, the terrible revelation that he had sacrificed his wife's health and happiness in his absorption in his work; that he had been oblivious of his most obvious obligations, and had been negligent, inconsiderate, and selfish. The fault was grave and the remorse agonising" (316). Froude's linking the two names in the passages quoted earlier, as well as in the implied comparison above, does not signify that he intended the analogy between Oedipus and Carlyle to be total or exact. Rather, he clearly demarcated the grounds of comparison. Each had an overwhelming, impetuous character and a mysterious secret; each endured a terrible personal catastrophe followed by a sudden, painful realization of sin; finally, each underwent a subsequent, if incomplete, change of personality in old age. We need not carry parallels further, for if we do, they become strained. Setting up an analogy between Oedipus and Carlyle enabled Froude to grasp something of the complexity of Carlyle's being without distorting it beyond recognizable dimensions. In understanding how Froude perceived Oedipus, we begin to understand how he perceived Carlyle.

In his essay "England's Forgotten Worthies" (1852), Froude expresses a view of old age that directly parallels his consideration of Carlyle as a modern Oedipus. He describes two kinds of old age. One he compares to "the slow-dropping mellow autumn of a rich glorious summer" and finds that "in the old man, nature has fulfilled her work." Such an old age, he concludes, "is beautiful, but not the most beautiful." Unqualified admiration he reserves for a nobler level of existence: "There is another life, hard, rough, and thorny, trodden with bleeding feet and aching brow; the life of which the cross is the symbol; a battle which no peace follows, this side the grave; . . . this is the highest life of man. Look back along the great names of history; there is none whose life has been other than this."[39] Although he refers to England's "forgotten worthies" of the sixteenth century, Froude intends his words to apply to "the great names of history." Elsewhere he writes that "the Greeks thought that the highest knowledge could be obtained only through pain and mortification,"[40] Oedipus knew both in abundance in his declining years. So did Carlyle.

No one else, not even Ruskin, took up Carlyle's opinions concerning man and society with the fervor and strong conviction of Froude. He envisioned Carlyle as a man who by sheer force of character dominated his contemporaries, whose gospel was needed to guide a troubled England, and whose vision of society would be vindicated a hundred years hence. Then in 1866 he saw a personal tragedy of immense proportions strike his hero. Carlyle was metamorphosed. To be sure, traits of the old Carlyle remained. He was still proud, domineering, at times rude and unthinking in personal relationships; but he now revealed depths of sorrow and repentance for his harsh treatment of Jane Carlyle that

15

only a person of heroic dimensions could draw upon. Thus, in alluding to Oedipus as he grapples with the paradoxes of Carlyle's character, Froude insinuates that Oedipus's strange career can in meaningful ways illuminate Carlyle's.

Nineteenth-century critics of drama, from Coleridge and Hazlitt at one end of the century to A. C. Bradley at the other, tended to focus on character and to judge it on ethical grounds. In the *Poetics* Aristotle postulated the concept of hamartia, the flaw, "great or small, moral or intellectual, without which the hero would not have fallen nor his character been a tragic one. . . . Aristotelian hamartia is not *any* shortcoming which may be found in a suffering hero; it is the defect which makes his character tragically imperfect."[41] Aristotle's concept of the tragic flaw fitted well into the Victorian tradition of analyzing character from ethical premises and guided interpretation of *Oedipus the King* into the twentieth century. Froude would have been familiar with it; most probably he would have endorsed it, as he would have endorsed the tragic pattern of life upon which the play insists. He would have agreed with many readers of Aristotle that in Oedipus's case his tragic flaw was hubris, or excessive pride, and that it led directly to his fall. Thus he envisaged a Carlyle possessed of hubris, sovereignly independent, inconsiderate of others' feelings, yet a great man. "Carlyle was Carlyle—proud as Lucifer before he fell," he wrote.[42] Interpreting for his own purposes Aristotle's observations on Oedipus, Froude saw Carlyle undergoing a fundamental experience of "recognition" and "reversal." "Recognition," wrote Aristotle, "as the name indicates, is a change from ignorance to knowledge. . . . 'Reversal of the situation' is a change by which the action veers round to its opposite. . . . The best form of recognition is coincident with a reversal of the situation, as in the *Oedipus*."[43] For Froude, Carlyle underwent an experience of Aristotelian recognition—a moment of intense vision following a lifetime of blindness; it coincided with a reversal, after which he sought to understand his life in the light of the revelatory experience. Carlyle's moment of vision was, in Froude's view, the realization that he had mistreated his wife. The regeneration of the fallen hero, which took place for Oedipus in the *Colonus*, took place for Carlyle in the prolonged suffering and repentance of the years following Jane Carlyle's death.

Oedipus thus becomes the key to the riddle of Carlyle's character in Froude's biography. Once we recognize that Oedipus provides the lineaments of Froude's portrait of Carlyle, we perceive more clearly why Carlyle emerges as a tragic figure in the life; and, in turn, we can assess more surely the validity of Froude's interpretation of his character.

Jane Welsh Carlyle also plays a major role in Froude's biography. Of her he wrote to a correspondent: "*She* is my special legacy."[44] Carlyle's reminiscence of his wife was, in Froude's view, "as sternly tragic, as profoundly pathetic as the great Theban drama."[45] But in viewing her life, he usually subsumes the Oedipus myth within another. In *My Relations with Carlyle,* he refers to the married life of the Carlyles as a "singular and tragical story";[46] to Ruskin he writes: "*Her* life was a tragedy."[47] The representation of Jane Welsh Carlyle as a tragic heroine, established in the first volume of the biography, carries over into the next three. Although Froude never specifically mentions that he had a model in mind for Jane Welsh, one heroine of Greek tragedy often hovered in his imagination as he wrote of her. She is Iphigenia, daughter of Agamemnon and a personage about whom Froude had thought long and hard.

Iphigenia is referred to only once in the biography, and then not by name. But the timing of the reference is crucial. In his first authorial (or choric) comment after narrating Jane's marriage to Carlyle on 17 October 1826, Froude writes: "The victory was won, but, as of old in Aulis, not without a victim" (201). It *was* a victory, for the life of the Carlyles together was a triumphant achievement of the human spirit. This Froude never denied. But the price of victory for Jane Carlyle was, in his view, undeservedly high. There was indeed a victim. "What was he, and what was his father's house," Froude had asked during the courtship, "that she should sacrifice herself for him?" (182). Before the courtship was over, he had answered this question unhesitatingly: "Men may sacrifice themselves, if they please, to imagined high duties and ambitions, but

they have no right to marry wives and sacrifice them"
(193).

From his essay "Sea Studies," written in 1874, we observe that Froude had pondered the meaning of Iphigenia
for his own time.[48] The conception of her character, which
he found in Euripides and analyzes in this essay, fascinated
him. Despite its title the essay is largely a study of Iphigenia
as the incarnation of duty. Froude prized this virtue above
all others and believed it to be the guiding principle behind
Jane Carlyle's existence with her husband. As she moved
toward the inevitable marriage, he looked ahead to the life
that followed: "The stern and powerful sense of duty in
these two remarkable persons held them true through a long
and trying life together to the course of elevated action
which they had both set before themselves. . . . Her character was braced by the contact with him, and through
the incessant self-denial which the determination that he
should do his very best inevitably exacted of her" (172).
And during Jane Carlyle's later years, Froude found "the
sense of duty acting as perpetual curb to her impatience"
(452). Iphigenia's behavior under duress he thought ex-
emplary of the duty and self-sacrifice that humanity needs,
and he drew upon it in dramatizing Jane Carlyle's character and ordeal. In the guise of Iphigenia, she became both
an individual and a representative heroine.

Froude wrote his life of Carlyle near the end of an era
that had seen countless women, from working-class girls in
their teens to higher-born maidens of every age, sacrificed
to male dominance or to male pleasure. If the figure of
Iphigenia appears frequently in Victorian literature, it is
more than still another instance of the pervasive influence of
classical mythology: it is because she symbolizes the condition of many Victorian women. She appears in poetry—
Browning's Pompilia, for example—but it is in a cluster of
major novels written in the decades before the publication
of Froude's biography that Iphigenia comes into her own.
With her behavior being the classic representation of duty
under duress, self-sacrifice became a major theme in Victorian fiction. Dickens conceived of a host of self-
denying heroines, Florence Dombey, Amy Dorrit, and
Louisa Gradgrind being among the most conspicuous of

those women who submit meekly to paternal authority;[49] George Eliot, from her earliest attempts in fiction to her culminating portrait in *Middlemarch* of Dorothea Brooke sacrificing herself for a surrogate father, agonized over heroines who find it difficult continually to endure, be silent, and suffocate; Thackeray in *Vanity Fair* had "a cheerful brass group of the sacrifice of Iphigenia" in the house of old Osborne who wishes to use his children for monetary gain;[50] Trollope turned to Iphigenia, playfully with Eleanor Harding in *The Warden*, seriously with Emily Lopez's purposeless sacrifice in *The Prime Minister*, to explore conflicts of motive within his heroines; Henry James drew upon residual associations with Iphigenia in *The Portrait of a Lady*, where Isabel Archer rebels against her unidentified urges, her destructive frustrations, and standards of value she considers false—only to submit and conform; but it was George Meredith, with his startlingly modern psychology, who composed upon the Iphigenia theme with greatest sophistication. In *The Egoist* Clara Middleton rapidly becomes aware that it is her fate to be sacrificed by her father and by force of circumstances to Sir Willoughby Patterne. Dr. Middleton, seeing his daughter looking at Sirius, remarks that "it was the star observed by King Agamemnon before the sacrifice in Aulis. You were thinking of that? But, my love, my Iphigenia, you have not a father who will insist on sacrificing you."[51] Alas, she has. Only her determination, coupled with timely aid from the man she does love, enables her to escape becoming a most unwilling Iphigenia. The unusualness of her rebellion against paternal authority, and against the artificial codes of conduct that threaten to envelop her, underlines the sad reality that in Victorian society Iphigenia's behavior was the norm against which women were judged. The implications of Froude's reference to "Aulis," coming where it does in the biography, would have been immediately picked up by alert contemporary readers.

Victorian writers defined the genres—history, epic, poetry, novel, drama—less rigidly than later writers; each genre drew upon others for enrichment. Whereas historians such as Macaulay and Carlyle announced their histories in tones that indicated epic intent, novelists such as Thackeray and Dickens used history to give their novels realistic depth. The Victorian novel benefited from this mixing of genres, and as with the novel, so with biography—at least a biography written by a former (and future) novelist, a sometime poet and fabulist, and a historian who designed his major work, *The History of England from the Fall of Wolsey to the Defeat of the Spanish Armada,* upon epic models. Froude's life of Carlyle is impressive as a work of literary art, not because its author wrote other biographies, but because his wide experience in literature led him to conceive biography as a form of literature related to and drawing upon other forms. Froude understood history (and thus biography) to be a form of drama, he allowed preconceptions absorbed from Greek tragedy to determine the manner in which events are shaped, he let his characters reveal themselves with the skill of a dramatist. When he turned to the figure of Iphigenia in Euripides to seize the essence of Jane Carlyle, he quite naturally thought to endow that characterization with some of the force and elemental power of classical tragedy.

Euripides' vision of life was close to Froude's own, or so Froude believed. The crisis of later Victorian England— social, political, religious, moral—reflected a loss of belief in values, a loss that Euripides had experienced in Athens during the extended trauma of the Peloponnesian War and its sordid aftermath. Froude, by nature a pessimist, regarded himself as a latter day Euripides, interpreting his age and upholding ideals of duty and self-sacrifice in times when, he felt, many valued them little or not at all. Of all the defeated and helpless victims in Euripides, it is Iphigenia whom he viewed as the key to understanding the human dilemma.

"Every act of man which can be called good is an act of sacrifice." So Froude prefaced his discussion of Iphigenia in "Sea Studies." It was "an act which the doer of it would have left undone had he not preferred some other person's benefit to his own." Fundamental to human life, in Froude's view, was "the obligation to sacrifice self."[52] "Sacrifice is the first element of religion,"[53] and, as Froude had written in his unfinished autobiography, "religion meant essentially 'doing our duty.' It was not to be itself an object of thought but a guide to action."⁵⁴ All his life he held to this position. Froude's views on self-sacrifice, though they receive their most elaborate expansion in "Sea Studies," emerge in a number of his other writings. "The essence of true nobility," he wrote in an essay entitled "The Science of History" (1864), "is neglect of self. Let the thought of self pass in, and the beauty of a great action is gone—like the bloom from a soiled flower."⁵⁵ The special distinction of the Greeks, he argued in a *Fraser's* piece, was that they realized "that all that was most excellent in human society was bought by the sacrifice of the few good to the many worthless."⁵⁶ Only if we recognize the pervasiveness of this belief in self-sacrifice in Froude's thought will we grasp why he understood Jane Welsh Carlyle's life as a self-willed tragedy of devotion, a sacrifice not for the "many worthless" but for a man in whose greatness her belief never wavered.

It can hardly surprise us that Froude considered the sacrifice of Iphigenia to be a central event in human history. It and the Old Testament story of Jephthah's daughter, he believed, "prepared the way in the end for the reception of the doctrine of the Christian Atonement,"⁵⁷ for each prefigured the ultimate victim—Christ. Iphigenia's path of devotion to an ideal beyond herself was one that others must follow if they were to develop the noble qualities in their own natures. We need not consider Froude's discussion of Iphigenia in the plays of Euripides, but simply note the chief result of his study: that her selfless sacrifice came to hold immense symbolic import in his thought.

Froude's conception of Iphigenia owes something to Goethe as well as to Euripides; he would have know *Iphigenia auf Tauris* since the 1840s, when he studied Goethe intensely and translated his *Elective Affinities*.⁵⁸ In this play Goethe depicted the ennobling and beautiful potential of woman and the excellence of pure human charity. The ideal of inner spiritual harmony and total abnegation that Iphigenia represented in ancient times incarnated what became a central theme for Goethe and one that he believed needed to be resurrected in the present. In her opening monologue Iphigenia laments: "How circumscribed is woman's happiness! / To be submissive even to a coarse husband / Is her duty and comfort."[59] Yet her sense of her "duty and comfort" enabled her to meet with unflinching determination the ordeal that lay before her, as in Froude's view it enabled Jane Carlyle to meet hers, first in becoming Carlyle's wife, then as a martyr (self-conscious and often complaining, be it admitted) to duty and self-denial.

Until 1880 Froude felt that he could not be truthful about the Carlyles' marriage,[60] but by 27 June of that year he had already written the entire first volume and three-fourths of the second (285). Thus he wrote nearly all of the first half of his biography under a conception of biographical responsibility quite different from that which governed the remainder. As Froude specifically states that he did not go back to the first volume to revise his narrative of the Carlyles' courtship and marriage, it seems reasonable to assume that in the final two volumes his portrayal of their relationship would be more direct and frank—as indeed it is. But in the earlier volumes it was only through suggestion and allusion that he could present what he considered to be the "tragedy" of Jane's marriage to Carlyle.

If Froude's relationship to Carlyle gradually emerges over the course of his narrative, our sense of him in relation to Jane Carlyle remains obscure. He saw her frequently, we must remember, only from the time he moved to London in 1861 until her death five years later, thus during a period of failing health and intense pain. Undoubtedly, his view of her as a long-suffering heroine, a modern Iphigenia, had subconsciously been formed during her lifetime, even if it did not crystallize until he read her correspondence in the 1870s. There he encountered a Jane Carlyle who had been as faithful to her father, John Welsh, as Iphigenia had been to hers, dutiful and obediently loving in life, reverent to his memory after death, and after her own death resting with him in the same tomb. But her devotion to John Welsh is insufficient in itself to explain the pervasive tenderness and sympathy with which Froude viewed her. Jane Carlyle liked to feel herself admired by younger men, and Froude, who genuinely appreciated her abilities, responded warmly to an intelligent woman less than twenty years older who treated him kindly. This attachment, which may be explained in Freudian terms but need not be, helps explain the distortion that crept into his portrayal of her, a distortion that had its roots in his distant past. Froude's childhood had been a Victorian nightmare. As a boy he had suffered from lack of love. His mother had died when he was two, his father was elderly and domineering, his admired but cruel elder brother Hurrell a bully, his school existence one disaster after another. We know little of these formative experiences, less about the love crisis of his young manhood, less still about the effect it had upon his later life. It is amazing that he came out of such an emotionally deprived childhood and adolescence as well adjusted as he was. Jane Carlyle does not impress one as a motherly figure, yet she evidently made Froude welcome at Cheyne Row. That welcome led him, when he came to interweave her life with that of her husband, to take her part in the frequent domestic quarrels he felt compelled to recount and led him also to see her fate within a context provided by the classical heroine he most admired. In important ways, of course, Froude's view of Jane Carlyle is naïve and sentimental. If she was a suffering Iphigenia, she was also an acclaimed hostess known for her brilliant conversation, her even more brilliant letters, looked up to by a circle of admiring friends, male and female. That Carlyle made it possible for her to live an exceptionally rich life Froude does not deny (e.g., 172), but he does not stress it sufficiently. One further reason why he did not remains to be mentioned.

Froude understood the passage in Carlyle's Journal in which he exclaims that no one will ever fathom his life in the light of conversations and correspondence with Geraldine Jewsbury alleging Carlyle's sexual impotence. She told him Carlyle was incapacitated for marriage. "I was not unprepared to hear this," Froude wrote Ruskin in 1886,

> for I had gathered as much from one of his letters. He says also in his Journal that there was a secret about his life unknown to his dearest friends.— Afterwards when Geraldine was in her last illness when she knew that she was dying, and had no more to do with idle gossip, she repeated this and gave me long & really terrible accounts of the life in Cheyne Row. . . . Here was the especial sting of the Lady Ashburton business for companionship was all that he had to give & this was transferred—.[61]

Believing this and yet not able to say so directly, Froude

sought to present his case partly through the device of the Greek chorus, partly through a hero of Oedipean complexity (and one deeply attached to his mother),[62] and partly through use of the Iphigenia myth. Once Jane Carlyle had made her "sacrifice," nothing more could avail. Froude closes his account of her courtship and marriage thus: "I well remember the bright assenting laugh with which she once responded to some words of mine when the propriety was being discussed of relaxing the marriage laws. I had said that the true way to look at marriage was as a discipline of character" (203).[63]

"For history to be written with the complete form of a drama," Froude wrote in "The Science of History,"

> doubtless is impossible; but there are periods, and these the periods, for the most part, of greatest interest to mankind, the history of which may be so written that the actors shall reveal their characters in their own words; where mind can be seen matched against mind, and the great passions of the epoch not simply be described as existing, but be exhibited at their white heat in the souls and hearts possessed by them. There are all the elements of drama—drama of the highest order—where the huge forces of the times are as the Grecian destiny.[64]

He believed, as we have noted, that "the inner nature of the persons of whom [history] speaks is the essential thing about them" (540). Froude had long observed that Carlyle presented his characters as participants in a drama. "Dramatists, novelists have drawn characters with similar vividness," he wrote, "but it is the inimitable distinction of Carlyle to have painted actual persons with as much life in them as novelists have given to their own inventions, to which they might ascribe what traits they pleased" (542). The writing of dramatic history that was also true history posed a challenge to the literary artist.

In examining Froude's life of Carlyle, one should give due weight to its literary and quasi-mythic sources of inspiration. They are the work's strength and simultaneously its weakness. Precisely because Froude was a literary artist he could, like Carlyle himself, take the raw material of the Carlyles' lives and shape it into a literary work. For the same reason he could leave out the countervailing testimony (as he did in writing his histories) in order to throw his thesis into bolder relief. "My own difficulties," he wrote a correspondent about the biography, "have arisen rather from the excess of material than the absence of it."[65] To transform chaos into cosmos, Froude chose from Greek tragedy dramatic models that gave shape and force to the tale he had to tell, but unfortunately curtailed, in some measure, the complex randomness and freedom of experience.

Tragedy, as practiced by the Greeks, is a relatively pure and concentrated form of art. Life's myriad complexity is distilled in it to an irreducible essence. Characters are shaped, situations are presented, to realize a dynamic interaction between character and situation upon which the dramatist focuses intently. In Froude's case his desire to shape his characters rendered them dramatically vivid, but his artistic technique, given that he was dealing not with legends but with real persons, inevitably led to distortion. In Froude we have always to balance the gain in dramatic intensity against the distortion. Thus the concentration and purity of line attained come at the price of heterogeneity. The horizons of the Carlylean world shrink enormously as the sprawling novel of their lives converges into a play by Sophocles or Racine.

It is perhaps unfortunate that to depict the lives of the Carlyles Froude did not choose as his model Shakespearean drama. Its multifaceted understanding of humanity in the form of numerous highly individualized characters would have better captured the heterogeneity of the Carlyles and their circle. And yet adopting Shakespearean drama as a model might have resulted in the biography never being written, since it would have required an extraordinary effort of mind to have recreated the Carlyles, their friends, and their age within manageable proportions. The purer form of Greek tragedy, with its sternness and inexorability, its few strong characters locked together under the aegis of a "Grecian destiny," did restrict Froude in limning his portraits, but it also allowed him to shape those portraits out of the overwhelming mass of materials he was confronted with. If the result is a somber work, one that usually fails to recognize the moments of sunshine in the lives of the Carlyles, it is also a work of stark dramatic power.

Critics have leveled many charges against Froude's achievement. Besides accusing him of misinterpreting the relationship between the Carlyles, they have asserted that he lacked a sense of humor (thus making insufficient allowance for Carlyle's own), that his mood was "too uniformly like that of a man driving a hearse,"[66] that he misunderstood Carlyle's religious position, that he misjudged Carlyle because he was an Englishman and Carlyle a Scot, that he was inaccurate, and that he even went so far as to distort evidence consciously. Although these charges are by and large unfair to Froude, this is not the place for a detailed consideration of them, especially as they have been dealt with, for the most part adequately, in Dunn's *Froude and Carlyle* and in the Sharples dissertation. Dunn, however, omits from consideration one area in which Froude falls down badly and that relates directly to his treatment of the Carlyles—namely, Carlyle's capacity for friendship. He enjoyed a number of close friendships and a wide circle of acquaintances all his life, yet one would hardly guess from Froude's narrative that Carlyle was a social and, often enough, a convivial being. By narrowing his focus to the relationship between the pair, Froude neglects the friendships, the depth and endurance of other personal ties. We miss the humor, Jane's as well as Carlyle's; we miss the avalanche of Carlyle's conversation, the tartness of Jane's as she brings her husband smartly to heel. We are not made as aware as we should be why the Carlyles' home was an intellectual mecca for Victorian England.

In defense of Froude's slighting this side of Carlyle's character, we must remember that he did not meet Carlyle until 1849, when Carlyle was fifty-three, and that he did not get to know him well until 1861, when Carlyle was sixty-five. He thus knew personally and intimately only the older Carlyle, the Sage of Chelsea. For the earlier Carlyle he relied on the mass of correspondence left to him for his use, and above all, it would seem, on the Journal. Doing so kept his narrative close to primary sources but also led to distortions in emphasis. Carlyle had a gift for exaggeration, a capacity in discussing ordinary matters to plumb the depths of pathos, and he frequently indulged himself. Instead of discounting this tendency in Carlyle, Froude interpreted too

26

literally what he read in the correspondence and elsewhere.[67] He also failed to take into account that after Carlyle married Jane Welsh they corresponded only when apart. Their letters indeed show that they could quarrel, but they also show that each had an extraordinarily deep trust and belief in the other. Because the day-to-day harmony that probably was theirs during much of their lives rarely emerges in the correspondence, it consequently does not often find its way into Froude's account. The biography becomes a requiem for a marriage. We rarely sense in Froude's pages that Carlyle had a deep love for his wife and that it was fully reciprocated.

Froude's portraits of the Carlyles came into being not because he was inaccurate, or misrepresented the evidence, or had a jaundiced mind, or bore them deliberate malice, but because he had strong artistic and dramatic instincts. What Harold Nicolson has called the "momentary ardour of his imagination"[68] occasionally overburdened his emphases and unbalanced his sense of proportion. Froude the artist betrayed Froude the biographer. He became trapped by the interpretation he had developed. His dramatic imagination became so enamored of the portrait he was painting that, more or less unconsciously, its traits assumed for him the features of reality. Inevitably, this artistic technique led him to falsify, to a degree, the life of his characters. Although his portraits of the Carlyles still largely retain their validity, the models that inspired them—Oedipus and Iphigenia as well as the other heroes of literature and life—in part predetermine their contours. Yet these same models give his portraits intense psychological life and, in the case of Carlyle as Oedipus and Jane Welsh Carlyle as Iphigenia, a distinct tragic reverberation. The vitality of this life nearly a hundred years after the publication of the biography indicates that Froude's portraits will continue to influence our conception of the Carlyles.

THE VISION OF THE HEROIC

Study of Froude's artistic techniques has shown us how his portraits of the Carlyles came into being, but it has not told us why. What in Froude's own psychology led him to this tragic vision of life? The beginnings of an answer to this

27

question obviously lie deep within his paradoxical, enigmatic nature. In order to explore that nature, we must first
turn to the greatest of all biographies in English—Boswell's
Life of Johnson.

The *Life of Johnson* looms on the horizon of English biography in the nineteenth century like a colossus. Froude was
aware of it as a model—here to be followed, there to be
avoided. On the whole, he maintained his distance. Rarely
does he portray Carlyle, as Boswell does Johnson, through
character-revealing anecdote or conversation. "In representing Carlyle's thoughts on men and things, I have confined myself as much as possible to his own words in his
journals and letters," he wrote in the biography. "To report
correctly the language of conversations, especially when
extended over a wide period, is almost an impossibility. The
listener, in spite of himself, adds something of his own in
colour, form, or substance" (630).[69]

But in one crucial dimension of the biographer's role
Boswell and Froude are alike: they regarded their subjects
from perspectives remarkably similar, since each thought
of himself as recording the deeds of a hero who towered far
above himself and the age. Boswell obviously does not wish
to convey the impression that he stands on a par with Johnson; Froude writes that he looked upon Carlyle "with admiration too complete for pleasant social relationship."[70]
Although he became more intimate with the Sage after the
death of Jane Carlyle, contemporaries noted that even then
he never took issue with his statements or ventured to contradict him. "The relation between Carlyle and Froude was
not what I should describe as friendship," wrote Moncure D.
Conway, who knew both well; "it was too strictly intellectual for that. I have often listened to their conversation, and
in no instance do I remember Froude's grappling with Carlyle even on a small point."[71] If we understand friendship
to imply a relationship in which each partner rests on approximately equal footing with the other, neither Boswell
nor Froude achieved this kind of friendship with his subject.
In all fairness, perhaps neither wished to. What then, we
ask, was the relationship each developed?

A *roseau pensant* vibrating in the winds of religious controversy that swept through Oxford in the early 1840s,
Froude seized upon Carlyle's doctrines—in particular, his

belief in the need for dominating heroes[72]—and with them remade his life. Carlyle became for him a fixed point in the whirl of flux, the star in the firmament by which he could guide himself through the shoals of doubt and despair. In an era when nearly everyone sought heroes, Froude was one of the fortunate few who had the satisfaction of seeing his ideal realized in life.[73] "I had, however, from the time when I became acquainted with his writings," he wrote of Carlyle in the biography, "looked on him as my own guide and master—so absolutely that I could have said: *'errare malo cum Platone . . . quam cum istis vera sentire'* " (532).[74] Froude was fond of repeating to himself a line adapted from Goethe: *"Mit deinem Meister zu irren ist dein Gewinn"* (ibid.).[75] His fidelity was total and, once established, never broken. Boswell, too, clung in Johnson to an ideal hero. "I looked at him," he wrote unabashedly in the *Tour to the Hebrides*, "as a man whose head is turning at sea looks at a rock or any fixed object."[76] Boswell chose Johnson, as Donald A. Stauffer has insisted, "because Johnson was a part of himself, the ideal part."[77] For this same reason Froude chose Carlyle. For each biographer his hero was his "rock," ultimately his savior.

William C. Dowling, in a recent study of the Boswellian hero, has pointed out the significance of the hero within Boswell's personal life and creative vision.[78] Although Froude does not figure in the study, Dowling's analysis of Boswell's conception of the hero applies largely to Froude's conception of Carlyle. Dowling considers, as well as the life, the *Tour to Corsica* and the *Tour to the Hebrides*. These earlier works "are usually classified as travel books," he observes,

> but both are really books about heroes, men who represent what Carlyle called "superior natures," and whose moral nature Boswell found a matter of considerable fascination. When the three narratives are taken together, a striking conclusion begins to emerge: behind Boswell's portrayal of Paoli and his two portrayals of Johnson there lies a single conception of heroic character, one which reaches beyond the particular narrative situation to a final vision of man's dilemma in the modern world.[79]

"Boswell's great subject," in Dowling's view, "is the hero in an unheroic world."

In developing a complicated appeal to the conventions of heroic literature and to a certain myth of the heroic past, each of his narratives also dramatizes the character of an age which has placed men like Johnson and Paoli in spiritual isolation. . . . The hero in a world where heroism is possible exists within a community of shared belief, for his personality and his actions always give expression to certain values which, taken together, sustain the society from which he has emerged. His role is thus ultimately symbolic. . . . When a society feels itself to be disintegrating, there is thus a nostalgia for heroes which is also a nostalgia for the community of shared belief.[80]

Johnson towers above his contemporaries as he towers above his age, "but not until the *Life*, where the disparity between hero and society is so radical as to become a metaphor of spiritual isolation, do its tragic implications emerge."[81] "Yet the *Life* also gives us a hero who, in his moral and intellectual nature, is superior to such a world."[82] In incident after incident,

we perceive his resemblance to the noble protagonists of epic and tragedy. . . . The *Life* is partly the story of Johnson's heroic resistance to these individual forces of moral anarchy, of course, but its larger theme concerns the cost of such resistance to mind and soul. . . . The affinity of the *Life* with formal tragedy lies in the story of Johnson's personal struggle and the concept of spiritual isolation which lies behind it. . . . From the beginning, Boswell's conception of the hero contained a potential for tragedy, but only in the *Life* does he emerge as a genuinely tragic figure.[83]

Carlyle, in Froude's narrative, also emerges as a genuinely tragic figure. In writing the life Froude called upon his greatest strength as a historian—his sense of the tragic. Believing that the Carlyles' life together was one of unutterable sadness, he wrote a history of it that is at its deepest level a tragedy and that moves us by its tragic power. Its author consciously intends his narrative to carry the symbolic truth and resonance of tragedy. Thus when Froude claims that history appeals to the "higher emotion,"[84] he means, in effect, the tragic emotions. Goethe and the German Romantics perceived that the Gothic cathedrals, like the works of nature, possessed "inner form," a form evolved from within, not imposed from without. A biography in outward appearance, Froude's life of Carlyle is, in its "inner form," a tragedy. Carlyle's existence, in Froude's view, "was as noble as his writings and may well stand as an example of integrity & simplicity to all English men of letters[.] We sorely need an example of this kind for our profession tends to vanity and is not a wholesome one."[85] He meant his readers to feel the emotions of pity and fear, to value his presentation of Carlyle as a moral exemplum, and to close his book with a vision of the heroic life for their own troubled times.

"In the epic," Dowling argues, "because it is the earliest literary form, we see the relationship between the hero and society as a paradigm of unified concern. . . . Tragedy, on the other hand, is usually about the breakdown of this relationship."[86] Given Froude's tragic sense of life and his pessimism regarding the future of English society, tragedy was the inevitable form in which to record both the destiny of Carlyle and the decline of that society. Earlier in his career he had written a work that he justly intended his readers to regard as an epic—the twelve-volume *History of England from the Fall of Wolsey to the Defeat of the Spanish Armada*. It chronicles the birth of a young, vigorous England. But even before he published his first volumes in 1856 he knew that "this once noble England," as he spoke of it in an early essay, existed no longer.[87] If epic was appropriate for a new state in its struggles to achieve greatness, tragedy was appropriate to record the decline of that state. In his two greatest works, Froude hymned its rise and its fall. Yet he believed, as Carlyle did, in the eventual phoenix-like rebirth of England at some indefinite time in the future. Carlyle's prophetic vision would again guide Englishmen, and through his biography Froude meant future generations to partake of that vision. In no contemporary biographies, he had said as early as 1850, did he find that "the ideal tendencies of this age can be discerned in their true form; not one, or hardly any one, which we could place in a young man's hands, with such warm confidence as would let us say of it—'Read that; there is a man—such a man as you ought to be.' "[88] Thirty years later Froude thought he was writing such a life.

Dowling speaks of "an internal dramatic principle" at work in the *Life of Johnson* that results from the conflict between the hero and the age. "This principle of tension" becomes "in Boswell . . . a highly serious metaphor for the moral isolation of an actual great man."[89] The hero exists in an antipathetic world, and he resists as best he can the influence of that world. Boswell thinks of his *Life* in terms of Homeric epic and invokes Plutarch as his model; Froude compares Carlyle to great figures of the past—Isaiah and Jeremiah, Dante and Faust—and introduces the controlling model of Greek tragedy. Each biographer evokes a sense of his hero under siege by the proponents of his own age.

Samuel Johnson, needing a core of stability in a changing world, resolutely held fast to Christian orthodoxy in spite of nagging doubts. "His elevated wish for more and more evidence for spirit," as Boswell writes, "in opposition to the groveling belief of materialism" becomes a pervasive theme in his *Life of Johnson*.[90] It takes many forms: his denunciations of Hume, Adam Smith, and Gibbon; his bursting forth, " 'Subordination is sadly broken down in this age' ";[91] his lament that his age had "so little truth";[92] and finally, his desperate cry, "I have lived to see things all as bad as they can be."[93]

One of the strengths of Froude's life of Carlyle, as of Boswell's life of Johnson, lies in the depiction of the movement of the hero's life *against* the times. Froude develops an internal tension similar to Boswell's as he portrays Carlyle in conflict with contemporary mores. The young Carlyle is set apart from his family to receive a university education; he revolts against their wish that he become a minister; he is repelled by university life and the materialistic society he finds in Edinburgh; he confronts the literary lions of London in 1824 only to heap scorn upon them; he visits Paris the same year only to excoriate French society; he cannot find an audience for his early essays or for *Sartor Resartus*; he resists the Whiggism of Jeffrey and the utilitarianism of Mill; he determines to express his own thoughts in his own way, indifferent that many find his style rebarbative; he takes upon himself the mantle of a prophet seemingly careless if few heed him. In his long life he remains resolutely himself, steadfast in his beliefs and values as the world swirls by him. "The strongest man can but retard the current partially and for a short hour," Carlyle had written of Johnson,[94] and Froude viewed Carlyle vigorously reacting to an age he found increasingly alien. Like the heroes of old to which he is compared, he drew strength from his combat with its corrupting influences. His tragic nature set him both apart from and against his times.

The Carlyle of Froude's biography becomes one of the last great manifestations of Victorian England's need for hero worship. Addicted as Froude was to pessimism, he found relief from contemplating the present by immersing himself in heroic ages of history. "Far off he seemed though very near at hand," wrote one observer of Froude in the 1880s.[95] It is tempting to speculate that in these moments he relived the past. With his pessimism went a belief in human greatness exemplified by the heroes of old. The deeper the pessimism became, the greater the need to plumb the past for redeeming heroes. We might characterize him as a pragmatic visionary.

Reading the Greek tragedians as a youth probably gave support to a tragic sense of life that may have been born with the man. By the 1840s a miserable adolescence and a disastrous experience in love had reinforced this perspective. Oxford deepened his pessimism. The controversial *Nemesis of Faith* he intended as a tragedy.[96] In letters Froude bewails the chaos and confusion around him. To Clough in 1852 he speaks of "these unheroic times."[97] Two years later he expresses to Max Müller his fatalism and his belief in self-abnegation:

> I do not share your feeling that suffering is proportional always to what we deserve. There is a use of suffering beyond the punishing our faults. I never knew of a really noble minded person from "the man of sorrows" down to Shakespear & Luther who had not a sad heart[.] It is good to desire happiness for ourselves but it is better to put off *ourselves* altogether, to accept what God sends & use it as best we can. . . . The *second best men* He does seem to me to make happy here. The best of all pass again into "the Shadow of death" even because they are the best.[98]

Froude had a "sad heart" himself, and he valued Carlyle for his. Suffering became a good in itself. We discern here the germ of his thinking about Iphigenia, in which she and her fate become a model for the best of suffering mankind to emulate. These are, to be sure, remarkably somber thoughts for a man still young. "Alas I am past forty," he wrote to Clough in 1858, "—and the best part of such years as may remain will have to pass not in pleasant imaginations but in the treadmill of mere work.— What is the good of it when it is done— The doing it is an enjoyment of a kind certainly because I take an interest in the thing."[99]

During the years Froude toiled over his biography of Carlyle the shadows grew deeper still. By the early 1880s "the disintegration of opinion" had become "so rapid that wise men and foolish are equally ignorant where the close of this waning century will find us."[100] Hostile attacks in the press, the possibility of a lawsuit with Alexander and Mary Carlyle, the deaths of several slightly older contemporaries, his awareness, above all, of the gradual collapse of the mid-Victorian ethos—all tended to increase his dejection. "Rule and precedent have no longer an existence," he wrote to Tupper two weeks before Carlyle died, "and the Church like all is dissolving into Chaos."[101] Carlyle's death affected him greatly. "You will understand me I am sure," he wrote William Smith the day after Carlyle died, "when I tell you that I cannot drive out for some little time— Carlyle has been to me for 30 years past a father buttress friend teacher—everything. . . . Of course I knew what was coming, but now when it has come the weight of what I have lost makes itself felt as what it really is."[102] The biography became, as we know, his *In Memoriam*. Several months later, to Milnes, he laments the death of another of those who had wrestled with problems of faith and doubt: "Alas for Stanley! Abiit ad plures [thus go they all]— The other place is rapidly absorbing all those whom we knew & valued most. . . . The next generation may be as good, (better for all that I know) but I cannot fit myself into the ways of theirs.— Carlyle Spedding Stanley, all within a few months gone— C. had a vague hope that there might be a something beyond. Spedding distinctly none. Stanley I cannot say."[103] Carlyle, too, had often met the world in a hostile and despairing mood, especially after the failure of the 1848 revolutions. By the 1860s when Froude came to know him well he had settled into a weary sadness. With Froude, less buoyant by nature, the hostility and despair appeared earlier, and the gloom, once there, rarely lifted.

If Froude wrote his biography of Carlyle for a later generation, he also had in mind the one then alive. Carlyle's message might not find vindication for a hundred years, but his contemporaries needed some reassurance to relieve the despair Froude believed they felt before the course of events. Many years as editor of *Fraser's*, many more as a professional man of letters writing for the periodical press, had taught Froude the importance of keeping before his readers' eyes present-day issues. He studs his narrative of the Carlyles with references to the burning religious and political questions of the day, to the perpetual problem of Ireland, to the rise (and virtues) of modern Germany, to the activities of such veterans as Gladstone and W. E. Forster. The times were unsettled, were indeed getting worse, and to those as pessimistic as he was about them, Froude held up Carlyle as a model of integrity and heroism. Here, at least, was a man who had not compromised himself with the age.

Froude is not alone of his generation in voicing disillusionment. Others at this time felt troubled by the present and feared what the future might bring. To take examples almost at random, Trollope thought he lived "in an age that was then surrendering itself to quick perdition" and shuddered before "the horrors of the present day";[104] Max Müller, in the year of Carlyle's death, found it "difficult to have patience with this life" and felt "more and more solitary—frightened almost when I see how I stand alone in my opinions and judgments";[105] and James Bryce a few years later drew ominous parallels between the British Empire and the Empire of the Augustan settlement.[106] The life of Carlyle was only part of a larger concern that Froude felt for his own society, particularly for its religious and political health, that found expression in other writings. As he toiled over Carlyle's biography, he turned also to write short lives of Bunyan and Luther (1880, 1883), viewing them as religious heroes standing, as Carlyle stood, above the decay and licentiousness of their times. A few years earlier he had turned to Caesar, whose biography he published in 1879; like his life of Carlyle, it too was intended in part as a tract for the times, for Froude explored in it the great man theme in the political sphere and held up to the present generation the possibility of enlightened Caesarism. A letter Froude sent to Lord Lytton at this time indicates the despairing mood in which he contemplated England's future:

> I used to think that some "Caesar" might arise out of it all— But a Caesar is possible only after a civil war, and the materials dont exist for a civil war[.] The aggressive power of Democracy is infinitely less strong now than it was 50 years ago. But the resisting power has diminished even more in proportion. What we are now witnessing is the universal precipitation of atoms which have lost all coherence.—[107]

When he realized that political reform would not occur, Froude turned to religious heroes. During the time he wrote the biography of Carlyle his need to find comfort in the past must have been especially great. All his writings of this period reveal intense concern, indeed involvement, with the condition of England. He was one of many who believed that Victorian society, outwardly healthy and prosperous, carried within itself the seeds of corruption and decline. And the process of decay, long begun, was irreversible.

Coupled with Froude's melancholy, with his desperate unease before the political and religious situation, was his belief that soon he would die. To Mark Pattison he wrote in 1857, "Next year I shall be perhaps two months at work in the Bodleian—if I am alive next year."[108] In his last decades Froude viewed himself as one constantly near death. Every work he undertook in the 1880s and 1890s he thought would be his last. He would rouse himself to one final heroic effort and then die. But, amazingly, he lived on, and hardly a year went by without an announcement in the press of a new work by him. When the first two volumes of his biography of Carlyle appeared he was in his mid-sixties. In letters he spoke of his desperate efforts to complete the work, and true to form he assumed it would be his last (82).[109] But it, too, among other writing and editorial obligations, he completed—nineteen-hundred pages published within four years of Carlyle's death. Nor did Froude's belief in his approaching end prevent him from leading an exceptionally full and vigorous life until the age of seventy-six and from producing a body of work any Victorian might envy. Lord Carnarvon described in 1878 the strange blend of exhaustion and energy that characterized Froude: "at times . . . he betrays an almost weariness of life: but at other times he is extraordinarily fresh and elastic."[110] In fairness to Froude we must recognize that in the early 1880s he worked under great pressures and that at this time he may have had more reason than usual to suppose that he had not long to live.

What Carlyle meant to him we perceive in a remarkable letter Froude wrote him on 10 July 1874, six weeks before he set out on a diplomatic mission for Lord Carnarvon to South Africa. He did not know whether he would return or, if he did, whether Carlyle would still be alive. I quote this letter virtually in its entirety, for in no other place does Froude express to Carlyle himself so clearly what he owed to him.

> The risks of life increase in a long journey like that which I have before me.— I should like to hear something of your plans that I may see you before I go.— You must give me directions about the sacred letters & Papers which you have trusted to my charge.— Whether you wish them to be returned to your custody during my absence—or whether they shall be locked up in a sealed parcel in Onslow Gardens [Froude's London residence], with instructions in case I never come back to be placed in such hands as you shall desire.
>
> If God so orders it, I will fulfil the trust which you have committed to me with such powers as I have.— No greater evidence of confidence was ever given by one man to another.— And in receiving it from *you* I am receiving it from one to whom no words of mine will ever convey the obligation which I feel—from one too whose writings I am certain have yet to do their work and form a new starting point for the spiritual hopes of mankind. To me, you & you only have appeared to see your way in the labyrinth of modern confusion— You have made it possible for me still to believe in truth & righteousness and the spiritual significance of life while creeds & systems have been falling to pieces.— As more & more our inherited formulas are seen to be incredible, so more & more the English speaking world will turn to you for light.— Centuries hence perhaps the meaning of your presence here will only be fully recognized. My own Self, whatever it be worth, was falling to wreck when I first came to know you. Since that time in whatever I have done or written I have endeavoured to keep you before my eyes—and at each step I have asked myself whether it was such as you would approve.— What you have been to me you have been to thousands of others[.] Now when I am about to part with you on this long & uncertain journey I feel compelled to tell you in

words what hitherto however imperfectly & unworthily I have tried
to shew you silently.— The journey itself is virtually yours. It is
only an attempt to give form to ideas which I have so often heard
you express.— . . . The thought of you will still be with me wherever I go to encourage guide & govern me.[111]

Before he left England Froude did spend time with Carlyle, and presumably the two men settled matters to their
mutual satisfaction.

Froude revered Tennyson almost as much as he did Carlyle. His correspondence with the laureate casts a revelatory light on both his belief in heroism and his attitude of
reverence toward Carlyle. Adrift at Oxford as a young
man, Froude had responded to their counsel on the great
religious and ethical questions. They understood that the
grounds of belief were uncertain, yet insisted upon the
need to find truth in what was left, to believe in it, and to
live by it. "Tennyson became the voice of this feeling in
poetry; Carlyle in what was called prose, though prose it
was not, but something by itself, with a form and melody
of its own," he wrote in the biography (418). For him
as for many others, Disraeli among them, Tennyson and
Carlyle were the two polestars of the literary world in the
nineteenth century. A letter to Hallam Tennyson of 7
June 1880 reveals Froude's dual vision of the hero:

Your father has two existences.— Spiritually he lives in all our
minds (in mine he has lived for nearly forty years)—in forms imperishable as diamonds which time & change have no powers
over. . . . Centuries will pass before we have another fullgrown
Poet. The seeds of them I suppose are sown and grow for a bit and
the reviews clap their hands. But they come to nothing. The moral
atmosphere is pestilential. The force which there is in the world is
all destruction and disintegration and heaven knows where any
organizing life will show itself again[.][112]

Tennyson was the last of Froude's heroes to die. He had
emerged as a great poet only because, as Froude told Hallam after his father's death, "he was born at the fit time
before the world had grown inflated with the vanity of
Progress, and there was still an atmosphere in which such
a soul could grow. There will be no such others," he concluded, "for many a long age."[113]

Carlyle also lived on two levels for Froude. On one, he
was the petty domestic tyrant, irritable and self-centered,

and this side of Carlyle Froude in all honesty felt obliged to reveal. On the other, he was an ideal whose existence was clothed "in forms imperishable as diamonds which time & change have no powers over." This was the Carlyle who awed his contemporaries by his powers of mind and who guided them by his prophetic vision. No one was like him, no one would come to replace him. The world would not again see a figure of his stature. With the loss of its great men, a civilization corrupt and heedless of its prophets would inevitably sink into chaos. But during Froude's lifetime, Tennyson as well as Carlyle had fueled his sense of human greatness and given credibility to his vision of the heroic.

STYLE

Froude is such a master of sustained exposition that it is difficult to put his biography down in one of its narrative stretches. Much of its effect, its hold upon the reader, lies in its style. Froude writes clearly, simply, usually with elegance, often with power, nearly always with irony. He conveys a relentless momentum to his narrative, a sense of event succeeding event, of time moving rapidly, and he does so as much through style as through his choice of incident or his depiction of character. In any consideration of the biography, we must ask, how did Froude create so compelling a narrative?

The "first aim" of style, Froude wrote in 1886, "should be to be simple and forcible."[114] Once he asserted that he had "never thought about style at any time in my life"; on another occasion he said that he rewrote everything once or twice over.[115] That the two statements do not necessarily contradict each other is suggested by the following observation. When asked in 1890 how to develop a good style, Froude advised: "If you sincerely desire to write nothing but what you really know or think, and to say that as clearly and as briefly as you can, style will come as a matter of course."[116] Not to be dull entailed writing with the conviction that one spoke the truth. What is needed is a natural fusion of thought and language; once the author has mastered his subject and disciplined his mode of expression, style emerges inevitably.

39

"Ornament for ornament's sake is always to be avoided," Froude insisted. "There is a rhythm in prose as well as in verse, but you must trust your ear for that."[117] Ornamentation in his own prose made him uneasy. A fantasy he published in *Fraser's* in 1879 entitled "A Siding at a Railway Station" suggests that, at least on occasion, Froude viewed his own style with nervous humility. He imagines his writings before the bar of ultimate judgment. "Pale and illegible became the fine-sounding paragraphs on which I had secretly prided myself. A few passages, however, survived here and there at long intervals. They were those on which I had laboured least and had almost forgotten."[118] Yet one who wrote as well as Froude did must have taken considerable pains with his style, pains of such compass that, as Meredith once said of Carlyle, "every word of a sentence should fall on the ear with the emphasis it carried in his mind."[119] By yoking directness of expression to simplicity of language, Froude developed a forceful style. The clarity of utterance characteristic of this style could only have come about, as Dunn observes, from an intense effort to express his thoughts in the plainest terms.[120]

But we cannot account for Froude's best passages by a policy of their being merely "simple and forcible." That is only the first aim of style. Not only is Froude a master of disciplined precision, but he is also a prose poet of impressive scope who orchestrates a whole range of tones through words. If the basic ground tone is the held trumpet of Carlyle's tragic character and Froude's melancholy awareness of it, other tones enter to provide contrast and relief. During Froude's formative years there prevailed what George Saintsbury calls the "standard style," exemplified, for example, by Southey, the style commonly utilized during the eighteenth and early nineteenth centuries.[121] Froude learned to master it early. Saintsbury also intimates that Ruskin's prose, which so influenced Charles Kingsley, left some trace upon Froude.[122] Although the first volumes of *Modern Painters* date from 1843 and the first passages of prose poetry in Froude date from his 1845 essay on Saint Neot, a more musical prose had already entered upon the scene at this time—one could cite De Quincey's experiments, for instance, which went back several decades. In my view, when Froude's prose achieves effects of rhythm and harmony comparable to Ruskin's or De Quincey's it is not because he imitates either but because he draws upon his own formidable natural gift for language.

Nor did he fall under the spell of Carlyle's style. "No great thing was ever, or will ever be done with ease, but with difficulty," Carlyle had written in "Sir Walter Scott"; the writer must meditate upon his subject, must let his thoughts mature with great care, and then write them out "rapidly at fit intervals, being ready to do it."[123] Froude observed this precept of Carlyle's but Carlyle's influence on his style probably did not extend much further. No two styles could be outwardly more unlike. Although Froude recognized that Carlyle's poetic prose had "a form and melody of its own" (418), by and large he shied away from imitating it, wisely if we judge by the performances of others who attempted Carlylese.[124]

Critics have invariably noted the affinities of Froude's style to the writings of his contempories at Oxford and, in particular, to those of John Henry Newman. Here attempts to trace a connection are more legitimate. Newman was, by Froude's own admission, one of the major influences upon his intellectual development. Reflecting upon the spell cast by Newman several decades after they had both left Oxford, Froude remembered him as "lightness itself—the lightness of elastic strength—and he was interesting because he never talked for talking's sake, but because he had something real to say."[125] Newman wrote the way he talked—and so did Froude. Herbert Paul, himself an Oxonian of a later generation, took up Froude's words in arguing that Newman and the Oriel Common Room together had given Froude's prose its particular characteristics.

There is the same ease, the same grace, the same lightness of elastic strength. Froude, like Newman, can pass from racy, colloquial vernacular, the talk of educated men who understand each other, to heights of genuine eloquence, where the resources of our grand old English tongue are drawn out to the full. His vocabulary was large and various. He was familiar with every device of rhetoric. He could play with every pipe in the language, and sound what stop he pleased. Oxford men used to talk very much in those days, and have talked more or less ever since, about the Oriel style.[126]

The "elastic strength" of this style drew upon the intangibles of Oxford, its centuries of tradition, its intellectual companionships, its classical and humanistic emphasis, its high valuation of the art of intelligent discourse. Such an education, followed by decades of writing for leading Victorian periodicals, had taught Froude how to write for a cultivated audience.

Both individual sentences and paragraphs demonstrate what Froude calls "rhythm in prose." This stylistic rhythm complements and occasionally overshadows his substance. Although Froude concentrates on shorter clauses and phrases, he varies his sentence structure by using many syntactical forms. But in one he may have no equal: the short sentence, or rather the sequence of short sentences. The subject-verb-object pattern is the basic unit, often disguised with additions so that it does not tire the reader by repetition. Nor does it have the jerky monotony often characteristic of this style. If a sequence of short sentences does not have internal variation. Froude will deliberately break the pattern in the last sentence. He utilizes short sentences most commonly to synthesize material. Late in 1824 Carlyle stood at the crossroads of his career:

> He had now seen London. He had seen Birmingham with its busy industries. He had seen Paris. He had been brought into contact with English intellectual life. He had conversed and measured strength with some of the leading men of letters of the day. He knew that he had talents which entitled him to a place among the best of them. But he was sick in body, and mentally he was a strange combination of pride and self-depreciation. (162)

Six short sentences vividly build up Carlyle's diversified experience; the seventh, veering in another direction, undercuts the momentum achieved—and lets the reader ponder the tension between the outward life and the inner man. George Washburn Smalley has well described the effect that Froude's paratactic sentences achieve: "Read Mr. Froude, or listen to him, and the result is the same; you perceive that he so employs the short sentence as to produce the sustained effect which the long one aims at—the easy movement, the unbroken flow, the rhythm, the never-failing charm. Alone he possesses it."[127]

Short sentences also quickly supply background information, recalling facts from Carlyle's past to explain the present. Often Froude mixes syntactical patterns skillfully to achieve a climax in which concentration of thought emerges in short, aphoristic sentences capped (as so often) by a colorful concluding metaphor. *Cromwell* had just appeared:

> He had drawn his breath when he ended his work in September. He had felt idyllic. He and his poor wife had climbed the hill together by a thorny road. He had arrived at the height of his fame. He was admired, praised, and honoured by all England and America; nothing, he said, could now be more natural than that they should sit still and look round them a little in quiet. Quiet, unhappily, was the one thing impossible. He admired quiet as he admired silence, only theoretically. Work was life to him. Idleness was torture. The cushion on which he tried to sit still was set with spines. (444)

If Froude appears more conscious of balance and rhythm than of vocabulary and imagery, still metaphors abound in his prose. Occasionally—as in the above—the metaphor may give the reader, as the "spines" did Carlyle, a mild start. Cactus imagery seems especially favored. Froude thus depicts the trying conditions under which Carlyle prepared his lectures on heroes: "Among such elements as these grew the magnificent addresses on great men and their import in this world. Fine flowers will grow where the thorns are sharpest; and the cactus does not lose its prickles, though planted in the kindliest soil" (389).

Even Froude's complex sentences retain the basic subject-verb-object pattern; these he often links skillfully by the connective "and." By giving prominence to "and," Froude's prose can produce almost infinite further differences of rhythmical effect. In 1848, when revolution threatened in England, Froude describes the situation thus: "The spring wore on, and the early summer came, and all eyes were watching, sometimes France and sometimes Ireland" (470). The repetition of "and" suggests the passing of time, that of "sometimes" keeps the synecdochic "eyes" moving from one country to another. The paratactic pattern is maintained, but has become hardly recognizable. When in 1853 a neighbor's cocks joined other annoyances to wreak havoc on Carlyle's nervous system, Froude notes laconically:

"The cocks were locked up next door, and the fireworks at Cremorne were silent, and the rain fell and cooled the July air; and Carlyle slept, and the universe became once more tolerable" (519). Here the sequence of "and" establishes an ironic effect as Carlyle's nerves are slyly equated with the state of the universe. A little later, after a recurrence of the cocks, we read, "Morning after morning the horrid clarions blew" (ibid.). Here the rhythm of the prose moves toward the overtly metrical as three iambs follow three trochees.

Froude's control of style extends from the sentence to the paragraph. Often constructed upon an intricate pattern of syntactical units and always designed with care, Froude's paragraphs demonstrate the economy with which he composed his narrative. He knew how to reveal character through anecdote: "Monckton Milnes had made his acquaintance, and invited him to breakfast. He [Carlyle] used to say that, if Christ was again on earth, Milnes would ask Him to breakfast, and the Clubs would all be talking of the 'good things' that Christ had said" (376). The paragraph's next and final sentence qualifies this impression of Milnes's conviviality. "But Milnes, then as always, had open eyes for genius, and reverence for it truer and deeper than most of his contemporaries." Here Froude's sense of "rhythm in prose," by focusing first on Milnes's surface charm, suggests multiple dimension in character by insisting upon inner worth. The paragraph, only three sentences long, holds together as a believable cameo of Milnes's personality. It hints, moreover, at the essential qualities of his relationship with Carlyle.

There remains the larger canvas made up of hundreds of paragraphs working cumulatively upon the reader. Froude prepares his audience to contemplate the main themes of his narrative by adumbrating them in passages whose importance can only be discerned in retrospect. Consider the biography's first paragraph:

The River Annan, rising above Moffat in Hartfell, descends from the mountains through a valley gradually widening and spreading out, as the fells are left behind, into the rich and well-cultivated district known as Annandale. Picturesque and broken in the upper part of its course, the stream, when it reaches the level

44

country, steals slowly among meadows and undulating wooded hills, till at the end of forty miles it falls into the Solway at Annan town. Annandale, famous always for its pasturage, suffered especially before the union of the kingdoms from border forays, the effects of which were long to be traced in a certain wildness of disposition in the inhabitants. Dumfriesshire, to which it belongs, was sternly Cameronian. Stories of the persecutions survived in the farmhouses as their most treasured historical traditions. Cameronian congregations lingered till the beginning of the present century, when they merged in other bodies of seceders from the established religion.

The first two sentences trace the river Annan from its source to its termination; the third speaks of the "wildness of disposition" of the inhabitants in this long-contested border region—and prepares us for Froude's reiterated emphasis on the wildness of Carlyle's own character; the fourth introduces us to the religious beliefs of Dumfriesshire that will, in considerable measure, determine the course of Carlyle's life and the mode of his prophetic utterance. In the fifth and sixth we learn of the tradition of dissent and protest into which the young Carlyle—himself raised as a Burgher Seceder—grew and matured. The religious isolation into which Carlyle was born foreshadows both his role as a prophet for his age and the solitude in which he would deliver his message to the world. He will remain incorruptibly true in his hatred of cant and sham and in his insistence upon the eventuality—and necessity —of a better life.

Reading this passage we gain a sense of the passing of time, from the seventeenth to the early nineteenth centuries and, by implication, on to the biographer's own present, three-quarters of a century later, in which he looks upon what has happened with an awareness that such ages of faith have now disappeared forever. As we think of Carlyle entering the world in such a context, we remember that he too perceived man within a similar time perspective, the present being "the conflux of two Eternities . . . made up of currents that issue from the remotest Past, and flow onwards into the remotest Future."[128] Froude's metaphor of the river links space with time: as the river flows from time past through time present into time future, it flows also down from the mountains into the plain, from the larger area of Annandale into the smaller of Dumfries-shire, before it joins the sea. Thus it unites Carlyle's life with the ongoing life of humanity, both the particular humanity present in southwestern Scotland and the larger family of mankind. In six economical sentences, rhythmically and syntactically in delicate balance, Froude not only has introduced us into a physical landscape, but has suggested what we may call the world of Carlyle's being.

A Victorian writing a Victorian life in the decade of Victoria's Golden Jubilee, Froude is also the first modern biographer. In his conception of the biographer's role, he inaugurates a new era. Froude "was the first to introduce into English biography the element of satire," Harold Nicolson affirmed in his 1928 lectures on *The Development of English Biography*. "The peculiar brand of sceptical detachment which we realise to be the main element in twentieth-century biography can first be recognised, although only in germinal form, in Froude's treatment of the Carlyles."[129] By "satire" we should understand Nicolson to mean something very close to "irony"; by "detachment" we should understand, not the distancing of oneself in order to write "objective" biography, but the liberty of the creative artist to speak about his subject freely and from a personal point of view. Froude does indeed write from such an individual perspective, and he maintains it through a pervasive use of irony. His employment of irony on different levels—in vocabulary, in commentary, in depiction of incident, and in dramatic portraiture—suggests the presence of a commanding intelligence that controls style as well as substance. Clearly it is impossible to consider his style without, at some point, dealing with the omnipresent irony.

Nicolson, to instance Froude's ironic stance, cites a passage in the biography from Carlyle's Journal of 7 July 1833. Carlyle was thirty-eight. He and his wife had lived at Craigenputtoch over five years and found themselves increasingly dissatisfied with their existence there. In the Journal Carlyle contemplates his destiny:

> On the whole, however, art thou not among the *vainest* of living men? At bottom, among the very *vainest*. Oh the sorry mad ambitions that lurk in thee! God deliver me from vanity, from self-conceit; the first sin of this universe, and the last—for I think it will *never* leave us? (284)

46

Froude prefaces this passage simply: "One discovery came on him as a startling surprise." He makes no further comment. He does not have to. Irony of style, even in the restricted sense of juxtaposition that Nicolson intends, is indeed a major component of Froude's method.

But Froude's ironic stance pervades his biography even more than Nicolson realized. His understanding of Froude's biographical method was perceptive but incomplete, limited by his own practice and by the climate of biography in the 1920s. Detachment achieved through style is only part of a method whose purpose was to reveal a subject's inner nature. I have already touched upon the ironic manner Froude adopts when he places himself in the role of the Greek chorus that comments at crucial moments upon the fortunes of his hero and heroine (10-11). We have also seen that when Froude endows Carlyle with traits of certain other heroes—for example, with the credulity of Owen Glendower or with the slavish devotion of Don Quixote (11-12)—he interjects a note of unmistakable irony. Neither of these techniques, however, exhausts the possibilities of revealing Carlyle's inner nature.

Froude can use irony either to distance himself from Carlyle or to achieve a perspective on him that differs from Carlyle's own; yet he often does so to bring us—ultimately—closer to his hero. Early in 1836 Carlyle, who was then toiling over *The French Revolution*, had reached a low point in his fortunes. Basil Montagu offered him a clerkship at £200 a year. A proud Carlyle politely, but firmly, refused. To his brother John, however, he gave vent to his indignation. "One other thing I could not but remark: the *faith* of Montagu—wishing me for his Clerk; thinking the Polar Bear, reduced to a state of dyspeptic dejection, might be safely trusted tending rabbits."[130] Froude comments:

> The "Polar Bear," it might have occurred to Carlyle, is a difficult beast to find accommodation for. People do not eagerly open their doors to such an inmate. Basil Montagu, doubtless, was not a wise man, and was unaware of the relative values of himself and the person that he thought of for a clerk. But, after all, situations suited for polar bears are not easily found outside the Zoological Gardens. (347)

By expanding Carlyle's metaphor, Froude underscores the

intractability of Carlyle's nature and his consequent isolation. He soaks his style in irony—so much so that it becomes difficult to isolate it precisely; irony appears in the interjections ("it might have occurred to Carlyle," "doubtless," "after all"), as well as in the narrative sequence of statements. Yet as so often the ironic effect has a purpose. The rest of the paragraph thoughtfully assesses Carlyle's position, concluding: "This small incident shows only how impossible it was at this time to do anything for Carlyle except what was actually done, to leave him to climb the precipices of life by his own unassisted strength" (ibid.). The irony of the first sentences, by preparing us unconsciously for the sobriety of the subsequent analysis, serves to open up a perspective upon Carlyle both understanding and shrewd. As the paragraph proceeds, the distance between Carlyle and his biographer gradually narrows until we find ourselves by its end in complete and unironic sympathy with Carlyle's position.

Elsewhere Froude observes Carlyle with ironic, yet tender, regard. This gentlest of ironies, pervasive yet varying greatly in mode of usage, is almost invisible in passages such as the following, where—significantly—Carlyle cooperates in the effect. The Sage had just returned from Scotland.

> His wife was at the Grange when he reached Cheyne Row. There was no one to receive him but her dog Nero, who after a moment's doubt barked enthusiastic reception, and "the cat" who "sat reflective, without sign of the smallest emotion more or less." He was obliged to Nero, he forgave the cat. He was delighted to be at home again. (499)

Usually irony is so much a part of Froude's presentation that style and substance merge indissolubly, as in the following instance in which the biographer brings to our attention Carlyle's horse Fritz. During the many years Carlyle toiled "in the valley of the shadow" of *Frederick*, he went riding on Fritz most afternoons. Without these rides in Fritz's company, Carlyle hardly knew how he would have written his history. Fritz was "a very clever fellow," he told Froude, and "was much attached to me, and understood my ways" (535). Each time Fritz reappears in the narrative, Froude reminds us of his intellect and devotion (e.g., 537, 572). When he finally becomes too old to support his master with security, we regret his departure as we would that of an old friend. Wit, fused with tenderness, causes Fritz to live in memory.

Somewhat more overt in its intended effect is a passage a few pages after Fritz is first introduced in which Froude plays with Carlyle's language. The Sage relished abstract nouns—the Immensities, the Eternities, and so forth. While staying with his sister Mary in 1858, he wrote in his Journal under 30 June: "The evening walks in the grey howl of the winds, by the loneliest places I can find, are like walks in Hades; yet there is something wholesome in them, something stern & grand: as if one had the Eternities for company in defect of suitabler" (543). Froude coolly observes: "The Eternities, however fond he was of their company, left him time to think of other things." Irony here renders Froude's more common-sense position and serves as an implicit comment on Carlyle's mode of thinking and expression. He may even expect his readers to remember that, if now Carlyle found the Eternities congenial, a moment ago Fritz had been the favored companion. Juxtaposing the two in our minds affords us relief as we follow Carlyle through the wearisome years of *Frederick*.

Only on a very few occasions does Froude's sense of tact fail him. In these moments irony becomes mere cleverness. In one, narrating an excursion by Carlyle into Wales to climb Mt. Snowdon, Froude writes: "They travelled light, for Carlyle took no baggage with him except a razor, a shaving-brush, a shirt, and a pocket-comb; 'tooth-brush' not mentioned, but we may hope forgotten in the inventory" (426). This observation deserves A. Carlyle's marginal notation "How clever!"[131] It *is* clever; it is also uncalled-for.[132] Yet such instances in the biography stand out as rare. That Froude occasionally indulges in a petty aside should not obscure the basic integrity of his presentation.

We return to where we began in our discussion of Froude's art, the need for the biographer to reveal his subject's inner nature. This can be done as well through style as by dramatic portraiture or by sympathetic hero worship. Froude developed a style that appeals as much to the heart as to the head. "Masculine vigour and feminine delicacy," John Skelton wrote of this prose, "blended in the expression of, what may be called, intellectual emotion."[133] "Intellectual emotion" suggests that Froude strove to achieve in his prose the effect of poetry, for the phrase is virtually identical to one he used to describe Shakespeare's impact. "Shakespeare is true to real experience," he wrote in "The Science of History." "The mystery of life he leaves as he finds it; and, in his most tremendous positions, he is addressing rather the intellectual emotions than the understanding."[134] History, of which biography was a part, was not only drama, then, but poetry. To render the great moments in a person's life, the biographer must subsume reality in myth, must transcend the "understanding" in order to present "real experience," must—above all—stir the "intellectual emotions" of his readers. He can best do so, in Froude's view, by writing a poetic prose, musical in its cadences, taut in its controlled power. Saintsbury speaks of this prose "as a perfect harmony of unpretentious music, adjusted to the matter that it conveys, and lingering on the ear that it reaches."[135] In other words, it is the prose of one who has the mind of a poet. Froude had insisted in an early essay on Homer that "the poet is the truest historian." Only the empathetic imagination of the poet can penetrate to the hidden recesses of the past. "Whatever is properly valuable in history," he continues, "the poet gives us— not events and names, but emotion, but action, but life. . . . Great men . . . lie beyond prose, and can only be really represented by the poet."[136]

Emotion, action, life—over these does Froude's prose, marvelously subtle and modulated, play so lovingly. He is himself one of the poets of humanity, nowhere more so than in the biography of Carlyle. In his deepest being as well as in his art, Froude was a Romantic, and, like other Romantics, he appealed to resources other than the intellectual. His style, full of emotional resonance, has a quality that has almost disappeared from modern prose. That quality is eloquence. Froude did not fear to strive for large effects. Occasionally he failed, more often he succeeded. And in the biography's great moments—the courtship of

Jane Welsh, his first meeting with Carlyle, the moving
final pages—he triumphed.

1. Frederic Harrison, *The Choice of Books* (London: Macmillan,
1886), p. 175.

2. Ibid., p. 176.

3. P. 79 of this volume. Hereafter page numbers in parentheses in
the Introduction refer to pages in this edition.

4. Froude's private statements to correspondents about his purpose
in writing the biography accord with his public pronouncements. To
Thomas Wentworth Higginson he wrote: "He was an extraordinary
man—extraordinary in his intellect & peculiar in his character. I should
be false to him and false to my duty if I were to trick him as a painted
idol for the mob to put in their temples like their Christs & Virgins"
(letter of ca. 1881, reproduced in Higginson, *Part of a Man's Life* [Bos-
ton and New York: Houghton, Mifflin, 1905], after p. 56). Compare the
similar comment to Frederic Ouvry: "I honoured and loved him above
all other men that I ever knew or shall know. It is my duty to show him
as he was & no life known to me will bear a Sterner Scrutiny. But he
wished—especially wished—his faults to be known. They are nothing,
amount to nothing, in the great balance of his qualities. But such as they
are they must be described.— Surely by no unfriendly hand" (12 May
1881, cited in K. J. Fielding, "Froude and Carlyle: Some New Considerations," in *Carlyle Past and Present: A Collection of New Essays*,
ed. K. J. Fielding and Rodger L. Tarr [London: Vision Press, 1976],
pp. 255–56).

5. See Dunn, *F and C*, p. 260 ff., and Hector C. Macpherson, *Thomas Carlyle* (Edinburgh and London: Oliphant Anderson & Ferrier,
[1896]), pp. 136–37. The third surviving sister was Jean Carlyle Aitken,
mother of Mary Aitken Carlyle.

6. 13 May 1884. MS: Bodleian Eng. lett. d. 100, fol. 240.

7. Froude to Cowley Powles, 26 September 1885, in Dunn, *Froude*,
2:535.

8. The Froude-Carlyle controversy constitutes one of the more sordid episodes in English literary history. The standard work on it remains Dunn, *F and C*, partisan to Froude but well-informed, well-
documented, and generally accurate. See also Edward Sharples, Jr.,
"Carlyle and His Readers: The Froude Controversy Once Again"
(Ph.D. dissertation, University of Rochester, 1964), less partisan but
tending to confirm Dunn's conclusions; Hyder E. Rollins, "Charles
Eliot Norton and Froude," *Journal of English and Germanic Philology*
57 (October 1958): 651-64; and G. B. Tennyson's balanced overview
in his chapter on Carlyle in *Victorian Prose: A Guide to Research*, ed.
David J. DeLaura (New York: Modern Language Association, 1973).

Recent opinion supports Froude on most disputed points. An exception is the Fielding essay (cited in note 4). I discuss Froude's inaccuracy and touch upon the controversy in the section on editorial procedures.

9. Preface to Lytton Strachey, *Eminent Victorians* (1918; rpt. London: Chatto & Windus, 1926), p. viii.

10. For a discussion of several of these dimensions of the biography, see A. O. J. Cockshut, *Truth to Life: The Art of Biography in the Nineteenth Century* (London: Collins, 1974), chap. 9.

11. Paul, p. 110.

12. 12 November 1889, in Dunn, *Froude*, 2:562.

13. Dated 1890, ibid., p. 569.

14. *Oxford Essays . . . 1855* (London: John W. Parker, [1855]), p. 78. For Froude's skepticism about "facts," see his *Short Studies*, 1:1, 13, 367–68.

15. 10 April [1886], in Viljoen, p. 46.

16. Froude to Frederick Locker, 30 August 1889, in Dunn, *Froude*, 2:562.

17. I. W. Dyer, *A Bibliography of Thomas Carlyle's Writings and Ana* (Portland, Me.: Southworth Press, 1928), p. 347.

18. Introduction to Froude, *Nemesis of Faith*, pp. xiv, xv. Conway's observations have especial value, coming as they do from a man who had read many of Froude's writings and who had known him well.

19. Froude interpreted "the Lady Ashburton business" through an elaborate analogy based on Spenser's *Faerie Queene*. The interrelationships that he drew among Lady Ashburton (Gloriana, Queen of Fairyland), Carlyle (the rustic Red Cross Knight, gallant but occasionally obtuse), and Jane Carlyle (Una, the faithful believer in him) were usually present in Froude's mind even when not pointed to directly in his narrative. Although he did not intend exact correlations, he probably expected his more discerning readers to envision a complex web of indirect associations between. the reality of the interlocking relationships and Spenser's poem and settings. For further discussion of these analogies, see my "Grecian Destiny: Froude's Portraits of the Carlyles," in *Carlyle and His Contemporaries*, pp. 324–31. Iris Origo presents a balanced discussion of "The Carlyles and the Ashburtons" in *A Measure of Love* (London: Jonathan Cape, 1957).

20. P. xiii.

21. *CL*, 3:249.

22. Ibid., p. 258.

23. Ibid., p. 266; 4:112.

24. *My Relations with Carlyle*, p. 22.

25. Use of the Greek chorus is only part of a larger control of narrative through irony, a subject that I take up more fully in the section on style.

26. The entry can only be that of 10 October 1843 or of 29 December 1848. See p. 321 and the accompanying note.

27. *CL*, 7:326.

28. Isaiah on p. 356 and elsewhere; Saint John on Patmos in *CL*, 5:141–42 and elsewhere; Saint Anthony in *CL*, 6:328; "Bedouin" on pp. 202, 302, and 417; and Faust in TC to JWC, 20 August 1839 (NLS, 610.41).

29. Isaiah or Jeremiah on p. 82; Athanasius in W. T. Stead, *The M.P. for Russia: Reminiscences and Correspondence of Madame Olga Novikoff*, 2 vols. (New York and London: Andrew Melrose, 1909), 2:328.

30. Prometheus on p. 561; "knight errant" on p. 278; Owen Glendower in an unpublished manuscript on Carlyle, composed by Froude but in Margaret Froude's hand, cited in chap. 16, n. 4 (MS: Beinecke Library, Yale); Dante on p. 317; for the rest, see below. Although not all of the above analogies occur in the biography itself, those that do are similar to those that do not.

31. Froude to Charles Graves, bishop of Limerick, 22 May [1884]. MS: Duke.

32. J. A. Froude, *Lord Beaconsfield* (London: Sampson, Low, 1890), p. 253; undated letter by Froude to Ewald Flügel in the latter's *Thomas Carlyle's Moral and Religious Development*, trans. J. G. Tyler (New York: M. L. Holbrook, 1891), p. xiii.

33. *My Relations with Carlyle*, p. 18.

34. Ibid., p. 19.

35. Froude to Mrs. Charles Kingsley, [October 1884], in Paul, p. 331. See also p. 318 below.

36. This and subsequent quotations in the paragraph are from *My Relations with Carlyle*, pp. 12, 13.

37. Ibid., p. 13.

38. Entry of 25 February 1887, in Dunn, *Froude*, 2:550.

39. *Short Studies*, 1:327.

40. "Lord Macaulay [a review of Trevelyan's *Life*]," *Fraser's Magazine* 93 (June 1876): 693.

41. H. D. F. Kitto, *Greek Tragedy: A Literary Study* (1939; rpt. Garden City, N.Y.: Doubleday-Anchor, 1954), p. 143.

42. Froude to John Murray [ca. 1880], in George Paston, *At John Murray's: Records of a Literary Circle, 1843–1892* (London: John Murray, 1932), p. 263.

43. Aristotle, *On the Art of Poetry* . . . , trans. S. H. Butcher and ed. Milton C. Nahm (New York: Liberal Arts Press, 1948), pp. 14, 15. I have quoted the passages slightly out of order.

44. Froude to G. J. Holyoake [1882], in Joseph McCabe, *Life and Letters of George Jacob Holyoake*, 2 vols. (London: Watts, 1908), 2:126.

45. *My Relations with Carlyle*, pp. 33-34.

46. Ibid., p. 17.

47. 1 May [1886], in Viljoen, p. 46.

48. *Short Studies*, 3:144-81.

49. In an interesting twist, Dickens has Florence Dombey always ready to sacrifice herself for her father—but the sacrifice is continually rejected by him. In chap. 47 Edith elopes and Mr. Dombey strikes Florence, precipitating her flight from his household. In the plate to this chapter, "Florence & Edith on the Staircase," Dickens underscores the brutality of the father's act by including a statue of Agamemnon, knife in hand, about to strike Iphigenia.

50. W. M. Thackeray, *Vanity Fair*, ed. Geoffrey and Kathleen Tillotson (Boston: Houghton Mifflin, 1963), p. 120. Thackeray depicts on the plate to chap. 13, "Mr Osborne's welcome to Amelia," that part of the chronometer showing Iphigenia about to be sacrificed by Agamemnon.

51. George Meredith, *The Egoist*, ed. Lionel Stevenson (Boston: Houghton Mifflin, 1958), p. 370. See also chap. 10, in which Clara, asked to wear the Patterne family jewels, inquires of Sir Willoughby, "Does one not look like a victim decked for the sacrifice—the garlanded heifer you see on Greek vases . . . ?" She concludes, "I have learnt, that the ideal of conduct for women is to subject their minds to the part of an accompaniment."

52. *Short Studies*, 3:166.

53. Ibid., p. 167.

54. Dunn, *Froude*, 1:20; see also Froude, *Nemesis of Faith*, p. 72.

55. *Short Studies*, 1:15. Similar statements mark Carlyle's writings; for example, in a letter of ca. 1 February 1831 to his sister Jean he states: "Humility is no mean feeling, but the highest, and only high one; the *denial of Self* it is, and therein is the beginning of all that is truly generous and noble" (*CL*, 5:225).

56. *Short Studies*, 3:168.

57. Ibid., p. 169.

58. See David J. DeLaura, "Froude's Anonymous Translation of Goethe," *Papers of the Bibliographical Society of America* 69 (1975): 187-96.

59. "Wie eng-gebunden ist des Weibes Glück! / Schon einem rauhen Gatten zu gehorchen, / Ist Pflicht und Trost."

60. *My Relations with Carlyle*, p. 30, and p. 619 below.

61. 29 November [1886], in Viljoen, pp. 65-66. In several letters of 1889-90 to Mrs. Alexander Ireland, who was working on what became the first separate biography of Jane Carlyle, Froude urged her to speak more candidly than he had spoken: "Mrs Carlyle ought to have been a wife and a mother—she was neither. . . . You leave the impression that

it was only a question of tempers—you may say that I have done the same. I allow it—but I did not seek the task which was laid on me. Had I undertaken to write Mrs Carlyles life myself I must have told the whole truth—or else when I found out how the matter stood, have let it alone. I know you cannot tell in plain words what was amiss—but you might indicate that there was only companionship" (11 October [1890]. MS: Beinecke Library, Yale). In an earlier letter Froude gave what was probably his final judgment: "The marriage was a most unfortunate one—yet I can hardly wish it had never been—as without her, Carlyle would never have been what he was" (20 September [1889]. MS: Beinecke Library, Yale).

62. For discussion of the Oedipean dimensions of Carlyle's relationship to his mother, see chap. 2, n. 3.

63. Any juxtaposition or reconciliation of the myths of Iphigenia and Oedipus in Froude's biography clearly fails. But need they be juxtaposed or reconciled? Froude does not, I think, intend them to be, but uses them rather to suggest dimensions of the Carlyles without implying total, or even dominant, parallelism, just as he uses other figures to suggest elements in their characters as disparate as Don Quixote's idealism and Una's fidelity. No analogy excludes any other. For Froude analogy was an artistic technique by which his readers might better perceive both the complexity and the inherent drama in the lives of his protagonists.

For a different perspective on the Carlyles' marriage, see chap. 8, n. 24.

64. *Short Studies*, 1:23.

65. Froude to G. J. Holyoake [1882], in McCabe, 2:126.

66. David Masson makes both points in *Carlyle Personally and in His Writings* (London: Macmillan, 1885), pp. 18, 17.

67. Ibid., pp. 30–31.

68. Harold Nicolson, *The Development of English Biography* (London: Hogarth Press, 1928), p. 129. A. C. Benson, in *Rambles and Reflections* (New York: G. P. Putnam's Sons, 1926), makes the same point in a different way: "Froude had a strong romantic element in him, and when he had made up his mind about a subject, he saw facts not as they were, but by the light of his own imagination. Froude was wholly incapable of deliberate distortion, but his subconscious mind was too strong for him" (p. 122).

69. After his father's death Hallam Tennyson asked Froude to tell him what he recalled of Carlyle and Tennyson together. Froude's answer suggests further reasons why he recorded so little of Carlyle's talk in the life. "I remember well seeing your father with Carlyle in Cheyne Row," he wrote Hallam,

—but I kept no notes of their conversation. It is long ago and I have experienced so often in myself and others the unconscious tendency to reconstruct scenes of this kind in memory till they lose all likeness to the past that I dare not try.

To attribute words which they did not use to such men as Carlyle and your father is a sin against the Holy Ghost.

Carlyle very often talked to me about your father, and of course you know how he admired and loved him— Even of their conversations however, which are more vividly present to me I should hesitate to write anything. Half the discourse attributed by S*t* John to Christ was probably so modelled by S*t* John's own mind that Christ would hardly have recognized his own speech in him. . . .

The difficulty in reproducing expressions of Carlyle is that he rarely praised any one without an acrid drop intermixed— Leave the drop out and you destroy the character of the words. Put it in, and you have a disagreeable taste. He used to complain of your fathers "indolence" in his own peculiar way. I entirely disagreed with him . . . but I am afraid to trust my memory as to what he said. (2 May 1893 or 1894. MS: Beinecke Library, Yale).

This reply indicates something of Froude's conscientiousness in wishing to present Carlyle's views fairly. His unwillingness to reproduce conversations imperfectly remembered led him to rely excessively on Carlyle's letters and Journal to render Carlyle's personality. Froude was not aware, as scholars now are, that Boswell took down at the time extensive notes and that he based the passages of Johnson's conversation in his *Life of Johnson* on them.

70. *My Relations with Carlyle*, p. 4.

71. Introduction to Froude, *Nemesis of Faith*, p. xiv. Conway expressed a similar opinion in his *Autobiography: Memories and Experiences*, 2 vols. (Boston and New York: Houghton, Mifflin & Co., 1904), 2:213. Yet Carlyle himself, in his last letter to Emerson, recognized the vigor of Froude's conversation: "Froude is coming to you in October. You will find him a most clear, friendly ingenious solid and excellent man. . . . He is the valuablest Friend I now have in England, nearly tho' not quite altogether the one man in talking with whom I can get any real profit or comfort" (2 April 1872, in Slater, *CEC*, p. 589).

72. "Believing mainly as I do in little other Political right than the right of the strongest" (Froude to A. H. Clough, [mid-1840s]. MS: Bodleian Eng. lett. c. 190, fol. 288). Various statements in the biography indicate that Froude came to a more subtle understanding of Carlyle's "might vs. right" concept than he reveals here.

73. For an astute analysis of the widespread hero worship pervading all levels of society, see Walter E. Houghton, *The Victorian Frame of Mind, 1830–1870* (New Haven: Yale University Press, 1957), chap. 12.

74. "I would rather be wrong with Plato than right with such men as these" (Cicero *Tusculan Disputations* 1. 17. 39). "Such men as these" were the Pythagoreans.

75. "To err with your Master is your reward," adapted from Goethe's "Sprichwörtlich," ca. 1810–12: "Willst du dir aber das Beste tun, /

So bleib nicht auf dir selber ruhn, / Sondern folg eines Meisters Sinn; / Mit ihm zu irren ist dir Gewinn."

76. James Boswell, *Journal of a Tour to the Hebrides with Samuel Johnson, LL.D., 1773*, ed. Frederick A. Pottle and Charles H. Bennett (New York: McGraw-Hill, 1961), p. 118.

77. Donald A. Stauffer, *The Art of Biography in Eighteenth Century England* (Princeton: Princeton University Press, 1941), p. 411.

78. William C. Dowling, "The Boswellian Hero," *Studies in Scottish Literature* 10 (October 1972): 79–93. The quotations I give from Dowling's fine article inevitably simplify a complex, interwoven argument.

79. Ibid., p., 80.

80. Ibid., pp. 80, 80–81, 82, 84.

81. Ibid., p. 87.

82. Ibid., p. 90.

83. Ibid., pp. 90, 91, 92.

84. In "The Science of History," *Short Studies*, 1:24.

85. Froude to Martin F. Tupper, 3 December [1882]. MS: University of Illinois. Letter quoted in part in Derek Hudson, *Martin Tupper: His Rise and Fall* (London: Constable, 1949), pp. 308–9. Froude in these comments harks back to the old Plutarchian ideal in biography, which taught suppression of uncomfortable and too revealing facts about the subject in order to set an "example of integrity & simplicity" before the eyes of readers. In actual practice Froude suppressed very little. See also *Short Studies*, 1:374.

86. Dowling, p. 81.

87. In "Suggestions on the best Means of teaching English History," *Oxford Essays . . . 1855*, p. 66.

88. "Representative Men," in *Short Studies*, 1:389.

89. Dowling, p. 85.

90. Boswell, *Life of Johnson*, p. 462.

91. Ibid., p. 924.

92. Ibid., p. 948.

93. Ibid., p. 1201 (but see Johnson's qualification of this view on p. 1288).

94. *Works*, 28:122.

95. Theocritus, speaking of Hylas, in *Idylls* 13. 1. 60, cited in John Churton Collins's account of an interview with Froude in L. C. Collins, *Life and Memoirs of John Churton Collins* (London and New York: John Lane, 1912), p. 89. I have quoted the translation in Dunn, *Froude*, 2:545.

96. Preface to the second edition. The two tales in *Shadows of the Clouds* (1847) also end tragically.

97. 16 May [1852]. MS: Bodleian Eng. lett. d. 177, fol. 61. Pub-

lished in *The Correspondence of Arthur Hugh Clough*, ed. Frederick L. Mulhauser, 2 vols. (Oxford: Clarendon, 1957), 1:311–12.

98. 13 February [1854]. MS: Bodleian Dep. d. 170, fols. 73v and 74r. The ellipsis points are Froude's.

99. 2 May [1858]. MS: Bodleian Eng. lett. e. 74, fol. 33. This attitude may suggest a chief reason for Froude's carelessness in small matters, for which see the discussion in "Editorial Procedures."

100. Preface (dated 6 November 1882), *Short Studies*, 4:v.

101. 17 January 1881. MS: Bodleian Eng. lett. e. 44, fol. 136.

102. 6 February 1881. MS: Humanities Research Center, University of Texas.

103. 31 July [1881]. MS: Houghton Papers, Trinity College, Cambridge. Published in part in James Pope-Hennessy, *Monckton Milnes: The Flight of Youth, 1851–1885* (New York: Farrar, Straus, & Cudahy, 1955), p. 248. J. Churton Collins records in 1886 that Froude "spoke very sadly and bitterly of human life and said that Shakespeare's and Homer's attitude was, Poor Devils, why be hard on them, they have so many miseries" (L. C. Collins, p. 88).

104. Anthony Trollope, *The Prime Minister*, Oxford World's Classics Edition, Double Volume (London: Oxford University Press, 1975), 1:176; 2:2. The novel was first published in 1876.

105. Diary entry, [2 May 1881], cited from Nirad C. Chaudhuri, *Scholar Extraordinary: The Life of Professor the Rt. Hon. Friedrich Max Müller, P.C.* (London: Chatto & Windus, 1974), p. 275.

106. In several of the *Studies in History and Jurisprudence*, 2 vols. (1901). John D. Rosenberg has explored the apocalyptic theme in Tennyson's *Idylls of the King*, but his discussion also has relevance for other late Victorian poems, including Gerard Manley Hopkins's "The Wreck of the Deutschland," James Thomson's "The City of Dreadful Night," and the poems of Yeats. See Rosenberg's *The Fall of Camelot: A Study of Tennyson's "Idylls of the King"* (Cambridge: Harvard University Press, Belknap Press, 1973), chap. 3 ("Timescape").

107. 30 May [1881?]. MS: Hon. David Lytton Cobbold and Hertfordshire County Council. Professor Robert Goetzman kindly drew my attention to this letter.

108. Dunn, *Froude*, 2:264.

109. See also Stead, *The M. P. for Russia*, 2:324.

110. Sir Arthur Hardinge, *The Life of Henry Howard Molyneux Herbert, Fourth Earl of Carnarvon*, 3 vols. (London and Edinburgh: Humphrey Milford, 1925), 3:15.

111. MS: Folger Shakespeare Library. I wish to thank Professor G. A. Cate for bringing this letter to my attention. Waldo H. Dunn published Carlyle's moving reply, dated 13 July 1874, in "Carlyle's Last Letters to Froude," *Twentieth Century* 160 (September 1956): 243–44.

112. MS: Tennyson Research Centre, City Library, Lincoln. Printed

with slight variations from the manuscript in [Hallam Tennyson,] *Alfred Lord Tennyson: A Memoir*, 2 vols. (London: Macmillan, 1897), 2:244.

113. 16 December [1892?]. MS: Tennyson Research Centre, City Library, Lincoln. Printed in *Tennyson: A Memoir*, 2:468, where it is dated "1894." The year 1892 (possibly 1893) is more likely (Froude died 20 October 1894). Tennyson's hero worship of Arthur Hallam would also have drawn Froude to him and his poetry.

114. Recorded in L. C. Collins, p. 85.

115. Froude to George Bainton [1889?], in the latter's *The Art of Authorship* (London: J. Clarke, 1890), p. 306; L. C. Collins, p. 85. "I never print anything which I have not written over twice if not thrice— and I always find something to correct," Froude wrote Mrs. Alexander Ireland on 11 October 1890 (MS: Beinecke Library, Yale).

116. Bainton, p. 307. Froude's attitude was also Matthew Arnold's. See Kenneth and Miriam Allott, eds., *Victorian Prose,, 1830–1880* (Harmondsworth, Middlesex: Penguin Books, 1956), p. xxi.

117. Bainton, p. 307.

118. *Short Studies*, 4:393–94.

119. Quoted from Clubbe, *Carlyle and His Contemporaries*, p. 262.

120. Dunn, *Froude*, 2:570.

121. See Saintsbury's discussions of Froude in the *History of English Prose Rhythm* (London: Macmillan & Co., 1912); in the two essays on style in *Collected Essays and Papers of George Saintsbury, 1875–1920*, 3 vols. (London and Toronto: J. M. Dent, 1923), vol. 3; and in *A History of Nineteenth Century Literature (1780–1895)* (New York: Macmillan, 1904).

122. *History of English Prose Rhythm*, p. 411.

123. *Works*, 29:79. See also *Reminiscences*, 2:41.

124. See essays by Gordon S. Haight and G. B. Tennyson in Clubbe, *Carlyle and His Contemporaries*, especially pp. 186 and 310. Kenneth Allott points, however, to a passage in Froude's *Nemesis of Faith* "strongly influenced by Carlyle" (*Victorian Prose*, p. xxxvi). It may also be argued that Froude's prose owes something to the paratactic style of much of *The French Revolution*, a book he admired greatly.

125. *Short Studies*, 4:199.

126. Paul, p. 61. Several passages in Froude's life of Carlyle betray signs of hasty writing. Yet few authors sustain, as Algernon Cecil has claimed in regard to Froude's *History of England*, so high a level of expression through so long a work. See Cecil's *Six Oxford Thinkers* (London: John Murray, 1908), p. 174.

127. George Washburn Smalley, *London Letters and Some Others*, 2 vols. (London: Macmillan, 1890), 2:105–6.

128. "Signs of the Times," *Works*, 27:59; Harrold, *Sartor*, pp. 65–66.

129. Nicolson, pp. 130, 135–35 (and 143). A disciple of Lytton Strachey, Nicolson wrote his lectures under the influence of *Eminent Victorians* and *Queen Victoria*.

130. 26 January 1836 (NLS, 520.50). See p. 444 for another instance of Froude's picking up Carlyle's always interesting animal imagery.

131. Notation in his copy of Froude's biography, now NLS, 753.

132. Donald J. Greene, in a rather different context, has discussed the motivation that may lurk behind such remarks. "Bruno Bettelheim reviewing Ernest Jones's biography of Freud," he writes, "called attention to the time-honoured tradition of the disciple subtly undercutting the master, pointing out (in the most reverent way) his little imperfections, bringing him down to the disciple's size or a little lower, making his teachings comprehensible to the masses by diluting them with his disciple's—as, Bettelheim complains, St. Paul did for Jesus. Perhaps he might also have cited Boswell on Johnson." Or, we might add, Froude on Carlyle. For Greene's statement, see "Reflections on a Literary Anniversary," in *Twentieth Century Interpretations of Boswell's Life of Johnson*, ed. James L. Clifford (Englewood Cliffs, N.J.: Prentice-Hall, 1970), pp. 100–101. Bettelheim's review of Jones's biography of Freud is in *The New Leader*, 19 May 1958.

133. John Skelton, *The Table-Talk of Shirley: Reminiscences of and Letters from Froude Thackeray Disraeli Browning Rossetti Kingsley Baynes Huxley Tyndall and Others* (Edinburgh and London: William Blackwood, 1895), p. 209.

134. *Short Studies*, 1:19.

135. *A History of Nineteenth Century Literature*, p. 252.

136. *Short Studies*, 1:337. "Homer" was first published in 1851.

Editorial Procedures

The first two volumes of Froude's biography, entitled *Thomas Carlyle: A History of the First Forty Years of His Life, 1795–1835*, appeared in 1882; the second two volumes, entitled *Thomas Carlyle: A History of His Life in London, 1834–1881*, appeared in 1884. Longmans, Green and Company published the four volumes. An authorized American edition, by Scribner's, also appeared; Harper's published unauthorized editions of all four volumes, G. Munroe of the first two. In 1890 Longmans put out a "New Edition" and in 1896 a "Cabinet Edition" (each several times reprinted).

By the end of 1884 Froude had returned the papers in his keeping to the Carlyle family. However, before he did so he and his daughter Margaret made a number of corrections in the biography, both in the texts of the quoted documents and in the narrative itself. The Beinecke Library at Yale holds Froude's personal copies of the Scribner edition of the first two volumes (1882) and of the Longmans edition of the second two (the latter of these two volumes is a second edition, dated 1885 but otherwise unchanged from the first edition). Corrections in volumes 1 and 2 are not in Froude's hand but in Margaret's. She caught a number of errors in the texts of her father's transcriptions (though still only a fraction of the total, judged by standards of modern textual editing); the texts for all four volumes I have myself corrected fully, as explained subsequently. Margaret also corrects her father's prose on points of style; such changes I have usually accepted if they eliminate misprints or remove ambiguity. Corrections in volume 3 are largely in Froude's hand and are both of texts quoted and of his own narrative. These alterations he made for the New Edition of 1890; from the smudges on the pages it is clear that the compositor set type for the edition from this copy. The corrections, almost exclusively stylistic, I have incorporated into my text as representing Froude's final thoughts; only a few have called for comment in the notes. Corrections in volume 4 are in Margaret Froude's hand; there are only two, and they have not been accepted. As far as I can determine, the New Edition of 1890 incorporates only the changes Froude made himself in volume 3.[1] Therefore, because the first London editions of 1882 and 1884 have far fewer printer's errors, I have based the text of this edition upon them.[2]

THE ABRIDGMENT

I have pruned Froude's biography to about three-eighths of its original length. Four stout volumes, running to nearly nineteen-hundred pages, have become one corpulent tome. Writing in the tradition of the Victorian life and letters, Froude felt obliged to publish as many of Carlyle's letters as he could include, but he took few pains to integrate the letters within his narrative. The book thus lends itself easily to abridgment since Froude often printed long extracts from Carlyle's letters and from his Journal—one from the Journal runs to nearly thirty pages—with usually not more than a sentence or two of introduction. Therefore, omitting a number of these extracts—most since published in more accurate texts—has the result both of reducing the bulk of quoted material and of increasing narrative flow.

I have attempted to compress Froude into reasonable compass while preserving the essence of his narrative. Given Froude's belief in the value of supporting firsthand material, the four volumes inevitably lack unity. This abridgment, shorn of great chunks of heaped-up documentation, does have a coherence that the original volumes lack. I have retained, however, enough from the letters of both Carlyles (and from Carlyle's Journal) to convey a vivid sense of the personalities of the two as reflected in their characteristic literary styles. In abridging the text,

EDITORIAL PROCEDURES

I have kept in mind the need to retain the comprehensiveness of Froude's presentation of Carlyle. Few—perhaps ten or fifteen percent at most—of Froude's own words have been cut, and no passages, I believe, of first importance. Thus, if I have abridged or omitted many of the longer extracts from Carlyle's letters and his Journal, I have included almost everything by Froude that bears on Carlyle. Inevitably, this abridged and somewhat revised Froude has taken on certain of the characteristics of a collaboration.

EDITORIAL POLICIES

Preparing this abridged version has necessitated a number of changes in the text. Absolute textual fidelity would have been a logical course to follow if I had been contemplating a complete edition of Froude's life of Carlyle. This is not the case—indeed, given the present economics of publishing, it is not likely to be the case for a long time—and thus I have felt free to depart whenever necessary from such a policy. Editorial decisions are usually debatable, most involve compromise (especially given the present quagmire in which editors of nineteenth-century texts work), and some of mine may be open to cavil. A reasonable compromise between faithfully reproducing Froude's narrative and achieving readability was necessary. The reader may be assured that I have long pondered the policies outlined in the following paragraphs.

TEXT OF THE BIOGRAPHY

I have reduced Froude's seventy-five chapters to thirty-one, breaking the narrative at logical divisions. The chapters in Froude's first two volumes have no titles; in the second two they remain untitled, but short summaries preface them. These I have dropped and instead have given each of the thirty-one chapters of the abridgment a title of my own devising, preceded by the years the chapter covers. Throughout I have tried to be fair to Froude's presentation and emphases and hope that I have not unduly fragmented his basic point of view.

Omissions within Froude's narrative have not been indicated. Absence of ellipsis points may be justified for the sake of the appearance of the page, which otherwise would have been studded with them. The reader may assume that any remaining ellipsis points are Froude's. Correcting Froude's quotations from Carlyle has required other minor changes. To achieve transitional smoothness I have occasionally (without altering basic meaning) omitted or changed a word in Froude—"had gone" to "went," "he" to "Jeffrey," etc. I have not called attention to these alterations with brackets. Changes of substance in Froude's text, however—those clearly necessitated by corrections made in the passages quoted from Carlyle—have been bracketed. For instance, I have dropped "for a month longer" and substituted "[until mid-August]." A few dates and figures I have silently corrected; here and there for clarity's sake I have inserted a date in brackets. Overworking *"sic"* has been avoided. I have enclosed in brackets the few necessary transition passages of my own.

Froude admitted to being a poor proofreader, and I have corrected a number of typographical errors in his narrative, tried to make his spelling and capitalization more consistent, and changed to roman type a few of the words that he, for one reason or another, italicized when current practice would not. Book and journal titles I have printed in italics instead of in the quotation marks Froude used; quotations of several lines or more I have set off. Occasionally, because of other changes, I have shortened Froude's sentences without indication. This, in turn, led to my shortening paragraphs. Some of these abridged paragraphs I have combined. I have also filled out proper names that Froude abbreviated, for instance, "Lord Ashburton" instead of his frequent "Lord A."; his "&c." has become "etc.," "MS" has become "manuscript." I have adopted standard spellings, such as "Descartes" for "Des Cartes," and have tried to reduce the number of inconsistencies, for example, the spelling of "judgement," which (as in Carlyle) is sometimes with the "e" and sometimes without; it is now Froude's more usual "judgement." Translations of words in foreign languages (except French) have been placed in brackets following the foreign words. I have corrected a few lapses in grammar in Froude's narrative (some pointed out by A. Carlyle); as with the typographical errors, perpetuating them would serve no useful purpose. Otherwise, I have not modernized the text and have left Froude's English spelling as it is. All told, I have probably made several thousand emendations, for the most part silently, in the hope of producing a book that neither scholars nor laymen will resent reading.

TEXT OF THE MATERIAL QUOTED BY FROUDE

I have included accurate texts of Carlyle's letters and journals, Jane Carlyle's letters, and the letters to the Carlyles quoted in Froude whenever I have been able to examine original manuscripts or Xerox copies of them at Duke University. If the document has been published, I give a reference to the best published text. Often the reader will find, however, that the text of a quotation differs—sometimes considerably—from the published source cited. In these cases he may assume that I am quoting directly from the manuscript. I have adopted this policy of giving whenever possible references to published texts for passages quoted from manuscript so that interested readers can check to see whether Froude is quoting in context. A few words in Carlyle I have made consistent after his more usual practice —"Craigenputtoch" always with an "h," "Comely" (not "Comley") Bank. I have also usually expanded Carlyle's abbreviations in his letters and in the Journal—"which" instead of "wh*h*," "humour" instead of "hum*r*," for example. The text for all passages from correspondence through 1834 reproduces that in the *Collected Letters of Thomas and Jane Welsh Carlyle*, the first four volumes of which (covering the years 1812–28) appeared in 1970, the three subsequent (covering 1829–34) in 1977.

Froude is reputed to be a notoriously inaccurate transcriber of documents. After identifying and correcting most of the manuscripts he quotes in his biography, I have found that reputation largely justified. With accurate texts of these documents now before him, the interested scholar can judge for himself the evidence upon which Froude based his opinions. He will find that Froude, though careless in transcribing, generally adhered to the facts of Car-

lyle's life as he found them in these documents. He will
also find that Froude usually distorted the material he
quoted less than several other contemporary editors of
Carlyle who attacked him for his carelessness.

When faced with the choice between giving Froude's often inaccurate quotations from Carlyle (perhaps recalled
from memory) and citing the passage directly, I have unhesitatingly quoted the passage whenever I could find it.
Thus quotation marks have been inserted or omitted as
necessary and in accordance with modern practice. Now
and again Froude deliberately left out words or phrases
within a passage—names of people, occasionally a revealing aside, more often incidental or supplementary information. Many of these comments are of no particular importance, but in all but a few instances I have restored
them. If a passage quoted by Froude has been subsequently published, I give a reference to the most reliable
text, the name of the correspondent (if the document is a
letter), and the date of the manuscript. If the passage has
not appeared other than in Froude, I give the name of the
correspondent (if the document is a letter), the date of the
manuscript (if known or ascertainable), and its location.
Dates in brackets are editorial inferences, either mine or
those of others. In addition, I have given National Library
of Scotland manuscript numbers for passages quoted by
Froude from letters held by that institution and still unpublished elsewhere. Since Froude's life remains one of the
important primary sources for the study of Carlyle, the
interested scholar can thus, with the information supplied,
investigate the evidence on which Froude based his statements. He will see that Froude's narrative often closely
follows Carlyle's own words. He can now, if he wishes,
check those words against the complete document to see
whether Froude is quoting in context. I think that in all but
a very few instances he is. Often where Froude has been
most controversial, it has turned out that he is quoting or
paraphrasing Carlyle or Jane Carlyle. The documentation provided in this edition should do a great deal toward restoring
the credibility of Froude's interpretation of many crucial
events in the lives of the Carlyles. Students of Carlyle will
of course continue to consult the original four volumes, but

even they should find useful the newly accurate texts, now identified and dated, of material quoted by Froude.

If I have failed to locate the source of a quotation, the reader should not assume that Froude made the passage up. For a number of quotations he obviously relied upon his memory, which was fallible. Some letters Froude did not date—or date accurately—or did not otherwise give sufficient indication of a passage's location within the huge mass of the Carlyle's papers for me to find it. Others I may have overlooked. A number we can reasonably attribute to conversations with Carlyle. The reader may assume that for these unfootnoted quotations (a small percentage of the total number) I have made a reasonably thorough search, as full as time and resources have permitted. For these quotations—with the exception of those from the Journal— he may also assume that he is reading unadulterated Froude. For a number of the quotations in the biography I offer what amounts to a radically new text: these include not only passages published in *Two Reminiscences of Thomas Carlyle*, but quotations from Carlyle's annotations of his wife's letters, from his Journal, and (most frequently) from his correspondence.

FROUDE AS EDITOR

I can offer no altogether convincing explanation why Froude transcribed texts so inaccurately: why he made no attempt, for example, to correlate the texts published in the final two volumes of his biography with those he had already published in his editions of the *Reminiscences* and of the *Letters and Memorials of Jane Welsh Carlyle*. I agree with Herbert Paul, who writes, "Two-thirds of Froude's mistakes would have been avoided . . . if [he] had had a keener eye for slips in his proofsheets, or had engaged competent assistance."[3] In reading a number of Froude's letters of this time, I have found that it takes practice to decode his hand, that words blend together, and that punctuation is uncertain. The original manuscript of the life of Carlyle, which has not survived, would undoubtedly have caused a typesetter problems. Froude does indeed seem to have read proof without assistance, though his publisher must assume the blame for deficiencies in the indexes to both sets of volumes.[4]

Froude attributed a large number of his errors in transcription to difficulty in reading Carlyle's later hand; but even if we grant that this hand is difficult, it is not impossible to read. It should not have posed an excessive hurdle for a man who had tested his strength against the manuscripts at Simancas. But although Froude's texts of Carlyle manuscripts reveal a number of minor differences when compared to the originals, they rarely mislead in matters of substance. Nor does this carelessness distort his portraits of the Carlyles. Froude may misread words often enough, but, unlike several subsequent editors, he rarely leaves words out—or sentences or paragraphs, for that matter. In his essay on Froude, Strachey wrote perceptively: "The Victorian public, unable to understand a form of hero worship which laid bare the faults of the hero, was appalled, and refused to believe what was the simple fact—that Froude's adoration was of so complete a kind that it shrank with horror from the notion of omitting a single wart from the portrait."[5] Strachey overstates the case: Froude *did* omit a few of the warts. But if he often quoted inaccurately, he almost always quoted fairly and in context. In this respect he is the most fearless of Victorians.

Froude's suffering from "constitutional inaccuracy," as Leslie Stephen put it,[6] remains part of the mystery of man. Something in his temperament did not permit him to revise thoroughly or correct his work extensively. It has been argued that Froude's weak vision after 1858 may have been at least partially responsible for his carelessness and errors, but this strikes me as more an apparent than a real cause.[7] A surer clue to Froude's frequent slips may be found in the 1858 letter to Clough, cited earlier, in which he laments that "the best part of such years as may remain will have to pass not in pleasant imaginations but in the treadmill of mere work.— What is the good of it when it is done."[8] The "treadmill of mere work" apparently did not always provide Froude with the satisfaction that his mentor Carlyle claimed for it. One who preferred "pleasant imaginations" may have been unwilling to discipline himself to precision in small matters.[9] Still, the corrections in the Beinecke copies of the biography, as well as the 1890 correspondence with Mary Aitken Carlyle mentioned in note 1, indicate that Froude made some effort to revise his text in the light of criticism. It seems fair to say that he tried to make the biography as good as he could and gave it more care than any of his other works.

EDITOR'S NOTES

My notes are not intended to provide a thorough annotation of Froude's text, which must await the first modern editing of the entire work. I have not attempted, even if it were possible to do so, to correct all his errors of fact or to arbitrate all his disputed interpretations. Rather, I have tried to correct the more blatant errors, point out some of his more controversial biases by suggesting alternate readings of the evidence, indicate (where significant) discoveries of later scholarship, and answer obvious questions that the reader is likely to have. I have also cited passages from Froude's letters whenever I felt they elucidated what he was doing in the biography. The life needs, of course, to be modified and supplemented in many places, for a vast amount of information about Carlyle and the Victorians has accumulated since Froude's day. Tempting as it might have been to add this material, in the end I would have submerged Froude's text beneath a sea of commentary, thus defeating my purpose of presenting the work basically on its own terms. The notes have been reduced from the original number and rigorously honed so that the main lines of Froude's exposition stand clear. That modern scholarship on Carlyle usually begins with Froude is sufficient testimony to the durability of his achievement. With the bibliographical aids presently available to students of the Victorian era, it did not make sense to overload Froude's text with supplementary information or to append extensive lists of later work. Bibliographers have served Carlyle well, and for further guidance the reader may consult the bibliographies dealing with secondary literature on Carlyle by Isaac W. Dyer, Carlisle Moore, Charles Richard Sanders, G. B. Tennyson, R. W. Dillon, and Rodger L. Tarr.[10]

In keeping with this policy of minimal interference, I have given few references to D. A. Wilson's massive six-volume biography of Carlyle, which supplements Froude with much detail. Several notes I have taken over from my edition of *Two Reminiscences of Thomas Carlyle*, others from the Duke-Edinburgh edition of *The Collected Letters of Thomas and Jane Welsh Carlyle*. The few notes by Froude that I have retained are so designated.

ANNOTATED COPY OF FROUDE'S LIFE
IN THE NATIONAL LIBRARY OF SCOTLAND

The National Library in Edinburgh holds the copy of the biography, catalogued under MS 751–754, that was owned by Carlyle's nephew Alexander Carlyle (1843–1931)—not to be confused with Carlyle's brother Alexander (1797–1876)— and his niece Mary Aitken Carlyle (ca. 1848–95). Alexander and Mary, first cousins, married in 1879. Alexander Carlyle (designated hereafter as A. Carlyle) annotated Froude's biography extensively, Mary Aitken Carlyle to a much lesser degree; in addition, they corrected the texts and supplied the dates (when not given by Froude) to many passages from Carlyle's letters and Journal. Their work has therefore been a great boon to me. Although Froude returned the final lot of the Carlyle papers in his possession to A. Carlyle and Mary late in 1884, only after the latter's death in 1895 did A. Carlyle begin "to make a careful study of the Carlyle papers which had now become mine alone and were a great responsibility to me."[11] Part of this responsibility involved preparing several editions of Carlyle's correspondence, but he also read and reread Froude's life, making abundant marginal comments as he went along and dating some of them. He seems to have written many observations in the years preceding 1904; the latest dated comment is 18 October 1928.

ANNOTATIONS BY A. CARLYLE AND
MARY AITKEN CARLYLE

I have included a selection of A. Carlyle's and Mary Aitken Carlyle's comments in this edition chiefly because several of them point out deficiencies in Froude's narrative of which the reader might not otherwise be aware. Others reveal A. Carlyle's humorous, crusty personality and indicate something of the dogmatic spirit with which he pursued his long controversy with Froude (and Froude's ghost). His comments are also worth having because he was, in his way, an able if not altogether scrupulous man and because he had at his fingertips a great deal of family lore. He does not have anything to say regarding Froude's interpretation of Carlyle's beliefs and writings but limits himself to matters of fact, family history, textual corrections, and a few major points at issue regarding Carlyle's biography, e.g., his marriage. The more important of these comments I have retained. They set Froude's narrative in a different perspective, one that is hostile but not always unfairly so. If some enterprising soul again undertakes an investigation of the Froude-Carlyle controversy, he should find A. Carlyle's statements—all hitherto unpublished—useful in clarifying matters in Carlyle's biography that still remain obscure. At the end of each volume of the biography, A. Carlyle lists Froude's chief "errors" of fact and interpretation, perhaps intending to refute them in detail at some later time (he never did). I have not included A. Carlyle's comments when, as is frequently the case, he has been proved wrong and Froude right or when both are clearly wrong. Nor have I usually included the many corrections of small points in Carlyle's biography, though I give a sampling to illustrate their nature.

TEXT OF PASSAGES FROM CARLYLE'S
JOURNAL QUOTED BY FROUDE

For my purposes, A. Carlyle's greatest service has been his correction and dating of the many passages from Carlyle's Journal that Froude published. He fills in blanks of names in Froude's text, restores Carlyle's distinctive punctuation and underscoring, and incorporates sentences and passages omitted by Froude. Although Charles Eliot Norton published in 1898 Carlyle's Journal through 1832 (under the title *Two Note Books of Thomas Carlyle*), scholars have had to rely on Froude's text for the years after 1832.

71

Froude remains the only one of Carlyle's biographers to have read Carlyle's Journal, and it seems fairly certain that if he had not published large segments from it in his biography, A. Carlyle would have preferred to destroy it.[12] That Froude had the courage to print so much of the Journal—and thus ensure its preservation—is not the least of our debts to him. Using A. Carlyle's copy of the biography as well as other sources made available to me, I have been able not only to identify many passages from Carlyle as being from the Journal but also to give them in substantially accurate texts.

THE FROUDE-CARLYLE CONTROVERSY

With the eruption of the controversy even before the publication of the first two volumes, Froude's life of Carlyle was prejudged by many. Only in recent years have we begun to acquire the historical perspective necessary to allow it to stand clear of all the often acrimonious debate that has pursued it for so long. Waldo H. Dunn's 1930 *Froude and Carlyle*, for all its deficiencies, has survived better than most works of scholarship that approach the half century. Granted that Dunn began his investigation with a bias in Froude's favor and was often rigid in his views, his knowledge of the material and the thoroughness with which he balanced the various claims and counterclaims far surpasses that of his predecessors—or successors. Most subsequent writers, as noted earlier, tend to confirm his conclusions. It can therefore be said that, in spite of the sometimes violent criticisms made by A. Carlyle and others, Froude's presentation of Carlyle's character is intelligent, informed, and responsible, weighted no doubt by his sympathy for Jane Carlyle, yet neither malicious nor essentially unjust to Carlyle, and animated by fair and ample recognition of his virtues.

1. With one other exception. In the "New Edition" Froude altered "gey ill to live wi' " to "gey ill to deal wi'," a slip pointed out to him by Moncure D. Conway (see chap. 3, n. 7). In 1890 there also occurred an exchange of correspondence (through lawyers) between Froude and

Mary Aitken Carlyle in which Froude requested permission to reexamine the Carlyle manuscripts in Mary's possession in order to prepare a second edition of the biography. Mary interposed difficulties that Froude found objectionable. After several exchanges (published in Dunn, *F and C*, pp. 332-36), the matter rested. See also ibid., pp. 85-86, 234.

2. As Froude's biography has an importance for Carlyle's life nearly equal to Boswell's for Johnson's, it is perhaps surprising that no annotated edition or abridgment of it has appeared before now. The pastiche of passages with occasional bridging commentary that Professor Frederick W. Hilles of Yale put together in 1939 for his classes in biography can reasonably be excepted, since the availability of this work was generally limited to Yale students. Froude published, in the *Nineteenth Century* 53 (July 1881): 1-42, a reduced version of the first 107 pages of his biography (pp. 85-125 of this edition).

3. Paul, p. 188.

4. "I revised the proofs with the originals [of the letters] at hand," Froude wrote to Mrs. Ireland on 8 February [1890] (MS: Beinecke Library, Yale). A postcard from Longmans' to Scribner's, dated 10 September 1884, indicates that the publisher was responsible for at least the index to the last two volumes of the biography (MS: Princeton [Scribner archive]).

5. Lytton Strachey, *Portraits in Miniature and Other Essays* (New York: Harcourt, Brace, 1931), pp. 194-95.

6. Leslie Stephen, *Studies of a Biographer*, 4 vols. (New York and London: G. P. Putnam's Sons, 1907), 3:207.

7. Sharples (cited above, n. 8), pp. 148, 224; based on Dunn, *Froude*, 2:271-72.

8. See pp. 33-34 and n. 99. J. Churton Collins records a similar comment by Froude: "You should remember that it must all perish and what is the good of taking so much pains: that is how I comfort myself" (L. C. Collins, p. 85).

9. In smoothing over Carlyle's prose by lessening the contrast between it and his own more flowing style, Froude may also have thought he was presenting a more readable narrative.

10. Dyer, *Bibliography of Thomas Carlyle's Writings and Ana;* Carlisle Moore, "Thomas Carlyle," in *The English Romantic Poets and Essayists: A Review of Research and Criticism*, ed. Carolyn W. Houtchens and Lawrence H. Houtchens, rev. ed. (New York: New York University Press, 1966), pp. 333-78; Charles Richard Sanders, "Thomas Carlyle," in *The New Cambridge Bibliography of English Literature*, vol. 3 (1800-1900), ed. George Watson (Cambridge: At the University Press, 1969), pp. 1248-70; Tennyson, *Victorian Prose*; R. W. Dillon, "A Centenary Bibliography of Carlylean Studies: 1928-1974," *Bulletin of Bibliography and Magazine Notes* 32 (October-December 1975): 133-56; and Rodger L. Tarr, *Thomas Carlyle: A Bibliography of*

English-Language Criticism, 1824–1974 (Charlottesville: University Press of Virginia, 1976).

11. "Jottings of Alexander Carlyle's Life and Work by Himself," p. 9 (NLS, 739).

12. See Clubbe, *Carlyle and His Contemporaries*, p. 342.

Froude's
Life of Carlyle

Froude's Preface

Mr. Carlyle expressed a desire in his will that of him no biography should be written. I find the same reluctance in his Journal. No one, he said, was likely to understand a history, the secret of which was unknown to his closest friends.[1] He hoped that his wishes would be respected.

Partly to take the place of a biography of himself, and partly for other reasons, he collected the letters of his wife— letters which covered the whole period of his life in London to the date of her death, when his own active work was finished. He prepared them for publication, adding notes and introductory explanations, as the last sacred duty which remained to him in the world. He intended it as a monument to a character of extreme beauty; while it would tell the public as much about himself as it could reasonably expect to learn.

These letters he placed in my hands eleven years ago, with materials for an Introduction which he was himself unable to complete.[2] He could do no more with it, he said. He could not make up his mind to direct positively the publication even of the letters themselves. He wished them to be published, but he left the decision to myself; and when I was reluctant to undertake the sole responsibility, he said that, if I was in doubt when the time came, I might consult his brother John and his friend Mr. Forster.

The Preface is for the first two volumes of the biography (1882).

Had he rested here, my duty would have been clear. The collection of letters, with the Memoir of Mrs. Carlyle which was to form part of the Introduction, would have been considered among us, and would have been either published or suppressed, as we might jointly determine. Mr. Carlyle's remaining papers would have been sealed up after his death, and by me at least no use would have been made of them.

Two years later, however, soon after he had made his will, Carlyle discovered that, whether he wished it or not, a life, or perhaps various lives, of himself would certainly appear when he was gone. When a man has exercised a large influence on the minds of his contemporaries, the world requires to know whether his own actions have corresponded with his teaching, and whether his moral and personal character entitles him to confidence. This is not idle curiosity; it is a legitimate demand. In proportion to a man's greatness is the scrutiny to which his conduct is submitted. Byron, Burns, Scott, Shelley, Rousseau, Voltaire, Goethe, Pope, Swift, are but instances, to which a hundred others might be added, showing that the public will not be satisfied without sifting the history of its men of genius to the last grain of fact which can be ascertained about them. The publicity of their private lives has been, is, and will be, either the reward or the penalty of their intellectual distinction. Carlyle knew that he could not escape. Since a "Life" of him there would certainly be, he wished it to be as authentic as possible. Besides the Memoir of Mrs. Carlyle, he had written several others, mainly autobiographical, not distinctly to be printed, but with no fixed purpose that they should not be printed.[3] These, with his journals and the whole of his correspondence, he made over to me, with unfettered discretion to use in any way that I might think good.

In the papers thus in my possession, Carlyle's history, external and spiritual, lay out before me as in a map. By recasting the entire material, by selecting chosen passages out of his own and his wife's letters, by exhibiting the fair and beautiful side of the story only, it would have been easy, without suppressing a single material point, to draw a picture of a faultless character. When the Devil's advocate has said his worst against Carlyle, he leaves a figure still of unblemished integrity, purity, loftiness of purpose, and inflexible resolution to do right, as of a man living consciously under his Maker's eye, and with his thoughts fixed on the account which he would have to render of his talents.

Of a person of whom malice must acknowledge so much as this, the prickly aspects might fairly be passed by in silence; and if I had studied my own comfort or the pleasure of my immediate readers, I should have produced a portrait as agreeable, and at least as faithful, as those of the favoured saints in the Catholic calendar. But it would have been a portrait without individuality—an ideal, or, in other words, an "idol," to be worshipped one day and thrown away the next. Least of all men could such idealising be ventured with Carlyle, to whom untruth of any kind was abominable. If he was to be known at all, he chose to be known as he was, with his angularities, his sharp speeches, his special peculiarities, meritorious or unmeritorious, precisely as they had actually been. He has himself laid down the conditions under which a biographer must do his work if he would do it honestly, without the fear of man before him; and in dealing with Carlyle's own memory I have felt myself bound to conform to his own rule. He shall speak for himself. I extract a passage from his review of Lockhart's *Life of Scott.*

> One thing we hear greatly blamed in Mr. Lockhart: that he has been too communicative, indiscreet, and has recorded much that ought to have lain suppressed. Persons are mentioned, and circumstances, not always of an ornamental sort. It would appear there is far less reticence than was looked for! Various persons, name and surname, have "received pain": nay, the very Hero of the Biography is rendered unheroic; unornamental facts of him, and of those he had to do with, being set forth in plain English: hence "personality," "indiscretion," or worse, "sanctities of private life," etc. etc. How delicate, decent is English Biography, bless its mealy mouth! A Damocles' sword of *Respectability* hangs forever over the poor English Life-writer (as it does over poor English Life in general), and reduces him to the verge of paralysis. Thus it has been said "there are no English lives worth reading except those of Players, who, by the nature of the case have bidden Respectability good-day." The English biographer has long felt that if in writing his Man's Biography, he wrote down

79

anything that could by possibility offend any man, he had written wrong. The plain consequence was, that, properly speaking, no biography whatever could be produced. The poor biographer, having the fear *not* of God before his eyes, was obliged to retire as it were into vacuum; and write in the most melancholy, straitened manner, with only vacuum for a result. Vain that he wrote, and that we kept reading volume on volume: there was no biography, but some vague ghost of a biography, white, stainless; without feature or substance; *vacuum*, as we say, and wind and shadow. . . .

Of all the praises copiously bestowed on [Mr. Lockhart's] Work, there is none in reality so creditable to him as this same censure, which has also been pretty copious. It is a censure better than a good many praises. He is found guilty of having said this and that, calculated not to be entirely pleasant to this man and that; in other words, calculated to give him and the thing he worked in a living set of features, not leave him vague, in the white beatified-ghost condition. Several men, as we hear, cry out, "See, there is something written not entirely pleasant to me!" Good friend, it is pity; but who can help it? They that will crowd about bonfires may, sometimes very fairly, get their beards singed; it is the price they pay for such illumination; natural twilight is safe and free to all. For our part, we hope all manner of biographies that are written in England will henceforth be written so. If it is fit that they be written otherwise, then it is still fitter that they be not written at all: to produce not things, but ghosts of things can never be the duty of man.

The biographer has this problem set before him: to delineate a likeness of the earthly pilgrimage of a man. He will compute well what profit is in it, and what disprofit; under which latter head this of offending any of his fellow-creatures will surely not be forgotten. Nay, this may so swell the disprofit side of his account, that many an enterprise of biography, otherwise promising, shall require to be renounced. But once taken up, the rule before all rules is to do *it*, not to do the ghost of it. In speaking of the man and men he has to deal with, he will of course keep all his charities about him; but all his eyes open. Far be it from him to set down aught *untrue*; nay, not to abstain from, and leave in oblivion, much that is true. But having found a thing or things essential for his subject, and well computed the for and against, he will in very deed set down such thing or things, nothing doubting,—*having*, we may say, the fear of God before his eyes, and no other fear whatever. Censure the biographer's prudence; dissent from the computation he made, or agree with it; be all malice of his, be all falsehood, nay, be all offensive avoidable inaccuracy, condemned and consumed; but know that by this plan only, executed as was possible, could the biographer hope to make a biography; and blame him not that he did what it had been the worst fault not to do. . . .

80

The other censure, of Scott being made unheroic, springs from
the same stem; and is, perhaps, a still more wonderful flower of it.
Your true hero must have no features, but be white, stainless, an
impersonal ghost-hero! But connected with this, there is a hypothesis now current . . . that Mr. Lockhart at heart has a dislike to
Scott, and has done his best in an underhand treacherous manner
to dishero him! Such hypothesis is actually current: he that has
ears may hear it now and then. On which astounding hypothesis,
if a word must be said, it can only be an apology for silence. . . .
For if Mr. Lockhart is fairly chargeable with any radical defect,
if on any side his insight entirely fails him, it seems even to be in
this, that Scott is altogether lovely to him; that Scott's greatness
spreads out for him on all hands beyond reach of eye; that his very
faults become beautiful . . . ; and of his worth there is no measure.[4]

I will make no comment on this passage further than to
say that I have considered the principles here laid down by
Carlyle to be strictly obligatory upon myself in dealing with
his own remains. The free judgements which he passed on
men and things were part of himself, and I have not felt
myself at liberty to suppress them. Remarks which could injure any man—and very few such ever fell from Carlyle's
lips—I omit, except where indispensable. Remarks which
are merely legitimate expressions of opinion I leave for the
most part as they stand. As an illustration of his own wishes
on this subject, I may mention that I consulted him about a
passage in one of Mrs. Carlyle's letters describing an eminent living person. Her judgement was more just than flattering, and I doubted the prudence of printing it. Carlyle
merely said, "It will do him no harm to know what a sensible woman thought of him."[5]

As to the biography generally, I found that I could not
myself write a formal life of Carlyle within measurable compass without taking to pieces his own Memoirs and the
collection of Mrs. Carlyle's letters; and this I could not think
it right to attempt. Mr. Forster and John Carlyle having
both died, the responsibility was left entirely to myself. A
few weeks before Mr. Carlyle's death, he asked me what I
meant to do. I told him that I proposed to publish the
Memoirs as soon as he was gone—those which form the
two volumes of the *Reminiscences*. Afterwards I said that
I would publish the letters about which I knew him to be
most anxious. He gave his full assent, merely adding that he

81

trusted everything to me. The Memoirs, he thought, had better appear immediately on his departure. He expected that people would then be talking about him, and that it would be well for them to have something authentic to guide them.[6]

These points being determined, the remainder of my task became simplified. Mrs. Carlyle's letters are a better history of the London life of herself and her husband than could be written either by me or by anyone. The connecting narrative is Carlyle's own, and to meddle with his work would be to spoil it. It was thus left to me to supply an account of his early life in Scotland, the greater part of which I had written while he was alive, and which is contained in the present volumes. The publication of the letters will follow at no distant period. Afterwards, if I live to do it, I shall add a brief account of his last years, when I was in constant intercourse with him.[7]

It may be said that I shall have thus produced no "Life," but only the materials for a "Life."[8] That is true. But I believe that I shall have given, notwithstanding, a real picture as far as it goes; and an adequate estimate of Carlyle's work in this world is not at present possible. He was a teacher and a prophet in the Jewish sense of the word. The prophecies of Isaiah and Jeremiah have become a part of the permanent spiritual inheritance of mankind, because events proved that they had interpreted correctly the signs of their own times, and their prophecies were fulfilled. Carlyle, like them, believed that he had a special message to deliver to the present age. Whether he was correct in that belief, and whether his message was a true message, remains to be seen. He has told us that our most cherished ideas of political liberty, with their kindred corollaries, are mere illusions, and that the progress which has seemed to go along with them is a progress towards anarchy and social dissolution. If he was wrong, he has misused his powers. The principles of his teaching are false. He has offered himself as a guide upon a road of which he had no knowledge; and his own desire for himself would be the speediest oblivion both of his person and his works. If, on the other hand, he has been right; if, like his great predecessors, he has read truly the tendencies of this modern age of ours, and his teaching is authenticated by facts, then Carlyle, too, will take his place among the inspired seers, and he will shine on, another fixed star in the intellectual sky.

Time only can show how this will be:

Days to come are the wisest witnesses.[9]

chapter one

1795–1814

Beginnings

The river Annan, rising above Moffat in Hartfell, descends from the mountains through a valley gradually widening and spreading out, as the fells are left behind, into the rich and well-cultivated district known as Annandale. Picturesque and broken in the upper part of its course, the stream, when it reaches the level country, steals slowly among meadows and undulating wooded hills, till at the end of forty miles it falls into the Solway at Annan town. Annandale, famous always for its pasturage, suffered especially before the union of the kingdoms from border forays, the effects of which were long to be traced in a certain wildness of disposition in the inhabitants. Dumfriesshire, to which it belongs, was sternly Cameronian. Stories of the persecutions survived in the farmhouses as their most treasured historical traditions. Cameronian congregations lingered till the beginning of the present century, when they merged in other bodies of seceders from the established religion.

In its hard fight for spiritual freedom Scotch Protestantism lost respect for kings and nobles, and looked to Christ rather than to earthly rulers; but before the Reformation all Scotland was clannish or feudal; and the Dumfriesshire yeomanry, like the rest, were organised under great noble families, whose pennon they followed, whose name they bore, and the remotest kindred with which, even to a tenth generation, they were proud to claim. Among the families of the western border the Carlyles were not the least distinguished.

85

They were originally English, and were called probably after Carlisle town. They came to Annandale with the Bruces in the time of David the Second. A Sir John Carlyle was created Lord Carlyle of Torthorwald in reward for a beating which he had given the English at Annan. Michael, the fourth lord, signed the Association Bond among the Protestant lords when Queen Mary was sent to Lochleven, being the only one among them, it was observed, who could not write his name. Their work was rough. They were rough men themselves, and with the change of times their importance declined. The title lapsed,[1] the estates were dissipated in lawsuits, and by the middle of the last century nothing remained of the Carlyles but one or two households in the neighbourhood of Burnswark who had inherited the name either through the adoption of their forefathers of the name of their leader, or by some descent of blood which had trickled down through younger sons.

In one of these families, in a house which his father, who was a mason, had built with his own hands, Thomas Carlyle was born on December 4, 1795. Ecclefechan, where his father lived, is a small market town on the east side of Annandale, six miles inland from the Solway, and about sixteen on the great north road from Carlisle. It consists of a single street, down one side of which, at that time, ran an open brook. The aspect, like that of most Scotch towns, is cold, but clean and orderly, with an air of thrifty comfort. The houses are plain, that in which the Carlyles lived alone having pretensions to originality. In appearance one, it is really double, a central arch dividing it. James Carlyle, Thomas Carlyle's father, occupied one part. His brother, who was his partner in trade, lived in the other.

Of their ancestors they knew nothing beyond the second generation. Tradition said that they had been long settled as farmers at Birrens, the Roman station at Middlebie (two miles from Ecclefechan). One of them, it was said, had been unjustly hanged on pretext of border cattle-stealing. The case was so cruel that the farm had been given as some compensation to the widow, and the family had continued to possess it till their title was questioned, and they were turned out, by the Duke of Queensberry. Whether this story was true or not, it is certain that James Carlyle's grand-

ARCHED HOUSE, ECCLEFECHAN. CARLYLE'S BIRTHPLACE. Photograph taken in the 1890s just after the planting of the beech trees that now tower over the brook in the foreground—"the little Kuhbach [cow-brook] gushing kindly by, among beech rows" of *Sartor Resartus*. "This umbrageous Man's-nest," Carlyle described it in *Sartor*. (Photograph by John Patrick, courtesy of the University of Edinburgh.)

STREET VIEW, ECCLEFECHAN. "Changes take place so slowly in Scottish villages that the Ecclefechan of to-day differs but little from the Ecclefechan of Carlyle's boyhood," wrote Henry C. Shelley in 1895 (*Literary By-paths in Old England*). Although the pace of life has accelerated in the twentieth century, this Dumfriesshire village remains much as it was in earlier times. The visitor can still see the Arched House (now protected by the National Trust) and the graves of the Carlyles in Ecclefechan Kirkyard. (Photograph by John Patrick, courtesy of the University of Edinburgh.)

mother lived at Middlebie in extreme poverty, and that she died in the early part of the last century, leaving two sons.[2] Thomas, the elder, was a carpenter, worked for some time at Lancaster, came home afterwards, and saw the Highlanders pass through Ecclefechan in 1745 on their way to England. Leaving his trade, he settled at a small farm called Brown-knowe, near Burnswark Hill, and, marrying a certain Mary Gillespie, produced four sons and two daughters. Of these sons James Carlyle was the second. The household life was in a high degree disorderly. Old Thomas Carlyle was formed after the border type, more given to fighting and wild adventure than to patient industry. "My Grandfather did not drink," his grandson says, but "he was a fiery man; irascible, indomitable: of the toughness and springiness of steel. An old market-brawl, called 'the Ecclefechan Dog-fight,' in which he was a principal, survives in tradition there to this day."[3] He was proud, poor, and discontented, leaving his family for the most part to shift for themselves. They were often without food or fuel; his sons were dressed in breeks made mostly of leather.

> They had to scramble ("scraffle!") for their very clothes and food. They knit, they thatched, for hire; above all they hunted. My Father had tried all these things, almost in boyhood. Every dell and *burngate* and *cleugh* of that district he had traversed, seeking hares and the like: he used to tell of these pilgrimages: once, I remember, his gun-flint was "tied on with a hatband." He was a *real* hunter, like a wild Indian, from Necessity. The hares' flesh was food: hare-skins (at some sixpence each) would accumulate into the purchase-money of a coat. . . . His hunting years were not useless to him. Misery was early training the rugged boy into a Stoic;—that, one day, there might be assurance of a Scottish Man.[4]

"Travelling tinkers," "Highland drovers," and such like were occasional guests at Brownknowe. Sandy Macleod, a pensioned soldier who had served under Wolfe, lived in an adjoining cottage, and had stories to tell of his adventures.[5] Old Thomas Carlyle, notwithstanding his rough, careless ways, was not without cultivation. He studied Anson's *Voyages*, and in his old age, strange to say, when his sons were growing into young men, he would sit with a neighbour over the fire, reading, much to their scandal, the *Arabian Nights*. They had become, James Carlyle especially, and his brothers through him, serious lads, and they were shocked to see two old men occupied on the edge of the grave with such idle vanities.[6]

Religion had been introduced into the house through another singular figure, John Orr, the schoolmaster of Hoddam, who was also by trade a shoemaker. Schoolmastering in those days fell to persons of clever irregular habits, who took it from taste partly, and also because other forms of business did not answer with them. Orr was a man of strong pious tendencies, but was given to drink. He would disappear for weeks into pothouses, and then come back to his friends shattered and remorseful. He, too, was a friend and visitor at Brownknowe, teaching the boys by day, sleeping in the room with them at night, and discussing arithmetical problems with their father. From him James Carlyle gained such knowledge as he had, part of it a knowledge of the Bible, which became the guiding principle of his life. The effect was soon visible on a remarkable occasion. While he was still a boy, he and three of his companions had met to play cards. There was some disagreement among them, when James Carlyle said that they were fools and worse for quarrelling over a probably sinful amusement. They threw the cards into the fire, and perhaps no one of the four, certainly not James Carlyle, ever touched a card again. Hitherto he and his brother had gleaned a subsistence on the skirts of settled life. They were now to find an entrance into regular occupation. James Carlyle was born in 1757.[7] In[8] 1773, when he was sixteen, a certain William Brown, a mason from Peebles, came into Annandale, became acquainted with the Carlyles, and married Thomas Carlyle's eldest daughter Fanny. He took her brothers as apprentices, and they became known before long as the most skilful and diligent workmen in the neighbourhood. James, though not the eldest, had the strongest character, and guided the rest. "They were (censoriously) noted for their brotherly affection, and coherence." They all prospered. They were noted also for their "hard sayings," and it must be said also, in their early manhood, for "hard *strikings*." They were warmly liked by those near them; "by those at a distance, viewed, as something dangerous to meddle with, something *not* to be meddled with."[9]

James Carlyle never spoke with pleasure of his young days, regarding them as "days of folly, perhaps sinful days"; but it was well known that he was strictly temperate, pure, abstemious, prudent, and industrious. Feared he was from his promptness of hand, but never aggressive, and using his strength only to put down rudeness and violence. On one occasion, says Carlyle, "a huge rude peasant was rudely defying and insulting the party my Father belonged to; the others quailed, and bore it, till he could bear it no longer; but clutches his rough adversary . . . by the two flanks, swings him with ireful force round in the air (hitting his feet against some open door), and hurls him to a distance —supine, lamed, vanquished and utterly humbled. . . . He would say of such things: 'I am wae to think on't'—wae from repentance: Happy who has nothing worse to repent of!"[10]

The apprenticeship over, the brothers began work on their own account, and with marked success; James Carlyle taking the lead. He built, as has been already said, a house for himself, which still stands in the street of Ecclefechan. His brothers occupied one part of it, he himself the other; and his father, the old Thomas, life now wearing out, came in from Brownknowe to live with them. James, perhaps the others, but James decisively, became an avowedly religious man. He had a maternal uncle, one Robert Brand, whose advice and example influenced him in this matter. Brand was a "vigorous Religionist," of strict Presbyterian type. From him James Carlyle received a definite faith, and made his profession as a "Burgher," a seceding sect which had separated from the Establishment as insufficiently in earnest for them. They had their humble meeting-house, "thatched with heath"; and for minister a certain John Johnston, from whom Carlyle himself learned afterwards his first Latin; "the priestliest man," he says, "I ever under any ecclesiastical guise was privileged to look upon."[11]

In 1791, having then a house of his own, James Carlyle married a distant cousin of the same name, Janet Carlyle. They had one son, John, and then she died of fever. Her long fair hair, which had been cut off in her illness, remained as a memorial of her in a drawer, into which the children

MARGARET AITKEN CARLYLE. "A pious mother, if there ever was one," Carlyle wrote of her after her death; "pious to God the Maker and to all He had made. Intellect, humour, softest pity, love, and, before all, perfect veracity in thought, in word, mind, and action; these were her characteristics, and had been now for above eighty-three years, in a humbly diligent, beneficent, and often toilsome and suffering life." The book in her right hand may be the Bible. In 1881 this painting hung in Carlyle's bedroom. (Portrait in oil by Maxwell of Dumfries, 1842, courtesy of the Carlyle House, Chelsea.)

afterwards looked with wondering awe. Two years after the husband married again Margaret Aitken, "a woman," says Carlyle, "of to me the fairest descent, that of the pious, the just and wise."[12] Her character will unfold itself as the story goes on. Thomas Carlyle was her first child, born December 4, 1795; she lived to see him at the height of his fame, known and honoured wherever the English language was spoken. To her care "for body and soul" he never ceased to say that he owed "endless gratitude."[13] After Thomas came eight others, three sons and five daughters, one of whom, Janet, so called after the first wife, died when she was a few months old.[14]

The family was prosperous, as Ecclefechan working life understood prosperity. In one year, his best, James Carlyle made in his business as much as £100. At worst he earned an artisan's substantial wages, and was thrifty and prudent. The children, as they passed out of infancy, ran about barefoot, but were otherwise cleanly clothed, and fed on oatmeal, milk, and potatoes. Our Carlyle learned to read from his mother too early for distinct remembrance; when he was five his father taught him arithmetic, and sent him with the other village boys to school. Like the Carlyles generally he had a violent temper. John, the son of the first marriage, lived usually with his grandfather, but came occasionally to visit his parents. Carlyle's earliest recollection is of throwing his little brown stool at his brother in a mad passion of rage, when he was scarcely more than two years old, breaking a leg of it, and feeling "for perhaps the first time, the united pangs of Loss and of Remorse."[15] The next impression which most affected him was the small round heap under the sheet upon a bed where his little sister lay dead. Death, too, he made acquaintance with in another memorable form. His father's eldest brother John died. "I remember the funeral; and perhaps a day before it, how an ill-behaving servant-wench to some crony of hers, lifted up the coverlid from off his pale, ghastly-befilleted head to show it her: unheeding of me, who was alone with them there, and to whom the sight gave a new pang of horror."[16] The grandfather followed next, closing finally his Anson and his *Arabian Nights*. He had a brother whose adventures had been remarkable. Francis Carlyle, so he was called, had been apprenticed to a shoemaker. He, too, when his time was out, had gone to England, to Bristol among other places, where he fell into drink and gambling. He lost all his money; one morning after an orgy he flung himself desperately out of bed and broke his leg. When he recovered he enlisted in a brig of war, distinguished himself by special gallantry in supporting his captain in a mutiny, and was rewarded with the command of a Solway revenue cutter. After many years of rough creditable service he retired on half-pay to his native village of Middlebie. There had been some family quarrel, and the brothers, though living close to one another, had held no intercourse. They were both of them above eighty years of age. The old Thomas being on his death-bed, the sea captain's heart relented. He was a grim, broad, fierce-looking man; "prototype of Smollett's Trunnion."[17] Being too unwieldy to walk, he was brought into Ecclefechan in a cart, and carried in a chair up the steep stairs to his dying brother's room. There he remained some twenty minutes, and came down again with a face which printed itself in the little Carlyle's memory. They saw him no more, and after a brief interval the old generation had disappeared.

Amidst such scenes our Carlyle struggled through his early boyhood.

> It was not a joyful life (what life is), yet a safe, quiet one; above most others (or any other I have witnessed) a wholesome one. We were taciturn rather than talkative; but if little were said, that little had generally a meaning. I cannot be thankful enough for my parents.[18]

[Carlyle spoke of his father as]

> Considerably the most . . . [remarkable man] I have ever met with in my journey thro' life. Sterling *veracity*, in thought, in word, and in deed; *courage* mostly quiet, but capable of blazing into fire-whirlwinds when needful: these, and such a flash of just *insight*, and of brief natural eloquence and emphasis, true to every feature, as I have never met with in any other man (myself included) were the leading features of him. "Humour," of a most grim Scandinavian type, he occasionally had; "wit" rarely or never, too serious for "wit." My excellent Mother, with perhaps the deeper *piety* in most senses, had also the most *sport*,—of what is called wit, humour &c. No man of my day, or hardly any man, can have had better parents.[19]

94

The Sunday services in Mr. Johnston's meeting-house were the events of the week. The congregation were "Dissenters" of a marked type, some of them coming from as far as Carlisle; another party, and among these at times a little eager boy, known afterwards as Edward Irving, appearing regularly from Annan.

Education is a passion in Scotland. It is the pride of every honourable peasant, if he has a son of any promise, to give him a chance of rising as a scholar. As a child Carlyle could not have failed to show that there was something unusual in him. The schoolmaster in Ecclefechan gave a good account of his progress in "figures." The minister reported favourably of his Latin. "Tom, I do not grudge thy schooling," his father said to him one day, "now when thy uncle Frank owns thee to be a better Arithmetician than himself."[20] It was decided that he should go to Annan Grammar School, and thence, if he prospered, to the University, with final outlook to the ministry.

He was a shy thoughtful boy, shrinking generally from rough companions, but with the hot temper of his race. His mother, naturally anxious for him, and fearing perhaps the family tendency, extracted a promise before parting with him that he would never return a blow, and, as might be expected, his first experiences of school were extremely miserable. Boys of genius are never well received by the common flock, and escape persecution only when they are able to defend themselves.

Sartor Resartus is generally mythic, but parts are historical, and among them the account of the first launch of Teufelsdröckh into the Hinterschlag Gymnasium. Hinterschlag (smite behind) is Annan. Thither, leaving home and his mother's side, Carlyle was taken by his father, being then in his tenth year, and "fluttering [with] boundless hopes," at Whitsuntide, 1806, to the school which was to be his first step into a higher life.

> Well do I still remember the red sunny Whitsuntide morning, when, trotting full of hope by the side of Father Andreas, I entered the main street of the place, and saw its steeple-clock (then striking Eight) and *Schuldthurm* (Jail), and the aproned or disaproned Burghers moving-in to breakfast: a little dog, in mad terror, was

THE ACADEMY, ANNAN. "Well do I still remember the red sunny Whitsuntide morning, when, trotting full of hope by the side of Father Andreas, I entered the main street of the place," Carlyle wrote in *Sartor* of his first day at the school to which he went, accompanied by his father, after previous study in Ecclefechan. He was ten years old. "'With my first view of the Hinterschlag [Smite-behind] Gymnasium,' writes he [Teufelsdröckh], 'my evil days began.'" (Photograph by John Patrick, courtesy of the University of Edinburgh.)

rushing past; for some human imps had tied a tin-kettle to its tail. . . . Fit emblem also of much that awaited myself, in that mischievous Den. . . .

"Alas, the kind beech-rows of Entepfuhl were hidden in the distance: I was among strangers, harshly, at best indifferently, disposed towards me; the young heart felt, for the first time, quite orphaned and alone." His schoolfellows . . . were . . . "mostly rude Boys, and obeyed the impulse of rude Nature, which bids the deer-herd fall upon any stricken hart, the duck-flock put to death any broken-winged brother or sister, and on all hands the strong tyrannise over the weak."[21]

Carlyle retained to the end of his days a painful and indeed resentful recollection of these school experiences of his. This, he said of the passage just quoted from *Sartor,* is *"true* . . . and not half of the truth."[22]

He had obeyed his mother's injunctions. He had courage in plenty to resent ill usage, but his promise was sacred. He was passionate, and often, probably, violent, but fight he would not, and everyone who knows English and Scotch life will understand what his fate must have been. One consequence was a near escape from drowning. The boys had all gone to bathe; the lonely child had stolen apart from the rest, where he could escape from being tormented. He found himself in a deep pool which had been dug out for a dock and had been filled with the tide. The mere accident of someone passing at the time saved him. At length he could bear his condition no longer; he turned on the biggest bully in the school and furiously kicked him; a battle followed in which he was beaten; but he left marks of his fists upon his adversary, which were not forgotten. He taught his companions to fear him, if only like Brasidas's mouse. He was persecuted no longer, but he carried away bitter and resentful recollections of what he had borne, which were never entirely obliterated.[23]

The teaching which Carlyle received at Annan, he says, was limited, and of its kind only moderately good. Elsewhere in a note I find the following account of his first teaching and school experience:

My Mother had taught me reading, I never remembered when. "Tom Donaldson's School" at Ecclefechan,—a severely correct young man, Tom; from Edinburgh College, one session probably; went afterwards to Manchester &c, & I never saw his face again,

97

tho' I still remember it well, as always merry & kind to me, tho' harsh & to the ill-deserving severe. Hoddam School afterwards; which then stood at the Kirk. "Sandy Beattie" (subsequently a Burgher Minister in Glasgow; I well remember his "examining" us that day) reported me "complete in English," age then about 7; that I must "go into Latin," or waste my time: Latin accordingly; with what enthusiasm! But the poor Schoolmaster did not himself know Latin; I gradually got altogether swamped and bewildered under him; reverend Mr Johnstone of Ecclefechan (or *first*, his son, home from College, and already teaching a young Nephew or Cousin, in a careless but intelligent manner) had to take me in hand; and, once pulled afloat again, I made rapid & sure way. . . .

Sartor here, in good part [for the years at Annan Academy, 1806–9]; not to be trusted in details! "Greek," for example, consisted of the *Alphabet* mainly; "Hebrew" is quite a *German* entity,—nobody in that region, except my reverend old Mr Johnstone, could have read one sentence of it to save his life. I did get to read Latin & French with fluency (Latin *quantity* was left a frightful chaos, and I had to learn it afterwards); some geometry, algebra (*arithmetic* thoroughly well), vague outlines of geography &c I did learn;—all the Books I could get were also devoured. . . . Mythically *true* is what Sartor says of his Schoolfellows, and not half of the truth. Unspeakable is the damage & defilement I got out of those unguided tyrannous cubs,—especially till I revolted against them, and gave stroke for stroke; as my pious Mother, in her great love of peace and of my best interests, spiritual chiefly, had imprudently forbidden me to do. One way and another I had never been so wretched as here in that School, and the first 2 years of my time in it still count among the miserable of my life. "Academies," "High Schools," "Instructors of Youth"—Oh ye unspeakable!—[24]

Of holidays we hear nothing, though holidays there must have been at Christmas[25] and Midsummer; little also of school friendships or amusements. For the last, in such shape as could have been found in boys of his class in Annan, Carlyle could have had little interest. He speaks warmly of his mathematical teacher, a certain Mr. Morley, from Cumberland, "whom I loved much, and who taught me well."[26] He had formed a comradeship with one or two boys of his own age, who were not entirely uncongenial to him; but only one incident is preserved which was of real moment. In his third school year Carlyle first consciously saw Edward Irving. Irving's family lived in Annan. He had himself been at the school, and had gone thence to the University of Edinburgh. He had distinguished himself there, gained prizes, and was otherwise honourably spoken of. Annan, both town and

school, was proud of the brilliant lad that they had produced. And Irving one day looked in upon the class room,
the masters out of compliment attending him. "Irving was
scrupulously dressed, black coat, ditto tight pantaloons in
the fashion of the day . . . and looked very neat, self-
possessed, and enviable: a flourishing slip of a youth; with
coal-black hair, swarthy clear complexion; very straight on
his feet; and, except for the glaring squint alone, decidedly
handsome."[27] The boys listened eagerly as he talked in a
free airy way about Edinburgh and its professors. A University man who has made a name for himself is infinitely
admirable to younger ones; he is not too far above them to
be comprehensible. They know what he has done, and they
hope distantly that they too one day may do the like. Of
course Irving did not distinguish Carlyle. He walked through
the rooms and disappeared.

The Hinterschlag Gymnasium was over soon after, and
Carlyle's future career was now to be decided on. The
Ecclefechan family life was not favourable to displays of pre-
cocious genius. Vanity was the last quality that such a man
as James Carlyle would encourage, and there was a severity
in his manner which effectively repressed any disposition to
it.

> We had all to complain that we *durst not* freely love [our father].
> His heart seemed as if walled in. . . . My Mother has owned to me
> that she could never understand him; that her affection, and . . .
> her admiration of him was obstructed: it seemed as if an atmosphere
> of Fear repelled us from him. To me it was especially so. . . . My
> heart and tongue played freely only with my Mother. He had an air
> of deepest gravity, even sternness. . . . He had the most entire
> and open contempt for all idle tattle, what he called "clatter."
> *Any* talk that had meaning in it he could listen to: what had *no*
> meaning in it, above all, what seemed false, he absolutely could
> and would not hear; but abruptly turned aside from it. . . . Long
> may we remember his "I don't believe thee;" his tongue-paralysing,
> cold, indifferent "Hah!"[28]

Besides fear, Carlyle, as he grew older, began to experience a certain awe of his father as of a person of altogether
superior qualities.

> None of us will ever forget that bold glowing style of his, flowing
> free from the untutored Soul; full of metaphors (though he knew
> not what a metaphor was), with all manner of potent words (which

99

he appropriated and applied with a *surprising* accuracy; . . . brief, energetic; and which . . . conveyed the most perfect picture, definite, clear not in ambitious *colours* but in full *white* sunlight. . . . Emphatic I have heard him beyond all men. In anger he had no need of oaths; his words were like sharp arrows that smote into the very heart.[29]

Such a father may easily have been alarming and slow to gain his children's confidence. He had silently observed his little Tom, however. The reports from the Annan masters were all favourable, and when the question rose what was to be done with him, he inclined to venture the University. The wise men of Ecclefechan shook their heads. "Educate a boy," said one of them, "and he grows up to despise his ignorant parents." Others said it was a risk, it was waste of money, there was a large family to be provided for, too much must not be spent upon one. James Carlyle had seen something in his boy's character which showed him that the risk, if risk there was, must be encountered; and to Edinburgh it was decided that Tom should go and be made a scholar of.

To English ears university life suggests splendid buildings, luxurious rooms, rich endowments as the reward of successful industry; as students, young men between nineteen and twenty-three with handsome allowances, spending each of them on an average double the largest income which James Carlyle had earned in any year of his life. Universities north of the Tweed had in those days no money prizes to offer, no fellowships and scholarships, nothing at all but an education, and a discipline in poverty and self-denial. The lads who went to them were the children, most of them, of parents as poor as Carlyle's father. They knew at what a cost the expense of sending them to college, relatively small as it was, could be afforded; and they went with the fixed purpose of making the very utmost of their time. Five months only of each year they could remain in their classes; for the rest of it they taught pupils themselves, or worked on the farm at home to pay for their own learning.

Each student, as a rule, was the most promising member of the family to which he belonged, and extraordinary confidence was placed in them. They were sent to Edinburgh, Glasgow, or wherever it might be, when they were mere boys of fourteen. They had no one to look after them either on their journey or when they came to the end. They walked from their homes, being unable to pay for coach-hire. They entered their own names at the college. They found their own humble lodgings, and were left entirely to their own capacity for self-conduct. The carriers brought them oatmeal, potatoes, and salt butter from the home farm, with a few eggs occasionally as a luxury. With their thrifty habits they required no other food. In the return cart their linen went back to their mothers to be washed and mended. Poverty protected them from temptations to vicious amusements. They formed their economical friendships; they shared their breakfasts and their thoughts, and had their clubs for conversation or discussion. When term was over they walked home in parties, each district having its little knot belonging to it; and known along the roads as University scholars, they were assured of entertainment on the way.

As a training in self-dependence no better education could have been found in these islands. If the teaching had been as good as the discipline of character, the Scotch universities might have competed with the world. The teaching was the weak part. There were no funds, either in the colleges or with the students, to provide personal instruction as at Oxford and Cambridge. The professors were individually excellent, but they had to teach large classes, and had no leisure to attend particularly to this or that promising pupil. The universities were opportunities to boys who were able to take advantage of them, and that was all.

Such was the life on which Carlyle was now to enter, and such were the circumstances of it. It was the November term 1809. He was to be fourteen on the fourth of the approaching December. Edinburgh is nearly one hundred miles from Ecclefechan.[30] He was to go on foot like the rest, under the guardianship of a boy named "Tom Smail," two or three years his senior, who had already been at college, and was held, therefore, to be a sufficient protector.

"Tom Smail" was a poor companion, very innocent, very conceited, an indifferent scholar. Carlyle in his own mind had a small opinion of him. The journey over the moors was a weary one, the elder lad stalking on generally ahead,

101

whistling an Irish tune; the younger given up to his bits of reflections in the silence of the hills. Twenty miles a day the boys walked, by Moffat and over Erikstane. They reached Edinburgh early one afternoon, got a lodging in Simon Square, got dinner, and sallied out again that "Palinurus Tom" might give the novice a glance of the great city.[31]

Of the University he says that he learned little there. In the Latin class he was under Professor Christison, "who had never noticed me while in his class, nor could distinguish me from another 'Mr. *Irving* Carlyle,' an older, considerably bigger boy, with flaming red hair, wild buck-teeth, and scorched complexion, and the *worst* Latinist of all my acquaintance."[32]

It was not much better with philosophy. " 'Dugald Stewart' had gone, the year before I entered: my Professional Lecturer was Thomas Brown; an eloquent acute little gentleman; full of enthusiasm about 'simple suggestion' & 'relative' ditto,—to me unprofitable utterly & bewildering & dispiriting 'as the autumn winds among the withered leaves.' "[33]

In mathematics only he made real progress. His temperament was impatient of uncertainties. He threw himself with delight into a form of knowledge in which the conclusions were indisputable, where at each step he could plant his foot with confidence. Professor Leslie (Sir John Leslie afterwards) discovered his talent and exerted himself to help him with a zeal of which Carlyle never afterwards ceased to speak with gratitude.[34]

Yet even in mathematics, on ground with which he was familiar, his shy nature was unfitted for display. He carried off no prizes.[35] He tried only once, and though he was notoriously superior to all his competitors the crowd and noise of the class room prevented him from even attempting to distinguish himself. I have heard him say late in life that his thoughts never came to him in proper form except when he was alone.

Sartor Resartus, I have already said, must not be followed too literally as a biographical authority. It is mythic, not historical. Nevertheless, as mythic it may be trusted for the general outlines.

Among eleven-hundred Christian youths, there will not be wanting
some eleven eager to learn. By collision with such, a certain
warmth, a certain polish was communicated; by instinct and happy
accident, I took less to rioting, . . . than to thinking and reading,
which latter also I was free to do. Nay from the chaos of that
Library, I succeeded in fishing-up more books than had been
known to the very keepers thereof. The foundation of a Literary
Life was hereby laid. I learned, on my own strength, to read
fluently in almost all cultivated languages, on almost all subjects
and sciences. . . . A certain groundplan of Human Nature and
Life began to fashion itself in me; . . . by additional experiments
might be corrected and indefinitely extended.[36]

The teaching at a university is but half what is learned
there; the other half, and the most important, is what young
men learn from one another. Carlyle's friends at Edinburgh, the eleven out of the eleven hundred, were of his own
rank of life, sons of peasants who had their own way to
make in life. From their letters, many of which have been
preserved, it is clear that they were clever good lads, distinctly superior to ordinary boys of their age, Carlyle himself holding the first place in their narrow circle. Their
lives were pure and simple. Nowhere in these letters is there
any jesting with vice, or light allusions to it. The boys wrote
to one another on the last novel of Scott or poem of Byron,
on the *Edinburgh Review*, on the war, on the fall of Napoleon, occasionally on geometrical problems, sermons,
college exercises, and divinity lectures, and again on innocent trifles, with sketches, now and then humorous and
bright, of Annandale life as it was seventy years ago. They
looked to Carlyle to direct their judgement and advise them
in difficulties. He was the prudent one of the party, able, if
money matters went wrong, to help them out of his humble
savings. He was already noted, too, for power of effective
speech—"far too sarcastic for so young a man" was what
elder people said of him. One of his correspondents [John
Edward Hill] addressed him always as "Jonathan," or
"Dean," or "Doctor," as if he was to be a second Swift.[37]
Others called him Parson, perhaps from his intended profession. All foretold future greatness to him of one kind or
another. They recognised that he was not like other young
men, that he was superior to other young men, in character

103

as well as intellect. "Knowing how you abhor all affectation" is an expression used to him when he was still a mere boy.

His destination was "the ministry," and for this, knowing how much his father and mother wished it, he tried to prepare himself. He was already conscious, however, "that he had not the least enthusiasm for that business, that even grave prohibitory doubts were gradually rising ahead. Formalism was not the pinching point, had there been the preliminary of belief forthcoming." "No Church, or speaking Entity whatever," he admitted, "can do without 'formulas'; but it must believe them first, if it would be honest!"[38]

chapter two

1814–1818

Teacher

Having finished his college course, Carlyle looked out for pupils to maintain himself. The ministry was still his formal destination, but several years had still to elapse before a final resolution would be necessary—four years if he remained in Edinburgh attending lectures in the Divinity Hall; six if he preferred to be a rural Divinity student, presenting himself once in every twelve months at the University and reading a discourse. He did not wish to hasten matters, and, the pupil business being precarious and the mathematical tutorship at Annan falling vacant, Carlyle offered for it and was elected by competition in 1814. He never liked teaching. The recommendation of the place was the sixty or seventy pounds a year of salary,[1] which relieved his father of further expense upon him, and enabled him to put by a little money every year, to be of use in future either to himself or his family. In other respects the life at Annan was only disagreeable to him. His tutor's work he did scrupulously well, but the society of a country town had no interest for him.[2] He would not visit. He lived alone, shutting himself up with his books, disliked the business more and more, and came finally to hate it. Annan, associated as it was with the odious memories of his schooldays, had indeed but one merit—that he was within reach of his family, especially of his mother, to whom he was attached with a real passion.[3]

His father had by this time[4] given up business at Ecclefechan, and had taken a farm in the neighbourhood. The great north road which runs through the village rises gradually into an upland treeless grass country. About two miles distant on the left-hand side as you go towards Lockerbie, there stands, about three hundred yards in from the road, a solitary low whitewashed cottage, with a few poor outbuildings attached to it. This is Mainhill, which was now for many years to be Carlyle's home, where he first learned German, studied *Faust* in a dry ditch, and completed his translation of *Wilhelm Meister*. The house itself is, or was when the Carlyles occupied it, of one story, and consisted of three rooms, a kitchen, a small bedroom, and a large one connected by a passage. The door opens into a square farmyard, on one side of which are stables, on the other side opposite the door the cow byres, on the third a washhouse and a dairy. The situation is high, utterly bleak and swept by all the winds. Not a tree shelters the premises; the fences are low, the wind permitting nothing to grow but stunted thorn. The view alone redeems the dreariness of the situation. On the left is the great hill of Burnswark. Broad Annandale stretches in front down to the Solway, which shines like a long silver riband; on the right is Hoddam Hill with the Tower of Repentance on its crest, and the wooded slopes which mark the line of the river. Beyond towers up Criffel, and in the far distance Skiddaw, and Saddleback, and Helvellyn, and the high Cumberland ridges on the track of the Roman wall. Here lived Carlyle's father and mother with their eight children, Carlyle himself spending his holidays with them; the old man and his younger sons cultivating the sour soil and winning a hard-earned living out of their toil, the mother and daughters doing the household work and minding cows and poultry, and taking their turn in the field with the rest in harvest time.

So two years passed away; Carlyle remaining at Annan. Of his own writing during this period there is little preserved, but his correspondence continued, and from his friends' letters glimpses can be gathered of his temper and occupations. He was mainly busy with mathematics, but he was reading incessantly, Hume's *Essays* among other books. He was looking out into the world, meditating on the fall of Napoleon, on the French Revolution, and thinking

MAINHILL. James Carlyle's first farm, taken in 1815 and for ten years the home of the Carlyle family. Here Carlyle returned each summer from Edinburgh. "There with my best of nurses and hostesses—my mother; blessed voiceless or low-voiced time, still sweet to me," he wrote in his *Reminiscences*. (Photograph by John Patrick, courtesy of the University of Edinburgh.)

much of the suffering in Scotland which followed the close
of the war. There were sarcastic sketches, too, of the families with which he was thrown in Annan. Robert Mitchell
(an Edinburgh student who had become master of a school
at Ruthwell)[5] rallies him on having reduced "the fair and
fat academicians" "into scorched, singed, and shrivelled
hags"; and hinting a warning "against the temper with
respect to this world which we are sometimes apt to entertain," he suggests that young men like him and his correspondent "ought to think how many are worse off than
they," "should be thankful for what they had, and not allow
imagination to create unreal distress."[6]

To another friend, Thomas Murray, author afterwards of
a history of Galloway, Carlyle had complained of his fate in
a light and less bitter spirit. To an epistle written in this tone
Murray replied with a description of Carlyle's style, which
deserves a place if but for the fulfilment of the prophecy
which it contains.

> I have had the pleasure of receiving My Dear Carlyle your very hu-
> morous and friendly letter—a letter remarkable for vivacity, a
> Shandean turn of expression and an affectionate pathos—which
> indicate a peculiar turn of mind—make sincerity doubly striking
> and wit doubly poignant. You flatter me with saying my letter
> was good but allow me to observe that among all my elegant and
> respectable correspondents there is none whose manner of letter-
> writing I so much envy as yours. A happy flow of language—either
> for pathos description or humour—and an easy and graceful cur-
> rent of ideas appropriate to every subject characterize your corre-
> spondence. This is not adulation—I speak what I think. . . .
> Your letters will always be a feast—a varied and exquisite re-
> past—and the time I hope will come—but I trust is far distant—
> when these our juvenile epistles will be read—probably applauded
> —by a generation unborn and that the name of *Carlyle at least* will
> be inseparably connected with the literary history of the nineteenth
> century.[7]

Murray kept Carlyle's answer to this far-seeing letter.

> —But—O Tom! what a foolish flattering creature tho[u] art! to
> talk of future eminence, and connection with the literary history
> of the Nineteenth century to such a one as me!— Alas! my good
> lad, when I and all my fancies, and reveries and speculation[s]
> shall have been swept over with the *besom of oblivion,* the lit-
> erary history of *No* century will know itself one jot the worse.—
> Yet think not that because I talk thus, I am careless about literary

fame. No! Heaven knows that ever since I have [been] able to form a wish—*the wish of being known* has been the foremost.[8]

These college companions were worthy and innocent young men; none of them, however, came to any high position, and Carlyle's career was now about to intersect with the life of a far more famous contemporary who flamed up a few years later into meridian splendour and then disappeared in delirium. Edward Irving was the son of a well-to-do burgess of Annan, by profession a tanner. Irving was five years older than Carlyle; he had preceded him at Annan School; he had gone thence to Edinburgh University, where he had specially distinguished himself, and had been selected afterwards to manage a school at Haddington, where his success as a teacher had been again conspicuous. Among his pupils at Haddington there was one gifted little girl who will be hereafter much heard of in these pages, Jane Baillie Welsh, daughter of a Dr. Welsh whose surgical fame was then great in that part of Scotland, a remarkable man who liked Irving and trusted his only child in his hands. The Haddington adventure had answered so well that Irving, after a year or two, was removed to a larger school at Kirkcaldy, where, though no fault was found with his teaching, he gave less complete satisfaction. A party among his patrons there thought him too severe with the boys, thought him proud, thought him this or that which they did not like. The dissentients resolved at last to have a second school of their own, to be managed in a different style, and they applied to the classical and mathematical professors at Edinburgh to recommend them a master. Professor Christison and Professor Leslie, who had noticed Carlyle more than he was aware of, had decided that he was the fittest person that they knew of; and in the summer of 1816 notice of the offered preferment was sent down to him at Annan.

He had seen Irving's face occasionally in Ecclefechan church, and once afterwards, as has been said, when Irving, fresh from his college distinctions, had looked in at Annan school; but they had no personal acquaintance, nor did Carlyle, while he was a master there, ever visit the Irving family. Of course, however, he was no stranger to the reputation of their brilliant son, with whose fame all Annandale was ringing, and with whom kind friends had compared him to his own disadvantage.

In the winter of 1815 Carlyle for the first time personally met Irving, and the beginning of the acquaintance was not promising. He was still pursuing his Divinity course. Candidates who could not attend the regular lectures at the University came up once a year and delivered an address of some kind in the Divinity Hall. One already he had given the first year of his Annan mastership—an English sermon on the text "Before I was afflicted I went astray." He calls it "a weak and flowery sentimental Piece," for which, however, he had been complimented by "comrades and Professors." His next was a discourse in Latin on the question whether there was or was not such a thing as "Natural Religion." This, too, he says was "weak enough."[9] It is lost, and nothing is left to show the view which he took about the matter. But here also he gave satisfaction, and was innocently pleased with himself. It was on this occasion that he fell in accidentally with Irving at a friend's rooms in Edinburgh, and there was a trifling skirmish of tongue between them, where Irving found the laugh turned against him.

A few months after came Carlyle's appointment to Kirkcaldy as Irving's quasi rival, and perhaps he felt a little uneasy as to the terms on which they might stand towards each other. His alarms, however, were pleasantly dispelled. He was to go to Kirkcaldy in the summer holidays of 1816 to see the people there and be seen by them before coming to a final arrangement with them. Adam Hope, one of the masters in Annan School, to whom Carlyle was much attached, and whose portrait he has painted, had just lost his wife. Carlyle had gone to sit with the old man in his sorrows, and unexpectedly fell in with Irving there, who had come on the same errand.

> If I had been in doubts about his reception of me . . . he quickly and for ever ended them, by a friendliness which, on wider scenes, might have been called chivalrous. At first sight he heartily shook my hand; welcomed me as if I had been a valued old acquaintance, almost a brother; and before my leaving . . . came up to me again, and with the frankest tone said, "You are coming to Kirkcaldy to look about you in a month or two: you know I am there; my house and all that I can do for you is yours;—two Annandale people must not be strangers in Fife!"— The "doubting Thomas"

durst not quite believe all this, so chivalrous was it; but felt
pleased and relieved by the fine and sincere tone of it; and thought to
himself, "Well, it would be pretty!"[10]

To Kirkcaldy, then, Carlyle went with hopes so far improved. How Irving kept his word; how warmly he received him; how he opened his house, his library, his heart to him; how they walked and talked together on Kirkcaldy Sands on the summer nights, and toured together in holiday time through the Highlands; how Carlyle found in him a most precious and affectionate companion at the most critical period of his life—all this he has himself described. The reader will find it for himself in the *Reminiscences* which he has left of the time.[11]

Correspondence with his family had commenced and was regularly continued from the day when Carlyle went first to college. The letters, however, which are preserved begin with his settlement at Kirkcaldy. From this time they are constant, regular, and, from the care with which they have been kept on both sides, are to be numbered in thousands. Father, mother, brothers, sisters, all wrote in their various styles, and all received answers. They were "a clannish folk" holding tight together, and Carlyle was looked up to as the scholar among them. Of these letters I can give but a few here and there, but they will bring before the eyes the Mainhill farm, and all that was going on there in a sturdy, pious, and honourable Annandale peasant's household.

Mrs. Carlyle could barely write at this time. She taught herself later in life for the pleasure of communicating with her son, between whom and herself there existed a special and passionate attachment of a quite peculiar kind. She was a severe Calvinist, and watched with the most affectionate anxiety over her children's spiritual welfare, her eldest boy's above all. The hope of her life was to see him a minister— a "priest" she would have called it—and she was already alarmed to know that he had no inclination that way.

The letters from the other members of the family were sent equally regularly whenever there was an opportunity, and give between them a perfect picture of healthy rustic life at the Mainhill farm—the brothers and sisters down to the lowest all hard at work, the little ones at school, the

EDWARD IRVING. "A man of noble faculties & qualities; the noblest, largest and brotherliest man, I still say, whom I have met with in my Life-journey," Carlyle wrote in the *Reminiscences* in 1866, more than thirty years after Irving's death. "But for Irving, I had never known what the communion of man with man means." This portrait hung in Carlyle's dressing room in Cheyne Row. (Courtesy of the Carlyle House, Chelsea.)

elders ploughing, reaping, tending cattle, or minding the dairy, and in the intervals reading history, reading Scott's novels, or, even trying at geometry, which was then Carlyle's own favourite study. In the summer of 1817 the mother had a severe illness, by which her mind was affected. It was necessary to place her for a few weeks under restraint away from home—a step no doubt just and necessary, but which she never wholly forgave, but resented in her own humorous way to the end of her life. The disorder soon passed off, however, and never returned.

Meanwhile Carlyle was less completely contented with his position at Kirkcaldy than he had let his mother suppose. For one thing he hated schoolmastering, and would, or thought he would, have preferred to work with his hands, while except Irving he had scarcely a friend in the place for whom he cared. His occupation shut him out from the best kind of society, which there, as elsewhere, had its exclusive rules. He was received, for Irving's sake, in the family of Mr. Martin, the minister; and was in some degree of intimacy there, liking Martin himself, and to some extent, but not much, his wife and daughters, to one of whom Irving had, perhaps too precipitately, become engaged. There were others also—Mr. Swan, a Kirkcaldy merchant, particularly—for whom he had a grateful remembrance; but it is clear, both from Irving's letters to him and from his own confession, that he was not popular either there or anywhere. Shy and reserved at one moment, at another sarcastically self-asserting, with forces working in him which he did not himself understand, and which still less could be understood by others, he could neither properly accommodate himself to the tone of Scotch provincial drawing-rooms, nor even to the business which he had especially to do. A man of genius can do the lowest work as well as the highest; but genius in the process of developing, combined with an irritable nervous system and a fiercely impatient temperament, was not happily occupied in teaching stupid lads the elements of Latin and arithmetic. Nor were matters mended when the Town Corporation, who were his masters, took upon them, as sometimes happened, to instruct or rebuke him.

Life, however, even under these hard circumstances, was

113

not without its romance. I borrow a passage from the *Reminiscences*:

> Some hospitable human firesides I found, and these were at intervals a fine little element; but in general we were but onlookers (the one real "Society," our books and our few selves);—not even with the bright "young ladies" (what was a sad feature) were we generally on speaking terms. By far the cleverest and brightest, however, an Ex-pupil of Irving's, and genealogically and otherwise (being poorish, proud, and well-bred) rather a kind of alien in the place, I did at last make acquaintance with (at Irving's first, I think, though she rarely came thither); some acquaintance;—and it might easily have been more, had she, and her Aunt, and our economic and other circumstances liked! She was of the fair-complexioned, softly elegant, softly grave, witty and comely type, and had a good deal of gracefulness, intelligence and other talent. . . . To me, who had only known her for a few months, and who within a twelve or fifteen months saw the last of her, she continued for perhaps some three years a figure hanging more or less in my fancy, on the usual romantic, or latterly quite elegiac and silent terms, and to this day there is in me a goodwill to her, a candid and gentle pity for her, if needed at all. She was of the Aberdeenshire Gordons . . . "Margaret Gordon," born I think in New Brunswick, where her Father, probably in some official post, had died young and poor,—her *accent* was prettily English, and her voice very fine. . . . A year or so after we heard the fair Margaret had married some rich insignificant Aberdeen Mr. Something; who afterwards got into Parliament, thence out "to Nova Scotia" (or *so*) "as Governor;" and I heard of her no more,—except that lately she was still living about Aberdeen, childless, as the "Dowager Lady,"——, her Mr. Something having got knighted before dying. Poor Margaret! Speak to her, since the "good-bye, then" at Kirkcaldy in 1819, I never did or could. I saw her, recognisably to me, here in her London time (1840 or so), *twice*, once with her maid in Piccadilly promenading, little altered; a second time, that same year or next, on horseback both of us, and *meeting* in the gate of Hyde Park, when her *eyes* (but that was all) said to me almost touchingly, "Yes, yes; that is you!"[12]

Margaret Gordon was the original, so far as there was an original, of Blumine in *Sartor Resartus*.[13] Two letters from her remain among Carlyle's papers, which show that on both sides their regard for each other had found expression.[14] Circumstances, however, and the unpromising appearance of Carlyle's situation and prospects, forbade an engagement between them, and acquit the aunt of needless harshness in peremptorily putting an end to their acquaintance.

chapter three

1818–1821

Spiritual Torment

Carlyle had by this time abandoned the thought of the "ministry" as his possible future profession—not without a struggle, for both his father's and his mother's hearts had been set upon it; but the "grave prohibitive doubts" which had risen in him of their own accord had been strengthened by Gibbon, whom he had found in Irving's library and eagerly devoured. Never at any time had he "the least inclination" for such an office, and his father, though deeply disappointed, was too genuine a man to offer the least remonstrance.[1] The "schoolmastering" too, after two years' experience of it, became intolerable. His disposition, at once shy and defiantly proud, had perplexed and displeased the Kirkcaldy burghers. Both he and Irving also fell into unpleasant collisions with them, and neither of the two was sufficiently docile to submit tamely to reproof. An opposition school had been set up which drew off the pupils, and finally they both concluded that they had had enough of it— "better *die* than be a Schoolmaster for one's living"[2]—and would seek some other means of supporting themselves. Carlyle had passed his summer holidays as usual at Mainhill (1818), where he had perhaps talked over his prospects with his family. On his return to Kirkcaldy in September he wrote to his father explaining his situation. He had saved about £90, on which, with his thrifty habits, he said that he could support himself in Edinburgh till he could "fall into some other way of doing." He could perhaps get a few mathematical pupils, and meantime could study for the bar.

The end was, that when December came Carlyle and Irving "kicked the schoolmaster functions over," removed to Edinburgh, and were adrift on the world. Irving had little to fear; he had money, friends, reputation; he had a profession, and was waiting only for "a call" to enter on his full privileges. Carlyle was far more unfavourably situated. He was poor, unpopular, comparatively unknown, or, if known, known only to be feared and even shunned. "In Edinburgh from my fellow creatures," he says, "little or nothing but *vinegar* was my reception—cup [i.e., a slight bow] when we happened to meet or pass near each other; —my own blame mainly, so proud, shy, poor, at once so insignificant-looking and so grim and sorrowful. That in *Sartor*, of the *'worm* trodden & proving a *torpedo*,' . . . is not wholly a fable; but did actually befal once or twice, as I still (with a kind of small not ungenial malice) can remember."[3] He had, however, as was said, nearly a hundred pounds, which he had saved out of his earnings; he had a consciousness of integrity worth more than gold to him. He had thrifty self-denying habits which made him content with the barest necessaries, and he resolutely faced his position. His family, though silently disapproving the step which he had taken and necessarily anxious about him, rendered what help they could. Once more the Ecclefechan carrier brought up the weekly or monthly supplies of oatmeal, cakes, butter, and, when needed, under-garments, returning with the dirty linen for the mother to wash and mend, and occasional presents which were never forgotten; while Carlyle, after a thought of civil engineering, for which his mathematical training gave him a passing inclination, sat down seriously, if not very assiduously, to study law.[4]

Carlyle had written a sermon on the salutary effects of "affliction," as his first exercise in the Divinity School. He was beginning now, in addition to the problem of living which he had to solve, to learn what affliction meant. He was attacked with dyspepsia, which never wholly left him, and in these early years soon assumed its most torturing form, like "a rat gnawing at the pit of his stomach." His disorder working on his natural irritability found escape in

116

expressions which showed, at any rate, that he was attaining a mastery of language. The pain made him furious; and in such a humour the commonest calamities of life became unbearable horrors.

While law lectures were being attended, the difficulty was to live. Pupils were a not very effective resource, and of his adventures in this department Carlyle gave ridiculous accounts. One, sometimes two, pupils were found willing to pay at the rate required [two guineas a month for an hour's instruction daily]. Dr. Brewster, afterwards Sir David, discovered Carlyle and gave him occasional employment on his [Edinburgh] Encyclopaedia. He was thus able to earn, as long as the session lasted, about two guineas a week, and on this he contrived to live without trenching on his capital.

Carlyle was thinking as much as his mother of religion, but the form in which his thoughts were running was not hers. He was painfully seeing that all things were not wholly as he had been taught to think them; the doubts which had stopped his divinity career were blackening into thunderclouds; and all his reflections were coloured by dyspepsia. "I . . . was entirely unknown in 'Edinburgh circles,' " he says; "solitary, 'eating my own heart,' fast losing my health, too; a prey, in fact, to nameless struggles and miseries, which have yet a kind of horror in them to my thought. Three weeks without *any* Sleep (from *im*possibility to be free of noise)." In fact he was entering on what he called "the three most miserable years of my life."[5] He would have been saved from much could he have resolutely thrown himself into his intended profession; but he soon came to hate it, as just then, perhaps, he would have hated anything.

Men who are out of humour with themselves often see their own condition reflected in the world outside them, and everything seems amiss because it is not well with themselves. But the state of Scotland and England also was well fitted to feed his discontent. The great war had been followed by a collapse. Wages were low, food at famine prices. Tens of thousands of artisans were out of work, their families were starving, and they themselves were growing mutinous. Even at home from his own sternly patient father, who never meddled with politics, he heard things not calculated to reconcile him to existing arrangements.

These early impressions can be traced through the whole of Carlyle's writings; the conviction was forced upon him that there was something vicious to the bottom in English and Scotch society, and that revolution in some form or other lay visibly ahead. So long as Irving remained in Edinburgh "the condition of the people" question was the constant subject of talk between him and Carlyle. They were both of them ardent, radical, indignant at the injustice which they witnessed, and as yet unconscious of the difficulty of mending it. Irving, however, he had seen little of since they had moved to Edinburgh, and he was left, for the most part, alone with his own thoughts. There had come upon him the trial which in these days awaits every man of high intellectual gifts and noble nature on their first actual acquaintance with human things—the question, far deeper than any mere political one, What is this world then, what is this human life, over which a just God is said to preside, but of whose presence or whose providence so few signs are visible? In happier ages religion silences scepticism if it cannot reply to its difficulties, and postpones the solution of the mystery to another stage of existence. Brought up in a pious family where religion was not talked about or emotionalised, but was accepted as the rule of thought and conduct, himself too instinctively upright, pure of heart, and reverent, Carlyle, like his parents, had accepted the Bible as a direct communication from Heaven. It made known the will of God, and the relation in which man stood to his Maker, as present facts like a law of nature, the truth of it, like the truth of gravitation, which man must act upon or immediately suffer the consequences. But religion, as revealed in the Bible, passes beyond present conduct, penetrates all forms of thought, and takes possession wherever it goes. It claims to control the intellect, to explain the past, and foretell the future. It has entered into poetry and art, and has been the interpreter of history. And thus there had grown round it a body of opinion, on all varieties of subjects, assumed to be authoritative; dogmas which science was contradicting; a history of events which it called infallible, yet which the canons of evidence, by which other histories

118

are tried and tested successfully, declared not to be infallible at all. To the Mainhill household the Westminster Confession was a full and complete account of the position of mankind and of the Being to whom they owed their existence. The Old and New Testament not only contained all spiritual truth necessary for guidance in word and deed, but every fact related in them was literally true. To doubt was not to mistake, but was to commit a sin of the deepest dye, and was a sure sign of a corrupted heart. Carlyle's wide study of modern literature had shown him that much of this had appeared to many of the strongest minds in Europe to be doubtful or even plainly incredible. Young men of genius are the first to feel the growing influences of their time, and on Carlyle they fell in their most painful form. Notwithstanding his pride, he was most modest and self-distrustful. He had been taught that want of faith was sin, yet, like a true Scot, he knew that he would peril his soul if he pretended to believe what his intellect told him was false. If any part of what was called Revelation was mistaken, how could he be assured of the rest? How could he tell that the moral part of it, to which the phenomena which he saw round him were in plain contradiction, was more than a "devout imagination"? Thus to poverty and dyspepsia there had been added the struggle which is always hardest in the noblest minds, which Job had known, and David, and Solomon, and Aeschylus, and Shakespeare, and Goethe. Where are the tokens of His presence? where are the signs of His coming? Is there, in this universe of things, any moral Providence at all? or is it the product of some force of the nature of which we can know nothing save only that "one event comes alike to all, to the good and to the evil, and that there is no difference"?

Commonplace persons, if assailed by such misgivings, thrust them aside, throw themselves into occupation, and leave doubt to settle itself. Carlyle could not. The importunacy of the overwhelming problem forbade him to settle himself either to law or any other business till he had wrestled down the misgivings which had grappled with him. The greatest of us have our weaknesses, and the Margaret Gordon business had perhaps intertwined itself with the spiritual torment. The result of it was that Carlyle was extremely

119

miserable, "tortured," as he says, "by the freaks of an imagination of extraordinary and wild activity."

He went home, as he had proposed, after the session [1819], but Mainhill was never a less happy home to him than it proved this summer. He could not conceal, perhaps he did not try to conceal, the condition of his mind; and to his family, to whom the truth of their creed was no more a matter of doubt than the presence of the sun in the sky, he must have seemed as if "possessed." He could not read; he wandered about the moors like a restless spirit. His mother was in agony about him. He was her darling, her pride, the apple of her eye, and she could not restrain her lamentations and remonstrances. His father, with supreme good judgement, left him to himself.

In November Carlyle was back at Edinburgh again, with his pupils and his law lectures, which he had not yet deserted, and still persuaded himself that he would persevere with. He did not find his friend; Irving had gone to Glasgow to be assistant to Dr. Chalmers; and the state of things which he found in the metropolis was not of a sort to improve his humour.

The law lectures went on, and Carlyle wrote to his mother about his progress with them. "The law," he said, "I find to be a most complicated subject; yet I like it pretty well, and feel that I shall like it better as I proceed. Its great charm in my eyes, is that no mean compliances are requisite for prospering in it."[6]

Reticence about his personal suffering was at no time one of his virtues. Dyspepsia had him by the throat. Even the minor ailments to which our flesh is heir, and which most of us bear in silence, the eloquence of his imagination flung into forms like the temptations of a saint. His mother had early described him as "gey ill to deal wi',"[7] and while in great things he was the most considerate and generous of men, in trifles he was intolerably irritable. Dyspepsia accounts for most of it. He did not know what was the matter with him, and when the fit was severe he drew pictures of his condition which frightened everyone belonging to him. He had sent his family in the middle of the winter a report of himself which made them think that he was seriously ill.[8]

The fright had been unnecessary. Dyspepsia, while it tortures body and mind, does little serious injury. The attack had passed off. With his family it was impossible for him to talk freely, and through this gloomy time he had but one friend, though this one was of priceless value. To Irving he had written out his discontent. He was now disgusted with law, and meant to abandon it.

The University term ends early in Scotland. The expenses of the six months which the students spend at college are paid for in many instances by the bodily labours of the other six. The end of April sees them all dispersed, the class rooms closed, the pupils no longer obtainable; and the law studies being finally abandoned, Carlyle had nothing more to do at Edinburgh, and migrated with the rest. He was going home; he offered himself for a visit to Irving at Glasgow on the way, and the proposal was warmly accepted.

Carlyle went to Glasgow, spent several days there, and noted, according to his habit, the outward signs of men and things. He saw the Glasgow merchants in the Tontine, he observed them, fine, clean, opulent, with their shining bald crowns and serene white heads, sauntering about or reading their newspapers. He criticised the dresses of the young ladies, for whom he had always an eye, remarking that with all their charms they had less taste in their adornments than were to be seen in Edinburgh drawing-rooms. He saw Chalmers too, and heard him preach. "Never preacher went so into one's heart." Some private talk, too, there was with Chalmers, "the Doctor" explaining to him "some scheme . . . for proving Christianity by its visible fitness for human nature 'all written in us already,' " he said, " 'as in *sympathetic ink*; Bible awakens it, and you can read!' "9

But the chief interest in the Glasgow visit lies less in itself than in what followed it—a conversation between two young, then unknown men, strolling alone together over a Scotch moor, seemingly the most trifling of incidents, a mere feather floating before the wind, yet, like the feather, marking the direction of the invisible tendency of human thought. Carlyle was to walk home to Ecclefechan. Irving had agreed to accompany him fifteen miles of his road, and

then leave him and return. They started early, and breakfasted on the way at the manse of a Mr. French. Carlyle
himself tells the rest.

> The talk had grown ever friendlier, more interesting: at length the
> declining sun said plainly, You must part. We sauntered slowly into
> the Glasgow-Muirkirk highway . . . masons were building at a
> wayside Cottage near by, or were packing up on ceasing for the
> day: we leant our backs to a dry stone fence . . . , and looking into
> the western radiance, continued in talk yet a while, loth both of us
> to go. It was here, just as the sun was sinking, [Irving] actually
> drew from me by degrees, in the softest manner, the confession that
> I did *not* think as he of Christian Religion, and that it was vain for
> me to expect I ever could or should. This, if this were so, he had pre-
> engaged to take *well* of me,—like an elder brother, if I would be
> frank with him;—and right loyally he did so, and to the end of his
> life we needed no concealments on that head; which was really a
> step gained. The sun was about setting, when we turned away, each
> on his own path. Irving would have had a good space *farther* to go
> than I . . . —perhaps fifteen or seventeen miles,—and would not
> be in Kent Street till towards midnight. But he feared no amount of
> walking; enjoyed it rather,—as did I in those young years.[10]

Nothing further has to be recorded of Carlyle's history
for some months. He remained quietly through the spring
and summer at Mainhill, occupied chiefly in reading. He
was beginning his acquaintance with German literature, his
friend Mr. Swan, of Kirkcaldy, who had correspondents at
Hamburg, providing him with books.[11] He was still writing
small articles, too, for Brewster's *Encyclopaedia*, unsatisfactory work, though better than none.[12]

August brought Irving to Annan for his summer holidays,
which opened possibilities of companionship again. Mainhill
was but seven miles off, and the friends met and wandered
together in the Mount Annan woods, Irving steadily cheering Carlyle with confident promises of ultimate success. In
September came an offer of a tutorship in a family, which
Irving urged him to accept.

Irving's judgement was perhaps at fault in this advice.
Carlyle, proud, irritable, and impatient as he was, could not
have remained a week in such a household. His ambition
(downtrodden as he might call himself) was greater than he
knew. At any rate the proposal came to nothing,[13] and with
the winter he was back once more at his lodgings in Edin-

burgh, determined to fight his way somehow, though in what direction he could not yet decide or see.

To his family Carlyle made the best of his situation; and indeed, so far as outward circumstances were concerned, there was no special cause for anxiety. His farmhouse training had made him indifferent to luxuries, and he was earning as much money as he required. It was not here that the pinch lay; it was in the still uncompleted "temptations in the wilderness," in the mental uncertainties which gave him neither peace nor respite. He had no friend in Edinburgh with whom he could exchange thoughts, and no society to amuse or distract him. And those who knew his condition best, the faithful Irving especially, became seriously alarmed for him. So keenly Irving felt the danger, that in December he even invited Carlyle to give up Edinburgh and be his own guest for an indefinite time at Glasgow.

Well might Carlyle cherish Irving's memory. Never had he or any man a truer-hearted, more generous friend. The offer could not be accepted. Carlyle was determined before all things to earn his own bread, and he would not abandon his pupil work. Christmas he did spend at Glasgow, but he was soon back again. He was corresponding now with London booksellers, offering a complete translation of Schiller for one thing, to which the answer had been an abrupt No.[14]

The gloomy period of Carlyle's life—a period on which he said that he ever looked back with a kind of horror—was drawing to its close, [and] the natural strength of his intellect was asserting itself. Better prospects were opening; more regular literary employment; an offer, if he chose to accept it, from his friend Mr. Swan, of a tutorship at least more satisfactory than the Yorkshire one. His mother's affection was more precious to him, however simply expressed, than any other form of earthly consolation.

Friends and family might console and advise, but Carlyle himself could alone conquer the spiritual maladies which were the real cause of his distraction. In June of this year 1821 was transacted what in *Sartor Resartus* he describes as his "conversion," or "new birth," when he authentically took "the Devil by the nose," when he began to achieve the convictions, positive and negative, by which the whole of his later life was governed.

Nothing in *"Sartor"* thereabouts is *fact* (symbolical *myth* all) except that of the *"incident* in the Rue St. Thomas de l'Enfer,"— which occurred quite literally to myself in Lieth [Leith] Walk, during those 3 weeks of total sleeplessness, in which almost my one solace was that of a daily bathe on the sands between Lieth and Portobello. Incident was as I went *down* (coming *up* I generally felt a little refreshed for the hour); I remember it well, & could go yet to about the place.[15]

As the incident is thus authenticated, I may borrow the words in which it is described, opening, as it does, a window into Carlyle's inmost heart.

"But for me, so strangely unprosperous had I been, the net-result of my Workings amounted as yet simply to—Nothing. How then could I believe in my Strength, when there was as yet no mirror to see it in? Ever did this agitating, yet, as I now perceive, quite frivolous question, remain to me insoluble: Hast thou a certain Faculty, a certain Worth, such even as the most have not; or art thou the completest Dullard of these modern times? Alas, the fearful Unbelief is unbelief in yourself; and how could I believe? Had not my first, last Faith in myself, when even to me the Heavens seemed laid open, and I dared to love, been all-too cruelly belied? The speculative Mystery of Life grew ever more mysterious to me: neither in the practical Mystery had I made the slightest progress, but been everywhere buffeted, foiled, and contemptuously cast out. A feeble unit in the middle of a threatening Infinitude, I seemed to have nothing given me but eyes, whereby to discern my own wretchedness. Invisible yet impenetrable walls, as of Enchantment, divided me from all living. . . . Now when I look back, it was a strange isolation I then lived in. The men and women around me, even speaking with me, were but Figures; I had, practically, forgotten that they were alive, that they were not merely automatic. In the midst of their crowded streets and assemblages, I walked solitary; and (except as it was my own heart, not another's, that I kept devouring) savage also, as the tiger in his jungle. Some comfort it would have been, could I, like a Faust, have fancied myself tempted and tormented of the Devil; for a Hell, as I imagine, without Life, though only diabolic Life, were more frightful: but in our age of Downpulling and Disbelief, the very Devil has been pulled down, you cannot so much as believe in a Devil. To me the Universe was all void of Life, of Purpose, of Volition, even of Hostility: it was one huge, dead, immeasurable Steam-engine, rolling on, in its dead indifference, to grind me limb from limb. O, the vast, gloomy, solitary Golgotha, and Mill of Death! Why was the Living banished thither companionless, conscious? Why, if there is no Devil; nay, unless the Devil is your God? . . .

"So had it lasted," concludes the Wanderer, "so had it lasted, as in bitter protracted Death-agony, through long years. The heart within me, unvisited by any heavenly dew-drop was smouldering in sulphurous, slow-consuming fire. Almost since earliest memory I had shed no tear; or once only when I, murmuring half-audibly, recited Faust's Death-song, that wild *Selig der den er im Siegesglanze findet* (Happy whom *he* finds in Battle's splendour), and thought that of this last Friend even I was not forsaken, that Destiny itself could not doom me not to die. Having no hope, neither had I any definite fear, were it of Man or of Devil; nay, I often felt as if it might be solacing, could the Arch-Devil himself, though in Tartarean terrors, but rise to me, that I might tell him a little of my mind. And yet, strangely enough, I lived in a continual, indefinite, pining fear; tremulous, pusillanimous, apprehensive of I knew not what; it seemed as if all things in the Heavens above and the Earth beneath would hurt me; as if the Heavens and the Earth were but boundless jaws of a devouring monster, wherein I, palpitating, waited to be devoured.

"Full of such humour . . . was I, one sultry Dog-day, after much perambulation, toiling along the dirty little *Rue Saint-Thomas de l'Enfer,* . . . in a close atmosphere, and over pavements hot as Nebuchadnezzar's Furnace; whereby doubtless my spirits were little cheered; when, all at once, there rose a Thought in me, and I asked myself: "What *art* thou afraid of? Wherefore, like a coward, dost thou for ever pip and whimper, and go cowering and trembling? Despicable biped! what is the sum-total of the worst that lies before thee? Death? Well, Death; and say the pangs of Tophet too, and all that the Devil and Man may, will or can do against thee! Hast thou not a heart; canst thou not suffer wha[t]soever it be; and, as a Child of Freedom, though outcast, trample Tophet itself under thy feet, while it consumes thee? Let it come, then; and I will meet it and defy it!" And as I so thought, there rushed like a stream of fire over my whole soul; and I shook base Fear away from me forever. I was strong, of unknown strength; a spirit, almost a god. Ever from that time, the temper of my misery was changed; not Fear or whining Sorrow was it, but Indignation and grim fire-eyed Defiance.

"Thus had the EVERLASTING NO (*das ewige Nein*) pealed authoritatively through all the recesses of my Being, of my ME; and then was it that my whole ME stood up, in native God-created majesty, and with emphasis recorded its Protest. Such a Protest, the most important transaction in Life, may that same Indignation and Defiance, in a psychological point of view, be fitly called. The Everlasting No had said: 'Behold, thou art fatherless, outcast, and the Universe is mine (the Devil's)'; to which my whole Me now made answer: '*I* am not thine, but Free, and forever hate thee!'

"It is from this hour I incline to date my spiritual New-birth, or Baphometic Fire-baptism; perhaps I directly thereupon began to be a Man."[16]

chapter four

1821

Jane Baillie Welsh

Craigenputtoch, craig, or whinstone hill of the puttocks,[1] is a high moorland farm on the watershed between Dumfriesshire and Galloway, sixteen miles from the town of Dumfries. The manor house, solid and gaunt, and built to stand for centuries, lies on a slope protected by a plantation of pines, and surrounded by a few acres of reclaimed grass land—a green island in the midst of heathery hills, sheepwalks, and undrained peat-bogs. A sterner spot is hardly to be found in Scotland. Here for many generations had resided a family of Welshes, holding the rank of small gentry. The eldest son bore always the same name—John Welsh had succeeded John Welsh as far back as tradition could record; the earliest John of whom authentic memory remained being the famous Welsh, the minister of Ayr, who married the daughter of John Knox.[2] This lady it was who, when her husband was banished, and when she was told by King James that he might return to Scotland if he would acknowledge the authority of bishops, raised her apron and said, "Please your Majesty I'd rather kep his head there." The king asked her who she was. "Knox and Welsh," he exclaimed, when she told him her parentage, "Knox and Welsh! The devil never made such a match as that." "It's right like, sir," said she, "for we never speered [asked] his advice."

A family with such an ancestry naturally showed remarkable qualities. "Several blackguards among them, but not one blockhead that I heard of,"[3] was the account of her kinsfolk given to Jane Welsh by her grandfather.

John Welsh [Jane's father] was the eldest of fourteen. He was born at Craigenputtoch in 1776, and spent his childish years there. Scotch lads learn early to take care of themselves. He was sent to Edinburgh University when a mere lad to study medicine. While attending the classes he drew attention to himself by his intelligence, and was taken as an apprentice by the celebrated John Bell. Dr. Bell saw his extraordinary merit, and in 1796, when he was but twenty, recommended him for a commission as regimental surgeon to the Perthshire Fencibles. This post he held for two years, and afterwards, in 1798, he succeeded either by purchase or otherwise to the local practice of the town and neighbourhood of Haddington. His reputation rose rapidly, and along with it he made a rapid fortune. To help his brothers and sisters he purchased Craigenputtoch from his father, without waiting till it came to him by inheritance. He paid off the encumbrances, and he intended eventually to retire thither when he should give up business.

In 1800 Dr. Welsh married, the wife whom he chose being a Welsh also, though of another family entirely unrelated to his own. She, too, if tradition might be trusted, came of famous blood. John Welsh was descended from Knox. Grace or Grizzie Welsh traced her pedigree through her mother, who was a Baillie, to Wallace. Her father was a well-to-do stock farmer, then living at Caplegill on Moffat Water. Walter Welsh (this was his name), when his daughter left him to go to Haddington, moved himself into Nithsdale, and took a farm then known as Templand, near Penfillan. Thus Jane Welsh's two grandfathers, old Walter and old John, Welshes both of them, though connected only through their children's marriage, became close neighbours and friends. Walter of Templand lived to a great age, and Carlyle after his marriage knew him well. He took to Carlyle, indeed, from the first, having but two faults to find with him, that he smoked tobacco and would not drink whisky punch; not that old Walter drank to excess himself, or at all cared for drinking, but he thought that total abstinence in a young man was a sign of conceit or affectation.

The beautiful Miss Baillie, Walter's wife, who came of Wallace, died early. Their son, called also John (the many John Welshes may cause some confusion in this biography unless the reader can remember the distinctions), went into business at Liverpool, and was prospering as a merchant there, when a partner who was to have been his brother-in-law proved dishonest, ran off with all the property that he could lay hands on, and left John Welsh to bankruptcy and a debt of £12,000. The creditors were lenient, knowing how the catastrophe had been brought about. John Welsh exerted himself, remade his fortune, and after eight years invited them all to dinner, where each found under his cover a cheque for the full amount of his claim. He was still living at Liverpool long after Carlyle settled in London with his niece, and will be heard of often in her correspondence.

His sister Grace, or Grizzie, was the wife of Dr. Welsh at Haddington. In appearance she was like her mother, tall, aquiline, and commanding. Dr. Welsh himself did not live to know Carlyle. He died in 1819, while still only forty-three, of a fever caught from a patient, [two] years before Carlyle's acquaintance with the family began. His daughter was so passionately attached to him, that she rarely mentioned his name even to her husband.

Such was the genealogy of the young lady to whom Carlyle was now about to be introduced by Irving, and who was afterwards to be his wife. Tradition traced her lineage to Knox and Wallace. Authentic history connected her with parents and kindred of singular, original, and strikingly superior quality. Jane Baillie Welsh was an only child, and was born in 1801. In her earliest years she showed that she was a girl of no common quality. She had black hair, large black eyes shining with soft mockery, pale complexion, broad forehead, nose not regularly formed, but mocking also like the eyes, figure slight, airy, and perfectly graceful. She was called beautiful, and beautiful she was even to the end of her life, if a face be beautiful which to look at is to admire. But beauty was only the second thought which her appearance suggested; the first was intellectual vivacity. Precious as she was to parents who had no other child, she was brought up with exceptional care. Strict obedience in essentials was the rule of the Haddington household. But the

stories of her young days show that there was no harsh interference with her natural playfulness. Occasional visits were
allowed to Templand, to her grandfather Walter, who was
especially fond of her. In that house she was called "Pen"
(short for Penfillan) to distinguish her from a second Jane
Welsh of the other family. On one of these occasions, when
she was six years old, her grandfather took her out for a ride
on a quiet little pony. When they had gone as far as was
desirable, Walter burring his r's and intoning his vowels as
usual said, "Now we will go back by So-and-so, 'to vary the
scene' (to vah-ry, properly 'to vah-*chy*' the *sha*ne)." "Where
did you ride to, Pen?" the company asked at dinner. "We
rode to *so*, then to *so*," answered she, punctually; "then
from *so*, returned by *so* 'to vah-chy the shane!' " at which,
says Carlyle, "the old man himself burst into his cheeriest
laugh at the mimicry of tiny little Pen."[4]

She was a collected little lady, with a fine readiness in
difficulties. The Welshes were the leading family at Haddington, and were prominent in the social entertainments
there. She learned rapidly the usual young lady's accomplishments—music, drawing, modern languages; and she had
an appetite for knowledge not easily to be satisfied. A
girl's education was not enough. She demanded to "learn
Latin like a boy." Her mother was against it. Her father, who
thought well of her talents, inclined to let her have her way.
The question was settled at last in a characteristic fashion
by herself. She found some lad in Haddington who introduced her to the mysteries of nouns of the first declension.
Having mastered her lesson, one night when she was
thought to be in bed, she had hidden herself under the
drawing-room table. When an opportunity offered, the
small voice was heard from below the cover, " '*Penna*, a
pen; *pennae*, of a pen;' etc." She crept out amidst the general amusement, ran to her father, and said, "I want to learn
Latin; please let me be a boy."[5] Haddington school was a
furlong's distance from her father's house. Boys and girls
were taught together there; and to this accordingly she was
sent.

A fiery temper there was in her too. Boys and girls were
kept for the most part in separate rooms at the school,[6] but
arithmetic and algebra, in which she was especially profi-

cient, they learnt together,—or perhaps she in her zeal for knowledge was made an exception. The boys were generally devoted to her, but differences rose now and then. A lad one day was impertinent. She doubled her little fist, struck him on the nose, and made it bleed. Fighting in school was punished by flogging. The master came in at the instant, saw the marks of the fray and asked who was the delinquent. All were silent. No one would betray a girl. The master threatened to *tawse* [whip] the whole school, and being a man of his word would have done it, when the small Jeannie looked up and said, "Please it was I." The master tried to look grave, failed entirely, and burst out laughing. He told her she was "a little deevil," and had no business there, and bade her "go her ways" to the girls' room.

Soon after this there was a change in the school management. Edward Irving, then fresh from college honours, came as master, and, along with the school, was trusted with the private education of Jane Welsh. Dr. Welsh had recognised his fine qualities, and took him into the intimacy of his household, where he was treated as an elder son. He watched over the little lady's studies, took her out with him on bright nights to show her the stars and teach her the movements of them. Irving was then a young man, and his pupil was a child. A few years were to make a difference. She worked with feverish eagerness, getting up at five in the morning and busy with her books at all hours. She was soon *dux* in mathematics.[7] Her tutor introduced her to "Virgil," and the effect of "Virgil" and of her other Latin studies was "to change her religion and make her into a sort of Pagan."

When she was fourteen she wrote a tragedy, rather inflated, but extraordinary for her age.[8] She never repeated the experiment, but for many years she continued to write poetry. She had inherited from her mother the gift of verse-making. Mrs. Welsh's lyrics were soft, sweet, passionate, musical, and nothing besides. Her daughter had less sweetness, but touched intellectual chords which her mother never reached.

She lost [her father], as has been said, at an age when she most needed his guiding hand. Had Dr. Welsh lived, her life would have been happier, whether more useful it is

130

unprofitable to conjecture. The patient from whom he caught the fever which killed him was at some distance from Haddington. She being then eighteen had accompanied him in the carriage in this his last drive, and it was for ever memorable to her. Carlyle writes:

> The usually tacit man, tacit especially about his bright Daughter's gifts and merits, took to talking with her that day, in a style quite new; told her she was a good girl, capable of being useful and precious to him and to the circle she would live in; that she must summon her utmost judgment and seriousness to choose her path, and *be* what he expected of her; that he did not think she had ever yet seen the Life-Partner that would be worthy of her; . . . in short that he expected her to be wise, as well as good-looking and good. All this in a tone and manner which filled her poor little heart with surprise, and a kind of sacred joy; coming from the man she of all men revered. Often she told me about this. For it was her last talk with him: on the morrow, perhaps that evening, certainly within a day or two, he caught from some poor old woman patient (who, I think, recovered of it) a typhus fever; which, under injudicious treatment, killed him in three or four days (September 1819):—and drowned the world for her in the very blackness of darkness. In effect, it was her first sorrow; and her greatest of all. It broke her health, permanently, within the next two or three years; and, in a sense, almost broke her heart. A Father so mourned and loved I have never seen: to the end of her life, his title even to me was "He" and "Him;" not above twice or thrice, quite in late years, did she ever mention (and then in what a sweet slow tone!), "my Father."[9]

After her father's death, Miss Welsh continued with her mother at Haddington. With the exception of some small annuity for his widow, Dr. Welsh had left everything belonging to him to his daughter. Craigenputtoch became hers; other money investments became hers; and though the property altogether was not large according to modern estimates of such things, it was sufficient as long as mother and child remained together to enable them to live with comfort and even elegance. Miss Welsh was now an heiress. Her wit and beauty added to her distinctions, and she was called the flower of Haddington. Her hand became an object of speculation. She had as many suitors as Penelope. They were eligible, many of them, in point of worldly station. Some afterwards distinguished themselves. She amused herself with them, but listened favourably to none, being protected perhaps by a secret attachment, which had grown up unconsciously between herself and her tutor. There were difficulties in the way which prevented them from acknowledging to one another, or even to themselves, the condition of their feelings. Edward Irving had been removed from Haddington to Kirkcaldy, where he had entered while Jane Welsh was still a child into a half-formed engagement with the daughter of the Kirkcaldy minister, Miss Isabella Martin.[10] In England young people often fancy themselves in love. They exchange vows which as they grow older are repented of, and are broken without harm to either party. In Scotland, perhaps as a remains of the ecclesiastical precontract which had legal validity, these connections had a more binding character. They could be dissolved by mutual consent; but if the consent of both was wanting, there was a moral stain on the person escaping from the bond. Irving had long been conscious that he had been too hasty, and was longing for release. But there was no encouragement on the side of the Martins. Marriage was out of the question till he had made a position for himself, and he had allowed the matter to drift on, since immediate decision was unnecessary. Jane Welsh meanwhile had grown into a woman. Irving, who was a constant visitor at Haddington, discovered when he looked into his heart that his real love was for his old pupil, and the feeling on her part was—the word is her own—"passionately" returned.[11] The mischief was done before they became aware of their danger. Irving's situation being explained, Miss Welsh refused to listen to any language but that of friendship from him until Miss Martin had set him free. Irving, too, was equally high principled, and was resolved to keep his word. But there was an unexpressed hope on both sides that he would not be held to it, and on these dangerous terms Irving continued to visit at Haddington, when he could be spared from his duties. Miss Welsh was working eagerly at literature, with an ambition of becoming an authoress, and winning name and fame. Unable or too much occupied himself to be of use to her, Irving thought of his friend Carlyle, who was living in obscurity and poverty at Edinburgh, as a fit person to assist and advise her. The acquaintance, he considered, would be mutually agreeable. He obtained leave from Mrs. Welsh to bring him over and introduce him. The introduction was effected a little before Carlyle had taken "the Devil by the nose," as he describes in *Sartor Resartus*;[12] and perhaps the first visit to Haddington had contributed to bringing him off victorious from that critical encounter.

> *June 1821* (probably about the middle of June),[13] Edward Irving, who was visiting & recreating about Edinburgh, one of his occasional Holiday Sallies from Glasgow, took me out to Haddington: we walked cheerily together, pleasantly and multifariously talking, not always by the highway, but meandering at our will (as has been explained elsewhere);—and about sunset of that same evening, I first saw Her who was to be so important to me thenceforth. A red dusky evening; the sky hanging huge & high, but dim as if with dust or drought over Irving & me, as we walked home to our Lodging in the George Inn. The visit lasted 3 or 4 days; and included Gilbert Burns and other Figures, besides the one fair Figure most of all important to me. We were often in her Mother's house; sat talking with the two for hours, almost every evening. I was in wretched health; had begun to be thoroughly *dyspeptic* (without Doctor to counsel me, or worse than without,—tho' a wise Dr might have greatly helped),—however I did my best. The beautiful, bright and earnest young Lady was intent on Literature, as the highest aim in life; and felt imprisoned in the dull element which yielded her no commerce in that kind, and would not even yield her Books to read. I obtained permission to send at least books from Edinburgh; Book-parcels naturally included bits of writing to and from;—and thus an acquaintance and correspondence was begun, which had hardly ever interruption, and no break at all while life lasted. She was often in Edinburgh on visit with her Mother, to "Uncle Robert in Northumberland Street," to "Old Mr Bradfute in George's Square"; and I had leave to call on these occasions,—which I zealously enough, if not too zealously sometimes, in my awkward way, took advantage of. I was not her declared lover; nor could she admit me as such, in my waste & uncertain posture of affairs & prospects: but we were becoming thoroughly acquainted with each other; and her tacit, hidden, but to me visible friendship for me was the happy island in my otherwise altogether dreary, vacant and forlorn existence in those years.[14]

Eager as the interest which Carlyle was taking in his new acquaintance, he did not allow it to affect the regulation of his life, or to drive him into the beaten roads of the established professions on which he could arrive at fortune. His zeal for mathematics had by this time cooled. He had travelled, as he said, into more "pregnant inquiries." Inquiry had led to doubt, and doubt had enfeebled and dispirited him till he had grappled with it and conquered it. Traditionary interpretations of things having finally broken down with him, he was now searching for some answer which he could believe to the great central question. What this world is, and what is man's business in it? Of classical literature he knew little, and that little had not attracted him. He was not living in ancient Greece or Rome, but in modern Europe, modern Scotland, with the added experiences and discoveries of eighteen centuries; and light, if light there was, could be looked for only in the writers of his own era. English literature was already widely familiar to him. He had read every book in Irving's library at Kirkcaldy, and his memory had the tenacity of steel. He had studied Italian and Spanish.[15] He had worked at D'Alembert and Diderot, Rousseau and Voltaire. Still unsatisfied, he had now fastened himself upon German, and was devouring Schiller and Goethe. Having abandoned the law, he was becoming conscious that literature must be the profession of his life. He did not suppose that he had any special gift for it. He told me long after, when at the height of his fame, that he had perhaps less capability for literature than for any other occupation. But he was ambitious to use his time to honourable purposes. He was impatient of the trodden ways which led only to money or to worldly fame, and literature was the single avenue which offered an opening into higher regions. The fate of those who had gone before him was not encouraging. "The biographies of English men of letters," he says somewhere, "are the wretchedest chapters in our history, except the Newgate Calendar." Germany, however, and especially modern Germany, could furnish brighter examples. Schiller first took hold of him: pure, innocent, consistent, clear as the sunlight, with a character in which calumny could detect neither spot nor stain. The situation of Schiller was not unlike his own. A youth of poverty, surrounded by obstructions; long difficulty in finding a road on which he could travel; bad health besides, and despondent fits, with which Carlyle himself was but too familiar. Yet with all this Schiller had conquered adversity. He had raised himself to the second, if not to the highest place, in the admiration of his countrymen; and there was not a single act in his whole career which his biographer would regret to record. Schiller had found his inherited beliefs break down under him, and had been left floating in uncertainties. But he had formed moral convictions of his own, independent of creeds and churches, and had governed his thought and conduct nobly by them. Nothing that he did required forgiveness, or even apology. No line ever fell from his pen which he could have wished unwritten when life was closing round him. Schiller's was thus an inspiriting figure to a young man tremulously launching himself on the same waters. His work was high and serene, clear and healthy to the last fibre, noble thought and noble feeling rendered into words with true artistic skill.

Nevertheless, the passionate questionings which were rising in Carlyle's mind could find no answer which would satisfy him in Schiller's prose or consolation in Schiller's lyrics. Schiller's nature was direct and simple rather than profound and many-sided. Kant had spoken the last word in philosophy to him. His emotions were generous, but seldom subtle or penetrating. He had never looked with a determined eye into the intellectual problems of humanity. He worked as an artist with composed vigour on subjects which suited his genius, and while his sentiments are lofty and his passion hearty and true, his speculative insight is limited. Thus Schiller is great, but not the greatest; and those who have gone to him for help in the enigmas social and spiritual which distract modern Europe, have found generally that they must look elsewhere. From Schiller Carlyle had turned to Goethe, and Goethe had opened a new world to him. Schiller believed in the principles for which Liberals had been fighting for three centuries. To him the enemy of human welfare was spiritual and political tyranny, and Don Carlos, William Tell, the revolt of the Netherlands, or the Thirty Years' War, were ready-made materials for his workshop. He was no vulgar politician. He soared far above the commonplaces of popular orators and controversialists. He was a poet, with a poet's sympathies. He could admire greatness of soul in a Duke of Friedland; he could feel for suffering if the sufferer was a Mary Stuart. But the broad articles of faith professed by the believers in liberal progress were Schiller's also, and he never doubted their efficacy for man's salvation. Goethe had no such beliefs—no beliefs of any kind which could be reduced to formulas. If he distrusted priests, he distrusted still more the *Freiheits Apostel*[16] and the philosophic critics. He had studied his age on all its sides. He had shared its misgivings; he had suffered from its diseases; he had measured its possibilities; he had severed himself from all illusions; and held fast to nothing but what he could definitely recognise as truth. In *Werther*, in *Faust*, in "Prometheus," Carlyle found that another as well as he had experienced the same emotions with which he was himself so familiar. In *Wilhelm Meister*, that menagerie of tame creatures, as Niebuhr called it, he saw a picture of society, accurate precisely because it was so tame, as it existed in middle-class European communities; the ardent, well-disposed youth launched into the middle of it, beginning his apprenticeship in the false charms of the provincial theatre, and led at last into a recognition of the divine meaning of Christianity. Goethe had trod the thorny path before Carlyle. He had not rushed into atheism. He had not sunk into superstition. He remained true to all that intellect could teach him, and after facing all the spiritual dragons he seemed to have risen victorious into an atmosphere of tranquil wisdom. On finishing his first perusal of *Meister*, and walking out at midnight into the streets of Edinburgh to think about it, Carlyle said to himself, "with a very mixed sentiment in other respects, we could not but feel that here lay more insight into the elements of human nature, and a more poetically perfect combining of these, than in all the other fictitious literature of our generation."[17]

Having been charged by Irving with the direction of Miss Welsh's studies, he at once introduced her to his German friends. Irving, of the nature of whose interest in her welfare Carlyle had no suspicion, was alarmed at what he had done. His own religious convictions were profound and sincere. He had occasioned unexpected mischief already with his "Virgil." He had laboured afterwards with all his energies to lead his pupil to think about Christianity as he thought himself, and when he heard of the books which she was set to read, he felt that he had been imprudent.

Irving identified "principle" with belief in the formulas of the Church, and therefore supposed Carlyle to be without it. He considered his friend no doubt to be playing with dangerous weapons, and likely to injure others with them besides himself. But Carlyle's principles when applied to the common duties of life were as rigid as Irving's. He had been struck by his new acquaintance at Haddington, but he was too wise to indulge in dreams of a nearer relation—which their respective positions seemed to put out of the question— and he was too much in earnest to allow himself to be disturbed in the course of life which he had adopted, or forget the dearer friends at Mainhill to whom he was so passionately attached. He had remained this summer in Edinburgh longer than usual, and he and Irving had meditated a small walking tour together at the end of it. Irving, however, was unable to take a holiday. Carlyle went home alone, walking as he always did, and sending his box by the carrier. For him, as for so many of his student countrymen, coaches were rarely tasted luxuries. They tramped over moor and road with their bundles on their shoulder, sleeping by the way at herdsmen's cottages; and journeys which to the rich would be a delightful adventure, were not less pleasing to the sons of Scottish peasants because forced on them by honest poverty. Mainhill had become again by this time the happiest of shelters to him, and between his family and himself the old clear affection and mutual trust had completely reestablished themselves. The passing cloud had risen only out of affectionate anxiety for his eternal well-being. Satisfied of the essential piety of his nature, his mother had been contented to believe that the differences between herself and her son were differences of expression merely, not of radical conviction. His father was beginning to be proud of him, and was sensible enough to leave him to his own guidance. Three quiet months were spent with his brothers and sisters while he was writing articles for Brewster's *Encyclopaedia*. In November he was in Edinburgh again with improving prospects.

chapter five

1822–1824

The Bullers. *Life of Schiller.*
Wilhelm Meister

An important change was now to take place in Carlyle's circumstances, which not only raised him above the need of writing articles for bread or hunting after pupils, but enabled him to give his brother the lift into the University which he had so ardently desired to give him. It came about in this way, through the instrumentality of his constant friend, Edward Irving. Irving's position at Glasgow, Carlyle says, was not an easy one. Theological Scotland was jealous of originality, and Irving was always inclined to take a road of his own. He said himself that "I have but toleration from the Wes[t]land Whigs—when praised it is with reservation often with cold and unprofitable admonition." Even Chalmers sometimes, in retailing the general opinion of him, "makes me feel all black in my prospects."[1] He was growing dispirited about himself, when, just at that time, he received an invitation to go to London on experimental trial. The Caledonian Chapel in Hatton Garden was in need of a minister. "Certain Glasgow people," who thought more favourably of Chalmers's assistant than their neighbours thought, or than Chalmers himself, named him to the trustees, and Irving was sent for that his "gifts" might be ascertained. The gifts proved to be what London wanted. He was brilliantly successful. There was no jealousy of originality in Hatton Garden, but ardent welcome rather to a man who had something new to say on so worn a subject as the Christian religion.

Great persons of all kinds were brought to the Caledonian

138

Chapel by the report of a new man of genius who really believed in Christianity. It happened that among the rest there came Mrs. Strachey, wife of a distinguished East Indian director, and her sister, Mrs. Charles Buller. Mr. Buller was also a retired Anglo-Indian of eminence. Mrs. Strachey was devout and evangelical, and had been led to Hatton Garden by genuine interest; Mrs. Buller had accompanied her in languid curiosity; she was struck, like the rest of the world, by Irving's evident ability, and she allowed herself to be afterwards introduced to him. She had three sons—one the Charles Buller who won so brilliant a place for himself in Parliament, and died as he was beginning to show to what a height he might have risen; another, Arthur, the Sir Arthur of coming years, an Indian judge; and a third, Reginald, who became a clergyman. Charles was then fifteen, having just left Harrow, and was intended perhaps for Cambridge; Arthur was a year or two younger, and Reginald was a child.[2] The Bullers were uncertain about the immediate education of the two elder boys. Mrs. Buller consulted Irving, and Irving recommended the University of Edinburgh, adding that he had a friend of remarkable quality there who would prove an excellent tutor for them. Mrs. Buller was prompt in her decisions, if not always stable in adhering to them. A negotiation was opened and was readily concluded. Carlyle's consent having been obtained, he was instructed to expect the arrival of his pupils as soon as arrangements could be made for their board. The family intended to follow, and reside themselves for a time in Scotland.

The salary was to be £200 a year. The offer, so desirable in many ways, came opportunely, and at Mainhill was warmly welcomed. The times were hard; the farm was yielding short returns. For once it was Carlyle who was to raise the spirits of the family. The young Bullers arrived at Edinburgh early in the spring. They lodged with a Dr. Fleming in George Square, Carlyle being in daily attendance.

Carlyle was now at ease in his circumstances. He could help his brother; he had no more money anxieties. He was living independently in his own rooms in Moray Street. His evenings were his own, and he had leisure to do what he

139

pleased. Yet it was not his nature to be contented. He was full of thoughts which were struggling for expression, and he was beginning that process of ineffectual labour so familiar to every man who has risen to any height in litera- ture, of trying to write something before he knew what the something was to be; of craving to give form to his ideas before those ideas had taken an organic shape. The result was necessarily failure, and along with it self-exasperation. He translated his Legendre easily enough, and made a suc- cessful book out of it; but he was aspiring to the production of an original work, and what it should be he could not decide. Now it was an essay on Faust, now a history of the English Commonwealth, now a novel to be written in con- cert with Miss Welsh. An article on Faust was finished, but it was crude and unsatisfactory.[3] The other schemes were commenced and thrown aside.

The correspondence with Haddington meanwhile grew more intimate. The relations between tutor and pupil devel- oped, or promised to develop, into literary partnership. Miss Welsh sent Carlyle her verses to examine and correct. Carlyle discussed his plans and views with her, and they proposed to write books in concert. But the friendship, at least on her part, was literary only. Carlyle, in one of his earliest letters to her, did indeed adopt something of the ordinary language of gallantry natural in a young man when addressing a beautiful young lady. But she gave him to understand immediately that such a tone was disagreeable to her, and that their intimacy could only continue on fraternal and sisterly terms. Carlyle obeyed without suspecting the reason. He had known that Irving was engaged to Miss Martin. It never occurred to him as possible that he could be thinking of anyone else, or anyone else of him.

As for Irving himself, the reception which he had met with in London was all that he could desire. A brilliant career appeared to be opening before him, and ardent and enthusi- astic as he was, he had allowed his future in all points to be coloured by his wishes. There could be no doubt that the Hatton Garden committee would confirm his London appointment. He would then be able to marry, and his fate would have to be immediately decided. He was to return to

140

Scotland in the spring to be ordained—he was as yet only in his noviciate; meanwhile he was in high spirits, and his letters were of the rosiest colour.

In March the trial period had ended. The trustees were satisfied; Irving was to be minister of the Hatton Garden chapel. He returned to Glasgow in March to prepare for his ordination [and there wrote to Carlyle].

> Some other things also that I cannot render even into language unto my own mind. There is an independence about my character, a want of resemblance with others, especially with others of my profession, that will cause me to be apprehended ill of. Yet I hope to come through honestly and creditably. God grant it.[4]

I am not writing Irving's history, save so far as it intersects with that of Carlyle, and I must hasten to the catastrophe of their unconscious rivalry. The "other things" which he could not render into language, the "independence of character which might cause him to be apprehended ill of," referred to his engagement, and to his intentions with respect to it. Miss Martin had been true to him through many years of tedious betrothal, and he was bound to her by the strictest obligations of honour and conscience. But it is only in novels that a hero can behave with entire propriety. Folded among Irving's letters to Miss Welsh is a passionate sonnet addressed to her, and on the other side of it (she had preserved his verses and so much of the accompanying letter as was written on the opposite page of the paper) a fragment, written evidently at this period, in which he told her that he was about to inform Miss Martin and her father of the condition of his feelings. It seems that he did so, and that the answer was unfavourable to his hopes. The Martins stood by their contract, as justice and Scotch custom entirely entitled them to do. Miss Welsh had refused to listen to his addresses until he was free; and Irving, though he confessed afterwards (I use his own words) that the struggle had almost "made his faith and principles to totter," submitted to the inevitable.[5]

I should not unveil a story so sacred in itself, and in which the public have no concern, merely to amuse their curiosity; but Mrs. Carlyle's character was profoundly affected by this early disappointment, and cannot be understood without a knowledge of it. Carlyle himself, though acquainted generally with the circumstances, never realised completely the intensity of the feeling which had been crushed. Irving's marriage was not to take place for a year, and it was still possible that something might happen in the interval. He went back to his place in London, flung himself into religious excitement as grosser natures go into drink, and took popularity by storm. The fashionable world rushed after him. The streets about Hatton Garden were blocked with carriages. His chapel was like a theatre, to which the admission was by tickets. Great statesmen went with the stream. Brougham, Canning, Mackintosh bespoke their seats, that they might hear the new actor on the theological stage. Irving concluded that he had a divine mission to re-establish practical Christianity. He felt himself honoured above all men, yet he bore his honours humbly, and in his quiet intervals his thoughts still flowed towards Haddington. Miss Welsh's husband he could not be; but he could still be her guide, her spiritual father—some link might remain which would give him an excuse for writing to her.

Though he seldom found time to write to Carlyle, he had not forgotten him. He was eager to see him in the position which of right belonged to him; especially to see him settled in London. "Scotland breeds men," he said, "but England rears them." He celebrated his friend's praises in London circles. He had spoken of him to Mr. Taylor, the proprietor of the *London Magazine*. Carlyle had meditated a series of "portraits of men of genius and character." Taylor, on Irving's recommendation, undertook to publish these sketches in monthly numbers, paying Carlyle sixteen guineas a sheet. Carlyle closed with the proposal, and a *Life of Schiller* was to be the first to appear. Irving's unwearied kindness unfortunately did not help him out of his own entanglements. The year passed, and then he married, and from that time the old, simple, unconscious Irving ceased to exist. His letters, once so genial and transparent, became verbose and stilted. Though "faith and principle" escaped unscathed, his intellect was shattered. He plunged deeper and deeper into the great ocean of unrealities. When his illusions failed him his health gave way, and after flaming for a few years as a world's wonder, he died, still young in age, worn out and broken-hearted. "There would have been no tongues," Mrs. Carlyle once said, "had Irving married me."[6]

Carlyle, meanwhile, was working with his pupils, and so far as circumstances went, had nothing to complain of. The boys gave him little trouble. He was no longer obliged to write articles for Brewster to support himself. The Legendre was well done—so well that he was himself pleased with it.

He ought to have been contented; but content was not in him. Small discomforts were exaggerated by his imagination till they actually became the monsters which his fancy represented. He was conscious of exceptional power of some kind, and was longing to make use of it, yet was unable as yet to find out what sort of power it was, or what to do with it.

In July the London season ended, and the parent Bullers arrived in Edinburgh with their youngest boy. They took a large house and settled for the autumn and winter. They made acquaintance with Carlyle, and there was immediate and agreeable recognition of one another's qualities, both on his side and theirs. Mrs. Buller was clever and cultivated. In her creed she was Manichaean. In her youth she had been a beauty, and was still handsome, and was in London the centre of an admiring circle of intellectual politicians and unbelieving Radicals. She was first amused, then charmed and really interested in a person so distinctly original and remarkable as her sons' tutor. Her husband, though of different quality, liked him equally well. Mr. Buller was practical and hard-headed; a Benthamite in theory, in theology negative and contemptuous. He had not much sympathy with literature, but he had a keen understanding; he could see faculty, and appreciate it whenever it was genuine, and he forgave Carlyle's imagination for the keenness of his sarcasms. Thus it was not only settled that he was to continue to be the tutor, but he was admitted into the family as a friend, and his presence was expected in the drawing-room in the evenings more often than he liked. The style of society was new to him, and he could not feel himself at ease. The habits of life were expensive, and the luxuries were not to his taste.

On the other hand, he found Mrs. Buller, naturally enough, "one of the most fascinating refined women I have ever seen." The "Goodman" he did not take to quite so readily, but he thought him at least "an honest worthy straightforward English Gentleman."[7] His comfort was considered in every way. They would have liked to have him reside in their house, but he wished to keep his lodgings in Moray Street, and no difficulty was made. Even his humours, which were not always under restraint, were endured without resentment.

Not the least of the advantages of this tutorship was the power which it gave Carlyle of being useful to his family. John Carlyle came in the autumn to live with him in Moray Street and attend the University lectures, Carlyle taking upon himself the expenses. With himself, too, all was going well. He had paid a hasty visit to Mainhill in October; where, perhaps, as was likely enough, in some of their midnight smokes together, he had revived the anxieties of his mother about his spiritual state. His constant effort was to throw his own thoughts into her language, and prevent her from distressing herself about him.

Taylor's offer for the *London Magazine* came to the help of his resolution [to write out the truth that was in him], and he began his *Life of Schiller* as the commencement of the intended series. Goethe was designed to follow. But the biography of Goethe was soon exchanged for a translation of *Wilhelm Meister*.

Thus opened the year 1823. The Buller connection continued to be agreeable. John Carlyle's companionship relieved the loneliness of the Edinburgh lodgings, while spare moments were occupied with writing letters to Miss Welsh or correcting her exercises.[8]

The family, young and old, often contributed their scraps to the carrier's budget. The youngest child of all, Jane,[9] called the Craw, or Crow, from her black hair, and not yet able even to write, was heard composing in bed in the morning, to be enclosed in her father's letter, "a scrap of doggerel from his affectionate sister Jane Carlyle."[10]

Of Carlyle's brothers, Alexander had the most natural genius. Of his sisters, the eldest, Margaret, had a tenderness, grace, and dignity of character which, if health and circumstances had been more kind, would have made her into a distinguished woman. But Jane was peculiar and original.

144

She, when the day's work was over, and the young men wandered out in the summer gloaming, would cling to "Tom's" hand and trot at his side, catching the jewelled sentences which dropped from his lips. She now, when he was far away, sent, among the rest, her little thoughts to him, composing the " 'meanest of the letter kind' "[11] instinctively in rhyme and metre; her sister Mary, who had better luck in having been at school, writing down the words for her.

"She must be a very singular *crow*," was Carlyle's observation on reading her characteristic lines.[12] "Meanest of the letter kind" became a family phrase, to be met with for many years when an indifferent composition seemed to require an apology. Carlyle, in return, thought always first of his mother. He must send her a present. She must tell him what she needed most. "Dear! Bairn," she might answer, "I want for nothing." But it was not allowed to serve. "Will you never understand that you cannot gratify me so much, by any plan you can take, as by enabling me to promote your comfort in any way within my power?"[13]

The Bullers after a winter's experience grew tired of Edinburgh, and in the spring of 1823 took Kinnaird House, a large handsome residence in Perthshire. Carlyle during the removal was allowed a holiday. He had been complaining of his health again. He had been working hard on *Schiller*, and was beginning his translation of *Meister*. Kinnaird House is a beautiful place in the midst of woods near Dunkeld on the Tay. Carlyle spent a week in Annandale, and rejoined the Bullers there at the end of May.

Of [his] friends, Miss Welsh was naturally the most frequently in his mind. Her relations with him were drifting gradually in the direction in which friendships between young men and young women usually do drift. She had no thought of marrying him, but she was flattered by his attachment. It amused her to see the most remarkable person that she had ever met with at her feet. His birth and position seemed to secure her against the possibility of any closer connection between them. Thus he had a trying time of it. In serious moments she would tell him that their meeting had made an epoch in her history, and had influenced her character and life. When the humour changed, she would ridicule his Annandale accent, turned his passionate expressions to scorn, and when she had toned him down again she would smile once more, and enchant him back into illusions. She played with him, frightened him away, drew him back, quarrelled with him, received him again into favour as the fancy took her, till at last the poor man said, "My own private idea is that you are a *witch*; or like Sapphira in the New Testament, concerning whom Dr Nimmo once preached in my hearing: 'It seems probable, my friends, that Annanias was tempted unto this by some demon *more wicked than his wife*.' "[14] At last, in the summer of 1823, just after he was settled at Kinnaird, she was staying in some house which she particularly disliked, and on this occasion, in a fit of impatience with her surroundings —for she dated a letter which she wrote to him thence, very characteristically, as from "Hell"[15]—she expressed a gratitude for Carlyle's affection for her, more warm than she had ever expressed before. He believed her serious, and supposed that she had promised to be his wife. She hastened to tell him, as explicitly as she could, that he had entirely mistaken her:

> My Friend I love you— I repeat it tho' I find the e[x]pression a rash one—all the best feelings of my nature are concerned in loving you— But were you my Brother I would love you the same, were I married to another I would love you the same. . . . Oh no! Your Friend I will be, your truest most devoted friend, while I breath[e] the breath of life; but your wife! never never! Not though you were as rich as Croesus, as honoured and renowned as you yet shall be—[16]

Carlyle took his rebuke manfully. "My heart," he said, "is too old by almost half a score of years, and made of sterner stuff than to break in junctures of that kind. . . . I have no idea of dying in the Arcadian shepherd style, for the disappointment of hopes which I never seriously entertained, or had no right to entertain seriously."[17] Could they have left matters thus, it had been better for both of them. Two diamonds do not easily form cup and socket.[18] But Irving was gone. Miss Welsh was romantic; and to assist and further the advance of a man of extraordinary genius, who was kept back from rising by outward circumstances, was not without attraction to her. Among her papers there is a curious correspondence which passed about this time

146

between herself and the family solicitor. Her mother had been left entirely dependent on her. Her marriage, she said, was possible, though not probable; and "she did not choose that her husband, if he was ever to be so disposed, should have it in his power to lessen her mother's income."[19] She executed an instrument, therefore, by which she transferred the whole of her property to her mother during Mrs. Welsh's life. By another she left it to Carlyle after her own and her mother's death. It was a generous act, which showed how far she had seen into his character and the future which lay before him, if he could have leisure to do justice to his talents. But it would have been happier for her and for him if she could have seen a little further, and had persevered in her refusal to add her person to her fortune.

Men of genius are "kittle [ticklish] folk," as the Scotch say. Carlyle had a strange temper, and from a child was "gey ill to deal wi'." When dyspepsia was upon him he spared no one, least of all those who were nearest and dearest to him. Dearly as he loved his brother John, yet he had spoken to him while they were lodging together in language which he was ashamed to remember. "Often in winter," he acknowledged ruefully to poor John, "when Satanas in the shape of bile was heavy upon me, I have said cruel things to thee, and bitterly tho' vainly do I recollect them: yet at bottom I hope you have never doubted that I loved you."[20] Penitence, however, sincere as it might be, was never followed by amendment, even to the very end of his life.

But enough will be heard hereafter on this sad subject. The life at Kinnaird went on smoothly. The translation of *Meister* prospered. An Edinburgh publisher undertook to publish it and pay well for it.

The Bullers, as he admitted, were most kind and considerate; yet he must have tried their patience. He was uneasy, restless, with dyspepsia and intellectual fever. He laid the blame on his position, and was already meditating to throw up his engagement. In better moments Carlyle recognised that the mischief was in himself, and that the spot did not exist upon earth where so sensitive a skin would not be irritated. Mrs. Buller must have been a most forbearing and discerning woman. She must have suffered, like everyone who came in contact with Carlyle, from his strange humours, but she had mind enough to see what he was, and was willing to endure much to keep such a man at her sons' side.

If Carlyle complained, his complaints were the impatience of a man who was working with all his might. If his dyspepsia did him no serious harm, it obstructed his efforts and made him miserable with pain. He had written the first part of *Schiller*, which was now coming out in the *London Magazine*. He was translating *Meister*, and his translation, though the production of a man who had taught himself with grammar and dictionary, and had never spoken a word of German, is yet one of the very best which has ever been made from one language into another. In everything which he undertook he never spared labour or slurred over a difficulty, but endeavoured with all his might to do his work faithfully. A journal which he kept intermittently at Kinnaird throws light into the inner regions of his mind, while it shows also how much he really suffered.[21] Deeply as he admired his German friends, his stern Scotch Calvinism found much in them that offended him. Goethe and even Schiller appeared to think that the hope of improvement for mankind lay in culture rather than morality—in aesthetics, in art, in poetry, in the drama, rather than in obedience to the old rugged rules of right and wrong; and this perplexed and displeased him.

There can be no doubt that Carlyle suffered and perhaps suffered excessively. It is equally certain that his sufferings were immensely aggravated by the treatment to which he was submitted. "A long hairy-eared jackass," as he called some eminent Edinburgh physician,[22] had ordered him to give up tobacco, but he had ordered him to take mercury, as well; and he told me that along with the mercury he must have swallowed whole hogsheads of castor oil. Much of his pain would be so accounted for; but of all the men whom I have ever seen, Carlyle was the least patient of the common woes of humanity. Nature had, in fact, given him a constitution of unusual strength. He saw his ailments through the lens of his imagination, so magnified by the metaphors in which he described them as to seem to him to be something supernatural; and if he was a torment to himself, he distracted every one with whom he came in contact. He had been to Edinburgh about the printing of *Meister*, and had slept in the lodgings which he had longed for at Kinnaird. "There was one of the public guardians," he says in a letter, "whose throat I could have cut that night. . . . He awoke me every half-hour throughout the night; his voice was loud, hideous and ear- and soul-piercing; resembling the voices of ten thousand gib-cats all molten into one terrific peal."[23]

I have dwelt more fully on these aspects of Carlyle's character than in themselves they deserve, because the irritability which he could not or would not try to control followed him through the greater part of his life. It was no light matter to take charge of such a person, as Miss Welsh was beginning to contemplate the possibility of doing. Nor can we blame the anxiety with which her mother was now regarding the closeness of the correspondence between Carlyle and her daughter. Extreme as was the undesirableness of such a marriage in a worldly point of view, it is to Mrs. Welsh's credit that inequality of social position was not the cause of her alarm, so much as the violence of temper which Carlyle could not restrain even before her. The fault, however, was of the surface merely, and Miss Welsh was not the only person who could see the essential quality of the nature which lay below. Mrs. Buller had suffered from Carlyle's humours as keenly as anyone, except, perhaps, her poor "sluttish harlots";[24] yet she was most anxious that he should remain with the family and have the exclusive training of her sons. They had been long enough at Kinnaird; their future plans were unsettled. They thought of a house in Cornwall, of a house in London, of travelling abroad, in all of which arrangements they desired to include Carlyle. At length it was settled—so far as Mrs. Buller could settle anything—that they were to stay where they were till the end of January, and then go for the season to London. Carlyle was to remain behind in Scotland till he had carried *Meister* through the press. Irving had invited him to be his guest at any time in the spring which might suit him, and further plans could then be arranged. For the moment his mind was taken off from his own sorrows by the need of helping his brothers. His brother Alick was starting in business as a farmer. Carlyle found himself in money, and refused to be thanked for it. "What any brethren of our father's house possess," he said, "I look on as common stock, from which all are entitled to draw whenever their convenience requires it. Feelings far nobler than pride are my guides in such matters."

He was already supporting John Carlyle at college, and not supporting only, but directing and advising. His counsels were always wise. As a son and brother his conduct in all essentials was faultlessly admirable.

He was looking forward to London, though far from sharing the enthusiastic expectations which Irving had formed for him. Irving, it seems, had imagined that his friend had but to present himself before the great world to carry it by storm as he had himself done, and when they met in the autumn had told him so. Carlyle was under no such illusion.

The Bullers went at last. Carlyle returned to his lodgings at Edinburgh, finished his *Schiller*, and was busy translating the last chapters of *Meister* while the first were being printed. Miss Welsh came into the city to stay with a friend. They met and quarrelled. She tormented her lover till he flung out of the room, banging the door behind him. A note of penitence followed. "I declare," she said, "I am very much of Mr Kemp's way of thinking, that 'certain persons are possessed of devils even in the present times.' Nothing less than a Devil (I am sure) could have tempted me to torment you and myself, as I did, on that unblessed day."[25] There was no engagement between them, and under existing circumstances there was to be none; but she shared Irving's conviction that Carlyle had but to be known to spring to fame and fortune; and his fortune, as soon as it was made, she was willing to promise to share with him. Strict secrecy was of course desired. Her mother and his mother were alone admitted to the great mystery; but the "sorrows of Teufelsdröckh," bodily and mental, were forgotten for at least three months.

Carlyle did not stay long in Edinburgh. He remained only till he had settled his business arrangements with Boyd, his publisher, and then went home to Mainhill to finish his translation of *Meister* there. He was to receive £180 on publication for the first edition. If a second edition was called for, Boyd was to pay him £250 for a thousand copies, and after that the book was to be Carlyle's own. "Any way, I am already paid sufficiently for all my labour," he said. "Am I a *genius* still? I was intended for a *horse-dealer* rather."[26] The sheets of *Meister* were sent to Haddington as they were printed. Miss Welsh refused to be interested in it, and thought more of the money which Carlyle was making than of the great Goethe and his novel. Carlyle admitted that she had much to say for her opinion.

> There is not properly speaking the smallest particle of *historical* interest in it, except what is connected with Mignon; and her you cannot see fully, till near the very end. Meister himself is perhaps one of the greatest *ganaches* [blockheads] that ever was created by quill and ink. I am going to write a fierce preface, disclaiming all concern with the literary or the moral merit of the work; grounding my claims to recompense or toleration on the fact that I have accurately copied a striking portrait of Goethe's mind, the strangest and in many points the greatest now extant. What a work! Bushels of dust and straws and feathers, with here and there a diamond of the purest water![27]

Carlyle was very happy at this time at Mainhill. He had found work that he could do, and had opened, as it seemed, successfully his literary career. The lady whom he had so long worshipped had given him hopes that his devotion might be rewarded. She had declined to find much beauty even in Mignon; but she might say what she pleased now without disturbing him.

In this mood Carlyle heard of the end of Lord Byron. He had spoken slightingly of Byron in his last letter; he often spoke in the same tone in his own later years; but he allowed no one else to take the same liberties. Perhaps in his heart he felt at four score much what he wrote when the news came from Missolonghi. Both he and Miss Welsh were equally affected. She wrote, "I was told it all at once in a room full of people, My God if they had said that the sun or the moon had gone out of the heavens it could not have struck me with the idea of a more awful and dreary blank in the creation than the words Byron is dead."[28] Carlyle answered:

> Poor Byron! Alas poor Byron! The news of his death came down upon my heart like a mass of lead; and yet, the thought of it sends a painful twinge thro' all my being, as if I had lost a brother! O God! That so many souls of mud and clay should fill up their

base existence to its utmost bound, and this, the noblest spirit in Europe, should sink before half his course was run! Late so full of fire, and generous passion, and proud purposes, and now forever dumb and cold! Poor Byron! And but a young man; still struggling amid the perplexities, and sorrows and aberrations, of a mind not arrived at maturity or settled in its proper place in life. Had he been spared to the age of three score and ten, what might he not have done, what might he not have been! But we shall hear his voice no more: I dreamed of seeing him and knowing him; but the curtain of everlasting night has hid him from our eyes. We shall go to him, he shall not return to us. Adieu my dear Jane! There is a blank in your heart, and a blank in mine, since this man passed away.[29]

chapter six

1824–1825

London

The time for Carlyle's departure for London had now arrived. A letter came from Mrs. Buller begging his immediate presence. *Meister* was finished and paid for. A presentation copy was secured for Mainhill, and there was no more reason for delay. The expedition was an epoch in Carlyle's life. There was, perhaps, no one of his age in Scotland or England who knew so much and had seen so little. He had read enormously—history, poetry, philosophy; the whole range of modern literature—French, German, and English—was more familiar to him, perhaps, than to any man living of his own age; while the digestive power by which all this spiritual food had been digested and converted into intellectual tissue was equally astonishing. And yet all this time he had never seen any town larger than Glasgow, or any cultivated society beyond what he had fallen in with at occasional dinners with Brewster, or with the Bullers at Kinnaird. London had hovered before him rather as a place of doubtful possibilities than of definite hope. The sanguine Irving would have persuaded him that it would open its arms to a new man of genius. Carlyle knew better. He had measured his own capabilities. He was painfully aware that they were not of the sort which would win easy recognition, and that if he made his way at all it would be slowly, and after desperate and prolonged exertion. He would never go to bed unknown and wake to find himself famous. His own disposition was rather towards some quiet place in Scotland, where with fresh air and plain food he could possess his soul in peace and work undisturbed and unconfused. Still London was to be seen and measured. He was to go by sea from Leith, and for the first week or two after his arrival he was to be Irving's guest at Pentonville. A few happy days were spent at Haddington, and on Sunday morning, June 5, he sailed—sailed literally. Steamers had begun to run, but were not yet popular; and the old yacht, safe if tedious, was still the usual mode of transit for ordinary travellers.

Carlyle has described in his *Reminiscences* his arrival in London, his reception in Irving's house, and his various adventures during his English visit.[1] When written evidence rises before us of what we said and did in early life, we find generally that memory has played false to us, and has so shaped and altered past scenes that our actions have become legendary even to ourselves. Goethe called his autobiography *Dichtung and Wahrheit*, being aware that facts stand in our recollection as trees, houses, mountains, rivers stand in the landscape; that lights and shadows change their places between sunrise and sunset, and that objects are grouped into new combinations as the point of vision alters. But none of these involuntary freaks of memory can be traced in Carlyle's *Reminiscences*. After two and forty years the scenes and persons which he describes remain as if photographed precisely as they are to be found in his contemporary letters. Nothing is changed. The images stand as they were first printed, the judgements are unmodified, and are often repeated in the same words. His matured and epitomised narrative may thus be trusted as an entirely authentic record of the scenes which are recorded at fuller length in the accounts which he sent at the time to his family and friends. With Irving he was better pleased than he expected. Uneasiness Carlyle had felt about him—never, indeed, that the simplicity and truth of Irving's disposition could be impaired or tarnished, but that he might be misled and confused by the surroundings in which he was to find him. "The orator," he wrote, "is mended since I saw him at Dunkeld: he begins to see that his honours are not supernatural; and his honest practical warmth of heart is again becoming the leading feature in his character."[2] He was thrown at once into Irving's circle, and made acquaintance with various persons whom he had previously heard celebrated. Mrs. Strachey, Mrs. Buller's sister, he admired the most. Her husband, too, he met and liked, and her niece, Miss Kirkpatrick. [He was soon introduced to the literary worthies of London—"Barry Cornwall," Allan Cunningham, Thomas Campbell—and, of course, made the pilgrimage to Highgate to meet Coleridge.]

Coleridge naturally was an object of more than curiosity. He was then at the height of his fame—poet, metaphysician, theologian, accomplished, or supposed to be accomplished, in the arts in which Carlyle was most anxious to excel. Carlyle himself had formed a high if not the highest opinion of the merits of Coleridge, who was now sitting up at Highgate receiving the homage of the intellectual world, and pouring out floods of eloquence on all who came to worship in a befitting state of mind. The befitting state was not universal even in those who sincerely loved the great man. Leigh Hunt and Lamb had sate one night in the Highgate drawing room for long hours listening to the oracle discoursing upon the Logos. Hunt, as they stood leaning over a stile in the moonlight, on their way home, said, "How strange that a man of such indisputable genius should talk such nonsense!" "Why, you see," said Lamb, stammering, "C-c-coleridge has so much f-f-fun in him." The finished portrait of Coleridge is found in Carlyle's *Life of Sterling*.[3] The original sketch is in a letter of the 24th of June to his brother John.

I have seen many . . . curiosities. Not the least of these I reckon Coleridge, the Kantean metaphysician and quondam Lake poet. I will tell you all about our interview *when we meet*. Figure a fat flabby incurvated personage, at once short, rotund and relaxed, with a watery mouth, a snuffy nose, a pair of strange brown timid yet earnest looking eyes, a high tapering brow, and a great bush of grey hair—you will have some faint idea of Coleridge. He is a kind, good soul, full of religion and affection, and poetry and animal magnetism. His cardinal sin is that he wants *will*; he has no resolution, he shrinks from pain or labour in any of its shapes. His very attitude bespeaks this: he never straightens his knee joints, he stoops with his fat ill shapen shoulders, and in walking he does not tread but shovel and slide—my father would call it *skluiffing*. He is also always busied to keep by strong and frequent inhalations the water of his mouth from overflowing; and his eyes

155

have a look of anxious impotence; he *would* do with all his heart, but he knows he dare not. The conversation of the man is much as I anticipated. A forest of thoughts; some true, many false, most part dubious, all of them ingenious in some degree. But there is not method in his talk; he wanders like a man sailing among many currents, whithersoever his lazy mind directs him—; and what is more unpleasant he preaches, or rather soliloquizes: he cannot speak; he can only "*tal-k*" (so he names it). Hence I found him unprofitable, even tedious: but we parted very good friends I promising to go back and see him some other evening—a promise I fully intend to keep. . . . I reckon him a man of great and useless genius—a strange not at all a great man.[4]

The Bullers were still uncertain about their future movements. One day they were to take a house at Boulogne, the next to settle in Cornwall, the next to remain in London, and send Carlyle with the boys into the country. As a temporary measure, ten days after his arrival he and Charles found themselves located in lodgings at Kew Green, which Carlyle soon grew weary of and Charles Buller hated; while Carlyle, though he appreciated, and at times even admired, Mrs. Buller's fine qualities, was not of a temper to submit to a woman's caprices.

Mrs. Page [his landlady] was unlike the dames who had driven Carlyle so distracted in Edinburgh, and the contrast between the respectful manners of English people and the hard familiarity of his countrywomen struck him agreeably. Time and progress have done their work, whether for good or evil, and it would at present be difficult to find reverential landladies either at Kew Green or anywhere in the British dominions; Kew Green has become vulgarised, and the grace has gone from it; the main points of the locality can be recognised from Carlyle's picture, but cockneys and cockney taste are now in possession. The suburban sojourn came to an early end, and with it Carlyle's relations with Mr. Buller and his family. He describes the close of the connection in words which did not express his deliberate feeling. He knew that he owed much to Mrs. Buller's kindness; and her own and Mr. Buller's regard for him survived in the form of strong friendship to the end of their lives. But he was irritated at the abruptness with which he conceived that he had been treated. He was proud and thin-skinned. [A] letter [to his mother] is dated from Irving's house at

Pentonville, which was again immediately opened to him, and contains the history of the Buller break-up, and of a new acquaintance which was about to take him to Birmingham. "My dear Mother" [he begins],

I suppose you are not expecting to hear from me so soon again, and still less to hear the news I have got to tell you. The last letter was dated from Kew Green; there will no more of mine be dated there: last time, I was complaining of the irresolute and foolish fluctuations of the Bullers; I shall never more have reason to complain of their proceedings, I am now free of them for ever and a day. . . . It was agreed that I should quit them—an arrangement not a little grievous to old Buller & his son, but nowise grievous to his wife, one of whose whims was Cambridge University; in which whim so long as she persists, she will be ready to stake her whole soul on the fulfilment of it. . . .

My movements for a while must be rather desultory. My first is to the northward. Among the worthy persons whom I have met with here is a Mr. Beddomes [Badams], a friend of Irvings, a graduate in medicine tho' his business is in chemical manufactories at Birmingham, where I understand he is rapidly realizing a fortune. This man one of the most sensible clear-headed persons I have ever met with seems also one of the kindest. After going about together for a day or two, talking about pictures, and stomach-disorders in the cure of which he is famous, and from which he once suffered four years of torment in person—what does the man do but propose that I should go up to Birmingham, and live a month with him that he might find out the make of me, and prescribe for my unfortunate inner man! . . . I have consented to go with him.[5]

Carlyle was now once more his own master, adrift from all engagements which made his time the property of others, and without means or prospect of support save what his pen could earn for him. Miss Welsh had expected with too sanguine ignorance that when his first writings had introduced him to the world, the world would rush forward to his assistance; that he would be seized upon for some public employment, or at worst would be encouraged by a sinecure. The world is in no such haste to recognise a man of original genius. Unless he runs with the stream, or with some one of the popular currents, every man's hand is at first against him. Rivals challenge his pretensions; his talents are denied; his aims are ridiculed; he is tried in the furnace of criticism, and it is well that it should be so. A man does not know himself what is in him till he has been

157

tested; far less can others know; and the metal which glitters most on the outside most often turns out to be but pinchbeck. A longer and more bitter apprenticeship lay upon Carlyle than even he, little sanguine as he was, might at this time have anticipated. His papers on Schiller had been well received and were to be collected into a volume; a contemptuous review of *Meister* by De Quincey appeared in the *London Magazine*, but the early sale was rapid. He had been well paid for the first specimens of jewels which he had brought out of the German mines. An endless vein remained unwrought, and the field was for the present his own. Thus he went down to Birmingham to his friend with a light heart, anxious chiefly about his health, and convinced that if he could mend his digestion, all else would be easy for him. Birmingham with its fiery furnaces and fiery politics was a new scene to him, and was like the opening of some fresh volume of human life. He has given so full a history of his experiences when he was Mr. Badams' guest that there is no occasion to dwell upon it. The visit lasted two months instead of one. His first impression of the place, as he described it in a letter to his brother, is worth preserving as a specimen of his powers of minute word-painting, and as a description of what Birmingham was sixty years ago.

Birmingham I have now tried for a reasonable time, and I cannot complain of being tired of it. As a town, it is pitiful enough; a mean congeries of bricks, including scarcely one or two large capitalists, some hundreds of minor ones, and perhaps a hundred and twenty thousand sooty artisans in metals & chemical produce. The streets are ill-built, ill-paved, always flimsy in their aspect, often poor, sometimes miserable. Not above one or two of them are paved with flag-stones at the sides; and to walk upon the little egg-shaped slipper flints that supply their place is something very like a pennance. Yet withal it is interesting, from some of the commons or lanes that spot or intersect the green woody undulating environs, to view this City of Tubal-cain. Torrents of thick smoke with ever and anon a burst of dingy flame are issuing from a thousand funnels; "a thousand hammers fall by turns on the red [i]ron of the furnace"; you hear the clank of innumerable steam-engines, the rumbling of vans and cars and the hum of men, interrupted by the sharper rattle of some canal-boat loading or disloading, or perhaps some fierce explosion where the cannon-founders are proving their new-made ware. I have seen their rolling mills; their polishing of teapots and buttons and gunbarrels, and fire-shovels and swords, and all manner of toys and tackle; I have looked into their ironworks (where 150,000 men are smelting the metal, in a district a few miles to the north), their coal mines—fit image of Avernus!— their tubs and vats (as large as country-churches) full of copperas and aquafortis and oil of vitriol; and the whole is not without its attractions as well as repulsions, of which when we meet I will preach to you at large.[6]

But all the while Carlyle's heart was in Scotland, at Haddington—and less at Haddington than at Mainhill. The strongest personal passion which he experienced through all his life was his affection for his mother. She was proud and wilful, as he. He had sent her, or offered her, more presents, and she had been angry with him. She had not been well, and she was impatient of doctors' regulations.

Eight weeks were passed with Badams, without, however, the advantage to Carlyle's health which he had looked for. There had been daily rides into the country, visits to all manner of interesting places—Hadley, Warwick, and Kenilworth. The society had been interesting, and Badams himself all that was kind and considerate. But the contempt of "drugs" which he had professed in London had been rather theoretic than practical; and the doses which had been administered perhaps of themselves accounted for the failure of other remedies. At the beginning of September an invitation came to Carlyle to join the Stracheys at Dover. The Irvings were to be of the party. Irving needed rest from his preaching. Mrs. Irving had been confined and had been recommended sea air for herself and her baby. The Stracheys and Miss Kirkpatrick had taken a house at Dover; the Irvings had lodgings of their own, but were to live with their friends, and Carlyle was to be included in the party. Mrs. Strachey was a very interesting person to him, still beautiful, younger than Mrs. Buller, and a remarkable contrast to her. Mrs. Buller was a sort of heathen; Mrs. Strachey was earnestly religious. She is "as unlike her" [Mrs. Buller], Carlyle told his mother, "as pure gold is to gilt copper: she is an earnest, determined, warm-hearted, religious matron, while the other is but a fluttering patroness of routs and operas."[7] An invitation to stay with her had many attractions for him.

The Dover visit, however, was accomplished, and the unexpected trip to Paris which grew out of it. For this, too, the reader is mainly referred to the *Reminiscences* which need no correction from contemporary letters; and to which those letters, though written when the scenes were fresh, can still add little, save a further evidence of the extreme accuracy of his memory.[8]

Mrs. Strachey came down [to Dover] after a few days. The little party was always together—walking on the beach or reading Fletcher's *Purple Island*. Mrs. Strachey herself was in full sympathy with Irving, if no one else was. Then her husband came, who was especially wanting in sympathy. The difference of sentiment became perceptible. The French coast lay invitingly opposite. The weather was beautiful. A trip to Paris was proposed and instantly decided on. Mr. Strachey, Miss Kirkpatrick, and Carlyle were to go. Mrs. Strachey and the Irvings were to stay behind. A travelling carriage was sent across the channel, post-horses were always ready on the Paris road, and Carlyle, who had but left Scotland for the first time four months before, and had been launched an entire novice into the world, was now to be among the scenes so long familiar to him as names. They went by Montreuil, Abbeville, Nampont, with Sterne's *Sentimental Journey* as a guide book, when Murray was unknown. They saw the Cathedral at Beauvais, for which Carlyle did not care at all; they saw French soldiers, for which he cared a great deal. He himself could speak a little French; Strachey, like more Englishmen, almost none. Montmorency reminded him of Rousseau. From Montmartre they looked down on Paris: "not a breath of smoke or dimness anywhere, every roof and dome and spire and chimney-top clearly visible, and the skylights sparkling like diamonds: I have never," he says, "since or before, seen so fine a view of a Town."[9] Carlyle, who could see and remember so much of Stratford, where he stayed only while the coach changed horses, coming on Paris fresh, with a mind like wax to receive impressions, yet tenacious as steel in preserving them, carried off recollections from his twelve days' sojourn in the French capital which never left him, and served him well in after years when he came to write about the Revolution. He saw the places of which he had read. He saw Louis Dix-huit lying in state, Charles Dix, Legendre (whose *Geometry* he had translated for Brewster), the

160

great Laplace, M. de Chézy the Persian professor. He heard
Cuvier lecture. He went to the Théâtre Français, and saw
and heard Talma in *Oedipe*. He listened to a sermon at
Ste. Geneviève. A more impressive sermon was a stern old
grey-haired corpse which he saw lying in the Morgue. He
saw the French people, and the ways and works of them,
which interested him most of all. These images, with glimpses of English travellers, were all crowded into the few
brief days of their stay; the richest in new ideas, new emotions, new pictures of human life, which Carlyle had yet experienced.

From the many letters which he wrote about it, I select
one to his brother John.

Of Paris I shall say nothing till we meet. It is the Vanity-fair of the
universe, and cannot be described in *many* letters. . . . With very
few exceptions the streets are narrow and crowded and unclean;
the kennel in the middle, and a lamp hanging over it here and
there, on a rope from side to side. There are no foot-paths; but an
everlasting press of carriages and carts, and dirty people hastening
to and fro among them, amidst a thousand *gare-gares!* and *sacrés*
and other oaths and admonitions; while by the side are men roast-
ing ches[t]nuts in their booths; fruit-shops, wine-shops, barbers, silk-
merchants selling *à Prix juste* (without cheating), *restaurateurs*,
cafés, traiteurs, magasins de bon-bons, billiard tables, *estaminets*
(gin-shops), *débits de tabac* (where you buy a cigar for a halfpenny,
and go out smoking it), and every species of *dépôt* and *entre-
pot* and *magasin* for the comfort and refreshment of the physical
part of the natural man; plying its vocation in the midst of noise
and stink, both of which it augments by its produce and its efforts to dispose of it. The *Palais Royal* is a spot unrivalled in the
world; the chosen abode of vanity and vice; the true palace of
the *tigre-singes* (tiger-apes) as Voltaire called his countrymen; a
place which I rejoice to think is separated from me by the girdle
of the ocean, and never likely to be copied in the British isles. I
dined in it often; and bought four little bone *étuis* (needle-cases)
at a frank (9-1/2 *d*) each for our four sisters at Mainhill. It is a sort
of emblem of the French character; the perfection of the physical
and fantastical part of our nature, with an absence of all that is
solid and substantial in the moral and often in the intellectual
part of it. Looking-glasses and trinkets and fricassées and gaming-
tables seem to be the life of a Frenchman; his home is a place
where he sleeps and dresses; he *lives* in the *salon du restaurateur* on
the *boulevards* or the garden of the *Palais royal*. Every room you
enter, destitute of carpet or fire, is expanded into boundlessness
by mirrors, and I should think about fifty thousand dice-boxes
are set a rattling every night (especially on Sundays) within the

161

walls of Paris. There the people sit and chatter, and fiddle away existence as if it were all a raree-shew; careless how it go, so they have excitement, *des sensations agréables*. Their palaces and picture-galleries and triumphal arches are the wonder of the Earth; but the stink of their streets is considerable, and you cannot walk on them without risking the fracture of your legs of [or] neck.[10]

Such was Carlyle's sudden visit to Paris—an incident of more importance to him than he knew at the moment. He complained before and he complained after of the hardness of fortune to him; but fortune in the shape of friends was throwing in his way what very few young men better connected in life have the happiness of so early falling in with. The expedition created no small excitement at Mainhill. The old people had grown up under the traditions of the war. For a son of theirs to go abroad at all was almost miraculous. When they heard that he was gone to Paris, "all the stoutness of their hearts" was required to bear it.

The holiday was over. Carlyle returned to London with the Stracheys, and settled himself in lodgings in Southampton Street, near Irving. Here at any rate he intended to stay till Schiller was off his hands complete in the form of the book. That accomplished, the problem of his future life remained to be encountered. What was he to do? He was adrift, with no settled occupation. To what should he turn his hand? Where should he resolve to live? He had now seen London. He had seen Birmingham with its busy industries. He had seen Paris. He had been brought into contact with English intellectual life. He had conversed and measured strength with some of the leading men of letters of the day. He knew that he had talents which entitled him to a place among the best of them. But he was sick in body, and mentally he was a strange combination of pride and self-depreciation. He was free as air, but free only, as it seemed to him, because of his insignificance,—because no one wanted his help. Most of us find our course determined by circumstances. We are saved by necessity from the infirmity of our own wills. No necessity interfered with Carlyle. He had the world before him with no limitations but his poverty, and he was entirely at sea. So far only he was determined, that he would never sell his soul to the

162

Devil, never speak what he did not wholly believe, never do what in his inmost heart he did not feel to be right, and that he would keep his independence, come what might.

Literature lay open. Nothing could hinder a man there save the unwillingness of publishers to take his wares; but of this there seemed to be no danger. *Meister* seemed to be coming to a second edition; the *Schiller*, such parts of it as had as yet appeared, had been favourably noticed; and Schiller's own example was specially encouraging. Schiller, like himself, had been intended for the ministry, had recoiled from it, had drifted, as he had done, into the initial stages of law, but had been unable to move in professional harness. Schiller, like himself again, had been afflicted with painful chronic disease, and, though it killed him early, his spirit had triumphed over his body. At the age at which Carlyle had now arrived, Schiller's name was known in every reading household in Germany, and his early plays had been translated into half the languages in Europe. Schiller, however, more fortunate than he, possessed the rare and glorious gift of poetry. Carlyle had tried poetry and had consciously failed. He had intellect enough. He had imagination—no lack of that, and the keenest and widest sensibilities; yet with a true instinct he had discovered that the special faculty which distinguishes the poet from other men, nature had not bestowed upon him. He had no correct metrical ear; the defect can be traced in the very best of his attempts, whether at translation or at original composition. He could shape his materials into verse, but without spontaneity, and instead of gaining beauty they lost their force and clearness. His prose at this time was, on the other hand, supremely excellent, little as he knew it. The sentences in his letters are perfectly shaped, and are pregnant with meaning. The more impassioned passages flow in rhythmical cadence like the sweetest tones of an organ. The style of the *Life of Schiller* is the style of his letters. He was not satisfied with it; he thought it "wretched," "bombastic," "not in the right vein." It was in fact simple. Few literary biographies in the English language equal it for grace, for brevity, for clearness of portraiture, and artist-like neglect of the unessentials. Goethe so clearly recognised its merits, that in 1830 it was to be translated under his direction into German, and edited with a preface by himself. While England and Scotland were giving Carlyle at best a few patronising nods, soon to change to anger and contempt, Goethe saw in this young unknown Scotchman the characteristics of a true man of genius, and spoke of him "as a new moral force, the extent and effects of which it was impossible to predict."[11]

The rewriting and arranging of the *Life of Schiller* was more tedious than Carlyle expected. It was not finished till the middle of winter, all which time Carlyle was alone in his London lodgings.

The correspondence with Miss Welsh had continued regularly since Carlyle left Scotland. Letters written under such circumstances are in their nature private, and so must for the most part remain. Miss Welsh, however, was necessarily a principal element in any scheme which Carlyle might form for his future life, and to her his views were exposed without the smallest reserve. The pensions or sinecures of which her too sanguine expection had dreamt, he had known from the first to be illusions. He must live, if he lived at all, by his own hand. He had begun to think that both for body and mind London was not the place for him. He had saved between two and three hundred pounds, beyond what he had spent upon his brothers. His tastes were of the simplest. The plainest house, the plainest food, the plainest dress, was all that he wanted. The literary men whom he had met with in the metropolis did not please him. Some, like Hazlitt, were selling their souls to the periodical press. Even in Campbell and Coleridge the finer powers were dormant or paralysed, under the spell it seemed of London and its influences. Southey and Wordsworth, who could give a better account of their abilities, had turned their backs upon the world with its vain distinctions and noisy flatteries, and were living far away among the lakes and mountains. [To Jane, Carlyle wrote of his London acquaintances.]

On the whole, however, [Irving] is among the best fellows in London; by far the best that I have met with. Thomas Campbell has a far clearer judgment, infinitely more taste and refinement; but there is no living well of thought or feeling in him; his head is a shop not a manufactory; and for his heart, it is as dry as a Greenock *kipper.* I saw him for the second time, the other night; I viewed him more clearly and in a kindlier light, but scarcely altered my opinion of him. He is not so much a man, as the Editor of a Magazine: his life is that of an exotic; he exists in London, as most Scotchmen do, like a shrub disrooted, and stuck into a bottle of water. Poor Campbell! There were good things in him too: but Fate has pressed too heavy on him, or he has resisted it too weakly. His poetic vein is failing or run out; he has a Port-Glasgow wife, and their only son is in a state of idiocy. I sympathized with him; I could have loved him, but he has forgot the way to love.— Little Procter here has set up house on the strength of his writing faculties, with his wife a daughter of the "Noble Lady" [Mrs. Anna Montagu]. He is a good-natured man, lively and ingenious; but essentially a Small.— Coleridge is sunk inextricably in the depths of putrescent indolence. Southey and Wordsworth have retired far from the din of this monstrous city. So has Thomas Moore. Whom have we left? The dwarf Opium-Eater (my Critic in the London Magazine) lives here in lodgings, with a wife and children living or starving on the scanty produce of his scribble, far off in Westmoreland. He carries a laudanum bottle in his pocket; and the venom of a wasp in his heart. . . . A rascal Maghean (or Mag*in*[n] who writes much of the blackguardism of Blackwood) his [has] been frying him to cinders on the gridiron of the *John Bull.* Poor Dequincey! He had twenty thousand pounds, and a liberal share of gifts from nature: vanity and opium have brought him to the state of "dog distract or monkey sick." If I could find him, it would give me pleasure to procure him one substantial beef-steak before he dies— Hazlitt is *writing* his way thro' France and Italy: the ginshops and pawnbrokers bewail his absence. Leigh Hunt writes "wishing caps" for the Examiner, and lives on the tightest of diets at Pisa.— But what shall I say of *you,* ye Theodore Hooks, ye Ma*jins,* and Darlys, and all the spotted fry that "report" and "get up" for the "Public Press"; that earn money by writing calumnies, and spend it in punch and other viler objects of debauchery? Filthiest and basest of the children of men! . . .

Such is the "Literary World" of London; indisputably the poorest part of its population at present.[12]

While in this humour with English men of letters, Carlyle was surprised and cheered by a letter from one of the same calling in another country, the man whom above all others he most honoured and admired, Goethe himself. He had sent a copy of his translation of *Meister* to Weimar, but no notice had been taken of it, and he had ceased to expect any. "It was almost like a message from Fairy Land; I could scarcely think that *this was* the real hand and signature of that mysterious personage, whose name had floated thro' my fancy, like a sort of spell, since boyhood; whose

GOETHE. Unbounded was Carlyle's reverence for the German sage, who stands behind his vision of the hero. Correspondence, begun in 1824, continued regularly from 1827 until Goethe's death in 1832. Carlyle earned Goethe's respect through his biography of Schiller, his translation of *Wilhelm Meister*, and his articles on German literature. Chiefly from Goethe's writings, *Wilhelm Meister* in particular, did Carlyle take strength to emerge from the Leith Walk "conversion" of 1822 described graphically in "The Everlasting No" of *Sartor*. "I then felt, and still feel, endlessly indebted to *Goethe* in the business," he wrote in the *Reminiscences*; "he, in his fashion, I perceived, had travelled the steep rocky road before me,—the first of the moderns." Carlyle's brother John sent him this engraving, a gift to Carlyle from Baron von Eichthal, from Munich in 1828. Underneath it Goethe had written in 1825: "Liegt dir Gestern klar und offen / Wirkst du Heute kräftig frey; / Kannst auch auf ein Morgen hoffen / Das nicht minder glücklich sey." Carlyle translated the lines thus: "Know'st thou *Yesterday*, its aim and reason; / Work'st thou well *Today*, for worthy things? / Calmly wait the Morrow's hidden season, / Need'st not fear what hap soe'er it brings." (Engraving by S. Bendixon after the painting by Carl Christian Vogel von Vogelstein, courtesy of the Carlyle House, Chelsea.)

thoughts had come to me in maturer years with almost the impressiveness of revelations."[13]

This is the first of several letters which Carlyle received from Goethe; the earliest token of the attention which he had commanded from the leader of modern literature, an attention which deepened into regard and admiration when the *Life of Schiller* reached Goethe's hands. The acquaintance which was to prove mutually interesting came of course to nothing. The momentary consequence which attached to him as the correspondent of the poet-minister of the Duke of Weimar disappeared in England, where he seemed no more than an insignificant struggling individual, below the notice of the privileged circles.

Goethe's letter was more than a compliment. Goethe, who did not throw away his words in unmeaning politenesses, had noticed Carlyle; and notice was more welcome from such a source than if it had come from ministers or kings. The master had spoken approvingly. The disciple was encouraged and invigorated. He had received an earnest that his intellectual career would not be a wholly unfruitful one. Pleasant as it was, however, it did not help the solution of the pressing problem, what was he immediately to do? The prospect of a farm in Scotland became more attractive the more he thought of it. Freedom, fresh air, plain food, and the society of healthy, pious people, unspoilt by the world and its contagion—with these life might be worth having and might be turned to noble uses. He had reflected much on his engagement with Miss Welsh. He had felt that perhaps he had done wrong in allowing her to entangle herself with a person whose future was so uncertain, and whose present schemes, even if realised successfully, would throw her, if she married him, into a situation so unlike what she had anticipated, so unlike the surroundings to which she had been accustomed. In his vehement way he had offered to release her if she wished it; and she had unhesitatingly refused. As little, however, was her ambition gratified with the prospect of being mistress of a Scotch farm. She had mocked at his proposal. She had pointed out with serious truth his own utter unfitness for a farmer's occupation. She had jestingly told him that she had land of her own at Craigenputtoch. The tenant was leaving. If he was bent on trying, let him try Craigenputtoch. He took her jest in earnest. Why should he not farm Craigenputtoch? Why should not she, as she was still willing to be his life companion, live with him there? Her father had been born in the old manor-house, and had intended to end his days there. To himself the moorland life would be only a continuance of the same happy mode of existence which he had known at Mainhill. In such a household, and in the discharge of the commonest duties, he had seen his mother become a very paragon of women. He did not understand, or he did not wish to understand, that a position which may be admirably suited to a person who has known no other, might be ill-adapted to one who had been bred in luxury and had never known a want uncared for. The longer he reflected on it, the more desirable the plan of taking Craigenputtoch appeared to him to be.

Miss Welsh, after having lost Irving, had consented to be Carlyle's wife as soon as he was in a fair position to marry, in the conviction that she was connecting herself with a man who was destined to become brilliantly distinguished, whom she honoured for his character and admired for his gifts, in whose society and in whose triumphs she would find a compensation for the disappointment of her earlier hopes. She was asked to be the mistress of a moorland farming establishment. Had she felt towards Carlyle as she had felt towards his friend, she would perhaps have encountered cheerfully any lot which was to be shared with the object of a passionate affection. But the indispensable feeling was absent. She was invited to relinquish her station in society, and resign comforts which habit had made necessary to her, and she was apparently to sacrifice at the same time the very expectations which had brought her to regard a marriage with Carlyle as a possibility. She knew better than he what was really implied in the situation which he offered her. She knew that if farming on a Scotch moor was to be a successful enterprise, it would not be by morning rides, metaphorical vituperation of "lazy hinds," and forenoons and evenings given up to poetry and philosophy. Both he and she would have to work with all their might, and with their own hands, with all their time and all their energy, to the extinction of every higher ambition. Carlyle himself also she knew to be entirely unfit for any such occupation.

168

The privations of it might be nothing to him, for he was used to them at home, but he would have to cease to be himself before he could submit patiently to a life of mechanical drudgery. She told him the truth with the merciless precision which on certain occasions distinguished her.

> Think of some more promising plan, than farming the most barren spot in the county of Dumfries-shire— What a thing that would be to be sure! you and I keeping house at Craigenputtoch! I would just as soon think of building myself a nest on the Bass-rock— nothing but your ignorance of the place saves you from the imputation of insanity for admitting such a thought. Depend upon it, you could not *exist* there a twelvemonth. For my part I would not spend a month on it with an Angel— Think of something else then— apply your industry to carry it into exffect[*sic*,] your talents to glid[e] over the inequality of our births and then—we will talk of marrying. If all this were realized I *think* I should have goodsense enough to abate something of my romantic ideal, and to content myself with stopping short on this side idolatry— At all events I will marry no one else— This is all the promise I can or will make. A positive engagement to marry a certain person at a certain time, at all haps and hazards[,] I have always considered the most rediculous thing on earth: it is either altogether useless or altogether miserable; if the parties continue faithfully attached to each other it is a mere ceremony—if otherwise it becomes a galling fetter reviting [riveting] them to wretchedness and only to be broken with disgrace.
>
> Such is the result of my deliberations on this very serious subject[.] You may approve of it or not; but you cannot either persuade me or convince me out of it— My decisions—when I *do* decide [—] are unalterable as the laws of the Medes & Persians— Write instantly and tell me that you are content to leave the event to time and destiny—and in the meanwhile to continue my Friend and Guardian which you have so long and so faithfully been—*and nothing more*—
>
> It would be more agreeable to etiquette, and perhaps also to prudence, that I should adopt no middle course in an affair such as this—that I should not for another instant encourage an affection I *may* never reward and a hope I *may* never fulfil; but cast your heart away from me at once since I cannot embrace the resolution which would give me a right to it for ever. This I would assuredly do if *you* were like the generality of lovers, or if it were still in my power to be happy independent of your affection but as it [is] neither etiquette nor prudence can obtain this of me. If there is any change to be made in the terms on which we have so long lived with one another; it must be made by *you* not *me*— I *cannot* make any[.][14]

An ordinary person who had ventured to make such a proposal as Miss Welsh had declined, would have been supremely foolish if he had supposed that it could be acceded to; or supremely selfish if he had possessed sufficient influence with the lady whom he was addressing to induce her to listen to it. But Carlyle was in every way peculiar. Selfish he was, if it be selfishness to be ready to sacrifice every person dependent on him, as completely as he sacrificed himself to the aims to which he had resolved to devote his life and talents. But these objects were of so rare a nature, that the person capable of pursuing and attaining them must be judged by a standard of his own. His rejoinder throws a light into the inmost constitution of his character. He thanked Miss Welsh for her candour; he was not offended at her resoluteness; but also, he said, he must himself be resolute. She showed that she did not understand him. He was simply conscious that he possessed powers for the use of which he was responsible, and he could not afford to allow those powers to run to waste any longer.

The functions of a biographer are, like the functions of a Greek chorus, occasionally at the important moments to throw in some moral remarks which seem to fit the situation.[15] The chorus would remark, perhaps, on the subtle forms of self-deception to which the human heart is liable, of the momentous nature of marriage, and how men and women plunge heedlessly into the net, thinking only of the satisfaction of their own immediate wishes. . . . Self-sacrifice it might say was a noble thing. But a sacrifice which one person might properly make, the other might have no reasonable right to ask or to allow. It would conclude, however, that the issues of human acts are in the hands of the gods, and would hope for the best in fear and trembling. Carlyle spoke of self-denial. The self-denial which he was prepared to make was the devotion of his whole life to the pursuit and setting forth of spiritual truth; throwing aside every meaner ambition. But apostles in St. Paul's opinion were better unwedded. The cause to which they give themselves leaves them little leisure to care for the things of their wives. To his mother Carlyle was so loving,

> That he might not beteem the winds of heaven
> Visit her face too roughly.[16]

This was love indeed—love that is lost in its object, and

thinks first and only how to guard and foster it. His wife he would expect to rise to his own level of disinterested self-surrender, and be content and happy in assisting him in the development of his own destiny; and this was selfishness—selfishness of a rare and elevated kind, but selfishness still; and it followed him throughout his married life. He awoke only to the consciousness of what he had been, when the knowledge would bring no more than unavailing remorse. He admired Miss Welsh; he loved her in a certain sense; but, like her, he was not *in love*.

He admired Miss Welsh. Her mind and temper suited him. He had allowed her image to intertwine itself with all his thoughts and emotions; but with love his feeling for her had nothing in common but the name. There is not a hint anywhere that he had contemplated as a remote possibility the usual consequence of a marriage—a family of children. He thought of a wife as a companion to himself who would make life easier and brighter to him. But this was all, and the images in which he dressed out the workings of his mind served only to hide their real character from himself.

Miss Welsh had been perfectly candid; and had she ended there, Carlyle—if persons in such situations were ever as wise as they ought to be—would have seen from [her] frank expression of her feelings that a marriage with himself was not likely to be a happy one for her. He had already dimly perceived that the essential condition was absent. She did not love him as she felt that she could love. As little, however, could she make up her mind to give him up or consent that, as he had said, they should "go forth upon our several paths."[17] She refused to believe that he could mean it. "How could I," she said, "*part* from the only living soul that understands me? I would marry you tomorrow rather! but then,—our parting would need to be brought about by death or some despensation [*sic*] of uncontrollable Providence—were *you* to will it, *to part* would no longer be bitter, the bitterness would be in thinking you unworthy."[18] Part with Carlyle, however, she would not, unless he himself wished it.

Thus matters drifted on to their consummation. The stern and powerful sense of duty in these two remarkable persons held them true through a long and trying life together to the course of elevated action which they had both set before themselves. He never swerved from the high aims to which he had resolved to devote himself. She, by never failing toil and watchfulness, alone made it possible for him to accomplish the work which he achieved. But we reap as we have sown. Those who seek for something more than happiness in this world must not complain if happiness is not their portion. She had the companionship of an extraordinary man. Her character was braced by the contact with him, and through the incessant self-denial which the determination that he should do his very best inevitably exacted of her. But she was not happy. Long years after, in the late evening of her laborious life, she said, "I married for ambition. Carlyle has exceeded all that my wildest hopes ever imagined of him—and I am miserable."[19]

chapter seven

1825–1826

Hoddam Hill

By the beginning of January the *Life of Schiller* was finished. Carlyle lingered in London for a few weeks longer. The London publishers had their eye on him, and made him various offers for fresh translations from the German; for a life of Voltaire; for other literary biographies. For each or all of these they were ready to give him, as they said, fair terms. He postponed his decision till these terms could be agreed on. Meanwhile he was as usual moody and discontented; in a hurry to be gone from London, and its "men of letters," whom he liked less and less.

To live in London and become enrolled in the unillustrious fellowship, Carlyle felt to be once for all impossible. But what was to be the alternative? Miss Welsh had condemned the farming project; but the opinion at Mainhill was not so unfavourable. If a good farm could be found, his brother Alexander was ready to undertake to set it going. His mother or a sister would manage the house and dairy. To his father, who was experienced in such matters, that Tom should take to them as he had done appeared neither wild nor unfeasible. He might, indeed, go back to Edinburgh and take pupils again. Mr. Buller was prepared to send his son Arthur to him, and go on with the £200 a-year. One of the Stracheys might come, and there were hopes of others; but Carlyle hated the drudgery of teaching, and was longing for fresh air and freedom.

The start of *Schiller* in the trade was less favourable than

173

had been looked for, and the offers from the booksellers for future work, when they came to be specified, were not satisfactory. Carlyle in consequence formed an ill opinion of these poor gentlemen.

He was more successful in making an arrangement with the publishers of *Wilhelm Meister* for further translations. It was arranged that he should furnish them with selections from Goethe, Tieck, Hoffmann, Jean Paul, and several others, enough to form the considerable book, which appeared in [early 1827], in four volumes, as *German Romance*. With this work definitely in prospect, which he felt that he could execute with ease as a mechanical task, Carlyle left London at the beginning of March, and left it with dry eyes. He regretted nothing in it but Irving; and Irving having taken now to interpretation of prophecy, and falling daily into yet wilder speculations, was almost lost to him. Their roads had long been divergent—Irving straying into the land of dreams, Carlyle into the hard region of unattractive truth, which as yet presented itself to him in its sternest form. The distance was becoming too wide for intimacy, although their affection for each other, fed on recollections of what had been, never failed either of them. Carlyle went down to Scotland, staying about [ten days] at Birmingham [with Badams], and [several more] at Manchester to see an old schoolfellow. When the coach brought him to Ecclefechan he found waiting for him his little sister Jane, the poetess, who had been daily watching for his arrival. "Her bonny little blush," he wrote long after, "and radiancy of look, when I let down the window and suddenly disclosed myself, are still present to me."[1]

His relation with his family was always beautiful. They had been busy for him in his absence, and had already secured what he was longing after. Two miles from Mainhill, on the brow of a hill, on the right as you look towards the Solway, stands an old ruined building with uncertain traditions attached to it, called the Tower of Repentance. Some singular story lies hidden in the name, but authentic record there is none. The Tower only remains visible far away from the high slopes which rise above Ecclefechan. Below the Tower is the farm-house of Hoddam Hill, with a few acres of tolerable land attached to it. The proprietor, General

174

HODDAM HILL, NEAR ECCLEFECHAN. The Carlyle family having outgrown the limited space at Mainhill, Mrs. Carlyle, with her sons Thomas and "Alick" and her two youngest daughters, moved in 1825 to a new farm, Hoddam Hill or Repentance Hill, where they were destined to remain only one year. "From the windows," Carlyle wrote, "there is such a view as Britain or the world could hardly have matched." James Carlyle stayed behind at Mainhill with the two oldest daughters. "With all its manifold petty troubles, this year at Hoddam Hill has a rustic beauty and dignity to me; and lies now like a not ignoble russet-coated Idyll in my memory; one of the quietest on the whole, and perhaps the most triumphantly important of my life." Thus wrote Carlyle in his reminiscence of Edward Irving. In this year and at this home he largely emerged from the spiritual crisis vividly portrayed in *Sartor*. The Tower of Repentance ("fit memorial for reflecting sinners," Carlyle wrote to Jane Welsh) is visible at the far left. (Photograph by John Patrick, courtesy of the University of Edinburgh.)

Sharpe, was the landlord of whom the Carlyles held Main-hill. It had been occupied by General Sharpe's factor; but the factor wishing to leave, they had taken it at the moderate rent of £100 a year for "Tom," and Alick was already busy putting in the crops, and the mother and sisters preparing the house to receive him. They would have made a home for him among themselves, and all from eldest to youngest would have done everything that affection could prompt to make him happy. But the narrow space, the early hours, the noises inseparable from the active work of a busy household, above all, the necessity of accommodating himself to the habits of a large family, were among the evils which he reckoned that he must avoid. He required a home of his own where he could be master of everything about him, and sit or move, sleep or rise, eat or fast, as he pleased, with no established order of things to interfere with him. Thus Hoddam Hill was taken for him, and there he prepared to settle himself.

Miss Welsh had promised that as soon as he was settled she would pay him and his mother a visit at Hoddam, that she might become acquainted with her future relations, and see with her eyes the kind of home which he was inviting her to share with him. His own imagination had made it into fairyland. [Living in] a country home among his own people was already telling on the inmost fibres of his nature, and soothing into sleep the unquiet spirits that tormented him.

I avoid as far as possible quoting passages from the *Reminiscences*, preferring the contemporary record of his letters which were written at the time; and because what is already there related does not need repeating. But in this year, when he was living among his own people, the letters are wanting, and one brief extract summing up the effects and experiences of the life at Hoddam may here be permitted.

> A neat compact little Farm, rent £100, which my Father had leased for me; on which was a prettyish-looking Cottage for dwelling-house . . . and from the windows, such a "view" (fifty miles in radius, from beyond Tyndale to beyond St. Bees, Solway Frith and all the Fells to Ingleborough inclusive) as Britain or the world could hardly have matched! Here the ploughing etc. was already in progress (which I often rode across to see); and here at term-day (26th May 1825) I established myself; set up my Books and bits of

176

implements *Lares*; and took to doing *German Romance* as my daily work; "ten pages daily" my stint, which, barring some rare accident, I faithfully accomplished. Brother Alick was my practical *farmer*; ever-kind and beloved Mother, with one of the little girls, was generally there,—Brother John, too, oftenest, who had just taken his degree;—these, with a little man and ditto maid, were our establishment. . . . This year at Hoddam Hill has a rustic beauty and dignity to me; and lies now like a not ignoble russet-coated Idyll in my memory; one of the quietest on the whole, and perhaps the most triumphantly important of my life. I lived very silent, diligent, had long solitary rides (on my wild Irish horse "Larry," good for the *dietetic* part);—my meditatings, musings and reflections were continual; thoughts went wandering (or travelling) through Eternity, through Time, and through Space, so far as poor I had scanned or known;—and were now, to my endless solacement, coming back with *tidings* to me! This year I found that I had conquered all my scepticisms, agonising doubtings, fearful wrestlings with the foul and vile and soul-murdering mud-Gods of my Epoch.[2]

The industry which Carlyle describes did not show itself immediately on his settlement at Hoddam. The excitement of the winter months had left him exhausted; and for the first few weeks at least he was recovering himself in an idleness which showed itself in the improvement of his humour.

Carlyle could not long be idle. The weariness passed off. He took up his translating work, and went on with it as he has related. An accident meanwhile precipitated the relations between himself and Miss Welsh, which had seemed likely to be long protracted, and, after threatening to separate them for ever, threw them more completely one upon the other.

When Irving first settled in London he had opened the secrets of his heart to a certain lady [Mrs. Anna D. B. Montagu] with whom he was very intimately acquainted. He had told her of his love for his old pupil, and she had drawn from him that the love had been returned. She had seen Irving sacrifice himself to duty, and she had heard that his resolution had been sustained by the person to whom the surrender of their mutual hopes had been as bitter as to himself. The lady was romantic, and had become profoundly interested. Flowing over with sympathy, she had herself commenced a correspondence with Haddington. To Car-

HODDAM CHURCH. "The sound of the Kirk-bell, once or twice on Sunday mornings (from Hoddam Kirk, about a mile off on the plain below me), was strangely touching,—like the departing voice of eighteen hundred years," Carlyle wrote in 1866 (*Reminiscences*). (Photograph by John Patrick, courtesy of the University of Edinburgh.)

lyle she wrote occasionally, because she really admired him. To Miss Welsh she introduced herself as one who was eager for her confidence, who was prepared to love her for the many excellences which she knew her to possess, and to administer balm to the wounds of her heart.

Miss Welsh did not respond very cordially to this effusive invitation. It was not her habit to seek for sympathy from strangers; but she replied in a letter which her new friend found extremely beautiful, and which stirred her interest still deeper. The lady imagined that her young correspondent was still pining in secret for her lost lover, and she was tempted to approach closer to the subject which had aroused her sympathies. She thought it would be well slightly to disparage Irving. She painted him as a person whose inconstancy did not deserve a prolonged and hopeless affection. She too had sought to find in him the dearest of friends; but he had other interests and other ambitions, and any woman who concentrated her heart upon him would be disappointed in the return which she might meet with.

The lady's motive was admirable. She thought that she could assist in reconciling Miss Welsh to her disappointment. In perfect innocence she wrote confidentially to Carlyle on the same subject. She regarded him simply as the intimate friend both of Miss Welsh and Irving. She assumed that he was acquainted with their secret history. She spoke of the affection which had existed between them as still unextinguished on either side. For the sake of both of them she wished that something might be done to put an end to idle regrets and vain imaginings. Nothing she thought could contribute more to disenchant Miss Welsh than a visit to herself in London, where she could see Irving as he was in his present surroundings.[3]

Miss Welsh had for two years never mentioned Irving to Carlyle except bitterly and contemptuously; so bitterly indeed that he had often been obliged to remonstrate. Had he been less singleminded, a tone so marked and acid might have roused his suspicions. But that Irving and she had been more than friends, if he had ever heard a hint of it, had passed out of his mind. Even the lady's letter failed to startle him. He mentioned merely, when he next wrote to her, that the writer laboured under some strange delusion

179

about her secret history, and had told him in a letter full of eloquence that her heart was with Irving in London.

Miss Welsh felt that she must at least satisfy her ecstatic acquaintance that she was not pining for another woman's husband. She was even more explicit. She had made up her mind to marry Carlyle. She told her intrusive correspondent so in plain words, desiring her only to keep her secret. The lady was thunderstruck. In ordinary life she was high-flown, and by those who did not know her might have been thought affected and unreal; but on occasions really serious she could feel and write like a wise woman. She knew that Miss Welsh could not love Carlyle. The motive could only be a generous hope of making life dearer, and want of health more endurable, to an honest and excellent man, while she might be seeking blindly to fill a void which was aching in her own heart. She required Miss Welsh, she most solemnly adjured her, to examine herself, and not allow one who had known much disappointment and many sorrows to discover by a comparison of his own feelings with hers that she had come to him with half a heart, and had mistaken compassion and the self-satisfaction of a generous act for a sentiment which could alone sustain her in a struggle through life. Supposing accident should set Irving free, supposing his love to have been indestructible and to have been surrendered only in obedience to duty, and supposing him, not knowing of this new engagement, to come back and claim the heart from which an adverse fate had separated him, what in such a case would her feeling be? If she could honestly say that she would still prefer Carlyle, then let her marry him, and the sooner the better. If, on the other hand, she was obliged to confess to herself that she could still find happiness where she had hoped to find it, Irving might still be lost to her; but in such a condition of mind she had no right to marry anyone else.

With characteristic integrity Mis Welch, on receiving this letter, instantly enclosed it to Carlyle. She had been under no obligation, at least until their marriage had been definitively determined on, to inform him of the extent of her attachment to Irving. But sincere as she was to a fault in the ordinary occasions of life, she had in this matter not only kept back the truth, but had purposely misled Carlyle

180

as to the nature of her feelings. She felt that she must make a full confession. She had deceived him—wilfully deceived him. She had even told him that she had never cared for Irving. "It was false," she said. She had loved him—"*once passionately loved him.*" For this she might be forgiven. "And if I showed weakness in loving one whom I knew to be engaged to another, I made amends in persuading him to marry the other and preserve his honour from reproach."[4] But she had disguised her real feelings, and for this she had no excuse. She who had felt herself Carlyle's superior in their late controversy, and had been able to rebuke him for selfishness, felt herself degraded and humbled in his eyes. If he chose to cast her off, she said that she could not say he was unjust; but her pride was broken; and very naturally, very touchingly, she added that he had never been so dear to her as at that moment when she was in danger of losing his affection and, what was still more precious to her, his respect.

If Carlyle had been made of common stuff, so unexpected a revelation might have tried his vanity. The actual effect was to awaken in him a sense of his own unworthiness. He perceived that Miss Welsh was probably accepting him only out of the motives which Mrs. Montagu suggested. His infirmities, mental and bodily, might make him an unfit companion for her or indeed for any woman. It would be better for her once for all to give him up. He knew, he said, that he could never make her happy. They might suffer at parting, but they would have obeyed their reason, and time would deaden the pain. No affection was unalterable or eternal. Men themselves, with all their passions, sank to dust and were consumed. He must imitate her sincerity. He said (and he spoke with perfect truth) that there was a strange, dark humour in him over which he had no control. If she thought they were " 'blue devils' " or "weak querulous wailings of a distempered mind,"[5] she would only show that she did not understand him. In a country town she had seen nothing of life, and had grasped at the shadows that passed by her. First, the rude, smoky fire of Edward Irving seemed to her a star from heaven; next, the quivering *ignis fatuus* of the soul that dwelt in himself. The world had a thousand noble hearts that she did not dream of.

What was he, and what was his father's house, that she should sacrifice herself for him?

It was not in nature—it was not at least in Miss Welsh's nature—that at such a time and under such circumstances she should reconsider her resolution. She was staying with her grandfather at Templand when these letters were interchanged. She determined to use the opportunity to pay the Carlyles her promised visit, see him in his own home and his own circle, and there face to face explain all the past and form some scheme for the immediate future. Like the lady in London, she felt that if the marriage was to be, or rather since the marriage was to be, the sooner it was over now the better for everyone. Carlyle was to have met her on the road, and was waiting with horses; but there had been a mistake. She was dropped by the coach the next morning at Kelhead Kilns, from which she sent him a little characteristic note.

> Good morning Sir— I am not at all to blame for your disappointment last night— The fault was partly your own and still more the Landlady's of the Commercial Inn as I shall presently demonstrate to you *viva voce*. In the mean time I have billeted myself in a snug little house by the wayside where I purpose remaining with all imaginable patience till you can make it convenient to come and fetch me, being afraid to proceed directly to Hoddam hill in case so sudden an apparition should throw the whole family into hysterics. If the Pony has any prior engagement never mind[.] I can make a shift to *walk* two miles in pleasant company— Any way pray make all possible dispatch, in case the owner of these premises should think I mean to make a regular settlement in them— Yours Jane[6]

The great secret, which had been known from the first to Mrs. Carlyle and suspected by the rest, was now the open property of the family; and all, old and young, with mixed feelings of delight and anxiety, were looking forward to the appearance of the lady who was soon to belong to them.

> She stayed with us above a week, happy, as was very evident, and making happy. Her demeanour among us I could define as unsurpassable; spontaneously perfect. From the first moment, all embarrassment, even my Mother's as tremulous and anxious as *she* naturally was . . . fled away without returning. Everybody felt the all-pervading simple grace, the perfect truth and perfect trustfulness of that beautiful, cheerful, intelligent and sprightly

creature; and everybody was put at his ease. The questionable visit
was a clear success on all hands.

She and I went riding about; the weather dry and grey,— nothing
ever going wrong with us;—my guidance taken as beyond criticism;
she ready for any pace, rapid or slow; melodious talk, of course, never
wanting. . . .

Of course she went to Mainhill. . . . She made complete acquaintance with my Father (whom she much esteemed and even
admired now and henceforth, a *reciprocal* feeling, strange enough!),
and with my two eldest Sisters, Margaret & Mary,—who now offi-
cially "kept house" with Father there. On the whole, she made
clear acquaintance with us all; saw, face to face, us, and the rugged
peasant element and way of life we had;—& was *not* afraid of it;
but recognized like her noble self, what of intrinsic worth it might
have, what of real human dignity. She charmed all hearts; and was
herself visibly glad and happy,—right loth to end those halcyon
days; 8 or perhaps 9, the utmost appointed sum of them.[7]

Two little anecdotes she used to tell of this visit, showing
that under peasant's dresses there was in the Carlyles the
essential sense of delicate high breeding. She was to use the
girls' room at Mainhill while there; and it was rude enough
in its equipments as they lived in it. Margaret Carlyle,
doing her little best, had spread on the deal table for a
cover a precious new shawl which some friend had given
her. More remarkable was her reception by the father.
When she appeared he was in his rough dress, called in
from his farm work on the occasion. The rest of the family
kissed her. The old man to her surprise drew back, and
soon left the room. In a few minutes he came back again,
fresh shaved and washed, and in his Sunday clothes. Now,
he said, if Miss Welsh allows it, I am in a condition to kiss
her too. When she left Hoddam, Carlyle attended her back
to Dumfries.

Miss Welsh had now seen with her own eyes the realities
of life in a small Scotch farm, and was no longer afraid of it.
She doubtless distrusted as much as ever Carlyle's fitness
in his own person for agricultural enterprises. But if his
brother would take the work off his hands he could himself
follow his own more proper occupations. She had recognised
the sterling worth of his peasant family, and for her own
part she was willing to share their method of existence,
sharply contrasted as it was with the elegance and relative

luxury of her home at Haddington. It was far otherwise with her mother. Mrs. Welsh's romantic days were not over. They were never over to the end of her life; but she had no romance about Carlyle. She knew better than her daughter how great the sacrifice would be, and the experience of fifty years had taught her that resolutions adopted in enthusiasm are often repented of when excitement has been succeeded by the wearing duties of hard every-day routine. She was a cultivated, proud, beautiful woman, who had ruled as queen in the society of a Scotch provincial town. Many suitors had presented themselves for her daughter's hand, unexceptionable in person, in fortune, in social standing. Miss Welsh's personal attractions, her talents, the fair if moderate fortune which, though for the present she had surrendered it, must be eventually her own, would have entitled her to choose among the most eligible matches in East Lothian. It was natural, it was inevitable, independent of selfish considerations, that she could not look without a shudder on this purposed marriage with the son of a poor Dumfriesshire farmer, who had no visible prospects and no profession, and whose abilities, however great they might be, seemed only to unfit him for any usual or profitable pursuit. Added to this, Carlyle himself had not attracted her. She was accustomed to rule, and Carlyle would not be ruled. She had obstinate humours, and Carlyle, who never checked his own irritabilities, was impatient and sarcastic when others ventured to be unreasonable. She had observed and justly dreaded the violence of his temper, which when he was provoked or thwarted would boil like a geyser. He might repent afterwards of these ebullitions; he usually did repent. But repentance could not take away the sting of the passionate expressions, which fastened in the memory by the metaphors with which they were barbed, especially as there was no amendment, and the offence was repeated on the next temptation. It will easily be conceived, therefore, that the meeting between mother and daughter after the Hoddam visit, and Miss Welsh's announcement of her final resolution, was extremely painful. Miss Welsh wrote to Carlyle an account of what had passed. His letter in reply bears the same emblem of the burning candle, with the motto,

184

"Terar dum prosim," which he had before sketched in his journal. He was fond of a design which represented human life to him under its sternest aspect.[8]

After the bright interlude of Miss Welsh's visit to Hoddam, life soon became as industrious as Carlyle has described. The mornings were spent in work over the German Tales, the afternoons in rides, Larry remaining still in favour notwithstanding his misdemeanours. In the evenings he and his mother perhaps smoked their pipes together, as they used to do at Mainhill, she in admiring anxiety labouring to rescue his soul from the temptations of the intellect; he satisfying her, for she was too willing to be satisfied, that they meant the same thing, though they expressed it in different languages. He was meditating a book, a real book of his own, not a translation, though he was still unable to fasten upon a subject; while the sense that he was in his own house, lord of it and lord of himself, and able if he pleased to shut his door against all comers, was delightful to him.

chapter eight

1826

Marriage

The life at Hoddam Hill, singularly happy while it lasted, and promising to last, was not after all of long continuance. Differences with the landlord, General Sharpe, rose to a quarrel, in which old Mr. Carlyle took his son's part. Hoddam Hill was given up; the lease of Mainhill, expiring at the same time, was not renewed, and the whole family, Carlyle himself with the rest, removed to Scotsbrig, a substantial farm in the neighbourhood of Ecclefechan, where the elder Carlyles remained to the end of their lives, and where their youngest son succeeded them.

The break-up at Hoddam precipitated the conclusion of Carlyle's protracted relations with Miss Welsh. He sums up briefly his recollections of the story of this year, which was in every way so momentous to him.

My *translation* work [*German Romance*] went steadily on;— the *pleasantest* kind of labour I ever had; could be done by *task*, in whatever humour or condition one was in: and was, day by day (ten pages a-day, I think) punctually and comfortably so performed. *Internally*, too, there were far higher things going on; a grand and *ever*-joyful victory getting itself achieved at last! The final chaining down, and trampling home, "for good," home into their caves forever, of all my *Spiritual Dragons*, which had wrought me such woe and, for a decade past, had made my life black and bitter: this year 1826 saw the end of all that. With such a feeling on my part as may be fancied. I found it to be, essentially, what Methodist people call their "Conversion," the deliverance of their soul from the Devil and the Pit; precisely enough that, in my new form;—and there burnt, accordingly, a sacred flame of joy in me, silent in my inmost being, as of one henceforth superior to Fate,

SCOTSBRIG. The Carlyle family was reunited in moving to Scotsbrig at Whitsuntide 1826. Here Carlyle's parents lived until they died, and James, the youngest son, continued tenant in it until 1880. Although Carlyle lived at the farm for only a few months before his marriage with Jane Baillie Welsh in October 1826, he made nearly annual returns to see his mother after he moved to London in 1834. (Photograph by John Patrick, courtesy of the University of Edinburgh.)

able to look down on *its* stupid injuries with pardon and contempt, almost with a kind of thanks and pity. This "holy joy," of which I kept silence, lasted sensibly in me for several years, in blessed counterpoise to sufferings and discouragements enough; nor has it proved what I can call fallacious at any time since. . . .

In brief, after much survey and consideration of the real interests and real feelings of both parties, I proposed, and it was gently acceded to, that *German Romance* once *done* (end of September or so), we should WED, settle at Edinburgh, in some small suburban House (details and preparations there all left to her kind Mother and her);—and thenceforth front our chances in the world, not as two lots, but as *one*. For better, for worse; till Death us part!

House in Comely Bank, suitable as possible, had been chosen; was being furnished from Haddington,—beautifully, perfectly and even richly, by Mrs Welsh's great skill in such matters, aided by her Daughter's which was also great,—and by the frank & *wordless* generosity of both, which surely was very great![1]

So Carlyle, at a distance of forty-two years, describes the prelude to his marriage—accurately so far as substance went, and with a frank acknowledgment of Mrs. Welsh's liberality, as the impression was left upon his memory. But, exactly and circumstantially as he remembered things which had struck and interested him, his memory was less tenacious of some particulars which he passed over at the time with less attention than perhaps they deserved, and thus allowed to drop out of his recollection. Details have to be told which will show him *not* on the most considerate side. They require to be mentioned for the distinct light which they throw on aspects of his character which affected materially his wife's happiness. There were some things which Carlyle was *constitutionally* incapable of apprehending, while again there are others which he apprehended perhaps with essential correctness, but on which men in general do not think as he thought. A man born to great place and great visible responsibilities in the world is allowed to consider first his position and his duties, and to regard other claims upon him as subordinate to these. A man born with extraordinary talents, which he has resolved to use for some great and generous purpose, may expect and demand the same privileges, but they are not so easily accorded to him. In the one instance it is assumed as a matter of course that secondary interests must be set aside; even in marriage the heir of a large estate consults the advantage of his family; his wife's pleasure, even his wife's comforts, must be postponed to the supposed demands of her husband's situation. The claims of a man of genius are less tolerantly dealt with; partly perhaps because it is held an impertinence in any man to pretend to genius till he has given proof of possessing it; partly because, if extraordinary gifts are rare, the power of appreciating them is equally rare, and a fixed purpose to make a noble use of them is rarer still. Men of literary faculty, it is idly supposed, can do their work anywhere in any circumstances; if the work is left undone the world does not know what it has lost; and thus, partly by their own fault, and partly by the world's mode of dealing with them, the biographies of men of letters are, as Carlyle says, for the most part the saddest chapter in the history of the human race except the Newgate Calendar.[2]

Carlyle, restless and feverish, was convinced that no real work could be got out of him till he was again in a home of his own, and till his affairs were settled on some permanent footing. His engagement, while it remained uncompleted, kept him anxious and irritated. Therefore he conceived that he must find some cottage suited to his circumstances, and that Miss Welsh ought to become immediately the mistress of it. He had money enough to begin housekeeping; he saw his way, he thought, to earning money enough to continue it on the scale in which he had himself been bred up—but it was on condition that the wife that he took to himself should do the work of a domestic servant as his own mother and sisters did; and he was never able to understand that a lady differently educated might herself, or her friends for her, find a difficulty in accepting such a situation. He was in love, so far as he understood what love meant. Like Hamlet he would have challenged Miss Welsh's other lovers "to weep, to fight, to fast, to tear themselves, to drink up Esil, eat a crocodile," or "be buried with her quick in the earth";[3] but when it came to the question how he was himself to do the work which he intended to do, he chose to go his own way, and expected others to accommodate themselves to it.

Plans had been suggested and efforts made to secure some permanent situation for him. A newspaper had been projected in Edinburgh, which Lockhart and Brewster were to have conducted with Carlyle under them. This would have been something; but Lockhart became editor of the *Quarterly Review,* and the project dropped. A Bavarian Minister had applied to Professor Leslie for someone who could teach English literature and science at Munich. Leslie offered this to Carlyle, but he declined it. He had set his mind upon a cottage outside Edinburgh, with a garden and high walls about it to shut out noise. This was all which he himself wanted. He did not care how poor it was so it was *his own,* entirely his own, safe from intruding fools.

Here he thought that he and his wife might set themselves up together and wish for nothing more. It did, indeed, at moments occur to him that, although he could be happy and rich in the midst of poverty, "for a woman to descend from Superfluity to live with a sick ill-natured man in Poverty, and *not* in wretchedness, would be the greatest miracle of all."[4] But though the thought came more than once, it would not abide. The miracle would perhaps be wrought; or indeed without a miracle his mother and sisters were happy, and why should anyone wish for more luxuries than they had?

Mrs. Welsh being left a widow, and with no other child, the pain of separation from her daughter was unusually great. Notwithstanding a certain number of caprices, there was a genuine and even passionate attachment between mother and daughter. It might have seemed that a separation was unnecessary, and that if Mrs. Welsh could endure to have Carlyle under her own roof, no difficulty on his side ought to have arisen. Mrs. Welsh indeed, romantically generous, desired to restore the property, and to go back and live with her father at Templand; but her daughter decided peremptorily that she would rather live with Carlyle in poverty all the days of her life sooner than encroach in the smallest degree on her mother's independence. She could expect no happiness, she said, if she failed in the first duty of her life. Her mother should keep the fortune, or else Miss Welsh refused to leave her.

All difficulties might be got over, the entire economic problem might be solved, if the family could be kept together. As soon as the marriage was known to be in contemplation this arrangement occurred to everyone who was interested in the Welshes' welfare as the most obviously desirable. Mrs. Welsh was as unhappy as ever at an alliance that she regarded as not imprudent only, but in the highest degree objectionable. Carlyle had neither family nor fortune nor prospect of preferment. He had no religion that she could comprehend, and she had seen him violent and unreasonable. He was the very last companion that she would have selected for herself. Yet for her daughter's sake she was willing to make an effort to like him, and, since the marriage was to be, either to live with her or to accept him as her son-in-law in her own house and in her own circle.

Her consent to take Carlyle into her family removed Miss Welsh's remaining scruples, and made her perfectly happy. It never occurred to her that Carlyle himself would refuse, and the reasons which he alleged might have made a less resolute woman pause before she committed herself further. "It is impossible," he said, "for two households to live as if they were one. . . . I shall never get any enjoyment of your company till you are all my own." Mrs. Welsh had a large acquaintance. He liked none of them, and her "visitors would [not] be diminished in number or bettered in quality." No! he must have the small house in Edinburgh; and "the moment I am master of a house, the first use I turn it to will be to slam the door of it on the face of nauseous intrusions."[5] It never occurred to him, as proved too fatally to be the case, that he would care little for "the right companionship" when he had got it; that he would be absorbed in his work; that, after all, his wife would see but little of him, and that little too often under trying conditions of temper; that her mother's companionship, and the "intrusions" of her mother's old friends, might add more to her comfort than it could possibly detract from his own.

However deeply she honoured her chosen husband, she could not hide from herself that he was selfish—extremely selfish. He had changed his mind indeed about the Edinburgh house almost as soon as he had made it up—he was only determined that he would not live with Mrs. Welsh.

[Jane Welsh jestingly, yet tearfully, summed up their respective positions:]

191

Suppose we take different roads, and try how that answers. There is Catherina Aurora Kirkpatrick, for instance, has fifty thousand pounds, and a princely lineage and "never was out of humour in her life"—with such a "singularly pleasing creature" and so much fine gold, you could hardly fail to find yourself admirably well off— While, I, on the other hand, might better my fortunes in many quarters; a certain, handsome stammering Englishman I know of would give his ears to carry me away South with him, my second-cousin too, the Dr. at Leeds has set up a fine establishment and writes to me that I am "the very first of my sex"—or, nearer home, I have an interesting young Widower in view, who has no scruple about making me Mother to his three small children, Bluestocking tho' I be— But what am I talking about? As if we were not already married,—alas, married past redemption! God knows, in that case, what is to become of us! at times I am so disheartened that I sit down and weep—and then at other times! oh Heaven![6]

Carlyle could just perceive that he had not been gracious, that Mrs. Welsh's offer had deserved "a more serious deliberation, and at the very least a more courteous refusal."[7] He could recognise also, proud as he was, that he had little to offer in his companionship which would be a compensation for the trials which it might bring with it.

You tell me that you often weep when you think what is to become of us. It is unwise in you to weep: if you are reconciled to be *my* wife (not the wife of an ideal *me*, but the simple actual prosaic *me*), there is nothing frightful in the future. I look into it with more and more confidence and composure. Alas! Jane you do not know me: it is not the poor, unknown, rejected Thomas Carlyle that you know, but the prospective rich known and admired. I am reconciled to my fate as it stands or promises to stand ere long: I have pronounced the word *unpraised* in all its cases and numbers; and find nothing terrific in it, even when it means *unmonied*, and by the mass of his Majesty's subjects *neglected* or even partially *contemned*. I thank Heaven I have other objects in my eye than either *their* pudding or their breath. This comes of the circumstance that my Apprenticeship is ending, and yours still going on. O Jane! Jane! I could weep too; for I love you in my deepest heart.

There are hard sayings, my beloved child; but I cannot spare them; and I hope, tho' bitter at first, they may not remain without wholesome influence.[8]

That Carlyle could contemplate with equanimity being unpraised, unmoneyed, and neglected all his life, that he required neither the world's "pudding" nor its "breath," and could be happy without them, was pardonable and perhaps commendable. That he should expect another person to share this unmoneyed, puddingless, and rather forlorn condition, was scarcely consistent with such lofty principles. Men may sacrifice themselves, if they please, to imagined high duties and ambitions, but they have no right to marry wives and sacrifice them. Nor were these "hard sayings" which could not be spared exactly to the point, when he had been roughly and discourteously rejecting proposals which would have made his *"unmonied"* situation of less importance.[9]

He had said that Miss Welsh did not know him, which was probably true; but it is likely also that he did not know himself. She had answered this last letter of his with telling him that she had chosen him for her husband, and should not alter her mind. Since this was so he immediately said, she had better "wed a wild man of the woods, and come and live with him in his cavern, in hope of better days."[10] The cavern was Scotsbrig. When it had been proposed that he should live with Mrs. Welsh at Haddington, he would by consenting have spared the separation of a mother from an only child, and would not perhaps have hurt his own intellect by an effort of self-denial. It appeared impossible to him, when Mrs. Welsh was in question, that two households could go on together. He was positive that he must be master in his own house, free from noise and interruption, and have fire and brimstone cooked for him if he pleased to order it. But the two households were not, it seemed, incompatible when one of them was his own family. If Miss Welsh would come to him at Scotsbrig, he would be "a new man"; "the bitterness of life would pass away like a forgotten tempest," and he and she "should walk in bright weather"[11] thenceforward to the end of their existence. This, too, was a mere delusion. The cause of his unrest was in himself; he would carry with him, wherever he might go or be, the wild passionate spirit, fevered with burning thoughts, which would make peace impossible, and cloud the fairest weather with intermittent tempests. Scotsbrig would not have frightened Miss Welsh. She must have perceived his inconsistency, though she did not allude to it. But if Carlyle had himself and his work to consider, she had her mother. Her answer was very beautiful.

Were happiness, then, the thing chiefly to be cared for, in this world; I would even put my hand in yours *now*, as you say, and so cut the gordian knot of our destiny at once. But, oh my Husband, have you not told me a thousand times and my conscience tells me also that happiness is only a secondary consideration—it must not . . . be sought out of the path of duty. . . . Should I do well to go into Paradise myself, and leave the Mother who bore me to break her heart? She is looking forward to my marriage with a more tranquil mind, in the hope that our separation is to be in a great measure nominal,—that by living wheresoever my Husband lives she may at least have every moment of my society which he can spare. And how would it be possible not to disappoint her in this hope, if I went to reside with your people in Annandale? *Her* presence *there* would be a perpetual cloud over our little world of love and peace. For the sake of all concerned it would be necessary to keep her quite apart from us—and apart from us—yet so near she would be the most wretched of Mothers, the most desolate woman in the world. Oh is it for *me* to make her so—*me* who am so unspeakably dear to her in spite of all her caprice, who am her only, only child—and her a widow—I love you Mr Carlyle, tenderly, devotedly as ever Woman loved; but I may not put my Mother away from me even for *your* sake— I cannot do it! I have lain awake whole nights . . . trying to reconcile this act with my conscience; but my conscience will have nothing to say to it—rejects it with indignation—

What is to be done then? Indeed, I see only one way of escape out of all these perplexities. Be patient with me while I tell you what it is.— My Mother, like myself, has ceased to find any contentment in this pitiful Haddington, and is bent on disposing of our house here as soon as may be and hiring one elsewhere. . . . now, why should it not be the vicinity of Edinburgh after all? and why should not you live with your wife in her Mothers house?[12]

The arrangement was at least as reasonable as that which he had himself proposed, and Carlyle, who was so passionately attached to his own mother, might have been expected to esteem and sympathise with Miss Welsh's affection for hers. At Scotsbrig he would have had no door of his own to slam against "nauseous intrusions"; his father, as long as he lived, would be master in his own house; while the self-control which would have been required of him, had he resided with Mrs. Welsh as a son-in-law, would have been a discipline which his own character especially needed. But he knew that he was "gey ill to deal wi'." His own family were used to him, and he in turn respected them, and could, within limits, conform to their ways. From others he would submit to no interference. He knew that he would not, and that it would be useless for him to try. He felt that he had not considered Mrs. Welsh as he ought to have done; but his consideration, even after he had recognised his fault, remained a most restricted quantity.

> Perhaps, as I have told you, Love, I may not yet have got to the bottom of this new plan so completely as I wished: but there is one thing that strikes me more and more, the longer I think of it. This the grand objection of all objections, the head and front of offence, the soul of all my counter-pleading; an objection which is too likely to overset the whole project. It may be stated in a word: *The Man should bear rule in the house and not the Woman.* This is an eternal axiom, the Law of Nature h[erself w]hich no mortal departs from unpunished. I have meditated on this ma[ny long] years, and every day it grows plainer to me: I must not and I cannot live in a house of which I am not head. I should be miserable myself, and make all about me miserable. Think not, Darling, that this comes of an imperious temper; that I shall be a harsh and tyrannical Husband to thee. God forbid! But it is the nature of a man that if he be controuled by any thing but his own Reason, he feels himself degraded; and incited, be it justly or not, to rebellion and discord. It is the nature of a woman again (for she is essentially *passive* not *active*) to cling to the man for support and direction, to comply with his humours, and feel pleasure in doing so, simply because they are his; to reverence while she loves him, to conquer him not by her force but her weakness, and perhaps (the cunning gipsy!) after all to command him by obeying him.[13]

The Greek chorus would have shaken its head ominously, and uttered its musical cautions, over the temper displayed in this letter. Yet it is perfectly true that Carlyle would have been an unbearable inmate of any house, except his father's, where his will was not absolute. "Gey ill to deal wi'," as his mother said. The condition which he made was perhaps not so much as communicated to Mrs. Welsh, for whom it would have furnished another text for a warning sermon. The *"judicious desperation"*[14] which Carlyle recommended to her daughter brought her to submit to going to live at Scotsbrig. Under the circumstances Mrs. Welsh, in desperation too, decided that the marriage should be celebrated immediately and an end made. She comforted herself with the thought that being at Templand with her father, she would at least be within reach, and could visit Scotsbrig as often as she pleased. Here, however, new difficulties arose. Carlyle, it seems, had made the proposition without so much as consulting his father and mother. They at least, if not he, were sensible, when they heard of it, of the unfitness of their household to receive a lady brought up as Miss Welsh had been. "Even in summer," they said, "it would be difficult for you to [live at Scotsbrig], in winter altogether impossible"; while the notion that Mrs. Welsh should ever be a visitor there seemed as impossible to Carlyle himself. He had deliberately intended to bring his wife into a circle where the suggestion of her mother's appearance was too extravagant to be entertained.

> You talked of your Mother visiting us! By Day and Night! it would astonish her to see this same household. O No, my Darling! Your Mother must not visit mine. What good were it? By an utmost exertion on the part of both, they might learn perhaps to tolerate each other, more probably to pity and partially dislike each other; better than mutual tolerance I could anticipate nothing from them.[15]

It is sad to read such words. Carlyle pretended that he knew Mrs. Welsh. Human creatures are not all equally unreasonable; and he knew as little of her as he said that her daughter knew of Scotsbrig. The two mothers, when the family connection brought them together, respected each other, could meet without difficulty, and part with a mutual regard which increased with acquaintance. Had the incompatibility been as real as he supposed, Carlyle's strange oblivion both of his intended wife's and his wife's mother's natural feelings would still be without excuse.

His mind was fixed, as men's minds are apt to be in such circumstances. He chose to have his own way, and since it was impossible for Miss Welsh to live at Scotsbrig, and as he had on his side determined that he would not live with Mrs. Welsh, some alternative had to be looked for. Once more he had an opportunity of showing his defective perception of common things. Mrs. Welsh had resolved to leave Haddington and to give up her house there immediately. The associations of the place after her daughter was gone would necessarily be most painful. All her friends, the social circle of which she had been the centre, regarded the marriage with Carlyle as an extraordinary *mésalliance*. To them he was known only as an eccentric farmer's son without profession or prospects, and their pity or their sympathy would be alike distressing. She had herself found him moody, violent, and imperious, and she at least could only regard his conduct as extremely selfish. Men in the situation of lovers often are selfish. It is only in novels that they are heroic or even considerate. It occurred to Carlyle that since Mrs. Welsh was going away the house at Haddington would do well for himself. There it stood, ready provided with all that was necessary. He recollected that Edinburgh was noisy and disagreeable, Haddington quiet, and connected with his own most pleasant recollections. It might have occurred to him that under such altered circumstances, where she would be surrounded by a number of acquaintances, to every one of whom her choice appeared like madness, Miss Welsh might object to living there as much as her mother. She made her objections as delicately as she could; but he pushed them aside as if they were mere disordered fancies; and the fear of "nauseous intrusions," which had before appeared so dreadful to him, he disposed of with the most summary serenity. "To me," he calmly wrote, "among the weightier evils and blessings of existence the evil of impertinent visitors and so forth seems but as the small drop of the bucket and an exceedingly little thing. I have nerve enough in me to dispatch that sort of deer forever by dozens in the day."[16]

"That sort of deer" were the companions who had grown up beside Miss Welsh for twenty years. She was obliged to tell him peremptorily that she would not hear of this plan. It would have been happier and perhaps better both for her and for him had she taken warning from the unconscious exhibition which he had made of his inner nature. After forty years of life with him—forty years of splendid labour, in which his essential conduct had been pure as snow, and unblemished by a serious fault, when she saw him at length rewarded by the honour and admiration of Europe and America—she had to preach nevertheless to her younger friends as the sad lesson of her own experience, "My dear, whatever you do, never marry a man of genius." The mountain-peaks of intellect are no homes for quiet people. Those who are cursed or blessed with lofty gifts and lofty purposes may be gods in their glory and their greatness, but are rarely tolerable as human companions. Carlyle consented to drop the Haddington proposal, not, however,

without showing that he thought Miss Welsh less wise
than he had hoped.

[Mother and daughter] settled the matter at last in their
own fashion. The Haddington establishment was broken up.
They moved to Edinburgh, and took the house in Comely
Bank which Carlyle mentioned. Mrs. Welsh undertook to
pay the rent, and the Haddington furniture was carried
thither. She proposed to remain there with her daughter till
October, and was then to remove finally to her father's
house at Templand, where the ceremony was to come off.
Carlyle when once married and settled in Edinburgh would
be in the way of any employment which might offer for him.
At Comely Bank, at any rate, Mrs. Welsh could be received
occasionally as a visitor. For immediate expenses of living
there was Carlyle's £200 and such additions to it as he could
earn.

Carlyle was supremely satisfied. The knotty problem
which had seemed so hopeless was now perfectly solved.
The great business having been once arranged, the rest of
the summer flew swiftly by. *German Romance* was finished,
and paid for the marriage expenses. The world was taken
into confidence by a formal announcement of what was
impending: Miss Welsh, writing for the first time to her
relations, sent a description of her intended husband to the
wife of her youngest uncle, Mrs. George Welsh. She was
not blinded by affection—no one ever less so in her circumstances. I have not kept back what I believe to have
been faults in Carlyle, and the lady to whom he was to be
married knew what they were better than anyone else can
know; yet here was her deliberate opinion of him. He stood
there such as he had made himself: a peasant's son who had
run about barefoot in Ecclefechan street, with no outward
advantages, worn with many troubles bodily and mental.
His life had been pure and without spot. He was an admirable son, a faithful and affectionate brother, in all private relations blamelessly innocent. He had splendid talents,
which he rather felt than understood; only he was determined, in the same high spirit and duty which had governed his personal conduct, to use them well, whatever they
might be, as a trust committed to him, and never, never to
sell his soul by travelling the primrose path to wealth and

198

distinction. If honour came to him, honour was to come unsought. I as if feel in dwelling on his wilfulness

> I did him wrong, being so majestical,
> To offer him the show of violence.[17]

But I learnt my duty from himself: to paint him as he was, to keep back nothing and extenuate nothing. I never knew a man whose reputation, take him for all in all, would emerge less scathed from so hard a scrutiny.

The wedding day drew on; not without (as was natural) more than the usual nervousness on both sides at the irrevocable step which was about to be ventured. Carlyle knew too well he was "a perverse mortal to deal with," that "the best resolutions make shipwreck in the sea of practice,"[18] and that "it was a chance if any woman could be happy with him." "The brightest moment of his existence," as in anticipation he had regarded his marriage, was within [four] weeks of him, yet he found himself "so splenetic, so sick, so sleepless, so void of hope, faith, charity, in short so altogether bad and worthless. I trust in Heaven I shall be better soon," he said; "a certain incident otherwise will wear a quite original aspect."[19] Clothes had to be provided, gloves thought of. Scotch custom not recognising licences in such cases, required that the names of the intending pair should be proclaimed in their respective churches; and this to both of them was intolerable. They were to be married in the morning at Templand church, and to go the same day to Comely Bank.

Jest as she would, however, Miss Welsh was frightened and Carlyle was frightened. They comforted one another as if they were going to be executed. Carlyle, on his side, tried to allay his fears of what Miss Welsh called "that odious ceremony" by reading Kant, and had reached the hundred and fiftieth page of the *Kritik der reinen Vernunft,* when he found that it was too abstruse for his condition, and that Scott's novels would answer better.[20] With this assistance he tried to look more cheerfully on the adventure.

So the long drama came to its conclusion. The banns were published, the clothes made, the gloves duly provided. The day was the 17th of October, 1826. Miss Welsh's final letter, informing Carlyle of the details to be observed, is

199

JANE WELSH CARLYLE, AGE 25. (From the miniature by Kenneth Mcleay, courtesy of the Scottish National Portrait Gallery.)

humorously headed, "The last Speech and *marrying* words of that unfortunate young woman Jane Baillie *Welsh.*"[21] [To which Carlyle replied:]

> Truly a most delightful and swan-like melody was in them; a tenderness and warm devoted trust, worthy of such a maiden bidding farewell to the (unmarried) Earth, of which she was the fairest ornament. . . . Let us pray to God that our holy purposes be not frustrated; let us trust in Him and in each other, and fear no evil that can befall us.[22]

They were married in the parish church of Templand in the quietest fashion, the minister officiating, John Carlyle the only other person present except Miss Welsh's family.[23]

Breakfast over, they drove off in a post-chaise. In the evening they arrived safely at Comely Bank.[24]

Regrets and speculations on "the might have beens" of life are proverbially vain. Nor is it certain that there is anything to regret. The married life of Carlyle and Jane Welsh was not happy in the roseate sense of happiness. In the fret and chafe of daily life the sharp edges of the facets of two diamonds remain keen, and they never wear into surfaces which harmoniously correspond. A man and a woman of exceptional originality and genius are proper mates for one another only if they have some other object before them besides happiness, and are content to do without it. For the forty years which these two extraordinary persons lived together, their essential conduct to the world and to each other was sternly upright. They had to encounter poverty in its most threatening aspect—poverty which they might at any moment have escaped if Carlyle would have sacrificed his intellectual integrity, would have carried his talents to the market, and written down to the level of the multitude. If he ever flagged, it was his wife who spurred him on; nor would she ever allow him to do less than his very best. She never flattered anyone, least of all her husband; and when she saw cause for it the sarcasms flashed out from her as the sparks fly from lacerated steel. Carlyle, on his side, did not find in his marriage the miraculous transformation of nature which he had promised himself. He remained lonely and dyspeptic, possessed by thoughts and convictions which struggled in him for utterance, and which could be fused and cast into form only (as I have heard him say) when his whole mind was like a furnace at white heat. The work which he has done is before the world, and the world has long acknowledged what it owes to him. It would not have been done as well, perhaps it would never have been done at all, if he had not had a woman at his side who would bear, without resenting it, the outbreaks of his dyspeptic humour, and would shield him from the petty troubles of a poor man's life—from vexations which would have irritated him to madness—by her own incessant toil.

The victory was won, but, as of old in Aulis, not without a victim.[25] Miss Welsh had looked forward to being Carlyle's intellectual companion, to sharing his thoughts and helping

201

him with his writings. She was not overrating her natural powers when she felt being equal to such a position and deserving it. The reality was not like the dream. Poor as they were, she had to work as a menial servant.[26] She, who had never known a wish ungratified for any object which money could buy; she, who had seen the rich of the land at her feet, and might have chosen among them at pleasure, with a weak frame withal which had never recovered from the shock of her father's death—she after all was obliged to slave and cook and wash and scour and mend shoes and clothes for many a weary year. Bravely she went through it all; and she would have gone through it cheerfully if she had been rewarded with ordinary gratitude. But if things were done rightly, Carlyle did not inquire who did them. Partly he was occupied, partly he was naturally undemonstrative, and partly she in generosity concealed from him the worst which she had to bear. The hardest part of all was that he did not see that there was occasion for any special acknowledgment. Poor men's wives had to work. She was a poor man's wife, and it was fit and natural that she should work. He had seen his mother and his sisters doing the drudgery of his father's household without expecting to be admired for doing it. Mrs. Carlyle's life was entirely lonely, save so far as she had other friends. He consulted her judgement about his writings, for he knew the value of it, but in his conceptions and elaborations he chose to be always by himself. He said truly that he was a Bedouin. When he was at work he could bear no one in the room; and, at least through middle life, he rode and walked alone, not choosing to have his thoughts interrupted. The slightest noise or movement at night shattered his nervous system; therefore he required a bedroom to himself; thus from the first she saw little of him, and as time went on less and less; and she, too, was human and irritable. Carlyle proved, as his mother had known him, "ill to deal wi'." Generous and kind as he was at heart, and as he always showed himself when he had leisure to reflect, "the Devil," as he had said, "continued to speak out of him in distempered sentences," and the bitter arrow was occasionally shot back.

Miss Welsh, it is probable, would have passed through life more pleasantly had she married someone in her own rank of life; Carlyle might have gone through it successfully with his mother or a sister to look after him. But, after all is said, trials and sufferings are only to be regretted when they have proved too severe to be borne. Though the lives of the Carlyles were not happy, yet if we look at them from the beginning to the end they were grandly beautiful. Neither of them probably under other conditions would have risen to as high an excellence as in fact they each achieved; and the main question is not how happy men and women have been in this world, but what they have made of themselves. I well remember the bright assenting laugh with which she once responded to some words of mine when the propriety was being discussed of relaxing the marriage laws. I had said that the true way to look at marriage was as a discipline of character.

chapter nine

1826–1828

Comely Bank

Married life had begun; and the first eighteen months of his new existence Carlyle afterwards looked back upon as the happiest that he had ever known. Yet the rest which he had expected did not come immediately. He could not rest without work, and work was yet to be found. Men think to mend their condition by a change of circumstances. They might as well hope to escape from their shadows. His wife was tender, careful, thoughtful, patient, but the spirit which possessed her husband, whether devil or angel he could hardly tell, still left him without peace.

One piece of good fortune the Carlyles had. He had some friends in Edinburgh and she many; and he was thus forced out of himself. He was not allowed after all to treat visitors as "nauseous intrusions." His wife had a genius for small evening entertainments; little tea parties such as in after days the survivors of us remember in Cheyne Row, over which she presided with a grace all her own, and where wit and humour were to be heard flashing as in no other house we ever found or hoped to find. These began in Edinburgh; and no one who had been once at Comely Bank refused a second invitation. Brewster came and De Quincey, penitent for his article on *Meister,* and Sir William Hamilton and Wilson (though Wilson for some reason was shy of Carlyle), and many more.

Already it seems his power of speech, unequalled so far as my experience goes by that of any other man, had begun to open itself. "Carlyle first, and all the rest nowhere," was the description of him by one of the best judges in London, when speaking of the great talkers of the day. His vast reading, his minute observation, his miraculously retentive memory, gave him something valuable to say on every subject which could be raised. What he took into his mind was dissolved and recrystallised into original combinations of his own. His writing, too, was as fluent as his speech. His early letters—even the most exquisitely finished sentences of them—are in an even and beautiful hand without erasure or alteration of a phrase. Words flowed from him with a completeness of form which no effort could improve. When he was excited it was like the eruption of a volcano, thunder and lightning, hot stones and smoke and ashes. He had a natural tendency to exaggeration, and although at such times his extraordinary metaphors and flashes of Titanesque humour made him always worth listening to, he was at his best when talking of history or poetry or biography, or of some contemporary person or incident which had either touched his sympathy or amused his delicate sense of absurdity. His laugh was from his whole nature, voice, eyes, and even his whole body. And there was never any malice in it. His own definition of humour, "a genial sympathy with the under side," was the definition also of his own feeling about all things and all persons, when it was himself that was speaking, and not what he called the devil that was occasionally in possession. In the long years that I was intimate with him I never heard him tell a malicious story or say a malicious word of any human being. His language was sometimes like the rolling of a great cathedral organ, sometimes like the softest flute-notes, sad or playful as the mood or the subject might be; and you listened—threw in, perhaps, an occasional word to show that you went along with him, but you were simply charmed, and listened on without caring to interrupt. Interruption, indeed, would answer little purpose, for Carlyle did not bear contradiction any better than Johnson. Contradiction would make him angry and unreasonable. He gave you a full picture of what was in his own mind, and you took it away with you and reflected on it.

This singular faculty—which, from Mrs. Carlyle's language, appears to have been shared in some degree by his

sister Jean—had been the spell which had won his wife, as
Othello's tales of his adventures won the heart of Desde-
mona; and it was already brightening the evenings at Comely
Bank. She on her side gives an imperfect idea of her own
occupations when she describes herself as busy with needle-
work and books and the piano. They kept but one servant,
and neither she nor her husband could endure either dirt or
disorder, while Carlyle's sensitive stomach required a more
delicate hand in the kitchen than belonged to a maid of all
work. The days of the loaf—her first baking adventure,
which she watched as Benvenuto Cellini watched his Perseus
—were not yet. Edinburgh bread was eatable, and it was not
till they were at Craigenputtoch that she took charge of the
oven. But Carlyle himself has already described her as making the damaged Scotsbrig eggs into custards and puddings.
When they married, Miss Jewsbury says,

> she resolved that he should never write for money, only when he
> wished it, when he had a message in his heart to deliver, [and]
> . . . she would make whatever money he gave her answer for all
> needful purposes. . . . She managed so well that comfort was
> never absent from her house, and no one looking on could have
> guessed whether they were rich or poor. . . . Whatever she had to
> do she did it with a peculiar personal grace that gave a charm
> to the most prosaic details. No one who in later years saw her lying on
> the sofa in broken health, and languor, would guess the amount of
> energetic hard work she had done in her life. . . . The first time
> she tried a pudding, she went into the kitchen and locked the door
> on herself, having got the servant out of the road. It was to be a
> suet pudding—not just a common suet pudding but something spe-
> cial—and it was good, being made with care by weight and mea-
> sure with exactness.[1]

Thus prettily Carlyle's married life began, the kind friends
at Scotsbrig sending weekly supplies by the carrier. But
even with Mrs. Carlyle to husband them the visible financial resources were ebbing and must soon come to low water;
and on this side the prospect resolutely refused to mend. As
he grew more composed, Carlyle thought of writing some
kind of didactic novel. He could not write a novel, any more
than he could write poetry. He had no *invention*. His genius
was for fact: to lay hold on truth, with all his intellect and
all his imagination. He could no more invent than he could
lie. The novel was a failure and eventually had to be burnt.[2]

The hope which had vaguely lingered of some regular and salaried appointment faded away. Overtures of various kinds to London publishers had met with no acceptance. *German Romance* was financially a failure also, and the Edinburgh publishers would make no future ventures. Under these conditions it is not wonderful that (resolved as he was never to get into money difficulties) Carlyle's mind reverted before long to his old scheme of settling at Craigenputtoch. He no longer thought of turning farmer himself. His wife's ridicule would have saved him from any rash enterprise of that kind. But his brother Alick was still willing to undertake the farm and to make a rent out of it. For himself he looked to it only as a cheap and quiet residence. His Hoddam experience had taught him the superior economy of a country life. At Craigenputtoch he could have his horse, pure air, milk diet, all really or theoretically essential to his health. Edinburgh society he considered was of no use to him; practical Edinburgh, he was equally sure, would do nothing for him; and away on the moors "he could go on with his literature and with his life-task generally in the absolute solitude and pure silence of nature, with nothing but loving and helpful faces round him under clearly improved omens."[3] To his wife he did recognise that the experiment would be unwelcome. She had told him before her marriage that she could not live a month at Craigenputtoch with an angel, while at Comely Bank she had little to suffer and something to enjoy.

Only one recommendation Craigenputtoch could have had to Mrs. Carlyle—that it was her own ancestral property, and that her father had been born there. Happily her mother, when the scheme was mentioned to her, approved heartily. Templand was but fifteen miles from Craigenputtoch gate, not more than a morning's ride, and frequent meetings could be looked forward to. The present tenant of Craigenputtoch was in arrears with his rent, and was allowing house and fences to go to ruin. Some change or other had become indispensable, and Mrs. Welsh was so anxious to have the Carlyles there that she undertook to put the rooms in repair and to pay the expenses of the move.

After a week or two of consideration Carlyle joined his brother Alick in the middle of April at Dumfries, Mrs.

Welsh paying her daughter a visit during his absence. They drove out together and examined the place, and the result was that the tenant was to go, while Carlyle was to enter into possession at Whitsuntide; the house was to be made habitable, and, unless some unforeseen good luck should befall Carlyle meanwhile, he and his wife were to follow when it was ready to receive them.

Alexander Carlyle, with his sister Mary, went into occupation of Craigenputtoch at Whitsuntide 1827. His brother had intended to join him before the end of the summer, but at this moment affairs in Edinburgh began to brighten and took a turn which seemed at one time likely to lead into an entirely new set of conditions. Carlyle had mentioned that he had a letter of introduction to Jeffrey. He had delayed presenting it, partly, perhaps, on account of the absolute silence with which some years before Jeffrey had received a volunteered contribution from him for the *Edinburgh Review*. Irving had urged the experiment, and it had been made. The manuscript was not only not accepted, but was neither acknowledged nor returned.[4] Carlyle naturally hesitated before making another advance where he had been repulsed so absolutely. He determined, however, shortly after his return from his Craigenputtoch visit, to try the experiment. He called on the great man and was kindly received. Jeffrey was struck with him; did not take particularly to his opinions; but perceived at once, as he frankly said to him, that "you are a man of Genius—and of original character and right heart," and that he would "be proud and happy to know more of you."[5] A day or two after he called with Mrs. Jeffrey at Comely Bank, and was as much—perhaps even more—attracted by the lady whom he found there, and whom he discovered to be some remote Scotch kinswoman. It was the beginning of a close and interesting intimacy, entered upon, on Jeffrey's part, with a genuine recognition of Carlyle's qualities and a desire to be useful to him, which, no doubt, would have assumed a practical form had he found his new friend amenable to influence or inclined to work in harness with the party to which Jeffrey belonged. But Jeffrey was a Benthamite on the surface, and underneath an Epicurean, with a good-humoured contempt for enthusiasm and high aspirations. Between him

FRANCIS JEFFREY. "A beautiful little man . . . and a bright island to me and mine in the sea of things," Carlyle wrote in his *Reminiscences*. Although surviving correspondence and Froude's narrative indicate utter incompatibility of viewpoint, Carlyle valued Jeffrey's human warmth and Jeffrey Carlyle's intellect. (Oil painting by Colvin Smith, courtesy of the Scottish National Portrait Gallery.)

and a man "so dreadfully in earnest"[6] as Carlyle, there could be little effective communion, and Carlyle soon ceased to hope, what at first he had allowed himself to expect, that Jeffrey might be the means of assisting him into some independent situation.

The immediate effect of the acquaintance, however, was Carlyle's admission, freely offered by the editor, into the *Edinburgh Review*, a matter just then of infinite benefit to him, drawing him off from didactic novels into writing the series of Essays, now so well known as the *Miscellanies*, in which he tried his wings for his higher flights, and which in themselves contain some of his finest thoughts and most brilliant pictures. His first contribution was to be for the number immediately to appear, and Jeffrey was eager to receive it.

"Jean Paul" was decided on, to be followed in the autumn by a more elaborate article on the general state of German literature. It was written at once, and forms the first of the *Miscellaneous Essays* in the collected edition of Carlyle's works. Carlyle's "style," which has been a rock of offence to so many people, has been attributed to his study of Jean Paul. No criticism could be worse founded. His style shaped itself as he gathered confidence in his own powers, and had its origin in his father's house in Annandale. His mode of expressing himself remained undistinguished by its special characteristics till he had ceased to occupy himself with the German poets.

> Edward Irving and his admiration of the Old Puritans & Elizabethans (whom, at heart, I never could entirely adore, tho' trying hard), his and everybody's doctrine on that head, played a much more important part than Jean Paul on my poor "style";—& the most important part by far was that of Nature, you would perhaps say, had you ever heard my Father speak, or very often heard my Mother & her inborn melodies of heart and of voice![7]

Carlyle's acquaintance with Wilson—"Christopher North"—had been slight, Wilson, perhaps, dreading his radicalism. In the course of the summer, however, accident threw them more closely together, and one of their meetings is thus described.

> Last night I supped with John Wilson, Professor of Moral Philosophy here, author of the "Isle of Palms," &c., a man of the

most fervid temperament, fond of all stimulating things, from tragic poetry down to whisky punch. He snuffed and smoked cigars
and drank liquors, and talked in the most indescribable style. . . .
Daylight came on us before we parted; indeed, it was towards
three o'clock as the Professor and I walked home, smoking as we
went. . . . But I expect to see Wilson in a more philosophic key
ere long; he has promised to call on me, and is, on the whole, a
man I should like to know better. Geniuses of any sort, especially
of so kindly a sort, are so very rare in this world.[8]

Another and yet brighter episode of this summer was a
second and far more remarkable letter from Goethe. Carlyle had sent the *Life of Schiller* to Weimar, and afterwards
the volumes of *German Romance*. They were acknowledged with a gracious interest which went infinitely beyond
his warmest hopes. There was not a letter only, but little
remembrances for himself and his wife; and better even than
the presents, a few lines of verse addressed to each of them.[9]

A still more charming, because unintended, compliment
was to follow from the same quarter. When the purposed
removal to Craigenputtoch came to be talked of among
Carlyle's Edinburgh friends, it seemed to them "considerably fantastic and unreasonable."

> Prospects in Edinburgh had begun to brighten economically and
> otherwise; the main origin of this was our acquaintance with the
> brilliant Jeffrey, a happy accident rather than a matter of fore-
> thought on either side. My poor article on Jean Paul, willingly
> enough admitted into his "Review," excited a considerable, though
> questionable, sensation in Edinburgh, as did the next still weightier
> discharge of "[State of] German Literature" in that
> unexpected vehicle, and at all events denoted me as a fit head for
> that kind of adventure.[10]

The article on German literature reached Weimar. It was
of course anonymous. Goethe read it, and, curious to know
the authorship of such an unexpected appearance, wrote to
Carlyle for information. "Can you tell me in confidence,"
he said, "who wrote the article in the *Edinburgh Review*,
No. XCII., October 1827, on the *State of German Literature*? Here, people believe it was Mr. Lockhart, Sir W.
Scott's son-in-law. Its earnestness and good feeling are
alike admirable."[11] Goethe could not be suspected of insincere politeness, and every sentence of the previous letter
was a genuine expression of true feeling; but this indirect

211

praise was so clearly undesigned that it was doubly encouraging.

Carlyle was still determined on Craigenputtoch, but various causes continued to detain him in Edinburgh. The acquaintance with Jeffrey ripened into a warm intimacy. Jeffrey was a frequent visitor in Comely Bank; the Carlyles were as often his guests at Craigcrook. They met interesting persons there, whose society was pleasant and valuable. Jeffrey was himself influential in the great world of politics, and hopes revived—never, perhaps, very ardently in Carlyle himself, but distinctly in his wife and among his friends— that he would be rescued by some fitting appointment from banishment to the Dumfriesshire moors. Carlyle was now famous in a limited circle, and might reasonably be selected for a professorship or other similar situation; while other possibilities opened on various sides to which it was at least his duty to attend. Meanwhile demands came in thick for fresh articles: Jeffrey wanted one on Tasso; the *Foreign Quarterly* wanted anything that he pleased to send, with liberal offers of pay. He could not afford at such a moment to be out of the reach of libraries, and therefore for the present he left his brother alone in the moorland home.

In the summer he and his wife ran down for a short holiday at Scotsbrig, giving a few brief days to Templand, and a glance at Craigenputtoch. By August they were again settled in Comely Bank. The Carlyles, as he said long before, were a clannish set, and clung tenaciously together. The partings after even so brief a visit were always sorrowful.

With reputation growing, and economics looking less gloomy, Carlyle's spirits were evidently rising. We hear no more of pain and sickness and bilious lamentations, and he looked about him in hope and comfort. The London University was getting itself established, offering opportunities for Nonconformist genius such as England had never before provided. Professors were wanted there in various departments of knowledge. He was advised to offer himself to be one of them, and he wrote to Irving to inquire, with no particular result.

In appointments to the London University, the great

Brougham, not yet Chancellor or peer, but member for Yorkshire, and greatest orator in the House of Commons, was likely to be omnipotent. Jeffrey, it was equally probable, would carry weight with Brougham; and Jeffrey, when Carlyle consulted him, expressed the utmost personal willingness to be of use to Carlyle. But his reply illustrates what Goethe had observed about Schiller, that genius rarely finds recognition from contemporaries as long as it can possibly be withheld. At all times, Jeffrey said, he would be willing to recommend Carlyle as a man of genius and learning; he did not conceal, however, that difficulties would lie in the way of his success in this especial enterprise. Carlyle, he said, was a sectary in taste and literature, and was inspired with the zeal by which sectaries were distinguished. He was inclined to magnify the special doctrines of his sect, and rather to aggravate than reconcile the differences which divided them from others. He confessed, therefore, that he doubted whether the patrons either would or ought to appoint such a person to such a charge. The sincerity and frankness of Carlyle's character increased the objection, for such a person would insist the more peremptorily on the articles of his philosophic creed—a creed which no one of the patrons adopted, and most of them regarded as damnable heresy. It was therefore but too likely that this would prove an insuperable obstacle. In all other respects Jeffrey considered Carlyle fully qualified, and likely, if appointed, to do great credit to the establishment. But he was afraid that Carlyle would not wish to disguise those singularities of opinion from which he foresaw the obstructions to his success; and as a further difficulty he added that the chair at which Carlyle was aiming had long been designed for Thomas Campbell, and would probably be given to him.

Jeffrey did what he could, perhaps not with very great ardour, but with vigour enough to save him from the charge of neglecting his friend. He went on a visit to Brougham in the autumn. He mentioned Carlyle, and in high terms of praise. He found Brougham, however, "singularly shy on the subject," and though the subject was introduced "half a dozen times" during Jeffrey's stay, Brougham was careful

213

"to evade it in a way that shewed" that he "did not wish to be pressed for an explicit answer even by an intimate friend."[12]

He came to know Brougham better in after years. There was probably no person in England less likely to recognise Carlyle's qualities; and the more distinguished Carlyle became, the more Brougham was sure to have congratulated himself on having kept his new University clear of such an influence. It must be admitted that the *"disesteem"* was equally marked on both sides.

Carlyle meanwhile did not rest on the vain imagination of help from others. He worked with all his might on the new line which had been opened to him, and here I have to mention one of those peculiarly honourable characteristics which meet us suddenly at all turns of his career. He had paid his brother's expenses at the University out of his salary as the Bullers' tutor. He was now poor himself with increased demands upon him, but the first use which he made of his slightly improved finances was to send John Carlyle to complete his education in the medical schools in Germany. He estimated John's talents with a brother's affection, and he was resolved to give him the best chances of distinguishing himself.[13] The cost was greater than he had calculated on, but he was not discouraged.

While Carlyle was taking care of his brother, an active interest was rising in Edinburgh about himself. Scotch people were beginning to see that a remarkable man had appeared among them, and that they ought not to let him slip through their hands. A new opening presented itself which he thus describes to his father: "there has been a fresh enterprize started for me: no less than the attempt to be successor to Dr Chalmers in the St. Andrews University!"[14]

Among those who encouraged Carlyle in this ambition, and lent active help, Jeffrey was now the first, and, besides general recommendations, wrote most strongly in his favour to Dr. Nicol, the Principal of the University. Equal testimonials, viewed by the intrinsic quality of the givers, to those which were collected or spontaneously offered on this occasion, were perhaps never presented by any candidate for a Scotch professorship. Goethe himself wrote one, which in these times might have carried the day; but Goethe was then only known in Scotland as a German dreamer. Carlyle, though again personally pretending indifference, exerted himself to the utmost, and was, perhaps, more anxious than he was aware of being.

There is a certain humour in the claims of Thomas Carlyle, supported by the most famous man of letters in Europe, being submitted to be tried in the scales by such a person as this. But so it was, and is, and perhaps must be, in constitutional countries, where high office may fall on the worthy, but rarely or never on the most worthy. It is difficult everywhere for the highest order of merit to find recognition. Under a system of popular election it is almost impossible.

After a few weeks the suspense was over. Carlyle was not appointed; someone else was; and someone else's church was made over to another someone else whom it was desirable to oblige; "and so the whole thing be rounded off in the neatest manner possible."[15] Such at least was Carlyle's account of what he understood to be the arrangement. Perhaps the "someone else" was a fitter person after all. Education in countries so jealous of novelty as Great Britain is, or at least was sixty years ago, follows naturally upon lines traced out by custom, and the conduct of it falls as a matter of course to persons who have never deviated from those lines. New truths are the nutriment of the world's progress. Men of genius discover them, insist upon them, prove them in the face of opposition, and if the genius is not merely a phosphorescent glitter, but an abiding light, their teaching enters in time into the University curriculum. But out of new ideas time alone can distinguish the sound and real from the illusive and imaginary; and it was enough that Carlyle was described as a man of original and extraordinary gifts to make college patrons shrink from contact with him.

Carlyle himself dimly felt that St. Andrew's might not be the best place for him. It seemed hard to refuse promotion to a man because he was too good for it, and no doubt he would have been pleased to be appointed. But for the work which Carlyle had to do a position of intellectual independence was indispensable, and his apprenticeship to poverty and hardship had to be prolonged still further to harden his nerves and perhaps to test his sincerity. The loss of this professorship may be regretted for Mrs. Carlyle's sake, who did not need the trials which lay before her. Carlyle himself in a University chair would have been famous in his day, and have risen to wealth and consequence, but he might not have been the Carlyle who has conquered a place for himself among the Immortals.

So ended the only fair prospect which ever was opened to him of entering any of the beaten roads of life; and fate having thus decided in spite of the loud remonstrance of all friends, of Jeffrey especially, Carlyle became once more bent on removing to Craigenputtoch. The repairs in the old house were hastened forward, that it might be ready for them in the spring.

The domestic scene in Comely Bank had been meantime brightened by the long-talked-of event of the visit of old Mrs. Carlyle to Edinburgh. In all her long life she had never yet been beyond Annandale, had never seen the interior of any better residence than a Scottish farmhouse. To the infinite heaven spread above the narrow circle of her horizon she had perhaps risen as near on wings of prayer and piety as any human being who was upon the earth beside her; but of the earth itself, of her own Scotland, she knew no more than could be descried from Burnswark Hill. She was to spend Christmas week at Comely Bank. She arrived at the beginning of December [and stayed about four weeks, seeing the sights of Edinburgh, yet anxious to return home to her work].

Eager as Carlyle was to be gone from Edinburgh, he confessed that in his wife's manner he had detected an unwillingness to bury herself in the moors. The evident weakness of her health alarmed him, and he could scarcely have forgotten the aversion with which she had received his first suggestion of making Craigenputtoch their home. For himself his mind was made up; and usually when Carlyle wished anything he was not easily impressed with objections to it. In this instance, however, he was evidently hesitating. Craigenputtoch, sixteen miles from the nearest town and the nearest doctor, cut off from the outer world through the winter months by snow and flood, in itself gaunt, grim, comfortless, and utterly solitary, was not a spot exactly suited to a

216

delicate and daintily nurtured woman. In the counter scale was her mother, living a few miles below in Nithsdale. But for this attraction Mrs. Carlyle would have declined the adventure altogether; as it was she trembled at the thought of it.

The house in Comely Bank was held only by the year. They were called on to determine whether they would take it for another twelve months or not. Before deciding they resolved to see Craigenputtoch together once more. Little Jean was left in charge at Edinburgh, and Carlyle and Mrs. Carlyle went down to Dumfriesshire. "My two nights at Craigenputtoch . . . I vividly enough recollect: Proofsheets of *Goethe's Helena* in my pocket; & Dumfries 'architects' to confer with! Scene grim enough, outlook too rather ditto; but resolution fixed enough."[16]

On a blusterous March day Craigenputtoch could not look to advantage. They left it still irresolute, and perhaps inclining to remain among their friends. But the question had been settled for them in their absence; on returning to Comely Bank they found that their landlord, not caring to wait longer till they had made up their minds, had let the house to another tenant, and that at all events they would have to leave it at Whitsuntide. This ended the uncertainty.

So ended the life at 21 Comely Bank—the first married home of the Carlyles; which began ominously, as a vessel rolls when first launched, threatening an overturn, and closed with improved health and spirits on Carlyle's part, and prospects which, if not brilliant, were encouraging and improving. He had been fairly introduced into the higher walks of his profession, and was noticed and talked about. Besides the two articles on Jean Paul and on German literature, he had written the paper on Werner, the essay on Goethe's "Helena," and the more elaborate and remarkable essay on Goethe himself, which now stand among the *Miscellanies*.[17] Goethe personally remained kind and attentive. He had studied Carlyle's intellectual temperament, and had used an expression about him in the St. Andrews testimonial which showed how clear an insight he had gained into the character of it. Carlyle was resting, he said, "on an original foundation," and was so happily constituted that he could "develop in himself the essentials of what is good and

217

beautiful"[18]—in himself, not out of contact with others. The work could be done, therefore, as well, or perhaps better, in solitude. Along with the testimonial had come a fresh set of presents, with more cards and verses and books, and with a remembrance of himself which Carlyle was to deliver to Sir Walter Scott.

This was the last of Comely Bank. A few days later the Carlyles were gone to the Dumfriesshire moorland where for seven years was now to be their dwelling-place.[19] Carlyle never spoke to Scott, as he hoped to do; nor did Sir Walter even acknowledge his letter. It seems that the medals and the letter to Scott from Goethe were entrusted to Wilson, by whom, or by Jeffrey, they were delivered to Scott on the arrival of the latter soon after in Edinburgh. Carlyle's letter, of which Wilson had also taken charge, was perhaps forgotten by him.[20]

chapter ten

1828

A Calvinist without the Theology

Goethe had said of Carlyle that he was fortunate in having in himself an originating principle of conviction, out of which he could develop the force that lay in him unassisted by other men.[1] Goethe had discerned what had not yet become articulately clear to Carlyle himself. But it is no less true that this principle of conviction was already active in his mind, underlying his thoughts on every subject which he touched. It is implied everywhere, though nowhere definitely stated in his published writings. We have arrived at a period when he had become master of his powers, when he began distinctly to utter the "poor message," as he sometimes called it, which he had to deliver to his contemporaries. From this time his opinions on details might vary, but the main structure of his philosophy remained unchanged. It is desirable, therefore, before pursuing further the story of his life, to describe briefly what the originating principle was. The secret of a man's nature lies in his religion, in what he really believes about this world, and his own place in it. What was Carlyle's religion? I am able to explain it, partly from his conversations with myself, but happily not from this source only, into which alien opinions might too probably intrude. There remain among his unpublished papers the fragments of two unfinished essays which he was never able to complete satisfactorily to himself, but which he told me were, and had been, an imperfect expression of his actual thoughts.

We have seen him confessing to Irving that he did not believe, as his friend did, in the Christian religion, and that it was vain to hope that he ever would so believe. He tells his mother, and he so continued to tell her as long as she lived, that their belief was essentially the same, although their language was different. Both these statements were true. He was a Calvinist without the theology. The materialistic theory of things—that intellect is a phenomenon of matter, that conscience is the growth of social convenience, and other kindred speculations, he utterly repudiated. Scepticism on the nature of right and wrong, as on man's responsibility to his Maker, never touched or tempted him. On the broad facts of the Divine government of the universe he was as well assured as Calvin himself; but he based his faith, not on a supposed revelation, or on fallible human authority. He had sought the evidence for it, where the foundations lie of all other forms of knowledge, in the experienced facts of things interpreted by the intelligence of man. Experienced fact was to him revelation, and the only true revelation. Historical religions, Christianity included, he believed to have been successive efforts of humanity, loyally and nobly made in the light of existing knowledge, to explain human duty, and to insist on the fulfilment of it; and the reading of the moral constitution and position of man, in the creed, for instance, of his own family, he believed to be truer far, incommensurably truer, than was to be found in the elaborate metaphysics of utilitarian ethics. In revelation, technically so called, revelation confirmed by historical miracles, he was unable to believe—he felt himself forbidden to believe—by the light that was in him. In other ages men had seen miracles where there were none, and had related them in perfect good faith in their eagerness to realise the divine presence in the world. They did not know enough of nature to be on their guard against alleged suspensions of its unvarying order. To Carlyle the universe was itself a miracle, and all its phenomena were equally in themselves incomprehensible. But the special miraculous occurrences of sacred history were not credible to him. "It is as certain as mathematics," he said to me late in his own life, "that no such thing ever has been or can be." He had learnt that effects succeeded causes uniformly and inexorably without intermission or interruption, and that tales of wonder were as little the true accounts of real occurrences as the theory of epicycles was a correct explanation of the movements of the planets.

So far his thoughts on this subject did not differ widely from those of his sceptical contemporaries, but his further conclusions not only were not their conclusions, but were opposed to them by whole diameters; for while he rejected the literal narrative of the sacred writers, he believed as strongly as any Jewish prophet or Catholic saint in the spiritual truths of religion. The effort of his life was to rescue and reassert those truths which were being dragged down by the weight with which they were encumbered. He explained his meaning by a remarkable illustration. He had not come (so far as he knew his own purpose) to destroy the law and the prophets, but to fulfil them, to expand the conception of religion with something wider, grander, and more glorious than the wildest enthusiasm had imagined.

The old world had believed that the earth was stationary, and that sun and stars moved round it as its guardian attendants. Science had discovered that sun and stars, if they had proper motion of their own, yet in respect of the earth were motionless, and that the varying aspect of the sky was due to the movements of the earth itself. The change was humbling to superficial vanity. "The stars in their courses" could no longer be supposed to fight against earthly warriors, or comets to foretell the havoc on fields of slaughter, or the fate and character of a prince to be affected by the constellation under which he was born. But if the conceit of the relative importance of man was diminished, his conception of the system of which he was a part had become immeasurably more magnificent; while every phenomenon which had been actually and faithfully observed remained unaffected. Sun and moon were still the earthly time-keepers; and the mariner still could guide his course across the ocean by the rising and setting of the same stars which Ulysses had watched upon his raft.

Carlyle conceived that a revolution precisely analogous to that which Galileo had wrought in our apprehension of the material heaven was silently in progress in our attitude towards spiritual phenomena.

221

The spiritual universe, like the visible, was the same yesterday, to-day, and for ever, and legends and theologies
were, like the astronomical theories of the Babylonians,
Egyptians, or Greeks, true so far as they were based on
facts, which entered largely into the composition of the worst
of them—true so far as they were the honest efforts of man's
intellect and conscience and imagination to interpret the
laws under which he was living, and regulate his life by
them. But underneath or beyond all these speculations lay
the facts of spiritual life, the moral and intellectual constitution of things as it actually was in eternal consistence. The
theories which dispensed with God and the soul Carlyle
utterly abhorred. It was not credible to him, he said, that
intellect and conscience could have been placed in him by a
Being which had none of its own. He rarely spoke of this.
The word God was too awful for common use, and he veiled
his meaning in metaphors to avoid it. But God to him was
the fact of facts. He looked on this whole system of visible
or spiritual phenomena as a manifestation of the will of God
in constant forces, forces not mechanical but dynamic, inter-
penetrating and controlling all existing things, from the
utmost bounds of space to the smallest granule on the
earth's surface, from the making of the world to the lightest
action of a man. God's law was everywhere: man's welfare
depended on the faithful reading of it. Society was but a
higher organism, no accidental agreement of individual persons or families to live together on conditions which they
could arrange for themselves, but a natural growth, the conditions of which were already inflexibly laid down. Human
life was like a garden, "to which the will was gardener,"
and the moral fruits and flowers, or the immoral poisonous
weeds, grew inevitably according as the rules already
appointed were discovered and obeyed, or slighted, overlooked, or defied. Nothing was indifferent. Every step
which a man could take was in the right direction or the
wrong. If in the right, the result was as it should be; if in the
wrong, the excuse of ignorance would not avail to prevent
the inevitable consequence.

These in themselves are but commonplace propositions
which no one denies in words; but Carlyle saw in the entire

tone of modern thought, that practically men no longer really believed them. They believed in expediency, in the rights of man, in government by majorities; as if they could make their laws for themselves. The law, did they but know it, was already made; and their wisdom, if they wished to prosper, was not to look for what was convenient to themselves, but for what had been decided already in Nature's chancery.

Many corollaries followed from such a creed when sincerely and passionately held. In arts and sciences the authority is the expert who understands his business. No one dreamt of discovering a longitude by the vote of a majority; and those who trusted to any such methods would learn that they had been fools by running upon the rocks. The science of life was no easier—was harder far than the science of navigation: the phenomena were infinitely more complex; and the consequences of error were infinitely more terrible. The rights of man, properly understood, meant the right of the wise to rule, and the right of the ignorant to be ruled. "The gospel of force," of the divine right of the strong, with which Carlyle has been so often taunted with teaching, merely meant that when a man has visibly exercised any great power in this world, it has been because he has truly and faithfully seen into the facts around him; seen them more accurately and interpreted them more correctly than his contemporaries. He has become in himself, as it were, one of nature's forces, imperatively insisting that certain things must be done. Success may blind him, and then he mis-sees the facts and comes to ruin. But while his strength remains he is strong through the working of a power greater than himself. The old Bible language that God raised up such and such a man for a special purpose represents a genuine truth.

But let us hear Carlyle himself. The following passages were written in 1852, more than twenty years after the time at which we have now arrived. Figure and argument were borrowed from new appliances which had sprung into being in the interval. But the thought expressed in them was as old as Hoddam Hill when they furnished the armour in which he encountered Apollyon. They are but broken thoughts, flung out as they presented themselves, and wanting the careful

touch with which Carlyle finished work which he himself
passed through the press; but I give them as they remain in
his own handwriting.

> The primary conception by rude nations, in regard to all great
> attainments and achievements by man, is that each was a miracle
> and the gift of the gods. Language was taught man by a Heavenly
> Power; Minerva gave him the olive, Neptune the Horse, Tripto-
> lemus taught him Agriculture, etc. etc. The effects of *optics* in
> this strange camera obscura of an existence are most of all singular!
> The grand centre of the modern revolution of ideas is even this. We
> begin to have a notion that all this *is* the effect of optics; and that the
> intrinsic fact is very different from our old conception of it. Not less
> "miraculous," not less divine; but with an altogether (totally) new
> (or hitherto unconceived) *species* of divineness, a divineness lying
> much nearer home than formerly. A divineness that does not come
> from Judea from Olympus, Asgard, Mt. Meru; but is in man him-
> self, in the heart of every living man. A grand revolution indeed;
> which is altering our ideas of Heaven and of Earth to an amazing
> extent in every particular whatsoever. From top to bottom our
> spiritual world, and all that depends on the same, which means
> nearly everything in the furniture of our life outward as well as in-
> ward, is as this idea advances undergoing change of the most
> essential sort,—is slowly getting "overturned," as they angrily say;
> which in the sense of being gradually turned over, and having its
> vertex set where its base used to be, is indisputably true; and means
> a "revolution" such as never was before, or at least since letters
> and recorded history existed among us never was.[2]

So far Carlyle had written, and then threw it aside as
unsatisfactory, as not adequately expressing his meaning,
and therefore not to be proceeded with. But a very intelligible meaning shines through it; and when I told him that
I had found and read it, he said that it contained his real
conviction, a conviction that lay at the bottom of all his
thoughts about man and man's doings in this world. A sense
lay upon him that this particular truth was one which he was
specially called on to insist upon, yet he could never get it
completely accomplished. On another loose sheet of rejected
manuscript I find the same idea stated somewhat differently:

> Singular what difficulty I have in getting my poor message deliv-
> ered to the world in this epoch: things I imperatively need still to
> say.
> 1.   That all history is a Bible—a thing stated in words by me more
> than once, and adopted in a sentimental way; but nobody can I bring
> fairly into it, nobody persuade to take it up practically as a *fact*.

2. Part of the "grand Unintelligible," that we are now learning spiritually too—that the earth *turns*, not the sun and heavenly spheres. One day the spiritual astronomers will find that *this* is the infinitely greater miracle. The universe is not an orrery, theological or other, but a universe; and instead of paltry theologic brass spindles for axis, &c., has laws of gravitation, laws of attraction and repulsion; is not a Ptolemaic but a Newtonian universe. As Humbolt's "Cosmos" to a fable of children, so will the new world be in comparison with what the old one was, &c.

3. And flowing out of this, that the work of genius is not *fiction* but fact. How dead are all people to that truth, recognising it in word merely, not in deed at all! . . .

Old piety was wont to say that God's judgments tracked the footsteps of the criminal; that all violation of the eternal laws, done in the deepest recesses or on the conspicuous high places of the world, was absolutely certain of its punishment. You could do no evil, you could do no good, but a god would repay it to you. It was as certain as that when you shot an arrow from the earth, gravitation would bring it back to the earth. The all-embracing law of right and wrong was as inflexible, as sure and exact, as that of gravitation. Furies with their serpent hair and infernal maddening torches followed Orestes who had murdered his mother. In the still deeper soul of modern Christendom there hung the tremendous image of a Doomsday—*Dies irae, dies illa*—when the All-just, without mercy now, with only terrific accuracy now, would judge the quick and the dead, and to each soul measure out the reward of his deeds done in the body—eternal Heaven to the good, to the bad eternal Hell. The Moslem too, and generally the Oriental peoples, who are of a more religious nature, have conceived it so, and taken it, not as a conceit, but as a terrible fact, and have studiously founded, or studiously tried to found, their practical existence upon the same.

My friend, it well behoves us to reflect how true essentially all this still is: that it continues, and will continue, fundamentally a fact in all essential particulars—its certainty, I say its infallible certainty, its absolute justness, and all the other particulars, the eternity itself included. He that has with his eyes and soul looked into nature from any point—and not merely into distracted theological, metaphysical, modern philosophical, or other cobweb representations of nature at second hand—will find this true, that only the vesture of it is changed for us; that the essence of it cannot change at all. Banish all miracles from it. Do not name the name of God; it is still true.

Once more it is in religion with us, as in astronomy—we know now that the earth moves. But it has not annihilated the stars for us; it has infinitely exalted and expanded the stars and universe. Once it seemed evident the sun did daily rise in the east; the big sun—a sun-god—did travel for us, driving his chariot over the crystal floor all days: at any rate the sun *went*. Now we find it is only the earth that goes. So too all mythologies, religious conceptions, &c., we begin to discover, are the necessary products of man's godmade mind.[3]

I need add little to these two fragments, save to repeat that they are the key to Carlyle's mind; that the thought which they contain, although nowhere more articulately written out, governed all his judgements of men and things. In this faith he had trampled down his own *"Spiritual Dragons."*[4] In this faith he interpreted human history, which history witnessed in turn to the truth of his convictions. He saw that now as much as ever the fate of nations depended not on their material development, but, as had been said in the Bible, and among all serious peoples, on the moral virtues, courage, veracity, purity, justice, and good sense. Nations where these were honoured prospered and became strong; nations which professed well with their lips, while their hearts were set on wealth and pleasure, were overtaken, as truly in modern Europe as in ancient Palestine, by the judgement of God.

"I should not have known what to make of this world at all," Carlyle once said to me, "if it had not been for the French Revolution."[5]

chapter eleven

1828–1830

First Years at Craigenputtoch

I have already described Craigenputtoch as the dreariest spot in all the British dominions. The nearest cottage is more than a mile from it; the elevation, seven hundred feet above the sea, stunts the trees and limits the garden produce to the hardiest vegetables. The house is gaunt and hungry-looking. It stands with the scanty fields attached as an island in a sea of morass. The landscape is unredeemed either by grace or grandeur, mere undulating hills of grass and heather, with peat bogs in the hollows between them. The belts of firs which now relieve the eye and furnish some kind of shelter were scarcely planted when the Carlyles were in possession. No wonder Mrs. Carlyle shuddered at the thought of making her home in so stern a solitude, delicate as she was, with a weak chest, and with the fatal nervous disorder of which she eventually died already beginning to show itself. Yet so it was to be. She had seen the place in March for the first time in her life, and then, probably, it had looked its very worst. But in May, when they came to settle, the aspect would have scarcely been mended. The spring is late in Scotland; on the high moors the trees are still bare. The fields are scarcely coloured with the first shoots of green, and winter lingers in the lengthening days as if unwilling to relax its grasp. To Mrs. Carlyle herself the adventure might well seem desperate. She concealed the extent of her anxiety from her husband, though not entirely from others. Jeffrey especially felt serious alarm. He feared not without reason that Carlyle was too

CRAIGENPUTTOCH. The house and extensive grounds had long been in the Welsh family, and to economize the Carlyles moved here in 1828. Visible in the foreground is the old carriage drive, up which Francis Jeffrey and his family came in a memorable visit that autumn. Carlyle wrote of Craigenputtoch in his *Reminiscences*: "I incline to think it the poor *best* place that could have been selected for the ripening into fixity and composure of anything useful which there may have been in me against the years that were coming." He retained to the end mixed feelings about the moorland home where he and his wife spent six years and where *Sartor* was written. (Photograph by John Patrick, courtesy of the University of Edinburgh.)

much occupied with his own thoughts to be trusted in such a situation with the charge of a delicate and high-spirited woman, who would not spare herself in the hard duties of her situation.[1]

The decision had been made, however, and was not to be reconsidered. Jeffrey could only hope that the exile to Siberia would be of short duration. When the furniture at Comely Bank was packed and despatched, he invited Mr. and Mrs. Carlyle to stay with him in Moray Place, while the carts were on the road. After two days they followed, and in the last week of May they were set down at the door of the house which was now to be their home. The one bright feature in the situation to Carlyle was the continual presence of his brother at the farm. The cottage in which Alexander Carlyle lived was attached to the premises; and the outdoor establishment of field, stall, and dairy servants was common to both households.

The carpenters and plasterers were at last dismissed. Craigenputtoch became tolerable, if not yet "cosmic," and as soon as all was quiet again, Carlyle settled himself to work. [An article on] Tasso was abandoned, or at least postponed, but the article on Burns was written—not so ungraciously, so far as regarded Lockhart, as the epithet "trivial" which had been applied to his book might have foreboded.[2] But it is rather on Burns himself than on his biographer's account of him that Carlyle's attention was concentrated. It is one of the very best of his essays, and was composed with an evidently peculiar interest, because the outward circumstances of Burns's life, his origin, his early surroundings, his situation as a man of genius born in a farmhouse not many miles distant, among the same people and the same associations as were so familiar to himself, could not fail to make him think often of himself while he was writing about his countryman. How this article was judged by the contemporary critics will be presently seen. For himself, it is too plain that before he came to the end of it the pastoral simplicities of the moorland had not cured Carlyle of his humours and hypochondrias. He had expected that change of scene would enable him to fling off his shadow. His shadow remained sticking to him; and the poor place where he had cast his lot had as usual to bear the blame of his disappointment. In his diary there stands a note: "Finished a Paper on *Burns*. September 16, 1828; at this Devil's Den, Craigenputtoch."[3]

Meanwhile, though he complained of hearing little from the world outside, his friends had not forgotten him. Letters came by the carrier from Dumfries, and the Saturday's post was the event of the week. Jeffrey especially was affectionate and assiduous. He reproached Carlyle for not writing to him, complained of being so soon forgotten, and evidently wished to keep his friend as close to him as possible. The papers on German literature had brought a pamphlet upon Jeffrey about Kant, from "some horrid German blockhead"; but he was patient under the affliction and forgave the cause. King's College had been set on foot in London on orthodox principles, under the patronage of the Duke of Wellington and the bishops. He offered to recommend Carlyle to them as Professor of Mysticism; although mysticism itself he said he should like less than ever if it turned such a man as Carlyle into a morbid misanthrope, which seemed to be its present effect. Sir Walter had received his medals and had acknowledged them; had spoken of Goethe as his master, and had said civil things of Carlyle, which was more than he had deserved.[4] Jeffrey cautioned Carlyle to be careful of the delicate companion who had been trusted to him; offered his services in any direction in which he could be of use, and throughout, and almost weekly, sent to one or other of the "hermits" some note or letter, short or long, but always sparkling, airy, and honestly affectionate. I am sorry that I am not at liberty to print these letters *in extenso*; for they would show that Jeffrey had a genuine regard and admiration for Carlyle, which was never completely appreciated. It was impossible from their relative positions that there should not be at least an appearance of patronage on Jeffrey's part. The reader has probably discovered that Carlyle was proud, and proud men never wholly forgive those to whom they feel themselves obliged.[5]

July this year had been intensely hot. Jeffrey had complained of being stifled in the courts, and for the moment had actually envied his friends their cool mountain breezes. The heat had been followed in August by rain. It had been "the wettest, warmest summer ever known." Alexander

Carlyle had been living hitherto with his brother, the cottage which he was to occupy with one of his sisters not being yet ready. The storms had delayed the masons; while the article on Burns was being written the premises were still littered with dirt, and Carlyle's impatience with small misfortunes perhaps had inspired the unpleasant epithet of Devil's Den with which he had already christened his home. He appears to have remained, however, in a—for him—tolerable humour.

The Jeffreys were to have come in September, while the weather was still fine, but they had gone first to the western Highlands, and their visit was put off till the next month. Meanwhile the article on Burns had been sent off, and before the appearance of the visitors at Craigenputtoch a sharp altercation had commenced between the editor and his contributor on certain portions of it, which was not easily ended. On the article itself the world has pronounced a more than favourable verdict. Goethe considered it so excellent that he translated long passages from it, and published them in his collected works; but, as Goethe had observed about Schiller, contemporaries always stumble at first over the writings of an original man. The novelty seems like presumption. The editor of the *Edinburgh Review* found the article long and diffuse, though he did not deny that it contained "much beauty and felicity of diction." He insisted that it must be cut down—cut down perhaps to half its dimensions. He was vexed with Carlyle for standing, as he supposed, in his own light, misusing his talents and throwing away his prospects. He took the opportunity of reading him a general lecture.

You will treat me as something worse than an ass I suppose when I say that I am firmly persuaded the great source of your extravagance, and of all that makes your writings intolerable to many —and ridiculous to not a few, is not so much any real peculiarity of opinions as an unlucky ambition to appear more original than you are—or the humbler and still more delusive hope of converting our English intellects to the creed of Germany—and being the apostle of another reformation— I wish to God I could persuade you to fling away these affections—and be contented to write like your famous countrymen of all ages—as long at least as you write *to* your countrymen and *for* them— The *nationality* for which you commend Burns so highly might teach you I think that there are nobler tasks for a man like you than to vamp up the vulgar

231

dreams of these Dousterswivels you are so anxious to cram down our throats—but which I venture to predict no good judge among us will swallow—and the nation at large speedily reject with loathing—[6]

So spoke the great literary authority of the day. The adventurous Prince who would win the golden water on the mountain's crest is always assailed by cries that he is a fool and must turn back, from the enchanted stones which litter the track on which he is ascending. They too have once gone on the same quest. They have wanted faith, and are become blocks of rock echoing commonplaces; and if the Prince turns his head to listen to them, he too becomes as they.[7] Jeffrey tried to sweeten his admonitions by compliments on the article upon Goethe; but here too he soon fell to scolding. "But tho' I admire," he said,

the talent of your paper, I am more and more convinced of the utter fallacy of your opinions—and the grossness of your idolatry. I predict too, with full and calm assurance, that your cause is quite hopeless—and that England *never will* admire—nor indeed endure your German divinities— It thinks better and more of them indeed at this moment than it ever will again— *Your* eloquence and ingenuity a little masks [sic] their dull extravagance and tiresome presumption—as soon as they appear in their own persons everybody will laugh and yawn. . . . I am really anxious to save you from this *foeda superstitio* [horrible fanaticism]— The only harm it has yet done you is to make you a little verbose and prone to exaggeration— There are strong symptoms of both in your Burns— I have tried to staunch the first but the latter is in the grain—and we must just risk the wonder and the ridicule it may bring on us—[8]

This was not merely the protest of an editor, but the reproach of a sincere friend. Jeffrey ardently desired to recommend Carlyle and to help him forward in the world. For Carlyle's own sake, and still more for the sake of his young and delicate relative, he was vexed and irritated that he should have buried himself at Craigenputtoch. He imagined, and in a certain sense with justice, that Carlyle looked on himself as the apostle of a new faith (to a clever man of the world the most absurd and provoking of illusions), which the solitude of the moors only tended to encourage.

With October the promised visit was accomplished. How he came with Mrs. Jeffrey and his daughter, how the big carriage stood wondering how it had got there in the rough farm-yard, how Carlyle and he rode about the country, with what astonishment he learnt that his dinner had been cooked for him by his hostess's own hands, how he delighted them all in the evenings with his brilliant anecdotes and mimicries—all this has been told elsewhere and need not be repeated.[9] Those two days were a sunny island in the general dreariness, an Indian summer before winter cut the Carlyles off from the outside world and wrapped them round with snow and desolation. During the greater part of the Jeffreys' stay controverted subjects were successfully avoided. But Carlyle's talk had none the less provoked Jeffrey. He himself, with a spiritual creed which sat easy on him, believed nevertheless that it was the business of a sensible man to make his way in the world, use his faculties to practical purposes, and provide for those who were dependent upon him. He saw his friend given over as he supposed to a self-delusion which approached near to foolish vanity, to have fallen in love with clouds like Ixiòn, and to be begetting chimaeras which he imagined to be divine truths. All this to a clear practical intelligence like that of Jeffrey was mere nonsense, and on the last night of his stay he ended a long argument in a tone of severe reproach for which he felt himself afterwards obliged to apologise. His excuse, if excuse was needed, was a genuine anxiety for Carlyle's welfare, and an equal alarm for his wife, whose delicacy, like enough, her husband was too much occupied with his own thoughts to consider sufficiently. "I cannot bring myself to think," he said in a letter which he wrote after he had left them, "that either you [or] Mrs. C. are *naturally* placed at Craigenputtoch—and tho' I *know* and reverence the feelings which have led you to fix there for the present, I must hope that it will not long be necessary to obey them in that retreat."[10]

The trouble with the article on Burns was not over. Jeffrey, as editor, had to consider the taste of the great Liberal party in literature and politics, and to disciples of Bentham, as indeed to the average reader of any political persuasion, Carlyle's views were neither welcome nor intelligible. When the proof sheets came, he found "the first portion of it all into shreds," "the body of a quadruped with the head of a bird; a man *shortened* by cutting out his thighs, and fixing the Knee-pans on the hips!"[11] Carlyle refused to let it appear "in such a horrid shape." He replaced the most important passages, and returned the sheets with an intimation that the paper might be cancelled, but should not be mutilated. Few editors would have been so forbearing as Jeffrey when so audaciously defied. He complained, but he acquiesced. He admitted that the article would do the *Review* credit, though it would be called tedious and sprawling by people of weight whose mouths he could have stopped. He had wished to be of use to Carlyle by keeping out of sight in the *Review* his mannerism and affectation; but if Carlyle persisted he might have his way.

Carlyle was touched; such kindness was more than he had looked for. The proud self-assertion was followed by humility and almost penitence, and the gentle tone in which he wrote conquered Jeffrey in turn. Jeffrey said that he admired and approved of Carlyle's letter to him in all aspects. The "candour and sweet blood" which was shown in it deserved the highest praise; and, as the dying pagan said in the play, "If these are Christian virtues I am Christian," so Jeffrey, hating as he did what he called Carlyle's mysticism, was ready to exclaim, if these were mystic virtues he was mystic. "But it is not so—the virtues are your own," he said,

and you possess them not in consequence of your mysticism but in spite of it— You shall have the proof sheets—and any thing you like— I really cannot chaffer with such a man or do anything to vex him—and you shall write mysticism for me too—if it will not be otherwise—and I will print it too, at all hazards—with few, very few and temperate corrections— I think you have a great deal of eloquence and talent—and might do considerable things, if— but no matter—I will not tire of you—and after all there are many more things I believe as to which we agree—than about which we differ—and the difference is not radical, but formal chiefly.[12]

So the winter settled down over Craigenputtoch. The weekly cart struggled up when possible from Dumfries with letters and parcels, but storms and rain made the communications more and more difficult. Old James Carlyle came over from Scotsbrig for a week after the Jeffreys went, an Edinburgh friend followed for three days more, and after that few faces save those of their own household were seen at the Carlyles' door. Happily for him he was fully employed. The *Foreign Review* and the *Edinburgh* gave him as much work as he could do. He had little need of money;

Scotsbrig supplied him with wheat flour and oatmeal, and the farm with milk and eggs and hams and poultry. There was little that needed buying save tea and sugar and tobacco; and his finances (for his articles were long and handsomely paid for) promised for a time to be on an easy footing in spite of the constant expenses of his brother John at Munich. There were two horses in the stable—Larry, the Irish horse of "genius," and Harry, Mrs. Carlyle's pony. In fine weather they occasionally rode or walked together. But the occasions grew rarer and rarer. Carlyle was essentially solitary. He went out in all weathers, indifferent to wet and, in spite of his imagined ill-health, impervious to cold. But he preferred to be alone with his thoughts, and Mrs. Carlyle was left at home to keep the house in proper order. She by education, and he by temperament, liked everything to be well kept and trim. He was extremely dainty about his food. He did not care for delicacies, but cleanliness and perfect cookery of common things he always insisted on, and if the porridge was smoked, or the bread heavy, or the butter less than perfect, or a plate or a dish ill-washed, he was entirely intolerable. Thus the necessary imperfections of Scotch farm-servant girls had to be supplemented by Mrs. Carlyle herself. She baked the bread, she dressed the dinner or saw it dressed, she cleaned the rooms. Among her other accomplishments she had to learn to milk the cows, in case the byre-woman should be out of the way, for fresh milk was the most essential article of Carlyle's diet. Nay, it might happen that she had to black the grates to the proper polish, or even scour the floors while Carlyle looked on encouragingly with his pipe. In addition to this she had charge of dairy and poultry; not herself necessarily making butter or killing fowls, but directing what was to be done and seeing that it was done properly. Her department, in short, was the whole establishment. This winter she was tolerably well, and as long as her health lasted she complained of nothing. Her one object was to keep Carlyle contented, to prevent him from being fretted by any petty annoyance, and prevent him also from knowing with how much labour to herself his own comfort was secured.

Thus the months passed on pleasantly. The "tempests,"

about which Jeffrey had been so anxious, howled over the moors, but did not much affect them. Carlyle's letters were written in fair spirits. The Devil's Den had become a tolerable home.

> This house (bating some outskirt things which must be left till Spring) is really a substantial, comfortable and even half-elegant house[.] I sit here in my little library, and laugh at the howling tempests, for there are green curtains and a clear fire and papered walls; the "old Kitchen" also is as tight a dining-room as you would wish for me, and has a black clean-barred grate, at which, when filled with Sanquhar coals, you might roast Boreas himself. The goodwife too is happy, and contented with me, and her solitude, which I believe is not to be equalled out of Sahara itself. You cannot figure the stillness of these moors in a November drizzle: nevertheless I walk often under cloud of night (in good Ecclefechan *clogs*) down as far as Carstammon-burn, [(]sometimes to Sandy-wells) conversing with the void heaven, in the most pleasant fashion. Besides Jane also has a pony now, which can canter to perfection even by the side of Larry! Tomorrow she is going over to Templand with it; and it is by her that I send this Letter. Grace, our servant, a tight, tidy, careful sharp-tempered woman is the only other inmate of the house. . . . I write hard all day; then Jane and I (both learning Spanish for the last month) read a chapter of Don Quixote between dinner and tea, and are already half thro' the first volume, and eager to persevere. After tea, I sometimes writ[e] again (being [*dre*]*adfully* slow at the business); and then generally go over to Alick and Ma[ry and] smoke my last pipe with them; and so end the day, having done little good perhaps [but] almost no ill that I could help to any creature of God's.[13]

When Carlyle was in good spirits, his wife had a pleasant time with him. "Ill to deal wi'," impatient, irritable over little things, that he always was; but he was charming, too; no conversation in my experience ever equalled his; and unless the evil spirit had possession of him, even his invectives when they burst out piled themselves into metaphors so extravagant that they ended in convulsions of laughter with his whole body and mind, and then all was well again. Their Spanish studies together were delightful to both. His writing was growing better and better. She —the most watchful and severest of critics,—who never praised where praise was not deserved, was happy in the fulfilment of her prophecies, and her hardest work was a delight to her when she could spare her husband's mind an anxiety or his stomach an indigestion. At Christmas she had a holiday, going down to her mother and grandfather at Templand. But while away among her own people her heart was on the Craig.

The first year of Craigenputtoch thus drew to an end. The storms of December were succeeded by frost, and the moors were bound fast in ice. Carlyle continued as busy as ever at what he called "the despicable craft of reviewing," but doing his very best with it. No slop-work ever dropped from his pen. He never wrote down a word which he had not weighed, or a sentence which he had not assured himself contained a truth. Every one of the articles composed on this bare hill-top has come to be reprinted unaltered, and most of them have a calmness too often absent from his later writings. Handsome pay, as I said, came in, but not more than was needed. Brother John was a constant expense; and even in the "Dunscore wilderness" life was impossible without money. "Alas," Carlyle said, "for the days when Diogenes could fit up his tub, and let the 'literary world' and all other worlds, except the only true one within his own soul, wag hither and thither at discretion!"[14]

Voltaire was now his subject. His mind was already turning with an unconscious fascination towards the French Revolution. He had perceived it to be the most noteworthy phenomenon of modern times. It was interesting to him, as an illustration of his conviction that untruthfulness and injustice were as surely followed by divine retribution as the idolatries and tyrannies of Biblical Egypt and Assyria; that the Power which men professed on Sundays to believe in was a living Power, the most real, the most tremendous of all facts. France had rejected the Reformation. Truth had been offered her in the shape of light, and she would not have it, and it was now to come to her as lightning. She had murdered her prophets. She had received instead of them the scoffing Encyclopaedists. Yet with these transcendental or "mystic" notions in his head, Carlyle could write about the most worldly of all men of genius, as himself a man of the world. He meets Voltaire on his own ground, follows him into his private history with sympathising amusement; falls into no fits of horror over his opinions or his immoral-

237

ities; but regards them as the natural outcome of the circumstances of the time. In Voltaire he sees the representative Frenchman of the age, whose function was to burn up unrealities, out of the ashes of which some more healthy verdure might eventually spring. He could not reverence Voltaire, but he could not hate him. How could he hate a man who had fought manfully against injustice in high places, and had himself many a time in private done kind and generous actions? To Carlyle, Voltaire was no apostle charged with any divine message of positive truth. Even in his crusade against what he believed to be false, Voltaire was not animated with a high and noble indignation. He was simply an instrument of destruction, enjoying his work with the pleasure of some mocking imp, yet preparing the way for the tremendous conflagration which was impending. There is, of course, audible in this article a deep undertone of feeling. Yet the language of it is free from everything like excited rhetoric. In the earlier part of his career Carlyle sympathised with and expected more from the distinctive functions of revolution than he was able to do after longer experience. "I thought," he once said to me, "that it was the abolition of rubbish. I find it has been only the kindling of a dunghill. The dry straw on the outside burns off; but the huge damp rotting mass remains where it was."

Thinking on these momentous subjects, Carlyle took his nightly walks on the frozen moor, the ground crisp under his feet, the stars shining over his head, and the hills of Dunscore (for advantage had been taken of the dryness of the air) "gleaming like Strombolis or Aetnas, with the burning of heath; otherwise this place is silent, solitary as Tadmor of the Wilderness. Yet the infinite Vault is over us, and this Earth, our little Ship of Space, is under us; and man is everywhere in his Makers eye and hand!"[15]

Of outward incidents meanwhile the Craigenputtoch history was almost entirely destitute. The year 1829 rolled by without interruption to the tranquil routine of daily life. John Carlyle came home from Germany and became sometimes his brother's guest till a situation as doctor could be found for him. Carlyle himself wrote and rode and planted potatoes. His wife's faculty for spreading grace about her had extended to the outside premises, and behind the shelter of the trees she had raised a rose garden. An old but strong and convenient gig was added to the establishment. When an article was finished Carlyle allowed himself a fortnight's holiday: he and Mrs. Carlyle driving off with Larry either to Templand or to Scotsbrig; the pipe and tobacco duly arranged under cover on the inner side of the splashboard. The Jeffreys passed through Dumfries in the summer. Their friends from the Craig drove down to see them, and were even meditating afterwards an expedition in the same style throughout England as far as Cornwall.

Carlyle was full of thoughts on the great social questions of the day. He wished to see with his own eyes the actual condition of the people of England, as they lived in their own homes. The plan had to be abandoned for want of means, but he had set his own heart upon it, and Mrs. Carlyle would have been glad too of a change from a solitude which was growing intolerably oppressive. Carlyle's ill humours had not come back, but he was occupied and indifferent. There is a letter from his wife to old Mrs. Carlyle at Scotsbrig, undated, but belonging evidently to March of this year, in which she complains of the loneliness. "Carlyle," she says, "never asks me to go with *him*, never even looks as if he desired my company."

One visitor, however, came to Craigenputtoch in the summer whose visit was more than welcome. Margaret, the eldest of Carlyle's sisters, had the superiority of mind and talent which belonged to her brother, and she had along with it an instinctive delicacy and nobleness of nature which had overcome the disadvantages of her education. She had become a most striking and interesting woman, but unhappily along with it she had shown symptoms of consumption. In the preceding autumn the family had been seriously alarmed about her. She had been ill all through the winter, but she had rallied with the return of warm weather. The cough ceased, the colour came back to her cheek, she was thought to have recovered entirely.

Life went on as usual; but the autumn brought anxieties of more than one description. The letters that remain are few, for his wife and his brother Alexander, to whom he wrote most confidentially, were both at Craigenputtoch, and his brother John also was for several months with him. He was trying to produce something better than review articles, and was engaged busily with an intended history of German literature, for which he had collected a large quantity of books. But John Carlyle, who was naturally listless, had to be stimulated to exertion, and was sent to London to look for employment. Employment would not come; perhaps was less assiduously looked for than it might have been. The expense of his maintenance fell on Carlyle, and the reviews were the only source to which he could look. More articles therefore had to be produced if a market could be found for them. Jeffrey, constant in his friendship, consulted the new editor of the *Edinburgh* [Macvey Napier], and various subjects were suggested and thought over. Carlyle proposed Napoleon, but another contributor was in the way. Jeffrey was in favour of Wycliffe, Luther, or "the Philosophy of the Reformation." Napier thought a striking article might be written on some poetical subject; but when Jeffrey hinted to him some of Carlyle's views on those topics, and how contemptuously he regarded all the modern English singers, the new editor "shuddered at the massacre of the innocents to which he had dreamt of exciting him." Still, for himself, Jeffrey thought that if Carlyle was in a relenting mood, and wished to exalt or mystify the world by a fine rhapsody on the divine art, he might be encouraged to try it.

Liking Jeffrey as Carlyle did, he was puzzled at so much interest being shown in him. He called it a mystery. Jeffrey humorously caught up the word, and accepted it as the highest compliment which Carlyle could pay. In a humbler sense, however, he was content to think it natural that one man of a kind heart should feel attracted towards another, and that signal purity and loftiness of character, joined to great talents and something of a romantic history, should excite interest and respect.

Jeffrey's anxiety to be of use did not end in recommendations to Napier. He knew how the Carlyles were situated in money matters. He knew that they were poor, and that their poverty had risen from a voluntary surrender of means which were properly their own, but which they would not touch while Mrs. Welsh was alive. He knew also that Carlyle had educated and was still supporting his brother out of his own slender earnings. He saw, as he supposed, a man of real brilliancy and genius weighed down and prevented from doing justice to himself by a drudgery which deprived him of the use of his more commanding talents; and with a generosity the merit of which was only exceeded by the delicacy with which the offer was made, he proposed that Carlyle should accept a small annuity from him. The whole matter he said should be an entire secret between them. He would tell no one—not even his wife. He bade Carlyle remember that he too would have been richer if he had not been himself a giver where there was less demand upon his liberality. He ought not to wish for a monopoly of generosity, and if he was really a religious man he must do as he would be done to; nor, he added, would he have made the offer did he not feel that in similar circumstances he would have freely accepted it himself. To show his confidence he enclosed £50, which he expected Carlyle to keep, and desired only to hear in reply that they had both done right.

Carlyle was grateful, but he was proud. He did not at the time, or perhaps ever, entirely misconstrue the spirit in which Jeffrey had volunteered to assist him; but it is hard, perhaps it is impossible, for a man to receive pecuniary help, or even the offer of pecuniary help, from a person who is not his relation without some sense that he is in a position of inferiority; and there is force in the objection to accepting favours which Carlyle thus describes, looking back over forty years:

> Jeffrey . . . generously offered to confer on me an annuity of £100;—which annual sum, had it fallen on me from the clouds, would have been of very high convenience at that time; but which I could not, for a moment, have dreamt of accepting as gift or subventionary help from any fellow-mortal. It was at once, in my handsomest, gratefullest, but brief and conclusive way [declined] from Jeffrey: "Republican equality the silently fixed law of human society at present; each man to live on his own resources, and have an *Equality* of economies with every other man; dangerous, and not possible except through cowardice or folly, to depart from said clear rule,—till perhaps a better era rise on us again!"[16]

If anyone thinks that Carlyle was deficient in gratitude, let him remember that gratitude is but one of many feelings which are equally legitimate and reputable. The gentleman commoner at Pembroke College meant only kindness when he left the boots at Johnson's door; but Johnson, so far from being grateful, flung the boots out of window, and has been praised by all mankind for it.[17]

The Fates this winter were doing their very worst to Carlyle. His wife had escaped harm from the first season at Craigenputtoch, but was not to be let off so easily a second time. All went well till the close of December; a fat goose had been killed for the new year's feast; when the snow fell and the frost came, and she caught a violent sore-throat, which threatened to end in diphtheria. There was no doctor nearer than Dumfries, and the road from the valley was hardly passable. Mrs. Welsh struggled up from Templand through the snow-drifts; care and nursing kept the enemy off, and the immediate danger in a few days was over; but the shock had left behind it a sense of insecurity, and the unsuitableness of such a home for so frail a frame became more than ever apparent.

It appears from the Journal that early in 1830 Carlyle had advanced so far with his "History of German Literature" that he was hoping soon to see it published and off his hands.[18] A first sketch of "Teufelsdröckh"[19]—the egg out of which *Sartor Resartus* was to grow—had been offered without result to London magazine editors. Proposals were made to him for a Life of Goethe. But on Goethe he had said all that for the present he wished to say. Luther was hanging before him as the subject which he wanted next to grapple, could he but find the means of doing it. But the preliminary reading necessary for such a work was wide and varied. The books required were not to be had at Craigenputtoch; and if the literary history could once be finished, and any moderate sum of money realised upon it, he meditated spending six months in Germany, taking Mrs. Carlyle with him, to collect materials. He had great hopes of what he could do with Luther. An editor had offered to bring it out in parts in a magazine, but Carlyle would not hear of this.

When I write that Book of the great German Lion, it shall be the best Book I have ever written, and go forth, I think, on its own legs. Do you know, we are actually talking of spending the next winter in Weimar; and preparing all the raw material of right *Luther*, there at the fountain-head. That, of course, if I can get this *History* done, and have the cash.[20]

Jeffrey started at the idea of the winter at Weimar—at

least for Mrs. Carlyle—and suggested that if it was carried out she should be left in his charge at Edinburgh. He was inclined, he said, to be jealous of the possible influence of Goethe, who had half bewitched her at a distance—unless indeed the spell was broken by the personal presence of him. But Jeffrey's fears were unnecesssary. There was no Weimar possible for Carlyle, and no Life of Luther. The unfortunate "German Literature" could not find a publisher who would so much as look at it. Boyd, who had brought out the volumes of *German Romance,* wrote that he would be proud to publish for Carlyle upon almost any other subject except German literature. He knew that in this department Carlyle was superior to any other author of the day, but the work proposed was not calculated to interest the British public. Every one of the books about German literature had been failures, most of them ruinous failures. The feeling in the public mind was that everything German was especially to be avoided, and with the highest esteem for Carlyle's talent he dared not make him an offer. Even cut up into articles he still found no one anxious to take it. There was still another hope. Carlyle's various essays had been greatly noticed and admired. An adventurous bookseller might perhaps be found who would bid for a collected edition of them. The suggestion took no effect however. The "Teufelsdröckh" had to be sent back from London, having created nothing but astonished dislike. Nothing was to be done therefore but to remain at Craigenputtoch and work on, hoping for better times. Fresh articles were written, a second on Jean Paul, a slight one on Madame de Staël, with the first of the two essays on history which are published in the *Miscellanies.* He was thus able to live, but not so far as money was concerned to overtake the time which he had spent over his unsaleable book; his finances remained sadly straitened, and he needed all his energy to fight on against discouragement.

The Carlyles as a family were passionately attached to each other. Margaret Carlyle's apparent recovery was as delusive as her sister-in-law had feared. In the winter she fell ill again; in the spring she was carried to Dumfries in the desperate hope that medical care might save her. Carlyle has written nothing more affecting than the account of her end in the *Reminiscences.*[21]

Margaret Carlyle sleeps in Ecclefechan churchyard. Her father followed soon, and was laid beside her. Then after him, but not for many years, the pious, tender, original, beautiful-minded mother. John Carlyle was the next of their children who rejoined them, and next he of whom I am now writing. The world and the world's business scatter families to the four winds, but they collect again in death. Alick lies far off in a Canadian resting-place; but in his last illness, when the memory wanders, he too had travelled in spirit back to Annandale and the old days when his brother was at college, and with the films of the last struggle closing over his eyes he asked anxiously "If Brother Tom were not coming back from Edinburgh tomorrow."[22]

The loss of this sister weighed heavily on Carlyle's spirits, and the disappointment about his book fretted him on the side to which he might naturally have turned to seek relief in work. Goethe's steady encouragement was of course inspiriting, but it brought no grist to the mill, and the problem of how he was to live was becoming extremely serious. Conscious though he was of exceptional powers, which the most grudging of his critics could not refuse to acknowledge, he was discovering to his cost that they were not marketable. He could not throw his thoughts into a shape for which the Sosii of the day would give him money. He had tried poetry, but his verse was cramped and unmelodious. He had tried to write stories, but his convictions were too intense for fiction. The dreadful earnestness of which Jeffrey complained[23] was again in his way, and he could have as little written an entertaining novel as St. Paul or St. John. His entire faculty—intellect and imagination alike—was directed upon the sternest problems of human life. It was not possible for him, like his friend at Craigcrook, to take up with the first creed that came to hand and make the best of it. He required something which he could really believe. Thus his thoughts refused to move in any common groove. He had himself to form the taste by which he could be appreciated, and when he spoke his words provoked the same antagonism which every original thinker is inevitably condemned to encounter—antagonism first in the form of wonder, and when the wonder ceased of irritation and angry enmity. He taught like one that had authority—a tone which men

244

naturally resent, and must resent, till the teacher has made his pretensions good. Every element was absent from his writing which would command popularity, the quality to which booksellers and review editors are obliged to look if they would live themselves. Carlyle's articles were magnetic enough, but with the magnetism which repelled, not which attracted. His faith in himself and in his own purposes never wavered; but it was becoming a subject of serious doubt to him whether he could make a living, even the humblest, by literature. The fair promises of the last year at Comely Bank had clouded over; instead of invitations to write, he was receiving cold answers to his own proposals. Editors, who had perhaps resented his haughty style, were making him "feel the difference," neglecting to pay him even for the articles which had been accepted and put in type.

chapter twelve

1830–1831

Craigenputtoch and the Writing of
Sartor Resartus

Trials had fallen sharply on Carlyle, entirely, as Jeffrey had said, through his own generosity. He had advanced £240 in the education and support of his brother John. He had found the capital to stock the farm at Craigenputtoch, and his brother Alick thus had received from him half as much more—small sums, as rich men estimate such matters, but wrung out by Carlyle as from the rock by desperate labour, and spared out of his own and his wife's necessities. John (perhaps ultimately Alexander, but of this I am not sure) honourably repaid his share of this debt in the better days which were coming to him, many years before fortune looked more kindly on Carlyle himself. But as yet John Carlyle was struggling almost penniless in London. Alick's farming at Craigenputtoch, which Carlyle had once rashly thought of undertaking for himself, had proved a disastrous failure, and was now to be abandoned. The pleasant family party there had to be broken up, and his brother was to lose the companionship which softened the dreariness of his solitude. Alick Carlyle had the family gift of humour. His letters show that had he been educated he too might have grown into something remarkable. Alick could laugh with all his heart and make others laugh. His departure changed the character of the whole scene. Carlyle himself grew discontented. An impatient Radicalism rings through his remarks on the things which were going on round him. The political world was shaken by the three glorious days in

Paris. England, following the example, was agitating for Reform, and a universal and increasing distress flung its ominous shadow over the whole working community. Reports of it all, leaking in through chance visitors, local newspapers, or letters of friends, combined with his own and his brother's indifferent and almost hopeless prospects, tended too naturally to encourage his gloomy tendencies. Ever on the watch to be of use to him, the warm-hearted Jeffrey was again at hand to seduce him into conformity with the dominant Liberal ways of thinking; that in the approaching storm he might at least open a road for himself to his own personal advancement. In August Jeffrey pressed his two friends in his most winning language to visit him at Craigcrook. Carlyle, he said, was doing nothing, and could employ himself no better than to come down with his blooming Eve out of his "blasted Paradise," and seek shelter in the lower world. To Mrs. Carlyle he promised roses and a blue sea, and broad shadows stretching over the fields. He said that he felt as if destined to do them real service, and could now succeed at last. Carlyle would not be persuaded; so in September the Jeffreys came again unlooked for to Craigenputtoch. Carlyle was with his family at Scotsbrig.

How brilliant Jeffrey was, how he delighted them all with his anecdotes, his mockeries, and his mimicries, Carlyle has amply confessed; and he has acknowledged the serious excellence which lay behind the light exterior. It was on this occasion that he sent £50 to Hazlitt which came too late and found poor Hazlitt dying. It was on this occasion that he renewed his generous offer to lift Carlyle for a time over his difficulties out of his own purse, and when he could not prevail, promised to help John Carlyle in London, give him introductions, and if possible launch him in his profession. He charged himself with the "Literary History," carried it off with him, and undertook to recommend it to Longman. From all this Jeffrey had nothing to gain: it was but the expression of hearty good will to Carlyle himself for his own sake and for the sake of his wife, in whom he had at least an equal interest. He wrote to her as cousin: what the exact relationship was I know not; but it was near enough, as he thought, to give him a right to watch over her

welfare; and the thought of Carlyle persisting, in the face
of imminent ruin, in what to him appeared a vain hallucina-
tion, and the thought still more of this delicate woman degraded to the duties of the mistress of a farmhouse, and
obliged to face another winter in so frightful a climate, was
simply horrible to him. She had not concealed from him
that she was not happy at Craigenputtoch; and the longer
he reflected upon it the more out of humour he became with
the obstinate philosopher who had doomed her to live there
under such conditions.

It is evident from his letters that he held Carlyle to be
gravely responsible. He respected many sides of his character, but he looked on him as under the influence of a
curious but most reprehensible vanity, which would not and
could not land him anywhere but in poverty and disappointment, while all the time the world was ready and eager to
open its arms and lavish its liberality upon him if he would
but consent to walk in its ways and be like other men. In
this humour nothing that Carlyle did would please him. He
quarrelled with the "Literary History." He disliked the
views in it; he found fault with the style. After reading it,
he had to say that he did not see how he could be of use
in the obstetrical department to which he had aspired in its
behalf.

Meanwhile, and in the midst of Jeffrey's animadversions,
Carlyle himself was about to take a higher flight. "I *have* a
Book in me that will cause ears to tingle."[1] Out of his discontent, out of his impatience with the hard circumstances
which crossed, thwarted, and pressed him, there was growing in his mind *Sartor Resartus*. He had thoughts ferment-
ing in him which were struggling to be uttered. He had
something real to say about the world and man's position
in it to which, could it but find fit expression, he knew
that attention must be paid. The "clothes philosophy,"
which had perhaps been all which his first sketch contained,
gave him the necessary form. His own history, inward and
outward, furnished substance, some slight invention being
all that was needed to disguise his literal individuality; and
in the autumn of the year he set himself down passionately
to work. Fast as he could throw his ideas upon paper the
material grew upon him. The origin of the book is still trace-

able in the half fused, tumultuous condition in which the metal was poured into the mould. With all his efforts in calmer times to give it artistic harmony he could never fully succeed. "There are but a few pages in it," he said to me, "which are rightly done." It is well perhaps that he did not succeed. The incompleteness of the smelting shows all the more the actual condition of his mind. If defective as a work of art, *Sartor* is for that very reason a revelation of Carlyle's individuality.

The idea had first struck him when on a visit with Mrs. Carlyle at Templand. Customs, institutions, religious creeds, what were they but *clothes* in which human creatures covered their native nakedness, and enabled men themselves to live harmoniously and decently together? Clothes, dress, changed with the times; they grew old, they were elaborate, they were simple; they varied with fashion or habit of life; they were the outward indicators of the inward and spiritual nature. The analogy gave the freest scope and play for the wilfullest and wildest humour. The "Teufelsdröckh," which we have seen seeking in vain for admission into London magazines, was but a first rude draft. Parts of this perhaps survive as they were originally written in the opening chapters. The single article, when it was returned to him, first expanded into two; *then* he determined to make a book of it, into which he could project his entire self. The *Foreign Quarterly* continued good to him. He could count on an occasional place in *Fraser's*. The part already written of his "Literary History," slit into separate articles, would keep him alive till the book was finished. He had been well paid for his *Life of Schiller*. If the execution corresponded to the conception, then *Sartor* would be ten times better.

On the 19th of October he described what he was about to his brother:

> For myself here I am leading the stillest life; musing amid the pale sunshine, or rude winds of October Tirl[shake]-the-trees, when I go walking in this almost ghastly solitude; and for the rest, writing with impetuosity. I think it not impossible that I may see you this winter in London! I mean to come whenever I can spare the money; that I may look about me again among men for a little. . . . What I am writing at is the strangest of all things. . . . A very singular piece, I assure you! It glances from Heaven to

CARLYLE'S STUDY, CRAIGENPUTTOCH. Here he wrote *Sartor Resartus* in 1830–31. "I will speak out what is in me, tho' far harder chances threatened," Carlyle wrote to his brother John on 17 July 1831; "I must to my *Dreck*, for the hours go." (Photograph by John Patrick, courtesy of the University of Edinburgh.)

Earth & back again in a strange satirical frenzy whether *fine* or not remains to be seen.[2]

Sartor was indeed a free-flowing torrent, the outbursting of emotions which as yet had found no escape. The discontent which in a lower shape was rushing into French Revolutions, Reform Bills, Emancipation Acts, Socialism, and Bristol riots and rick burnings, had driven Carlyle into far deeper inquiries—inquiries into the how and why of these convulsions of the surface. The Hebrew spiritual robes he conceived were no longer suitable, and that this had something to do with it. The Hebrew clothes had become "old clothes"—not the fresh wrought garments adapted to man's real wants, but sold at second-hand, and gaping at all their seams. Radical also politically Carlyle was at this time. The constitution of society, as he looked at it, was unjust from end to end. The workers were starving; the idle were revelling in luxury. Radicalism, as he understood it, meant the return of Astraea—an approach to equity in the apportionment of good and evil in this world; and on the intellectual side, if not encouragement of truth, at least the withdrawal of exclusive public support of what was not true, or only partially true. He did then actually suppose that the Reform Bill meant something of that kind; that it was a genuine effort of honourable men to clear the air of imposture. He had not realised, what life afterwards taught him, that the work of centuries was not to be accomplished by a single political change, and that the Reform Bill was but a singeing of the dungheap. Even then he was no believer in the miraculous effects to be expected from an extended suffrage. He knew well enough that the welfare of the State, like the welfare of everything else, required that the wise and good should govern, and the unwise and selfish should be governed; that of all methods of discovering and promoting your wise man the voice of the mob was the least promising, and that if Reform meant only liberty, and the abolition of all authority, just or unjust, we might be worse off perhaps than we were already. But he was impatient and restless; stung no doubt by resentment at the alternative offered to himself either to become a humbug or to be beaten from the field by starvation; and the memorable epitaph on Count Zaehdarm and his achievements in this world showed in what direction his intellectual passions were running.[3]

It seems that when Jeffrey was at Craigenputtoch Carlyle must have opened his mind to him on these matters, and still more fully in some letter afterwards. Jeffrey, who was a Whig of the Whigs, who believed in liberty, but by liberty meant the right of every man to do as he pleased with his own as long as he did not interfere with his neighbour, had been made seriously angry. Mysticism was a pardonable illusion, provoking enough while it lasted, but likely to clear off, as the morning mist when the sun rises higher above the horizon; but these political views, taken up especially by a man so determined and so passionately in earnest as Carlyle, were another thing, and an infinitely more dangerous thing. Reform within moderate limits was well enough, but these new opinions if they led to anything must lead to revolution. Jeffrey believed that they were wild and impracticable; that if ever misguided missionaries of sedition could by eloquence and resolute persistence persuade the multitude to adopt notions subversive of the rights of property, the result could only be universal ruin. His regard and even esteem for Carlyle seem to have sensibly diminished from this time. He half feared him for the mischief which he might do, half gave him up as beyond help—at least as beyond help from himself. He continued friendly. He was still willing to help Carlyle within the limits which his conscience allowed, but from this moment the desire to push him forward in the politico-literary world cooled down or altogether ceased.

He tried the effect, however, of one more lecture, the traces of which are visible in *Sartor*. He had a horror of Radicalism, he said. It was nothing but the old feud against property, made formidable by the intelligence and conceit of those who had none. . . . Carlyle's views either meant the destruction of the right of property altogether, and the establishment of a universal co-operative system—and this no one in his senses could contemplate—or they were nonsense. Anything short of the abolition of property, sumptuary laws, limitation of the accumulation of fortunes, compulsory charity, or redivision of land, would not make the poor better off, but would make all poor; would lead to the destruction of all luxury, elegance, art, and intellectual culture, and reduce men to a set of savages scrambling for animal subsistence. The institution of property brought some evils with it, and a revolting spectacle of inequality. But to touch it would entail evils still greater; for though the poor suffered, their lot was only what the lot of the great mass of mankind must necessarily be under every conceivable condition. They would escape the pain of seeing others better off than they were, but they would be no better off themselves, while they would lose the mental improvement which to a certain extent spread downwards through society as long as culture existed anywhere, and at the same time the hope and chance of rising to a higher level, which was itself enjoyment even if it were never realised. Rich men after all spent most of their income on the poor. Except a small waste of food on their servants and horses, they were mere distributors among frugal and industrious workmen.

If Carlyle meant to be a politician, Jeffrey begged him to set about it modestly and patiently, and submit to study the questions a little under those who had studied them longer. If he was a Radical, why did he keep two horses himself, producing nothing and consuming the food of six human creatures, that his own diaphragm might be healthily agitated? Riding-horses interfered with the subsistence of men five hundred times more than the unfortunate partridges.[4] So again Carlyle had adopted the Radical objections to machinery. Jeffrey inquired if he meant to burn carts and ploughs—nay, even spades too, for spades were but machines? Perhaps he would end by only allowing men to work with *one* hand, that the available work might employ a larger number of persons. Yet for such aims as these Carlyle thought a Radical insurrection justifiable and its success to be desired. The very first enactments of a successful revolution would be in this spirit: the overseers of the poor would be ordered to give twelve or twenty shillings to every man who could not, or said he could not, earn as much by the labour to which he had been accustomed.

Speculations on these and kindred subjects are found scattered up and down in *Sartor*. Jeffrey was crediting Carlyle with extravagances which it is impossible that even in his then bitter humour he could have seriously entertained. He was far enough from desiring insurrection, although a conviction did lie at the very bottom of his mind that incurably unjust societies would find in insurrection and conflagration their natural consummation and end. But it is likely that he talked with fierce exaggeration on such subjects. He always did talk so. It is likely, too, that he had come to some hasty conclusions on the intractable problems of social life, and believed changes to be possible and useful which fuller knowledge of mankind showed him to be dreams. Before a just allotment of wages in this world could be arrived at—just payment according to real desert —he perceived at last that mankind must be themselves made just, and that such a transformation is no work of a political revolution. Carlyle too had been attracted to the St. Simonians. He had even in a letter to Goethe expressed some interest and hope in them; and the wise old man had warned him off from the dangerous illusion. "Von der Société St. Simonienne bitte Sich fern zu halten," Goethe had said, "From the Society of the St. Simonians I entreat you to hold yourself clear."[5] Jeffrey's practical sense had probably suggested difficulties to Carlyle which he had overlooked; and Goethe carried more weight with him than Jeffrey. Sartor may have been improved by their remonstrances; yet there lie in it the germs of all Carlyle's future teaching—a clear statement of problems of the gravest import, which cry for a solution, which insist on a solution, yet on which political economy and Whig political philosophy fail utterly to throw the slighest light. I will mention one to which Carlyle to his latest hour was continually returning. Jeffrey was a Malthusian. He had a horror and dread of over-population. Sartor answers him with a scorn which recalls Swift's famous suggestion of a remedy for the distresses of Ireland.[6]

When Carlyle published his views on "the Nigger question," his friends on both sides of the Atlantic were astonished and outraged. Yet the thought in that pamphlet and the thought in Sartor is precisely the same. When a man can be taught to work and made to work, he has a distinct value in the world appreciable by money like the value of a horse. In the state of liberty where he belongs to nobody, and his industry cannot be calculated upon, he makes his father poorer when he is born. Slavery might be a bad system, but under it a child was worth at least as much as a foal, and the master was interested in rearing it. Abolish slavery and substitute anarchy in the place of it, and the parents, themselves hardly able to keep body and soul together, will bless God when a timely fever relieves them of a troublesome charge.

This fact, for fact it is, still waits for elucidation, and I often heard Carlyle refer to it; yet he was always able to see "the other side." No Hengst or Alaric had risen in the fifty years which had passed since he had written *Sartor*; yet not long before his death he was talking to me of America and of the success with which the surplus population of Europe had been carried across the sea and distributed over that enormous continent. Frederick himself, he said, could not have done it better, even with absolute power and unlimited resources, than it had "done itself" by the mere action of unfettered liberty.

A change meanwhile came over the face of English politics. Lord Grey became Prime Minister, and Brougham Chancellor, and all Britain was wild over Reform and the coming millennium. Jeffrey went into Parliament and was rewarded for his long services by being taken into the new Government as Lord Advocate. Of course he had to remove to London, and his letters, which henceforward were addressed chiefly to Mrs. Carlyle, were filled with accounts of Cabinet meetings, dinners, Parliamentary speeches—all for the present going merry as a marriage bell. Carlyle at Craigenputtoch continued steady to his work. His money difficulties seemed likely to mend a little. Napier was overcoming his terror, and might perhaps take articles again from him for the *Edinburgh*. The new *Westminster* was open to him. The *Foreign Quarterly* had not deserted him, and between them and *Fraser's* he might still find room enough at his disposal. The "Literary History" was cut up as had been proposed; the best parts of it were published in the coming year in the form of Essays, and now constitute the greater part of the third volume of the *Miscellanies*. A second paper on Schiller, and another on Jean Paul, both of which had been for some time seeking in vain for an editor who would take them, were admitted into the *Foreign Review* and *Fraser's*. Sufficient money was thus ultimately obtained to secure the household from starvation. But some months passed before these arrangements could be completed, and *Sartor* had to go on with the prospect still gloomy in the extreme. Irving had seen and glanced over the first sketch of it when it was in London, and had sent a favourable opinion.

Alick Carlyle was to leave Craigenputtoch at Whitsuntide, a neighbouring grazier having offered the full rent for the farm, which Alick was unable to afford.[7] Where he was to go and what was to become of him was the great family anxiety.

Both brothers were virtually thrown upon his hands, while he seemingly was scarce able to take care of himself and his wife. When Alick was gone he and she would be left "literally *unter vier Augen* [to ourselves], alone among the whinstone desarts; within fifteen miles not one creature that we can so much as speak to";[8] and *Sartor* was to be written under such conditions. Another winter at Craigenputtoch in absolute solitude was a prospect too formidable to be faced. They calculated that with the utmost economy they might have £50 in hand by the end of the summer; "Teufelsdröckh" could by that time be finished. Mrs. Carlyle could stay and take care of Craigenputtoch, while Carlyle himself would visit "the great Beehive and Waspnest"[9] of London, find a publisher for his book, and then see whether there was any other outlook for him.

Meanwhile the affairs of the poor Doctor were coming to extremity. Excellent advice might be given from Craigenputtoch; but advice now was all that could be afforded. Even his magazine articles, for which he had been rebuked for writing, could not be sold after all. It was time clearly for a *deus ex mâchina* to appear and help him. Happily there was a *deus* in London able and willing to do it in the shape of Jeffrey. Though he had failed in inducing Carlyle to accept pecuniary help from him, he could not be prevented from assisting his brother, and giving him or lending him some subvention till something better could be arranged. Here, too, Carlyle's pride took alarm. It was pain and humiliation to him that any member of his family should subsist on the bounty of a stranger. He had a just horror of debt. The unlucky John himself fell in for bitter observations upon his indolence. John, he said, should come down to Scotland and live with him. There was shelter for him and food enough, such as it was. He did not choose that a brother of his should be degraded by accepting obligations. But this time Jeffrey refused to listen. It might be very wrong, he admitted, for a man to sit waiting by the pool till an angel stirred the water, but it was not necessarily right therefore that because he could not immediately find employment in his profession, he should renounce his chances and sit down to eat potatoes and read German at Craigenputtoch. He had no disposition to throw away money without a prospect of doing good with it, but he knew no better use to which it could be put than in floating an industrious man over the shoals into a fair way of doing good for himself. Even towards Carlyle, angry as he had been, his genuine kindness obliged him to relent. If only he would not be so impracticable and so arrogant! If only he could be persuaded that he was not an inspired being, and destined to be the founder of a new religion! But a solitary life and a bad stomach had so spoilt him, all but the heart, that he despaired of being able to mend him.

Jeffrey was so evidently sincere that even Carlyle could object no longer on his brother's account. "My Pride," he said, "were true Pride, savage, satanic and utterly damnable, if it offered any opposition to such a project, where my own Brother and his future happiness may be concerned."[10] Jeffrey did not mean to confine himself to immediate assistance with his purse. He was determined to find, if possible, some active work for John. Nothing could be done immediately, for he was obliged to leave London on election business. Help in money at least was to be given as soon as he returned.

At Craigenputtoch the most desperate pinch was not yet over. One slip of the "Literary History" came out in the April number of the *Edinburgh* in the form of a review of Taylor's *Historic Survey of German Poetry*, but payment for it was delayed or forgotten. Meanwhile the farm-horses had been sold. Old Larry, doing double duty on the road and in the cart, had laid himself down and died—died from overwork.[11] So clever was Larry, so humorous, that it was as if the last human friend had been taken away. The pony had been parted with also, though it was recovered afterwards; and before payment came from Napier for the article they were in real extremity. Alick by his four years of occupation was out of pocket £300. These were the saddest days which Carlyle had ever known.

The summer came, and the Dunscore moors grew beautiful in the dry warm season. "So still, so pure are the air, the foliage, the herbage and everything round us," that he said, he "might (if Arcadianly given) almost fancy that the yellow butter-cups were Asphodel, and the whole scene a portion of Hades—some outskirt of the Elysian portion. . . . the very perfection of solitude."[12] Between the softness of the scene and the apparent hopelessness of his prospects, Carlyle's own heart seems for a moment to have failed. He wrote to Jeffrey in extreme depression, as if he felt he had lost the game, and that there was nothing for it but to turn cynic and live and die in silence. The letter I have not seen, and I do not know whether it has been preserved, but Jeffrey's answer shows what the tone of it must have been. "The cynic tub," "the primitive lot of man," Jeffrey frankly called an unseemly and unworthy romance. If Carlyle did not care for himself, he ought to think of his young and delicate wife, whose great heart and willing martyrdom would make the sacrifice more agonising in the end. It was not necessary. He should have aid—effective aid; and if he pleased he might repay it some day ten times over. Something should be found for him to do neither unglorious nor unprofitable. He was fit for many things, and there were more tasks in the world fit for him than he was willing to believe. He complimented him on his last article in the *Edinburgh*. Empson had praised it warmly. Macaulay and several others, who had laughed at his "Signs of the Times," had been struck with its force and originality. If he would but give himself fair play, if he could but believe that men might differ from him without being in damnable error, he would make his way to the front without difficulty. If Jeffrey had been the most tender of brothers he could not have written more kindly. Carlyle if one of the proudest was also one of the humblest of mortals. He replied that he "felt ready to work at ANY honest thing whatsoever"; that he "did not see that Literature could support an *honest* man otherwise than *à la Diogenes.*" In this fashion he "meant to experiment, if *nothing* else could be found, which however, thro all channels of investigation, I was minded to try."[13]

It is not easy to see precisely what kind of employment Jeffrey had really in view for Carlyle. At one time no doubt he had thought of recommending him strongly to the Government. At another he had confessedly thought of him as his own successor on the *Edinburgh Review*. But he had been frightened at Carlyle's Radicalism. He had been offended at his arrogance. Perhaps he thought that it indicated fundamental unsoundness of mind. He little conjectured that the person for whom he was concerning himself was really one of the most remarkable men in Europe, destined to make a deeper impression upon his contemporaries than any thinker then alive. This was not to be expected; but it must be supposed that he was wishing rather to try the sincerity of Carlyle's professions than that he was really serious in what he now suggested. He gave a list of possible situations: a clerkship at the Excise or the Board of Longitude or the Record Office, or a librarianship at the British Museum, or some secretaryship in a merchant's house of business. He asked him which of these he would detest the least, that he might know before he applied for it.

Poor Carlyle! It was a bitter draught which was being commended to his lips. But he was very meek; he answered that he would gratefully accept any one of them; but even such posts as these he thought in his despondency to be beyond his reach. He was like the pilgrim in the valley of humiliation. "I do not expect," he told John, "that he will be able to accomplish anything for me. I must even get thro' life *without a trade*, always in poverty, as far better men have done. Our want is the want of *Faith*. Jesus of Nazareth was not poor tho' he had not where to lay his head. Socrates was rich enough.— I have a deep, irrevocable all-comprehending Ernulphus Curse to read upon—GIGMAN-ITY; that is the Baal Worship of this time."[14]

The picture of Carlyle's condition—poor, almost without hope, the companions which had made the charm of his solitude—his brother Alick, his horse Larry—all gone or going, the place itself disenchanted—has now a peculiar interest, for it was under these conditions that *Sartor Resartus* was composed. A wild sorrow sounds through its sentences like the wind over the strings of an aeolian harp. Pride, too, at intervals fiercely defiant, yet yielding to the inevitable, as if the stern lesson had done its work. Carlyle's pride needed breaking. His reluctance to allow his brother to accept help from Jeffrey had only plunged him into worse perplexities. John had borrowed money, hoping that his articles would enable him to repay it. The articles had not been accepted, and the hope had proved a quicksand. Other friends were willing to lend what was required, but he would take nothing more; and the only resource left was to draw again upon Carlyle's almost exhausted funds.

Once more [to John] on the 17th of the same month:

> I am labouring at *Teufel* with considerable impetuosity and calculate that unless accidents intervene, I may be actually ready to get under way about the end of the month. But there will not be a minute to lose. I sometimes think the Book *will* prove a kind of medicinal Assafoetida for the pudding Stomach of England, and produce new secretions there. *Iacta est alea* [The die is cast]! I will speak out what is in me, tho' far harder chances threatened. I have no other trade, no other strength, or portion in this Earth. Be it so. . . . Courage! Courage! *Tapferkeit*, "deliberate valour" is God's highest gift, and comes not without trial to any. Times will mend: or if Times never mend, then in the Devil's name, let them stay as they are, or grow worse, and *we* will mend.— I know but one true wretchedness, the Want of Work (Want of Wages is comparatively trifling); which want, however, in such a world as this Planet of ours, *cannot* be permanent—unless we continue blind therein. . . . I must to my *Dreck*, for the hours go: *Gott mit Dir* [God be with you]![15]

It was a sad, stern time to these struggling brothers; and it is with a feeling like what the Scots mean by *wae* that one reads the letters that Jeffrey was writing during the worst of it to Mrs. Carlyle. He had done what he was allowed to do. Perhaps he thought they understood their own matters best; and it was not easy to thrust his services on so proud a person as Mrs. Carlyle's husband, when they were treated so cavalierly; but he did not choose to let the correspondence fall, and to her he continued to write lightly and brilliantly on London gaieties and his own exploits in the

House of Commons. The tone of these letters must have been out of harmony with the heavy hearts at Craigenputtoch, but he was still acting as a real friend and remained on the watch for opportunities to be of use, if not to Carlyle himself, yet at least to his brother.

So July ran out and *Sartor* was finished, and Carlyle prepared to start, with the manuscript and the yet unpublished sections of the "Literary History" in his portmanteau, to find a publisher for one or both of them; to find also, if possible, some humble employment to which his past work might have recommended him; to launch himself, at any rate, into the great world, and light on something among its floating possibilities to save him from drowning, which of late had seemed likely to be his fate. With Craigenputtoch as a home he believed that he had finally done. The farm which was to have helped him to subsist had proved a failure, and had passed to strangers. Living retired in those remote moorlands, he had experienced too painfully that from articles in reviews he could count on no regular revenue, while the labour lost in the writing led to nothing. Work of such a kind, if it was to be profitable, must become an intellectual prostitution and to escape from this was the chief object of his London journey. He had so far swallowed his pride as to accept after all a loan of £50 from Jeffrey for his expenses. The sums due to him would provide food and lodging during his stay. Such hopes as he still may have entertained of the realisation of his old dream of making a mark in the world lay in the manuscript of *Sartor*. "It is a work of genius, dear," Mrs. Carlyle said to him as she finished the last page—she whose judgement was unerring, who flattered no one, and least of all her husband. A work of genius! Yes; but of genius so original that a conventional world, measuring by established rules, could not fail to regard it as a monster. Originality, from the necessity of its nature, offends at its first appearance. Certain ways of acting, thinking, and speaking are in possession of the field and claim to be the only legitimate ways. A man of genius strikes into a road of his own, and the first estimate of such a man has been, is, and always will be, unfavourable. Carlyle knew that he had done his best, and he knew the

261

worth of it. He had yet to learn how hard a battle still lay ahead of him before that worth could be recognised by others. Jeffrey compared him to Parson Adams going to seek his fortune with his manuscript in his pocket. Charles Buller, more hopeful, foretold gold and glory. Jeffrey, at any rate, had made it possible for him to go; and, let it be added, John Carlyle, notwithstanding his struggles to avoid obligations, had been forced to accept pecuniary help from the same kind hand.

chapter thirteen

1831–1832

Eight Months in London

[On 4 August Carlyle left Craigenputtoch and, after taking several coaches and enduring various adventures, arrived in London on the tenth. For a while it seemed as if the prestigious house of Murray might, on the strength of Jeffrey's recommendation, publish *Sartor*. In London Carlyle saw old friends again with varying degrees of satisfaction: Mrs. Strachey, Charles Buller, Irving, Badams, Allan Cunningham, the Montagus. He met Godwin and Sir John Bowring. Murray delayed a decision on *Sartor*—it turned out that he never read the manuscript—and Carlyle in disgust finally took it back. Fraser offered to publish it—but only if Carlyle would "give *him* a sum not exceeding £150 sterling!" Carlyle refused, "strode thro' these streets, carrying Teufelsdreck openly in my hand,"[1] and took it to Longman, who also declined it. Jeffrey consented to take charge of the manuscript and promised to try to persuade Murray to look at it again.]

Carlyle, little sanguine as he was, had a right to be surprised at the difficulty of finding a publisher for his book. Seven years before he had received a hundred pounds for his *Life of Schiller*. It had been successful in England. It had been translated into German under the eye of Goethe himself. *Sartor* Carlyle reckoned to be at least three times as good, and no one seemed inclined to look at it.

Meanwhile, on another side of his affairs the prospect unexpectedly brightened. His brother had been the heaviest of his anxieties. A great lady, the Countess of Clare, was going abroad and required a travelling physician. Jeffrey heard of it, and with more real practical kindness than Carlyle in his impatience had been inclined to credit him with, successfully recommended John Carlyle to her. The arrangements were swiftly concluded. The struggling, penniless John was lifted at once into a situation of responsibility and security, with a salary [300 guineas a year] which placed him far beyond need of further help, and promised to enable him to repay at no distant time both his debt to Jeffrey, and all the money which Carlyle had laid out for him. Here was more than compensation for the other disappointments. Not only Carlyle had no longer to feel that he must divide his poor earnings to provide for his brother's wants in London, but he could look without anxiety on his own situation. He even thought himself permitted, instead of returning to Craigenputtoch, to propose that Mrs. Carlyle should join him in London without the help of Mrs. Montagu. He was making friends; he was being talked about as a new phenomenon of a consequence as yet unknown. Review and magazine editors were recovering heart, and again seeking his assistance. He could write his articles as well in a London lodging as in the snowy solitudes of Dunscore, while he could look about him and weigh at more leisure the possibilities of finally removing thither.

[Murray finally agreed to] "print a small edition (750 copies) of *Dreck*, on the half-profits system (that is I getting *nothing*, but also *giving* nothing) after which the sole copyright of the Book is to be mine. Which offer he makes partly out of love to 'your Ludship [Jeffrey],' chiefly from 'my great opinion of the originality' &c &c."[2]

Anticipating slightly, I may finish here the adventures of *Sartor* or *Dreck*, and for the present have done with it. Murray at Jeffrey's instance had agreed to take the book on the terms which Carlyle mentioned—not, however, particularly willingly. Jeffrey himself, who had good practical knowledge of such things, thought that it was "too much of the nature of a rhapsody to command success or respectful attention."[3] Murray perhaps rather wished to attach to himself a young man of unquestionable genius, whose works might be profitable hereafter, than expected much from this immediate enterprise. He decided to run the risk, however. The manuscript was sent to the printer, and a page was set in type for consideration, when poor Murray, already repenting of what he had done, heard that while he was hesitating *Sartor* had been offered to Longman, and had been declined by him. He snatched at the escape, and tried to end his bargain. He professed to think, and perhaps he really thought, that he had been treated unfairly.

[Several exchanges of letters followed, Murray declining to print *Sartor* until he could "get it read by some literary friend,"[4] Carlyle replying formally that if Murray repented of his bargain he could return the manuscript.]

The result was the letter from the "bookseller," enclosing the critical communication from his literary adviser, which Carlyle with pardonable malice attached as an Appendix to *Sartor* when it was ultimately published, and which has been thus preserved as a singular evidence of critical fallibility. But neither is Murray to be blamed in the matter nor his critic. Their business was to ascertain whether the book, if published, would pay for the printing; and it was quite certain, both that the taste which could appreciate Carlyle did not exist till he himself created it, and that to *Sartor*, beautiful and brilliant as it now seems, the world would then have remained blind. Carlyle himself, proud, scornful, knowing if no one else knew the value of the estimate of "the gentleman in the highest class of men of letters"[5] who had been consulted in the matter, judged Murray after his fashion far too harshly.

Carlyle was not alone in his contempt for the existing literary taste. Macvey Napier, to whom he had expressed an opinion that the public had been for some time "fed with froth," and was getting tired of it, agreed that he saw "no indications in that vast body, of any appetite for solid aliments." Nay, he added, I "am thoroughly convinced, that were another Gibbon to appear, & produce another such work as the *Decline & Fall*, the half of an impression of 750 copies would be left to load the shelves of its Publisher."[6]

The article on Luther which Carlyle had offered for the *Edinburgh* could not get itself accepted. Napier recognised that Luther was a noble subject, but he could not spare space for the effective treatment of it. He recommended instead a review of Thomas Hope's book on Man; and Carlyle, accepting the change, made Hope the text for the paper which he called "Characteristics." This essay, more profound and far-reaching even than *Sartor*, was written in these autumn weeks in London.

Mrs. Carlyle arrived in London on the first of October, a good deal shattered by the journey and the charge of the miscellaneous cargo of luggage which she had brought with her: oatmeal, hams, butter, etc., supplied by the generous Scotsbrig to lighten the expense of the London winter. George Irving's lodgings, being found to contain bugs, were exchanged for others. John Carlyle departed with Lady Clare for Italy. Carlyle and his wife quartered themselves at Ampton Street, turning out of Gray's Inn Road, where they had two comfortable rooms in the house of an excellent family named Miles, who belonged to Irving's congregation. Here friends came to see them: Mill, Empson, later on Leigh Hunt, drawn by the article on Hope ("Characteristics") which Carlyle was now assiduously writing, Jeffrey, and afterwards many more, the Carlyles going out into society, and reconnoitring literary London. Mrs. Carlyle in her way was as brilliant as her husband was in his own; she attracting every one, he wondered at as a prodigy, which the world was yet uncertain whether it was to love or execrate.

[Among those Carlyle met was Charles Lamb, whom he judged harshly:]

Charles Lamb I sincerely believe to be in some considerable degree *insane*. A more pitiful, rickety, grasping, staggering, stammering Tom fool I do not know. He is witty by denying truisms, and abjuring good manners. His speech wriggles hither and thither with an incessant painful fluctuation; not an opinion in it or a fact or even a phrase that you can thank him for: more like a convulsion fit than natural systole and diastole. —Besides he is now a confirmed shameless drunkard; *asks* vehemently for gin-and-water in strangers houses; tipples till he is utterly mad, and is only not thrown out of doors because he is too much despised for taking such trouble with him. Poor Lamb! Poor England where such a despicable abortion is named genius! —He said: There are just two things I regret in English History; first that Guy Faux's Plot did not take effect (there would have been so glorious an *explo-*

sion); second, that the Royalists did not hang Milton (then we might have laughed at them); &c. &c. *Armer Teufel* [*poor devil*]!⁷

Carlyle did not know at this time the tragedy lying behind the life of Charles Lamb, which explained or extenuated his faults. Yet this extravagantly harsh estimate is repeated—scarcely qualified—in a sketch written nearly forty years after.

> Among the scrambling miscellany of notables and quasi-notables that hovered about us, Leigh Hunt . . . was probably the best; poor Charles Lamb . . . the worst. He was sinking into drink, poor creature; his fraction of "humour" &c I recognised, and recognise, but never could accept for a great thing,—genuine, but an essentially small and *Cockney* thing;—and now with *gin* &c superadded, one had to say, "Genius"? This is not *genius*, but *diluted insanity*: please remove this![8]

The gentle Elia deserved a kinder judgement. Carlyle considered "humour" to be the characteristic of the highest order of mind. He had heard Lamb extravagantly praised, perhaps, for this particular quality, and he was provoked to find it combined with habits which his own stern Calvinism was unable to tolerate.

[Edward Irving was, in Carlyle's eyes, well advanced on the long road of his decline. Carlyle wrote to his mother:]

> I daresay you have not yet seen in the newspapers, but will soon see something extraordinary about poor Edward Irving. His friends here are all much grieved about him. For many months, he has been puddling and muddling in the midst of certain insane jargoning of hysterical women, and crackbrained enthusiasts, who start up from time to time in public companies, and utter confused Stuff, mostly "Ohs" and "Ahs" and absurd interjections about "the Body of Jesus"; they also pretend to "work miracles," and have raised more than one weak bedrid woman, and cured people of "Nerves," or as they themselves say, "cast Devils out of them." All which poor Irving is pleased to consider as the "work of the Spirit"; and to *janner* [talk foolishly] about at great length, as making *his* Church the peculiarly blessed of Heaven, and equal to or greater than the primitive one at Corinth! This, greatly to my sorrow, and that of many, has gone on privately for a good while, with increasing vigour; but last Sabbath, it burst out publickly in the open Church; for one of the "Prophetesses" (a woman on the verge of derangement) started up in the time of worship, and began to "speak with tongues"; and as the thing was encouraged by Irving, there were some three or four fresh hands who started up in the evening sermon, and began their ragings;

267

whereupon the whole congregation got into foul uproar, some groaning, some laughing, some shrieking, not a few falling into swoons: more like a Bedlam than a Christian Church.[9]

Carlyle did attempt, as he has related in the *Reminiscences*, and as he tells in his letters,[10] to drag Irving back from the precipice; but it proved as vain as he had feared; and all that he could do was but to stand aside and watch the ruin of his true and noble-minded friend. The last touch was added to the tragedy by the presence of Mrs. Carlyle to witness the catastrophe.

Meanwhile London was filling again after the holidays; and the autumn brought back old faces of other friends whom Carlyle was glad to see again. The Bullers were among the earliest arrivals. Charles Buller, then beginning his brief and brilliant career, was an advanced Radical in politics, and equally advanced in matters of speculation. He had not yet found a creed, as he had said, which he could even wish to believe true. He had a generous scorn of affectation, and did not choose, like many of his contemporaries, to wear a mask of veiled hypocrisy. The hen is terrified when the ducklings she has hatched take to water. Mrs. Buller, indeed, shared her son's feelings and felt no alarm; but her sister, Mrs. Strachey, who, a good religious woman, was shocked at a freedom less common then than it is now, because it could be less safely avowed, and in despair of help from the professional authorities, to whom she knew that her nephew would not listen, she turned to Carlyle, whose opinions she perhaps imperfectly understood, but of whose piety of heart she was assured.

Carlyle was extremely fond of Charles Buller. He was the only person of distinction or promise of distinction with whom he came in contact that he heartily admired; and he, too, had regretted to see his old pupil rushing off into the ways of agnosticism. Well he knew that no man ever came, or ever could come, to any greatness in this world in irreverent occupation with the mere phenomena of earth. The agnostic doctrines, he once said to me, were to appearance like the finest flour, from which you might expect the most excellent bread; but when you came to feed on it you found it was powdered glass and you had been eating the deadliest poison. What he valued in Buller was his hatred of cant, his frank contempt of insincere professions. But refusal even to appear to conform with opinions which the world holds it decent to profess, is but the clearing of the soil from weeds. Carlyle, without waiting to be urged by Mrs. Strachey, had long been labouring to sow the seeds in Buller of a nobler belief; but a faith which can stand the wear and tear of work cannot be taught like a mathematical problem, and if Carlyle had shown Mrs. Strachey the condition of his own mind, she would scarcely have applied to him for assistance. Buller died before it had been seen to what seed sown such a mind as his might eventually have grown.

A great catastrophe was now impending in Carlyle's life. His father had been ailing for more than two years, sometimes recovering a little, then relapsing again; and after each oscillation he had visibly sunk to a lower level. The family anticipated no immediate danger, but he had himself been steadily contemplating the end as fast approaching him.

The old man at parting with his son in the summer gave him some money out of a drawer with the peculiar manner which the Scotch call *fey*—the sign of death when a man does something which is unlike himself. Carlyle paid no particular attention to it, however, till the meaning of the unusual action was afterwards made intelligible to him. The reports from Scotsbrig in the autumn and early winter had been more favourable than usual.

Napier unexpectedly and even gratefully accepted "Characteristics." He confessed that he could not understand it; but everything which Carlyle wrote, he said, had the indisputable stamp of genius upon it, and was therefore most welcome to the *Edinburgh Review*. Lytton Bulwer pressed for an article on Frederick the Great; [Abraham] Hayward was anxious that a final article should be written on Goethe, to punish Wilson for his outrages against the great German in the *Noctes Ambrosianae*. Hayward, too, had done Carlyle a still more seasonable service, for he had induced Dr. Lardner to promise to take Carlyle's "History of German Literature" for the *Cabinet Encyclopaedia*. The articles on the subject which had al-

269

ready appeared were to form part of it; some new matter was to be added to round off the story; and the whole was to be bound up into a *Zur Geschichte* [*Historical Sketch*], for which Carlyle was to receive £300. To Hayward then and always he was heartily grateful for this piece of service, though eventually, as will be seen, it came to nothing. These brightening prospects were saddened by the deaths of various eminent persons whom he held in honour. Dr. Becker died of cholera at Berlin, then Hegel from cholera also; and still worse, his old friend Mr. Strachey, whom he had met lately in full health, was seized with inflammation of the lungs, and was carried off in a few days.

Worst of all—the worse because entirely unlooked for—came fatal news from Scotsbrig [announcing the death of his father on 22 January 1832].

> Fie! 'tis a fault to heaven,
> A fault against the dead, a fault to nature,
> To reason most absurd, whose common theme
> Is death of fathers, and who still hath cried,
> From the first corse till he that died to-day,
> "This must be so."[11]

Yet being so common, it was still "particular" to Carlyle. The entire family were knit together with an extremely peculiar bond. Their affections, if not limited within their own circle, yet were reserved for one another in their tenderest form. Friendship the Carlyles might have for others; their love was for those of their own household; while again, independently of his feeling as a son, Carlyle saw, or believed he saw, in his father personal qualities of the rarest and loftiest kind. Though the old man had no sense of poetry, Carlyle deliberately says that if he had been asked whether his father or Robert Burns had the finest intellect, he could not have answered. Carlyle's style, which has been so much wondered at, was learnt in the Annandale farmhouse; and beyond the intellect there was an inflexible integrity, in word and deed, which Carlyle honoured above all human qualities. The aspect in which he regarded human life, the unalterable conviction that justice and truth are the only bases on which successful conduct, either private or public, can be safely rested, he had derived from his father, and it was the root of all that was great in himself. Being unable to be present at the funeral, he spent the intervening days in composing the memoir which has been published as the first of his *Reminiscences*.[12]

A few weeks only now remained of Carlyle's stay in London. The great change at Scotsbrig recommended, and perhaps required, his presence in Scotland. His brother Alick had finally left Craigenputtoch to settle on a farm elsewhere, and the house on the moor could not be left unprotected. In London itself he had nothing further to detain him. He had failed in the object which had chiefly brought him there. *Sartor Resartus* had to lie unpublished in his desk. On the other hand, he had made new and valuable acquaintances—John Mill, Leigh Hunt, Hayward, Lytton Bulwer—for the first three of whom at least he entertained considerable respect. He had been courted more than ever by magazines. Owing to the effect of his personal presence, he had as much work before him as he was able to undertake, and by Hayward's help Dr. Lardner was likely to accept on favourable terms his "Literary History." He had learnt, once for all, that of promotion to any fixed employment there was no hope for him. Literature was and was to be the task of his life. But the doubt of being able to maintain himself honourably by it was apparently removed. His thrifty farmhouse habits made the smallest certain income sufficient for his wants. His wife had parted cheerfully with the luxuries in which she had been bred, and was the most perfect of economical stewardesses. His brother John was now in circumstances to repay the cost of his education, and thus for two years at least he saw his way clearly before him. Some editorship or share of editorship might have been attainable had he cared to seek such a thing; but the conditions of the London literary profession disinclined him to any close connection with it; and he had adjusted his relations with Napier, Fraser, Lytton Bulwer, and the rest, on terms more satisfactory to himself than complimentary to them. With Napier he was on a really pleasant footing. The "Characteristics" had been published without a word being altered or omitted. He liked Napier, and excepted him from his general censures. He was now writing his review of Croker's [edition of Boswell's] *Life of Johnson*, which he had promised Fraser as

Yours faithfully,

T. Carlyle.

THOMAS CARLYLE IN 1832. Pencil drawing, showing him full length leaning against a pillar, made by Daniel Maclise (signed "Alfred Croquis del*t*") for inclusion in the series of portraits of contributors to *Fraser's Magazine*. Carlyle was a frequent contributor at this time, and *Sartor* first appeared in the journal in 1833–34. At first Carlyle thought that Maclise's drawing had "little or no resemblance: except in the hair, coat, and boots." Later he found that it "had a very considerable likeness. Done from life in Fraser's back-parlour in about twenty minutes." (From an engraving in the editor's possession.)

the last piece of work which he was to do in London. "So this is the way I have adjusted myself," he wrote: "I say, will *you* or your Dog's carrion-cart take this Article of mine, and sell it *unchanged*? With the Carrion-cart itself I have and can have no personal concern. For Fraser I am partly bound as to this piece on *Johnson*: Bulwer if he want anything on similar terms, and I feel unoccupied, he shall have it; otherwise not."[13] In such scornful humour he prepared to retreat once more for another two years to his whinstone castle, and turn his back on London and the literary world.

My *attitude* towards literary London is almost exactly what I could wish: great respect, even love from some few; much matter of thought given me for instruction and high edification by the very baseness and ignorance of the many. . . . I dined at Magazine Fraser[']s some five weeks ago; saw Lockhart, Galt, Cunningham, Hogg: G[alt] has since sent me a Book (new, and worth little)[;] he is a broad gawsie Greenock man, old-growing, loveable with pity: L[ockhart] a dandiacal not without force, but barren and unfruitful; Hogg utterly a singing *Goose*, whom also I pitied and loved. The conversation was about the basest I ever assisted in. The Scotch here afterwards got up a brutish thing by way of "Burns's dinner," which has since been called the "Hogg dinner"; to the number of 500: famished Gluttony, Quackery and Stupidity were the elements of the work, which has been laughed at much. . . . Procter regards me as a proud Mystic; I him (mostly) as a worn-out Dud: so we walk on separate roads. The other Montagues are mostly mere *simulacra*, and not edifying ones. Peace be to all such. . . . Of male favourites Mill stands at the top: Jeffrey from his levity a good deal lower; yet he is ever kind, and pleasant to see hopping round one. . . . I saw Irving yesternight. . . . He is still goodnatured and patient; but enveloped in the vain sound of the "Tongues": I am glad to think he will not go utterly *mad* (not madder than a Don Quixote was); but his intellect seems quietly settling into a superstitious *caput mortuum*; he has no longer any opinion to deliver worth listening to on any secular matter.[14]

chapter fourteen

1832–1833

Later Years at Craigenputtoch

The Carlyles left London on the 25th of March. They returned to Scotland by Liverpool, staying a few days with
Mr. Welsh in Maryland Street, and then going on as they
had come by the Annan steamer. Mrs. Carlyle suffered
frightfully from sea-sickness. She endured the voyage for
economy's sake; but she was in bad health and in worse
spirits. The Craigenputtoch exile, dreary and disheartening,
was again to be taken up; the prospect of release once
more clouded over. Her life was the dreariest of slaveries
to household cares and toil. She was without society, except on an occasional visit from a sister-in-law or a rare
week or so with her mother at Templand. Carlyle, intensely occupied with his thoughts and his writing, was unable to bear the presence of a second person when busy at
his desk. He sat alone, walked alone, generally rode alone.
It was necessary for him some time or other in the day to
discharge in talk the volume of thought which oppressed
him. But it was in vehement soliloquy, to which his wife
listened with admiration perhaps, but admiration dulled by
the constant repetition of the dose, and without relief or
comfort from it. The evenings in London, with the brilliant
little circle which had gathered about them, served only to
intensify the gloom of the desolate moor, which her nerves,
already shattered with illness, were in no condition to encounter. Carlyle observed these symptoms less than he
ought to have done. His own health, fiercely as at times he
complained of it, was essentially robust. He was doing his

own duty with his utmost energy. His wife considered it to be part of hers to conceal from him how hard her own share of the burden had become. Her high principles enabled her to go through with it; but the dreams of intellectual companionship with a man of genius in which she had entered on her marriage had long disappeared; and she settled down into her place again with a heavy heart. Her courage never gave way; but she had a bad time of it. They stayed a fortnight at Scotsbrig, where they heard the news of Goethe's death. At the middle of April they were on the moor once more, and Carlyle was again at his work. The "Characteristics" and the article on Johnson had been received with the warmest admiration from the increasing circle of young intellectual men who were looking up to him as their teacher, and with wonder and applause from the reading London world. He sat down with fresh heart to new efforts. "The Death of Goethe" was written immediately on his return for Lytton Bulwer. *Das Mährchen,* "The Tale," so called in Germany, as if there were no other fit to be compared with it, was translated for *Fraser's* with its singular explanatory notes. His great concluding article on Goethe himself, on Goethe's position and meaning in European history, had to be written next for the *Foreign Quarterly*; another for the *Edinburgh* on Ebenezer Elliott, the Corn-law Rhymer; and lastly the essay on Diderot, for which he had been collecting materials in London. He had added to his correspondents the new friend John Mill, between whom and himself there had sprung up an ardent attachment.

His letters to Mill are not preserved, but Mill's to him remain.[1] Between Jeffrey and Mrs. Carlyle also the communication began again, Mrs. Carlyle apparently telling her cousin more of her inner state of feeling than she pleased to show to anyone else. Jeffrey had been an almost daily visitor in Ampton Street: he saw and felt for her situation, he regarded himself as, in a sense, her guardian, and he insisted that she should keep him regularly informed of her condition. In London he had observed that she was extremely delicate; that the prospect of a return to Craigenputtoch was intolerable to her. Carlyle's views and Carlyle's actions provoked him more and more. He thought him as visionary as the Astronomer in *Rasselas,* and confessed that he was irritated at seeing him throwing away his talent and his prospects.

Carlyle, after his reception in London circles, was less than ever inclined to listen to Jeffrey's protests. If in the midst of his speculations he could have spared a moment to study his wife's condition, the state of things at Craigenputtoch might have been less satisfactory to him. He was extremely fond of her: more fond, perhaps, of her than of any other living person except his mother. But it was his peculiarity, that if matters were well with himself, it never occurred to him that they could be going ill with anyone else; and, on the other hand, if he was uncomfortable, he required everybody to be uncomfortable along with him. After a week of restlessness he was at his work in vigorous spirits—especially happy because he found that he could supply Larry's place, and again afford to keep a horse.

Pleasant letters came from London. John Mill, young, ingenuous, and susceptible, had been profoundly impressed by Carlyle. He had an instinct for recognising truth in any form in which it might be presented to him. Charles Buller had foretold that although Mill's and Carlyle's methods of thought were as wide asunder as the poles, they would understand and appreciate each other. They sympathised in a common indignation at the existing condition of society, in a common contempt for the insincere professions with which men were veiling from themselves and from one another their emptiness of spiritual belief; and neither Mill nor Carlyle as yet realised how far apart their respective principles would eventually draw them. The review of Boswell's *Life of Johnson* had delighted Mill. He had read it so often that he could almost repeat it from end to end. He recognised the immense superiority of intellectual honesty to intellectual power. He recognised the shallowness and feebleness of modern thought in the midst of its cant of progress. He professed himself a humble disciple of Carlyle, eager to be convinced (which as yet he admitted that he was not) of the greatness of Goethe; eager to admit with innocent modesty Carlyle's own superiority to himself.

[His Journal] shows how powerfully Carlyle's intellect was working, how he was cutting out an original road for himself, far away from the Radicalism of the day. But it is in the nature of such thoughts that they draw off a man's attention from what is round him, and prevent him from attending to the thousand little things and the many great things of which the commonplaces of life are composed. Vocal as he was—pouring out whatever was in him in a stream of talk for hours together—he was not the cheerfullest of companions. He spoke much of *hope,* but he was never hopeful. The world was not moving to his mind. His anticipations were habitually gloomy. The persons with whom he had come in contact fell short of the demands which the sternness of his temper was inclined to make on them, from the drudge who had ill-cleaned a vegetable dish, to the man of letters who had written a silly article, or the Phaeton who was driving the State chariot through the wrong constellations. Thus, although indigestion, which interfered with his working, recalled his impatience to himself, he could leave his wife to ill-health and toil, assuming that all was well as long as she did not complain; and it was plain to every one of her friends, before it was suspected by her husband, that the hard, solitary life on the moor was trying severely both her constitution and her nerves.

Carlyle saw, and yet was blind. If she suffered she concealed her trials from him, lest his work should suffer also. But she took refuge in a kind of stoicism, which was but a thin disguise for disappointment and at times for misery. It was a sad fate for a person so bright and gifted; and if she could endure it for herself, others, and especially Jeffrey, were not inclined to endure it for her. Jeffrey had been often in Ampton Street, claiming the privileged intimacy of a cousin.[2] Eyes so keen as the Lord Advocate's could not fail to see how things were going with her. She herself perhaps did not hide from him that the thought of being again immured in Craigenputtoch was horrible to her. Liking and even honouring Carlyle as he did, he did not like his faults, and the Lord Advocate was slightly irritated at the reception which Carlyle had met with in London, as tending to confirm him in the illusion that he was a prophet of a new religion. He continued to write to Mrs. Carlyle tenderly and even passionately, as he would have written to a daughter

277

of his own. It was intolerable to him to think of her with her fine talents lost to all the enjoyments that belonged to her age and character, and provoking to feel that it was owing to moody fancies too long cherished, and fantastic opinions engendered and fed in solitude. She made the best of her position, as she always did.

To him his cousin's situation had no relieving feature, for he believed that Carlyle was entered on a course which would end only less ruinously than Irving's—that he was sacrificing his own prospects, as well as his wife's happiness, to arrogant illusions. The fact was not as Jeffrey saw it. Carlyle was a knight errant, on the noblest quest which can animate a man. He was on the right road, though it was a hard one; but the lot of the poor lady who was dragged along at his bridle-rein to be the humble minister of his necessities was scarcely less tragic. One comfort she had— he had recovered her pony for her, and she could occasionally ride with him. His mother came now and then to Craigenputtoch to stay for a few days; or when a bit of work was done they would themselves drive over to Scotsbrig.

So passed the summer. The Goethe paper (which did not please him: "these are no days for speaking of Goethe")[3] being finished and despatched, Carlyle took up Diderot. Diderot's works, five and twenty large volumes of them, were to be read through before he could put pen to paper. He could read with extraordinary perseverance from nine in the morning till ten at night without intermission save for his meals and his pipes. The twelfth of August brought the grouse shooting and young Welsh relations with guns, who drove him out of his house and sent him on a few days' riding tour about the country. On returning he at once let the shooting of Craigenputtoch, that he might be troubled with such visitors no more. A small domestic catastrophe followed, the maid-servant having misconducted herself and having to be sent away at an hour's notice. "O Mother! Mother!" exclaimed Carlyle in telling her the story, "what trouble the Devil does give us; how *busy he* is wheresoever men are! I could not have fancied this unhappy shameless heartless creature would have proved herself so; but she was long known for a person that did not *speak the*

278

truth, and of such (as I have often remarked) there *never* comes good."[4]

Meanwhile he "stuck," as he said, "like a *burr* to my reading, and managed a volume every lawful day. On Sabbath I read to my assembled household [his wife, the maid, and the stableboy], in the Book of Genesis."[5] And so the time wore on.

In the middle of October, the Diderot article being finished, the Carlyles made an expedition into Annandale. They stayed for a day or two at Templand. Carlyle, "having nothing better to do," rode over, with Dr. Russell, of Thornhill, to Morton Castle, "a respectable old ruin; looked sternly expressive, striking enough, in the pale October evening." The castle had belonged to the Randolphs, and had been uninhabited for two centuries. The court was then a cattlefold. In the distance they saw the remains of the old Church of Kilbride, where Dr. Russell told Carlyle, "there still lies, open and loose on the wall, a circular piece of iron framing once used for supporting the baptismal ewer: protected for these hundred and fifty years by a superstitious feeling alone." Leaving Templand, they drove round by Loch Ettrick, Kirkmichael, and Lockerby, stopping to visit Alexander Carlyle in his new farm, and thence to Scotsbrig. Here the inscription was to be fixed on old Mr. Carlyle's grave in Ecclefechan churchyard. It was the last light of dusk when they arrived at the spot where Carlyle himself is now lying. "Gloomy empire of TIME!" he wrote, after looking at it. "How all had changed, changed; nothing stood still but some old Tombstones with their crossstones, which I remembered from boyhood. Their strange *süss-schauerliche* [bittersweet] effect on me. Our House where we had once all *lived* was within stone cast; but this too knew us no more again at all forever."[6] After ten days they returned to Craigenputtoch, bringing "sister Jane" with them, who was followed afterwards by the mother. The winter they meditated spending in Edinburgh.

Jeffrey's relations with Carlyle might be cooling. To his cousin his affection was as warm as ever, though they seemed to enjoy tormenting each other. He had been long silent, finding a correspondence which could not help Mrs. Carlyle exceedingly painful. He had been busy getting himself returned for Edinburgh; but something more than this—impatience, provocation, and conscious inability to do any good—had stopped his pen. Now, however, he heard that the Carlyles were actually coming to Edinburgh, and the news brought a letter from him of warm anticipation.

The journey, which had been arranged for the beginning of December, was delayed by the illness of Mrs. Carlyle's grandfather, her mother's father, old Mr. Welsh of Templand, which ended in death. Mrs. Carlyle went down to assist in nursing him, leaving her husband alone with his mother at Craigenputtoch, himself busy in charge of the household economies, which his mother, either out of respect for her daughter-in-law, or in fear of her, declined to meddle with. He had to congratulate himself that the establishment was not on fire; nevertheless, he wrote that his "Coadjutor's return will bring blessings with it."[7] The illness, however, ended fatally, and she could not come back to him till it was over.

Sick of Craigenputtoch, sick of solitude, sick with thoughts of many kinds for which he could as yet find no proper utterance, Carlyle went to Edinburgh [in January 1833] to find books and hear the sound of human voices. Books he found in the Advocates' Library, books in plenty upon every subject; on the one subject, especially, which had now hold of his imagination. The French Revolution had long interested him, as illustrating signally his own conclusions on the Divine government of the world. Since he had written upon Diderot, that tremendous convulsion had risen before him more and more vividly as a portent which it was necessary for him to understand. He had read Thiers' history lately. Mill, who had been a careful student of the Revolution, furnished him with memoirs, pamphlets, and newspapers. But these only increased his thirst.

In the Advocates' Library at Edinburgh he was able to look round his subject, and examine it before and after; to look especially to scattered spiritual and personal phenomena; to look into Mirabeau's life, and Danton's, and Madame Roland's; among side pictures to observe Cagliostro's history, and as growing out of it the melodrama of

280

"The Diamond Necklace." All this Carlyle devoured with voracity, and the winter so spent in Edinburgh was of immeasurable moment to him. Under other aspects the place was unfortunately less agreeable than he had expected to find it. In his choice of a future residence he had been hesitating between London and Edinburgh. In his choice of a subject on which to write he had been doubting between "The French Revolution" and "John Knox and the Scotch Reformation." On both these points a few weeks' experience of the modern Athens decided him. Edinburgh society was not to his mind. He discerned, probably not for the first time in human history, that a prophet is not readily acknowledged in his own country. No circle of disciples gathered round him as they had done in Ampton Street. His lodgings proved inconvenient, and even worse. Neither he nor his wife could sleep for the watchman telling the hours in the street. When they moved into a back room they were disturbed by noises overhead. A woman, it appeared, of the worst character, was nightly entertaining her friends there. They could do with little money in Craigenputtoch; life in Edinburgh, even on humble terms, was expensive. Napier was remiss in his payments for the articles in the *Edinburgh Review*. He was generally six months in arrear. He paid only after repeated dunning, and then on a scale of growing illiberality. These, however, were minor evils, and might have been endured. They had gone up with light hearts, in evident hope that they would find Edinburgh an agreeable change from the moors. Carlyle himself thought that, with his increasing reputation, his own country would now, perhaps, do something for him.

For the first week or two Edinburgh itself was not disagreeable. "The transi[t]ion is so singular from bare solitary moors, with only myself for company, to crowded streets and the converse of men." The streets themselves were "orderly and airy." "The reek generally of *Auld Reekie* seems the clearness of mountain tops compared to the horrible vapours of London."[8] Friends came about them, Jeffrey, Sir William Hamilton, Harry Inglis, and many more, "all kind and courteous"; but their way of thinking was not Carlyle's way of thinking, "the things they a[re] running the race for are no prizes to me," and "I feel myself singularly a stranger among them. . . . The men stare at me when I give voice; I listen when they have the word, 'with a sigh or a smile.' "[9] Then came another disappointment. A Professorship at Glasgow was vacant. Jeffrey, as Lord Advocate, had the appointment, or a power of recommending which would be as emphatic as a *congé d'élire*. Carlyle gave Jeffrey a hint about it, but Jeffrey left for London directly after, and Carlyle instinctively felt that he was not to have it. "My own private impression," he said, "is that I shall never get any promotion in this world; and happy shall I be if Providence enable me only to stand *my own* friend. That is (or should be) all the prayer I offer to Heaven."[10]

Carlyle had for some time spoken cheerfully of his wife, as not well, but as better than she had been. He observed nothing, as through his life he never did observe anything, about her which called away his attention from his work and from what was round him. A characteristic postscript in her own hand gives a sadly different picture of her condition.

> In truth I am always so sick now and so heartless that I cannot apply myself to any mental effort without a push from Necessity. . . . Indeed for the last year I have not made an inch of way but sat whimpering on a mile stone alamenting over the roughness of the road— If you would come home and set my *"interior"* to rights it would wonderfully facilitate the problem of living for me—but perhaps it is best for me that it should *not* be made easier.[11]

Edinburgh society pleased less the longer the Carlyles stayed. The fault partially, perhaps, was in Carlyle's own spiritual palate, which neither that nor anything was likely to please.

> As for the people here they are very kind, and would give us three "dinners" for one that we can eat: otherwise I must admit them to be rather a barren set of men. The spirit of Mammon rules all their world; Whig, Tory, Radical, all are alike of the earth earthy: they look upon me as a strong well-intending, utterly misguided man, who must needs run his head against posts yet. They are very right.[12]

To Mill he had written a letter full of discontent, and looking, in the absence of comfort in Edinburgh society about him, for sympathy from his friend. But Mill rather needed comfort for himself than was in a situation to console others. He, like many others, had expected that the Reform Bill would bring the Millennium, and the Millennium was as far off as ever.

To his mother, whatever his humour, Carlyle wrote regularly. To her, more than even to his brother, he showed his real heart. She was never satisfied without knowing the smallest incidents of his life and occupation; and he, on his part, was on the watch for opportunities to give her pleasure. He had sent her from Edinburgh a copy of *Thomas à Kempis*, with an introduction by Chalmers. The introduction he considered "wholly, or in great part, a *dud.*" Of the book itself he says: "No Book, I believe, except the Bible, has been so universally read and loved by Christians of all tongues and sects: it gives me pleasure to fancy that the Christian heart of my good Mother may also derive nourishment and strengthening from what has already nourished and strengthened so many."[13] In Edinburgh he described himself as at home, yet not at home; unable to gather out of the place or its inhabitants the sustenance which he had looked for.

The four months' experience of Edinburgh had convinced Carlyle that there at least could be no permanent home for him. If driven to leave his "castle on the moor," it must be for London—only London. In April he found that he had gathered sufficient materials for his article on the Diamond Necklace, which he could work up at Craigenputtoch. At the beginning of May he was again in Annandale on his way home, Mrs. Carlyle miserably ill, and craving like a wounded wild animal to creep away out of human sight. "I left Edinburgh," he wrote, "with the grieved heart customary to me on visits thither; a wretched *infidel* place; not one man that could forward you cooperate with you in any useful thing."[14]

The work which Carlyle had done in the winter had more than paid his modest expenses. He was still undetermined how next to proceed, and felt a need of rest and reflection. It seemed, he said, as if "outwardly and inwardly a kind of closing of the First Act goes on with me; the second as yet quite *un*opened."[15] Means to go on upon were found in the hitherto unfortunate Teufelsdröckh. Unable to find an accoucheur who would introduce him to the world complete, he was to be cut in pieces and produced limb by limb in *Fraser's Magazine*. Fraser, however, who had hitherto paid Carlyle twenty guineas a sheet for his articles (five guineas more than he paid any other contributor), had to stipulate for paying no more than twelve upon this unlucky venture.[16] Ten sheets were to be allotted to *Teufel* in ten successive numbers. Thus *Sartor Resartus* was to find its way into print at last in this and the following year, and sufficient money was provided for the Craigenputtoch house-keeping for another twelve months.

The summer so begun was a useful and not unpleasant one. John Carlyle, returning from Italy, spent two months of it in his brother's house, intending at the end of them to rejoin Lady Clare and go again abroad with her. There were occasional visits to Scotsbrig. Many books were read, chiefly about the French Revolution, while from the Journal it appears that Carlyle was putting himself through a severe cross-examination, discovering, for one thing, that he was too intolerant, "my own private discontent mingl[ing] considerably with my zeal against evil-doers," too contemptuously indifferent to those who were "not forwarding me on my course"; wanting in courtesy, and "given to far too much emphasis in the expression of my convictions." It was necessary for him to ascertain what his special powers were, and what were the limits of them. "I begin to suspect," he wrote, "only that I have no *poetic* talent whatsoever; but of this too am nowise absolutely *sure*. It still seems as if a whole magazine of Faculty lay in me, all undeveloped; held in thraldom by the meanest physical and economical causes."

One discovery came on him as a startling surprise.

On the whole, however, art thou not among the *vainest* of living men? At bottom, among the very *vainest*. Oh the sorry mad ambitions that lurk in thee! God deliver me from vanity, from self-conceit; the first sin of this universe, and the last—for I think it will *never* leave us?[17]

Mrs. Carlyle continued ill and out of spirits, benefiting less than she had hoped from her brother-in-law's skill in medicine, yet contriving now and then to sketch in her humorous way the accidents of the moorland existence.

John Carlyle remained at Craigenputtoch [until mid-August], and then left it to return with Lady Clare to Italy. Carlyle saw him off in the Liverpool steamer from Annan, and went back to solitude and work. He says that he was invariably sick and miserable before he could write to any real purpose. His first attempt at "The Diamond Necklace" had failed, and he had laid it aside. The entries in his Journal show more than usual despondency.

[One] entry in the Journal is in another handwriting. It is merely a name—"Ralph Waldo Emerson."

The Carlyles were sitting alone at dinner on a Sunday afternoon at the end of August when a Dumfries carriage drove to the door, and there stepped out of it a young American then unknown to fame, but whose influence in his own country equals that of Carlyle in ours, and whose name stands connected with his wherever the English language is spoken. Emerson, the younger of the two, had just broken his Unitarian fetters, and was looking out and round him like a young eagle longing for light. He had read Carlyle's articles and had discerned with the instinct of genius that here was a voice speaking real and fiery convictions, and no longer echoes and conventionalisms. He had come to Europe to study its social and spiritual phenomena; and to the young Emerson, as to the old Goethe, the most important of them appeared to be Carlyle. He had obtained an introduction to him from John Mill, in London, armed with which he had come off to Scotland. Mill had prepared Carlyle for his possible appearance not very favourably, and perhaps recognised in after years the fallibility of his judgement. Carlyle made no such mistake. The fact itself of a young American having been so affected by his writings as to have sought him out in the Dunscore moors, was a homage of the kind which he could especially value and appreciate. The acquaintance then begun to their mutual pleasure ripened into a deep friendship, which has remained unclouded in spite of wide divergences of opinion throughout their working lives, and continues warm as ever, at the moment when I am writing these words (June 27, 1880), when the labours of both of them are over, and they wait in

RALPH WALDO EMERSON. A surprise visit paid by Emerson to Craigenputtoch in August 1833—an encounter vividly evoked in the first chapter of Emerson's *English Traits*—inaugurated a friendship that lasted throughout their lives. (Courtesy of the Carlyle House, Chelsea.)

age and infirmity to be called away from a world to which they have given freely all that they had to give.

Emerson's visit at this moment is particularly welcome, since it gives the only sketch we have of Carlyle's life at Craigenputtoch as it was seen by others.

From Edinburgh I went to the Highlands. On my return I came from Glasgow to Dumfries, and being intent on delivering a letter which I had brought from Rome, inquired for Craigenputtoch. It was a farm in Nithsdale, in the parish of Dunscore, sixteen miles distant. No public coach passed near it, so I took a private carriage from the inn. I found the house amid desolate heathery hills, where the lonely scholar nourished his mighty heart. Carlyle was a man from his youth, an author who did not need to hide from his readers, and as absolute a man of the world, unknown and exiled on that hill-farm, as if holding on his own terms what is best in London. He was tall and gaunt, with a cliff-like brow, self-possessed and holding his extraordinary powers of conversation in easy command; clinging to his northern accent with evident relish; full of lively anecdote and with a streaming humor which floated every thing he looked upon. . . .

He had names of his own for all the matters familiar to his discourse. Blackwood's was the "sand magazine"; Fraser's nearer approach to possibility of life was the "mud magazine"; a piece of road near by, that marked some failed enterprise, was the "grave of the last sixpence." When too much praise of any genius annoyed him he professed hugely to admire the talent shown by his pig. He had spent much time and contrivance in confining the poor beast to one enclosure in his pen, but pig, by great strokes of judgment, had found out how to let a board down, and had foiled him. For all that he still thought man the most plastic little fellow in the planet, and he liked Nero's death, *"Qualis Artifex pereo!* [What an artificer dies in me!]" better than most history. He worships a man that will manifest any truth to him. At one time he had inquired and read a good deal about America. . . .

We talked of books. Plato he does not read, and he disparaged Socrates; and, when pressed, persisted in making Mirabeau a hero. Gibbon he called the "splendid bridge from the old world to the new." His own reading had been multifarious. Tristram Shandy was one of his first books after Robinson Crusoe, and Robertson's America an early favorite. Rousseau's Confessions had discovered to him that he was not a dunce; and it was now ten years since he had learned German, by the advice of a man who told him he would find in that language what he wanted. . . .

He still returned to English pauperism, the crowded country, the selfish abdication by public men of all that public persons should perform. Government should direct poor men what to do. Poor Irish folk come wandering over these moors. My dame makes it a rule to give to every son of Adam bread to eat, and supplies his wants to the next house. But here are thousands of acres which might give them all meat, and nobody to bid these poor Irish go to the moor and till it. They burned the stacks and so found a way to force the rich people to attend to them.

We went out to walk over long hills, and looked at Criffel, then without his cap, and down into Wordsworth's country. There we sat down and talked of the immortality of the soul. It was not Carlyle's fault that we talked on that topic, for he had the natural disinclination of every nimble spirit to bruise itself against walls, and did not like to place himself where no step can be taken. But he was honest and true, and cognizant of the subtile links that bind ages together, and saw how every event affects all the future. "Christ died on the tree; that built Dunscore kirk yonder; that brought you and me together. Time has only a relative existence."

He was already turning his eyes towards London with a scholar's appreciation. London is the heart of the world, he said, wonderful only from the mass of human beings. He liked the huge machine. Each keeps its own round. The baker's boy brings muffins to the window at a fixed hour every day, and that is all the Londoner knows or wishes to know on the subject. But it turned out good men. He named certain individuals, especially one man of letters, his friend, the best mind he knew, whom London had well served.[18]

Emerson stayed for a night and was gone in the morning, seeking other notabilities. Carlyle liked him well. Two days later he writes to his mother:

Our third happiness was the arrival of a certain young unknown Friend named Emerson from Boston in the United States, who turned aside so far from his British French and Italian travels, to see me here! He had an introduction from Mill and a Frenchman (Baron d'Eichthal's Nephew) whom John knew in Rome. Of course we could do no other than welcome him; the rather as he seemed to be one of the most loveable creatures in himself we had ever looked on. He staid till next day with us, and talked and heard talk to his heart's content, and left us all really sad to part with him. Jane says, it is the first journey ever since Noah's Deluge under-taken to Craigenputtoch for such a purpose. In any case, we *had* a cheerful day from it, and ought to be thankful.[19]

During these months, the autumn of 1833 and the begin-ning of the year which followed, a close correspondence was maintained between Carlyle and John Mill. Carlyle's part of it I have not seen, but on both sides the letters must have been of the deepest interest. Thinly sprinkled with information about common friends, they related almost entirely to the deepest questions which concern humanity; and the letters of Mill are remarkable for simplicity, hu-

THE CAIRN HEIGHTS, ABOVE CRAIGENPUTTOCH. The house lies hidden among the trees. Carlyle took Emerson on a long walk over the hills during Emerson's twenty-four hour visit in August 1833. "There we sat down and talked of the immortality of the soul," Emerson recalled in *English Traits*. (Photograph by John Patrick, courtesy of the University of Edinburgh.)

mility, and the most disinterested desire for truth. He had
much to learn about Carlyle; he was not quick to understand character, and was distressed to find, as their communications became more intimate, how widely their views
were divided. He had been bred a utilitarian. He had been
taught that virtue led necessarily to happiness, and was
perplexed at Carlyle's insistence on *Entsagen* (renunciation
of personal happiness) as essential to noble action. He had
been surprised that Carlyle liked Emerson, who had appeared to him perhaps a visionary. Carlyle, intending to
write another book, was hesitating between a life of John
Knox and the French Revolution. Either subject would
give him the opportunity, which he wanted, of expressing
his spiritual convictions. His inclination at this moment was
towards the history of his own country, and he had recommended Mill to write on the Revolution. Mill felt that it
would be difficult if not impossible for him, without expressing completely his views on Christianity, which the condition of public feeling in England would not allow him to do.
He spoke tenderly and reverently of the personal character
of the Founder of Christianity, and on this part of the subject he wrote as if he was confident that Carlyle agreed
with him. But, below the truth of any particular religion,
there lay the harder problem of the existence and providence
of God, and here it seemed that Carlyle had a positive
faith, while Mill had no more than a sense of probability.
Carlyle admitted that so far as external evidence went, the
Being of God was a supposition inadequately proved. The
grounds of certainty which Carlyle found in himself, Mill,
much as he desired to share Carlyle's belief, confessed that
he was unable to recognise. So again with the soul. There
was no proof that it perished with the body, but again
there was no proof that it did not. Duty was the deepest of
all realities, but the origin of duty, for all Mill could tell,
might be the tendency of right action to promote the general happiness of mankind. Such general happiness doubtless could best be promoted by each person developing his
own powers. Carlyle insisted that every man had a special
task assigned to him, which it was his business to discover;
but the question remained, by whom and how the task was
assigned; and the truth might only be that men in fact were

born with various qualities, and that the general good was most effectually promoted by the special cultivation of those qualities.

I have alluded to the correspondence only because it turned the balance in Carlyle's mind, sent him immediately back again to Marie Antoinette and the Diamond Necklace, and decided for him that he should himself undertake the work which was to make his name famous.

When John Carlyle left Craigenputtoch to rejoin Lady Clare, the parting between the brothers had been exceptionally sad. The popularity with Review editors which had followed Carlyle's appearance in London was as brief as it had been sudden. His haughty tone towards them, and his theory of the "Dog's carrion-cart"[20] as a description of the periodicals of the day, could not have recommended him to their favour. The article on Goethe was received unfavourably, Cochrane said with unqualified disapproval. *Sartor,* when it began to appear in *Fraser's* piecemeal, met a still harder judgement. No one could tell what to make of it. The writer was considered a literary maniac, and the unlucky editor was dreading the ruin of his magazine. The brothers had doubtless talked earnestly enough of the threatening prospect. John, who owed all that he had and was to his brother's care of him, and was in prosperous circumstances, was leaving that brother to loneliness and depression, and to a future on which no light was breaking anywhere.

[Carlyle wrote to Cochrane, editor of the *Foreign Quarterly Review,* asking him whether he would take his article on the Saint-Simonians or "The Diamond Necklace."]

The answer was unfavourable. All editors, from this time forward, gave Carlyle a cold shoulder till the appearance of *The French Revolution.* After the first astonishment with which his articles had been received, the world generally had settled into the view taken at Edinburgh, that fine talents, which no one had denied him, were being hopelessly thrown away—that what he had to say was extravagant nonsense. Whigs, Tories, and Radicals were for once agreed. He was, in real truth, a Bohemian, whose hand was against every man, and every man's hand, but too naturally, was against him, and the battle was sadly unequal. If Carlyle had possessed the peculiar musical quality which makes the form of poetry, his thoughts would have swept into popularity as rapidly and as widely as Byron's. But his verse was wooden. Rhymes and metre were to him no wings on which to soar to the empyrean. Happy for him in the end that it was so. Poetry in these days is read for pleasure. It is not taken to heart as practical truth. Carlyle's mission was that of a prophet and teacher—and a prophet's lessons can only be driven home by prose.

The dejected tone so visible in [his Journal] entries was due to no idle speculative distress, but to the menacing aspect which circumstances were beginning to assume. The editors and booksellers were too evidently growing shy; and unless articles could find insertion or books be paid for, no literary life for Carlyle would long be possible. Employment of some other kind, however humble and distasteful, would have to be sought for and accepted. Anything, even the meanest, would be preferable to courting popularity, and writing less than the very best that he could; writing *"duds,"* as he called it, to please the popular taste. An experienced publisher once said to me: "Sir, if you wish to write a book which will sell, consider the ladies'-maids. Please the ladies'-maids, you please the great reading world." Carlyle would not, could not, write for ladies'-maids.

The dreary monotony of the Craigenputtoch life on those terms was interrupted in November by interesting changes in the family arrangements. The Carlyles, as has been more than once said, were a family whose warmest affections were confined to their own circle. Jean, the youngest sister, the "little crow," was about to be married to her cousin, James Aitken who had once lived at Scotsbrig, and was now a rising tradesman in Dumfries; a house-painter by occupation, of superior sort, and possessed of talents in that department which with better opportunities might have raised him to eminence as an artist. "James Aitken," Carlyle wrote, "is . . . certainly an ingenious, clever kind of fellow, with fair prospects, no bad habit, and perhaps *very* great skill in his craft. I saw a copied *Ruysdael,* of his doing, which certainly amazed me."[21] The "crow" had not followed up the poetical promise of her childhood. She had educated herself into a clear, somewhat stern, well-informed and

292

sensible woman. Hard Annandale farm-work had left her no
time for more. But, like all the Carlyles, she was of a rugged,
independent temper. Jean, her mother said, was outgrowing
the contracted limits of the Scotsbrig household. Her marriage consequently gave satisfaction to all parties. Carlyle
himself was present at the ceremony: "a cold mutton-pie,
of gigantic dimensions" was consumed for the breakfast;
"the stirrup-cup" was drunk, Carlyle joining, and this
domestic matter was happily ended.[22]

But Jean's marriage was not all. James Carlyle, the
youngest brother, who carried on the Scotsbrig farm, had a
similar scheme on foot, and had for himself fallen in love;
"nothing almost, since Werter's time, has equalled the
intensity of his devotion in that quarter."[23] He, too, was
eager to be married; but as this arrangement would affect
his mother's position, Carlyle, as the eldest of the family,
had to interfere to prevent precipitancy. All was well settled
in the following spring, Carlyle making fresh sacrifices to
bring it about. His brother Alick owed him more than £200.
This, if it could be paid, or when it could be paid, was to
be added to his younger brother's fortune. His mother was
either to continue at Scotsbrig, or some new home was to be
found for her, which Carlyle himself thought preferable.
His letter to the intending bridegroom will be read with an
interest which extends beyond its immediate subject.

> I understand what wonderful felicities young men like you ex-
> pect from marriage; I know too (for it is a truth as old as the world)
> that such expectations hold out but for a little while. I shall re-
> joice much (such is my experience of the world) if in your new
> situation you feel *as* happy as in the old; say nothing of happier.
> But, in any case, do I not know that you will never (whatever
> happen) venture on any such solemn engagement with a direct
> Duty to fly in the face of? The Duty namely of doing to your dear
> Mother and your dear Sisters *as you would wish that they should
> do to you.* Believe me, my dear Brother, wait; half a year for such
> an object is not long! If you ever repent so doing, blame me for
> it.—[24]

Carlyle, perhaps, judged of possibilities by his own recollections. *He,* when it would have added much to his own
wife's happiness, and might have shielded her entirely from
the worst of her sufferings, had refused peremptorily to
live with her mother, or let her live with them, except on

impossible terms. He knew himself and his peremptory disposition, and in that instance was probably right. His own
mother happily found such an arrangement *not* impossible.
Her son married [Isabella Calvert], and she did not leave
her home, but lived out there her long and honoured life,
and ended it under the old roof.

chapter fifteen

1834

From Craigenputtoch to London

The economical situation of the Carlyles at Craigenput-toch grew daily more pressing. The editors gave no sign of desiring any further articles. "Teufelsdröckh" was still coming out in *Fraser's*; but the public verdict upon it was almost universally unfavourable. "The Diamond Neck-lace," which in my opinion is the very finest illustration of Carlyle's literary power, had been refused in its first form by the editor of the *Foreign Quarterly*. Fevered as he was with the burning thoughts which were consuming his very soul, which he felt instinctively, if once expressed, would make their mark on the mind of his country, Carlyle yet knew that his first duty was to provide honest mainte-nance for himself and his wife—somewhere and by some means; if not in England or Scotland, then in America. His aims in this direction were of the very humblest, not going beyond St. Paul's. With "food and raiment" both he and his wife could be well content. But even for these, the sup-plies to be derived from literature threatened to fail, and what to do next he knew not. In this situation he learnt from a paragraph in a newspaper that a new Astronomy Professorship was about to be established in Edinburgh. Some Rhetoric chair was also likely to be immediately va-cant. One or other of these, especially the first, he thought that Jeffrey could, if he wished, procure for him. Hith-erto all attempts to enter on the established roads of life had failed. He had little hopes that another would succeed; but he thought it to be his duty to make the attempt. He was justly conscious of his qualifications. The mathematical ability which he had shown in earlier times had been so remarkable as to have drawn the attention of Legendre. Though by the high standard by which he habitually tried himself Carlyle could speak, and did speak, of his own capabilities with mere contempt, yet he was above the affectation of pretending to believe that any really fitter candidate was likely to offer himself. "I will this day write to Jeffrey about it," he says in his Journal on the 11th of January. "Any hope? Little. Any care of it? Also not much. Let us *do what we can*. The issues not with *us*." He cared perhaps more than he had acknowledged to himself. He allowed his imagination to rest on a possible future, where, delivered from the fiery unrest which was distracting him, he might spend the remainder of his life in the calm and calming study of the stars and their movements. It was a last effort to lay down the burden which had been laid upon him, yet not a cowardly effort—rather a wise and laudable one—undertaken as it was in submission to the Higher Will.

It failed—failed with an emphasis of which the effects can be traced in Carlyle's reminiscence of his connection with Jeffrey. He condemns especially the tone of Jeffrey, which he thought both ungenerous and insincere. Insincere it certainly was, if Jeffrey had any real influence, for he said that he had none, and if he had already secured the appointment for his own secretary, for he said that he had not recommended his secretary. It may have been ungenerous if, as Carlyle suspected, Jeffrey had resented some remarks in the article on Diderot as directed against himself, for he endeavoured to lay the blame of unfitness for promotion upon Carlyle himself.

The doubt which Jeffrey pretended to feel, whether Carlyle was equal to the duties of handling delicate instruments without injuring them, cannot have been quite sincere. The supposition that a man of supreme intellectual qualification could fail in mastering a mere mechanical operation could only have originated in irritation. Carlyle already possessed a scientific knowledge of his subject. A few days' instruction might easily have taught him the mere manual exercise. It is possible, too, that if Jeffrey had gone out of his way to represent to Airy and Herschel, with whom the choice rested, what Carlyle's qualities really were, he might have saved to a Scotch university Scotland's greatest son, who would have made the School of Astronomy at Edinburgh famous throughout Europe, and have saved Scotland the scandal of neglect of him till his fame made neglect impossible.

In fairness to Jeffrey, however, whose own name will be remembered in connection with Carlyle as his first literary friend, we must put the Lord Advocate's case in his own way. If he was mistaken, he was mistaken about Carlyle's character with all the world. Everyone in Jeffrey's high Whig circle, the Broughams and Macaulays and such like, thought of Carlyle as he did. High original genius is always ridiculed on its first appearance; most of all by those who have won themselves the highest reputation in working on the established lines. Genius only commands recognition when it has created the taste which is to appreciate it. Carlyle acknowledged that "no more *un*promotable man than thou is perhaps extant at present."[1]

In the first week in December [1833, Jeffrey] had written affectionately to Mrs. Carlyle and kindly to Carlyle himself, pressing them to pay him a visit at Craigcrook. He professed and assuredly felt (for his active kindness in the past years places his sincerity above suspicion) a continued interest in Carlyle, some provocation, some admiration, and a genuine desire for his happiness. Carlyle thought that he did not please Jeffrey because he was "so dreadfully in earnest."[2] The expression had in fact been used by Jeffrey; but what really offended and estranged him was Carlyle's extraordinary arrogance—a fault of which no one who knew Carlyle, or who has ever read his letters, can possibly acquit him. He *was* superior to the people that he came in contact with. He knew that he was, and being incapable of disguise or affectation, he let it be seen in every sentence that he spoke or wrote. It was arrogance, but not the arrogance of a fool, swollen with conceit and vapour, but the arrogance of Aristotle's "man of lofty soul," "who being of great merit," knows that he is so, and chooses to be so regarded. It was not that Carlyle ever said to himself that he was wiser than others. When it came to introspection, never had anyone a lower opinion of himself; but let him be crossed in argument, let some rash person, whoever he might be, dare to contradict him, and Johnson himself was not more rude, disdainful, and imperious; and this quality in him had very naturally displeased Jeffrey, and had served to blind him, at least in some degree, to the actual greatness of Carlyle's powers. In this letter Jeffrey frankly admitted that he disliked the wrangling to which Carlyle treated him. Never having had much of a creed himself, he thought he had daily less; and having no tendency to dogmatism and no impatience of indecision, he thought zeal for creeds and anxiety about positive opinions more and more ludicrous. In fact, he regarded discussions which aimed at more than exercising the faculties and exposing intolerance very tiresome and foolish.

But for all that he invited Carlyle with genuine heartiness to come down from his mountains and join the Christmas party at Craigcrook. Carlyle professed to be a lover of his fellow-creatures. Jeffrey said he had no patience with a philanthropy that drew people into the desert and made them fly from the face of man.

The good-humoured tone of his letter, and the pleasant banter of it, ending as it did with reiterated professions of a willingness to serve Carlyle if an opportunity offered, made it natural on Carlyle's part to apply to him when an opportunity did present itself immediately after. Jeffrey's letter had been written on December 8. Three weeks later the news of the intended Astronomy Professorship reached Craigenputtoch, while Carlyle was told also that Jeffrey would probably have the decisive voice in the appointment. Carlyle wrote to him at once to ask for his good word, and there came by return of post the answer which he calls the "Fishwoman-shriek,"[3] and which it is clear that he never forgave. For some reason—for the reason, possibly, which Carlyle surmised, that he expected the situation to be given to his own secretary—Jeffrey was certainly put out by being taken thus at his word when he had volunteered to be of use.

Impatiently, and even abruptly, he told Carlyle that he had no chance of getting the Astronomy Chair, and that it would be idle for him (Jeffrey) to ask for it. The appointment was entirely out of his own sphere, and he would be laughed at if he interfered. As a matter of fact, the most promising candidate was his secretary, a gentleman who had already been nominated for the Observatory at the Cape, and wished to go through some preliminary observing work at Edinburgh. But this gentleman, he said, had not applied to him for a recommendation, but trusted to his own merits. It was matter of notoriety that no testimonial would be looked at except from persons of weight and authority in that particular branch of science, and he was perfectly certain—indeed he *knew*—that the Government would be entirely guided by their opinions. The place would be given, and it was difficult to say that it ought not to be given, according to the recommendations of Herschel, Airy, Babbage, and six or seven other men of unquestionable eminence in the astronomical department, without the least regard to unprofessional advisers. If Carlyle could satisfy *them* that he was the fittest person for the place, he might be sure of obtaining it; if he could not, he might be equally sure that it was needless to think of it. Whether Carlyle's scientific qualifications were such that he would be able to satisfy them, Jeffrey would not pretend to judge. But he added a further reason for thinking that Carlyle had no chance of success. He had had no practice in observing, and nobody would be appointed who was not both practised and of acknowledged skill.

Had Jeffrey stopped here, Carlyle would have had no right to complain. But Jeffrey went beyond what was necessary in using the occasion to give Carlyle a lecture. He was very sorry, he said; but the disappointment revived and increased the regret which he had always felt, that Carlyle was without the occupation, and consequent independence, of some regular profession. The profession of *teacher* was, no doubt, a useful and noble one; but it could not be exercised unless a man had something to teach which was thought worth learning, and in a way that was thought agreeable; and neither of those conditions was fulfilled by Carlyle. Jeffrey frankly said that he could not set much value on paradoxes and exaggerations, and no man ever did more than Carlyle to obstruct the success of his doctrines by the tone in which he set them forth. It was arrogant, obscure vituperation, and carried no conviction. It might impress weak, fanciful minds, but it would only revolt calm, candid, and thoughtful persons. It might seem harsh to speak as he was doing; but he was speaking the truth, and Carlyle was being taught by experience to know that it was the truth. Never, never would he find or make the world friendly to him if he persisted in addressing it in so extravagant a tone. One thing he was glad to find, that Carlyle was growing tired of solitude. He would be on his way to amendment if he would live gently, humbly, and, if possible, gaily, with other men; let him once fairly come down from the barren and misty eminence where he had his bodily abode, and he would soon be reconciled to a no less salutary intellectual subsidence.

Disagreeable as language of this kind might be to Carlyle, it was, after all, not unnatural from Jeffrey's point of view; and there was still nothing in it which he was entitled to resent: certainly nothing of the "Fishwoman." It was the language of a sensible man of the world who had long earnestly endeavoured to befriend Carlyle, and had been thwarted by peculiarities in Carlyle's conduct and character which had neutralised all his efforts. There was, in fact, very little in what Jeffrey said which Carlyle in his note-book was not often saying to and of himself. We must look further to explain the deep, ineffaceable resentment which Carlyle evidently nourished against Jeffrey for his behaviour on this occasion. The Astronomical chair was not the only situation vacant to which Carlyle believed that he might aspire. There was a Rhetoric chair—whether at Edinburgh or in London University, I am not certain.[4] To this it appears that there had been some allusion, for Jeffrey went on to say that if he was himself the patron of that chair he would appoint Carlyle, though not without misgivings. But the University Commissioners had decided that the Rhetoric chair was not to be refilled unless some man of great and established reputation was willing to accept it, and such a man Jeffrey said he could not in his conscience declare Carlyle to be. Had it been Macaulay that was the candidate, then, indeed, the Commissioners would see their way. Macaulay was the greatest of living Englishmen, not excepting the great Brougham himself. But Carlyle was—Carlyle. It was melancholy and provoking to feel

300

that perversions and absurdities (for as such alone he could regard Carlyle's peculiar methods and doctrines) were heaping up obstacles against his obtaining either the public position or the general respect to which his talents and his diligence would have otherwise entitled him. As long as society remained as it was and thought as it did, there was not the least chance of his ever being admitted as a teacher into any regular seminary.

There was no occasion for Jeffrey to have written with such extreme harshness. If he felt obliged to expostulate, he might have dressed his censures in a kinder form. To Carlyle such language was doubly wounding, for he was under obligations to Jeffrey, which his pride already endured with difficulty, and the tone of condescending superiority was infinitely galling. He was conscious, too, that Jeffrey did not understand him. His extravagances, as Jeffrey considered them, were but efforts to express thoughts of immeasurable consequence. From his boyhood upwards he had struggled to use his faculties honestly for the best purposes; to consider only what was true and good, and never to be led astray by any worldly interest; and for reward every door of preferment was closed in his face, and poverty and absolute want seemed advancing to overwhelm him. If he was tried in the fire, if he bore the worse that the world could do to him and came out at last triumphant, let those who think that they would have behaved better blame Carlyle for his occasional bursts of impatience and resentment. High-toned moral lectures were the harder to bear because Goethe far off in Germany could recognise in the same qualities at which Jeffrey was railing the workings of true original genius.

Even so it is strange that Carlyle, after the victory had long been won, when his trials were all over and he was standing on the highest point of literary fame, known, honoured, and admired over two continents, should have nourished still an evident grudge against the poor Lord Advocate, especially as, after the appearance of *The French Revolution*, Jeffrey had freely and without reserve acknowledged that he had all along been wrong in his judgement of Carlyle. One expression casually let fall at the end of one of Jeffrey's letters, to which I need not do more than allude, contains a possible explanation. Jeffrey was always gentlemanlike, and it is not conceivable that he intended to affront Carlyle, but Carlyle may have taken the words to himself in a sense which they were not meant to bear; and a misunderstanding, to which self-respect would have forbidden him to refer, may have infected his recollections of a friend whom he had once cordially esteemed, and to whom both he and his brothers were under obligations which could hardly be overrated. But this is mere conjecture.[5] It may be simply that Jeffrey had once led Carlyle to hope for his assistance in obtaining promotion in the world, and that when an opportunity seemed to offer itself, the assistance was not given.

Never any more did Carlyle seek admission into the beaten tracks of established industry. He was impatient of harness, and had felt all along that no official situation was fit for him, or he fit for it. He would have endeavoured loyally to do his duty in any position in which he might be placed. Never would he have accepted employment merely for its salary, going through the perfunctory forms, and reserving his best powers for other occupations. Anything which he undertook to do he would have done with all his might; but he would have carried into it the stern integrity which refused to bend to conventional exigencies. His tenure of office, whether of professor's chair or of office under government, would probably have been brief and would have come to a violent end. He never offered himself again, and in later times when a professorship might have been found for him at Edinburgh, he refused to be nominated. He called himself a Bedouin, and a Bedouin he was; a free lance owing no allegiance save to his Maker and his own conscience.

On receiving Jeffrey's letter, he adjusted himself resolutely and without complaining to the facts as they stood. He determined to make one more attempt, either at Craigenputtoch or elsewhere, to conquer a place for himself, and earn an honest livelihood as an English man of letters. If that failed, he had privately made up his mind to try his fortune in America, where he had learnt from Emerson, and where he himself instinctively felt, that he might expect more favourable hearing. He was in no hurry. In all that he

302

did he acted with a deliberate circumspection scarcely to have been looked for in so irritable a man. The words *"judicious desperation,"*[6] by which he describes the principle on which he guided his earlier life, are exactly appropriate.

Including Fraser's payments for "Teufelsdröckh" he was possessed of about two hundred pounds, and until his brother John could repay him the sums which had been advanced for his education, he had no definite prospect of earning any more—a very serious outlook, but he did not allow it to discompose him. At any rate he had no debts; never had a debt in his life except the fifty pounds which he had borrowed from Jeffrey, and this with the Advocate's loan to his brother was now cleared off. "The Diamond Necklace" had proved unsaleable, but he worked quietly upon it, making additions and alterations as new books came in. He was not solitary this winter. In some respects he was worse off than if he had been solitary. With characteristic kindness he had taken charge of the young Scotchman whom he had met in London, William Glen, gifted, accomplished, with the fragments in him of a true man of genius, but with symptoms showing themselves of approaching insanity, in which after a year or two he sank into total eclipse. With Glen, half for his friend's sake, he read Homer and mathematics. Glen, who was a good scholar, taught Carlyle Greek. Carlyle taught Glen Newtonian geometry; in the intervals studying hard at French Revolution history.

[In the first months of 1834, Carlyle tried to set afoot various literary projects—all in vain. Amidst increasing despair he and Jane, as he recorded in his Journal, began to speak "seriously of setting off for London to take up our abode there next Whitsunday. Nothing but the wretchedest, forsaken, discontented existence here, where almost your whole energy is spent in keeping yourself from flying out into exasperation."[7] The decision to strike out for London once made, plans to leave Craigenputtoch matured apace.] "The ships were burnt,"[8] two busy months being spent in burning them—disposing of old books, old bedsteads, kitchen things, all the rubbish of the establishment. The cows and poultry were sold. Mrs. Carlyle's pony was sent to Scotsbrig. Friends in London were busy looking out for houses.

Carlyle, unable to work in the confusion, grew unbearable, naturally enough, to himself and everyone, and finally, at the beginning of May, rushed off alone, believing that house letting in London was conducted on the same rule as in Edinburgh, and that unless he could secure a home for himself at Whitsuntide he would have to wait till the year had gone round. In this hurried fashion he took his own departure, leaving his wife to pack what they did not intend to part with, and to follow at her leisure when the new habitation had been decided on. Mill had sent his warmest congratulations when he learnt that the final resolution had been taken. Carlyle settled himself while house hunting at his old lodgings in Ampton Street.

Thus the six years' imprisonment on the Dumfriesshire moors came to an end. To Carlyle himself they had been years of inestimable value. If we compare the essay on Jean Paul, which he wrote at Comely Bank, with "The Diamond Necklace," his last work at Craigenputtoch, we see the leap from promise to fulfilment, from the immature energy of youth to the full intellectual strength of completed manhood. The solitude had compelled him to digest his thoughts. In *Sartor* he had relieved his soul of its perilous secretions by throwing out of himself his personal sufferings and physical and spiritual experience. He had read omnivorously far and wide. His memory was a magazine of facts gathered over the whole surface of European literature and history. The multiplied allusions in every page of his later essays, so easy, so unlaboured, reveal the wealth which he had accumulated, and the fulness of his command over his possessions. His religious faith had gained solidity. His confidence in the soundness of his own convictions was no longer clouded with the shadow of a doubt. *The French Revolution*, the most powerful of all his works, and the only one which has the character of a work of art, was the production of the mind which he brought with him from Craigenputtoch, undisturbed by the contradictions and excitements of London society and London triumphs. He had been tried in the furnace. Poverty, mortification, and disappointment had done their work upon him, and he had risen above them elevated, purified, and strengthened. Even the arrogance and self-assertion which Lord Jeffrey supposed to have been developed in him by living away from conflict with other minds, had been rather tamed than encouraged by his lonely meditations. It was rather collision with those who differed with him which fostered his imperiousness; for Carlyle rarely met with an antagonist whom he could not overbear with the torrent of his metaphors, whilst to himself his note-books show that he read many a lecture on humility.

He had laid in, too, on the moors a stock of robust health.[9] Lamentations over indigestion and want of sleep are almost totally absent from the letters written from Craigenputtoch. The simple, natural life, the wholesome air, the daily rides or drives, the pure food—milk, cream, eggs, oatmeal, the best of their kind—had restored completely the functions of a stomach never, perhaps, so far wrong as he had imagined. Carlyle had ceased to complain on this head, and in a person so extremely vocal when anything was amiss with him, silence is the best evidence that there was nothing to complain of. On the moors, as at Mainhill, at Edinburgh, or in London afterwards, he was always impatient, moody, irritable, violent. These humours were in his nature, and could no more be separated from them than his body could leap off its shadow. But, intolerable as he had found Craigenputtoch in the later years of his residence there, he looked back to it afterwards as the happiest and wholesomest home that he had ever known. He could do fully twice as much work there, he said, as he could ever do afterwards in London; and many a time, when sick of fame and clatter and interruption, he longed to return to it.

To Mrs. Carlyle Craigenputtoch had been a less salutary home. She might have borne the climate, and even benefited by it, if the other conditions had been less ungenial. But her life there, to begin with, had been a life of menial drudgery, unsolaced (for she could have endured and even enjoyed mere hardship) by more than an occasional word of encouragement or sympathy or compassion from her husband. To him it seemed perfectly natural that what his mother did at Scotsbrig his wife should do for him. Every household duty fell upon her, either directly, or in supplying the shortcomings of a Scotch maid-of-all-work. She had to cook, to sew, to scour, to clean; to gallop down alone to

Dumfries if anything was wanted; to keep the house, and even on occasions to milk the cows. Miss Jewsbury has preserved many anecdotes of the Craigenputtoch life, showing how hard a time her friend had of it there.[10] Carlyle, though disposed at first to dismiss these memories as legends, yet admitted on reflection that for all there was a certain foundation. The errors, if any, can be no more than the slight alterations of form which stories naturally receive in repetition. A lady brought up in luxury has been educated into physical unfitness for so sharp a discipline. Mrs. Carlyle's bodily health never recovered from the strain of those six years. The trial to her mind and to her nervous system was still more severe. Nature had given her, along with a powerful understanding, a disposition singularly bright and buoyant. The Irving disappointment had been a blow to her; but wounds which do not kill are cured. They leave a scar, but the pain ceases. It was long over, and if Carlyle had been a real companion to her, she would have been as happy with him as wives usually are. But he was not a companion at all. When he was busy she rarely so much as saw him, save, as he himself pathetically tells, when she would steal into his dressing-room in the morning when he was shaving, to secure that little of his society. The loneliness of Craigenputtoch was dreadful to her. Her hard work, perhaps, had so far something of a blessing in it, that it was a relief from the intolerable pressure. For months together, especially after Alick Carlyle had gone, they never saw the face of guest or passing stranger. So still the moors were, that she could hear the sheep nibbling the grass a quarter of a mile off. For the many weeks when the snow was on the ground she could not stir beyond the garden, or even beyond her door. She had no great thoughts, as Carlyle had, to occupy her with the administration of the universe. He had deranged the faith in which she had been brought up, but he had not inoculated her with his own; and a dull gloom, sinking at last almost to apathy, fell upon her spirits. She fought against it, like a brave woman as she was.

Carlyle himself recognised occasionally that she was not happy. Intentionally unkind it was not in his nature to be. After his mother, he loved his wife better than anyone in the world. He was only occupied, unperceiving, negligent;

and when he *did* see that anything was wrong with her, he was at once the tenderest of husbands.

Those who have studied Carlyle's writings as they ought to be studied, know that shrewd practical sense underlies always his metaphorical extravagances. In matters of business he was the most prudent of men. He had left his wife at Craigenputtoch to pack up, and had plunged, himself, into the whirlpool of househunting. He very soon discovered that there was no hurry, and that he was not the best judge in such matters. He understood—the second best form of wisdom—that he did not understand, and forbore to come to any resolution till Mrs. Carlyle could join him.

Carlyle had not been idle—had walked, as he said, till his feet were lamed under him. He had searched in Brompton, in Kensington, about the Regent's Park. He had seen many houses more or less desirable, more or less objectionable. For himself he inclined on the whole to one which Leigh Hunt had found for him near the river in Chelsea. Leigh Hunt lived with his singular family at No. 4 Upper Cheyne Row. About sixty yards off, about the middle of Great Cheyne Row, which runs at right angles to the other, there was a house which fixed his attention. Twice he went over it. "It is notable," he said, "how at every new visit, your opinion gets a little hitch the *contrary* way from its former tendency; imagination has outgone the reality. I nevertheless still feel a great liking for this excellent old House. . . . Chelsea is unfashionable; it was once the resort of the Court and great, however; hence numerous old houses in it, at once cheap and excellent."[11]

A third inspection produced a fuller description—description of the place as it was fifty years ago, and not wholly incorrect of its present condition; for Cheyne Row has changed less than most other streets in London. The Embankment had yet forty years to wait.

> The street . . . runs down upon the River, which I suppose you might see, by stretching out your neck from our front windows, at a distance of 50 yards on the left. We are called "Cheyne Row" proper (pronounced, *Chainie Row*), and are a "genteel neighbourhood," two old Ladies on one side, unknown character on the other but with "pianos." . . . Backwards, a Garden (the size of our back one at Comely Bank) with trees &c, in bad culture;

beyond this green hayfields and tree-avenues (once a Bishop's
pleasure-grounds) an unpicturesque, yet rather cheerful outlook.
The House itself is eminent, antique; wainscotted to the very
ceiling, and has been all new-painted and repaired; broadish stair,
with massive balustrade (in the old style) corniced and as thick as
one's thigh; floors firm as a rock, wood of them here and there
worm-eaten, yet capable of cleanness, and still with thrice the
strength of a modern floor. And then as to room, Goody! . . .
Three stories besides the sunk story; in every one of them *three*
apartments in depth (something like 40 feet in all). . . . Rent
£35! . . . Chelsea is a singular, heterogeneous kind of spot; very
dirty and confused in some places, quite beautiful in others;
abounding with antiquities and the traces of great men: Sir T.
More, Steele, Smollett, &c &c. Our Row (which for the last three
doors or so is a *street,* and none of the noblest) runs out upon a
beautiful "Parade" (perhaps they call it) running along the shore
of the River; shops &c, a broad highway, with huge shady trees;
boats lying moored, and a smell of shipping and tar; Battersea
Bridge (of wood) a few yards off; the broad River, with white-
trowsered, white-shirted Cockneys dashing by like arrows in their
long Canoes of Boats; beyond, the green beautiful knolls of
Surr[e]y with their villages: on the whole a most artificial,
green-painted, yet lively, fresh, almost opera-looking business,
such as you can fancy. . . . Finally, Chelsea abounds more than
any place in *Omnibii* . . . , and they take you to Coventry-street
(within a mile of this) for six-pence. Revolve all this in thy fancy
and judgement, my child; and see what thou canst make of it.[12]

Carlyle was not long left alone. Mrs. Carlyle arrived—she
came by Annan steamer and the coach from Liverpool at
the beginning of June; old Mrs. Carlyle, standing with a
crowd on the Annan pier, waving her handkerchief as the
vessel moved away. Carlyle, as he returned from his walk
to his lodgings in Ampton Street, was received by the chirp-
ing of little Chico, the canary bird; his wife resting after her
journey in bed. They had been fortunate in securing a
remarkable woman, who was more a friend and a companion
than a servant, to help them through their first difficulties
—Bessy Barnet, the daughter of Mr. Badams's housekeeper
at Birmingham, whom Carlyle had known there as a child.
Badams was now dead, and this Bessy, who had remained
with him to the last, now attached herself to Carlyle for
the sake of her late master. The Chelsea house was seen by
Mrs. Carlyle, and after some hesitation was approved; and
three days after they had taken possession of their future
home, and Pickford's vans were at the door unloading the
furniture from Craigenputtoch.

5 CHEYNE ROW (RENUMBERED 24 IN THE 1870s). The Carlyles went to London in 1834 and lived in the same house for the rest of their lives. The attic soundproof room is visible. (Postcard photograph, courtesy of the National Trust.)

The auspices under which the new life began were altogether favourable. The weather was fine; the cherries were ripening on a tree in the garden. Carlyle got his garden tools to work and repaired the borders, and set in slips of jessamine and gooseberry bushes brought from Scotland. To his mother, who was curious about the minutest details, he reported:

> We lie safe down in a little bend of the river, away from all the great roads; have air and quiet hardly inferior to Craigenputtoch, an outlook from the back windows into mere leafy regions, with here and there a red high-peaked old roof looking thro'; and see nothing of London, except by day the summits of St. Paul's Cathedral and Westminster Abbey, and by night the gleam of the great Babylon affronting the peaceful skies.[13]

The French Revolution had been finally decided on as the subject for the next book, and was to be set about immediately; Fraser having offered, not indeed to give money for it, but to do what neither he nor any other publisher would venture for *Sartor*—take the risk of printing it. Mill furnished volumes on the subject in "barrowfuls." Leigh Hunt was a pleasant immediate neighbour, and an increasing circle of Radical notabilities began to court Carlyle's society. There was money enough to last for a year at least. In a year he hoped that his book might be finished; that he might then give lectures; that either then or before some editorship might fall to him—the editorship, perhaps (for it is evident that he hoped for it) of Mill's and Molesworth's new Radical *Review*.[14] Thus at the outset he was—for him —tolerably cheerful.

The first letters from London would seem to indicate that Carlyle was tolerably "hefted" to his new home and condition; but the desponding mood was never long absent. Happy those to whom nature has given good animal spirits. There is no fairy gift equal to this for helping a man to fight his way, and animal spirits Carlyle never had. He had the keenest sense of the ridiculous; but humour and sadness are inseparable properties of the same nature; his constitutional unhopefulness soon returned upon him, and was taking deeper hold than he cared to let others see. The good effects of this change wore off in a few weeks: the old enemy was in possession again, and the entries in his diary were more desponding than even at Craigen-puttoch.

How to keep living was the problem. *The French Revolution*, Carlyle thought at this time, must be a mere sketch; finished and sold by the following spring if he was to escape entire bankruptcy. He had hoped more than he knew for the editorship of the new *Review*. It had been given to [W. J.] Fox, "as the safer man."

No doubt it was hard to bear. By Mill, if by no one else, Carlyle thought that he was recognised and appreciated; and Mill had preferred Fox to him. The *Review* fared as Carlyle expected: lived its short day as long as Molesworth's money held out, and then withered. Perhaps, as he said, "With him it had not been so." Yet no one who knows how such things are managed could blame Mill. To the bookselling world Carlyle's name, since the appearance of *Sartor Resartus* in *Fraser's*, had become an abomination, and so far was Mill from really altering his own estimate of Carlyle that he offered to publish "The Diamond Necklace" as a book "at his own expense . . . that he might have the pleasure and profit of reviewing it!"[15] Carlyle at bottom understood that it could not have been otherwise, and that essentially it was better for him as it was. Through his own thrift and his wife's skill, the extremity of poverty never really came, and his time and faculties were left unencumbered for his own work. Even of Fox himself, whom he met at a dinner-party, he could speak kindly; not unappreciatively. The cloud lifted now and then, oftener probably than his diary would lead one to suppose. Carlyle's sense of the ridiculous—stronger than that of any contemporary man—was the complement to his dejection. In his better moments he could see and enjoy the brighter side of his position.

So passed on the first summer of Carlyle's life in London. "The weather," he says, "was very hot; *defying* it (in hard almost brimless *hat*, which was *obbligato* in that time of slavery) did sometimes throw me into colic." In the British Museum lay concealed somewhere a "collection of *French Pamphlets*" on the Revolution, "the completest of its sort in the world," which, after six weeks' wrestle with officiality, he was obliged to find "*in*accessible"[16] to him. Idle obstruction will put the most enduring of men now and then out of patience, and Carlyle was not enduring in such matters; but his wife was able on the first of September to send to Scotsbrig a very tolerable picture of his condition. Carlyle's letter under the same cover communicates that the writing of *The French Revolution* was actually begun.

John Carlyle meanwhile was prospering with Lady Clare, and was in a position to return to his brother the generosity of earlier days. It was perfectly true, as Carlyle had said, that what any one of the family possessed the others were free to share with him. In September John sent home £130 for his mother. The expected provision barrels from Scotsbrig were long in arriving, and Carlyle had to quicken the family movements in the end of October by a representation of the state of things to which he and his wife were reduced.

For the rest, life went on without much variety. Bessy Barnet left Cheyne Row after two months, being obliged to return to her mother, and they had to find another servant among the London maids of all work. Carlyle crushed down his dispiritment; found at any rate that "nothing like the *deep sulkiness* of Craigenputtoch" troubled him in London. "I see always that I am in the right workshop, had I but got acquainted with the *tools* properly."[17] "Teufelsdröckh," circulating in a stitched-up form made out of the sheets of *Fraser's,* was being read, a few persons really admiring it; the generality turning up their eyes in speechless amazement. Irving had departed, having gone to Scotland, where he was reported as lying ill at Glasgow, and, to Carlyle's very deep distress, likely to die.

Among minor adventures, Carlyle was present at the burning of the Houses of Parliament. "The crowd," he says, "was quiet, rather [gratified] than otherwise; *whew'd* and whistled when the breeze came as if to encourage it: 'there's a *flare-up* . . . for the House O' Lords!'—'A judgement for the Poor-Law Bill!'—'There go their *hacts*' (acts)! —such exclamations seemed to be the prevailing ones. A man *sorry* I did not anywhere see."[18] "About a month before this date [21 November 1834]," Carlyle wrote years later,

Edward Irving rode to the door one evening, came in and staid with us some 20 minutes; the one call we ever had of him here,— his farewell call before setting out to ride towards Glasgow, as the Doctors, helpless otherwise, had ordered. He was very friendly, calm and affectionate; chivalrously courteous to Her (as I remember), "Ah, yes," looking round the room, "you are like an Eve, make every place you live in beautiful!" He was not sad in manner; but was at heart, as you could notice, serious, even solemn. Darkness at hand, & the weather damp, he could not loiter. I saw him mount at the door; watched till he turned the first corner (close by the Rector's garden-door),—and had vanished from us for altogether. He died at Glasgow before the end of December coming.[19]

Irving was dead, and with it closed the last chapter of Jane Welsh's early romance. Much might be said of the effect of it both on Irving and on her. The characters of neither of them escaped unscathed by the passionate love which had once existed between them. But all that is gone, and concerns the world no longer. I will add only an affectionately sorrowful letter which Carlyle wrote at the time to his mother when the news from Glasgow came.

Poor Edward Irving, as you have heard, has ended his pilgrimage. I had been expecting that issue; but not so soon; the news of his death, which Fraser the Bookseller (once a hearer of his) communicated quite on a sudden, struck me deeply; and the *wae* feeling of what it has all been, and what it has all ended in, kept increasing with me for the next ten days. . . . I am very sad about him: ten years ago (when I was first here), what a rushing and running; his house never empty of idle or half-earnest wondering people with their carriages and equipments: and *now*,— alas, it is all *gone*, marched on like a deceitful vision, and all is emptiness, desertion, and his place knows him no more! He was *a good man* too; that I do heartily believe: his faults we may hope were abundantly expiated in *this* life; and now his memory, as that of the just ought, shall be hallowed with us. One thing with another, I have not found another such man. I shall never forget these last times I saw him: I longed much to help him, to deliver him; but could not do it. My poor first Friend, my first and best! —— Bookseller Fraser applied to me to write a word about him; which I did.[20]

Tenderly, beautifully, Carlyle could feel for his friend. No more touching "funeral oration" was ever uttered over a lost companion than in the brief paper of which here he spoke;[21] and his heart at the time was heavy for himself also. He had almost lost hope. At no past period of his life does the Journal show more despondency than in this autumn and winter. He might repeat his mother's words to himself, "tine heart, tine a' [break heart, break all]." But the heart was near "tined" for all that.

[1 January] 1835. Twelve o'clock has just struck; the last hour of 1834, the first of a new year. Bells ringing (to me dolefully); a wet wind blustering; my wife in bed (very unhappily ill of a foot which a puddle of a maid scalded three weeks ago); I, after a day of *fruit*less toil, reading and re-reading about that Versailles "6th of October" still. It is long since I have written anything here. The future looks too black round me, the present too doleful, unfriendly. I am too sick at heart (wearied, wasted in body) to complain—even to myself. My first friend Edward Irving is dead; above three weeks ago. I am friendless here; or as good as that.[22]

With these words I close the story of Carlyle's apprenticeship. His training was over. He was now a master in his craft, on the eve, though he did not know it, of universal recognition as an original and extraordinary man. Henceforward his life was in his works. The outward incidents of it will be related in his wife's letters and in his own explanatory notes.[23] My part has been to follow him from the peasant's home in which he was born and nurtured to the steps of the great position which he was afterwards to occupy; to describe his trials and his struggles, and the effect of them upon his mind and disposition. But no one, especially no one of so rugged and angular a character, sees the lights and shadows precisely as others see them. When a man of letters has exercised an influence so vast over successive generations of thinkers, the world has a right to know the minutest particulars of his life; and the sovereigns of literature can no more escape from the fierce light which beats upon a throne, than the kings and ministers who have ruled the destinies of states and empires. Carlyle had no such high estimate of his own consequence. His poor fortunes he considered to be of moment to no one but himself; but he knew that the world would demand an account of him, and with characteristic unreserve he placed his journals and his correspondence in my hands with no instructions save that I should tell the truth about him, and if shadows there were, that least of all should I conceal them.

314

If in this part of my duty I have erred at all, I have erred in excess, not in defect. It is the nature of men to dwell on the faults of those who stand above them. They are comforted by perceiving that the person whom they have heard so much admired was but of common clay after all. The life of no man, authentically told, will ever be found free from fault. Carlyle has been seen in these volumes fighting for thirty-nine years—fighting with poverty, with dyspepsia, with intellectual temptations, with neglect or obstruction from his fellow mortals. Their ways were not his ways. His attitude was not different only from their attitude, but was a condemnation of it, and it was not to be expected that they would look kindly on him. His existence hitherto had been a prolonged battle; a man does not carry himself in such conflicts so wisely and warily that he can come out of them unscathed; and Carlyle carried scars from his wounds both on his mind and on his temper. He had stood aloof from parties; he had fought his way alone. He was fierce and uncompromising. To those who saw but the outside of him he appeared scornful, imperious, and arrogant. He was stern in his judgement of others. The sins of passion he could pardon, but the sins of insincerity, or half-sincerity, he could never pardon. He would not condescend to the conventional politenesses which remove the friction between man and man. He called things by their right names, and in a dialect edged with sarcasm. Thus he was often harsh when he ought to have been merciful; he was contemptuous where he had no right to despise; and in his estimate of motives and actions was often unjust and mistaken. He, too, who was so severe with others had weaknesses of his own of which he was unconscious in the excess of his self-confidence. He was proud—one may say savagely proud. It was a noble determination in him that he would depend upon himself alone; but he would not only accept no obligation, but he resented the offer of help to himself or to anyone belonging to him as if it had been an insult. He never wholly pardoned Jeffrey for having made his brother's fortune. His temper had been ungovernable from his childhood; he had the irritability of a dyspeptic man of genius; and when the Devil, as he called it, had possession of him, those whose comfort he ought most to have studied were the most exposed to the storm: he who preached so wisely *"Do the Duty which lies nearest thee,"*[24] forgot his own instructions, and made no adequate effort to cast the Devil out. Nay, more: there broke upon him in his late years, like a flash of lightning from heaven, the terrible revelation that he had sacrificed his wife's health and happiness in his absorption in his work; that he had been oblivious of his most obvious obligations, and had been negligent, inconsiderate, and selfish. The fault was grave and the remorse agonising. For many years after she had left him, when we passed the spot in our walks where she was last seen alive, he would bare his grey head in the wind and rain—his features wrung with unavailing sorrow. Let all this be acknowledged; and let those who know themselves to be without either these sins, or others as bad as these, freely cast stones at Carlyle.

But there is the other side of the account. In the weightier matters of the law Carlyle's life had been without speck or flaw. From his earliest years, in the home at Ecclefechan, at school, at college, in every incident or recorded aspect of him, we see invariably the same purity, the same innocence of heart, and uprightness and integrity of action. As a child, as a boy, as a man, he had been true in word and honest and just in deed. There is no trace, not the slightest, of levity or folly. He sought his friends among the worthiest of his fellow-students, and to those friends he was from the first a special object of respect and admiration. His letters, even in early youth, were so remarkable that they were preserved as treasures by his correspondents. In the thousands which I have read, either written to Carlyle or written by him, I have found no sentence of his own which he could have wished unwritten, or, through all those trying years of incipient manhood, a single action alluded to by others which those most jealous of his memory need regret to read, or his biographer need desire to conceal. Which of us would not shiver at the thought if his own life were to be exposed to the same dreadful ordeal, and his own letters, or the letters of others written about him, were searched through for the sins of his youth? These, it may be said, are but negative virtues. But his positive qualities were scarcely less beautiful. Nowhere is a man known better than in his own family. No disguise is

316

possible there; and he whom father and mother, brother and sister love, we may be sure has deserved to be loved.

Among the many remarkable characteristics of the Carlyle household, whether at Mainhill or Scotsbrig, was the passionate affection which existed among them and the special love which they all felt for "Tom." Well might Jeffrey say that Carlyle would not have known poverty if he had not been himself a giver. His own habits were Spartan in their simplicity, and from the moment when he began to earn his small salary as an usher at Annan, the savings of his thrift were spent in presents to his father and mother and in helping to educate his brother. I too can bear witness that the same generous disposition remained with him to the end. In his later years he had an abundant income, but he never added to his own comforts or luxuries. His name was not seen on charity lists, but he gave away every year perhaps half what he received. I was myself in some instances employed by him to examine into the circumstances of persons who had applied to him for help. The stern censor was in these instances the kindest of Samaritans. It was enough if a man or woman was miserable. He did not look too curiously into the causes of it. I was astonished at the profuseness with which he often gave to persons little worthy of his liberality.

Nor was there even in those more trying cases where men were prospering beyond their merits any malice or permanent ill-will. He was constitutionally atrabilious and scornful; but the bitterness with which he would speak of such persons was on the surface merely. "Poor devil," he would say of some successful political Philistine, "after all, if we looked into the history of him, we should find how it all came about." He was always sad: often gloomy in the extreme. Men of genius rarely take cheerful views of life. They see too clearly. Dante and Isaiah were not probably exhilarating companions; but Carlyle, when unpossessed and in his natural humour, was gentle, forbearing, and generous.

If his character as a man was thus nobly upright, so he employed his time and his talents with the same high sense of responsibility—not to make himself great, or honoured, or admired, but as a trust committed to him for his Maker's purposes. "What can you say of Carlyle," said Mr. Ruskin to me, "but that he was born in the clouds and struck by the lightning?"—"struck by the lightning"—not meant for happiness, but for other ends; a stern fate which nevertheless in the modern world, as in the ancient, is the portion dealt out to some individuals on whom the heavens have been pleased to set their mark. Gifted as he knew himself to be with unusual abilities, he might have risen to distinction on any one of the beaten roads of life, and have won rank and wealth for himself. He glanced at the Church, he glanced at the Bar, but there was something working in him like the Δαίμων [daimon] of Socrates, which warned him off with an imperious admonition, and insisted on being obeyed. Men who fancy that they have a "mission" in this world are usually intoxicated by vanity, and their ambition is in the inverse ratio of their strength to give effect to it. But in Carlyle the sense of having a mission was the growth of the actual presence in him of the necessary powers. Certain associations, certain aspects of human life and duty, had forced themselves upon him as truths of immeasurable consequence which the world was forgetting. He was a *vates*, a seer. He perceived things which others did not see, and which it was his business to force them to see. He regarded himself as being charged actually and really with a message which he was to deliver to mankind, and, like other prophets, he was "straitened" till his work was accomplished. A Goethe could speak in verse, and charm the world into listening to him by the melody of his voice. The deep undertones of Carlyle's music could not modulate themselves under rhyme and metre. For the new matter which he had to utter he had to create a new form corresponding to it. He had no pulpit from which to preach, and through literature alone had he any access to the world which he was to address. Even "a man of letters" must live while he writes, and Carlyle had imposed conditions upon himself which might make the very keeping himself alive impossible; for his function was sacred to him, and he had laid down as a fixed rule that he would never write merely to please, never for money, that he would never write anything save when specially moved to write by an impulse from within; above all, never to set down a sentence which he did not in his heart believe to be true, and to spare no labour till his work to the last fibre was as good as he could possibly make it.

These were rare qualities in a modern writer whose bread depended on his pen, and such as might well compensate for worse faults than spleen and hasty temper. He had not starved, but he had come within measurable distance of starvation. Nature is a sharp schoolmistress, and when she is training a man of genius for a great moral purpose, she takes care by "the constitution of things" that he shall not escape discipline. More than once better hopes had appeared to be dawning. But the sky had again clouded, and at the time of the removal to London the prospect was all but hopeless. No man is bound to fight for ever against proved impossibilities. *The French Revolution* was to be the last effort. If this failed Carlyle had resolved to give up the game, abandon literature, buy spade and rifle and make for the backwoods of America. "You are not fit for that either, my fine fellow,"[25] he had sorrowfully to say to himself. Still he meant to try. America might prove a kinder friend to him than England had been, in some form or other. Worse it could not prove.

For two years the writing of that book occupied him. The material grew on his hands, and the first volume, for the cause mentioned in the *Reminiscences*, had to be written a second time.[26] All the mornings he was at his desk; in the afternoons he took his solitary walks in Hyde Park, seeing the brilliant equipages and the knights and dames of fashion prancing gaily along the Row. He did not envy them. He would not have changed existences with the brightest of these fortune's favourites if the wealth of England had been poured into the scale. But he did think that his own lot was hard, so willing was he to do anything for an honest living, yet with every door closed against him. "Not one of you," he said to himself as he looked at them, "could do what I am doing, and it concerns you too, if you did but know it."[27]

They did not know it and they have not known it. Fifty years have passed since Carlyle was writing *The French Revolution*. The children of fashion still canter under the elms of the Park, as their fathers and mothers were cantering then, and no sounds of danger have yet been audible to flutter the Mayfair dove-cotes. "They call me a great man now," Carlyle said to me a few days before he died, "but not one believes what I have told them." But if they did not believe the prophet, they could worship the new star which was about to rise. The Annandale peasant boy was to be the wonder of the London world. He had wrought himself into a personality which all were to be compelled to admire, and in whom a few recognised, like Goethe, the advent of a new moral force the effects of which it was impossible to predict.[28]

chapter sixteen

1834

On Carlyle's Biography

In Carlyle's Journal I find written, on the 10th of October, 1843, the following words:

> One Horne writes last night about "notes for a biography" in some beggarly *"spirit of the age"* or other rubbish-basket he is about editing!— Re-jected, *nem. con.* What have I to do with their Spirits of the Age? To have my Life surveyed and commented upon by all men, even wisely, is no object with me, but rather the opposite; how much less to have it done *unwisely.* The world has no business with my Life; the world will never know my Life, if it should write and read a hundred "biographies" of me: the main *facts* of it even are known, and are like to be known, to myself alone of created men. The "goose-goddess" which they call "Fame" —*ach Gott!*

And again, December 29, 1848:

> Darwin said to Jane, the other day, in his quizzing-serious manner, "Who will write Carlyle's Life?" The word, reported to me, set me thinking how *impossible* it was, and would forever remain, for any creature to write my "Life"; the *chief* elements of my little destiny have all along lain deep below view or surmise, and never will or can be known to any Son of Adam. I would say to my Biographer, if any fool undertook such a task, "Forbear, poor fool; let no Life of *me* be written; let me and my bewildered wrestlings lie buried here, and be forgotten swiftly of all the world. If thou write, it will be mere delusions and hallucinations. The confused world never understood, nor will understand, me and my poor affairs; not even the persons nearest me could guess at them; —nor was it found indispensable; nor is it *now*, for any but an idle purpose, profitable, were it even possible. Silence,—and go thy ways elsewhither!"[1]

Reluctantly, and only when he found that his wishes would not and could not be respected, Carlyle requested me to undertake the task which he had thus described as hopeless; and placed materials in my hands which would make the creation of a true likeness of him, if still difficult, yet no longer as impossible as he had declared it to be. Higher confidence was never placed by any man in another. I had not sought it, but I did not refuse to accept it. I felt myself only more strictly bound than men in such circumstances usually are, to discharge the duty which I was undertaking with the fidelity which I knew to be expected from me. Had I considered my own comfort or my own interest, I should have sifted out or passed lightly over the delicate features in the story. It would have been as easy as it would have been agreeable for me to construct a picture, with every detail strictly accurate, of an almost perfect character. An account so written would have been read with immediate pleasure. Carlyle would have been admired and applauded, and the biographer, if he had not shared in the praise, would at least have escaped censure. He would have followed in the track marked out for him by a custom which is all but universal. When a popular statesman dies, or a popular soldier or clergyman, his faults are forgotten, his virtues only are remembered in his epitaph. Everyone has some frailties, but the merits and not the frailties are what interest the world; and with great men of the ordinary kind whose names and influence will not survive their own generation, to leave out the shadow, and record solely what is bright and attractive, is not only permissible, but is a right and honourable instinct. The good should be frankly acknowledged with no churlish qualifications. But the pleasure which we feel, and the honour which we seek to confer, are avenged, wherever truth is concealed, in the case of the exceptional few who are to become historical and belong to the immortals. The sharpest scrutiny is the condition of enduring fame. Every circumstance which can be ascertained about them is eventually dragged into light. If blank spaces are left, they are filled by rumour or conjecture. When the generation which knew them is gone, there is no more tenderness in dealing with them; and if their friends have been indiscreetly reserved, idle tales which survive in tradition become stereotyped into facts. Thus the characters of many of our greatest men, as they stand in history, are left blackened by groundless calumnies, or credited with imaginary excellences, a prey to be torn in pieces by rival critics, with clear evidence wanting, and prepossessions fixed on one side or the other by dislike or sympathy.

Had I taken the course which the "natural man" would have recommended, I should have given no faithful account of Carlyle. I should have created "delusions and hallucinations" of the precise kind which he who was the truest of men most deprecated and dreaded; and I should have done it not innocently and in ignorance, but with deliberate insincerity, after my attention had been specially directed by his own generous openness to the points which I should have left unnoticed. I should have been unjust first to myself— for I should have failed in what I knew to be my duty as a biographer. I should have been unjust secondly to the public. Carlyle exerted for many years an almost unbounded influence on the mind of educated England. His writings are now spread over the whole English-speaking world. They are studied with eagerness and confidence by millions who have looked and look to him not for amusement, but for moral guidance, and those millions have a right to know what manner of man he really was. It may be, and I for one think it will be, that when time has levelled accidental distinctions, when the perspective has altered, and the foremost figures of this century are seen in their true proportions, Carlyle will tower far above all his contemporaries, and will then be the one person of them about whom the coming generations will care most to be informed. But whether I estimate his importance rightly or wrongly, he has played a part which entitles everyone to demand a complete account of his character. He has come forward as a teacher of mankind. He has claimed "he taught them as *one* having authority, and not as the scribes."[2] He has denounced as empty illusion the most favourite convictions of the age. No concealment is permissible about a man who could thus take on himself the character of a prophet and speak to it in so imperious a tone.

Lastly, I should have been unjust to Carlyle himself and

to everyone who believed and has believed in him. To have been reticent would have implied that there was something to hide, and, taking Carlyle all in all, there never was a man—I at least never knew of one—whose conduct in life would better bear the fiercest light which can be thrown upon it. In the grave matters of the law he walked for eighty-five years unblemished by a single moral spot. There are no "sins of youth" to be apologized for. In no instance did he ever deviate even for a moment from the strictest lines of integrity. He had his own way to make in life, and when he had chosen his profession, he had to depend on popularity for the bread which he was to eat. But although more than once he was within sight of starvation he would never do less than his very best. He never wrote an idle word, he never wrote or spoke any single sentence which he did not with his whole heart believe to be true.[3] Conscious though he was that he had talents above those of common men, he sought neither rank nor fortune for himself. When he became famous and moved as an equal among the great of the land, he was content to earn the wages of an artisan, and kept to the simple habits in which he had been bred in his father's house. He might have had a pension had he stooped to ask for it; but he chose to maintain himself by his own industry, and when a pension was offered him it was declined. He despised luxury; he was thrifty and even severe in the economy of his own household; but in the times of his greatest poverty he had always something to spare for those who were dear to him. When money came at last, and it came only when he was old and infirm, he added nothing to his own comforts, but was lavishly generous with it to others. Tender-hearted and affectionate he was beyond all men whom I have ever known. His faults, which in his late remorse he exaggerated, as men of noblest natures are most apt to do, his impatience, his irritability, his singular melancholy, which made him at times distressing as a companion, were the effects of temperament first, and of a peculiarly sensitive organisation; and secondly of absorption in his work and of his determination to do that work as well as it could possibly be done. Such faults as these were but as the vapours which hang about a mountain, inseparable from the nature of the man. They have to be told because without them his character cannot be

324

understood, and because they affected others as well as himself.[4] But they do not blemish the essential greatness of his character, and when he is fully known he will not be loved or admired the less because he had infirmities like the rest of us. Carlyle's was not the imperious grandeur which has risen superior to weakness and reigns cold and impassive in distant majesty. The fire in his soul burnt red to the end, and sparks flew from it which fell hot on those about him, not always pleasant, not always hitting the right spot or the right person; but it was pure fire notwithstanding, fire of genuine and noble passion, of genuine love for all that was good, and genuine indignation at what was mean or base or contemptible. His life was not a happy one, and there were features in it for which, as he looked back, he bitterly reproached himself. But there are many, perhaps the majority of us, who sin deeper every day of their lives in these very points in which Carlyle sinned, and without Carlyle's excuses, who do not know that they have anything to repent of. The more completely it is understood, the more his character will be seen to answer to his intellectual teaching. The one is the counterpart of the other. There was no falsehood and there was no concealment in him. The same true nature showed itself in his life and in his words. He acted as he spoke from his heart, and those who have admired his writings will equally admire himself when they see him in his actual likeness.

I, for myself, concluded, though not till after long hesitation, that there should be no reserve, and therefore I have practised none. I have published his own autobiographical fragments. I have published an account of his early years from his Letters and Journals. I have published the Letters and Memorials of his wife which describe (from one aspect) his life in London as long as she remained with him. I supposed for a time that if to these I added my personal recollections of him, my task would be sufficiently accomplished; but I have thought it better on longer consideration to complete his biography as I began it. He himself quotes a saying of Goethe that on the lives of remarkable men ink and paper should least be spared. I must leave no materials unused to complete the portrait which I attempt to draw.

chapter seventeen

1834–1836

London and the Writing of
The French Revolution

In the summer of 1834 Carlyle left Craigenputtoch and its
solitary moors and removed to London, there to make a last
experiment whether it would be possible for him to abide by
literature as a profession, or whether he must seek another
employment and perhaps another country. I have already
told how he set up his modest establishment in Cheyne
Row in the house where he was to remain till he died. He
had some £200 in money for immediate necessities; of distinct prospects he had none at all. He had made a reputation by his articles in reviews as a man of marked ability.
He had been well received on his visit to London in 1831–32,
and was an object of admiring interest to a number of young
men who were themselves afterwards to become famous,
to John Mill, to Charles Buller, to Charles Austin, Sir
William Molesworth, and the advanced section of the
Philosophic Radicals, and he doubtless hoped that when he
was seen and more widely known, some editorship, secretaryship, or analogous employment might fall in his way,
which would enable him to live. Even Brougham and
Macaulay and the orthodox Whigs of the *Edinburgh Review* admitted his talents, though they disliked the use
which he made of them, and would have taken him up and
provided for him if he would have allowed Jeffrey to put
him into harness. But harness it was impossible for him to
wear, even harness as light as was required by booksellers
and editors. They had wondered at him and tried him, but
since the appearance of *Sartor* they had turned their backs

upon him as hopeless, and had closed in his face the door of periodical literature. He was impracticable, unpersuadable, unmalleable, as independent and wilful as if he were an eldest son and the heir of a peerage. He had created no "public" of his own; the public which existed could not understand his writings and would not buy them, nor could he be induced so much as to attempt to please it; and thus it was that in Cheyne Row he was more neglected than he had been in Scotland. No one seemed to want his services, no one applied to him for contributions. At the Bullers' house, at the Austins', and in a gradually increasing circle, he went into society and was stared at as if he were a strange wild animal. His conversational powers were extraordinary. His unsparing veracity, his singular insight, struck everyone who came in contact with him, but were more startling than agreeable. He was unobtrusive, but when asked for his opinion he gave it in his metaphoric manner, and when contradicted was contemptuous and overbearing, "far too sarcastic for a young man,"[1] too sarcastic by far for the vanity of those whom he mortified. A worse fault was that he refused to attach himself to any existing sect, either religious or political. He abhorred cant in all its forms, and as cant in some shape gathers about every organised body of English opinion, he made many enemies and few friends; and those few, fearful of the consequences, were shy of confessing themselves his disciples. Month after month went by, and no opening presented itself of which he was able to avail himself. Molesworth founded a radical *Review*, but the management of it was not offered to Carlyle, though he hoped it might be offered. His money flowed away, and with the end of it would end also the prospect of making a livelihood in London.

I said no opening of which he could avail himself, but one opening there was which if he had chosen would have led him on to fortune, and which any one but Carlyle would have grasped at. In the small number of men who had studied *Sartor* seriously, and had discovered the golden veins in that rugged quartz rock, was John Sterling, then fresh from Cambridge and newly ordained a clergyman, of vehement but most noble nature, who though far from agreeing with Carlyle, though shrinking from and even hating,

327

so impetuous was he, many of Carlyle's opinions, yet saw also that he was a man like none that he had yet fallen in with, a man not only brilliantly gifted, but differing from the common run of people in this, that he would not lie, that he would not equivocate, that he would say always what he actually thought, careless whether he pleased or offended. Such a quality, rare always, and especially rare in those who are poor and unfriended, could not but recommend the possessor of it to the brave and generous Sterling. He introduced Carlyle to his father, who was then the guiding genius of the *Times;* and the great editor of the first periodical of the world offered Carlyle work there, of course on the implied conditions. When a man enlists in the army, his soul as well as his body belong to his commanding officer. He is to be no judge of the cause for which he has to fight. His enemies are chosen for him and not by himself. His duty is to obey orders and to ask no questions. Carlyle, though with poverty at his door, and entire penury visible in the near future, turned away from a proposal which might have tempted men who had less excuse for yielding to it. He was already the sworn soldier of another chief. His allegiance from first to last was to *truth,* truth as it presented itself to his own intellect and his own conscience. He could not, would not, advocate what he did not believe; he would not march in the same regiment with those who did advocate what he disbelieved; nor would he consent to suppress his own convictions when he chose to make them known. By this resolution not the *Times* only, but the whole world of party life and party action, was necessarily closed against him. Organisation of any kind in free communities is only possible where individuals will forget their differences in general agreement. Carlyle, as he said himself, was fated to be an Ishmaelite, his hand against every man and every man's hand against him; and Ishmaelites, if they are to prosper at all in such a society as ours, and escape being trampled under the horses' hoofs, require better material sources behind them than a fast-shrinking capital of £200.

One occupation, and one only, absorbed Carlyle's time and thought during these first years of his London life, the writing his history of the French Revolution. He had studied it at Craigenputtoch. He had written as a preliminary flight, and as if to try his wings, the exquisite sketch of the episode of the Diamond Necklace, which lay in his desk still unpublished. He had written *round* the subject, on Voltaire, on Diderot, and on Cagliostro. The wild tornado in which the French monarchy perished had fascinated his attention, because it illustrated to him in all its features such theory as he had been able to form of the laws under which this world is ruled, and he had determined to throw it out of himself if afterwards he was to abandon literature for ever. His mind had been formed in his father's house upon the Old Testament and the Presbyterian creed, and, far as he had wandered and deeply as he had read, the original lesson had remained indelible.

To the Scotch people and to the Puritan part of the English, the Jewish history contained a faithful account of the dealings of God with man in all countries and in all ages. As long as men kept God's commandments it was well with them; when they forgot God's commandments and followed after wealth and enjoyment, the wrath of God fell upon them. Commerce, manufactures, intellectual enlightenment, political liberty, outward pretences of religiosity, all that modern nations mean when they speak of wealth and progress and improvement, were but Moloch or Astarte in a new disguise, and now as then it was impossible to serve God and Baal. In some form or other retribution would come, wherever the hearts of men were set on material prosperity.

To this simple creed Carlyle adhered as the central principle of all his thoughts. The outward shell of it had broken. He had ceased to believe in miracles and supernatural interpositions. But to him the natural was the supernatural, and the tales of signs and wonders had risen out of the efforts of men to realise the deepest of truths to themselves. The Jewish history was the symbol of all history. All nations in all ages were under the same dispensation. We did not come into the world with rights which we were entitled to claim, but with duties which we were ordered to do. Rights men had none, save to be governed justly. Duties waited for them everywhere. Their business was to find what those duties were and faithfully fulfil them. So and

329

only so the commonweal could prosper, only so would they be working in harmony with nature, only so would nature answer them with peace and happiness. Of forms of government, "that which was best administered was best." Any form would answer where there was justice between man and man. Constitutions, Bills of Rights, and such like were no substitutes for justice, and could not further justice, till men were themselves just. They must *seek first* God's kingdom, they must be loyally obedient to the law which was written in their consciences; or though miracles had ceased, or had never been, there were forces in the universe terrible as the thunders of Sinai or Assyrian armies, which would bring them to their senses or else destroy them. The French Revolution was the last and most signal example of "God's revenge." The world was not made that the rich might enjoy themselves while the poor toiled and suffered. On such terms society itself was not allowed to exist. The film of habit on which it rested would burst through, and hunger and fury would rise up and bring to judgement the unhappy ones whose business it had been to guide and govern, and had not guided and had not governed.

England and Scotland were not yet like France, yet doubtless these impressions in Carlyle had originated in scenes which he had himself witnessed. The years which had followed the great war had been a time of severe suffering, especially in the North. It had been borne on the whole with silent patience, but the fact remained that hundreds of thousands of labourers and artisans had been out of work and their families starving while bread had been made artificially dear by the corn laws; and the gentry meanwhile had collected their rents and shot their grouse and their partridges, with a deep unconsciousness that anything else was demanded of them. That such an arrangement was not just—that it was entirely contrary, for one thing, to what was taught in the religion which everyone professed to believe—had early become evident to Carlyle, and not to him only, but to those whose opinions he most respected. His father, though too wise a man to meddle in active politics, would sternly say that the existing state of things could not last and ought not to last. His mother, pious and devout though she was, yet was a fiery Radical to the end of her days. Radicalism lay in the blood of the Scotch Calvinists, a bitter inheritance from the Covenanters. Carlyle felt it all to his heart; but he had thought too long and knew too much to believe in the dreams of the Radicals of politics. In them lay revolution, feasts of reason, and a reign of terror. Goethe had taught him the meaning and the worth of the apostles of freedom. They might destroy, but they could never build again. For the sick body and sick soul of modern Europe there was but one remedy, the old remedy of the Jewish prophets, repentance and moral amendment. All men high and low, wise and unwise, must call back into their minds the meaning of the word "duty"; must put away their cant and hypocrisy, their selfishness and appetite for pleasure, and speak truth and do justice. Without this, all tinkering of the constitution, all growth of wealth, though it rained ingots, would avail nothing.

France was the latest instance of the action of the general law. France of all modern nations had been the greatest sinner, and France had been brought to open judgement. She had been offered light at the Reformation, she would not have it, and it had returned upon her as lightning. She had murdered her Colignys. She had preferred to live for pleasure and intellectual enlightenment, with a sham for a religion, which she maintained and herself disbelieved. The palaces and châteaux had been distinguished by the splendour of dissipation. The poor had asked for bread and had been scornfully told to eat grass. The Annandale masons in old James Carlyle's time had dined on grass in silence; the French peasantry had borne with the tyranny of their princes and seigneurs, patient as long as patience was possible, and submitting as sheep to be annually sheared for their masters' pleasure; but the duty of subjects and the duty of rulers answer one to the other, and the question, sooner or later inevitable in such cases, began to be asked, what this aristocracy, these splendid units were, for whom thousands were sacrificed, these nobles who regarded the earth as their hunting ground, these priests who drew such lavish wages for teaching what they knew to be untrue—an ominous enquiry which is never made till fact has

answered it already. False nobles, false priests, once detected, could not be allowed to remain. Unfortunately it
did not occur to the French nation that when the false
nobles and the false priests were shaken off they would
need true nobles and true priests. The new creed rose,
which has since become so popular, that every man can be
his own ruler and his own teacher. The notion that one man
was superior to another and had a right to lead or govern
him was looked upon as a cunning fiction that had been
submitted to for a time by credulity. All men were brothers of one family, born with the same inalienable right to
freedom. The right had only to be acknowledged and respected, and the denial of it made treason to humanity,
and Astraea would then return, and earth would be again
a Paradise. This was the new Evangel. It was tried, and was
tried with the guillotine as its minister, but no millennium
arrived. The first article was false. Men were not equal,
but infinitely unequal, and the attempt to build upon an
untrue hypothesis could end only as all such attempts must
end. The Revolution did not mean emancipation from authority, because the authority of the wise and good over
fools and knaves was the first condition of natural human
society. What it did mean was the bringing great offenders
to justice, who for generation after generation had prospered in iniquity. Crown, nobles, prelates, seigneurs, they
and the lies which they had taught and fattened on were
burnt up as by an eruption from the nether deep, and of
them at least the weary world was made quit.

It was thus that Carlyle regarded the great convulsion
which shook Europe at the close of the last century. He believed that the fate of France would be the fate of all nations whose hearts were set on material things—who for religion were content with decent unrealities, satisfying their
consciences with outward professions—treating God as if he
were indeed, in Milton's words, "a buzzard idol."[2] God
would not be mocked. The poor wretches called mankind lay
in fact under a tremendous dispensation which would exact
an account of them for their misdoings to the smallest fibre.
Every folly, every false word, or unjust deed was a sin
against the universe, of which the consequences would remain, though the guilt might be purged by repentance. The

thought of these things was a weight upon his heart, and he could not rest till he was delivered of it. England just then was rushing along in the enthusiasm of Reform, and the warning was needed. His own future was a blank. He had no notion what was to become of him, how or where he was to live, on what he was to live. His immediate duty was to write down his convictions on this the greatest of all human problems, and *The History of the French Revolution* was the shape in which these convictions crystallised.

Let the reader therefore picture Carlyle to himself, as settled down to this work within a few months after his arrival in London. He was now thirty-nine years old, in the prime of his intellectual strength. His condition, his feelings, his circumstances, and the outward elements of his life are noted down in the letters and journals from which I shall now make extracts.

My Book *cannot* get on, though I stick to it like a burr. Why should I say Peace, Peace, where there is no peace? May God grant me strength to do or to endure aright what is appointed me in this coming now commenced division of Time. Let me *not* despair. Nay I do not in general. Enough to-night; for I am *done!* Peace be to my Mother, and all my loved ones that yet live! What a noisy inanity is this world.—[3]

Saturday. 7*th* February 1835.— The First Book of the French Revolution is finished.[4] . . . Soul and body both very *sick*; yet I have a kind of sacred defiance *trötzend das Schicksal* [in spite of fate]. It has become clear to me that I *have* honestly more force and faculty in me than belongs to the most I see; also it was always clear that no honestly exerted force *can* be utterly lost; were it long years after I am dead, in regions far distant from this, under names far different from thine, the seed thou sowest *will* spring. The great difficulty is to keep one's own *self* in right balance: not despondent, not exasperated defiant; free and clear. O for faith! Food and raiment thou hast never lacked and shalt not.

Nevertheless it is now some three and twenty months since I have earned one penny by my craft of literature: be this recorded as a fact and document for the Literary History of this time. I have been *ready* to work; I am abler than ever to work; know no fault I have committed: and yet so it stands. To *ask* able editors to employ you will not improve but worsen the matter: you are like a spinster waiting to be married; . . . I have some serious thoughts of quitting this Periodical craft one good time for all: *it* is not synonymous with a life of wisdom; when want is approaching, one must have done with whims. If literature will refuse me both bread

and a stomach to digest bread with, then surely the case is growing clear.

So Carlyle's first winter in London was passing away.
His prospects were blank, and the society in which he
moved gave him no particular pleasure, but it was good of
its kind, and was perhaps more agreeable to him than he
knew. His money would hold out till the book was done at
the rate at which it was progressing. The first volume was
finished. On the whole he was not dissatisfied with it. It
was the best that he could do, and he was for him, in moderately fair spirits. But the strain was sharp; his "labour-
pains" with his books were always severe. He had first to
see that the material was pure, with no dross of lies in it,
and then to fuse it all into white heat before it would run
into the mould, and he was in no condition to bear any
fresh burden. Alas for him, he had a stern taskmistress.
Providence or destiny (he himself always believed in Providence, without reason as he admitted, or even against
reason) meant to try him to the utmost. Not only was all
employment closed in his face, save what he could make
for himself, but it was as if something said "Even this too
you shall not do till we have proved your mettle to the last."
A catastrophe was to overtake him, which for a moment
fairly broke his spirit, so cruel it seemed—for the moment,
but for the moment only. It served in fact to show how admirably, though in little things so querulous and irritable,
he could behave under real misfortunes.

John Mill, then his closest and most valuable friend,
was ardently interested in the growth of the new book. He
borrowed the manuscript as it was thrown off, that he
might make notes and suggestions, either for Carlyle's use,
or as material for an early review. The completed first
volume was in his hands for this purpose, when one evening, the 6th of March, 1835, as Carlyle was sitting with his
wife, "toiling along like a *Nigger*"⁵ at the Feast of Pikes,
a rap was heard at the door, a hurried step came up the
stairs, and Mill entered deadly pale, and at first unable to
speak. "Why, Mill," said Carlyle, "what ails ye, man?
What is it?" Staggering, and supported by Carlyle's arm,
Mill gasped out to Mrs. Carlyle to go down and speak to
some one who was in a carriage in the street. Both Carlyle

and she thought that a thing which they had long feared must have actually happened, and that Mill had come to announce it and to take leave of them.[6] So genuine was the alarm that the truth when it came out was a relief. Carlyle led his friend to a seat "the very picture of despair." He then learnt in broken sentences that his manuscript, "left . . . out (too carelessly)" after it had been read, was, "except some three or four bits of leaves," irrevocably "*destroyed.*"[7] That was all, nothing worse; but it was ugly news enough, and the uglier the more the meaning of it was realised. Carlyle wrote always in a highly wrought quasi-automatic condition both of mind and nerves. He read till he was full of his subject. His notes, when they were done with, were thrown aside and destroyed; and of this unfortunate volume, which he had produced as if "possessed" while he was about it, he could remember nothing. Not only were the fruits of "five months of steadfast occasionally excessive and always sickly and painful toil"[8] gone irretrievably, but the spirit in which he had worked seemed to have fled too, not to be recalled; worse than all, his work had been measured carefully against his resources, and the household purse might now be empty before the loss could be made good. The carriage and its occupant drove off—and it would have been better had Mill gone too after he had told his tale, for the forlorn pair wished to be alone together in the face of such a calamity. But Carlyle, whose first thought was of what Mill must be suffering, made light of it, and talked of indifferent things, and Mill stayed and talked too—stayed, I believe, two hours. At length he left them. Mrs. Carlyle told me that the first words her husband uttered as the door closed were: "Well, Mill, poor fellow, is terribly cut up; we must endeavour to hide from him how very serious this business is to us."

The money part of the injury Mill was able to repair. He knew Carlyle's circumstances. He begged, and at last passionately entreated, Carlyle not to punish him by making him feel that he had occasioned real distress to friends whom he so much honoured; and he enclosed a cheque for £200, the smallest sum which he thought that he could offer. Carlyle returned it; but, his financial condition requiring that he should lay his pride aside, he intimated that he would accept half, as representing the wages of five months' labour. To this Mill unwillingly consented. He sent a hundred pounds, and, so far as money went, Carlyle was in the same position as when he began to write. He was not aware till he tried it what difficulty he would find in replacing what had been destroyed; and he was able to write to his brother of what had happened, before he did try again, as of a thing which had ceased to distress him.

For Mill's sake the misadventure was not spoken of in London. Carlyle had been idle for a week or two till he could muster strength to set to work again, and had gone into society as much as he could to distract himself. He was a frequent guest at Henry Taylor's, "a good man," he said, "whose *laugh* reminds me of poor Irving's."[9] At Taylor's he had met Southey. Shortly after the accident he met Wordsworth at the same house.

> I did not expect much; but got mostly what I expected. The old man has a fine shrewdness and naturalness in his expression of face (a long Cumberland figure); one finds also a kind of *sincerity* in his speech: but for prolixity, thinness, endless dilution it excels all the other speech I had heard from mortal. A genuine man (which is much) but also essentially a *small* genuine man: nothing perhaps is sadder (of the glad kind) than the *unbounded* laudation of such a man; sad proof of the *rarity* of such. I fancy however he has fallen into the garrulity of age, and is not what he was: also that his environment (and rural Prophethood) has hurt him much. He seems impatient that even Shakespear should be admired: "so much out of my own pocket"! The shake of hand he gives you is feckless, egoistical; I rather fancy he *loves* nothing in the world so much as one could wish. When I compare that man with a great man,—alas, he is like dwindling into a contemptibility. Jean Paul (for example), neither was he *great,* could have worn him as a finger-ring.[10]

To resolve to rewrite the burnt volume was easier than to do it. The *"Fête des Piques"* at which Carlyle had been engaged was leisurely finished. He then turned back to the death of Louis XV, the most impressive passage in the whole book as he eventually finished it, but he found that it would not prosper with him.

There was no hope now of the promised summer holiday when John Carlyle was to come home from Italy, and *The French Revolution* was to have been finished, and the brothers to have gone to Scotland together and settled their future plans in family council. Holidays were not now to be thought of, at least till the loss was made good. Then, as always when in real trouble, Carlyle faced his difficulties like a man. The household at Chelsea was never closer drawn together than in these times of trial.

Carlyle was brave; his *Heldin* [heroine, i.e., Jane] cheering him with word and look, his brother strong upon his own feet and heartily affectionate. But he needed all that affection could do for him. The "accelerated speed"[11] slackened to slow, and then to no motion at all. He sat daily at his desk, but his imagination would not work. Early in May, for the days passed heavily, and he lost the count of them, he notes "that I never at any period of my life, felt more thoroughly disconsolate, beaten-down, powerless than now. Simply *impossible* it seems that I should *ever* do that weariest miserablest of tasks." A man can rewrite what he has known; but he cannot rewrite what he has felt. Emotion forcibly recalled is artificial, and, unless spontaneous, is hateful. He laboured on "with the feeling of a man swimming in a rarer and rarer element." At length there was no element at all. "My will," he said, "is not conquered; but my vacuum of element to swim in seems complete." He locked up his papers, drove the subject out of his mind, and sat for a fortnight reading novels, English, French, German—anything that came to hand. "In this determination too," he thought, "there may be instruction for me."[12] It was the first of the kind that he had ever deliberately formed. He would keep up his heart. He would be idle, he would rest. He would try, if the word was not a mockery, to enjoy himself.

Another effect of Carlyle's enforced period of idleness was that he saw more of his friends, and of one especially, whose interest in himself had first amused and then attracted him. John Sterling, young, eager, enthusiastic, had been caught by the Radical epidemic on the spiritual side. Hating lies as much as Carlyle hated them, and plunging like a high-bred colt under the conventional harness of a clergyman, he believed, nevertheless, as many others then believed, that the Christian religion would again become the instrument of a great spiritual renovation. While the

337

Tractarians were reviving mediaevalism at Oxford, Sterling, Maurice, Julius Hare, and a circle of Cambridge liberals were looking to Luther, and through Luther to Neander and Schleiermacher, to bring "revelation" into harmony with intellect, and restore its ascendency as a guide into a new era. Coleridge was the high priest of this new prospect for humanity. It was a beautiful hope, though not destined to be realised. Sterling, who was gifted beyond the rest, was among the first to see how much a movement of this kind must mean, if it meant anything at all. He had an instinctive sympathy with genius and earnestness wherever he found it. In the author of *Sartor Resartus* he discovered these qualities, while his contemporaries were blind to them. I have already mentioned that he sought Carlyle's acquaintance, and procured him the offer of employment on the *Times*. His admiration was not diminished when that offer was declined. He missed no opportunity of becoming more intimate with him, and he hoped that he might himself be the instrument of bringing Carlyle to a clearer faith. Carlyle, once better instructed in the great Christian verities, might become a second and a greater Knox.

"[I] have seen," Carlyle writes in this same May, "a good deal of that young Clergyman (singular *clergy*man!) during these two weeks: a sanguine, light, loving man; of whom to me nothing but good seems likely to come; to himself a *mixture* (unluckily) of good and evil."[13] Of good and evil—for Carlyle, clearer-eyed than his friend, foresaw the consequences. Frederick Maurice, Sterling's brother-in-law, on the occasion of the agitation about subscription to the Thirty-nine Articles, had written a pamphlet extremely characteristic of him, to show that subscription was not a bondage, as foolish people called it, but a deliverance from bondage; that the Articles properly read were the great charter of spiritual liberty and reasonable belief. Sterling lent the pamphlet to Carlyle, who examined it, respectfully recognising that "an earnest man's earnest word was worth reading; but," he said, "my verdict lay in these four lines of jingle; which I, virtuously, spared Sterling the sight of:

Thirty-nine English Articles,
Ye wondrous little particles,

338

Did God shape His universe really by *you?*
In that case, I swear it,
And solemnly declare it,
This logic of M[aurice]'s is true.''[14]

Carlyle afterwards came to know Maurice, esteemed him, and personally liked him, as all his acquaintance did. But the "verdict" was unchanged. As a thinker he found him confused, wearisome, ineffectual; and he thought no better of the whole business in which he was engaged. An amalgam of "Christian verities" and modern critical philosophy was, and could be nothing else but, poisonous insincerity. This same opinion in respectful language he had to convey to Sterling, if he was required to give one. But he never voluntarily introduced such subjects, and Sterling's anxiety to improve Carlyle was not limited to the circle of theology. Sterling was a cultivated and classical scholar; he was disturbed by Carlyle's style, which offended him as it offended the world. This style, which has been such a stone of stumbling, originated, he has often said to myself, in the old farmhouse at Annandale. The humour of it came from his mother. The form was his father's common mode of speech, and had been adopted by himself for its brevity and emphasis. He was aware of its singularity and feared that it might be mistaken for affectation, but it was a natural growth, with this merit among others, that it is the clearest of styles. No sentence leaves the reader in doubt of its meaning. Sterling's objections, however, had been vehement. Carlyle admitted that there was foundation for them, but defended himself.

> Your objections as to phraseology and style have good grounds to stand on; many of them indeed are considerations to which I myself was not blind; which there (unluckily) were no means of doing more than nodding to as one passed. A man has but a certain strength; imperfections cling to him, which if he wait till he have brushed off entirely, he will spin for ever on his axis, advancing nowhither. Know thy thought, *believe* it; front Heaven and Earth with it,—in whatsoever *words* nature and art have made readiest for thee. . . . If one has thoughts not hitherto uttered in English Books, I see nothing for it but that you must use words *not* found ther[e], must *make* words,—with moderation and discretion, of course. . . . But finally do you reckon this really a time for Purism of Style; or that Style (mere dictionary style) has much to do with the worth or unworth of a Book? I do not:

339

with whole ragged battalions of Scott's-novel Scotch, with Irish, German, French, and even Newspaper Cockney (when "Literature" is little other than a Newspaper) storming in on us, and the whole structure of our Johnsonian English breaking up from its foundations,—revolution *there* as visible as everywhere else.[15]

"The style; ah, the style!" Carlyle notes nevertheless, as if he was uneasy about it; for in *The French Revolution* the peculiarities of it were more marked than even in *Sartor:*

> These poor people seem to think a style can be put off or put on not like a *skin* but like a coat! Now I refer it to Sterling himself (enemy as he is), whether a skin be not verily the product and close kinsfellow of all that lies under it; exact type of the nature of the beast: *not* to be plucked off without flaying and death? The Public is an old woman: let her maunder and mumble.[16]

Sterling was not satisfied, and again persisted in his remonstrances. *"Das wird zu lang* [this is becoming too protracted],"* Carlyle said; "I made *it* [the letter] into matches";[17] not loving his friend the less for advice which was faithfully given, but knowing in himself that he could not and ought not to attend to it. The *style* was and is the *skin*—an essential part of the living organisation.

But besides the style, Sterling had deeper complaints to make. He insisted on the defects of Carlyle's spiritual belief, being perhaps led on into the subject by the failure of Maurice's eloquence. *Sartor* was still the text. It had been ridiculed in *Fraser's* when it first appeared. It had been republished and admired in America, but in England so far it had met with almost entire neglect. Why should this have been? It was obviously a remarkable book, the most remarkable perhaps which had been published for many years.

> You ask, how it comes that none of the "leading minds" of this country . . . have given the Clothes-Philosophy any response? Why, my good friend, not one of them has had the happiness of seeing it! It issued thro' one of the main *cloacas* of Periodical Literature, where no leading mind, I fancy, looks, if he can help it: the poor Book cannot be destroyed by fire or other violence now, but solely by the *general* law of Destiny; and *I* have nothing more to do with it henceforth. . . . Meanwhile, do not suppose the poor Book has *not* been responded to; for the historical fact is, I could show very curious response to it here; not ungratifying, and fully three times as much as I counted on, as the wretched farrago itself deserved.[18]

Meanwhile the fortnight's idleness expired; he went to work again over his lost volume, but became "so sick" that he still made little progress. Emerson continued to press him to move for good and all to America, where he would find many friends and a congenial audience for his teaching; and more than once he thought of leaving the unlucky thing unwritten and of acting on Emerson's advice. He was very weary, and the books with which he tried to distract himself had no charm.

It was significant of a growing misgiving on Carlyle's part that he had mistaken his profession, and that as a man of letters—as a true and honest man of letters—he could not live. Everything was against him. No one wanted him; no one believed his report; and even Fate itself was now warning him off with menacing finger.

It was a mere chance at this time that *The French Revolution* and literature with it were not flung aside for good and all, and that the Carlyle whom the world knows had never been. If Charles Buller, or Molesworth, or any other leading Radical who had seen his worth, had told the Government that if they meant to begin in earnest on the education of the people, here was the man for them, Carlyle would have closed at once with the offer. The effort of writing, always great (for he wrote, as his brother said, "with his heart's blood"[19] in a state of fevered tension), the indifference of the world to his past work, his uncertain future, his actual poverty, had already burdened him beyond his strength. He always doubted whether he had any special talent for literature. He was conscious of possessing considerable powers, but he would have preferred at all times to have found a use for them in action. And everything was now conspiring to drive him into another career. If nothing could be found for him at home, America was opening its arms. He could lecture for a season in New England, save sufficient money, and then draw away into the wilderness, to build a new Scotsbrig in the western forest. So the possibility presented itself to him in this interval of enforced helplessness. He would go away and struggle with the stream no more. And yet at the bottom of his mind, as he told me, something said to him, "My good fellow, you are not fit for that either." Perhaps he

341

felt that when he was once across the water, America would at any rate be a better mother to him than England, would find what he was suited for, and would not let his faculties be wasted.

As writing seemed impossible, Carlyle had determined to go to Scotland after all. Lady Clare had meant to be in England soon after midsummer, bringing John Carlyle with her. John was now the great man of the family, the man of income, the travelled doctor from Italy, the companion of a peeress. His arrival was looked forward to at Scotsbrig with natural eagerness. Carlyle and he were to go down together and consult with their mother about future plans. Mrs. Carlyle would go with them to pay a visit to her mother. The journey might be an expense, but John was rich, and the fares to Edinburgh by steamer were not considerable. In the gloom that hung over Chelsea this prospect had been the one streak of sunshine—and unhappily it was all clouded over. Lady Clare could not come home after all, and John was obliged to remain with her, though with a promise of leave of absence in the autumn. At Radical Scotsbrig there was indignation enough at a fine lady's caprices destroying other people's pleasures. Carlyle more gently could *"pity* the heart that suffers, whether it beat under silk or under sackcloth"[20] for Lady Clare's life was not a happy one. He collected his energy. To soften his wife's disappointment, he invited Mrs. Welsh to come immediately on a long visit to Cheyne Row. Like his father he resolved to "gar [compel] himself," finish the burnt volume in spite of everything, and to think no more of Scotland till it was done. The sudden change gave him back his strength.

Things after this began to brighten. Mrs. Welsh came up to cheer her daughter, whose heart had almost failed like her husband's, for she had no fancy for an American forest. Carlyle went vigorously to work, and at last successfully. In ten days he had made substantial progress, though with "immense difficulty" still. "It is and continues the most ungrateful, intolerable of all tasks."[21] But he felt that he was getting on with it, and recovered his peace of mind. He even began to be interested again in the subject itself, which had become for the time entirely distasteful to him, and to regret that he could not satisfy himself better in his treatment of it. Notwithstanding his defence of his style to Sterling, he wished the skin were less "rhinoceros-like."

Gradually the story which he was engaged in telling got possession of him again. The terrible scenes of the Revolution seized his imagination, haunting him as he walked about the streets. London and its giddy whirl of life, that too might become as Paris had been. Ah! and what was it all but a pageant passing from darkness into darkness? The *world* often, indeed generally looks quite spectral, sometimes (as in Regent-Street, the other night; my *nerves* being all shattered), quite *hideous*, discordant, almost infernal."[22]

Amidst such "spectral" feelings the writing of *The French Revolution* went on. By August 10 Carlyle was within sight of the end of the unfortunate volume which had cost him so dear, and could form a notion of what he had done. His wife, an excellent judge, considered the second version better than the first. Carlyle himself thought it worse, but not much worse; at any rate he was relieved from the load, and could look forward to finishing the rest. Sometimes he thought the book would produce an effect; but he had hoped the same from *Sartor*, and he did not choose to be sanguine a second time. On September 23 he was able to tell his brother that the last line of the volume was actually written, that he was entirely exhausted and was going to Annandale to recover himself.

In the first week in October Carlyle started for his old home, not in a smack, though he had so purposed, but in a steamer to Newcastle, whence there was easy access, though railways as yet were not, to Carlisle and Annandale. His letters and diary give no bright picture of his first year's experience in London, and fate had dealt hardly with him; but he had gained much notwithstanding. His strong personality had drawn attention wherever he had been seen. He had been invited with his wife into cultivated circles, literary and political. The Sterlings were not the only new friends whom they had made. Their poverty was unconcealed; there was no sham in either of the Carlyles, and there were many persons anxious to help them in any form in which help could be accepted. Presents of all kinds, hampers of wine, and suchlike poured in upon them. Carlyle did not speak of these things. He did not feel them less than other people, but he was chary of polite expressions which are so often but half sincere, and he often seemed indifferent or ungracious when at heart he was warmly grateful. Mrs. Carlyle, when disappointed of her trip to Scotland, had been carried off into the country by the Sterlings for a week or two. In August Mrs. Welsh came, and stayed on while Carlyle was away. She was a gifted woman, a little too sentimental for her sarcastic daughter, and troublesome with her caprices. They loved each other dearly and even passionately. They quarrelled daily and made it up again. Mrs. Carlyle, like her husband, was not easy to live with. But on the whole they were happy to be together again after so long a separation. They had friends of their own who gathered about them in Carlyle's absence. Mrs. Carlyle occupied herself in learning Italian, painting and arranging the rooms, negotiating a sofa out of her scanty allowance, preparing a pleasant surprise when he should come back to his work. He on his part was not left to chew his own reflections. He was to provide the winter stock of bacon and hams and potatoes and meal at Scotsbrig. He was to find a Scotch lass for a servant and bring her back with him. He was to dispose of the rest of the Craigenputtoch stock which had been left unsold, all excellent antidotes against spectral visions. He had his old Annandale relations to see again, in whose fortunes he was eagerly interested, and to write long stories about them to his brother John. In such occupation, varied with daily talks and smokes with his mother, and in feeding himself into health on milk or porridge, Carlyle passed his holiday.

The holiday lasted but four weeks, and Carlyle was again at his work at Chelsea. He was still restless, of course, with so heavy a load upon him; but he did his best to be cheerful under it. Her chief resources were the Sterlings and the Italian lessons, and as long as she was well in health her spirits did not fail. Him, too, the Sterlings' friendship helped much to encourage; but he was absorbed in his writing and could think of little else.

[Parliament had addressed itself to the question of national education. Carlyle thought himself fit to write on the subject and hoped for a government appointment, but] nothing came of the national education scheme.[23] Carlyle was not a person to push himself into notice. Either Buller and his other friends did not exert themselves for him, or they tried and failed; governments, in fact, do not look out for servants among men who are speculating about the nature of the universe. Then as always the doors leading into regular employment remained closed. From his mother as far as possible he concealed his anxieties. But she knew him too well to be deceived. She, too, was heavy at heart for her idolised son, less on account of his uncertain prospects than for the want of faith, as she considered it, which was the real cause of his trouble. He told her always that essentially he thought as she did, but she could hardly believe it; and though she no longer argued or remonstrated, yet she dwelt in her letters to him, in her own simple way, on the sources of her own consolation.

It was very difficult for Carlyle (as he told me) to speak with or write to his mother directly about religion. She quieted her anxieties as well as she could by recognising the deep unquestionable piety of her son's nature. It was on the worldly side, after all, that there was real cause for alarm. The little stock of money would be gone now in a few months; and then what was to be done? America seemed the only resource. Yet to allow such a man to expatriate himself—a man, too, who would be contented with the barest necessaries of life—because in England he could not live, would be a shame and a scandal; and various schemes for keeping him were talked over among his friends. The difficulty was that he was himself so stubborn and impracticable. He would not write in the *Times*, because the *Times* was committed to a great political party, and Carlyle would have nothing to do with parties. Shortly after he came back from Scotland, he was offered the editorship of a newspaper at Lichfield. This was unacceptable for the same reason; and if he could have himself consented, his wife would not. She could never persuade herself that her husband would fail to rise to greatness on his own lines, or allow him to take an inferior situation.

A more singular proposition reached Carlyle from another quarter, kindly meant perhaps, but set forward with an air of patronage which the humblest of men would have resented unless at the last extremity; and humility was certainly not one of Carlyle's qualities. The Basil Montagus had been among the first friends to whom he had been introduced by Irving when he came to London in 1824. Great things had been then expected of him on Irving's report. Mrs. Montagu had interested herself deeply in all his concerns. She had been initiated into the romance of Jane Welsh's early life, and it was by her interference (which had never been wholly forgiven) that her marriage with Carlyle had been precipitated.[24] For some years a correspondence had been kept up, somewhat inflated on Mrs. Montagu's side, but showing real kindness and a real wish to be of use. The acquaintance had continued after the Carlyles settled in Chelsea, but Mrs. Montagu's advances had not been very warmly received, and were suspected, perhaps unjustly, of not being completely sincere. The sympathetic letter which she had ventured to write to Mrs. Carlyle on Irving's death had been received rather with resentment than satisfaction. Still the Montagus remained in the circle of Carlyle's friends. They were aware of his circumstances, and were anxious to help him if they knew how to set about it. It was with some pleasure, and perhaps with some remorse at the doubts which he had entertained of the sincerity of their regard, that Carlyle learned that Basil Montagu had a situation in view for him which, if he liked it, he might have—a situation, he was told, which would secure him a sufficient income, and would leave him time besides for his own writing. The particulars were reserved to be explained at a personal interview. Carlyle had been so eager, chiefly for his wife's sake, to find something to hold on to, that he would not let the smallest plank drift by without examining it. He had a vague misgiving, but he blamed himself for his distrust. The interview took place, and the contempt with which he describes Mr. Montagu's proposition is actually savage.

> Basil Montagu had within the last six months a Life-benefaction all cut and dried for me; needing little but acceptance,—no, it depended on the measure of gratitude, whether it *was* to be ready for me or for another: a Clerkship under him at the rate of £200 a-year; whereby a man, lecturing also in Mechanics' Institutes in the evening, and doing etceteras, might live! I listened with grave fixed eyes to the Sovereign of Quacks as he *mewed* out all the fine sentimentalities he had stuffed into this beggarly account of empty boxes (for which

too I had been sent trotting many miles of pavement, tho' I knew from the beginning it could be only moonshine): and with grave thanks, for this potentiality of a Clerkship, took my leave that night; and next morning, all still in the potential mood, sent an *indicative* Threepenny. . . . One other thing I could not but remark: the *faith* of Montagu—wishing *me* for his Clerk; thinking the Polar Bear, reduced to a state of dyspeptic dejection, might be safely trusted tending Rabbits! Greater faith I have not found in Israel.— Let us leave these people: they shall hardly again cost me even an "exchange of Threepennies."[25]

The "Polar Bear," it might have occurred to Carlyle, is a difficult beast to find accommodation for. People do not eagerly open their doors to such an inmate. Basil Montagu, doubtless, was not a wise man, and was unaware of the relative values of himself and the person that he thought of for a clerk. But, after all, situations suited for polar bears are not easily found outside the Zoological Gardens. It was not Basil Montagu's fault that he was not a person of superior quality. He knew that Carlyle was looking anxiously for employment with a fixed salary, and a clerkship in his office had, in his eyes, nothing degrading in it. Except in a country like Prussia, where a discerning government is on the look-out always for men of superior intellect, and knows what to do with them, the most gifted genius must begin upon the lowest step of the ladder.[26] The proposal was of course an absurd one, and the scorn with which it was received was only too natural; but this small incident shows only how impossible it was at this time to do anything for Carlyle except what was actually done, to leave him to climb the precipices of life by his own unassisted strength.

Thus, throughout this year 1836, he remained fixed at his work in Cheyne Row. He wrote all the morning. In the afternoon he walked, sometimes with Mill or Sterling, more often alone, making his own reflections.

Mrs. Carlyle was confined through the winter and spring with a dangerous cough. He himself, though he complained, was fairly well; nothing was essentially the matter, but he slept badly from overwork, "gaeing stavering [stumbling] aboot the hoose at night," as the Scotch maid said, restless alike in mind and body. When he paused from his book to write a letter or a note in his Journal, it was to discover a state of nerves irritated by the contrast between his actual performance and the sense of what he was trying to accomplish. The ease which he expected when the lost volume was recovered had not been found. The toil was severe as ever.

At the back of Carlyle's house in Cheyne Row is a strip of garden, a grass plot, a few trees and flowerbeds along the walls, where are (or were) some bits of jessamine and a gooseberry-bush or two, transported from Haddington and Craigenputtoch. Here, when spring came on, Carlyle used to dig and plant and keep the grass trim and tidy. Sterling must have seen him with his spade there when he drew the picture of Collins in "The Onyx Ring," which is evidently designed for Carlyle.[27] The digging must have been more of a relaxation for him than the walks, where the thinking and talking went on without interruption. Very welcome and a real relief was the arrival of his brother John at last in the middle of April. Lady Clare could not part with him in the autumn, but she had come now herself, bringing the doctor with her, and had allowed him three months' leave of absence. Half his holiday was to be spent in Cheyne Row. The second volume of *The French Revolution* was finished, and Carlyle gave himself up to the full enjoyment of his brother's company. He had six weeks of real rest and pleasure; for his curiosity was insatiable, and John, just from Italy, could tell him infinite things which he wanted to know. Scotsbrig, of course, had claims which were to be respected. When these weeks were over, John had to go north, and Carlyle attended him down the river to the Hull steamer.

"Very cheering to me, poor Jack," he writes when alone at home again; "I feel without him 'quite orphaned and alone.'"[28] Alone, and at the mercy again of the evil spirits whom "Jack's" round face had kept at a distance.

The old, old story: genius, the divine gift which men so envy and admire, which is supposed to lift its possessor to a throne among the gods, gives him, with the intensity of insight, intensity of spiritual suffering. His laurel wreath is a crown of thorns. To all men Carlyle preached the duty of "consuming their own smoke," and faithfully he fulfilled his own injunction. He wrote no *Leiden des jungen Werthers*, no musical *Childe Harold*, to relieve his own heart by inviting the world to weep with him. So far as the world was concerned, he bore his pains in silence, and only in his

THE GARDEN. When the Carlyles first moved to then unfashionable Chelsea, they could see the spires of the London churches across the intervening fields. "The garden," wrote Carlyle, "is of admirable comfort to me, in the smoking way: I can wander about in dressing gown and straw hat in it, as of old, and take my pipe in peace." Mrs. Carlyle's dog Nero, frequently mentioned in her letters, is buried at the far end. (A Gordon Fraser card, published for the National Trust.)

Journal left any written record of them. At home, however, he could not always be reticent; and his sick wife, whose spirits needed raising, missed John's companionship as much as her husband. The household economics became so pressing that the book had to be suspended for a couple of weeks while Carlyle wrote the article on Mirabeau, now printed among the *Miscellanies,* for Mill's Review.[29] Some fifty pounds was made by this; but by the time the article was finished, Mrs. Carlyle became so ill that she felt that unless she could get away to her mother "she would surely die." Carlyle himself could not think of moving, unless for a day or two to a friend in the neighborhood of London; but everything was done that circumstances permitted. She went first to her uncle at Liverpool, meaning to proceed (for economy) by the Annan steamer, though in her weak state she dreaded a sea voyage. She was sent forward by the coach. John Carlyle met her and carried her on to her mother at Templand, who had a "purse . . . filled with sovereigns"[30] ready for her as a birthday present (July 14). Carlyle himself wrote to her daily, making the best of his condition that she might have as little anxiety as possible on his account.

It has pleased Carlyle to admit the world behind the scenes of his domestic life.[31] He has allowed us to see that all was not as well there as it might have been, and in his own generous remorse he has taken the blame upon himself. No one, however, can read these letters, or ten thousand others like them, without recognising the affectionate tenderness which lay at the bottom of his nature. No one also can read between the lines without observing that poverty and dispiritment and the burden of a task too heavy for him was not all that Carlyle had to bear. She on her part, no doubt, had much to put up with. It was not easy to live with a husband subject to strange fits of passion and depression; often as unreasonable as a child, and with a Titanesque power of making mountains out of molehills. But she might have seen more clearly than she did, in these deliberate expressions of his feeling, the soundness of his judgement, and the genuine simple truth and loyalty of his heart. Let those married pairs who never knew a quarrel, whose days run on unruffled by a breeze, be grateful that their lot has been cast in pleasant circumstances, for otherwise their experience will have been different. Let them be grateful that they are not persons of "genius" or blessed or cursed with sarcastic tongues. The disorder which had driven Mrs. Carlyle to Scotland was mental as well as bodily. The best remedy for it lay, after all, at home; and she came back, as she said after two months' absence, " 'a sadder and a wiser' woman."[32]

She had returned mended in spirits. John had gone two days before, and was on his way to Italy again, but the effects remained of his cheery presence, and all things were looking better. The article on Mirabeau was printed, and had given satisfaction. "The Diamond Necklace" was to come out in parts in *Fraser's* and bring in a little money. Carlyle had never written anything more beautiful; and it speaks indifferently for English criticism that about this, when it appeared, the newspapers were as scornful as they had been about *Sartor*—a bad omen for *The French Revolution*, for "The Diamond Necklace" was a preliminary chapter of the same drama. But the opinions of the newspapers had long become matters of indifference. The financial pressure would be relieved at any rate, and the air in Cheyne Row, within doors and without, was like a still autumn afternoon, when the equinoctials have done blowing.

As the end of the book came in view, the question—what next? began to present itself. It was as morning twilight after a long night, and surrounding objects showed in their natural form. Evidently Carlyle did not expect that it would bring him money or directly better his fortunes. All that he looked for was to have acquitted his conscience by writing it: he would then quit literature and seek other work. The alternative, indeed, did not seem to be left to him—literature as a profession, followed with a sacred sense of responsibility (and without such a sense he could have nothing to do with it), refused a living to himself and his wife. For her sake as well as his own, he must try something else. He was in no hurry to choose. His plan, so far as he could form one, was that, as soon as the book was published, his wife should return for a while to her mother. He, like his own Teufelsdröckh, would take staff in hand, travel on foot about the world like a mediaeval monk, look about him, and then decide.

Ten years before, he had formed large hopes of what he might do and become as a man of letters. He concluded now that he had failed.

So the year wore out, and in this humour *The French Revolution* was finished. The last sentence was written on the 12th of January, 1837, on a damp evening, just as light was failing.[33] Carlyle gave the manuscript to his wife to read, and went out to walk. Before leaving the house he said to her: "I know not whether this book is worth anything, nor what the world will do with it, or misdo, or entirely forbear to do (as is likeliest), but this I could tell the world: You have not had for a hundred years any book that came more direct and flamingly from the heart of a living man; do with it what you like, you———."[34] Five days later he announced the event to Sterling, who was spending the winter at Bordeaux.

> Five days ago I finished, about ten o'clock at night; and really was ready both to weep and to pray,—but did not do either, at least not visibly or audibly. The Bookseller has it, and the Printer has it; I expect the first sheet tomorrow: in not many weeks more, I can hope to wash my hands of it forever and a day. It is a thing disgusting to me by the faults of it; the merits of which, for it is not without merits, will not be seen for a long time. It is a wild savage Book, itself a kind of French Revolution;—which perhaps, if Providence have so ordered it, the world had better *not* accept when offered it? With all my heart! What I do know of it is that it has come hot out of my own soul; born in blackness whirlwind and sorrow; that no man, for a long while, has stood speaking so completely alone under the Eternal Azure, in the character of man only; or is likely for a long while so to stand:—finally that it has come as near to choking the life out of me as any task I should like to undertake for some years to come; which also is an immense comfort, indeed the greatest of all. . . .
>
> I will repeat you again the little Song that goes humming thro' my head, very frequently in these times; the only modern *Psalm* I have met with for long:
>
> > The Future hides in it
> > Gladness and sorrow;
> > We press still thorow,
> > Nought that abides in it
> > Daunting us,—onward.
> >
> > And solemn before us,
> > Veiled, the dark Portal,
> > Goal of all mortal:—
> > Stars silent rest o'er us,
> > Graves under us silent!

But heard are the Voices,—
Heard are the Sages,
The Worlds and the Ages:
"Choose well; your choice is
Brief and yet endless:

Here eyes do regard you,
In Eternity's stillness;
Here is all fulness,
Ye brave, to reward you;
Work, and despair not."

Is it not a piece of Psalmody that? It seems to me like a piece of marching-music of the great brave Teutonic Kindred as they march through the waste of TIME,—through that section of Eternity *they* were appointed for; *oben die Sterne* and *unten die Gräber*, with the *Stimmen der Geister*, the *Stimmen der Meister*! Let us all sing it, and march on cheerful of heart. "We bid you hope";[35] so say the voices. Do they not?[36]

chapter eighteen

1837–1838

The French Revolution. Lectures on
German Literature. Lectures on
European Literature

I have been thus particular in describing the conditions
under which *The French Revolution* was composed, because this book gave Carlyle at a single step his unique
position as an English man of letters, and because it is in
many respects the most perfect of all his writings. In his
other works the sense of form is defective. He throws out
brilliant detached pictures, and large masses of thought,
each in itself inimitably clear. There is everywhere a unity
of purpose, with powerful final effects. But events are not
left to tell their own story. He appears continually in his
own person, instructing, commenting, informing the reader
at every step of his own opinion. His method of composition
is so original that it cannot be tried by common rules. The
want of art is even useful for the purposes which he has generally in view: but it interferes with the simplicity of a genuine historical narrative. *The French Revolution* is not open
to this objection. It stands alone in artistic regularity and
completeness. It is a prose poem with a distinct beginning,
a middle, an end. It opens with the crash of a corrupt system, and a dream of liberty which was to bring with it a
reign of peace and happiness and universal love. It pursues
its way through the failure of visionary hopes into regicide
and terror, and the regeneration of mankind by the guillotine. It has been called an *epic*.[1] It is rather an Aeschylean
drama composed of facts literally true, in which the Furies
are seen once more walking on this prosaic earth and shaking their serpent hair.

The form is quite peculiar, unlike that of any history ever written before, or probably to be written again. No one can imitate Carlyle who does not sincerely feel as Carlyle felt. But it is complete in itself. The story takes shape as it grows, a definite organic creation, with no dead or needless matter anywhere disfiguring or adhering to it, as if the metal had been smelted in a furnace seven times heated, till every particle of dross had been burnt away. As in all living things, there is the central idea, the animating principle round which the matter gathers and developes into shape. Carlyle was writing what he believed would be his last word to his countrymen. He was not looking forward to fame or fortune, or to making a position for himself in the world. He belonged to no political party, and was engaged in the defence of no theory or interest. For many years he had been studying painfully the mystery of human life, wholly and solely that he might arrive at some kind of truth about it and understand his own duty. He had no belief in the virtue of special "Constitutions." He was neither Tory, nor Whig, nor Radical, nor Socialist, nor any other "ist." He had stripped himself of "formulas, as of poisonou[s] Nessus' shirts," and flung them fiercely away from him, finding "formulas" in these days to be mostly lies agreed to be believed.[2] In the record of God's law, as he had been able to read it, he had found no commendation of "symbols of faith," of church organisation, or methods of government. He wrote, as he said to Sterling, "in the character of man"[3] only; and of a man without earthly objects, without earthly prospects, who had been sternly handled by fate and circumstances, and was left alone with the elements, as Prometheus on the rock of Caucasus. Struggling thus in pain and sorrow, he desired to tell the modern world that, destitute as it and its affairs appeared to be of Divine guidance, God or justice was still in the middle of it, sternly inexorable as ever; that modern nations were as entirely governed by God's law as the Israelites had been in Palestine—laws self-acting and inflicting their own penalties, if man neglected or defied them. And these laws were substantially the same as those on the Tables delivered in thunder on Mount Sinai. You shall reverence your Almighty Maker. You shall speak truth. You shall do justice to your fellow-man. If you set

355

truth aside for conventional and convenient lies; if you prefer your own pleasure, your own will, your own ambition,
to purity and manliness and justice, and submission to your
Maker's commands, then are whirlwinds still provided in
the constitution of things which will blow you to atoms.
Philistines, Assyrians, Babylonians, were the whips which
were provided for the Israelites. Germans and Huns swept
away the Roman sensualists. Modern society, though out of
fear of barbarian conquerors, breeds in its own heart the
instruments of its punishment. The hungry and injured millions will rise up and bring to justice their guilty rulers,
themselves little better than those whom they throw down,
themselves powerless to rebuild out of the ruins any abiding city; but powerful to destroy, powerful to dash in pieces
the corrupt institutions which have been the shelter and
the instrument of oppression.

And Carlyle *believed* this—believed it singly and simply
as Isaiah believed it, not as a mode of speech to be used
in pulpits by eloquent preachers, but as actual literal fact,
as a real account of the true living relations between man
and his Maker. The established forms, creeds, liturgies,
articles of faith, were but as the shell round the kernel.
The shell in these days of ours had rotted away, and men
supposed that, because the shell was gone, the entire conception had been but a dream. It was no dream. The kernel
could not rot. It was the vital force by which human existence in this planet was controlled, and would be controlled
to the end.

In this conviction he wrote his spectral *History of the
French Revolution*.[4] Spectral, for the actors in it appear
without their earthly clothes: men and women in their natural characters, but as in some vast phantasmagoria, with
the supernatural shining through them, working in fancy
their own wills or their own imagination; in reality, the mere
instruments of a superior power, infernal or divine, whose
awful presence is felt while it is unseen.

To give form to his conception, Carlyle possessed all
the qualities of a supreme dramatic poet, except command
of metre. He has indeed a metre, or rather a melody, of his
own. The style which troubled others, and troubled himself
when he thought about it, was perhaps the best possible to

356

convey thoughts which were often like the spurting of volcanic fire; but it was inharmonious, rough-hewn, and savage. It may be said, too, that he had no "invention." But he refused to allow that any real poet had ever "invented." The poet had to represent truths, not *lies*, or the polite form of lies called fiction. Homer, Dante, believed themselves to be describing real persons and real things. Carlyle "created" nothing; but with a real subject before him he was the greatest of historical painters. He took all pains first to obtain an authentic account of the facts. Then, with a few sharp lines, he could describe face, figure, character, action, with a complete insight never rivalled except by Tacitus, and with a certain sympathy, a perennial flashing of humour, of which Tacitus has none. He produces a gallery of human portraits each so distinctly drawn, that whenever studied it can never be forgotten. He possessed besides another quality, the rarest of all, and the most precious, an inflexible love of truth. It was first a moral principle with him; but he had also an intellectual curiosity to know everything exactly as it was. Independently of moral objections to lies, Carlyle always held that the fact, if you knew it, was more interesting than the most picturesque of fictions, and thus his historical workmanship is sound to the core. He spared himself no trouble in investigating; and all his effort was to delineate accurately what he had found. Dig where you will in Carlyle's writings, you never come to water. Politicians have complained that Carlyle shows no insight into constitutional principles, that he writes as if he were contemptuous of them or indifferent to them. Revolutionists have complained of his scorn of Robespierre, and of his tenderness to Marie Antoinette. Catholics find Holy Church spoken of without sufficient respect, and Tories find kings and nobles stripped of their fine clothes and treated as vulgar clay. But Constitutions had no place in Carlyle's Decalogue. He did not find it written there that one form of government is in itself better than another. He held with Pope:

> For Forms of Government let fools contest;
> Whate'er is best administered is best.[5]

His sympathies were with purity, justice, truthfulness, man-

357

ly courage, on whichever side he found them. His scorn was for personal cowardice, or cant, or hollow places of any kind in the character of men; and when nations are split into parties, wisdom or folly, virtue or vice, is not the exclusive property of one or the other.

A book written from such a point of view had no "public" prepared for it. When it appeared, partisans on both sides were offended; and to the reading multitude who wish merely to be amused without the trouble of thinking, it had no attraction till they learned its merits from others. But to the chosen few, to those who had eyes of their own to see with, and manliness enough to recognise when a living man was speaking to them, to those who had real intellect, and could therefore acknowledge intellect and welcome it whether they agreed or not with the writer's opinions, the high quality of *The French Revolution* became apparent instantly, and Carlyle was at once looked up to, by some who themselves were looked up to by the world, as a man of extraordinary gifts; perhaps as the highest among them all. Dickens carried a copy of it with him wherever he went. Southey read it six times over. Thackeray reviewed it enthusiastically. Even Jeffrey generously admitted that Carlyle had succeeded upon lines on which he had himself foretold inevitable failure. The orthodox political philosophers, Macaulay, Hallam, Brougham, though they perceived that Carlyle's views were the condemnation of their own, though they felt instinctively that he was their most dangerous enemy, yet could not any longer despise him. They with the rest were obliged to admit that there had arisen a new star, of baleful perhaps and ominous aspect, but a star of the first magnitude in English literature.

But six months had still to pass before the book could be published, and I am anticipating. Carlyle had been so long inured to disappointment, that he expected nothing from the world but continued indifference. His only anxiety was to be done with the thing, and it had still to be printed and corrected. The economical crisis had been postponed. Life could be protracted at Cheyne Row for another six months on the proceeds of "Mirabeau" and "The Diamond Necklace."

Printing a book is like varnishing a picture. Faults and

merits both become more conspicuous. Carlyle, who was hard to please with his own work, and had called it worth nothing while in progress, found it in the proofs better than he expected. He made no foul copy of it or of anything that he wrote in these early days. The sentences completed themselves in his head before he threw them upon paper, and only verbal alterations were afterwards necessary; but he omitted many things in his proof sheets, redivided his books and chapters, and sharpened the lights and shadows.

Meantime the economic problem, though postponed, was still unsolved. The book was finished, but no money could be expected from it, at least for a considerable time; and, unless something could be done, it was likely that London, and perhaps England, would lose Carlyle just at the moment when they were learning the nature of the man to whom they were refusing ordinary maintenance. His circumstances were no secret. His friends were doubtless aware that he had been invited to lecture in America. A large number of persons, more or less influential, knew vaguely that he was a remarkable man, and some of them cast about for means to prevent such a scandal. One of the most anxious and active, be it recorded to her honour, was Harriet Martineau.[6]

To Miss Martineau, to Miss [Jane] Wilson, another accomplished lady friend, and to several more, it occurred that if Carlyle could be wanted to lecture in Boston, he might equally well lecture in London. If he could speak as well in public as he could talk in private, he could not fail of success; and money, a little, but enough, might be realised in this way. The Royal Institution was first thought of, but the pay at the Royal Institution was small, and the list, besides, was full for the year. The bold ladies turned their disappointment to better advantage. Carlyle gave a grumbling consent. They canvassed their acquaintance. They found two hundred persons ready each to subscribe a guinea to hear a course of lectures from him in a room engaged for himself only. *The French Revolution* was not to appear till the summer. That so many lords and ladies and other notabilities should have given their names for such a purpose implies that Carlyle's earlier writings had already made an impression. London society loves novelties, but it expects that the novelties shall be entertaining, and does not go into a thing of this kind entirely on hazard. Carlyle was spared all trouble. All that he had to do was to prepare something to say; and Willis's Rooms were engaged for him, the lectures to begin on May 1. He shuddered, for he hated display, but he felt that he must not reject an opening so opportunely made for him. He had no leisure for any special study, but he was full of knowledge of a thousand kinds. He chose the subject which came most conveniently for him, since he had worked so hard upon it at Craigenputtoch—German literature. There were to be six lectures in all. A prospectus was drawn up and printed, intimating that on such and such days Thomas Carlyle would deliver addresses:

I. Of the Teutonic People. German Language. Affinities. ULFILA. Northern Immigrations. The *Nibelungen Song*.

II. The Minne-singers. The Didactic: Tauler, Boner, Hugo von Trimberg: *Gesta Romanorum*. *Tyll Eulenspiegel*; *Reynard the Fox*; *Theuerdank*, by KAISER MAX. Legend of *Faust*; Popular Legends. Universities. The Reformation: LUTHER; ULRICH HUTTEN.

III. The Master-singers: HANS SACHS. Jacob Böhme. Decay of German Literature: ANTON ULRICH, Duke of Brunswick; OPITZ; Loga; Hoffmanswaldau; Thomasius. LEIBNITZ; Maskov; Liskov.

IV. Resuscitation of German Literature: LESSING; KLOPSTOCK. Leipsig: Rabener, Gellert, Ramler, Gleim; Schubart, Kleist. The Swiss: Haller; Bodmer; Gessner; Lavater. Efflorescence of German Literature: *Werter*; *Götz von Berlichingen*. Bürger; Voss; the Stollbergs. HEYNE; WINKELMANN.

V. Characteristics of new German Literature: Growth and Decay of Opinions; *Faust*. Philosophy: Mendelsohn, Hamann: KANT; FICHTE; SCHELLING. Art and Belief: GOETHE.

VI. The Drama: SCHILLER. *The Robbers*; *Wilhelm Tell*.

360

Pseudo-Drama: Klinger; Iffland; Kotzebue; Klingemann; Werner; Müllner; Grillparzer. Romance: LUDWIG TIECK; NOVALIS. Pseudo-Romance: Hoffmann. Poetry and General Literature: HERDER; WIELAND. The Schlegels. Maler Müller; Johannes von Müller. JEAN PAUL FRIEDRICH RICHTER. Results; Anticipations.[7]

A copious bill of fare! A more experienced hand would have spread the subjects of any one of these lectures into the necessary six, watering them duly to the palate of fashionable audiences. But Carlyle, if he undertook anything, chose to do it in a way that he could think of without shame. He was sulky and even alarmed, for he did not intend to *read*. He had undertaken to speak, and *speak* he would, or else fail altogether.

There was additional anxiety. Mrs. Carlyle in the cold spring weather had caught an influenza, and was seriously ill again. The alarm passed off; a change of weather carried away the influenza; Mrs. Welsh came up, and was most welcome, though the occasion of the summons was gone.

All thoughts in Cheyne Row were now directed to the lectures. Carlyle had never spoken in public, save a few words once at a dinner at Dumfries. With all his self-assertion he was naturally a shy man, and only those who are either perfectly un-selfconscious or perfectly impudent can look without alarm to a first appearance on a platform. As the appointed day approached, there was a good deal of anxiety among his friends. Men of high sincerity seldom speak well. It was an art to which they do not incline, being careful about truth, and knowing how difficult it is to adhere to truth in rapid and excited delivery. With skill and training even a sincere man can speak tolerably without telling many lies; but he is weighted heavily against competitors who care for nothing but effect. Carlyle, quoting Goethe, compared speech-making to swimming. It is more like skating. When a man stands on skates upon ice for the first time, his feet seem to have no hold under him; he feels that if he stirs he will fall; he does fall; the spectators laugh; he is ashamed and angry at himself; he plunges off somehow, and finds soon that if he is not afraid he can at least go forward. This much the sincere man arrives at on the platform without extraordinary difficulty; and if he has any truth to utter he can contrive to utter it, so that wise hearers will understand him. The curving and winding, the graceful sweeps this way and that way in endless convolutions, he leaves to the oratorical expert, with whom he has no desire to put himself in competition.

Nobody could feel assured that something strange might not happen. One acquaintance was afraid he would spoil all by beginning with "Gentlemen and ladies," putting the ladies last. It was more likely, his wife said, that he would begin with "Men and women," or with "Fool creatures come hither for diversion."

In point of fact, Carlyle acted like himself—not like other people, for that he could not do. He had the usual difficulties. Even when he was at ease, his speech, if he was in earnest, was not smooth and flowing, but turbid like a river in a flood. In the lecture-room he had the invariable preliminary fear of breaking down. He had to pause often before words would come, for he was scrupulous to say nothing which he did not mean. When he became excited, he spoke with a broad Annandale accent and with the abrupt manners which he had learnt in his father's house. But the end of it was that the lectures were excellent in themselves and delivered with strange impressiveness. Though unpolished, he was a gentleman in every fibre of him, never to be mistaken for anything else; and the final effect was the same as that which was produced by his writings, that here was a new man with something singular to say which well deserved attention. Of the first lecture Carlyle writes:

It was a sad planless jumble . . . but full enough of new matter, and of a furious determination on the poor Lecturer's part not to break down. Plenty of incondite stuff, accordingly, there was; new, and in a strangely new dialect and tone: the audience intelligent, partly fashionable, was very good to me; and seemed, in spite of the jumbled state of things, to feel it entertaining, even interesting. I pitied myself, so agitated, terrified, driven desperate and furious! But I found I had no remedy, necessity compelling.[8]

When all was over, he sent a full account to his brother:

As to the Lectures . . . the thing went off not without effect; and I have great cause to be thankful that I am so handsomely

362

quit of it. The audience, composed of mere quality and notabilities, was very humane to me; they seemed indeed to be not a little astonished at the wild Annandale voice which occasionally got high and earnest; in these cases they sat as still under me as stones. I had, I think, 200 and odd. The pecuniary net-result is £135, the expenses being great. . . . But the ulterior issues of it may by possibility be less inconsiderable. It seems possible I may get into [a] kind of way of lecturing or otherwise speaking direct to my fellow-creatures; and so get delivered out of this awful quagmire of difficulties in which you have so long seen me struggle and wriggle.[9]

Mrs. Carlyle adds a P.S.

I do not find that my husband has given you any adequate notion of the success of his lectures; but you will make large allowances for the known modesty of the man. Nothing that he has ever tried seems to me to have carried such conviction to the public heart that he is a real man of genius·and worth being kept alive at a moderate rate. Lecturing were surely an easier profession than authorship. We shall see. My cough is quite gon[e] and there [is] no consumption about me at present—I expect to grow strong now that he has nothing more to worry him.[10]

Miss Wilson and Miss Martineau had done well for Carlyle with their lecture adventure. They had brought him directly under the public eye at an important moment of his life; but far more than that, they had solved the problem whether it was possible for him to continue in London and follow his trade. £135, to the modest household in Cheyne Row, was not only, as Carlyle called it, "financial safety" for a year to come, but it was wealth and luxury. Another course had been promised for the season following, the profits of which could hardly be less, and with a safe income of £150 a year the thrifty pair would feel superior to fortune. At all events the heavy veil on the future had now lifted. There would be no more talk of the American backwoods, or of a walk over Europe like Teufelsdröckh. No "roup" (heavy mist) need be feared in Cheyne Row, or even such pinch of penury as had been already experienced there. Life and labour were now made possible on honest terms, and literary recognition, if it was to come at all, could be waited for without starvation. It was as if some cursed enchanter's spell had been broken. How the fetters had galled, Carlyle hardly knew till he began to stretch his limbs in freedom. *The French Revolution* was published immediately afterwards. It was not "subscribed for" among the booksellers. The author's name was unknown to most of them, and the rest had no belief in him. The book itself, style and matter, was so new, so unlike anything that had ever been seen before, that the few who read it knew not what to say or think. The reviewers were puzzled. Such a fabric could not be appraised at once like a specimen from a familiar loom. The sale at first was slow, almost nothing; but Carlyle was not dissatisfied with the few opinions which reached him. "Some," he said, "condemn me, as is very natural, for 'affectation.' Others are hearty, even passionate (as Mill) in their estimation. On the whole it strikes me as not unlikely that the Book may take some hold of the English People, and do them and itself a little good."[11] One letter especially pleased him. "Jeffrey," he said, "writes me . . . full of good augury, of praise and blame, and how I shall infallibly be much praised and much blamed, and on the whole carry my point; really a kind hearty Letter from the little man."[12] This was well enough, but months would pass before anything could be gathered like a general verdict; and Carlyle, after the long strain, was sinking into lassitude.

[On 21 June] Carlyle fled to Scotland fairly broken down. He had fought and won his long battle. The reaction had come, and his strangely organised nervous system was shattered. He went by sea from Liverpool to Annan. His brother Alick had come to meet him at Annan pier, and together they walked up to Ecclefechan. The view from the road across the Solway to the Cumberland mountains is one of the most beautiful in the island. The brother having some business in a cottage, Carlyle was left alone leaning on a milestone and looking back on the scene. "Tartarus itself," he says, "and the pale kingdoms of Dis could not have been more preternatural to me. . . . Most stern, gloomy, sad, grand, yet terrible, yet steeped in woe!"[13] The spot had been familiar to him from childhood. The impression was not a momentary emotion, but abode with him for many years. Let not the impatient reader call it affectation or exaggeration. If he does, he will know nothing of Carlyle. These spectral visions were part of his nature, and always haunted him when his mind had been overstrained. He stayed at Scotsbrig two months, wholly idle, reading novels, smoking pipes in the garden with his mother, hearing notices of his book from a distance, but not looking for them or caring about them. "The weather," he says in a letter,

after a long miserable spring, is the beautifullest I ever saw; the trees wave peaceful music in front of my window here, which is shoved up to the very top; Mother is washing in the kitchen apartment to my left; the sound of Jamie building his Peat-stack is audible; and they are stirring beat-potatoes down below. . . . My souls one wish is to be left alone; to hear the rustle of the trees, the gushing of the burn, and lie vacant as ugly and stupid as I like. There is soothing and healing for me in the green solitude of these simple spaces. I bless myself that the broiling horror of London is far, far. . . . "A favourable review in the *Chronicle*," . . . a "favourable review in the L. and Westminister," &c&c: no one of them have I yet set eye on. I find it, a bottom, hurtful to look after the like: one has a prurient titillability in that kind; extremely despicable; which it is better wholly to steer clear of.[14]

To his wife he wrote regularly, but in a tone somewhat constrained. Spenser's knight, sorely wounded in his fight with the dragon, fell back under the enchanted tree whence

flowd, as from a well,
A trickling streame of Balme, most soveraine . . .
Life and long health that gratious ointment gave,
And deadly woundes could heale, and reare againe
The senselesse corse appointed for the grave.
Into that same he fell: which did from death him save.[15]

What that tree was to the bleeding warrior, the poor Annandale farmhouse, its quiet innocence, and the affectionate kindred there, proved then as always to Carlyle, for he too had been fighting dragons and been heavily beaten upon.

Autumn, as usual, brought back the migratory London flocks, and among them Carlyle. He found his wife better in health, delighted to have him again at her side, and in lightened humour altogether. She knew, though he, so little vain was he, had failed as yet to understand it, that he had returned to a changed position, that he was no longer lonely and neglected, but had taken his natural place among the great writers of his day. Popular he might not be. Popularity with the multitude he had to wait for many a year; but he was acknowledged by all whose judgement carried weight with it to have become actually what Goethe had long ago foretold that he would be—a new moral force in Europe, the extent of which could not be foreseen, but must be great and might be immeasurable. He was still poor, wretchedly poor according to the modern standard. But the Carlyles did not think about standards, and on that score had no more anxieties. He had no work on hand or immediate desire for any. He was able to tell his brother John that, "having no *Book* to write this year, I shall not feel so fretted, shall not fret any one: there will be a cheerfuller household than of old."[16] An article on Sir Walter Scott had been promised to Mill, and a subject had to be thought of for the next Spring's lectures. Both of these would be easy tasks. Meanwhile, he discovered that his wife was right. "I am to be considered as a kind of successful man. The poor Book has done me real service; and in very truth had been abundantly reviewed and talked about and belauded far more than I had any expectation of. Neither, apparently, is it yet done."[17] He sent to Scotsbrig cheery accounts of himself. "I find John Sterling here," he said, "and many friends; all kinder each than the other to me[;] with talk and locomotion the days pass cheerfully till I rest, and gird myself together again. They make a great talk about the Book; which seems to have succeeded in a far higher degree than I looked for. . . . Everybody is astonished at every other bodys being pleased with this wonderful performance!"[18]

The Scott article was written as it appears unaltered in the *Miscellanies*. Carlyle was not himself pleased with it, and found the task at one moment *disgusting*.[19] He began it with indifference. The "steam got . . . *up*," and he fell into what he called "the old sham-happy nervously excited mood,—too well known to me!"[20] The world was satisfied, and what such a man as Carlyle had deliberately to say about Scott will always be read with interest; but he evidently did not take to the subject with cordial sympathy. A man so sternly in earnest could never forgive Sir Walter for squandering such splendid gifts on amusing people, and for creating a universal taste for amusement of that description. He did not perhaps improve his humour by reading, while he was writing the paper, the strongest imaginable contrast to the "Waverley Novels," Dante's *Inferno*. He found Dante "uphill work," "but a great and enduring thing." It is "worth noting," he says with a glance at Scott, "how *loth* we are to read great works; how much more willingly we cross our legs, back to candles, feet to fire, over some *Pickwick* or lowest trash of that nature! The reason is, we are very indolent, very wearied forlorn; and read oftenest chiefly that we may forget ourselves. Consider what Popularity, in that case, must mean!"[21]

Signs appeared, nevertheless, that the public could now find something, either amusement or instruction, or pleasure of some kind, in Carlyle's own writings. *The French Revolution* had made an alteration in this respect. The publishers spoke to him about reprinting *Sartor*, about "an edition of his collected articles." The question had become one of terms only, for the risk could be ventured. "Changed times," as he half-bitterly observed to his mother.

> Fraser the other day sent for me, to propose that he should reprint Teufelsdröckh and my Review Articles collected into volumes. The wind is changed there, at any rate! The last time he heard of Teufelsdröckh and the proposal to print it, he shrieked at the very notion. Seriously, it is good news this; an infallible sign that the other Book, the F. Revolution, prospers: nay still better, a sign that I shall either now or some time get a little cash by these poor scattered Papers. I have resolved that Fraser, for his old scream's sake, and for my own sake, shall not have the printing of the volumes without some very respectable sum of money now:—he should have done it formerly, and not screamed![22]

Internally at his own home things were going brightly with Carlyle. It was the coldest winter remembered in England, Murphy's winter, when the Thames was frozen from Oxford to Reading; but his wife remained well without signs of cough, and from all sides came signs of goodwill for the "great writer" who was now become famous. Scotsbrig sent its barrels of meal and butter. "Alick," who, farming having gone ill with him, had started a shop in Ecclefechan, sent an offering of first-rate tobacco. "Poor Alick," his brother said, "the first of his shop-goods; we received them with a most wistful thankfulness, glad and *wae*."[23] This was no more than usual; but Peers and Cabinet Ministers began to show a wish for a nearer acquaintance with a man who was so much talked of, and a singular compliment was paid him which later history makes really remarkable. "Some people here," he said, "are beginning to imitate my style, and such like. The French Revolution I knew from the first to be *savage*, an orson of a book; but the people have seen that it has a genuineness in it; and in consideration of that, have pardoned all the rest."[24]

Among the established "great," the first who held out a hand was Mr. Spring Rice, Lord Monteagle, afterwards Chancellor of the Exchequer in the Liberal Ministry. Spring Rice was a statesman of the strict official school, not given to Carlylean modes of thinking; but he was ready to welcome a man of genius, however little he might agree with him. His eldest son, Stephen Spring Rice, who died before his father, being untied to officiality, could admire more freely; and one at least of his sisters had been a subscriber to the lectures on German literature. Accordingly there came an invitation to Cheyne Row to an evening party. Carlyle would have refused, but his wife insisted that he should go. "It was a brilliant-looking thing," he said; "all very polite; marchionesses &c, 'with feelings exactly like ours (as my dear Mother said of the Foreign persons in *Wilhelm Meister*)."[25]

"Literature," so the fates had decided, was to remain Carlyle's profession.[26] He had meant to abandon it, but the cord which held him to his desk, though strained, had not broken. Yet it was a "bad best," he thought, for any man, more trying to the moral nature, and in his own case, so modestly he rated his powers, less likely to be useful, than any other honest occupation. He would still have gladly entered the public service if employment had been offered him, as offered it would have been, in any country but England, to a man who had shown ability so marked. He was acknowledged as a man of genius, and in England it is assumed that for a man of genius no place can be found. He is too good for a low situation. He is likely to be troublesome in a higher one, and is thus the one man distinctly unpromotable. *Foenum habet in cornu* [i.e., he is dangerous][27]— avoid him above all men. Carlyle had to accept his lot, since such had been ordered for him. But his distaste continued, and extended to other members of the craft who were now courting his acquaintance. He found them *bores*, a class of persons for whom he had the least charity.

> It often strikes me as a question whether there ought to be any such thing as a literary man at all. He is surely the wretchedest of all sorts

of men. I wish with the heart occasionally I had never been one. I cannot say I have ever seen a member of the guild whose life seems to me enviable. A *man*, a Goethe, will be a man on paper too; but it is a questionable life for him.[28]

Let young men who are dreaming of literary eminence as the laurel wreath of their existence reflect on these words. Let them win a place for themselves as high as Carlyle won, they will find that he was speaking no more than the truth, and will wish, when it is too late, that they had been wise in time. Literature—were it even poetry—is but the shadow of action; the action the reality, the poetry an echo. The *Odyssey* is but the ghost of Ulysses—immortal, but a ghost still; and Homer himself would have said in some moods with his own Achilles—

> Rather would I in the sun's warmth divine
> Serve a poor churl who drags his days in grief,
> Than the whole lordship of the dead were mine.[29]

Jeffrey, while congratulating his friend on the success of *The French Revolution*, yet could see that the business of an author was not the happiest or the most healthful for a person of Carlyle's temper. Contact with the common things of life would make him more tolerant of a world which if not perfect was better than it had ever been before, and would give him a better chance of mending it, while he despised it less.[30] But it was not to be, and even to Carlyle authorship was better than idleness. When he was idle the acids ate into the coating of his soul.[31] The first set of lectures Carlyle had been obliged to deliver out of his acquired knowledge, having no leisure to do more. For the second he prepared carefully, especially the Greek and Roman parts. Classics are not the strong point of an Edinburgh education, and the little which he had learned there was rusty. "I have read Thucydides, Herodotus," he wrote in April; "part of Niebuhr, Michelet &c.,—the latter two with small fruit and much disappointment, the former two not. . . . I should have several good things to say and do very well were I in health, were I *in brass* [in a brazen mood]."[32] But trouble had come into Cheyne Row again. Without any definite ailment, Mrs. Carlyle seemed unwell in mind and body. There was even a thought of sending her to Italy when the lectures were over, if there were means to do it. Carlyle even thought of going thither himself, or at any rate of leaving London altogether.

[His letters of the time] indicate no pleasant condition of mind, not a condition in which it could have been agreeable to take to the platform again and deliver lectures. But Carlyle could command himself when necessary, however severe the burden that was weighing upon him. This time he succeeded brilliantly, far better than on his first experiment. The lectures were reported in the *Examiner* and other papers, and can be recovered there by the curious.[33] He did not himself reprint them, attaching no importance to what he called "a detestable mixture of Prophecy and Playactorism."[34]

[The course was of twelve lectures divided into four periods of three lectures each. The first lecture was "of literature in general"; the second, on the Greeks from Homer through "Aeschylus to Socrates," illustrated the "Decline of the Greeks"; the third, on the Romans, closed the first period. The fourth and fifth lectures were on the Middle Ages—particularly, as might be expected, on German literature—and on Dante. "Yesterday," wrote Carlyle in his Journal, "lectured on Cervantes and the Spaniards. A hurried, loose-flowing, but earnest, wide-reaching sort of thing; which the people liked better than I." On 31 May he wrote: "Lecture on Luther and the Reformation; then on Shakespeare and John Knox (my best hitherto); finally on Voltaire and French scepticism,—the worst, as I compute, of all. To-morrow is to be Lecture tenth on Johnson, &c: there are then but two remaining."[35] The final two lectures treated "Consummation of Scepticism—Wertherism—The French Revolution" and "Of Modern German Literature—Goethe and His Works."]

The lecture course was perhaps too prolonged. Twelve orations such as Carlyle was delivering were beyond the strength of any man who meant every word that he uttered. It ended, however, with a blaze of fireworks—people "weeping" at the passionately earnest tone in which for once they heard themselves addressed. The money result was nearly £300, after all expenses had been paid. "A great blessing," as Carlyle said, "for a man that has been hunted by the squalid spectre of Beggary."[36] There were prospects of improved finances from other quarters too. Notwithstanding all the talk about *The French Revolution*, nothing yet had been realised for it in England, but Emerson held out hopes of remittances on the American edition. *Sartor*, "poor beast," as Mrs. Carlyle called it,[37] was at last coming out in a volume, and there was still a talk of reprinting the essays. But Carlyle was worn out. Fame brought its accompaniments of invitations to dinner which could not be all refused; the dinners brought indigestions; and the dog days brought heat, and heat and indigestion together made sleep impossible.

chapter nineteen

1838-1840

Interest in Cromwell. Lectures on the
Revolutions of Modern Europe. *Chartism.*
Lectures on Heroes and Hero-Worship

Carlyle's annual migrations were like those of Mrs. Primrose from the blue room to the brown—from London to Scotland.[1] Thither almost always, seldom anywhere else. He had
meant to stay all through the summer in Chelsea, but an
invitation from his friends, the Ferguses at Kirkcaldy,
tempted him, and in the middle of August he went by Leith
steamer to the old place where he had taught little boys, and
fallen in love with Miss Gordon, and rambled with Edward
Irving. It was "melodiously interesting," he said. He bathed
on the old sands. He had a horse which carried him through
the old familiar scenes. While at Kirkcaldy he crossed to
Edinburgh and called on Jeffrey.

After a week or two in Fife he made for Scotsbrig, where
news met him that £50 had been sent from America as a
royalty on the edition of *The French Revolution,* and that
more would follow. "What a touching thing is that!" he
said. "One prays that the blessing of him that was *rather
ill off* may be with them, these good friends of mine. Courage, my Goody! I begin to feel as if one might grow to be
moderately content with a Lot like mine."[2]

[When he returned to London] evidences were waiting
for him that he was becoming a person of consequence notwithstanding. Presents had been sent by various admirers.
There was good news from America. The English edition of
The French Revolution was almost sold, and another would
be called for, while there were numberless applications from
review editors for articles if he would please to supply them.

CARLYLE IN 1838. Of this portrait Carlyle wrote: "Really rather good,—infinitely better than common. . . . A likeness as of one in doleful dumps, with its mouth all *sheyled* [twisted awry] and its eyes looking fiercely out: meant to be very tragical." (Engraving by J. C. Armytage from the portrait in oil by Samuel Laurence; from a copy of this engraving in the editor's possession.)

Another £50 had come from Boston, and he had been meditating an indulgence for himself out of all this prosperity in the shape of a horse, nothing keeping him in health so much as riding.

Out of the suggestions made by editors for articles one especially had attracted Carlyle. Mill had asked him to write on Cromwell for the *London and Westminster.* There is nothing in his journals or letters to show that Cromwell had been

hitherto an interesting figure to him.[3] An allusion in one of
his Craigenputtoch papers shows that he then shared the
popular prevailing opinions on the subject. He agreed, however, to Mill's proposal, and was preparing to begin with it
when the negotiation was broken off in a manner specially
affronting. Mill had gone abroad, leaving Mr. Robertson to
manage the *Review*. Robertson, whom Carlyle had hitherto
liked, wrote to him coolly to say that he need not go on, for
"he meant to do Cromwell himself."[4] Carlyle was very
angry. It was this incident which determined him to throw
himself seriously into the history of the Commonwealth, and
to expose himself no more to cavalier treatment from "able
editors." His connection with the *London and Westminster*
at once ended. From this moment he began to think seriously
of a life of Oliver Cromwell as his next important undertaking, whatever he might have to do meanwhile in the way of
lectures or shorter papers.

Want of books was his great difficulty, with such a subject
on hand as the Commonwealth. His Cambridge friends had
come to his help by giving him the use of the books in the
University Library, and sending them up for him to read.
Very kind on their part, as he felt, "considering what a sulky
[fel]low I am."[5] But he needed resources of which he could
avail himself more freely. The British Museum was, of
course, open to him; but he required to have his authorities
at hand, where his own writing-tackle lay round him, where
he could refer to them at any moment, and for this purpose
the circulating libraries were useless. New novels, travels,
biographies, the annual growth of literature which today was
and tomorrow was cast into the oven—these he could get; but
the records of genuine knowledge, where the permanent
thoughts and doings of mankind lay embalmed, were to be
found for the most part only on the shelves of great institutions, could be read only there, and could not be taken out.
Long before, when at Craigenputtoch, it had occurred to him
that a county town like Dumfries, which maintained a gaol,
might equally maintain a public library. He was once at Oxford in the library of All Souls' College, one of the best in
England, and one (in my day at least) so little used that, if
a book was missed from its place, the whole college was in
consternation. Carlyle, looking wistfully at the ranged folios,

exclaimed: "Ah books, books! you will have a poor account to give of yourselves at the day of judgment. Here have you been kept warm and dry, with good coats on your backs, and a good roof over your heads; and whom have ye made any better or any wiser than he was before?" Cambridge, more liberal than Oxford, did lend out volumes with fit securities for their safety, and from this source Carlyle obtained his Clarendon and Rushworth; but he determined to try whether a public lending library of authentic worth could not be instituted in London. He has been talked of vaguely as "unpractical." No one living had a more practical business talent when he had an object in view for which such a faculty was required. He set on foot an agitation. The end was recognised as good. Influential men took up the question, and it was carried through, and the result was the infinitely valuable institution known as the "London Library" in St. James's Square. Let the tens of thousands who, it is to be hoped, are "made better and wiser" by the books collected there remember that they owe the privilege entirely to Carlyle. The germ of it lay in that original reflection of his on the presence of a gaol and the absence of a library in Dumfries. His successful effort to realise it in London began in this winter of 1839.[6]

Meanwhile a third remittance from America on the *Revolution* brought the whole sum which he had received from his Boston friends to £150. He felt it deeply, for as yet "not a sixpence could be realised here in one's own country."[7] In acknowledging the receipt, he said that he had never received money of which he was more proud, "sent me . . . almost by miracle."[8] He showed the draft to Fraser, his English publisher, and told him he ought to blush.

Few men cared less about such things than Carlyle did as long as penury was kept from his door. Apart from his business with the London Library, he was wholly occupied with the records of the Commonwealth, and here are the first impressions which he formed.

> I have read a good many volumes about Cromwell and his time; I have a good many more to read. Whether a book will come of it or not, still more *when* such will come, are questions as yet. The pabulum this subject yields me is not very great; I find it far inferior in interest to my French subject: but on the whole I want to get

acquainted with England (a great secret to me always hitherto), and I may as well begin here as elsewhere. There are but two very remarkable men in the Period visible as yet: Cromwell and Montrose. The rest verge towards wearisomeness; indeed the whole subject is Dutch-built, heavy-bottomed; with an internal fire and significance indeed, but extremely wrapt in buckram and lead. We shall see.[9]

Seldom had Carlyle seemed in better spirits than now. For once his outer world was going well with him. He had occasional fits of dyspepsia, which, indeed, seemed to afflict him most when he had least that was real to complain of. He was disappointed about Montrose for one thing. He had intended, naturally enough as a Scotchman, to make a principal figure of Montrose, and had found that he could not, that it was impossible to discover what Montrose was really like.[10] But the dyspepsia was the main evil—dyspepsia and London society, which interested him more than he would allow, and was the cause of the disorder.

Monckton Milnes had made his acquaintance, and invited him to breakfast. He used to say that, if Christ was again on earth, Milnes would ask Him to breakfast, and the Clubs would all be talking of the "good things" that Christ had said. But Milnes, then as always, had open eyes for genius, and reverence for it truer and deeper than most of his contemporaries.

More important by far to Carlyle was the "certain Baring" with whom he was to dine at Bath House.[11] It is the first notice of his introduction to the brilliant circle in which he was afterwards to be so intimate. Mr. Baring, later known as Lord Ashburton, became the closest friend that he had. Lady Harriet became his Gloriana, or Queen of Fairy Land, and exercised a strange influence over him for good and evil.[12] But this lay undreamed of in the future, when he wrote his account of the dinner.

> It was one of the most elevated things I had ever seen; Lords, Ladyships and other the like high personages, several of them auditors of mine in the last Lecturing season. The Lady of the House, one Lady Harriet Baring, I had to sit and talk with specially for a long long while; one of the cleverest creatures I have met with, full of mirth and spirit,—not very beautiful to look upon.[13]

And again, in another letter: "The Lady . . . kept me talking an hour or more up stairs, 'a cleva' devil,' *belle-laide,*

376

HARRIET LADY ASHBURTON. This seated, half-length portrait suggests the imperial manner of the first Lady Ashburton—the "Gloriana" of Froude's narrative. (Courtesy of the Carlyle House, Chelsea.)

full of wit, and the most like a dame of quality of all I have yet seen."[14]

The lectures had to be provided for, but the subject chosen, the Revolutions of Modern Europe, was one on which Carlyle could speak without special preparation. An English edition of the *Miscellanies* was coming out at last, and money was to be paid for it. He was thus able to lie upon his oars till Cromwell or some other topic took active possession.

CARLYLE IN 1839. This left profile lithograph was made from a sketch done by D'Orsay in Lady Blessington's drawing room in May 1839. Carlyle described it as "a fine portrait . . . dashed off in some twenty minutes." D'Orsay's original sketch, dated May 1839, is now in the attic study of the Carlyle House. (Drawn by Alfred D'Orsay and engraved by J. Sartain; from a copy of the engraving in the editor's possession.)

May brought the lectures at the old rooms in Edwardes Street. They did not please Carlyle, and, perhaps, were not really among his fine utterances. In *The French Revolution* he had given his best thoughts on the subject in his best manner. He could now only repeat himself, more or less rhetorically, with a varying text. Mrs. Carlyle herself did not think that her husband was doing justice to himself. He was unwell for one thing. But the success was distinct as ever; the audience bursting into ejaculations of surprise and pleasure. The "Splendids!" "Devilish fines!" "Most trues!" all indicating that on their side there was no disappointment. His own account of the matter indicates far less satisfaction.

> The Lectures . . . are over; with tolerable *éclat*, with a clear gain of very nearly £200, which latter is the only altogether comfortable part of the business. My audience was visibly more numerous than ever, and of more distinguished people; my sorrow in delivery was less, my *remorse* after delivery was much greater. I gave one very bad lecture (as I thought), the last but one; it was on the French Revolution. I was dispirited, in miserable health, my audience mainly Tory could not be expected to sympathize with me; in short, I felt, after it was over, "like a man that had been robbing henroosts." In which circumstance I, the day before my finale,—hired a swift horse, galloped out to Harrow and back again, went in [a] kind of rage to the room next day, and made, on Sansculottism itself, very considerably the nearest appro[ach] to a good Lecture they ever got out of me; carried the whole business glowing after me, and ended half an hour beyond my time with universal decisive applause, sufficient for the occasion.[15]

The *"remorse"* was genuine, for Carlyle in his heart disapproved of these displays and detested them. Yet he, too, had become aware of the strange sensation of seeing a crowd of people hanging upon his words, and yielding themselves like an instrument for him to play upon. There is an irresistible feeling of proud delight in such situations. If not intoxicated, he was excited; and Emerson writing at the same moment to press him to show himself in Boston, he did think for a second or two of going over for the autumn "to *learn* the business of extempore speaking."[16] Had he gone it might have been the ruin of him, for he had all the qualities which with practice would have made him a splendid orator. But he was wise in time, and set himself to a worthier enterprise—not yet Cromwell, but something which stood in the way of Cromwell—and insisted on being dealt with before he could settle upon history. All his life he had been meditating on the problem of the working-man's existence in this country at the present epoch; how wealth was growing, but the human toilers grew none the better, mentally or bodily— not better, only more numerous, and liable, on any check to trade, to sink into squalor and famine. He had seen the Glasgow riots in 1819. He had heard his father talk of the poor masons, dining silently upon water and water-cresses. His letters are full of reflections on such things, sad or indignant, as the humour might be. He was himself a working-man's son. He had been bred in a peasant home, and all his sympathies were with his own class. He was not a revolutionist; he knew well that violence would be no remedy; that there lay only madness and deeper misery. But the fact remained, portending frightful issues. The Reform Bill was to have mended matters, but the Reform Bill had gone by and the poor were none the happier. The power of the State had been shifted from the aristocracy to the mill-owners, and merchants, and shopkeepers. That was all. The handicraftsman remained where he was, or was sinking, rather, into an unowned Arab, to whom "freedom" meant freedom to work if the employer had work to offer him conveniently to himself, or else freedom to starve. The fruit of such a state of society as this was the Sansculottism on which he had been lecturing, and he felt that he must put his thoughts upon it in a permanent form. He had no faith in political remedies, in extended suffrages, recognition of "the rights of man," etc.—absolutely none. That was the road on which the French had gone; and, if tried in England, it would end as it ended with them—in anarchy, and hunger, and fury. The root of the mischief was the forgetfulness on the part of the upper classes, increasing now to flat denial, that they owed any duty to those under them beyond the payment of contract wages at the market price. The Liberal theory, as formulated in Political Economy, was that everyone should attend exclusively to his own interests, and that the best of all possible worlds would be the certain result. His own conviction was that the result would be the worst of all possible worlds, a world in which human life, such a life as human beings ought to live, would become impossible. People talked of Progress. To him there was no progress except "moral progress," a clearer recognition of the duties which stood face to face with every man at each moment of his life, and the neglect of which would be his destruction. He was appalled at the contrast between the principles on which men practically acted and those which on Sundays they professed to believe; at the ever-increasing luxury in rich men's palaces, and the wretchedness, without hope of escape, of the millions without whom that luxury could not have been. Such a state of things, he thought, might continue for a time among a people naturally well disposed and accustomed to submission; but it could not last for ever. The Maker of the world would not allow it. The angry slaves of toil would rise and burn the palaces, as the French peasantry had burnt the châteaux. The only remedy was the old one—to touch the conscience or the fears of those whom he regarded as responsible. He felt that he must write something about all that, though it was not easy to see how or where. Such a message as he had to give would be welcome neither to Liberals nor Conservatives. The Political Economists believed that since the Reform Bill all was going as it should go, and required only to be let alone; the more the rich enjoyed themselves, the more employment there would be, and high and low would be benefited alike. The Noble Lords and gentry were happy in their hounds and their game-preserves, and had lost the sense that rank and wealth meant anything save privilege for idle amusement. Not to either of these, nor to their organs in the press, could Carlyle be welcome. He was called a Radical, and Radical he was, if to require a change in the souls, and hearts, and habits of life of men was to be a Radical. But perhaps no one in England more entirely disbelieved every single article of the orthodox Radical creed. He had more in common with the Tories than with their rivals, and was prepared, if such a strange ally pleased them, to let it so appear. "Guess what immediate project I am on," he wrote to his brother, when the lectures were over:

> that of writing an Article *on the working classes* for the *Quarterly!* It is verily so: I offered to do the thing for Mill about a year ago; he durst not; I felt a kind of call and monition of duty to do it, wrote to Lockhart accordingly, was altogether invitingly answered, had a long interview with the man yesterday, found him a person of sense, goodbreeding, even kindness, and great consentaneity of opinion with myself on this matter, am to get books from him tomorrow; and so shall forthwith set about telling Conservatives a thing or two about the claims [,] condition, rights and mights of the working orders of men! Jane is very glad; partly from a kind of spite at the *Blödsinnigkeit* [idiocy] of Mill and his wooden set. The Radicals, as

381

they stand now, are dead and gone, I apprehend,—owing to their heartless stupidity on that very matter. . . . It is not to be out till Autumn[,] that being the time for "things requiring thought," as Lockhart says; I shall have much to read and inquire, but in fine I shall get the thing off my hands, and have my heart clear about it.[17]

What came of this project will be seen. One result of it, however, was a singular relation which grew up between Carlyle and Lockhart. They lived in different circles; they did not meet often, or correspond often; but Carlyle ever after spoke of Lockhart as he seldom spoke of any man; and such letters of Lockhart's to Carlyle as survive show a trusting confidence extremely remarkable in a man who was so chary of his esteem.

In general society Carlyle was mixing more and more, important persons seeking his acquaintance. He met Webster, the famous American, at breakfast one morning, and has left a portrait of this noticeable politician. "I will warrant him," he says,

> one of the stiffest logic-buffers and Parliamentary athletes anywhere to be met with in our world at present. A grim, tall broad-bottomed, yellow-skinned man, with brows like precipitous cliffs, and huge black dull wearied unwear-able-looking eyes under them; amorphous projecting nose; and the angriest shut mou[th] I have anywhere seen;—a droop on the sides of the upper lip is quite mastiff-like, magnificen[t] to look upon, it is so quiet withal. I guess [I] should like ill to be that man's nigger! However, he is a right clever man in his way; and has a husky sort of fun in him too;— drawls, [in] a handfast didactic manner, about "our republican institutions" &c &c, and so plays *his* p[art.][18]

Another memorable notability Carlyle came across at this time, who struck him much, and the attraction was mutual— Connop Thirlwall, afterwards Bishop of St. David's, then under a cloud in the ecclesiastic world, as "suspect" of heresy. Of this great man more will be heard hereafter. Their first meeting was at James Spedding's rooms in Lincoln's Inn Fields; "very pleasant; free and easy; with windows flung up, and tobacco ad libitum." He found the future bishop "a most sarcastic, sceptical, but strongheaded, strong-hearted man, whom I have a real liking for." The orthodox side of the conversation was maintained, it seems, by Milnes, who "gave us dilettante Catholicism, and endured Thirlwall's tobacco."[19]

382

One more pleasant incident befell Carlyle before the dog-days and the annual migration. He was known to wish for a horse, and yet to hesitate whether such an indulgence was permissible to a person financially situated as he was. Mr. Marshall, of Leeds, whose name has been already mentioned, heard of it; and Mr. Marshall's son appeared one day in Cheyne Row, with a message that his father had a mare for which he had no use, and would be pleased if Carlyle would accept her. The offer was made with the utmost delicacy. If he was leaving town, and did not immediately need such an article, they would keep her at grass till he returned. It was represented, in fact, as a convenience to them, as well as a possible pleasure to him. The gift was nothing in itself, for Mr. Marshall was a man of vast wealth; but it was a handsome sign of consideration and good-feeling, and was gratefully recognised as such. The mare became Carlyle's. She was called "Citoyenne," after *The French Revolution*. The expense would be something, but would be repaid by increase of health. Mrs. Carlyle said "it is . . . like my 'buying a *laying hen,* and giving it to some deserving person;—accept it, dear!' "[20]

A still nearer friend had also been taking thought for his comfort. He was going to Scotland, and this year his wife was going with him. The faithful, thoughtful John had sent £30 privately to his brother Alick at Ecclefechan, to provide a horse and gig, that Carlyle and she might drive about together as with the old *clatch* at Craigenputtoch—a beautiful action on the part of John. They went north in the middle of July, going first to Nithsdale to stay with Mrs. Welsh at Templand. Mrs. Welsh, too, had been considering what she could do to gratify her son-in-law, and had invited his mother over from Scotsbrig to meet him. Mrs. Carlyle was not well at Templand, and could not much enjoy herself; but Carlyle was like a boy out of school. He and his old mother drove about in John's gig together, or wandered through the shrubberies, smoking their pipes together, like a pair of lovers—as indeed they were. Later on, when he grew impatient again, he called the life which he was leading "sluggish ignoble solitude,"[21] but it was as near an approach as he ever knew to what is meant by happiness. This summer nothing went wrong with him. When the Templand visit was over, he removed to Scotsbrig and there stayed, turning over his intended article.

The holiday lasted two months only. *Wilhelm Meister* was now to be republished, and he was wanted at home. The railway had just been opened from Preston to London; and on this return journey he made his first experience of the new mode of locomotion.

> The whirl thro' the confused darkness on those steam wings was one of the strangest things I have experienced. Hissing and dashing on, one knew not whither, we saw the gleam of towns in the distance, unknown towns; we went over the tops of towns (one town or village I saw clearly with its chimney heads vainly stretching up towards us); *under* the stars, not *under* the clouds but among them; out of one vehicle then into another, snorting, roaring we flew;—the likest thing to a Faust's flight on the Devil's mantle[; or] as if some huge steam nightbird had flung you on its back, and were sweeping thro' unknown space with you, most probably towards London![22]

A pleasant surprise waited for Carlyle on his return to London—an article upon him by Sterling in the *Westminster Review*.[23] Sterling's admiration was steadily growing—admiration alike for his friend's intellect and character. It was the first public acknowledgment of Carlyle's "magnitude" which had been made. Sterling's appreciation, when read now, rather seems to fall short of the truth than to exceed it. But now is now, and then was then—and a man's heart beats when he learns, for the first time, that a brother man admires and loves him. If Carlyle was proud, he had no vanity, and he allowed no vanity to grow in him. He set himself to his article for Lockhart.

Under these conditions, and riding every day, Carlyle contrived to finish without fret or fume the hypothetical article for the *Quarterly*—for the *Quarterly* as had been proposed, yet, as it grew under his hand, he felt but too surely that in those pages it could find no place. Could the Tory party five-and-forty years ago have accepted Carlyle for their prophet, they would not be where they are now. Heat and motion, the men of science tell us, are modes of the same force, which may take one form or the other, but not both at once. So it is with social greatness. The Noble Lord may live in idleness and luxury, or he may have political power, but he must choose between them. If he prefer the first, he will not keep the second. Carlyle saw too plainly that for him in that quarter there would be no willing audience.

It proved as he expected with the *Quarterly*. Lockhart probably agreed with every word that Carlyle had written, but to admit a lighted rocket of that kind into the Conservative arsenal might have shattered the whole concern. "The Tory *Quarterly Review* people kept it for a week; and then, seemingly not without reluctance, sent it back, saying, 'We dare not.' "[24] It was then shown to Mill, who was unexpectedly delighted with it. The *Westminster Review* was coming to an end. Mill was now willing to publish *Chartism* "in his *final* Number, as a kind of final shout; that he might sink like a *Vengeur* battle-ship, with a broadside at the water's-edge!"[25] Carlyle might have consented; but his wife, and his brother John, who was in England, insisted that the thing was too good for a fate so ignoble. The *Westminster Review* was nothing to him, that he should sink along with it. This was his own opinion too, which for Mill's sake he had been ready to waive. "In short, I think of publishing this piece, which I have called '*Chartism,*' which is all about the Poor and their rights and wrongs, as a little separate Book. . . . Fraser will print it; 'halving' the profits. It may be out, probably, by the end of this month."[26]

The book was not long, the printers were expeditious, and before the year was out *Chartism* was added to the list of Carlyle's published works. The sale was rapid, an edition of a thousand copies being sold immediately—and the large lump of leaven was thrown into the general trough to ferment there and work as it could. *Meister*, the most unlike it of all imaginable creations, was republished at the same time. The collected *Miscellanies* were also passing through the press.

Chartism was loudly noticed; "considerable reviewing . . . but very *daft* reviewing."[27] Men wondered; how could they choose but wonder, when a writer of evident power stripped bare the social disease, told them that their remedies were quack remedies, and their progress was progress to dissolution? The Liberal journals, finding their "formulas" disbelieved in, clamoured that Carlyle was unorthodox; no Radical, but a wolf in sheep's clothing. Yet what he said was true, and could not be denied to be true. "They approve generally . . . ," he said, "but regret very much that I am—a Tory! Stranger Tory, in my opinion, has not been fallen in with in these latter generations."[28] Again a few weeks later (February 11): "The people are beginning to discover (wise men as they are!) that I am not a 'Tory,' ah no; but one of the deepest tho' perhaps the quietest of all the radicals now extant in the world; a thing productive of small comfort to several persons! 'They have said, and they will say, and let them say' &c. &c."[29]

He, too, had had his say. The burden on his soul which lay between him and other work had been thrown off. Now was time to take up the Commonwealth in earnest; but other subjects were again rising between Carlyle and the Commonwealth. One more, and this the final, course of lectures was to be delivered this spring; and it was to contain something of more consequence than its predecessors, something which he could wish to preserve. By the side of *laissez-faire* and "democracy" in politics there was growing up a popular philosophy analogous to it. The civilisation of mankind, it was maintained (though Mr. Buckle had not yet risen to throw the theory into shape), expanded naturally with the growth of knowledge.[30] Knowledge spread over the world like light, and though great men, as they were called, might be a few inches taller than their fellows, and so catch the rays a few days or years before the rest, yet the rays did not come from them, but from the common source of increasing illumination. Great men were not essentially superior to common men. They were the creatures of their age, not the creators of it, scarcely even its guides; and the course of things would have been very much the same if this or that person who had happened to become famous had never existed. Such a view was flattering to the millions who were to be invited to self-government. It was the natural corollary of the theory that all men were equal and possessed an equal right to have their opinions represented. It was the exact opposite of the opinion of Carlyle, who held that the welfare of mankind depended more on virtue than on scientific discoveries; and that scientific discoveries themselves which were worth the name were achievable only by truthfulness and manliness. The immense mass of men he believed to be poor creatures, poor in heart and poor in intellect, incapable of making any progress at all if left to their own devices, though with a natural loyalty, if not distracted into self-conceit, to those who were wiser and better than themselves. Every advance which humanity had made was due to special individuals supremely gifted in mind and character, whom Providence sent among them at favoured epochs. It was not true, then or ever, that men were equal. They were infinitely unequal—unequal in intelligence, and still more unequal in moral purpose. So far from being able to guide or govern themselves, their one chance of improvement lay in their submitting to their natural superiors, either by their free will, or else by compulsion. This was the principle which he proposed to illustrate in a set of discourses upon "Heroes and Hero-Worship."

> I am beginning seriously to meditate my *Course of Lectures*, and have even, or seem to have, the *primordium* of a subject in me,—tho' not nameable as yet. And the dinners, routs, callers, confusions; inevitable to a certain length in this mad summer quarter here! *Ay de mi*, I wish I were far from it: no health lies for me in that, for body or for soul; welfare, at least the absence of *ill*-fare and semi-delirium is possible for me in solitude only! Solitude is indeed sad as Golgotha; but it is not mad like Bedlam. "O, the Devil burn it, there is no pleasing of *you*, strike where one will."[31]

"The Devil burn it, there is no pleasing of *you!*" was the saying of an Irish corporal who was flogging some ill-deserver. Whether he hit him high or hit him low, the victim was equally dissatisfied.[32] Carlyle complained when alone, and complained when driven into the world; dinner parties cost him his sleep, damaged his digestion, damaged his temper. Yet when he went into society no one enjoyed it more or created more enjoyment. The record of adventures of this kind alternates with groans over the consequent sufferings. He was the keenest of observers; the game was not worth the candle to him, but he gathered out of it what he could. Here is an account of a dinner at the Stanleys' in Dover Street.

> There at the dear cost of a shattered set of nerves, and head set whirling for the next eight and forty hours, I did see Lords and Lions. Lord Holland and Lady, Normanby &c; and then for soirée up stairs, Morpeth, Lansdown[e], French Guizot, the Queen of Beauty &c. Nay *Pickwick* too was of the dinner-party, I mean Dickens; tho' they did not seem to heed him over much. He is a fine little fellow, Boz, as I think; clear blue intelligent eyes, eyebrows

387

that he arches amazingly, large protrusive rather loose mouth,—a face of the most extreme *mobility*, which he shuttles about, eyebrows, eyes, mouth and all, in a very singular manner while speaking; surmount this with a loose coil of common-coloured hair, and set it on a small compact figure, very small, and dressed rather *à la d'Orsay* than well: this is Pickwick;—for the rest a quiet shrewd-looking little fellow, who seems to guess pretty well what he is, and what others are.[33]

Letters came to him from strangers low and high who were finding in his writings guidance through their own intellectual perplexities. Dr. Arnold, of Rugby, wrote that "ever since I had read your History of the French Revolution, I have longed to become acquainted with you; because I found in that book an understanding of the true nature of history, such as it delighted my heart to meet with. . . . The wisdom of the book, as well as its singular eloquence and poetry, was such a treasure to me as I have rarely met with, and am not at all likely to meet with again."[34] A poor Paisley weaver thanked him, in a yet more welcome if ill-spelt missive, for having taught him that "man does not live by demonstration, but by faith. The world had been to him for a long time a deserted temple. Carlyle's writings had restored the significance of things to him, and his voice had been as the voice of a beneficent spiritual father."[35] This was worthier homage than the flattering worship of London frivolity which injured health and temper. "I pass my days under the abominablest pressure of physical misery,—a man foiled[?]! I mean to ride diligently for three complete months, *try* faithfully whether in that way my insupportable burden and imprisonment cannot be alleviated into at least the old degree of endurability; and failing *that*,—I shall pray God to aid me in the requisite decisive measures; for positively my life is black and hateful to me."[36]

"Physical misery" was not the worst, for it was an old failing of Carlyle's that when he was uncomfortable he could not keep it to himself, and made more of it than the reality justified. Long before, when with the Bullers at Kinnaird, he had terrified his family with accounts of his tortures from dyspepsia, and had told them afterwards they should have known that when he cried "murder" he was not always being killed.[37] His wife suffered perhaps more than he from colds and pains and sleeplessness; when her husband was dilating upon his own sorrows, he often forgot hers, or made them worse by worry. Charming, witty, brilliant, affectionately playful as she naturally was, she had "a hot temper," as Carlyle had said, and a tongue, when she was angry, like a cat's, which would take the skin off at a touch. Here is a brief entry in Carlyle's Journal significant of much.[38]

> *April* 23, 1840.—Work ruined for this day;—imprudently expressed complaints in the morning filled all the sky with clouds;—portending *grave* issues? or only inane ones? I am sick, and very miserable. I have kept riding for the last two months; my health seems hardly to improve. I have been *throwing* my Lectures upon paper; Lectures "On Heroes." I know not what will come of them: in twelve days we shall see! *Miscellanies* out; and *Chartism* (second thousand). . . . *If* I were a little healthier, ah me, all were well!

Among such elements as these grew the magnificent addresses on great men and their import in this world. Fine flowers will grow where the thorns are sharpest; and the cactus does not lose its prickles, though planted in the kindliest soil. London did not suit Carlyle, but would any other place have suited him better?

Of the delivery of this course of lectures we have a more particular account than of the rest, for he wrote regularly, while they were proceeding, to his mother. The first was on the Hero as God, Odin being the representative figure; Odin, and not Another, for obvious reasons; but in this, as in everything, Carlyle was Norse to the heart. [The second lecture was on the Hero as Prophet.]

> It was on *Mahomet*; I had bishops and all kinds of people among my hearers; I gave them to know that the poor Arab had points about him which it were good for all of them to imitate; that probably *they* were more of quacks than he,—that, in short, it was altogether a new kind of thing they were hearing today! The people seemed greatly astonished, and greatly pleased; I vomited it forth on them like wild Annandale grapeshot.[39]

The third and fourth lectures were on the Hero as Poet, Dante and Shakespeare being the representatives; and the Hero as Priest, with Luther and Knox. [The fifth lecture was on the Hero as Man of Letters, with Johnson, Rousseau, and Burns taken as models; the sixth and last presented the Hero as King, and discussed Cromwell, Napoleon, and Modern Revolution.] This was Carlyle's last appearance on the platform. He never spoke in public again till twenty-six years after, when he addressed the students in Edinburgh. His better nature disapproved of these exhibitions.

He had thought, as has been seen, of repeating the experiment in America. He knew well enough that if he resolutely tried he could succeed. But to succeed he knew also that he would have to part with his natural modesty, the noblest part of him, as of every man. He must part, too, with his love of truth. The orator, in the rush and flow of words, cannot always speak truth, cannot even try to speak truth; for he speaks to an audience which reacts upon him, and he learns as he goes on to utter, not the facts as he knows them to be, but the facts shaped and twisted to please his hearers. He shut his ears therefore to the treacherous siren, and turned back to his proper function. The lectures on Heroes were to be written out and made into a book. This was the occupation which he had laid out for himself for the summer; and there was to be no change to the North till "this bit of work was accomplished."

In the midst of his work he was still pushing forward the London Library. On June 24, a meeting was held at the Freemasons' Tavern. Lord Eliot was in the chair; Lords Montague, Howick, and Lyttelton—Milman, Milnes, Cornewall Lewis, John Forster, Helps, Bulwer, Gladstone, James Spedding, George Venables—all men who were then in the first rank, or afterwards rose into it, were gathered together by Carlyle's efforts. Thirlwall warmly interested himself. Carlyle represented that, of the innumerable evils of England, "there was no remediable worse one than its condition as to books," "a condition worthier of Dahomey than of England."[40] He could bear his mournful testimony that he never, in his whole life, had for one month complete access to books—such access as he would have had in Germany, in France, or anywhere else in the civilised earth. Books were written, not for rich men, but for all men. Every human being had by the nature of the case a *right* to hear what other wise human beings had spoken to him. It was one of the rights of man, and a cruel injustice if denied.

The defect grew out of the condition of the English mind. England hitherto had supposed that the Bible had contained everything which it was indispensable for man to know; and Bibles were within the reach of the humblest. But England

JOHN FORSTER. One of Carlyle's closest friends, as well as one of Dickens's, with whom he is more usually associated. Carlyle chose Forster to be, with his own brother John, one of the two original executors of his will. On this photograph Carlyle wrote: "John Forster (man of letters, &c &c),—very like." (Courtesy of the Columbia University Libraries.)

was growing, growing it knew not into what, but visibly
needing further help. The meeting agreed unanimously that
a library should be established. Subscription lists were
opened and swiftly filled. Competent persons were chosen
to collect books; a house was purchased. The thing was done,
and done most admirably, yet Carlyle himself remained miserable as ever. "Alas," he wrote on July 3, "I get so dyspeptical, melancholic, half-mad in the London Summer, all
courage to do anything but hold my peace fades away; I
dwindle into the pusillanimity of the ninth part of a tailor;
feel as I had nothing I could do but 'die in my hole like a
poisoned rat.' "[41] It was true, indeed, that he had a special
reason for lamentation at that particular moment. He had
been summoned to serve as a special juryman at Westminster. He appealed to Buller to deliver him. Buller told
him there *was* a way of escape if he liked to use it—"he
could be registered as a Dissenting preacher."[42] He had to
go, and the worst of it was he had to go for nothing,
"neither of my cases coming on,"[43] and the futility was a
text for fresh indignation.

If destiny in the shape of officials afflicted with one hand,
it sometimes brought anodynes in the other. One evening,
when he came home from his walk, he found Tennyson sitting with Mrs. Carlyle in the garden, smoking comfortably.
He admired and almost loved Tennyson. He says:

> A fine large-featured, dim-eyed, bronze-coloured, shaggyheaded
> man is Alfred; dusty, smoky, free-and-easy: who swims, outwardly
> and inwardly, with great composure in an inarticulate element of
> tranquil chaos and tobacco-smoke; great now and then when he
> does emerge: a most restful, brotherly, solidhearted man.[44]

Such a visit was the best of medicine.

The summer number of the *Edinburgh Review* was announced. He had heard that he was to be "annihilated,"
and that Macaulay was to be the executioner—the real writer
was Herman Merivale—and it was under this false impression that he remarked on the article when he read it:
"Macaulay's Article is not so bad; on the whole rather
interesting to me, and flattering rather than otherwise."[45]

He was undeceived about the authorship of this article.
"I was glad to hear" this, he said; of Macaulay he had still
considerable hopes.[46] The *Quarterly* had also an article, the

writer being William Sewell, a High Church leader on his own account, and then a rising star in the Oxford world.[47] Merivale had been ponderous and politico-economic; Sewell was astonishing, as indeed the whole Oxford movement was, to Carlyle.

Reputation in America brought visitors to Cheyne Row from that country—a young, unnamed Boston lady, among others, whom he called a "diseased rosebud."[48] Happily America yielded something else than "sweet sensibility." It yielded handsome sums of money; and, before the summer was over, he had received from that quarter as much as £400. There was an honourable sense across the Atlantic that, although novelists etc. might be fair prey, Carlyle ought to be treated honestly. About money there was no more anxiety.

It was now August. The Lectures on Heroes were by this time nearly written out. He had taken no holiday; but, as the end was now in sight, he allowed himself a week's riding tour in Sussex on "Citoyenne." Herstmonceaux and Julius Hare's parsonage was the furthest point which he reached, returning without misadventure by Tunbridge and Sevenoaks. He rode better than his loose seat seemed to promise. Mrs. Carlyle described to us, some years after, in her husband's presence, his setting out on this expedition; she drew him in her finest style of mockery—his cloak, his knapsack, his broadbrimmed hat, his preparation of pipes, etc.—comparing him to Dr. Syntax.[49] He laughed as loud as any of us: it was impossible not to laugh; but it struck me, even then, that the wit, however brilliant, was rather untender.

On August 23, late in the afternoon, he had substantially finished his work, and he went out, as he always did on these occasions, to compose himself by a walk.

the tea was up before I would stir from the spot; it was towards sunset when I first got out into the air, with the feeling of a finished man. *Finished* . . . in more than one sense! Eviting crowds and highways, I went along Battersea Bridge, and thence by a wondrous path, across cow-fields, mud-ditches, river-embankments, over a waste expanse of what attempted to pass for country,—wondrous enough in the darkening dusk, especially as I had never been there before, and the very road was uncertain! I had left my watch and purse; I had a good stick in my hand. Boat-people sat drinking about the Red House; Steamers snorting about the river, each with a lantern at their nose; old women sat in strange old cottages, trim-

393

ming their evening fire; bewildered-looking mysterious coke furnaces (with a very bad smell) glowed, at one place, I knew not why;
Windmills stood silent; blackguards, whores and *Miscellanei*
sauntered; harmless all; Chelsea lights burnt many-hued bright,
over water, in the distance,—under the great sky of silver, under the
great still Twilight: so I wandered, full of thoughts, or of things that
I could not *think*.[50]

Ruskin himself, when working most deliberately, never drew
a more exquisite picture in words than this unstudied reflection of a passing experience. In such mood the lectures were
completed, and, as usual, Carlyle was entirely dissatisfied
with them.

The hope had clung to him of being still able to go to Scotland in the early autumn. John Carlyle was there at this time
—an additional attraction. His plan had been "to take shipping, to find again there was an everlasting fresh sea water,
rivers, mountains, simple peaceful men; that God's universe was not an accursed, dusty, deafening distraction of a
cockneydom." But the weather broke up early this season,
and he found that he must stay where he was.

When the winter set in, Carlyle was still at home, deep in
Commonwealth tracts and history. It was stiff work; he did
not find he could make "great progress in this new enterprise." "My interest in it threatens sometimes to decline and
die!" He found it "not tenth part such a subject as the
French Revolution; nor can the art of man ever make such a
Book out of it."[51]

chapter twenty

1841–1842

Geraldine Jewsbury. Scotland.
Friendship with John Sterling.
Deaths of Mrs. Welsh and Dr. Arnold.
Tour of Belgium. Ely Cathedral and
Oliver Cromwell

Mrs. Carlyle, writing at the end of 1840, says of the state of things in Cheyne Row: "Carlyle is reading voraciously great folios preparatory to writing a new book—for the rest he growls away much in the old style—but one gets to feel a certain indifference to his growling—if one did not, it would be the worse for one."[1]

One asks with wonder why he found existence (such as it had become to him) so intolerable; why he seemed to suffer so much more under the small ills of life than when he had to face real troubles in his first years in London. He was now successful far beyond his hopes. The fashionable world admired and flattered him. The cleverest men had recognised his genius, and accepted him as their equal or superior. He was listened to with respect by all; and, far more valuable to him, he was believed in by a fast-increasing circle as a dear and honoured teacher. His money anxieties were over. If his liver occasionally troubled him, livers trouble most of us as we advance in life, and his actual constitution was a great deal stronger than that of ordinary men. As to outward annoyances, the world is so made that there will be such things, but they do not destroy the peace of our lives. Foolish people intrude upon us. Official people force us to do many things which we do not want to do, from sitting on juries to payment of rates and taxes. We express our opinion on such nuisances perhaps with imprecatory emphasis, but we bear them and forget them. Why could not Carlyle, with fame and honour and troops of friends, and the gates of a great career flung open before him, and a great intellect and a conscience unharassed by a single act which he need regret, bear and forget too? Why, indeed! The only answer is that Carlyle was Carlyle; and a man to whom the figures he met in the streets looked suddenly like spectres, who felt like a spectre himself, and in the green flowery earth, with the sky bending over it, could see "Tartarus itself and the pale kingdoms of Dis,"[2] was not to be expected to think and act like any other human being.

Fraser came to terms about the same time for the lectures on "Hero Worship." They were set in type, and he liked them a great deal better when he read them in proof. "It is," he said, "a *gowsterous* [boisterous] determined speaking out of the truth about several things; the people will be no worse for it at present! The astonishment of many of them is likely to be considerable."[3]

The *Miscellanies, Sartor,* and the other books were selling well, and fresh editions were wanted. Young people in earnest about their souls had begun to write to him, thanking him for delivering them from Egypt, begging to be allowed to come to Cheyne Row and see the face and hear the voice of one who had done such great things for them. Amongst the rest came Miss Geraldine Jewsbury, a Manchester lady, afterwards famous as a novelist, and the closest friend of Carlyle's wife; then fresh to life, eager to use it nobly, and looking passionately for some one to guide her. Carlyle's first impressions were unusually favourable.

> Miss Jewsbury, our fair Pilgrimess, is coming again tomorrow; and then departs for the North. She is one of the most interesting young women I have seen for years. Clear delicate sense and courage looking out of her small sylph figure;—a most heroic-looking damsel.[4]

The next impression was less satisfactory, though the young lady was still found interesting.

> *Que deviendra-t-elle?* A notable young woman; victim of much that *she* did not make; seeking passionately for some "paradise to be gained by battle,"—fancying George Sand &c and all that "Literature of Desperation," can help her thitherward! In the world there are few sadder sicklier phenomena for me than that George Sand and the response she meets with.[5]

For Madame Sand and all her works, for all sentimental,

GERALDINE JEWSBURY. This mid-Victorian novelist, an admirer of Jane as well as of Carlyle, became an intimate of the Cheyne Row household in the early 1840s. Carlyle described her in 1841: "Clear delicate sense and courage looking out of her small sylph figure;—a most heroic-looking damsel." From her testimony— not always reliable—Froude in part shaped his interpretation of the Carlyles' domestic relationship. This photograph was taken in April 1855. (Courtesy of the Columbia University Libraries.)

indecent literature whatsoever, Carlyle's dislike amounted to loathing. He calls it somewhere "a *new* astonishing Phallus-Worship," "with Balzac, Sue and Company for Evangelists, and Madame Sand for Virgin."[6] Emerson, who admired this great French celebrity, complained to me once of Carlyle's want of charity about her. Emerson had been insisting to him on her high qualities, and could get for answer nothing except that she was a great—improper female. Geraldine Jewsbury's inclination that way had not recommended her, nor did her own early novels, *Zoe, The Half-Sisters*, etc., tend to restore her to favour. But she worked through all this. In a long and trying intimacy she won and kept the affectionate confidence of the Cheyne Row household, and on his wife's death Geraldine was the first of her friends to whom he turned for support.[7]

Meanwhile Whitelocke and Rushworth did not grow more digestible. The proofs of *Hero Worship* were finished. The want of rest in the past summer had upset Carlyle's internal system. Work he could not; and at Easter he was glad to accept an invitation from Milnes to accompany him to his father's house at Fryston, in Yorkshire. His letters give a graphic and attractive picture of the Fryston circle.

The James Marshalls dined one evening at Fryston, Mrs. James Marshall being the Miss Spring Rice who was mentioned above as an attendant at the lectures. They lived at Headingly, near Leeds, and pressed Carlyle to pay them a visit when he left Fryston. He said he was "a waiter on Providence," and could not say what he could do, but decided eventually to go. The Fryston visit lasted a fortnight. "Alas," he says, on closing his account of it, "we were at Church on Sunday; Roebuck (much tamer than before) was here again, with lawyers, with louts;—'this way leads not to peace!' Yet I actually slept last night (for the first time) without rising to smoke!"[8]

Life in great English country houses may be as well spent as life elsewhere by the owners of them who have occupations to attend to. For visitors, when large numbers are brought together, some practice is required if they are to enjoy the elaborate idleness. The habits of such places as Fryston and Headingly, to which he went afterwards, were as yet a new experience to Carlyle.

Two pleasant days were spent with the Marshalls, and then Carlyle pursued his way. He had nothing definite to do. He was taking holiday with set purpose, and being so far north he went on by Liverpool, and by steamer thence to Dumfriesshire. His mother had been slightly ailing, and he was glad to be with her till she recovered. But he was among his own people, no longer under restraint as among strangers, and he grew restless and "atrabilious." "The stillness of this region," he wrote when at Scotsbrig, "would be a kind of Heaven for me, could I get it enjoyed. But I have no home here; I am growing weary of the perfect idleness: like that 'everlasting Jew,' I must *weiter, weiter, weiter* [onward, onward, onward]!"⁹ Accordingly in May he was in Cheyne Row again, but in no very improved condition. "My sickness is more than of body; it is of mind too, and my own blame. I ought to know *what I am going to work at*: all lies there! . . . Despicable mortal! Know thy own mind; go then and *do* it —in silence."¹⁰ He could not do it; he could not work, he could not rest. There was no help for it; he had to do what in the past year he knew he must do, allow himself a season of complete rest and sea air. The weather grew hot, and London intolerable. He went back to Scotsbrig, and took a cottage at Newby close to Annan, on the Solway, for the summer. Mrs. Carlyle came down with a maid who was to act as cook for them. They were to take possession at the end of July.

He had made so little secret of his dislike of London, and his wish to leave it, that when he was so much absent this season a report went abroad that he had finally gone, and Sterling had written to him to inquire. He told his friend, in answer, that for the present he had merely taken a cottage for the summer; for the rest "I never had any thought, only vague rebellious impulses, blind longings and *vellietés.*" "I do not think," he said, "I shall leave London for a while yet! I might readily go farther and fare worse; indeed in no other corner of the Earth have I ever been able to get any kind of reasonable social existence at all; everywhere else I have been a kind of exceptional anomalous anonymous product of Nature,—provoked and provoking in a very foolish unprofitable way."¹¹

399

The Newby lodgings were arranged, and he and his wife were settled in them. Rest was the object, the most desireable and the least attainable. He was determined to have nothing to say to his fellow-creatures. There he was, in the very centre of his oldest acquaintances. Not a place or a name or a person but was familiar to him from his boyhood. At Annan he had been at school. At the same school he had been an usher.[12] Annan was Irving's home, and Irving's relations were all round him. Yet he visited no one, he recognised no one, he allowed no one to speak to him, and he wandered in the dusk like a restless spirit amidst the scenes of his early dreams and his early sufferings. The month at Newby over, he stayed another week at Scotsbrig with his mother, went for a few days to the Speddings in Cumberland, thence with his wife, before going back to London, to see Miss Martineau at Tynemouth. At last, in the end of September, he was at home again, the long holiday over, to which he had looked forward so eagerly.

> *Ought* I to write now of Oliver Cromwell? *Gott weiss;* I cannot yet see clearly: I have been scrawling somewhat during the last week; but entirely without effect. Go on, go on! Do I not see *so much* clearly? Why complain of wanting light? It is courage, energy, perseverance, that I want.
> How many things of mine have already passed into public action! I can see them, with small exultation; really almost with a kind of sorrow,—so *little* light, how enormous is the darkness that renders *it* noticeable![13]

This extract explains the difficulty Carlyle had in beginning *Cromwell.* He felt that he had something to say, something which he ought to say about the present time to the present age; something of infinite importance to it. England as he saw it was saturated with cant, dosed to surfeit with doctrines half true only or not true at all, doctrines religious, doctrines moral, doctrines political, till the once noble and at heart still noble English character was losing its truth, its simplicity, its energy, its integrity. Between England as it was and England as it might yet rouse itself to be, and as it once had been, there was to Carlyle visible an infinite difference. Jeffrey had told him that, though things were not as they should be, they were better than they had ever been before. This, in Carlyle's opinion, was one of those commonly received falsehoods which were working like poison in the blood. England could never have grown to be what it was if there had been no more sincerity in Englishmen, no more hold on fact and truth, than he perceived in his own contemporaries. The "progress" so loudly talked of was progress downwards, and rapid and easy because it was downwards. There was not a statesman who could do honestly what he thought to be right and keep his office; not a member of Parliament who could vote by his conscience and keep his seat; not a clergyman who could hope for promotion if he spoke what he really believed; hardly anyone of any kind in any occupation who could earn a living if he only tried to do his work as well as it could be done; and the result of it all was that the very souls of men were being poisoned with universal mendacity. *Chartism* had been a partial relief, but the very attention which it had met with was an invitation to say more, and he had an inward impulse which was forcing him on to say it. How? was the question. The *Westminster Review* had collapsed. He thought for a time that he might have some Review of his own where he could teach what he called "believing Radicalism," in opposition to Political Economy and Parliamentary Radicalism. Of this he could make nothing. He could not find men enough with sufficient stuff in them to work with him. Thus all this autumn he was hanging restless, unable to settle his mind on *Cromwell*; unable to decide in what other direction to turn.

An interesting incident, though it led to nothing, lightened the close of this year. In the old days at Comely Bank and Craigenputtoch, Carlyle had desired nothing so much as a professorship at one or other of the Scotch universities. The door had been shut in his face, sometimes contemptuously. He was now famous, and the young Edinburgh students, having looked into his lectures on Heroes, began to think that, whatever might be the opinions of the authorities and patrons, they for their part would consider lectures such as those a good exchange for what was provided for them. A "History chair" was about to be established. A party of them, represented by a Mr. Duniface, presented a requisition to the Faculty of Advocates to appoint Carlyle. The *Scotsman* backed them up, and Mr. Duniface wrote to him to ask if he would consent to be nominated. Seven years before, such an offer would have had a warm welcome from him. Now he was gratified to find himself so respected by the students. But then was then, and now was now [and he refused the offer].

Sterling was spending the winter of 1841–1842 at Falmouth. His chest was weak. He had tried the West Indies, he had tried Madeira, he had tried the south of France, with no permanent benefit. He was now trying whether the mild air of the south of Cornwall might not answer at least as well, and spare him another banishment abroad. It was here and at this time that I became myself acquainted with Sterling. I did not see him often, but in the occasional interviews which I had with him he said some things which I could never forget, and which affected all my subsequent life. Among the rest, he taught me to know what Carlyle was. I had read *The French Revolution,* had wondered at it like my contemporaries, but had not known what to make of it. Sterling made me understand that it was written by the greatest of living thinkers, if by the side of Carlyle any other person deserved to be called a thinker at all. He showed me, I remember, some of Carlyle's letters to him, which have curiously come back into my hands after more than forty years. Looking over these letters now, I find at the beginning of this year some interesting remarks about Emerson, with whom also Sterling had fallen into some kind of correspondence. Besides his own *Essays,* Emerson had sent over copies of the *Dial,* the organ then of intellectual Liberal New England. Carlyle had not liked the *Dial,* which he thought high-flown, often even absurd. Yet it had something about it, too, which struck him as uncommon.

But the chief substance of these letters is about Sterling's own work. He had just written *Strafford,* and had sent the manuscript to be read at Cheyne Row. Carlyle, when asked for his opinion, gave it faithfully. He never flattered. He said honestly and completely what he really thought. His verdict on Sterling's tragedy was not and could not be favourable. He could find no true image of Strafford there, or of Strafford's surroundings. He had been himself studying for two years the antecedents of the Civil War. He had first thought Montrose to have been the greatest man

402

on Charles's side. He had found that it was not Montrose, it was Wentworth; but Wentworth, as he conceived him, was not in Sterling's play. Even the form did not please him, though on this he confessed himself an inadequate judge.

But from his own work and from Sterling's and all concerns of his own he was called away at this moment by a blow which fell upon his wife, a blow so severe that it had but one alleviation. It showed her the intensity of the affection with which she was regarded by her husband. Her mother, Mrs. Welsh, had now resided alone for several years at her old home at Templand in Nithsdale, where the Carlyles had been married. Her father, Walter Welsh, and the two aunts had gone one after the other. Except for the occasional visits to Cheyne Row, Mrs. Welsh had lived on there by herself in easy circumstances, for she had the rent of Craigenputtoch as well as her own jointure,[14] and, to all natural expectation, with many years of life still before her. The mother and daughter were passionately attached, yet on the daughter's part perhaps the passion lay in an intense sense of duty; for their habits did not suit, and their characters were strongly contrasted. Mrs. Welsh was enthusiastic, sentimental, Byronic. Mrs. Carlyle was fiery and generous, but with a keen sarcastic understanding; Mrs. Welsh was accustomed to rule; Mrs. Carlyle declined to be ruled when her judgement was unconvinced; and thus, as will have been seen, in spite of their mutual affection, they were seldom much together without a collision. Carlyle's caution— "Hadere nicht mit deinem [sic] Mutter, Liebstes. Trage, trage! Es wird bald enden! [Do not quarrel with your mother, dearest. Be patient, be patient! It will soon be over!]"[15]—tells its own story. Mrs. Carlyle, as well as her husband, was not an easy person to live with. She had a terrible habit of speaking out the exact truth, cut as clear as with a graving tool, on occasions, too, when without harm it might have been left unspoken.

Mrs. Welsh had been as well as usual. There had been nothing in her condition to suggest alarm since the summer when the Carlyles had been in Annandale. On February 23 Mrs. Carlyle had written her a letter, little dreaming that it was to be the last which she was ever to write to her, describing in her usual keen style the state of things in Cheyne Row.

> I am continuing to mend. If I could only get a good sleep, I should be quite recovered; but, alas! we are gone to the devil again in the sleeping department. That dreadful woman next door, instead of putting away the cock which we so pathetically appealed against, has produced another. . . . they crow and screech not only from daylight, but from midnight, and so near that it goes through one's head every time like a sword. The night before last they woke me every quarter of an hour, but I slept some in the intervals; for they had not succeeded in rousing *him* above. But last night they had him up at three. He went to bed again, and got some sleep after, the "horrors" not recommencing their efforts till five; but I, listening every minute for a new screech that would send him down a second time and prepare such wretchedness for the day, could sleep no more. . . .
>
> This despicable nuisance is not at all unlikely to drive us out of the house after all, just when he had reconciled himself to stay in it. How one is vexed with little things in this life! The great evils one triumphs over bravely, but the little eat away one's heart.

An "evil" greater than she had yet known since her father was taken away hung over Mrs. Carlyle while she was writing this letter. Five days later there came news from Templand, like a bolt out of the blue sky, that Mrs. Welsh had been struck by apoplexy and was dangerously ill. Mrs. Carlyle, utterly unfit for travelling, "almost out of herself," flew to Euston Square and caught the first train to Liverpool. At Liverpool, at her uncle's house, she learnt that all was over, and that she would never see her mother more. She was carried to bed unconscious. When she recovered her senses she would have risen and gone on; but her uncle would not let her risk her own life, and to have proceeded in her existing condition would as likely as not have been fatal to her. Extreme, intense in everything, she could only think of her own shortcomings, of how her mother was gone now, and could never forgive her. The strongest natures suffer worst from remorse. Only a strong nature, perhaps, can know what remorse means. Mrs. Carlyle had surrendered her fortune to her mother, but the recollection of this could be no comfort; she would have hated herself if such a thought had occurred to her. Carlyle knew what she would be suffering. The fatal news had been sent on to him in London. He who could be driven into frenzy if a cock crew near him at midnight, had no sorrow to spare for himself in the presence of real calamity.

Mrs. Carlyle lay ill in Liverpool, unable to stir, and unpermitted to write. He himself felt that he must go, and he went without waiting to hear more. As it was, he was too late for the funeral, which had for some reason been hurried; but his brother James, with the instinct of good feeling, had gone of his own accord from Ecclefechan to represent him. Carlyle was sole executor, and there were business affairs requiring attention which might detain him several weeks. He was a few hours with his wife at Liverpool on his way, and then went on, taking his wife's cousin Helen with him to assist in the many arrangements which would require a woman's hand. Everything was, of course, left to Mrs. Carlyle, and her own property was returned to her. It was not large, from £200 to £300 a year;[16] but, with such habits as hers and her husband's, it was independence, and even wealth.

But this was the last recollection which occurred to Carlyle. He travelled down on the box of the mail in a half-dreamy state, seeing familiar faces at Annan and Dumfries, and along the road, but taking no heed of them. Templand, when he reached it, was a haunted place. There he had been married; there he had often spent his holidays when he could come down from Craigenputtoch; there he had conceived *Sartor*; there two years before his own mother and he had smoked their pipes together in the shrubbery. It was from Templand that he had rushed away desperate in the twilight of a summer morning and seen the herons fishing in the river pools.[17] A thousand memories hung about the place, which was now standing desolate. During the six weeks while he remained there he wrote daily to his wife, and every one of these letters contained something tenderly beautiful.

In the quiet at Templand, and among such solemn surroundings, London and its noisy vanities, its dinners and its hencoops, did not seem more beautiful to Carlyle. More than ever he prayed to be away from it. At that house it was evident that Mrs. Carlyle could not bear the thought of living. But there was Craigenputtoch not far off, towards which he had often been wistfully looking. Of this, too, hitherto she had refused to hear so much as a mention; but it was now her own, and her objection might be less.

Carlyle took his leave of Templand, and went to pass a few quiet days with his mother. At Scotsbrig ordinary subjects resumed their interest, and Carlyle began to think again, though not very heartily, of his own work. Tedious business still detained him in Dumfriesshire. He could not leave till he had disposed of the lease of Templand. The agents of the noble Duke could not, consistently with their master's dignity, be rapid in their resolutions.

He had small respect for dukes and such-like, and perhaps Templand would not have answered with him if he had kept it; but he had a curious pride also in his own family. There was reason to believe that his own father was the actual representative of the Lords Carlyle of Torthorwald; and, though he laughed when he spoke of it, he was clearly not displeased to know that he had noble blood in him. Rustic as he was in habits, dress, and complexion, he had a knightly, chivalrous temperament, and fine natural courtesy; another sure sign of good breeding was his hand, which was small, perfectly shaped, with long fine fingers and aristocratic finger-nails. He knew well enough, however, that with him, as he was, pedigrees and such-like had nothing to do. The descent which he prized was the descent from pious and worthy parents, and the fortunes and misfortunes of the neighbouring peasant families were of more real interest to him than aristocratic genealogies.

It was on Carlyle's return from Scotland that he paid the visit to Rugby of which Dean Stanley speaks in his life of Dr. Arnold.[18] Arnold, it will be remembered, had written to Carlyle after reading *The French Revolution*. He had sympathised warmly also with his tract on *Chartism*, and his views as to the mights or rights of English working men. Cromwell, who was to be the next subject, was equally interesting to Arnold; and hearing that Carlyle would be passing Rugby, he begged him to pause on the way, when they could examine Naseby field together.

Carlyle, on his side, had much personal respect for the great Arnold—for Arnold himself as a man, though very little for his opinions. He saw men of ability all round him professing orthodoxy and holding office in the Church, while they regarded it merely as an institution of general expediency, with which their private convictions had nothing to do. Such men aimed only at success in the world, and if they chose to sell their souls for it, the article which they parted with was of no particular value. But Arnold was of a higher stamp. While a Liberal in politics and philosophy, and an historical student, he imagined himself a real believer in the Christian religion, and Carlyle was well assured that to men of Arnold's principles it had no ground to stand on, and that the clear-sighted among them would, before long, have to choose between an honest abandonment of an untenable position and a trifling with their own understandings, which must soon degenerate into conscious insincerity. Arnold, Carlyle once said to me, was happy in being taken away before the alternative was forced upon him. He died, in fact, six weeks after the visit.

The season was not over when Carlyle was again at home after his long absence, but the sad occupations of the spring, and the sad thoughts which they had brought with them, disinclined him for society. The summer opened with heat. He had a room arranged for him at the top of his house at the back, looking over gardens and red roofs and trees, with the river and its barges on his right hand, and the Abbey in the distance. There he sate and smoked, and read books on Cromwell, the sight of Naseby having brought the subject back out of the "the abysses." Forster's volumes were not sent back to him. Visitors were not admitted, or were left to be entertained in the drawing-room.

Of friends the most actively anxious to be kind were Mr. and Mrs. Charles Buller, with whom Carlyle had been at Kinnaird. Their eldest son, Charles, who had been his pupil, was now in the front rank in the House of Commons. Reginald, the youngest, had a living at Troston, in Suffolk, with a roomy parsonage. His father and mother had arranged to spend July and August there, and they pressed Mrs. Carlyle to go with them for change of scene. Mrs. Carlyle gratefully consented. She liked Mrs. Buller, and the Bullers' ways suited her. It was settled that they were to go first, and she was to follow. Carlyle's own movements were left doubtful. He, after so long an interruption of his work, did not wish to move again immediately; but he was very grateful to Mrs.

407

Buller for her kindness to his wife, and when she asked him in return to go to the House of Commons to hear her son speak, he could not refuse. He had never been there before; I believe he never went again; but it was a thing to see once, and though the sight did not inspire him with reverence, he was amused.

This single glance into the legislative sanctuary satisfied Carlyle's curiosity. Once, in after years, on some invitation from a northern borough, he did for a few moments contemplate the possibility of himself belonging to it; but it was for a moment only, and then with no more than a purpose of telling Parliament his opinion of its merits. For it was his fixed conviction that in that place lay not the strength of England, but the weakness of England, and that in time it would become a question which of the two would strangle the life out of the other. Of the debating department in the managment of the affairs of this country he never spoke without contempt. In the administration of them there was still vigour inherited through the traditions of a great past, and kept alive in the spirit of the public service. The navy especially continued a reality. Having seen the House of Commons, he was next to have a sight of a Queen's ship on a small scale, and of naval discipline.

The thing came about in this way. He could not work in the hot weather, and doubtless lamented as loud as usual about it. Stephen Spring Rice, Commissioner of Customs, was going in an Admirality yacht to Ostend on public business. The days of steam were not yet. The yacht, a cutter of the largest size, was lying in Margate roads. Spring Rice and his younger brother were to join her by a Thames steamer on August 5, and the night before they invited Carlyle to go with them. Had there been time to consider, he would have answered "impossible." But the proposal came suddenly. Mrs. Carlyle, who was herself going to Troston, strongly urged its acceptance. The expedition was not to occupy more than four or five days. Carlyle was always well at sea. In short, he agreed, and the result was summed up in a narrative, written in his very best style, which he termed "The Shortest Tour on Record."[19] He was well, he was in good humour; he was flung suddenly among scenes and people entirely new. Of all men whom I have ever

408

known, he had the greatest power of taking in and remembering the minute particulars of what he saw and heard, and of then reproducing them in language. The tour, if one of the shortest, is also therefore one of the most vivid.

His wife was still at Cheyne Row when he came back. The day after—August 11—she went off on the promised visit to the Bullers at Troston, of which she gives an account so humorous in the *Letters and Memorials*.[20] Her husband stayed behind with a half purpose of following her at the end of the month, and occupied himself in writing down the story of his flight into the other world, the lightest and brightest of all tourist diaries. He gave five days to it, seeing few visitors in his wife's absence.

[On the last day of August] he followed his wife into Suffolk. Charles Buller, who was to have met him at Troston, had not arrived, and, to use the time profitably, he obtained "a horse of the completest Rosinante species," and set off for a ride through Oliver Cromwell's country. His first halt was at Ely. He arrived in the evening, and walked into the cathedral, which, though fresh from Bruges and Ghent, he called "one of the most impressive buildings I have ever in my life seen." It was empty apparently. No living thing was to be seen in the whole vast building but a solitary sparrow, when suddenly some invisible hand touched the organ, and the rolling sounds, soft, sweet, and solemn, went pealing through the solitary aisles. He was greatly affected. He had come to look at the spot where Oliver had called down out of his reading-desk a refractory High Church clergyman, and he had encountered a scene which seemed a rebuke to his fierceness. "I believe," he said,

this Ely Cathedral is one of the "finest," as they call it, in all England, and from me also few masses of architecture could win more admiration; but I recoil everywhere from treating these things as a *dilettantism* at all; the impressions they give me are too deep and sad to have anything to do with the shape of stones. Tonight, as the heaving bellows blew, and the yellow sunshine streamed in thro' those high windows, and my footfalls and the poor country lad's were the only sounds from below, I looked aloft, and my eyes filled with very tears to look at all this, and remember beside it (wedded to it now, and *reconciled* with it for me) Oliver Cromwell's, "Cease your fooling, and come out, sir!" In these two antagonisms lie what volumes of meaning![21]

409

OLIVER CROMWELL. Carlyle first saw this early copy of a painting by Sir Peter Lely in September 1842 in the hall of Sidney Sussex College, Cambridge. In 1868 he recalled it as "the first real *Oliver Cromwell* . . . real not fictitious & imaginary, as above nine-tenths of them are,—which was vouchsafed me. Nothing so excellent had I ever seen before." This was his favorite portrait of the man whom he considered England's greatest hero and whose reputation his edition with "elucidations" of the *Letters and Speeches* did much to rehabilitate. A number of other portraits of Cromwell hang in the Carlyle House today, including a replica of his death mask. (Courtesy of Sidney Sussex College, Cambridge.)

Cromwell had been Carlyle's first thought in this riding expedition, but other subjects, as I have said, were rising between him and the Commonwealth. At St. Ives he had seen and noted more than Cromwell's farm. He had seen St. Ives poorhouse, and the paupers sitting enchanted in the sun, willing to work, but with no work provided for them. In his Journal for the 25th of October he mentions that he has been reading Eadmer, and Jocelyn de Brakelonde's Chronicle, and been meditating on the old monks' life in St. Edmund's monastery. Round these, as an incipient motive, another book was shaping itself in his mind, and making *Cromwell* impossible till this should be done.

1842–1843

Past and Present. Tour of
Cromwell's Battlefields

No Cromwell will ever come out of me in this world. I dare not even
try Cromwell.[1]

Carlyle *was* to try Cromwell, and was to clothe the ghost
with body again, impossible as the operation seemed; but he
had to raise another ghost first—an old Catholic ghost—before he could practise on the Puritans.

Events move so fast in this century, one crowding another
out of sight, that most of us who were alive in 1842 have
forgotten how menacing public affairs were looking in the
autumn of that year. Trade was slack, owing, it was said, to
the corn-laws, and hundreds of thousands of operatives were
out of work. Bread was dear, owing certainly to the corn-
laws, and actual famine was in the northern towns; while
the noble lords and gentlemen were shooting their grouse as
usual. There was no insurrection, but the "hands," unwillingly idle, gathered in the streets in dumb protest. The poor-
houses overflowed, and could hold no more; local riots
brought out the yeomanry, landowners and farmers, to put
down the artisans, who were short of bread for their families, lest foreign competition should bring down rents and
farmers' profits. Town and country were ranked against
each other for the last time. Never any more was such a
scene to be witnessed in England.

In his Suffolk ride Carlyle had seen similar scenes of
misery. Indignation blazed up in him at the sight of England
with its enormous wealth and haggard poverty; the earth

would not endure it, he thought. The rage of famished millions, held in check only by the invisible restraints of habit and traditional order, would boil over at last. In England, as in France, if the favoured classes did not look better to their ways, revolution would and must come; and if it could create nothing, might at least shatter society to pieces. His *Chartism* had been read and wondered over, but his prophecies had been laughed at, and the symptoms had grown worse. The corn-laws, it is to be remembered, were still standing. If they had continued to stand, if the growl of the hungry people had not been heard and the meaning of it discerned, most of us think that revolution would have come, and that Carlyle's view of the matter was right.

Between him and all other work, dragging off his mind from it, lay this condition of England question. Even if the dread of revolution was a chimaera, the degradation of the once great English people, absorbed, all of them, in a rage for gold and pleasure, was itself sufficient to stir his fury. He believed that every man had a special duty to do in this world. If he had been asked what specially he conceived his own duty to be, he would have said that it was to force men to realise once more that the world was actually governed by a just God; that the old familiar story acknowledged everywhere in words on Sundays, and disregarded or denied openly on week-days, was, after all, true. His writings, every one of them, his essays, his lectures, his *History of the French Revolution*, his *Cromwell*, even his *Frederick*, were to the same purpose and on the same text—that truth must be spoken and justice must be done; on any other conditions no real commonwealth, no common welfare, is permitted or possible. Political economy maintained that the distribution of the profits of industry depended on natural laws, with which morality had nothing to do. Carlyle insisted that morality was everywhere, through the whole range of human action. As long as men were allowed to believe that their business in this world was each to struggle for as large a share as he could get of earthly good things, they were living in a delusion with hearts poisoned and intellect misled. Those who seemed to prosper under such methods, and piled up huge fortunes, would gather no good out of them. The multitude whose own toil produced what they were forbidden to share would sooner or later present their bill for payment, and demand a reckoning.

Men say that he was an idle croaker, and that events have proved it. All was really going well. The bubbles on the surface were only the signs of the depth and power of the stream. There has been no revolution, no anarchy; wealth has enormously increased; the working men are better off than ever they were, etc. etc.

In part, yes. But how much has been done meanwhile of what he recommended? and how much of that is due to the effect which he himself produced? The corn-laws have been repealed, and this alone he said at the time would give us a respite of thirty years to set our house in order. *Laissez-faire* has been broken in upon by factory acts, education acts, land acts, emigration schemes, schemes and acts on all sides of us, that patience and industry may be snatched from the "grinding" of "natural laws." The "dismal science" has been relegated to "Jupiter and Saturn";[2] and these efforts have served as lightning-conductors. If we are safe now, we should rather thank him who, more than any other man, forced open the eyes of our legislators.

Forty years ago people were saying with Jeffrey that it was true that there were many lies in the world, and much injustice, but then it had always been so. Our forefathers had been as ill off as we, and probably—nay, certainly—worse off. Carlyle had insisted that no nation could have grown at all, still less have grown to England's stature, unless truer theories of man's claims on man had once been believed and acted on. Whigs and Radicals assured him that the older methods, so far as they differed from ours, were less just and less wise; that, although the artisans and labourers might be ill off occasionally, they were freer, happier, better clothed, better lodged, more enlightened, than in any previous age, and they challenged him to point to a time in English history which could honestly be preferred to the present. Jocelyn's Chronicle coming accidentally across him, with its singularly vivid picture of English life in the twelfth century, gave him the impulse which he needed to answer them, and *Past and Present* was written off with singular ease in the first seven weeks of 1843.[3] His heart was in his subject. He got the book completed, strange to say, without preliminary labour-pangs, and without leaving in his correspondence, during the process of birth, a single cry of complaint. The style shows no trace of rapid composition, unless in the white-heat intensity of expression, nor is it savage and scornful anywhere, but rather (for Carlyle) candid and considerate. The arrangement is awkward—as awkward as that of *Sartor*—for indeed there is no arrangement at all; and yet, as a whole, the book made a more immediate mark than anything which Carlyle had hitherto written. Prophetic utterances seldom fall into harmonious form; they do not need it, and they will not bear it.

Past and Present appeared at the beginning of April 1843, and created at once admiration and a storm of anger. It was the first public protest against the "Sacred Science" which its chief professors have since discovered to be no science, yet which then was accepted, even by the very clergy, whose teaching it made ridiculous, as being irrefragable as Euclid. The idol is dead now, and may be laughed at with impunity. It was then in its shrine above the altar, and to doubt was to be damned—by all the newspapers. In *Chartism* Carlyle had said that the real aim of all modern revolutionary movements was to recover for the free working man the condition which he had lost when he ceased to be a serf. The present book was a fuller insistence upon the same truth. The world's chief glory was the having ended slavery, the having raised the toiler with his hands to the rank and dignity of a free man; and Carlyle had to say that, under the gospel of political economy and free contract, the toiler in question had lost the substance and been fooled with the shadow. Gurth, born thrall of Cedric the Saxon, had his share of the bacon. The serf was, at least, as well cared for by his master as a horse or a cow. Under free contract he remained the slave of nature, which would kill him if he could not feed himself; he was as much as ever forced to work under the whip of hunger; while he was an ownerless vagrant, to be employed at competitive wages, the lowest that would keep him alive, as long as employment was to be had, and to be turned adrift to pine in a workhouse when it was no longer any one's interest to employ him. A cow, a horse, a pig, even a canary bird, was worth a price in the market, was worth feeding and preserving. The free labourer, except at such times as there

415

happened to be a demand for him, was worth nothing. The rich, while this gospel was believed in, might grow richer; but the poor must remain poor always, without hope for themselves, without prospect for their children, more truly slaves, in spite of their freedom, and even in consequence of their freedom, in a country so densely peopled as England, than the Carolina nigger. The picture was set out with the irony of which Carlyle was so unrivalled a master, with the indignation of which irony is the *art*.

With the existing state of things the book begins; with the existing state of things, and the only possible remedies for it, the book ends; in the middle stands in contrast the ancient English life under the early Plantagenet kings, before freedom in the modern sense had begun to exist; and the picture of St. Edmund's Abbey and its monks, which is thus drawn, is without a rival in modern literature. As to the relative merits of that age and ours there will be different opinions. We know so well where the collar galls our own necks, that we think anyone better off whose shoulder does not suffer at that particular point. Nor did Carlyle insist on drawing comparisons, being content to describe real flesh-and-blood human beings as they were then, and as they are now, and to leave us to our own reflections.

On the whole, perhaps we shall agree with what Lockhart answered, when Carlyle sent his book to him. Lockhart said he could accept none of his friend's inferences, except one, "that we are all wrong and all like to be damned. . . . Thou hast done a book such as no other living man could do or dream of doing"; that it had made him conscious of life and feeling as he had never been before; and that, finally, he wished Carlyle would write something more about the middle ages, write some romance, if he liked. He had more power of putting life into the dry bones than anyone but Scott; and that, as nothing could be less like Scott's manner of doing it than Carlyle's, there could be no suspicion of imitation.[4]

But it is unnecessary for me to review or criticise further a work which has been read so universally, and as to which no two persons are likely entirely to think alike. I shall endeavour rather at this point to describe something of the effect which Carlyle was producing among his contemporaries. *Past and Present* completes the cycle of writings which were in his first style, and by which he most influenced the thought of his time. He was a Bedouin, as he said of himself, a rough child of the desert. His hand had been against every man, and every man's hand against him. He had offended men of all political parties, and every professor of a recognised form of religion. He had offended Tories by his Radicalism, and Radicals by his scorn of their formulas. He had offended High Churchmen by his Protestantism, and Low Churchmen by his evident unorthodoxy. No sect or following could claim him as belonging to them; if they did, some rough utterance would soon undeceive them. Yet all had acknowledged that here was a man of extraordinary intellectual gifts and of inflexible veracity. If his style was anomalous, it was brilliant. No such humourist had been known in England since Swift; and the humour, while as searching as the great Dean's, was infinitely more genial. Those who were most angry with Carlyle could not deny that much that he said was true. In spite of political economy, all had to admit there was such a thing as justice; that it was the duty of men to abstain from lying a great deal more than they did. "A new thinker," in Emerson's phrase, "had been let loose upon the planet";[5] the representatives of the Religiones Licitae, the conventional varieties of permitted practice and speculation, found themselves encountered by a novel element which would assimilate with none of them, which disturbed all their digestions, yet which they equally could not ignore.

This on the surface. But there were circumstances in the time which made Carlyle's mode of thought exceptionally interesting, to young men especially whose convictions were unformed and whose line of life was yet undetermined for them. It was an era of new ideas, of swift if silent spiritual revolution. Reform in Parliament was the symbol of a general hope for the introduction of a new and better order of things. The Church had broken away from her old anchorage. The squire parsons, with their sleepy services, were to serve no longer. Among the middle classes there was the Evangelical revival. The Catholic revival at Oxford had convulsed the University, and had set half the educated men and women in England speculating on the authority of the priesthood, and the essential meaning of Christianity. All were agreed to have done with compromise and conventionalities. Again the critical and inquiring spirit which had been checked by the French Revolution had awakened from the sleep of half a century. Physical science, now that it was creating railroads, bridging the Atlantic with steamships, and giving proof of capacity which could no longer be sneered at, was forming a philosophy of the earth and its inhabitants, agitating and inconvenient to orthodoxy, yet difficult to deal with. Benthamism was taking possession of dominions which religion had claimed hitherto as its own, was interpreting morality in a way of its own, and directing political action. Modern history, modern languages and literature, with which Englishmen hitherto had been contented to have the slightest acquaintance, were pushing their way into school and college and private families, forcing us into contact with opinions as to the most serious subjects entirely different from our own. We were told to inquire; but to inquire like Descartes with a preconceived resolution that the orthodox conclusion must come out true— an excellent rule for those who can follow it, which all unhappily cannot do. To those who inquired with open minds it appeared that things which good and learned men were doubting about must be themselves doubtful. Thus all round us, the intellectual lightships had broken from their moorings, and it was then a new and trying experience. The present generation which has grown up in an open spiritual ocean, which has got used to it and has learned to swim for itself, will never know what it was to find the lights all drifting, the compasses all awry, and nothing left to steer by except the stars.

In this condition the best and bravest of my own contemporaries determined to have done with insincerity, to find ground under their feet, to let the uncertain remain uncertain, but to learn how much and what we could honestly regard as true, and believe that and live by it. Tennyson became the voice of this feeling in poetry; Carlyle in what was called prose, though prose it was not, but something by itself, with a form and melody of its own. Tennyson's poems, the group of poems which closed with *In Memoriam*, became to many of us what *The Christian Year* was to orthodox

418

Churchmen. We read them, and they became part of our minds, the expression in exquisite language of the feelings which were working in ourselves. Carlyle stood beside him as a prophet and teacher; and to the young, the generous, to everyone who took life seriously, who wished to make an honourable use of it, and could not be content with sitting down and making money, his words were like the morning reveille. The middle-aged and experienced who have outgrown their enthusiasm, who have learnt what a real power money is, and how inconvenient the absence of it, may forego a higher creed; may believe without much difficulty that utilitarianism is the only basis of morals; that mind is a product of organised matter; that our wisest course is to make ourselves comfortable in this world, whatever may become of the next. Others of nobler nature who would care little for their comforts may come at last, after long reflection on this world, to the sad conclusion that nothing can be known about it; that the external powers, whatever they may be, are indifferent to human action or human welfare.

For *there is* no remembrance of the wise more than of the fool. . . . And how dieth the wise *man?* as the fool.[6]

To such an opinion some men, and those not the worst, may be driven after weary observation of life. But the young will never believe it; or, if they do, they have been young only in name. Young men have a conscience, in which they recognise the voice of God in their hearts. They have hope. They have love and admiration for generous and noble actions, which tell them that there is more in this world than material things which they can see and handle. They have an intellect, and they cannot conceive that it was given to them by a force which had none of its own. Amidst the controversies, the arguments, the doubts, the crowding uncertainties of forty years ago, Carlyle's voice was to the young generation of Englishmen like the sound of "ten thousand trumpets" in their ears, as the Knight of Grange said of John Knox.[7] They had been taught to believe in a living God. Alas! it had seemed as if the life might be other moods and tenses, but not in the present indicative. They heard of what He had done in the past, of what He would do in the future, of what it was wished that He might do, of what we were to pray to Him that He would do. Carlyle was the first to make us see

419

His actual and active presence *now* in this working world, not in rhetoric and fine sentiments, not in problematic miracles at Lourdes or La Salette, but in clear letters of fire which all might read, written over the entire surface of human experience. To him God's existence was not an arguable probability, a fact dependent for its certainty on Church authority, or on Apostolic succession, or on so-called histories which might possibly prove to be no more than legends; but an awful reality to which the fates of nations, the fate of each individual man, bore perpetual witness. Here and only here lay the sanction and the meaning of the word duty. We were to do our work, not because it would prove expedient and we should be rewarded for doing it, but because we were bound to do it by our Master's orders. We were to be just and true, because God abhorred wrong and hated lies, and because an account of our deeds and words was literally demanded and exacted from us. And the lesson came from one who seemed "to speak with authority and not as the Scribes,"[8] as if what he said was absolute certainty beyond question or cavil.

Religious teachers, indeed, had said the same thing, but they had so stifled the practical bearing of their creed under their doctrines and traditions, that honest men had found a difficulty in listening to them. In Carlyle's writings dogma and tradition had melted like a mist, and the awful central fact burnt clear once more in the midst of heaven. Nor could anyone doubt Carlyle's power, or Carlyle's sincerity. He was no founder of a sect bent on glorifying his own personality. He was no spiritual janissary maintaining a cause which he was paid to defend. He was simply a man of high original genius and boundless acquirements, speaking out with his whole heart the convictions at which he had himself arrived in the disinterested search after truth. If we asked who he was, we heard that his character was like his teaching; that he was a peasant's son, brought up in poverty, and was now leading a pure, simple life in a small house in London, seeking no promotion for himself, and content with the wages of an artisan.

I am speaking chiefly of the effect of Carlyle in the circles in which I was myself moving. To others he was recommended by his bold attitude on the traditionary formulas, the defenders of which, though they could no longer use stake or gibbet, yet could still ruin their antagonists' fortunes and command them to submit or starve. Mere negations, whether of Voltaire or Hume or David Strauss, or whoever it might be, he valued little. To him it was a small thing comparatively to know that this or that theory of things was false. The important matter was not to know what was untrue, but what was true. He never put lance in rest simply for unorthodoxy. False as the priestly mummeries at Bruges might be, he could not wish them away to make room for materialism which was falser than they. Yet he had not concealed that he had small faith in bishops, small faith in verbal inspirations or articles of religion, small concern for the baptismal or other controversies then convulsing the Church of England; and such side cuts and slashes were welcome to the Theological Liberals, who found him so far on their side.

The Radicals, again, might resent his want of reverence for liberty, for political economy, and such like; but he could denounce corn-laws and game-preserving aristocrats with a scorn which the most eloquent of them might envy. In the practical objects at which he was aiming, he was more Radical than they were. They feared him, but they found him useful.

There were others again who were attracted by the quality which Jeffrey so much deprecated. That he was so "dreadfully in earnest," that he could not sit down quietly and enjoy himself "without a theory of the universe in which he could believe," was not an offense, but a recommendation. Some people cannot help being in earnest, cannot help requiring a real belief, if life is not to become intolerable to them. Add to this the novelty of Carlyle's mode of speech, his singularly original humour and imagery; add also the impressiveness of his personal presence, as reported by those who had been privileged to see him, and we have an explanation of the universal curiosity which began to be felt about the Prophet of Cheyne Row, and the fascination which he exercised over a certain class of minds in the days of the Melbourne Ministry and the agitation over the *Tracts for the Times*.

I, for one (if I may so far speak of myself), was saved by Carlyle's writings from Positivism, or Romanism, or Atheism, or any other of the creeds or no creeds which in those

421

ERASMUS DARWIN. Darwin was frequently in the Carlyles' company in the 1840s and 1850s. Carlyle described him in his *Reminiscences* as "one of the sincerest, naturally truest, and most modest of men. Elder brother of Charles Darwin . . . to whom I rather prefer him for intellect, had not his health quite doomed him to silence and patient idleness." This photograph is dated 8 June 1856. (Courtesy of the Columbia University Libraries.)

years were whirling us about in Oxford like leaves in an autumn storm.[9] The controversies of the place had unsettled the faith which we had inherited. The alternatives were being thrust upon us of believing nothing, or believing everything which superstition, disguised as Church authority, had been pleased to impose; or, as a third course, and a worse one, of acquiescing, for worldly convenience, in the established order of things, which had been made intellectually incredible. Carlyle taught me a creed which I could then accept as really true; which I have held ever since, with increasing confidence, as the interpretation of my existence and the guide of my conduct, so far as I have been able to act up to it. Then and always I looked, and have looked, to him as my master. In a long personal intimacy of over thirty years, I learnt to reverence the man as profoundly as I honoured the teacher. But of this I need say no more, and can now go on with the story.

John Carlyle was in Cheyne Row when *Past and Present* came out, and was a stay and comfort to his brother in the lassitude which always followed the publication of a book. He had left the Duke of Buccleuch. Lady Clare had wished him to go back with her to Italy, but for this he had no inclination. An opening had presented itself in London. Lord Jeffrey had recommended him to Lady Holland as physician in attendance, and that distinguished lady had been favourably inclined; but Carlyle, when John consulted him, considered "that she was a wretched, unreasonable, tyrannous old creature,"[10] of whom it would be wise for John to steer clear. As a guest at Chelsea he was welcome always, both to his brother and his sister-in-law: good humoured, genial, always a sunny presence in a house where sunshine was needed.[11] The book sold fast.

Cromwell, however, was still not immediately executable. Tired as he was with the efforts of the winter, he was less than ever able to face the London season, especially as increasing popularity increased people's eagerness to see him. An admirer—a Mr. [Charles] Redwood, a solicitor— living at Llandough, a few miles from Cardiff, had long humbly desired that Carlyle would pay him a visit. An invitation coming at the same time from Bishop Thirlwall, at St.

David's, which could be fitted in with the other, he decided to lay his work by for the present, and make acquaintance with new friends and a new part of the country. Mr. Redwood, who had no literary pretensions, engaged that he should not be made a show of, promised perfect quiet, sea-bathing, a horse if he wished to ride, and the absence of all society, except of himself and his old mother. These temptations were sufficient. On July 3 he left London by train from Paddington to Bristol. A day or two were to be given to acquaintances at Clifton, and thence he was to proceed by a Cardiff steamer. All was strange to him. He had never before been in the South or West of England; and his impressions, coming fresh, formed themselves into pictures, which he threw down in his letters to his wife. The house in Cheyne Row was cleaned and painted during his absence, his wife superintending. On such occasions he was himself better out of the way.

Almost a fortnight was given to Llandough. His friends were all kindness and attention, and their efforts were grate-fully appreciated; but the truth must be told—Carlyle required more than simple, quiet people had to give him. He was bored. He reproached himself, but he could not help it. Mr. Redwood was engaged all day in his office at Cow-bridge. His guest was left mainly to himself—to ride about the neighbourhood, to bathe, to lie under the trees on the lawn and smoke, precisely what he had fancied that he had desired. "The whole country is of a totally *somnolent* nature, not ill fitted for a man that has come out to see if he can find any sleep!"[12] He amused himself tolerably with his wife's letters and with Tieck's *Vittoria Accorombona*, which she had provided him with, and begged him to read. He could not approve, however, of this singular book: "a dreadful piece of work on Tieck's part!"[13] he called it. But occasionally his poor host, to show his respect, absented himself from his own work to do the honours of the country, and Carlyle required all his self-command not to be uncivil.

Occasional spurts of complaint over dulness lie scattered in these Llandough letters; but Carlyle knew good people when he saw them. The Redwoods had left him to himself with unobtrusive kindliness. They had not shown him off to their acquaintances. They had thought only what they could do for the comfort of an honoured guest— a mode of treatment very different from what he had sometimes experienced. "They are a terrible set of fellows," he said, "those open-mouthed wondering gawpies, who lodge you for the sake of looking at you: that is horrible." It was not, however, with alarm on this score that he entered on his next visiting adventure. He would have preferred certainly that such a man as Thirlwall should not have stooped to be made a bishop of, but he claimed no right to judge a man who was evidently of superior quality. How far he actually knew Thirlwall's opinions about religion I cannot say. At all events, he thought he knew them. Thirlwall had sought Carlyle's acquaintance, and had voluntarily conversed with him on serious subjects. Carlyle was looking forward now with curiosity to see how a man who, as he believed, thought much as he did himself, was wearing his anomalous dignities.

> I was warmly welcomed; tho' my Bishop did seem a little uneasy too, but how could he help it! I got with much pomp an extremely bad and late dish of tea; then plenty of good talk till midnight, and a room at the farther wing of the house, still as the heart of wildernesses, where after some smoking &c, I did at last sink into sleep. . . . My Bishop, I can discern, is a right solid honest hearted man, full of knowledge and sense; excessively *delicate* withal, and in spite of his positive temper almost *timid*; no wonder he is a little embarrassed with me, till he feel gradually that I have not come here to eat him, or make scenes in his still house![14]

> With the Bishop himself I, keeping a strict guard on my mode of utterance, not mode of thinking, get on extremely well; find him . . . very strangely *swathed*; on the whole right good company; and so we fare along, in all manner of discourse, and even laugh a good deal together. Could I but sleep!—but, then, I never can![15]

The expression "strangely *swathed*" implies that he had found the Bishop not entirely sympathetic; and perhaps he had not remembered sufficiently how beliefs linger honestly in the ablest mind, though the mode of thought be fatally at variance with them.

However this may have been, the visit was over, and Carlyle went his way. His plan was to go first to Gloucester and Worcester to look at the battle-fields; afterwards to go to Scotland, through Liverpool, to see his mother; then to make a tour with his brother John in North Wales; and finally, before returning to London, to examine the ground of Oliver's great fight at Dunbar. The railway train carried him past the hills where "the Gloucester Puritans saw Essex's signal fires and notice that help was nigh." The scene of the last battle of the Civil War was to have a closer inspection. "Wor'ster," he writes, "was three miles off the Station, westward. . . . From Severn Bridge I could see the *ground* of Oliver's battle; it was a most brief survey: a poor labourer whom I consulted 'had *heerd* of sitch a thing,' wished to God 'we had another Oliver, sir; times is dreadful bad!' "[16]

At Liverpool Carlyle was warmly welcomed by his wife's uncle, in Maryland Street. He found his brother John waiting for him there. They arranged to wait where they were for a day or two, and then to make their expedition into North Wales together before the days began to shorten.

The North Wales tour was brief. The brothers went in a steamer from Liverpool to Bangor, and thence to Llanberis, again in a "tub-gig," or Welsh car. They travelled light, for Carlyle took no baggage with him except a razor, a shaving-brush, a shirt, and a pocket-comb; "tooth-brush" not mentioned, but we may hope forgotten in the inventory.[17] They slept at Llanberis, and the next day went up Snowdon. The summit was thick in mist. They met two other parties there coming up from the other side of the mountain "like ghosts of parties escorted by their Charons." They descended to Beddgelert, and thence drove down to Tremadoc, where they were entertained by a London friend, one of the Chorleys, who had a house at that place. Carlyle began to feel already that he had had enough of it, to tire of his "tumblings" and to find that he did not "at bottom care two-pence for all the picturesqueness in the world."[18] One night sufficed for Tremadoc. They returned thence straight to Liverpool, and were again in Maryland Street on August 1.

Mrs. Carlyle had been suffering from heat and her exertions in house repairs, and her husband thought it possible that he might take a seaside lodging at Formby, at the mouth of the Mersey, where they could remain together for the rest of the summer. Formby had the advantage of being near Seaforth, where the Paulets lived, with whom Mrs. Carlyle had already become intimate. Mr. Paulet was a merchant, a sensible, well-informed, good kind of man. Mrs. Paulet, young, gifted, and beautiful, was one of Carlyle's most enthusiastic admirers. The neighbourhood of such friends as these was an attraction; but the place when examined into was found desolate and shelterless. The experiment of lodgings at Newby had not been successful, so Mrs. Carlyle was left to take care of herself, which she was well able to do, and her husband made off for Scotland by his usual sea route to Annan. Misadventures continued to persecute him on his travels, or rather travelling itself was one persistent misadventure, for he could never allow for the necessities of things. The steamer, to begin with, left Liverpool at three in the morning. When he went on board "it was . . . *Chaos*; cloudy, dim, bewildered . . . altogether like a nasty damp, clammy Dream of Confusion, dirt, impediment and general nightmare."[19] In the morning there was some amendment. [After a journey of several days] he lay still for a month at Scotsbrig doing nothing save a little miscellaneous reading, and hiding himself from human sight.

Carlyle's time in the North was running out; he had still to see Dunbar battle-field, and he had arranged his movements that he should see it on Oliver's own 3rd of September, the day of the Dunbar fight, the day of the Worcester fight, and the day of his death. One or two small duties remained to be discharged first in Dumfriesshire. His wife had asked him to go once more to Thornhill and Templand to see after her mother's old servants, and to visit also the grave in Crawford Churchyard. To Crawford he was willing to go; from Templand he shrank as too painful. In leaving it, he thought that he had bid adieu to the old scenes for ever. Still this and anything he was ready to undertake if it would give her any pleasure. Most tender, most affectionate, were the terms in which he gave his promise to go. He did go. He distributed presents among the old people, who in Mrs. Welsh had lost their best friend. Finally, he went also to the churchyard.

> The day was windless, the earth all still. Grey mist rested on the tops of the green hills, the vacant brown moors; *silence* as of Eternity rested over the world. It was like a journey thro' the Kingdoms of the Dead; one Hall of Spirits till I got past Crawford. . . . I was as a spirit, in the land of spirits, called land of the living.

427

> At Crawford, Dearest,—I was on a *sacred* spot; one of the two
> *sacredest* in all the world: I was at Her Grave! . . . I mean to go
> and see your brave Father's Grave too; and I will speak no word
> about it; you shall hold it for done without my speaking.[20]

This was written from Edinburgh on September 2. The
3rd was to be given to Dunbar, and along with Dunbar was
to be combined the pilgrimage to that last solemn spot to
which he referred with so fine delicacy. Without staying to
see any Edinburgh acquaintance except David Laing, he
went on direct to Haddington, where he was to be the guest
of his wife's old and dear friends, the Miss Donaldsons of
Sunny Bank. The thoughts which he had brought from
Crawford attended him still as he came among the scenes of
Mrs. Carlyle's childhood, where he and she had first looked
in each other's faces.

> These two days the image of my dear little Jeannie has hovered
> incessantly about me, waking and sleeping; in a sad, yet almost
> celestial manner; like the spirit, I might say, of a beautiful Dream.
> These were the streets and places where she ran about, a merry
> eager little fairy of a child;—and it is all gone away from her now,
> and she from it; and of all her possessions poor I am, as it were,
> all that remain to her! My Dearest, while I live, one soul to trust in
> shall not be wanting. My poor little Jeannie, how solemn is is
> [*sic*] this *Hall of the Past*; beautiful and mournful; the miraculous
> River of Existence rolling its grand course here, as elsewhere in
> the most prophetic places; now ever as of old: godlike tho' dark
> with death.[21]

Carlyle feeling and writing with such exquisite tenderness,
and Carlyle a fortnight later when he was in Cheyne Row
making a domestic earthquake and driving his wife distracted because a piano sounded too loud in the adjoining
house, are beings so different, that it seemed as if his soul
was divided, like the Dioscuri, as if one part of it was in
heaven, and the other in the place opposite to heaven.[22]
But the misery had its origin in the same sensitiveness of
nature which was so tremulously alive to soft and delicate
emotion. Men of genius have acuter feelings than common
men; they are like the wind-harp, which answers to the
breath that touches it, now low and sweet, now rising into
wild swell or angry scream, as the strings are swept by some
passing gust.

The rest of this letter describes the expedition to Dunbar,
and is written at a more ordinary pitch.

At Dunbar I found the battleground much more recognisable than any I had yet seen; indeed altogether what one would call clear: it is at the foot, and farther eastward along the slope, of the Hill they call the *Doun* that the Scots stood, Cromwell at Broxmouth (Duke of Roxburgh's place) and "saw the sun rise over the sea," and quoted a certain Psalm. I had the conviction that I stood on the very ground.— Having time to spare (for dinner was at six) I surveyed the old castle, washed my feet in the sea (smoking the while), took an image of Dunbar with me as I could; and then set my face to the wind and the *stour* [dust-storm] which had by this time risen to a quite tempestuous pitch.[23]

Duties all finished, there remained now to get back to Chelsea. The cheapest, and to Carlyle the pleasantest, way was by sea. A day could be given to Edinburgh, two to the Ferguses at Kirkcaldy. Thence he could go to Mr. Erskine and stay at Linlathen till the 15th, when a steamer would sail from Dundee. After the sight of the battle-fields, the "Cromwell" enterprise seemed no longer impossible. He was longing to be at home and at work; "at home with Goody and her new house and her old heart." The boat would be forty-five hours on the way. He would be at Chelsea by the 19th, and "his long pilgrimage be ended." He had seen many things in the course of it, but "nothing half as good as his own Goody." In the most amiable mood he called on everyone that he knew in Edinburgh—called on his wife's aunts at Morningside, called on Jeffrey at Craigcrook, to whom he was always grateful as his first active friend. "I found the old phenomena somewhat in a deteriorated state. The little Duke had lamed his *shin*; sits lean, disconsolate, irritable, talkative and argumentative as ever, with his foot laid on a stool: poor old fellow, I talked with him, him chiefly, till two o'clock, and then they drove me off homewards in their carriage."[24]

The days with Erskine in his quiet house at Linlathen were an enjoyment and amusement. Erskine officiating as a country gentleman, as chief commander of a squire's mansion, was a novel spectacle, the most gentle of men and yet obliged to put on the air of authority, and "doing it dreadfully ill." But Carlyle's thoughts were riveted on home. He had been irritable and troublesome before he went away in the summer. He was returning with the sense that in Cheyne Row only was paradise, where he would never be impatient again.

chapter twenty-two

1843–1846

Cromwell. Death of Sterling.
Publication of *Oliver Cromwell's
Letters and Speeches.*
Friendship with the Ashburtons

Alas for the infirmity of mortal resolution! Between the
fool and the man of genius there is at least this symptom of
their common humanity. Carlyle came home with the fixed
determination to be amiable and good and make his wife
happy. No one who reads his letters to her can doubt of his
perfect confidence in her, or of his childlike affection for
her. She was the one person in the world besides his mother
whose character he completely admired, whose judgement
he completely respected, whose happiness he was most
anxious to secure; but he came home to drive her immediately distracted, not by unkindness—for unkind he could
not be—but through inability to endure with ordinary
patience the smallest inconveniences of life. These were
times when Carlyle was like a child, and like a very naughty
one.

During the three months of his absence the house in Cheyne
Row had undergone a "thorough repair." This process,
which the dirt of London makes necessary every four or
five years, is usually undergone in the absence of the
owners. Mrs. Carlyle, feeble and out of health as she was,
had remained, to spare her husband expense, through the
paint and noise, directing everything herself, and restoring
everything to order and cleanliness at a minimum of cost.
The walls had been painted or papered, the floors washed,
the beds taken to pieces and remade, the injured furniture
mended. With her own hands she had newly covered chairs

and sofas, and stitched carpets and curtains; while for Carlyle himself she had arranged a library exactly in the form which he had declared before that it was essential to his peace that his own working-room should have. For three days he was satisfied, and acknowledged "a certain admiration." Unfortunately when at heart he was really most gratified, his acknowledgments were limited; he was shy of showing feeling, and even those who knew him best and understood his ways were often hurt by his apparent indifference. He had admitted that the house had been altered for the better, but on the fourth morning the young lady next door began upon her fatal piano, and then the tempest burst out which Mrs. Carlyle describes with such pathetic humour.[1] First he insisted that he would have a room made for himself on the roof where no sound could enter. When shown how much this would cost, he chose to have his rooms altered below—partitions made or taken down—new fireplaces introduced. Again the house was filled with dust and workmen; saws grating and hammers clattering, and poor Carlyle in the midst of it, "at sight of the uproar he had raised, was all but wringing his hands and tearing his hair."[2] And after all it was not the piano, or very little the piano. It is in ourselves that we are this or that, and the young lady might have played her fingers off, and he would never have heard her, had his work once been set going, and he absorbed in it. But go it would not, except fitfully and unsatisfactorily; his materials were all accumulated; he had seen all that he needed to see, yet his task still seemed impossible. The tumult in the house was appeased: another writing-room was arranged; the unfortunate young lady was brought to silence. *Past and Present* was done and out of the way. The dinner-hour was changed to the middle of the day to improve the biliary condition.[3] No result came. He walked about the streets to distract himself.

So Carlyle had been when he began *The French Revolution*. So it was, is, and must be with every serious man when he is first starting upon any great literary work. "Sport of every wind" he seems to himself, for every trifle, piano or what not, distracts him. Sterling was in London, then on the edge of his last fatal illness. In the Journal of October 23 Carlyle enters:

> Methinks I am a hieroglyphic bat
> Skim o'er the zenith in a slipshod hat;
> And to shed infant's blood, with horrid strides
> A damn'd potato on a whirlwind rides!

> Fabulously attributed to Nat Lee in Bedlam; composed, I imagine, by John Sterling, who gave it me yesterday.

After this he seemed to make progress. "Have been making an endeavour one other time to begin writing on Cromwell. Dare not say I have yet begun. All beginning is difficult!"[4] Many pages were covered, with writing of a sort. Mrs. Carlyle, on November 28, describes him as "over head and ears in Cromwell," and "lost to humanity for the time being."[5] That he could believe himself started gave some peace to her; but he was trying to make a consecutive history of the Commonwealth, and, as he told me afterwards, "he could not get the subject rightly taken hold of." There was no seed fitly planted and organically growing; and the further he went, the less satisfied he was with himself. He used to say that he had no genius for literature. Yet no one understood better what true literary work really was, or was less contented to do it indifferently.

One of his difficulties lay in his extreme conscientiousness. No sentence would be ever deliberately set down on paper without his assuring himself, if it related to a fact, that he had exhausted every means of ascertaining that the fact was true as he proposed to tell it; or, if it was to contain a sentiment or opinion, without weighing it to see if it was pure metal and not cant or insincere profession. This, however, lay in his nature, and, though it might give him trouble, would give him no anxiety. But his misgiving was that he was creating no living organic work, but a dead manufactured one, and this was intolerable. He flung aside at last all that he had done, burnt part of it, as he said, locked away the rest, and began again, as he told his mother, "on another side."[6] He gave up the notion of writing a regular history. He would make the person of Oliver Cromwell the centre of his composition, collect and edit, with introductions and connecting fragments of narrative, the extant letters and

speeches of Oliver himself—this, at least, as a first operation—a plain and comparatively easy one. When it was
finished, he told me that he found to his surprise that he had
finished all which he had to say upon the subject, and might
so leave it.

The dissatisfaction of Carlyle with his own work, as long
as he was engaged upon it, is a continuous feature in his
character. "The French Revolution was worth nothing."
"To have done with it" was the chief desire which he had. "To
have done with it" was his chief desire again now. "To have
done with it" was the yet more passionate cry in the prolonged agony of *Frederick.* The art of composition was merely
painful to him, so conscious was he always of the distance
between the fact as he could represent it and the fact as it
actually was. He could be proud when he measured himself
against other men; but his estimate of his merit, considered
abstractedly, was utterly low. His faults disgusted him; his
excellences he could not recognise; and when the work was
done and printed, he was surprised to find it so much better
than he had thought.

It is always so. The better a man is morally, the less conscious he is of his virtues. The greater the artist, the more
aware he must be of his shortcomings. If excellence is to be
its own only reward, poor excellence is in a bad way; for the
more there is of it, the less aware of itself it is allowed to be.
There is and must be, however, a certain comfort in the sense
that a man is doing a right thing, if not well, yet as well as
he can.

There was to be no Scotland for Carlyle this year. The
starting with *Cromwell* had been so hard that he did not
mean to pause over it till it was done; and an occasional rest
of a day or two at the houses of friends near London was all
that he intended to allow himself. It was his wife's turn to
have a holiday. She had not been in the North since she had
lost her mother. All the last summer had been spent with the
workmen in Cheyne Row. In autumn and winter she had
been ill as usual with coughs, sleeplessness, and nervous
headaches. As long as the cold weather lasted she had not been
well for a single day, and only her indomitable spirit seemed
to keep her alive at all. She never complained—perhaps for-
tunately—as with Carlyle to suffer in any way was to com-

plain loudly and immediately, and when complaint was absent he never realised that there could be occasion for it. Anyway she was now to have a holiday. She was to go first to her uncle at Liverpool, then to the Paulets at Seaforth, then to stay with Geraldine Jewsbury at Manchester; then, if she wished, to go to Scotland. She was always economical, and travelled at smallest cost. Money matters no longer, happily, required such narrow attention as in former years. Her letters (or parts of them) describing her adventures are published in the *Letters and Memorials*.[7] Carlyle, busy as he was, made time to write to her regularly, with light affectionate amusing sketches of his visitors or the news of the day; most particularly of the progress of the new acquaintance which was to have so serious an influence on her own future peace. . . . Mr. and Lady Harriet Baring, whom he had met two years previously, were now both of them becoming his intimate friends. From Mr. Baring there are many letters preserved among Carlyle's papers. They exhibit not only respect and esteem, but the strongest personal confidence and affection, which increased with fuller knowledge, and ceased only with death. They show, too, a fuller understanding of, and agreement with, Carlyle's general views than are to be found in almost any of those of his other correspondents. From Lady Harriet, too, there are abundance of notes, terse, clear, and peremptory, rather like the commands of a sovereign than the easy communications of friendship. She was herself gifted, witty, unconventional, seeing men and things much as they were, and treating them accordingly. She recognised the immense superiority of Carlyle to everyone else who came about her. She admired his intellect; she delighted in his humour. He at first enjoyed the society of a person who never bored him, who had a straight eye, a keen tongue, a disdain of nonsense, a majestic arrogance. As they became more intimate, the great lady affected his imagination. He was gratified at finding himself appreciated by a brilliant woman, who ruled supreme over half of London society. She became Gloriana, Queen of Fairyland, and he, with a true vein of chivalry in him, became her rustic Red Cross Knight, who, if he could, would have gladly led his own *Una* into the same enchanting ser-

434

vice.[8] The "Una," unfortunately, had no inclination for such a distinguished bondage.

Some misgiving may have crossed Carlyle's mind that too near an intimacy in these great circles might not be profitable to him. As long as social distinctions survive, an evenness of position is a condition of healthy friendship; and though genius is said to level artificial inequalities, it creates inequalities of another kind, which rather complicate the situation than simplify it. However this may have been, hard work and the London heat tired him out by the end of the summer. He was invited to stay at the Grange, a beautiful place belonging to the Barings in Hampshire, and as the visit was to be a short one he went. Mr. Baring's father, the Lord Ashburton of the American Treaty, still lived and reigned there. He had heard of Carlyle, and wished to make his acquaintance, as his Transatlantic wife did also. The Grange, in September especially, was the perfection of an English country palace. The habits of it did not suit Carlyle. He was off his sleep, woke early, could get no breakfast till ten, and no food but cigars and sunshine. But the park was beautiful, the riding delightful, "the solitude and silence divine."[9] He tried to be amused and happy, and succeeded tolerably.

While this new acquaintance was rising up into Carlyle's sky, another was setting or had set. News were waiting for him when he returned to Cheyne Row, which melted the Grange and its grandeurs into bodiless vapour. John Sterling was dead. Of all the friends whom Carlyle had won to himself since he came to London, there was none that he valued as he valued this one. Sterling had been his spiritual pupil, his first, and also his noblest and best. Consumption had set its fatal mark upon him. His spirit had risen against it and defied it. He had fled for life in successive winters to Italy, to France, and then to Falmouth and to Italy again. If not better, there had been no sign that he was becoming definitely worse. He had lately settled at Ventnor, in the Isle of Wight. He had added to his house; he had hoped, as his friends had hoped before for him, that years of useful energy might still be granted to him. It seemed impossible that a soul so gifted, so brilliant, so generous, should have been sent upon the earth merely to show how richly it had been endowed, and to pass away while its promise was but half fulfilled. But in this past summer he had been visibly declining. To himself, if to no one else, it had become sternly certain that the end was now near; and on August 10 he had written the letter of farewell, printed by Carlyle in his lost friend's biography, which I am therefore at liberty to transfer to these pages.

> Hillside Ventnor
> Aug 10—44.

> My dear Carlyle— For the first time for many months it seems possible to send you a few words merely however for Remembrance & Farewell. On higher matters there is nothing to say. I tread the common road into the great darkness without any thought of Fear & with very much Hope. Certainty indeed I have none. With regard to You and Me I cannot begin to write having nothing for it but to keep shut the lid of those secrets with all the iron weights that are in my power. Towards Me it is still more true than towards England—that no one has Been & Done like you. Heaven help you! If I can lend a hand when I am *there* that will not be wanting.— It is all very strange but not one hundredth part so sad as it seems to the standers by.
> Your wife knows my mind towards her & will believe it without asseverations.

> Yours to the last
> John Sterling.[10]

Sterling lingered for six weeks after writing this. He had been apparently dying more than once already, and yet had rallied. Carlyle could not believe that he was to lose him, and hoped that it might be so again. But it was not so to be. On September 18, within a day of Carlyle's return from the Grange, his friend was dead.

Sterling's death was the severest shock which Carlyle had yet experienced. Perhaps the presence of a real sorrow saved him from fretting over the smaller troubles of life. He threw himself the more determinately into his work. All the remainder of this year and all the next till the close of the summer he stayed at home, as far as possible alone, and seeing few friends in London except the Barings. His wife had been improved by her excursion. She had been moderately well since her return. Strong she never was; but for her the season had been a fair one. In July 1845, the end of *Crom-*

well was coming definitely in sight. She could be spared at home, and went off again to her relations at Liverpool. Carlyle had another horse—"Black Duncan" this one was called.[11] He rode daily, and sent regular bulletins to his "Necessary Evil."[12]

> The truth is, I have this very moment *ended* Oliver: hang it, he is ended thrums and all! I have nothing more to write on the subject; only mountains of wreck to burn. Not up to the chin in Paper-clippings, and chaotic litter, hatefuller to me than to most; I am to have a swept floor now again![13]

Thus was finished the first edition of the *Letters and Speeches of Oliver Cromwell*—the first edition—for other letters, other material of various kinds, came afterwards and had to be woven in with the rest; but essentially the thing was done on which Carlyle had been labouring for five years; and a few words may now be given to it.

This book is, in my opinion, by far the most important contribution to English history which has been made in the present century.[14] Carlyle was the first to break the crust which has overlaid the subject of Cromwell since the Restoration, and to make Cromwell and Cromwell's age again intelligible to mankind. Anyone who will read what was written about him before Carlyle's work appeared, and what has been written since, will perceive how great was the achievement. The enthusiast, led away by ambition, and degenerating into the hypocrite, the received figure of the established legend, is gone for ever. We may retain each our own opinion about Cromwell, we may think that he did well or that he did ill, that he was wise or unwise; but we see the real man. We can entertain no shadow of doubt about the genuineness of the portrait; and, with the clear sight of Oliver himself, we have a new conception of the Civil War and of its consequences. The book itself carries marks of the difficulty with which it was written. It has no clear continuity; large gaps are left in the story. Contrary to his own rule, that the historian should confine himself to the facts, with the minimum of commentary, Carlyle breaks in repeatedly in his own person, pats his friends upon the back, expands, applauds, criticises to an extent which most readers would wish more limited. This, however, is to be remembered, that

437

he was reproducing letters and speeches, of which both the thought and the language were obsolete—obsolete, or worse than obsolete, for most of it had degenerated into cant, insincere in everyone who uses such expressions now, and therefore suggesting insincerity in those who used them then. Perhaps he allowed too little for our ability to think for ourselves. But he had seen how fatally through this particular cause the character of the Commonwealth leaders had been obscured, and, if he erred at all, he erred on the right side. It is his supreme merit that he first understood the speeches made by Cromwell in Parliament, and enabled us to understand them. Printed as they had hitherto been, they could only confirm the impression, either that the Protector's own mind was hopelessly confused, or that he purposely concealed what was in it. Carlyle has shown that they were perfectly genuine speeches, not eloquent, as modern parliamentary speeches are, or aspire to be thought; but the faithful expressions of a most real and determined meaning, about which those who listened to him could have been left in no doubt at all. Such a feat was nothing less than extraordinary. It was not a "whitewashing," as attempts of this kind are often scornfully and sometimes deservedly called. It was the recovery of a true human figure of immense historical consequence from below two centuries of accumulated slander and misconception, and the work was completely done. No hammering or criticising has produced the least effect upon it. There once more Cromwell stands actually before us, and henceforth will stand, as he was when he lived upon the earth. He may be loved or he may be hated, as he was both loved and hated in his own time; but we shall love or hate the man himself, not a shadow or a caricature any more.

Detailed criticism of the book, or of any part of it, would be out of place in a biography, and I shall not attempt such a thing. I may mention, however, what Carlyle told me of the effect upon his own mind of his long study of the Commonwealth and its fortunes.

Many persons still believe that, if the army had not pushed the quarrel to extremities, if the "unpurged" Parliament had been allowed to complete its treaty with the King, the constitutional fruits of the struggle might have been secured more completely than they actually were; that the violent reaction would never have taken place which was provoked by the King's execution; that the Church of England could and would have then been completely reformed and made Protestant in form and substance; the pseudo-Catholicism— Episcopacy, Liturgy, and Ritual—which has wrought us all so much woe being swept clean from off the stage.

Speculations on what might have been are easy. We see what actually happened; what would have happened we can only guess. Charles, it is certain, was false—how false is now only completely known when the secret negotiations of himself and the Queen with the Catholic Powers have been brought to light. No promises which he had made would have bound him one moment beyond the time when he could safely break them; nor could anyone say what the composition of a new House of Commons might be after the next election. Taking the country through, the Royalists and the Moderates together were in the majority in point of numbers, and Cromwell's conclusion was that, so far as religion was concerned, the cause for which he and the army had fought would be utterly lost if the treaty was carried out. Wearied England, satisfied with having secured control of the purse strings, would hand over the sour fanatics to Charles's revenge. Carlyle was satisfied that Cromwell was right, and he drew from it a general inference of the incapacity of a popular assembly to guide successfully and permanently the destinies of this or any other country. No such body of men was ever seen gathered together in national council as those who constituted the Long Parliament. They were the pick and flower of God-fearing England, men of sovereign ability, of the purest patriotism—a senate of kings. If they failed, if they had to be prevented by armed force from destroying themselves and the interests committed to them, no other Parliament here or anywhere was likely to do better. Any pilot or council of pilots might answer, with smooth water and fair winds; but Parliaments, when circumstances were critical, could only talk, as their name denoted. Their resolutions would be half-hearted, their action a compromise between conflicting opinions, and therefore uncertain, inadequate, alternately rash or feeble, certain to end in disaster at all critical times when a clear eye and a firm hand was needed at the helm.

This was one inference which Carlyle drew. Another was on the rights of so-called "majorities." He had been bred a Radical, and a Radical he remained to the last, in the sense that he believed the entire existing form of human society, with its extremes of poverty and wealth, to be an accursed thing, which Providence would not allow to endure. He had been on the side of Catholic emancipation, hoping that the wretched Irish peasantry might get some justice by it. He had welcomed the Reform Bill, imagining it to mean that England was looking in earnest for her wisest men, and would give them power to mend what was amiss. He had found, as he said, that it was but the burning off the dry edges of the straw on the dunghill; that the huge, damp, putrid mass remained rotting where it was, and thus would remain, for anything that an extended suffrage would do to cure it. No result had come of the Reform Bill that he could care for. The thing needed was wisdom. Parliaments reflected the character of those who returned them. The lower the franchise, the less wisdom you were likely to find; and after each change in that direction the Parliament returned was less fit, not more fit, than its predecessor. In politics as in all else, Carlyle insisted always that there was a *right* way of doing things and a *wrong* way; that by following the *right* way alone could any good end be arrived at; and that it was as foolish to suppose that the *right* way of managing the affairs of a nation could be ascertained by a majority of votes, as the right way of discovering the longitude, of cultivating the soil, of healing diseases, or of exercising any one of the million arts on which our existence and welfare depend.

This conclusion he had arrived at, ever since he had seen what came and did not come of the Reform Bill of 1832; and it had prevented him from interesting himself in contemporary politics. But Cromwell's history had shown him that the *right* way had other means of asserting itself besides oratory and ballot-boxes and polling booths. The world was so constructed that the strongest, whether they were more or fewer, were the constituted rulers of this world. It must be so, unless the gods interfered, because there was no appeal. If one man was stronger than all the rest of mankind combined, he would rule all mankind. They would be unable to help themselves. But the world was also so constructed,

440

owing to the nature of the Maker of it, that superior strength was found in the long run to lie with those who had the right on their side. A good cause gave most valour to its defenders; and it was from this, and this alone, the supremacy of good over evil was maintained. Right-minded men would bear much rather than disturb existing arrangements—would submit to kings, to aristocracies, to majorities, as long as submission was possible; but, if driven to the alternative of seeing all that they valued perish or trying other methods, they would prove that, though they might be outvoted in the count of heads, they were not outvoted in the court of destiny. Superior justice in the cause made superior men—men who would make it good in spite of numbers. The best were the strongest, and so in the end would always prove, "considering who had made them strong." Behind all constitutions, never so popular, lay an ultimate appeal to force. Majorities, as such, had no more right to rule than kings, or nobles, or any other persons or groups of persons, to whom circumstances might have given temporary power. The right to rule lay with those who were right in mind and heart, whenever they chose to assert themselves. If they tried and failed, it proved only that they were not right *enough* at that particular time. But, in fact, no honest effort ever did fail; it bore its part in the eventual settlement. The strong thing, in the main, was the right thing, because the world was not the Devil's; and the final issue would be found to prove it whenever the question was raised. Society was in a healthy condition only when authority was in the hands of those most fit to exercise it. As long as kings and nobles were kings and nobles indeed, superior in heart and character, the people willingly submitted to them, and gave them strength by their own support. When they forgot the meaning of their position, lived for ambition and pleasure, and so ceased to be superior, their strength passed from them, and with their strength their authority. That was what happened, and was happening still, in England. There being no longer any superiority of class over class, the integers of society were falling into anarchy, and, to avoid quarrelling, might agree for a time to decide their differences by a majority of votes; but it could be but for a time only, unless all that was great and noble in humanity was to disappear for ever; for the good and the wise were few, and the selfish and the ignorant were many; the many would choose to represent them men like themselves, not men superior to themselves; and, under pain of destruction, it was indispensable that means must be found by which the good and wise should be brought to the front, and not the others. Nature had her means of doing it, and in extremity would not fail to use them.[15]

In some such frame of mind Carlyle was left after he had finished his *Cromwell*. I have described in my own words what, in his abrupt and scornful dialect, he often expressed to me. He was never a Conservative, for he recognised that, unless there was a change, impossible except by miracle, in the habits and character of the wealthy classes, the gods themselves could not save them. But the Radical creed of liberty, equality, and government by majority of votes, he considered the most absurd superstition which had ever bewitched the human imagination—at least, outside Africa.

Cromwell thus disposed of, he was off for Scotland, "wishing," as he said, to be amiable, but dreadfully bilious, and almost sick of his life, if there were not hopes of improvement. He joined his wife at Seaforth, stayed a day or two[16] with the Paulets there, and then, leaving Mrs. Carlyle to return and take care of the house in Cheyne Row, he made his way on by the usual sea route to Annan and Scotsbrig.

His mother was now fast growing weaker. She brightened up at letters from her daughter-in-law, or on visits from her illustrious son, whom all the world was talking of; but "all had grown old" about her, except her affection, which seemed younger than ever. Carlyle, while at Scotsbrig, was her constant companion, drove her about in the old gig, carried her down to see his sister Mary at Annan, or his sister Jean at Dumfries; and so the days passed on with autumnal composure, sad but not unhappy. Now and then troublesome proof-sheets came, which would stir the bile a little. But he kept himself patient, found "a day of Humiliation and Reflexion sometimes" "not useless to me,"[17] and grumbled little. "All work," he said, "if it be nobly done, is about alike;—really so: one has not reward out of it, except even that same: the *spirit* it was done in. That is blessed, or that is accursed; that always."[18] The world was saying that he was a great man. He did not believe it. Mrs. Paulet had written some wildly flattering letter, calling him "the greatest man in Europe." "Good Heavens," he said of this; "he feels himself in general the smallest man in Annandale almost! Being very bilious, confused and sleepless, let him never trouble his head about what magnitude he is of."[19] As to his *deserts*, he deserved, if it came to that, "to be in Purgatory!"[20]

Men of genius who make a mark themselves in literature, in art or science, or in any way which brings their name before the world, find ready admittance into the higher social circles; but the *entrée* is granted less readily to their wives and daughters. Where this arrangement is allowed, the feeling on both sides is a vulgar one; the great lady is desirous merely that a person who is talked about shall be seen in her reception rooms, and is not anxious to burden herself with an acquaintance with his inferior connections. The gifted individual is vain of appearing in the list of guests at aristocratic mansions, and is careless of the slight upon his family. The Barings were infinitely superior to paltry distinctions of this kind, nor would Carlyle have cared for their acquaintance if they had not been. He was far too proud in himself, and he had too high a respect for his wife, to visit in lordly saloons where she would be unwelcome. Mr. Baring had called on Mrs. Carlyle, had seen her often, and had cordially admired her. With Lady Harriet, though they had probably met, there had not yet been an opportunity of intimacy; but Carlyle was most anxious that his wife, too, should be appreciated as she deserved to be by a lady whom he himself so much admired. Mrs. Buller, an experienced woman of the world, who knew both Lady Harriet and Mrs. Carlyle, was convinced that they would not suit each other, and that no good would come from an attempt to bring them into close connection. To Carlyle Mrs. Buller's forebodings seemed absurd. With all his knowledge, he was innocent of insight into the subtleties of women's feelings, and it was with unmixed pleasure that he heard of a visit of his wife to Bath House on her own account, soon after her return.

The first impressions had apparently been favourable on both sides. Mrs. Carlyle wrote brightly to him both about the Bath House affair and everything else. Her letters during his absence were exceptionally lively and entertaining.

443

Cromwell done with, he was beginning to consider to what next he should put his hand, and *Frederick the Great* was already hanging before him as a possibility. He had read Preuss's book in the year preceding. He was now meditating an expedition to Berlin to learn more about this "greatest of modern men." His stay in Scotland was to be short. After a fortnight of it he was thinking about his return. How it was to be was the question. The railway from London only reached to Preston, and the alternative was equally horrible —the coach from Carlisle thither or the steamer to Liverpool. One day he thought he would go "to the whale" again, and say to it, "Swallow me at once," "thou doest it at once." The whale ultimately proved the least desirable of the various monsters. He chose the coach, and was at home again just when *Cromwell* was appearing.

The reception of it was, as might be expected, in the highest degree favourable. There was little to offend, and every one was ready to welcome a fair picture of the great Protector. The sale was rapid, and after a few months, as the interest grew, fresh materials were contributed from unexpected quarters, to be added in new editions. For the moment, however, Carlyle was left idle. He came back to find literally that he had nothing to do. *Frederick* was still but a thought, and of all conditions that of want of occupation was what he was least fitted to endure. He had drawn his breath when he ended his work in September. He had felt idyllic. He and his poor wife had climbed the hill together by a thorny road. He had arrived at the height of his fame. He was admired, praised, and honoured by all England and America; nothing, he said, could now be more natural than that they should sit still and look round them a little in quiet. Quiet, unhappily, was the one thing impossible. He admired quiet as he admired silence, only theoretically. Work was life to him. Idleness was torture. The cushion on which he tried to sit still was set with spines. Mrs. Carlyle says briefly that after he came back "she was kept in a sort of worry." The remedy which was tried was worse than the disease. Mr. Baring and Lady Harriet invited them both for a long visit to Bay House, near Alverstoke in Hampshire. They went in the middle of November and remained till the end of the year. Carlyle, to some moderate extent, seems to have enjoyed himself—certainly his wife did not.

To Mrs. Carlyle the visit was neither pleasant nor useful, probably the opposite of both. Mrs. Buller was turning out a true prophet. Mrs. Carlyle and Lady Harriet did not suit each other. Mrs. Carlyle did not shut her eyes to the noble lady's distinguished qualities: but even these qualities themselves might be an obstacle to cordial intimacy. People do not usually take to those who excel in the points where they have themselves been accustomed to reign supreme. Mrs. Carlyle knew that she was far cleverer than the general run of lady adorers who worshipped her husband. She knew also that he was aware of her superiority; that, by her talent as well as her character, she had a hold upon him entirely her own, and that he only laughed goodnaturedly at the homage they paid him. But she could not feel as easy about Lady Harriet. She saw that Carlyle admired her brilliancy, and was gratified by her queenly esteem. To speak of jealousy in the ordinary sense would be extravagantly absurd; but there are many forms of jealousy, and the position of a wife, when her husband is an intimate friend of another woman, is a difficult and delicate one. If there is confidence and affection between the ladies themselves, or if the friend has a proper perception of a wife's probable susceptibilities, and is careful to prevent them from being wounded, or if the wife herself is indifferent and incapable of resentment, all is well, and the relation may be delightful. In the present case there were none of these conditions. No one could suspect Lady Harriet Baring of intending to hurt Mrs. Carlyle; but either she never observed her discomfort, or she thought it too ridiculous to notice. She doubtless tried in her own lofty way to be kind to Mrs. Carlyle, and Mrs. Carlyle, for her husband's sake, tried to like Lady Harriet. But it did not answer on either side, and in such cases it is best to leave things to take their natural course. When two people do not agree, it is a mistake to force them into intimacy. They should remain on the footing of neutral acquaintance, and are more likely to grow into friends the less the direct effort to make them so. Gloriana may have a man for a subject without impairing his dignity—a woman in such a position becomes a dependent. Carlyle unfortunately could not see the distinction. To such a lady a certain homage seemed to be due; and if his wife resisted, he was angry. When Lady Harriet required her presence, she told John Carlyle that she was

445

obliged to go, or the lady would quarrel with her, "and that meant a quarrel with her husband." The Red Cross Knight was brought to evil thoughts of his "Una" by the enchantments of Archimage. To a proud fiery woman like Mrs. Carlyle the sense that Lady Harriet could come in any way between her husband and herself was intolerable.

Things had not come to this point during the Bay House visit, but were tending fast in that direction, and were soon to reach it.

In February 1846 a new edition was needed of the *Cromwell*. Fresh letters of Oliver had been sent which required to be inserted according to date; a process, Carlyle said, "requiring one's most exquisite talent as of shoe-cobbling, really, that kind of talent carried to a high pitch."[21]

The Barings were at Addiscombe in the spring, and it was arranged that Mrs. Carlyle should be with them there for the benefit of country air; he remaining at his work, but joining them on Saturdays and Sundays. She could not sleep, she did not like it. He who had meant everything for the best, tried to comfort her as well as he could.

Evidently he was labouring at his task under complications of worry and trouble. Perhaps both he and she would have been better off after all at Craigenputtoch. The "stitching and cobbling," however, was gone through with. *Cromwell* thus enlarged was now in its final form; and as soon as it was done, he took a step in connection with it which, I believe, he never took before or after with any of his writings: he presented a copy of it to the Prime Minister. Sir Robert Peel had hitherto been no favourite of his, neither Peel nor any one of the existing generation of statesmen; Sir Jabesh Windbag in *Past and Present* representing his generic conception of them. But Peel was now repealing the corn-laws; not talking of it, but doing it; and imperilling in one righteous act his own political fortune. That had something of greatness in it, especially with Carlyle, who had believed heroic sacrifice of self to be an impossible virtue in a Parliamentary leader. He discovered Peel to be a real man.

It was hard on Carlyle that, while engaged with work into which he was throwing his entire heart and soul, he should be disturbed and perplexed with domestic confusions. But it was his fate—a fate, perhaps, which could not be avoided; and those confusions were to grow and gather into a thick black cloud which overshadowed his life for many weary years. When Mrs. Carlyle returned to him from Addiscombe, it was, as she said, "with the mind of me all churned into froth"[22]—not a pleasant condition. Carlyle, in spite of his good resolutions, was occasionally "a little *'ill haired.'* "[23] At last things went utterly awry. She set off alone to the Paulets at the beginning of July. There was a violent scene when they parted. Her words, if seldom smoother than oil, were "very swords" when she was really angry. She did not write on her arrival, as she had promised to do.[24]

Among Mrs. Carlyle's papers are two letters—the first of them dated only July, yet in answer to one which she must have written before leaving London, showing that in her distress she had taken the strong step of consulting a friend on the course which she ought to follow. Happily she could have consulted no one who could have advised her more wisely.

> Awake, arise, dear friend! Beset by pain or not, we must go on with a sad smile and a practical encouragement from one another. We have something of our own to care about, something godlike that we must not yield to any living creature, whoever it be. Your life proves an empty thing, you say! Empty! Do not blaspheme. Have you never done good? Have you never loved? . . . Can't you trust Him a little longer? How long will you remain at Seaforth? Does he himself propose to go anywhere? I was coming to see you on Saturday. Write if and when it does good even homoeopathically to you, and be assured that to me it will always do.
>
> Ever yours,
> Joseph Mazzini

Either this letter or her own reflections led Mrs. Carlyle, after a day's delay, to write softly to her husband. He, poor man, as innocent of any thought of wrong, as incapable of understanding what he had done to raise such a tornado, as my Uncle Toby himself could have been, was almost piteously grateful.

On July 13 he wrote, enclosing his never-forgotten birthday present, "a poor little Card-case, a small memorial of Bastille-day, and of another day also very important to me and thee!"[25] This is the letter of which she speaks so touchingly in her reply,[26] the letter which had been delayed at the Seaforth post-office. She, agitated by a thousand thoughts, had feared that he had let the day pass without

GIUSEPPE MAZZINI. A slim, handsome man with a melodious voice and dark penetrating eyes, passionately dedicated to the cause of Italian liberty and the triumph of Republican principles, Mazzini was a particular favorite of Jane Carlyle's. Carlyle thought him impractical and visionary but gave him his respect. (Courtesy of the Columbia University Libraries.)

writing to her, and she had been thrown into a "tumult of wretchedness."[27] She had written again, it appears, to Mazzini; for from him, too, came another letter, tenderly sympathetic, yet wise and supremely honourable to him. No ghostly confessor could have been more judicious.

The birthday present, and the words which had come with it, ought to have made all well; and yet it did not, for the cause remained. The condition into which she had wrought herself through her husband's Gloriana worship would have been ridiculous if it had not been so tragic—tragic even in its absurdity, and tragic in its consequences. Fault there was little on any side. Want of judgement, perhaps, and want of perception; that was all. Carlyle had formed an acquaintance which he valued and she disliked, because she fancied that a shadow had risen between herself and him, which was taking from her part of what belonged to her. A few hearty words, a simple laugh, and the nightmare would have vanished. But neither laugh nor spoken word of any such salutary kind had been possible. Carlyle in such matters had no more skill than the Knight of La Mancha would have had. He was very shy, for one thing. He wrote with exquisite tenderness. In conversation he shrank from expressions of affection, even at moments when he felt most deeply. On the other hand, he was keenly sensitive to what he thought unreasonable or silly. He was easily provoked; and his irritation would burst out in spurts of angry metaphor, not to be forgotten from their very point and force. Thus his letters failed in producing their full effect from their contrast with remembered expressions which had meant nothing; while, again, he might himself naturally feel impatient when called on to abandon friends whose high character he admired, and who had been singularly kind to him, for a cause which he knew to be a preposterous creation of a disordered fancy, and which, in yielding, he would have acknowledged tacitly to have been just. A "man of genius," especially one whose function it was to detect and expose chimaeras, ought to have contrived better. Some strange mismanagement there must have been to have created such a condition of things. Yet "a man of genius" is no better off in such situations than an ordinary mortal. He was confronted with a problem which a person with a thousandth fraction of his abilities, either of brain or heart, would have solved in a moment by a smile; yet he wandered from mistake to mistake.

He had to tell her that a plan had been arranged for the Barings to go to the Highlands, that it had been proposed that he should accompany them, that he did not think he would, but that possibly he might.

He was struggling in a cobweb, and was not on the way to extricate himself. That a man of genius should enjoy the society of a brilliant and gifted lady of high rank was "just and laudable," as he called it.[28] It was natural, too, if not laudable, that Mrs. Carlyle should not be equally interested in a person who rivalled her in her own domain. She, for her own part, had no wish to be intimate with a great lady who could have no interest in her. Carlyle made the mistake of trying to force her into a position which she detested; and every step which he took in this direction only made the irritation greater.

His plans for the summer had been laid out independent of the Highland tour. He was to go first to his mother at Scotsbrig for a few days, and afterwards to run across to Ireland. The "Young Ireland" movement, the precursor of the Home Rule movement, was just then rising into heat. Charles Gavan Duffy, of the *Nation* newspaper, with others of the leaders, had sought him out in London in consequence of what he had written in *Chartism* about Irish misgovernment. He had promised to go over, when he had leisure, and see what they were doing. Had he confined himself to this programme, he would have given time for the waves to go down; but he went for a day or two to see his wife at Seaforth on his way to Scotland. It then appeared that he had engaged to meet the Barings after all, and that Mrs. Carlyle herself was pressed to join their party. His letters after he reached Scotsbrig show that the barometer was still at "stormy."

It is ludicrous to contrast with all this tempest the fate of the expedition which was the occasion of it. The projected tour with Mr. Baring and Lady Harriet lasted but five days, and was as melancholy as Mrs. Carlyle could have desired. They went from Carlisle to Moffat, sleeping in "noisy cabins in confused whisky inns,"[29] and in the worst of weather. The lady was cross; Mr. Baring only pa-

CHARLES GAVAN DUFFY. Duffy was the chief of a group of Young Irelanders whom Carlyle knew. Carlyle toured Ireland in his company in 1846 and 1849. Later Duffy emigrated to Australia, but returned to England in old age, and after Carlyle's death he wrote one of the most enlightening books on him by a contemporary—his *Conversations with Carlyle*. (Photograph by Elliott & Fry, courtesy of the Columbia University Libraries.)

tient and good-humoured. They had designed a visit to Drumlanrig: but "the Buccleuch household gave notice that it had *hooping-cough*,"[30] and were not to be approached; and Beattock, near Moffat, was the furthest point of the journey.

They had one fine day, which was given to Moffat and the neighbourhood, and then parted, the Barings to go on to the Highlands, Carlyle to retreat to Scotsbrig again—to "sleep . . . and practical sense and the free use of tobacco,"[31] and to prepare for his trip to Ireland. Mrs. Carlyle was in no spirits for Haddington, and returned alone to her own resting-place in Cheyne Row, after a day or two with Miss Jewsbury at Manchester. So the "weighty matter," which had called up such a storm, was over, and the gale had blown itself out. She, like a sensible woman, crushed down her own dissatisfaction. The intimacy was to go on upon whatever terms Carlyle pleased, and she resigned herself to take a part in it, since there was no reasonable cause to be alleged for cessation or interruption. But the wound fretted inwardly and would not heal. She and her husband had quarrelled often enough before—they had quarrelled and made it up again, for they had both hot tempers and sharp tongues—but there had been at bottom a genuine and hearty confidence in each other, a strong sincere affection, resting on mutual respect and mutual admiration. The feeling remained essentially unbroken, but the fine edge of it had suffered. Small occasions of provocation constantly recurred. Mrs. Carlyle consented to stay with Lady Harriet and submit to her authority as often and as much as she required; the sense of duty acting as perpetual curb to her impatience. But the wound burst out at intervals, embittering Carlyle's life, and saddening a disposition which did not need further clouds upon it. She wrote to him while he was at Scotsbrig about indifferent things in the spirit of the resolution which she had made, and he, man-like, believed that all was well again.[32]

chapter twenty-three

1846–1849

Ireland. Margaret Fuller. The Ashburtons.
"Exodus from Houndsditch." Revolutions of
1848 in Europe. Macaulay. Peel.
Visit to the Grange. Death of
Charles Buller. Froude's First
Meeting with Carlyle

Ireland had long been an anxious subject of Carlyle's meditations. It was the weak point of English constitutional
government. The Constitution was the natural growth of
the English mind and character. We had imposed it upon
the Irish in the confident belief that a system which answered among ourselves must be excellent in itself, and be
equally suited for every other country and people. Carlyle's conviction was that even for England it was something temporary in itself, an historical phenomenon which
in time would cease to answer its purpose even where it
originated, and that Ireland was the weak spot, where the
failure was first becoming evident. He had wished to see
the unfortunate island with his own eyes, now particularly
when its normal wretchedness was accentuated by the
potato blight and famine. He had no present leisure for a
detailed survey, but he had resolved at least to look at it if
only for a few days.

On the last of August he left Scotsbrig, went to Dumfries, and thence made a hasty visit to Craigenputtoch,
which was now his own property, and where there was business to be attended to. From Dumfries he went by coach
to Ayr and Ardrossan, from which a steamer carried him
at night to Belfast. Gavan Duffy and John Mitchel had
arranged to meet him at Drogheda. The drive thither from
Belfast was full of instruction; the scene all *new* to him;
the story of the country written in ruined cabins and uncul-
tivated fields, the air poisoned with the fatal smell of the

poisoned potato. He had an agreeable companion on the coach in a clever young Dublin man, who pleased him well. Drogheda must have had impressive associations for him. There is no finer passage in his *Cromwell* than his description of the stern business once enacted there. But he did not stay to look for traces of Oliver. He missed his two friends through a mistake at the Post Office, and hurried on by railway to Dublin, where he stopped at the Imperial Hotel in Sackville Street. Here for a day or two he was alone. He had come for a glance at Ireland, and that was all which he got.

The Young Irelanders had waited at Drogheda, and only discovered their guest at last at Dundrum, to which he had gone to some address which Mr. Duffy had given him. There he was entertained at a large dinner-party. "Young Ireland almost in mass." The novelist Carleton was there, "a genuine bit of Ould Ireland." They "talked, and dined, and drank liquids of various strength."[1] Carlyle was scornful. The Young Irelanders fought fiercely with him for their own views; but they liked him and he liked them, wild and unhopeful as he knew their projects to be. He could not see even the surface of Ireland without recognising that there was a curse upon it of some kind, and these young enthusiasts were at least conscious of the fact, and were not crying "Peace" when there was none. The next day he dined with one of them; then, perhaps, the most notorious. "Poor Mitchel!" Carlyle said afterwards, "I told him he would most likely be hanged, but I told him too they could not hang the immortal part of him."

On the last day of his stay he was taken for a drive, one of the most beautiful in the world, by the Dargle and Powerscourt, and round through the Glen of the Downs to Bray. Before entering the Dublin mountains, they crossed the low rich meadows of the old Pale, the longest in English occupation, a fertile oasis in the general wretchedness. I have heard that he said, looking over the thick green grass and well-trimmed fences and the herds of cattle fattening there, "Ah, Duffy, there you see the hoof of the bloody Saxon." This was his final excursion, a pleasant taste in the mouth to end with. The same evening his friends saw him on board the steamer at Kingstown; and in the early

454

morning of September 9 he was sitting smoking a cigar before the door of his wife's uncle's house in Liverpool till the household should awake and let him in.

He had looked on Ireland, and that was all; but he had seen enough to make intelligible to him all that followed. When he came again, three years later, the bubble had burst. Europe was in revolution; the dry Irish tinder had kindled, and a rebellion which was a blaze of straw had ended in a cabbage garden. Duffy, Mitchel, and others of that bright Dundrum party had stood at the bar to be tried for treason. Duffy narrowly escaped. The rest were exiled, scattered over the world, and lost to Ireland for ever. Mitchel has lately died in America. The "immortal part" of him still works in the Phoenix Park and in dynamite conspiracies; what will come of it has yet to be seen.

In London, when he was again settled there, he had nothing of importance to attend to. No fresh work had risen upon him. There had been trouble with servants. The establishment at Cheyne Row consisted of a single maid-of-all-work, and to find a woman who would take such a place, and yet satisfy a master and mistress so sensitive to disorder, material or moral, was no easy matter. Mrs. Carlyle has related her afflictions on this score;[2] just then they had been particularly severe, and she had been worried into illness. The "fame" from *Cromwell* had made Carlyle himself a greater object of curiosity than ever. He did not like being an object of curiosity. "Yesternight there came a bevy of Americans from Emerson; one Margaret Fuller the chief figure of them: a strange *lilting* lean old-maid, not nearly such a bore as I expected."[3]

Margaret Fuller, then on her way to Italy to be married to a Count Ossoli there, and to be afterwards tragically drowned, has left an account of this meeting with Carlyle, and being an external view of him and by a clever woman, it deserves a place here. Her first evening at Cheyne Row, she says, "delighted" her. Carlyle "was in a very sweet humour,—full of wit and pathos, without being overbearing and oppressive." She was "carried away with the rich flow of his discourse; and the hearty, noble earnestness of his personal being brought back the charm which once was upon his writing, before she wearied of it." She admired his Scotch dialect, "his way of singing his great full sentences, so that each one was like the stanza of a narrative ballad." "He talked of the present state of things in England, giving light, witty sketches of the men of the day . . . and some sweet, homely stories he told of things he had known among the Scotch peasantry. . . . There never was anything so witty as his description of ——— ———.[4] It was enough to kill one with laughing." Carlyle "is not ashamed to laugh, when he is amused, but goes on in a cordial human fashion."

On a second visit the humour was less sweet, though "more brilliant," and Miss Fuller was obliged to disagree with everything that he said.

> The worst of hearing Carlyle [she says, and she is very correct in this] is that you cannot interrupt him. I understand the habit and power of haranguing have increased very much upon him, so that you are a perfect prisoner when he has once got hold of you. To interrupt him is a physical impossibility. If you get a chance to remonstrate for a moment, he raises his voice and bears you down. True, he does you no injustice, and, with his admirable penetration, sees the disclaimer in your mind, so that you are not morally delinquent; but it is not pleasant to be unable to utter it.

This was not the last meeting, for the Carlyles in turn spent an evening with their new American acquaintances. Mazzini was there, whom Miss Fuller admired especially, and had perceived also to be "a dear friend of Mrs. C." Mazzini's presence, she writes, "gave the conversation a turn to 'progress' and ideal subjects, and C. was fluent in invectives on all our 'rose-water imbecilities.' . . . Mazzini, after some vain efforts to remonstrate, became very sad. Mrs. C. said to me, 'These are but opinions to Carlyle; but to Mazzini, who has given his all, and helped bring his friends to the scaffold, in pursuit of such subjects, it is a matter of life and death.' "

> All Carlyle's talk, that evening, was a defence of mere force, —success the test of right;—if people would not behave well, put collars round their necks;—find a hero, and let them be his slaves, &c. It was very Titanic, and anti-celestial. I wish the last evening had been more melodious. However, I bid Carlyle farewell with feelings of the warmest friendship and admiration. We cannot feel otherwise to a great and noble nature, whether it harmonize with our own or not. I never appreciated the work he has done for

his age till I saw England. I could not. You must stand in the shadow of that mountain of shams, to know how hard it is to cast light across it.[5]

Cheyne Row being made uncomfortable by change of servants, an invitation to Carlyle and his wife to stay at the Grange was accepted without objection on either side. Objections on that score were not to be raised any more. Mrs. Carlyle liked old Lord and Lady Ashburton well, and the Grange was one of the pleasantest houses in England. But it proved to be one of the great autumn gatherings which were a mere reproduction of London society. The visit lasted a fortnight, and gave little pleasure to either of them. The men were shooting all day; the women dispersed to their rooms in the forenoon, met at luncheon, strolled or rode in the afternoon; none of them *did* anything, and Carlyle was a fish out of water.

The Grange was Lord Ashburton's, his son, Mr. Baring, and Lady Harriet living (as has been seen), when not in London or Addiscombe, at Bay House, near Alverstoke. Mrs. Carlyle, after the Grange visit, became very ill, confined to bed for three weeks with cough and incessant headache. The new servant did not udnerstand her business. Carlyle himself was "very *idle*, reading nothing but wearisome trivialities, and not writing at all."[6] Lady Harriet, when Mrs. Carlyle became able to move, proposed that she and her husband should spend a month with her at Bay House for change of air. Mr. Baring had many engagements, and for part of the time she would be alone. Carlyle, writing to his brother about it, said that he did not regard this scheme "as quite unquestionable," and so had rather held back, but "Jane, having engaged for it, will go thro' with the affair."[7] Lady Harriet was most attentive; she secured them a separate compartment on the railway. Her carriage was waiting at the station with rugs, wrappings, and hot-water bottles. They went in the middle of January.

February brought other visitors, Buller, Milnes, etc. Lady Anne Charteris, who lived near Bay House, came often to sit with Mrs. Carlyle and play chess with her. On the 15th, when the month was near out, he could send a good account to his mother. "Jane has greatly improved in

457

health; indeed she is now about as well as usual; and we hope may now do well henceforth."[8]

Ireland weighed heavily on his thoughts. Each post brought news this spring of a land stricken with death. He had seen the place, and could realise what was passing there. Tens of thousands were perishing, and the wretched people, having lost their potatoes, were refusing even to plough. "They say, 'Why should we raise a crop? Our Landlords will come and take it all; we shall get fed by the Government any way! . . . ' On the whole, I think there never was seen such a scene as that of Ireland."[9] He longed to write something on it, but felt that he did not yet see through the problem. Nay, he believed an equal catastrophe lay over England herself, if she did not mend her ways. It was to this that he must next direct himself, when he could determine how; but there was no longer any immediate need to write anything. He would pause and consider. *Frederick* was still far off, nearer subjects were more pressing.

With the hot weather came a visit to Addiscombe—visits to the Barings, at one place or another, continually recuring, in which Mrs. Carlyle was as often as possible included. There is nothing to be said, save that Lady Harriet's attentions to her were unremitting. Carlyle himself was still what he called idle, i.e., incessantly reading all kinds of books, and watching the signs of the times. At the end of July he took his wife to Matlock for change of air. At Matlock they were joined by the now famous W. E. Forster, then one of his ardent admirers, and accompanied him to his house at Rawdon, whence Carlyle sent his mother, as usual, an account of his adventures.[10]

He might now have had his choice among the great houses of the land if he had cared to visit them, but he steadily reserved every available autumn for his mother. The week at Rawdon being over, his wife went home, and [in August] he made for Scotsbrig, pausing at Manchester with Miss Jewsbury and her brother Frank to see iron works and cotton mills; to talk with some of the leaders of the working men, who were studying his writings with passionate interest, and himself to be stared at in the Jewsbury drawing-room by the idle and curious. The most in-

458

teresting of his Manchester adventures was a day at Rochdale, when he made acquaintance with Mr. Jacob Bright and his distinguished brother.

The Mills, O the fetid fuzzy, deafening ill-ventilated mills! And, in Sharp's cyclopean Smithy, do you remember the poor "Grinders"? Sitting underground, in a damp dark place, some dozen of them: over their screeching stone-cylinders; from every cylinder a sheet of yellow *fire* issuing, the principal light of the place;—and the men, I was told, and they themselves knew it, and "did not mind it," were all or mostly *killed* before their time, the lungs being ruined by the metal and stone dust! Those poor fellows, in their paper caps, with their roaring grindstones and their yellow *cricflammes* of fire, all grinding themselves so quickly to death, will never go out of my memory.—In signing my name, as I was made to do, on quitting that Sharp Establishment, whose name, think you, stood next, to be succeeded by mine? In a fine flowing character, JENNY LIND's! Dickens and the other Player Squadron (wanting Forster, I think) stood on the same page. Adieu to Manchester, and its poor grinders and spinners! I will tell you about Bright and Brightdom and the Rochdale Bright Mill, some other day. *Jacob* Bright, the younger man, and actual manager at Rochdale, rather pleased me: a kind of delicacy in his heavy features when you saw them by daylight,—at all events, a decided element of "hero-worship," which of course went for much! But *John* Bright, the Anti-cornlaw Member, who had come across to meet me, with his squat stout body, with his cock-nose and pugnacious eyes, and Barclay-Fox Quaker collar,—John and I discorded in our views not a little! And in fact the result was that I got to talking, occasionally in the *Annandale* accent, and communicated large masses of my views to the Brights and Brightesses, and shook peaceable Brightdom as with a passing earthquake,—and I doubt left a very questionable impression of myself there! The poor young ladies (Quaker or Ex-Quaker), with their "abolition of Capital Punishment"—Ach Gott! I had a great *remorse* of it all that evening; but now begin almost to think I served them right. Any way, *we cannot help it.* So there it, and Lancashire in general, may lie, for the present.[11]

At Scotsbrig, when he reached it, he sank into what he called "stagnation and magnetic sleep." "Grey hazy dispiritment, fit for nothing but tobacco and silence." "In my own country I am as solitary as in a foreign land; and have more than ever, in looking over it, the feelings of a ghost!" Even with his mother he could talk less freely than usual, for he found her "terribly sensitive on *the Semitic* side of things,"[12] and he was beginning to think that he must write something about that—the "Exodus from Hounds-

JOHN BRIGHT. Victorian reformer, manufacturer, and M.P. Carlyle visited the Rochdale mill owned by Bright and his brother Jacob in 1847. Sparks flew at this encounter between two of the most self-willed of contemporaries. "But *John* Bright, the Anti-cornlaw Member," Carlyle wrote to Jane in Chelsea on 13 September, "who had come across to meet me, with his squat stout body, with his cock-nose and pugnacious eyes, and Barclay-Fox Quaker collar,—John and I discorded in our views not a little! And in fact the result was that I got to talking, occasionally in the *Annandale* accent, and communicated large masses of my views to the Brights and Brightesses, and shook peaceable Brightdom as with a passing earthquake,—and I doubt left a very questionable impression of myself there!" (Photograph by W. and D. Downey, courtesy of the Columbia University Libraries.)

ditch," as he termed it, being a first essential step towards all improvement. The news from Ireland disgusted him, "Meagher of the Sword"[13] talking open treason.

He wandered about the moors at night, "the driving clouds and moaning winds my only company." Even these were not impressive, "for my heart is shrunk into its cell, and refuses to be impressed." He "said silently to the muddy universe, however, 'Yes, thou art true, then; the fact is no better than *so*; let me recognise the fact, and admit it and adopt it.' "[14]

He had reasons for uneasiness besides the state of the universe. His wife had been ill again. Lady Harriet Baring, hearing she was alone in Cheyne Row, had carried her off to Addiscombe, and little guessing the state of her mind, and under the impression that she was hypochondriacal, had put her under a course of bracing. She wanted wine when she was exhausted; Lady Harriet thought wine unwholesome. She was not allowed to go to bed when tortured with headache. She suffered from cold, and lighted a fire in her bedroom. Fires were not allowed at Addiscombe so early in the autumn, and the housemaid removed the coals. Lady Harriet meant only to be kind, but was herself heaping fuel on a fire of a more dangerous sort. Carlyle himself was relieved when he heard that she was "home again, out of that constrained lodging." "My mother's rage," he wrote, "has been considerable, ever since she heard of it, 'That the puir craitur could na get a bit *fire!*' Not so much as a bit of fire, 'for a' their grandeur!' Money, if it exclude but things which are apt to go with the *want* of it, is of small value,—to the possessor or to others."[15] True enough! but one asks with wonder why he could not tell Lady Harriet plainly that, if she wished for his wife's friendship, she must treat her differently; why he insisted on the continuance of an intimacy which could never become an affectionate one, instead of accepting and adopting the facts, as a condition of the mud in the universe. His mother was full of tenderness for her forlorn daughter-in-law. She insisted, when Carlyle was going home, on sending her "a pair of coarse knit stockings (tho' I said you could never wear them), and two missionary Narratives, which even I could not have be[en] persuaded to read!" He was to write his wife's name in them at Chelsea, and say, "from her old withered Mother."[16]

Two bad nights before his departure sent him off in a dreary condition. "Ah me!" he exclaimed. "My poor old Mother; poor old Annandale, poor old *Life* in general! And in that shattered state of the nerves all stands before one with such a glaring ghastliness of hideous reality."[17]

It is curious that a man with such powerful practical sense should have indulged such feelings. It was "the nature of the beast," as he often said, but he was evidently much disturbed. He was at home by the second week in October, where an unexpected pleasure was waiting for him. His friend Emerson had arrived from Boston. Between Emerson and him there had been affectionate correspondence ever since they had met at Craigenputtoch. Emerson had arranged for the publication of his books in the United States, and had made his rights respected there. He in turn had introduced Emerson's *Essays* to the English world by a preface, and now Emerson had come in person to show himself as a lecturer on English platforms. I remember this visit. I already knew Emerson by his writings; I then learnt to know him personally, for he came to see us at Oxford, and his conversation, perhaps unknown to himself, had an influence on my after life. On his first landing he was a guest at Cheyne Row, and then went away to Manchester. "I rather think," Carlyle wrote shortly after, "his popularity is not very great hitherto; his doctrines are too *airy* and thin for the solid practical heads of the Lancashire region. We had immense talking with him here; but found he did not give us much to chew the cud upon,—found in fact that he came with the *rake* rather than the *shovel*. He is a pure high-minded man, but I think his talent is not quite so high as I had anticipated."[18]

A far more important thing was what Carlyle was next to do himself, for as long as he was idle he was certain to be miserable—and he had been idle now for more than a year. He brought out another edition of his *Miscellanies* this autumn. *The French Revolution* was going into another edition also. For this and the *Miscellanies* he was paid £600. So that he could say "I am pretty well in funds at present,—not chased about, as I used to be, by the haggard shade of Beggary; which is a great relief to me, now when I am growing old! I am very thankful for my poverty; and for my deliverance from it in good time."[19]

In January came an indispensable visit to the Barings. Mrs. Carlyle was to have gone, and they were to have stayed four weeks; but the winter was cold; she was feeble, and afraid of a chill. Wish to go she of course had none; and though Lady Harriet wrote warmly pressing letters, she insisted on remaining at home. Carlyle went, but if he describes his condition correctly, he could hardly have been an agreeable guest. For him there was no peace but in work, and life in such houses was organised idleness. To his mother he speaks of himself as wandering disconsolately on the shore watching the gangs of Portsmouth convicts; to his wife as *"unslept,* dyspeptic, bewildered."[20] He was worried, he said, with "the idleness, the folly, the cackling and noise." Milnes was his best resource. Milnes had come, and the Taylors and Bullers and Bear Ellice, and the usual circle; but it would not do. He was sickly, dispirited, unwell. "We are a pretty society, but a distracted one. Ten days of such, with a cold to help, is about enough, *I guess!"*[21]

Enough it proved; he could stand no more of it, and fled home. But it is impossible not to ask "What was Carlyle doing in such a galley?" Why was he there at all?[22] It is with real relief that I approach the end of the half-enchanted state into which he had fallen after *Cromwell.* It had been a trying time, both for his wife and for him.

Some time while the Jew Bill was before Parliament, and the fate of it doubtful, Baron Rothschild wrote to ask him to write a pamphlet in its favour, and intimated that he might name any sum which he liked to ask as payment. I inquired how he had answered. "Well," he said, "I had to tell him it couldn't be; but I observed, too, that I could not conceive why he and his friends, who were supposed to be looking out for the coming of Shiloh, should be seeking seats in a Gentile legislature." I asked what Baron Rothschild had said to that. "Why," Carlyle said, "he seemed to think the coming of Shiloh was a dubious business, and that meanwhile, &c. &c."

The Journal had remained almost a blank for four years,

EDWARD ELLICE. The Carlyles frequently met "Bear" Ellice, Whig politician and M.P., at the Ashburtons'. The nickname of "Bear" derives not from his ferocity but from his connection with the Northwest fur trade. Carlyle termed this photograph "very like." (Courtesy of the Columbia University Libraries.)

only a few trifling notes having been jotted down in it, but it now contains a long and extremely interesting entry. The real Carlyle is to be especially looked for in this book, for it contains his dialogues with his own heart.

> Schemes of *Books* (to be now set about? alas!)
> *Exodus from Houndsditch.* That, alas! is *im*possible as yet; tho' it is the gist of all writings and wise books, I sometimes think; the goal to be wisely aimed at, as the first of all for us. Out of Houndsditch, indeed:—ah *were* we but *out,* and had our own along with us! But they that come out hitherto, come in a state of brutal nakedness; scandalous mutilation; and impartial bystanders say sorrowfully, "Return, rather; it is better even to return!"[23]

The Exodus from Houndsditch Carlyle saw to be then impossible—impossible; and yet the essential preliminary of true spiritual recovery. The "Hebrew old clothes"[24] were attached so closely to pious natures that to tear off the wrapping would be to leave their souls to perish in spiritual nakedness; and were so bound up with the national moral convictions that the sense of duty could not be separated from a belief in the technical inspiration of the Bible. And yet Carlyle knew that it could do no good to anyone to believe what was untrue; and he knew also that since science had made known to us the real relation between this globe of ours and the stupendous universe, no man whose mind and heart were sound could any longer sincerely believe in the Christian creed. The most that such a man could arrive at was to persuade himself by refined reasonings that it might perhaps be true, that it could not be proved false, and that therefore he might profess it openly from the lips outwards with a clear conscience. But the convictions which govern the practical lives of men are not remote possibilities, but concrete certainties. As long as the "Holy Place" in their souls is left in possession of powerless opinions, they are practically without God in this world. The "wealth of nations" comes to mean material abundance, and individual duty an obligation to make money; while intellect, not caring to waste itself on shadows, constructs philosophies to show that God is no necessity at all. Carlyle's faith, on the other hand, was that without a spiritual belief—a belief in a Divine Being, in the knowledge of whom and obedience to whom mortal welfare alone consisted—the human race must degenerate into brutes. He longed, therefore, that the windows of the shrine should be washed clean, and the light of heaven let into it. The longer the acknowledgment of the facts regarding inspiration, etc., was delayed, the more hollow grew the established creeds, the falser the professional advocates of the creeds, the more ungodly the life and philosophy of the world.

Why, then, did he find it *im*possible to speak plainly on this momentous subject? Because, as he had said of the poor priests at Bruges, because, false as they were, there was nothing to take their places if they were cast out by the Gospel of Progress, which was falser even than they.[25] God Himself would in due time build a new temple for Himself above the ruins of the old beliefs. He himself, meanwhile, would do ill to wound simple hearts like that of his poor old mother. His resolution was often hardly tested. Often he would exclaim fiercely against "detestable idolatries." Often, on the appearance of some more than usually insincere episcopal manifesto, he would wish the Bishops and all their works dead as Etruscan soothsayers. But the other mood was the more prevalent. He spoke to me once with loathing of Renan's *Vie de Jêsus*. I asked if he thought a true life could be written. He said, "Yes, certainly, if it were right to do it; but it is not."

The Exodus, nevertheless, always lay before him as a thing that would have to be, if men were ever to recover their spiritual stature. "The ancient mythologies (religions)," he says in his Journal, "were merely religious readings of the Histories of Antiquity,—genial apprehensions and genial (that is always *divine*) representations of the Events of Earthly Life,—such as occur yet, only that we have no 'geniality' to take them up with, nothing but stupidity to take them up with! . . . *Exodus from Houndsditch* I believe to be the first beginning of such deliverance."[26]

Almost forty years have passed since these words were written, and we still wait to be delivered. Nay, some think that we need no deliverance—"upward and back to their fountains the sacred rivers are stealing."[27] The water of life is again flowing in the old fountains. It may be so. The

Ark of the Church has been repainted and gilded and decorated, and with architecture and coloured windows, and choral services, and incense, and candlesticks, and symbolic uniforms for mystic officiators, seemingly the dying body has been electrified into a semblance of animation. Is this life or merely galvanism? There are other signs not favourable to the pretensions of the Church revivalists. The air has cleared. It is no longer a sin to say what one thinks, and power no longer weights the scale in favour of orthodoxy. Forty years ago the law said to a clergyman, "You shall teach what the formulas prescribe, whether you believe it or not, and you shall stay at your post, even though you know that you disbelieve it; for you shall enter no other profession; you shall teach this, or you shall starve." That is gone, and much else is gone. Men are allowed to think and speak as they will without being punished by social ostracism. Truth must stand henceforth by its own strength, and what is really incredible will cease to be believed. Very much of the change in this happy direction is due to Carlyle's influence; in this direction, and perhaps also in the other, for every serious man, of every shade of opinion, had to thank him for the loud trumpet notes which had awakened the age out of its sleep.

One or other of the subjects for a new book on which we saw Carlyle to be meditating would probably have been now selected, when suddenly, like a bolt out of the sky, came the Revolution of February 24 at Paris. The other nations of Europe followed suit, the kings, as Carlyle expressed it, "running about like a gang of coiners when the police had come among them." Ireland blazed out. English Chartists talked of "physical force." The air seemed charged with lightning, threatening the foundations of modern society. So extraordinary a phenomenon surprised Carlyle less than it surprised most of his contemporaries. It confirmed what he had been saying for many years. The universal dungheap had caught fire again. Imposture was bankrupt once more, and "shams" this time, it was to be hoped, would be finished off in earnest. He did not believe in immediate convulsion in England; but he did believe that, unless England took warning and mended her ways, her turn would come.

The state of Europe was too interesting and too obscure to permit composure for writing. For the four months of that spring, the papers each morning announced some fresh convulsion, and the coolest thinkers could only look on and watch. When the Young Ireland deputation went to Paris to ask the Provisional Government to give a lift to the Irish Republic, war with France was at one moment on the cards.

London parties in an "era of revolutions" were excited and exciting. The leading men came out with their opinions with less reserve. Carlyle had frequently met Macaulay in drawing-rooms; but they had rather avoided each other. He had been much struck, many years before, with the "Essay on Milton"; indeed to the last he always spoke respectfully of Macaulay; but when two men of positive temperament hold views diametrically opposite, and neither can entertain even a suspicion that the other may accidentally be right, conversation between them is usually disagreeable. Thus they had not sought for any closer acquaintance, and common friends had not tried to bring them together. It happened now and then, however, that they were guests at the same table.

> Friday last at Lord Mahon's to breakfast: Macaulay, Lord and Lady Ashley &c. there. Niagara of eloquent commonplace talk from Macaulay: "very goodnatured man"; man cased in official mail of proof; stood my impatient fire-explosions with much patience, merely hissing a little steam up, and continued his Niagara —supply-and-demand, power ruinous to powerful himself, *impossibility* of Government doing more than keep the peace, suicidal distraction of new French Republic &c &c. Essentially irremediable *commonplace* nature of the man: all that ever was in him now gone to the tongue. A squat, thickset, low-browed, short, and now rather potbellied, grizzled little man of fifty: these be thy gods, O Israel![28]

A far more interesting meeting was with Sir Robert Peel, "one of the few men in England whom I have still any curiosity to see."[29] Peel had known him by sight since the present of *Cromwell*, and had given him looks of recognition when they met in the streets. The Barings brought about a personal acquaintance, which increased till Peel's death. It began at a dinner at Bath House.

> Went also to the Peel enterprise; sat next Sir Robert;—an evening

not unpleasant to remember. Peel is a finely made man; of strong, not heavy, rather of elegant, stature; stands straight, head slightly thrown back, and eyelids modestly drooping: every way mild and gentle, yet with less of that fixed smile than the portraits give him. He is towards sixty; and, tho' not broken at all, carries, especially in his complexion when you are *near* him, marks of that age. Clear strong blue eyes, which *kindle* on occasion. Voice extremely good; low-toned, something of *cooing* in it, rustic-affectionate, honest, mildly persuasive. Spoke about French Revolutions, new and old; well read in all that; had *seen* General Dumouriez &c. Reserved, seemingly by nature; obtrudes nothing of *diplomatic* reserve. On the contrary, a vein of mild *fun* in him; real sensibility to the ludicrous; which feature I liked best of all: nothing in that slight inspection, seemed to promise better in him than his laugh. . . . Shall I see the Premier again? I consider him by far our first Public Man, which indeed is saying little; and hope that England, in these frightful times, may still get some good of him.[30]

Not seeing his way to a book upon Democracy, Carlyle wrote a good many newspaper articles this spring; chiefly in the *Examiner* and the *Spectator*, to deliver his soul. Even Fonblanque and Rintoul (the editors), friendly though they were to him, could not allow him his full swing. "There is no established journal," he said, "that can stand my articles, no single one they would not blow the bottom out of." More than ever he wished to have some periodical of his own, which would belong to no party, and where he could hit out all around.

The theory that the title of governments in this world is "the consent of the governed" will lead by-and-by, if it lasts long enough, to very curious conclusions. As a theory it was held even in 1848 by speculative Liberal thinkers; but the old English temper was still dominant whenever there was necessity for action. Parliament was still able and willing to pass a Treason Felony Act through its three readings in one afternoon, and teach Chartists and Irish rebels that these islands were not to be swept into the Revolution. But that spirit, Carlyle saw, must abate with the development of Democracy. The will of the people, shifting and uncertain as the weather, would make an end of authoritative action. And yet such a government as he desired to see could be the product only of revolution of another kind. He said often that the Roman Republic was allowed so long a day because on emergencies the constitution was suspended by a dictatorship. Dictatorships might end as they ended at Rome, in becoming perpetual—and to this he would not have objected, if the right man could be found; but he was alone in his opinion, and for the time it was useless to speak of such a mighty transformation scene.

The spring wore on, and the early summer came, and all eyes were watching, sometimes France and sometimes Ireland. Events followed swiftly in Paris. The government fell into the hands of the Party of Order, the moderate Republicans; and the workmen, who had been struggling for the "organisation of labour," determined to fight for it. Out of this came the three tremendous days of June, the sternest battle ever fought in a modern city.

Emerson's curiosity had taken him to Paris in May, to see how Progress and Liberty were getting on. He had visited Oxford also, where he had been entertained at Oriel by my dear friend, Arthur Clough. He had breakfasted in Common Room, where several of us were struck by a likeness in his face to that of one once so familiar in the same spot, who had passed now into another fold—John Henry Newman.[31] Figure and features were both like Newman's. He was like a ghost of Newman born into a new element. The Oxford visit over, Emerson went back to London to finish his lectures. I heard the last of them (at the Polytechnic, I think), and there first saw Carlyle, whom Clough pointed out to me. We were sitting close behind him, and I had no sight of his face; but I heard his loud, kindly, contemptuous laugh when the lecturer ended; for, indeed, what Emerson said was, in Carlyle's word, "rather moonshiny."[32]

He was to sail for Boston in the week following. Before he left, he and Carlyle went on a small expedition together into Wiltshire, to look at Stonehenge—they two, the latest products of modern thought, and Stonehenge, the silent monument of an age all trace of which, save that one circle of stone, has perished.[33]

The sun of freedom which had risen so augustly on February 24 had been swiftly clouded. Carlyle had not expected definite good from it, and ought not to have been disappointed; yet he had not looked for a collapse so swift and so complete. He had thought that something would have been gained for poor mankind from such a breakdown of sham governments. Europe had revolted against them, but the earthquake, alas! had been transient. The sham powers, temporal and spiritual, had been shaken in their seats; but the shock passed, and they had crept back again. Cant, insincerity, imposture, and practical injustice ruled once more in the name of order. He was not entirely cast down. He was still convinced that so wild a burst of passion must have meant something, and the "something" in time would be seen; but the fog had settled back thick as before, probably for another long interval. Before two years were over, France saw Louis Napoleon and the Second Empire, with the Catholic Church supporting. French bayonets again propped up the Pope, who, in the strength of them, was to declare himself infallible. England rested contented with Laissez-faire and the "Dismal Science." In Ireland were famine and famine-fever; for remedy an Encumbered Estates Act; whole villages unroofed by fire or crowbar; two millions of the miserable people flying across the Atlantic with curses on the Anglo-Saxon in their mouths; the Anglo-Saxons themselves blessing Providence for ridding them so cheaply of the Irish difficulty. He saw clearly enough that there was no cure here for the diseases of which modern society was sick. Behind an order so restored could grow only the elements of mischief to come, and he was sickened at the self-satisfied complaisance with which the upper classes in England and everywhere welcomed the victory of the reaction. The day of reckoning would come whether they believed it or not, and the longer judgement was delayed the heavier it would be. They had another chance allowed them, that was all.

What Carlyle could do or say it was not easy for him to decide. No advice of his would find attention in the existing humour. the turn which things were taking, the proved impotence of English Chartism especially, seemed to justify the impatience with which practical politicians had hitherto listened to him. It would be a waste of words to go

471

on denouncing "shams" when "shams" everywhere were receiving a new lease of life. He stayed in London through the summer, Mrs. Carlyle with him, but doing nothing.

In all humours, light or heavy, he could count on the unshaken affection of his friends the Barings. A change in this last year had passed over their worldly situation. The old Lord had died in May, and Mr. Baring was now Lord Ashburton.

In September there was to be a great gathering of distinguished persons at the Grange under its new ownership, and the Carlyles, as this year he had not gone to Scotland, were invited for a long autumn visit. He hesitated to join the brilliant circle. "There are Marquises of Landsdown Ministers &c &c talked of; but I have found by experience *they* do not differ from little people, except in the *clothing and mounting.*"[34] He went, however, and his wife went with him.

Charles Buller was at the party at the Grange, brilliant as usual. In this winter he suddenly died through the blundering of an unskilful surgeon. Buller was one of the few real friends that Carlyle had left in the world, and was cut off in this sudden way just when the highest political distinctions were coming within his reach. His witty humour had for a time made his prospects doubtful. The House of Commons likes to be amused, but does not raise its jesters into Cabinets. Buller said he owed his success to Peel. He had been going on in his usual way one night when Peel said, "If the honourable member for Liskeard will cease for a moment from making a buffoon of himself, I will, &c." For these sharp words Buller was for ever grateful to Peel. He achieved afterwards the highest kind of Parliamentary reputation. A great career had opened before him, and now it was ended. Carlyle felt his loss deeply. He wrote a most beautiful elegy, which was published in the *Examiner*[35] in time for Buller's poor mother to read it. Then she died, too, of pure grief. Her husband had gone before, and the family with whom Carlyle had once been so intimately connected came to an end together.[36] It was a sad season altogether.

The winter went by with no work accomplished or begun, beyond the revising *Cromwell* for a third edition, as it

472

was still selling rapidly. "I find the Book is well liked," he could say, "and silently making its way into the heart of the country; which is a result I am very thankful for."[37]

The book had been too well liked, indeed; for it had created a set of enthusiastic admirers who wanted now to have a statue of the great Protector, or, at least, some public memorial of him. Carlyle was of Cato's opinion in that matter. He preferred that men should rather ask where Oliver's statue was than see it as one of the anomalous images which are scattered over the metropolis.

Ireland, of all the topics on which he had meditated writing, remained painfully fascinating. He had looked at the beggarly scene, he had seen the blighted fields, the ragged misery of the wretched race who were suffering for others' sins as well as for their own. Since that brief visit of his the famine had been followed by the famine-fever, and the flight of millions from a land which was smitten with a curse. Those ardent young men with whom he had dined at Dundrum were working as felons in the docks at Bermuda. Gavan Duffy, after a near escape from the same fate, had been a guest in Cheyne Row; and the story which he had to tell of cabins torn down by crowbars, and shivering families, turned out of their miserable homes, dying in the ditches by the roadside, had touched Carlyle to the very heart. He was furious at the economical commonplaces with which England was consoling itself. He regarded Ireland as "the *breaking* point of the huge suppuration which all British and all European society now is."[38] He determined to see it again, look at it further and more fully, "that ragged body of a diseased soul," and then write something about it which might move his country into a better sense of its obligations. So earnest he was that he struggled seriously to find some plainer form of speech, better suited to the world's comprehension, which they might read, not to wonder at, but to take to their hearts for practical guidance.

It was while Carlyle was preparing for an Irish tour that I myself became first personally acquainted with him. He had heard of me from Arthur Clough, who left Oxford when I left it. We had felt, both of us, that, thinking as we did, we were out of place in an Article-signing

JAMES ANTHONY FROUDE. Froude read Carlyle's major works in the early 1840s, fell under his influence, but did not meet him until June 1849—a meeting graphically related in the biography. He became, with Ruskin, the most steadfast of Carlyle's disciples. Carlyle told Emerson in 1872 that Froude was "the valuablest Friend I now have in England." (Courtesy of the Columbia University Libraries.)

University, and we had resigned our Fellowships. Of Clough Carlyle had formed the very highest opinion, as no one who knew him could fail to do. His pure beautiful character, his genial humour, his perfect truthfulness, alike of heart and intellect—an integrity which had led him to sacrifice a distinguished position and brilliant prospects, and had brought him to London to gather a living as he could from under the hoofs of the horses in the streets—these together had recommended Clough to Carlyle as a diamond sifted out of the general rubbish-heap. Of me, with good reason, he was inclined to think far less favourably. I had written something, not wisely, in which heterodoxy was flavoured with the sentimentalism which he so intensely detested.[39] He had said of me that I ought to burn my own smoke, and not trouble other people's nostrils with it. Nevertheless, he was willing to see what I was like. James Spedding took me down to Cheyne Row one evening in the middle of June. We found him sitting after dinner, with his pipe, in the small flagged court between the house and the garden. He was studying without much satisfaction the Life of St. Patrick by Jocelyn of Ferns in the *Acta Sanctorum*. He was trying to form a notion of what Ireland had been like before Danes or Saxons had meddled with it, when it was said to have been the chosen home of learning and piety, and had sent out missionaries to convert Northern Europe. His author was not assisting him. The Life of St. Patrick as given by Jocelyn is as much a biography of a real man as the story of Jack the Giant-killer. When we arrived Carlyle had just been reading how an Irish marauder had stolen a goat and eaten it, and the Saint had convicted him by making the goat bleat in his stomach. He spoke of it with rough disgust; and then we talked of Ireland generally, of which I had some local knowledge.

He was then fifty-four years old; tall (about five feet eleven), thin, but at that time upright with no signs of the later stoop. His body was angular, his face beardless, such as it is represented in Woolner's medallion, which is by far the best likeness of him in the days of his strength. His head was extremely long, with the chin thrust forward; the neck was thin; the mouth firmly closed, the under lip

CARLYLE IN 1851. This medallion by Thomas Woolner, the sculptor-poet of the Pre-Raphaelite movement, captures the projecting lower lip—a physiognomical trait Carlyle valued as signifying grit and determination. The medallion recalls Lady Eastlake's description of Carlyle: "The head of a thinker, the eye of a lover, and the mouth of a peasant." Froude thought it "by far the best likeness of him in the days of his strength." (Courtesy of the Scottish National Portrait Gallery.)

slightly projecting; the hair grizzled and thick and bushy. His eyes, which grew lighter with age, were then of a deep violet,[40] with fire burning at the bottom of them, which flashed out at the least excitement. The face was altogether more striking, most impressive every way. And I did not admire him the less because he treated me—I cannot say unkindly, but shortly and sternly. I saw then what I saw ever after—that no one need look for conventional politeness from Carlyle—he would hear the exact truth from him, and nothing else.

We went afterwards into the dining-room, where Mrs.

Carlyle gave us tea. Her features were not regular, but I thought I had never seen a more interesting-looking woman. Her hair was raven black, her eyes dark, soft, sad, with dangerous light in them. Carlyle's talk was rich, full, and scornful; hers delicately mocking. She was fond of Spedding, and kept up a quick, sparkling conversation with him, telling stories at her husband's expense, at which he laughed himself as heartily as we did.

It struck me then, and I found always afterwards, that false sentiment, insincerity, cant of any kind would find no quarter, either from wife or husband; and that one must speak truth only, and, if possible, think truth only, if one wished to be admitted into that house on terms of friendship. They told me that I might come again. I did not then live in London, and had few opportunities; but if the chance offered, I never missed it.[41]

chapter twenty-four

1849–1850

Second Tour of Ireland. *Latter-Day Pamphlets.* Peel and Wellington

Carlyle's purpose of writing a book on Ireland was not to be fulfilled. He went thither. He travelled through the four provinces. After his return he jotted down a hurried account of his experiences; but that was all the contribution which he was able to make for the solution of a problem which he found at once too easy and too hopeless. Ireland is an enchanted country. There is a land ready, as any land ever was, to answer to cultivation. There is a people ready to cultivate it, to thrive, and cover the surface of it with happy, prosperous homes, if ruled, like other nations, by methods which suit their temperament. If the Anglo-Saxons had set about governing Ireland with the singleness of aim with which they govern India or build their own railways, a few seasons at any time would have seen the end of its misery and discontent. But the Anglo-Saxons have never approached Ireland in any such spirit. They have had the welfare of Ireland on their lips. In their hearts they have thought only of England's welfare, or of what in some narrow prejudice they deemed to be such, of England's religious interests, commercial interests, political interests. So it was when Henry II set up Popery there. So it was when Elizabeth set up the Protestant Establishment there. So it is now when the leaders of the English Liberals again destroy that Establishment to secure the Irish votes to their party in Parliament.[1] The curse which has made that wretched island the world's by-word is not in Ireland in itself, but in the inability of its conquerors to recognise that, if they take away a nation's liberty, they may not use it as the plaything of their own selfishness or their own factions. For seven hundred years they have followed on the same lines: the principle the same, however opposite the action. As it was in the days of Strongbow, so it is to-day; and "healing measures," ushered in no matter with what pomp of eloquence or parade of justice, remain, and will remain, a mockery. Carlyle soon saw how it was. To write on Ireland, as if a remedy could be found there, while the poisonous fountain still flowed at Westminster unpurified, would be labour vain as spinning ropes of moonshine. He noted down what he had seen, and then dismissed the unhappy subject from his mind; giving his manuscript to a friend as something of which he desired to hear no more for ever. It was published after his death,[2] and the briefest summary of what to himself had no value is all that need concern us here. He left London on the 30th of June in a Dublin steamboat. He could sleep sound at sea, and therefore preferred "long sea" to land when the choice was offered him. Running past the Isle of Wight, he saw in the distance Sterling's house at Ventnor; he saw Plymouth, Falmouth, the Land's End. Then, crossing St. George's Channel, he came on the Irish coast at Wexford, where the chief scenes of the Rebellion of 1798 stand clear against the sky.

At Dublin he met Gavan Duffy again; stayed several days; saw various notabilities—Petrie, the antiquarian, among others whose high merit he at once recognised; declined an invitation from the Viceroy, and on the 8th (a Sunday), Dublin and the neighbourhood being done with, he started for the south.

Owing to the magic companionship of Mr. Duffy, he met and talked freely with priests and patriots. Lord Monteagle's introductions secured him attention from the Anglo-Irish gentry. He was entertained at the Castle at Lismore, saw Waterford, Youghal, Castlemartyr, and then Cork, where he encountered "one of the *two* sons of Adam" who, "some 15 years ago had . . . with Emerson of America" "encouraged poor bookseller Fraser, and didn't discourage him, to go *on* with '*Teufelsdröckh*,' "[3]

479

a priest, a Father O'Shea, to whom for this at least he was grateful.

Killarney was the next stage; beauty and squalor there, as everywhere, sadly linked to one another. Near Killarney he stayed with Sir William Beecher and his interesting wife;[4] good people, but strong upholders of the Anglo-Irish Church, which, however great its merits otherwise, had made little of missionary work among the Catholic Celts. He wished well to all English institutions in Ireland, but he had a fixed conviction that the Anglo-Catholic Church at least, both there and everywhere, was unequal to its work.

Limerick, Clare, Lough Derg on the Shannon, Galway, Castlebar, Westport—these were the successive points of the journey. At Westport was a workhouse and "human swinery has here reached its *acme*: 30,000 paupers in this union, population supposed to be about 60,000. . . . Abomination of desolation; what *can* you make of it!"[5] Thence, through the dreariest parts of Mayo, he drove on to Ballina, where he found Forster, of Rawdon, waiting for him—W. E. Forster, then young and earnest, and eager to master in Carlyle's company the enigma which he took in hand as Chief Secretary three years ago (1881, etc.), with what success the world by this time knows.[6] Carlyle, at least, is not responsible for the failure, certain as mathematics, of the Irish Land Act. Forster perhaps discovered at the time that he would find little to suit him in Carlyle's views of the matter. They soon parted. Carlyle hastened on to Donegal to see a remarkable experiment which was then being attempted there. Lord George Hill was endeavouring to show at Gweedore that, with proper resources of intellect, energy, and money wisely expended, a section of Ireland could be lifted out of its misery even under the existing conditions of English administration.

His distinct conclusion was that this too, like all else of the kind, was building a house out of sand. He went to Gweedore; he stayed with Lord George; he saw all that he was doing or trying to do, and he perceived, with a clearness which the event has justified, that the persuasive charitable method of raising lost men out of the dirt and leading them of their own accord into the ways that they should go, was, in Ireland at least, doomed to fail from the beginning.

It would be interesting to compare Carlyle's tour, or any modern tour, in Ireland, with Arthur Young's, something over a hundred years ago—before Grattan's constitution, the Volunteers, the glorious liberties of 1782, Catholic emancipation, and the rest that has followed. Carlyle found but one Lord George Hill hopelessly struggling with impossibilities; Arthur Young found not one, but many peers and gentlemen working effectively in the face of English discouragement: draining, planting, building, making large districts, now all "gone back to bog" again, habitable by human beings, and successfully accomplishing at least a part of the work which they were set to do. All that is not waste and wilderness in Ireland is really the work of these poor men.

From Gweedore to Derry was an easy journey. There his travels were to end; he was to find a steamer which would take him to Scotland. Five weeks had passed since he landed.

On the 7th, Carlyle was in his own land again, having left the "huge suppuration"[7] to suppurate more and more till it burst, he feeling that any true speech upon it would be like speaking to deaf winds.

His wife had meanwhile gone to Scotland on her own account. She had spent three singularly interesting days at Haddington (which she has herself described),[8] where she wandered like a returned spirit about the home of her childhood. She had gone thence to her relations at Auchtertool, in Fife, and was there staying when her husband was at Gweedore.

Carlyle stayed quiet at Scotsbrig, meditating on the break-down of the proposed Irish book, and uncertain what he should turn to instead. He had promised to join the Ashburtons in the course of the autumn at a Highland shooting-box. Shooting parties were out of his line altogether, but perhaps he did not object to seeing for once what such a thing was like. Scotsbrig, too, was not agreeing with him.

He remained there till the end of August, and then

481

started on his expedition. Glen Truim, to which he was bound, was in the far North, in Macpherson of Clunie's country. The railroad was yet unfinished, and the journey —long and tedious—had to be transacted by coach. He was going against the grain. Perhaps his wife thought that he would have done more wisely to decline. He stopped on the way at Auchtertool to see her; "had," he says, "a miserable enough hugger-mugger time. My own blame; none others' so much—saw that always."[9] Certainly, as the event proved, he would have been better off out of the way of the "gunner bodies."[10] If he was miserable in Fife, he was far from happy with his grand friends in Glen Truim.

The Ashburtons were as attentive to Carlyle's peculiarities as it was possible to be. No prince's confessor, in the ages of faith, could have more consideration shown him than he in this restricted mansion. The best apartment was made over to him as soon as it was vacant. A special dinner was arranged for him at his own hour. But he was out of his element. "Patientia! I have known now what Highland shooting-paradises are; and one experiment, I should think, will be about enough!"[11]

Poor "shooting paradise"! It answered the purpose it was intended for. Work, even to the aristocracy, is exacting in these days. Pleasure is even more exacting; and unless they could rough it now and then in primitive fashion and artificial plainness of living, they would sink under the burden of their splendours and the weariness of their duties. Carlyle had no business in such a scene. He never fired off a gun in his life. He never lived in habitual luxury, and therefore could not enjoy the absence of common conveniences. He was out of humour with what he saw. He was out of humour with himself for being a part of it. Three weeks of solitude at Scotsbrig, to which he hastened to retreat, scarcely repaired his sufferings at Glen Truim.

The three months of holiday were thus spent—strange holidays. But a man carries his shadow clinging to him, and cannot part with it, except in a novel.[12] He was now driven by accumulation of discontent to disburden his heart of its secretions. During the last two revolutionary years he had covered many sheets with his reflections. At the bottom of his whole nature lay abhorrence of falsehood. To see facts as they actually were, and, if that was impossible, at least to desire to see them, to be sincere with his own soul, and to speak to others exactly what he himself believed, was to him the highest of all human duties. Therefore he detested cant with a perfect hatred. Cant was organised hypocrisy, the art of making things seem what they were not; an art so deadly that it killed the very souls of those who practised it, carrying them beyond the stage of conscious falsehood into a belief in their own illusions, and reducing them to the wretchedest of possible conditions, that of being sincerely insincere. With cant of this kind he saw all Europe, all America, overrun; but beyond all, his own England appeared to him to be drenched in cant—cant religious, cant political, cant moral, cant artistic, cant everywhere and in everything.

Religion, a religion that was true, meant a rule of conduct according to the law of God. Religion, as it existed in England, had become a thing of opinion, of emotion flowing over into benevolence as an imagined substitute for justice. Over the conduct of men in their ordinary business it had ceased to operate at all, and therefore, to Carlyle, it was a hollow appearance, a word without force or controlling power in it Religion was obligation, a command which bound men to duty, as something which they were compelled to do under tremendous penalties. The modern world, even the religious part of it, had supposed that the grand aim was to abolish compulsion, to establish universal freedom, leaving each man to the light of his own conscience or his own will. Freedom—that was the word—the glorious birthright which, once realised, was to turn earth into paradise. And this was cant; and those who were loudest about it could not themselves believe it, but could only pretend to believe it. In a conditioned existence like ours, freedom was impossible. To the race as a race, the alternative was work or starvation—all were bound to work in their several ways; some must work or all would die; and the result of the boasted political liberty was an arrangement where the cunning or the strong appropriated the lion's share of the harvest without working, while the multitude lived on by toil, and toiled to get the means of living. That was the actual outcome of the doctrine of liberty, as seen in existing society; nor in fact to any kind of man any-where was freedom possible in the popular sense of the word. Each one of us was compassed round with restric-tions on his personal will, and the wills even of the strong-est were slaves to inclination. The serf whose visible fetters were struck off was a serf still under the law of nature. He might change his master, but a master he must have of some kind, or die; and to speak of "emancipation" in and by itself, as any mighty gain or step in progress, was the wildest of illusions. No "progress" would or could be made on the lines of Radicals or philanthropists. The "liberty," the only liberty, attainable by the multitude of ignorant mortals, was in being guided or else compelled by some one wiser than themselves. They gained nothing if they ex-changed the bondage to man for bondage to the devil. It was assumed in the talk of the day that "emancipation" created manliness, self-respect, improvement of character. To Carlyle, who looked at facts, all this was wind. Those "grinders," for instance, whom he had seen in that Man-chester cellar, earning high wages, that they might live merrily for a year or two, and die at the end of them—were they improved?[13] Was freedom to kill themselves for drink such a blessed thing? Were they really better off than slaves who were at least as well cared for as their master's cattle? The cant on this subject enraged him. He, starting from the other *pole*, believing not in the rights of man, but in the duties of man, could see nothing in it but detestable selfishness disguised in the plumage of angels—a shameful substitute for the neglect of the human ties by which man was bound to man. *"Facit indignatio versum* [Indignation makes the verse]."[14] Wrath with the things which he saw around him inspired the Roman poet; wrath drove Carlyle into writing the *Latter-Day Pamphlets*.

A paper on the Negro or Nigger question, properly the first of the *Latter-Day Pamphlets*, was Carlyle's declara-tion of war against modern Radicalism.[15] Hitherto, though his orthodoxy was questionable, and Radicals had been glad to claim him as belonging to them; and if Radicalism meant an opinion that modern society required to be reconstituted from the root, he had been, was, and remained the most thoroughgoing of them all. His objection was to the cant of Radicalism; the philosophy of it, bred of "Philanthropic Liberalism and the Dismal Science,"[16] the purport of which was to cast the atoms of human society adrift, mocked with the name of liberty, to sink or swim as they could. Negro emancipation had been the special boast and glory of the new theory of universal happiness. The twenty millions of indemnity and the free West Indies had been chanted and celebrated for a quarter of a century from press and platform. Weekly, almost daily, the English newspapers were crowing over the Americans, flinging in their teeth the Declaration of Independence, blowing up in America itself a flame which was ripening towards a furious war, while the result of the experiment so far had been the material ruin of colonies once the most precious that we had, and the moral ruin of the blacks themselves, who were rotting away in sensuous idleness amidst the wrecks of the plantations. He was touching the shield with the point of his lance when he chose this sacredly sensitive subject for his first onslaught. He did not mean that the "Niggers" should have been kept as cattle, and sold as cattle at their owners' pleasure. He did mean that they ought to have been treated as human beings, for whose souls and bodies the whites were responsible; that they should have been placed in a position suited to their capacity, like that of the English serf under the Plantagenets; protected against ill-usage by law; attached to the soil; not allowed to be idle, but cared for themselves, their wives and their children, in health, in sickness, and in old age.

He said all this; but he said it fiercely, scornfully, in the tone which could least conciliate attention. Black Quashee and his friends were spattered with ridicule which stung the more from the justice of it.

I once asked Carlyle if he had ever thought of going into Parliament, for I knew that the opportunity must have been offered him. "Well," he said. "I did think of it at the time of the *Latter-Day Pamphlets*. I felt that nothing could prevent me from getting up in the House and saying all that." He was powerful, but he was not powerful *enough* to have discharged with his single voice the vast volume of conventional electricity with which the collective wisdom of the nation was, and remains, charged. It is better that his

485

thoughts should have been committed to enduring print, where they remain to be reviewed hereafter by the light of fact.

The article on the "Nigger question" gave, as might have been expected, universal offence. Many of his old admirers drew back after this, and "walked no more with him." John Mill replied fiercely in the same magazine.[17] They had long ceased to be intimate; they were henceforth "rent asunder," not to be again united. Each went his own course; but neither Mill nor Carlyle forgot that they had once been friends, and each to the last spoke of the other with affectionate regret.

The *Pamphlets* commenced at the beginning of 1850, and went on month after month, each separately published, no magazine daring to become responsible for them. The first was on "The Present Time," on the advent and prospects of Democracy. The revolutions of 1848 had been the bankruptcy of falsehood, "a universal tumbling of Impostors and of Impostures into the street!"[18] The problem left before the world was how nations were hereafter to be governed. The English people imagined that it could be done by "suffrages" and the ballot-box; a system under which St. Paul and Judas Iscariot would each have an equal vote, and one would have as much power as the other. This was like saying that when a ship was going on a voyage round the world the crew were to be brought together to elect their own officers, and vote the course which was to be followed.

> Unanimity on board ship;—yes, indeed, the ship's crew may be very unanimous, which doubtless, for the time being, will be very comfortable to the ship's crew, and to their Phantasm Captain if they have one: but if the tack they unanimously steer upon is guiding them into the belly of the Abyss, it will not profit them much!—Ships accordingly do not use the ballot-box at all; and they reject the Phantasm species of Captains: one wishes much some other Entities,—*since all entities lie under the same rigorous set of laws*,—could be brought to show as much wisdom, and sense at least of self-preservation, the *first* command of Nature.[19]

The words in italics contain the essence of Carlyle's teaching. If they are true, the inference is equally true that in Democracy there can be no finality. If the laws are fixed under which nations are allowed to prosper, men fittest by capacity and experience to read those laws must be placed in command, and the ballot-box never will and never can select the fittest; it will select the *sham* fittest, or the *un*fittest. The suffrage, the right of every man to a voice in the selection of his rulers, was, and is, the first article of the Radical Magna Charta, the *articulus-stantis vel cadentis Reipublicae* [the article of the standing, or falling, republic], and is so accepted by every modern Liberal statesman. Carlyle met it with a denial as complete and scornful as Luther flung at Tetzel and his Indulgences —not, however, with the same approval from those whom he addressed. Luther found the grass dry and ready to kindle. The belief which Carlyle assailed was alive and green with hope and vigour.

The second pamphlet, on "Model Prisons," was as savage as the first. Society, conscious at heart that it was itself unjust, and did not mean to mend itself, was developing out of its uneasiness a universal "Scoundrel Protection" sentiment. Society was concluding that inequalities of condition were inevitable; that those who suffered under them, and rebelled, could not fairly be punished, but were to be looked upon as misguided brethren suffering under mental disorders, to be cured in moral hospitals, called by euphemism Houses of Correction. "Pity for human calamity," the pamphlet said, "is very beautiful; but the deep oblivion of the Law of Right and Wrong; this indiscriminate mashing-up of Right and Wrong into a patent treacle' of the Philanthropic movement, is by no means beautiful at all."[20]

Wishing to see the system at work with his own eyes, Carlyle had visited the Millbank Penitentiary. He found 1,200 prisoners, "notable murderesses among them," in airy apartments of perfect cleanliness, comfortably warmed and clothed, quietly, and not too severely, picking oakum; their diet, bread, soup, meat, all superlatively excellent. He saw a literary Chartist rebel in a private court, master of his own time and spiritual resources; and he felt that he himself, "so left with paper and ink, and all taxes and botherations shut-out from me, could have written such a Book as no reader will here ever get of me." He looked at felon after felon. He saw "ape-faces, imp-faces, angry dog-faces, heavy sullen ox-faces; degraded under-foot perverse creatures, sons of *in*docility, greedy mutinous darkness." To give the owners of such faces their "due" could be attempted only where there was an effort to give every one his due, and to be fair all round; and as this was not to be thought of, they were to be reclaimed by "the method of love." "Hopeless forevermore such a project." And these fine hospitals were maintained by rates levied on the honest outside, who were struggling to support themselves without becoming felons—"Rates on the poor servant of God and of Her Majesty, who still serves both in his way . . . to boil right soup for the Devil's declared Elect!"[21]

He did not expect that his protests would be attended to then, but in twenty years he thought there might be more agreement with him. This, like many other prophecies of his, has proved true. We hang and flog now with small outcry and small compunction. But the ferocity with which he struck right and left at honoured names, the contempt which he heaped on an amiable, if not a wise experiment, gave an impression of his own character as false as it was unpleasant. He was really the most tender-hearted of men. His savageness was but affection turned sour, and what he said was the opposite of what he did. Many a time I have remonstrated when I saw him give a shilling to some wretch with "Devil's elect" on his forehead. "No doubt he is a son of Gehenna," Carlyle would say; "but you can see it is very low water with him. This modern life hardens our hearts more than it should."

On the *Pamphlets* rushed. The third was on Downing Street and Modern Government. Lord John Russell, I remember, plaintively spoke of it in the House of Commons. The fourth was on "The New Downing Street, such as it might and ought to become." The fifth, on "Stump Oratory," was perhaps the most important of the set, for it touched a problem of moment then, and now every day becoming of greater moment; for the necessary tendency of Democracy is to throw the power of the State into the hands of eloquent speakers, and eloquent speakers have never since the world began been wise statesmen. Carlyle had not read Aristotle's *Politics,* but he had arrived in his own road at Aristotle's conclusions. All forms of government, Aristotle says, are ruined by parasites and flatterers. The parasite of the monarch is the favourite who flatters his vanity and hides the truth from him. The parasite of a democracy is the orator; the people are his masters, and he rules by pleasing them. He dares not tell them unpleasant truths, lest he lose his popularity; he must call their passions emotions of justice, and their prejudices conclusions of reason. He dares not look facts in the face, and facts prove too strong for him.[22] To the end of his life Carlyle thought with extreme anxiety on this subject, and, as will be seen, had more to say about it.

I need not follow the *Pamphlets* in detail. There were to have been twelve originally; one, I think, on the "Exodus from Houndsditch," for he occasionally reproached himself afterwards for over-reticence on that subject. He was not likely to have been deterred by fear of giving offence. But the arguments against speaking out about it were always as present with him as the arguments for openness. Perhaps he concluded, on the whole, that the good which he might do would not outbalance the pain he would inflict. The series, at any rate, ended with the eighth—upon "Jesuitism," a word to which he gave a wider significance than technically belongs to it. England supposed that it had repudiated sufficiently Ignatius Loyola and the Company of Jesus; but, little as England knew it, Ignatius's peculiar doctrines had gone into its heart, and were pouring through all its veins and arteries. Jesuitism to Carlyle was the deliberate shutting of the eyes to truth; the deliberate insincerity which, if persisted in, becomes itself sincere. You choose to tell a lie because, for various reasons, it is convenient; you defend it with argument—till at length you are given over to believe it—and the religious side of your mind being thus penally paralysed; morality becomes talk and conscience becomes emotion; and your actual life has no authoritative guide left but personal selfishness. Thus, by the side of a profession of Christianity, England had adopted for a working creed Political Economy, which is the contradictory of Christianity, imagining that it could believe both together. Christianity tells us that we are not to care for the things of the earth. Political economy is concerned with nothing else. Christianity says that the desire to make money is the root of all evil. Political economy says that the more each man struggles to "make money" the better for the commonwealth. Christianity says that it is the business of the magistrate to execute justice and maintain truth. Political economy (or the system of government founded upon it) limits "justice" to the keeping of the peace, declares that the magistrate has nothing to do with maintaining *truth*, and that every man must be left free to hold his own opinions and advance his own interests in any way that he pleases, short of fraud and violence.

Jesuitism, or the art of finding reasons for whatever we wish to believe, had enabled Englishmen to persuade themselves that both these theories of life could be true at the same time. They kept one for Sundays, the other for the working days; and the practical moral code thus evolved, Carlyle throws out in a wild freak of humour, comparable only to the memorable epitaph on the famous Baron in *Sartor Resartus*.[23]

[The *Latter-Day Pamphlets* were] written thirty-three years ago, when political economy was our sovereign political science. As the centre of gravity of political power has changed, the science has changed along with it. Statesmen have discovered that *laissez-faire*, though doubtless true in a better state of existence, is inapplicable to our imperfect planet. They have attempted, with Irish Land Bills, etc., to regulate in some degree the distribution of the hog's wash, and will doubtless, as democracy extends, do more in that direction. But when the *Pamphlets* appeared, this and the other doctrines enunciated in them were received with astonished indignation. "Carlyle taken to whisky" was the popular impression; or perhaps he had gone mad. *Punch,* the most friendly to him of all the London periodicals, protested affectionately. The delinquent was brought up for trial before him, I think for injuring his reputation. He was admonished, but stood impenitent, and even "called the worthy magistrate (*Mr. Punch*) a 'windbag,' a 'serf of flunkeydom,' and 'an ape of the Dead Sea.' "[24] I suppose it was Thackeray who wrote this, or some other kind friend, who feared, like Emerson, "that the world would turn its back on him."[25] He was under no illusion himself as to the effect which he was producing.

The outcry, curiously, had no effect on the sale of Carlyle's works. He had a certain public, slowly growing, which bought everything that he published. The praise of the newspapers never, he told me, sensibly increased the circulation; their blame never sensibly diminished it. His unknown disciples believed in him as a teacher whom they were to learn from, not to criticise. There were then about three thousand who bought his books. Now, who can say how many there are? He, for himself, had delivered his soul, and was comparatively at rest.

In the intervals between Carlyle's larger works, a discharge of spiritual bile was always necessary. Modern English life, and the opinions popularly current among men, were a constant provocation to him. The one object of everyone (a very few chosen souls excepted) seemed to be to make money, and with money increase his own idle luxury. The talk of people, whether written or spoken, was an extravagant and never-ceasing laudation of an age which was content to be so employed, as if the like of it had never been seen upon earth before. The thinkers in their closets, the politicians on platform or in Parliament, reviews and magazines, weekly newspapers and dailies, sang all the same note, that there had never since the world began been a time when the English part of mankind had been happier or better than they were then. They had only to be let alone, to have more and more liberty, and fix their eyes steadily on "increasing the quantity of attainable hog's wash,"[26] and there would be such a world as no philosophy had ever dreamt of. Something of this kind really was the prevalent creed thirty years ago, under the sudden increase of wealth which set in with railways and free trade; and to Carlyle it appeared a false creed throughout, from principle to inference. In his judgement the common weal of men and nations depended on their characters; and the road which we had to travel, if we were to make a good end, was the same as the Christian pilgrim had travelled on his way to the Celestial City, no primrose path thither having been yet made by God or man. The austerer virtues —manliness, thrift, simplicity, self-denial—were dispensed

491

with in the boasted progress. There was no demand for these, no need of them. The heaven aspired after was enjoyment, and the passport thither was only money. Let there be only money enough, and the gate lay open. He could not believe this doctrine. He abhorred it from the bottom of his soul. Such a heaven was no heaven for a man. The boasted prosperity would sooner or later be overtaken by "God's judgement." Especially he was angry when he saw men to whom nature had given talents lending themselves to this accursed persuasion; statesmen, theologians, philosophers composedly swimming with the stream, careless of truth, or with no longer any measure of truth except their own advantage. Some who had eyes were afraid to open them; others, and the most, had deliberately extinguished their eyes. They used their faculties only to dress the popular theories in plausible language, and were carried away by their own eloquence, till they actually believed what they were saying. Respect for fact they had none. Fact to them was the view of things conventionally received, or what the world and they together agreed to admit.

That the facts either of religion or politics were *not* such as bishops and statesmen represented them to be, was frightfully evident to Carlyle, and he could not be silent if he wished. Thus, after he had written *The French Revolution, Chartism* had to come out of him, and *Past and Present,* before he could settle to *Cromwell,. Cromwell* done, the fierce acid had accumulated again and had been discharged in the *Latter-Day Pamphlets*—discharged, however, still imperfectly, for his whole soul was loaded with bilious indignation. Many an evening, about this time, I heard him flinging off the matter intended for the rest of the series which had been left unwritten, pouring out, for hours together, a torrent of sulphurous denunciation. No one could check him. If anyone tried contradiction, the cataract rose against the obstacle till it rushed over it and drowned it. But, in general, his listeners sate silent. The imagery, his wild play of humour, the immense knowledge always evident in the grotesque forms which it assumed, were in themselves so dazzling and so entertaining, that we lost the use of our own faculties till it was over. He did

492

not like making these displays, and avoided them when he could; but he was easily provoked, and when excited could not restrain himself. Whether he expected to make converts by the *Pamphlets*, I cannot say. His sentences, perhaps, fell here and there like seeds, and grew to something in minds that could receive them. In the general hostility, he was experiencing the invariable fate of all men who see what is coming before those who are about them see it; and he lived to see most of the unpalatable doctrines which the *Pamphlets* contained verified by painful experience and practically acted on.

In the midst of the storm which he had raised, he was surprised agreeably by an invitation to dine with Sir Robert Peel. He had liked Peel ever since he had met him at Lord Ashburton's. Peel, who had read his books, had been struck equally with him, and wished to know more of him. The dinner was in the second week of May. [Among the guests was the Bishop of Oxford, Samuel Wilberforce.]

Carlyle had probably encountered the Bishop of Oxford before, at the Ashburtons; but this meeting at Sir Robert Peel's was the beginning of an intimacy which grew up between these singularly opposite men, who, in spite of differences, discovered that they thought, at bottom, on serious subjects, very much alike. The Bishop once told me he considered Carlyle a most eminently religious man. "Ah, Sam!" said Carlyle to me one day, "he is a very clever fellow; I do not hate him near as much as I fear I ought to do."

Once again, a few days later, Carlyle met Peel at a dinner at Bath House—"a real statesman" as he now discerned him to be

> Fresh and hearty; delicate, gentle, yet frank manners; a kindly man,—his *reserve,* as to all great or public matters, sits him quite naturally, and enhances your respect. A warm sense of *fun,* a vein really of genuine broad drollery looks thro' this "statesman" (such I really guess he is); the hopefullest feature I could clearly *see* in this last interview or the other. . . . At tea, talked to us, readily on slight hint from me, about Byron (*Birron* he called him), and their old schooldays—kindly reminiscences, agreeable to hear at first hand, tho' nothing new in them to us.[27]

At Bath House also, this season, Carlyle was to meet

493

(though without an introduction) a man whom he regarded with freer admiration than he had learnt to feel even for Peel. He was tempted to a ball there, the first and last occasion on which he was ever present at such a scene. He was anxious to see the thing for once, and he saw along with it the hero of Waterloo.

> By far the most interesting figure present was the old Duke of Wellington, who appeared between 12 and 1, and slowly glided thro' the rooms. Truly a beautiful old man; I had never seen till now how beautiful, and what an expression of graceful simplicity, veracity, and nobleness there is about the old hero when you see him close at hand. His very size had hitherto deceived me: he is a shortish slightish figure, about 5 feet 8; of good breadth however, and *all* muscle or bone;—his legs I think must be the short part of him, for certainly on horseback at least I have always taken him to be tall. Eyes beautiful light-blue, full of mild valour, with infinitely more faculty and geniality than I had fancied before. The face wholly gentle, wise, valiant and venerable; the voice too as I again heard, is *aquiline*, a clear, perfectly equable (*un*cracked, that is), and perhaps almost musical, but essentially *tenor* or almost treble voice. Eighty-two, I understand. He glided slowly along, slightly saluting this and the other; clean, clear fresh as the June Evening itself; till the silver-buckle of his stock vanished into the door of the next room (to make, I suppose, *one* round of the place), and I saw him no more. Except Dr. Chalmers I have not for many years seen so beautiful an old man.[28]

In his early Radical days, Carlyle had spoken scornfully, as usual, of Peel and Wellington, not distinguishing them from the herd of average politicians. He was learning to know them better, to recognise better, perhaps, how great a man must essentially be who can accomplish anything good under the existing limitations. But the knowledge came too late to ripen into practical acquaintance. Wellington's sun was setting, Peel was actually gone in a few weeks from the dinner at Bath House, and Wellington had passed that singular eulogy upon him in the House of Lords—singular, but most instructive commentary on the political life of our days, as if Peel was the only public man of whom such a character could be given. "He had never known him tell a deliberate falsehood."

The last great English statesman—the last great constitutional statesman perhaps that England will ever have—died through a fall from his horse in the middle of this summer, 1850.

Wednesday morning Post reported "Sir Robert died last night" (I think about 9): *Eheu! Eheu!*

Great expressions of "national sorrow," really a serious expression of regret in the public; an affectionate appreciation of this man, which he himself was far from being sure of or aware of while he lived. I myself have said nothing; hardly know what to think: feel only in general that I have now no definite hope of peaceable improvement for this country; that the one "Statesman" we had (or the least similitude of a statesman so far as I know or can guess) is suddenly snatched away from us.[29]

Great men die, like little men; "there is no difference," and the world goes its way without them. Parliament was to "wriggle on" with no longer any Peel to guide; "the wen," as Cobbett called London,[30] was to double its already overgrown, monstrous bulk, and Carlyle had still thirty years before him to watch and shudder at its extending. But from this time he cared little about contemporary politics, which he regarded as beating the wind. What *he* himself was next to do was a problem to him which he did not see his way through. Some time or other he meant to write a *Life of Sterling*, but as yet he had not sufficient composure. Up to this time he had perhaps some hope or purpose of being employed actively in public life. All idea of this kind, if he ever seriously entertained it, had now vanished. As a writer of books, and as this only, he was to make his mark on his generation, but what book was to be written next was entirely vague to him. The house in Chelsea required paint and whitewash again—a process which, for everyone's sake, it was desirable that he should not be present to witness. His friend, Mr. Redwood, again invited him to South Wales. He had been dreadfully "bored" there; but he was affected, too, by Redwood's loyal attachment. He agreed to go to him for a week or two, and intended afterwards to make his way into Scotland.

On the way to Cardiff, he spent a night with Savage Landor, who was then living apart from his family in Bath.

Dinner was *elaborate*-simple; the brave Landor forced me to talk far too much, and we did very near a bottle of claret besides two glasses of sherry,—far too much liquor and excitement for a poor fellow like me! However, he was really stirring company; a proud, irascible, trenchant, yet generous veracious and very dignified old man. Quite a ducal or royal man, in the temper of him; reminded me something of old Sterling, except that for Irish blarney, you must substitute a fund of Welsh choler.[31]

Mr. Redwood was no longer at Llandough, but had moved to Boverton, a place at no great distance. Boverton was nearer to the sea, and the daily bathe could be effected without difficulty. The cocks, cuddies, etc., were as troublesome as usual, though perhaps less so than Carlyle's vivid anathemas on the poor creatures would lead one to suppose. His host entertained him with more honour than he would have paid to a prince or an archbishop, and Carlyle could not but be grateful.

Carlyle would have been the most perfect of guide-book writers. Nothing escaped his observation; and he never rested till he had learnt all that could be known about any place which he visited: first and foremost, the meaning of the name of it, if it was uncommon or suggestive. His daily letters to Chelsea were full of descriptions of the neighbourhood, all singularly vivid.

The house-cleaning at Chelsea was complicated by the misconduct of servants. Mrs. Carlyle was struggling in the midst of it all, happy that her husband was away, but wishing perhaps that he would show himself a little more appreciative of what she was undergoing. No one ever laid himself more open to being misunderstood in such matters than Carlyle did. He was the gratefullest of men, but, from a shy reluctance to speak of his feelings, he left his gratitude unuttered. He seemed to take whatever was done for him as a matter of course, and to growl if anything was not to his mind. It was only in his letters that he showed what was really in his heart.

He stayed three weeks at Boverton, and then gratefully took leave. "The good Redwood," as he called his host, died the year following, and he never saw him again. His route to Scotsbrig was, as usual, by the Liverpool and Annan steamer. The discomforts of his journey were not different from other people's in similar circumstances. It was the traveller who was different; and his miseries, comical as they sound, were real enough to so sensitive a sufferer. He sent a history of them to Chelsea on his arrival. "I am," he said, "a very unthankful, ill conditioned, bilious, wayward and heart-worn son of Adam, I do suspect!—Well, you shall hear all my complaints. . . . To whom can we complain, if not to one another, after all?"[32] He had reached Liverpool without misadventure. He had gone on board late in the evening. The night, as the vessel ran down the Mersey, was soft and beautiful. He walked and smoked for an hour on deck, and then went in search of his sleeping-place.

> "This way the *gents' cabin*, sir!" And in truth it was almost worth a little voyage to see such a cabin of *gents*; for never in all my travels had I seen the like before, nor probably shall again. The little crib of a place which I had glanced at two hours before, and found six beds in, had now developed itself, by hinge-*shelves* [(]which in the day were parts of *sofas*) and iron *brackets* into the practical sleeping-place of at least sixteen of the gent species; there they all lay, my crib the only empty one; a pile of clothes up to the very ceiling, and all round it, gent packed on gent, few inches between the nose of one gent and the nape of the other gent's neck,—not a particle of air, all orifices closed;—five or six of said gents already raging and snoring; and a smell—*ach Gott*, I suppose it must resemble that of the Slave-ships in the middle passage:—it was positively *immoral* to think of sleeping in such a receptacle of abominations.[33]

He sought the deck again; but the night turned to rain, and the deck of a steamer in wet and darkness is not delightful, even in August: [he became] "a sublime spectacle of misfortune, appealing to Goody and Posterity." When the vessel reached Annan, and "I got flung out into the street," the unfortunate "Jonah" could but address a silent word of thanks to the Merciful Power.[34] At Scotsbrig he could do as he liked—be silent from morning till night, wander about alone among the hills, see no one, and be nursed in mind and body by the kindest hands; but he was out of order in one as well as the other. The reaction after the *Pamphlets* was now telling upon him.

The evident uncertainty as to his future occupations which appears in his letters, taken with what he told me of his thoughts of public life at the time of his *Pamphlets*, confirms me in my impression that he had nourished some practical hopes from those Pamphlets, and had imagined that he might perhaps be himself invited to assist in carrying out some of the changes which he had there insisted on. Such hopes, if he had formed them, he must have seen by this time were utterly groundless. Whatever improvements might be attempted, no statesman would ever call on him to take part in the process. To this, which was now a certainty, he had to

497

endeavour to adjust himself; but he was in low spirits—unusually low, even for him.

It was in this humour that Carlyle read *Alton Locke,* which Kingsley sent him. I well remember the gratification with which Kingsley showed me his approving criticism; and it speaks volumes for the merit of that book that at such a time Carlyle could take pleasure in it. Little did either of us then guess in what a depth of depression it had found him. The cloud lifted after a while; but these fits when they came were entirely disabling. Robust constitutional strength, which is half of it insensibility, was not among the gifts which Nature had bestowed on Carlyle. His strength was moral; it lay in an unalterable resolution to do what was right and to speak what was true—a strength nobly sufficient for the broad direction of his life and intellect, but leaving him a helpless victim of the small vexations which prey like mosquitoes on the nerves of unfortunate men of genius. Sometimes, indeed, by the help of Providence, his irritations neutralised one another. In his steady thrift, he had his clothes made for him in Annandale, the cloth bought at Dumfries and made up by an Ecclefechan tailor. His wardrobe required refitting before his return to London, and the need of attending to it proved an antidote to his present miseries.

With the end of September London and Cheyne Row came in sight again. The repairs were finished. At Scotsbrig, when the clothes had come in, he found himself "a distempered human soul, that had *slept ill,* and has been terribly dadded about of late! A phenomenon probably not quite unfamiliar to your observation."[35] He had thought of a trip to Iona before going home, but the season was too far advanced. A short visit was to be managed to his friends in Cumberland. Then he would hasten back, and be as amiable as he could when he arrived. Mrs. Carlyle, in one of the saddest of her sad letters, had regretted that her company had become so useless to him.[36] "Oh my Dear," he said, "if you could but cease being 'conscious' of what your company is to me;—the consciousness is *all* the malady in that: ah me, ah me! But that too will mend, if it please God."[37]

On the 27th of September he parted sorrowfully from his mother at Scotsbrig, after a wild midnight walk in wind and rain the evening before.[38] Three days were given to the

Speddings at Keswick, and thence, on pressing invitation, he went to the Marshalls at Coniston, where he met the Tennysons, then lately married. Neither of these visits brought much comfort. Mr. Spedding had gone with the rest of the world in disapproving the *Latter-Day Pamphlets*. At the Marshalls' he was prevented from sleeping by "poultry, children and flunkeys."[39]

He announced that he could not stay, that he must leave the next day, etc. Every attention was paid him. His room was changed. Not a sound was allowed to disturb him. He had a sound sleep, woke to find "a great alteration in me," with the sun shining over lakes and mountains; and then he thought he would stay "another day, and still other days" if he were asked. But he had been so peremptory that his host thought it uncourteous to press him further, and then he discovered that he was not wanted, "nothing except the *name* of me which was already got." Mr. Marshall himself accompanied him to the Windermere station, "forcing me to talk, which was small favour";[40] and the express train swept him back to London. Men of genius are "kittle" [ticklish] guests, and, of all such, Carlyle was the "kittlest."

His wife was at the Grange when he reached Cheyne Row. There was no one to receive him but her dog Nero, who after a moment's doubt barked enthusiastic reception, and "the cat" who "sat reflective, without sign of the smallest emotion more or less." He was obliged to Nero, he forgave the cat. He was delighted to be at home again. The improvements in the house called out his enthusiastic approbation. "O Goody," he exclaimed, "incomparable Artist Goody! It is really a 'series of glad surprises'; and this noble *grate* upstairs here:—all good and best, my bonny little Artistkin! Really it is clever and wise to a degree: and I admit it is pity you were not here to show it me yourself; but I shall find it all out too. Thank you, thank you, a thousand times."[41]

Mrs. Carlyle was distracted at his return in her own absence. She insisted that she must go to him at once; but she had been gaining strength at the Grange, and the Ashburtons begged her to stay on. Carlyle urged it too. With pretty delicacy he said, as if learning a lesson from her being away, "I shall know better than I ever did what the comfort to *me* is of being received by you, when I arrive worn out, and you welcome me with your old smiles, and the light of a human fire and human home!"[42] As she persisted that she must go back, he accepted Lady Ashburton's proposal that he should himself join his wife for a week or two before finally settling in for the winter; and it was not till the middle of October that they were together again in their own home.[43]

chapter twenty-five

1851–1852

Reviews of the *Latter-Day Pamphlets.*
The Life of John Sterling. Scotsbrig and
Paris. Work on *Frederick the Great* and
First Tour of Germany

There is a condition familiar to men of letters, and I suppose to artists of all descriptions, which may be called a moulting state. The imagination, exhausted by long efforts, sheds its feathers, and mind and body remain sick and dispirited till they grow again. Carlyle was thus moulting after the *Latter-Day Pamphlets.* He was eager to write, but his ideas were shapeless. His wings would not lift him. He was chained to the ground. Unable to produce anything, he began to read voraciously; he bought a copy of the *Annual Register;* he worked entirely through it, finding there "a great quantity of agreeable and not quite useless reading."[1] He read Sophocles with profound admiration. His friends came about Cheyne Row, eager to see him after his absence. They were welcome in a sense, but "alas!" he confessed, "nobody comes whose talk is half so good to me as silence; I fly out of the way of everybody, and would much rather smoke a pipe of wholesome tobacco than talk to any one in London just now! Nay their talk is often rather an offence to me; and I murmur to myself, 'Why open one's lips for *such* a purpose?' "[2]

The autumn quarterlies were busy upon the *Pamphlets,* and the shrieking tone was considerably modified. A review of them by Masson in the *North British Review* distinctly pleased Carlyle. A review in the *Dublin* he found "excellently serious," and conjectured that it came from some Anglican pervert or convert. It was written, I believe, by Dr. Ward.[3] The Catholics naturally found points of sympathy in so scornful a denunciation of modern notions about liberty. Carlyle and they believed alike in the divine right of wisdom to govern folly. "The wise man's eyes *are* in his head; but the fool walketh in darkness."[4] This article provided him "with interesting reflexions . . . for a day or two."[5] But books were his chief resource in these months.

At intervals he thought of writing something. "Ireland" came back upon him occasionally as still a possibility. A theory of education on the plan of Goethe's *Wanderjahre* would give him scope to say something not wholly useless. These were the two subjects which looked least contemptible. There was English history too: "the *Conqueror,* the *Battle of Towton,* Sir Simon de Montfort." "What," he asked himself, *"can* be done with a British Museum under Gorgons and fat Pedants, with a world so *sunk* as ours, and alas with a soul so sunk and subdued to its element as mine seems to be! *Voyons, voyons* (on another Paper); *au moins taisons-nous* [Let us see, let us see . . . at least let us be silent]!'"[6]

Notwithstanding the hopes and resolutions which Carlyle had brought back with him from Scotland, the domestic atmosphere was not clear in Cheyne Row, and had not been clear since his return. Nothing need be said about this. It added to his other discomforts—that was all.

At the end of January he went off again to the Grange, alone this time, to meet an interesting party there; Thirlwall, Milnes, the Stanleys, Sir John Simeon, Trench, then Dean of Westminster, and several others. He might have enjoyed himself if his spirits had been in better order; "the conversation is a thought more solid (thanks chiefly to the Bishop) than is usual." One evening it took a remarkable form, and as he more than once described the scene to me, I quote what he says about it in a letter.

> Last night there was a dreadful onslaught made on, what shall I say? properly the *Church* in presence of Trench and the Bishop: Trench affected to be very busy reading, and managed extremely well; the Bishop was also grand and rationally manful,—intrinsically *agreeing* with almost everything I said. Poor fat Simeon, a gentleman in search of a religion, sate stupent in the whirlpool of heterodox hail, and seemed to feel if his head were on his shoulders. This is an extraordinary epoch of the world, with a witness![7]

It was perhaps as an effect of this singular piece of talk, at any rate in discharge of a long-recognised duty, that Carlyle, on returning home, set about his long-meditated life of John Sterling. To leave Sterling any longer as an anatomical subject for the religious newspapers was treason to his friend's memory. He had waited, partly from want of composure, partly that the dust might settle a little; and now, having leisure on his hands, and being otherwise in the right mood, he re-read Sterling's letters, collected information from surviving relatives, and without difficulty—indeed, with entire ease and rapidity—he produced in three months what is perhaps the most beautiful biography in the English language. His own mind for the past year had been restless and agitated, but no restlessness can be traced in the *Life of Sterling*. The scorn, the pride, the indignation of the *Pamphlets* lie hushed down under a stream of quiet affection. The tone is calm and tender. Here, more than in any of the rest of his writings, he could give play, without a jarring note, to the gentlest qualities of his heart and intellect. It was necessary for him to express himself more plainly than he had hitherto done on the received religious creeds; but he wrote without mockery, without exasperation, as if his angry emotions were subdued to the element in which he was working. A friend's grave was no place for theological controversy, and though he allowed his humour free play, it was real play, nowhere savagely contemptuous. Sterling's life had been a short one. His history was rather that of the formation of a beautiful character than of accomplished achievement; at once, the most difficult to delineate, yet the most instructive if delineated successfully. The aim of the biographer was to lift the subject beyond the sordid element of religious exasperations; yet it was on Sterling's "religion," in the noble meaning of the word, that the entire interest turned. Growing to manhood in an atmosphere of Radicalism, political and speculative, Sterling had come in contact with the enthusiasts of European revolution. He had involved himself in a movement in which accident only prevented him from being personally engaged, and which ended in the destruction of his friends. In the depression which followed he had fallen under the influence of Coleridge. He had learnt from Coleridge that the key of the mystery of the universe lay, after all, with the Church creed rightly understood, and that, by an intellectual legerdemain, uncertainties could be converted into certainties. The process by which the wonderful transformation was to be effected, Carlyle himself had heard from the prophet's own lips, and had heard without conviction when Irving long before had taken him to Highgate to worship.

Carlyle for himself had refused to follow Coleridge into these airy speculations. He for one dared not play with truth, and he regarded his metaphysical conjuring as cowardly unmanliness, fatal to honesty of heart, and useful only to enable cravens, who in their souls knew better, to close their eyes to fact.

He held sternly to what his conscience told him, and would not listen to the Coleridgean siren. But many did listen, and ran upon the fatal shore. Intellectual clergymen especially, who had been troubled in their minds, imagined that they found help and comfort there. If, as they had been told, it was a sin to disbelieve the Church's creed, then the creed itself must rest on something beyond probability and the balance of evidence. Why not, then, on Coleridge's *"reason"*? It was a serious thing, besides, to have a profession to which they were committed for the means of living, and which the law forbade them to change. Thus, at the time when Carlyle was writing this book, a whole flight of clergy, with Frederick Maurice at their head and Kingsley for lieutenant, were preaching regeneration on Coleridge's principles, and persuading themselves that "the sacred river could run backwards after all."[8] Sterling, before them, had been carried away by the same illusion. In his enthusiasm, he took orders; a few months' experience sufficed to show so true an intelligence that the Highgate philosophy was "bottled moonshine"; and Carlyle draws the picture of him, not, like Julius Hare, as of "a vanquished doubter," but as "a victorious believer," resolutely shaking himself clear of artificial spider-webs—holding fast with all his powers to what he knew to be true and good, and living for that, and that only.[9]

Something of the high purpose which Carlyle assigns to Sterling was perhaps reflected from himself, as with a lover's portrait of his mistress; yet his account of him is essentially as true as it is affectionate. He did not give his esteem easily, and when it was given it was nobly deserved.

I well remember the effect which the book produced when it appeared. He himself valued it little, and even doubted whether it was worth publishing. As a piece of literary work it was more admired than anything which he had yet written. The calmness was a general surprise. He had a tranquil command of his subject, and his treatment of it was exquisitely delicate. He was no longer censuring the world as a prophet, but delighting it as an artist. The secular part of society pardoned the fierceness with which he had trampled on them for so beautiful an evidence of the tenderness of his real heart. The religious world was not so well satisfied. Anglicans, Protestants, Catholics had hoped from *Cromwell*, and even from the *Pamphlets*, that, as against spiritual Radicalism, he would be on their side. They found themselves entirely mistaken. "Does not believe in us either, then?" was the cry. "Not one of the *religiones licitae* [accepted observances] will this man acknowledge." Frederick Maurice's friends were the most displeased of all. The irreverence with which he had treated Coleridge was not to be forgiven. From all that section of Illuminati who had hitherto believed themselves his admirers, he had cut himself off for ever, and, as a teacher, he was left without disciples, save a poor handful who had longed for such an utterance from him. He himself gathered no conscious pleasure from what he had done. "A poor tatter of a thing," he called it, valuable only as an honest tribute of affection to a lost friend. It was so always. The execution of all his work fell so far short of his intention that when completed it seemed to be worth nothing.

[Carlyle's chief] uneasiness was about the "immense masses of things"[10] on which he wanted to write, and project after project rose and faded before he could see his way. The "Exodus from Houndsditch" was still one of them; ought he, or ought he not, to be explicit in that great matter, and sketch the outlines of a creed which might hereafter be sincerely believed?

Attempt to work it out Carlyle did in the two fragments on "Spiritual Optics" which I printed in the second volume of his early life.[11] He there seems to say that something of the sort was expected of him, and even obligatory upon him. But either he felt that the age was not ripe, or he could not develop the idea satisfactorily, and he left what he had written to mature in some other mind. "Few men," he says at this time, "were ever more puzzled to find their road than I am just now. Be silent! Look and seek!" His test of progress—of the moral worth of his own or any other age —was the *men* that it produced. He admired most of all things in this world single-minded and sincere people, who believed honestly what they professed to believe, and lived it out in their actions. Properly, he admired nothing else, and his special genius lay in depicting such ages and persons.

A new cant came up at this epoch to put him out of patience—Prince Albert's Grand Industrial Exhibition and Palace of Aladdin in Hyde Park, a temple for the consecration of commerce, etc., with the Archbishop of Canterbury for fugleman, a contrivance which was to bring in a new era, and do for mankind what Christianity had tried and failed to do. For such a thing as this Carlyle could have no feeling but contempt.

When summer came, and the Exhibition opened, London grew intolerable. The enthusiasm for this new patent invention to regenerate the human race was altogether too much for him. He fled to Malvern for the water-cure, and became, with his wife, for a few weeks the guest of Dr. Gully, who, long years afterwards, was brought back so terribly to his remembrance.[12] After long wavering he was beginning seriously to think of Frederick the Great as his next subject; if not a hero to his mind, yet at heart a man who had played a lofty part in Europe without stooping to conventional cant. With Frederick looming before him he went to cool his fever in the Malvern waters. The disease was not in his body, loudly as he complained of it. The bathing, packing, drinking proved useless—worse, in his opinion, than useless. He "found by degrees that water, taken as medicine, was the most destructive drug he had ever tried." He "had paid his tax to contemporary stupor." That was all. Gully himself, who would take no fees from him, he had not disliked, and was grateful for his hospitality. He stayed a month in all. His wife went to her friends in Manchester; he hastened to hide himself in Scotsbrig, full of gloom and heaviness, and totally out of health.

He found his mother not ill, but visibly sinking. She had divined that all was not as well in Cheyne Row as it ought to be. Why had not Mrs. Carlyle come too, to see her before she died? She said over and over again, "I wad ha' liked well to see Janie ance mair!"[13] All else was still and peaceful. The air, the home faces, the honest, old-fashioned life, did for him what Malvern and Gully could not do. The noise of the outside world reached him only as an echo, and he was only provoked a little when its disturbances came into his close neighbourhood.

Scotsbrig lasted three weeks. There had been an old arrangement that Carlyle should spend a few days at Paris with the Ashburtons. Lord and Lady Ashburton were now there, and wrote to summon him to join them. At such a command the effort seemed not impossible. He went to London, joined Browning at the South Eastern Railway station, and the same evening found him at Meurice's. The first forty-eight hours were tolerable: "nothing to *do* in Paris except 'amuse' myself," which he thought could be borne for a day or two. Lord Ashburton of course saw everyone that was worth seeing. Thiers came the second afternoon "and talked *immense* quantities of watery enough vain matter." Thiers was followed by two other " 'Men of Letters,' " "one Mérimée, one Laborde: *nichts zu bedeuten* [of no consequence]."[14] The third and fourth nights sleep unfortunately failed, with the usual consequences. He grew desperate, found that he had "never made such a fruitless jump into a red-sea of mud before." The last remains of his patience vanished when Mérimée dared to say that he thought "Goethe an inferior French apprentice."[15] This was enough of literature. He packed his bag and fled home to Chelsea.[16]

For several years now, with the exception of the short interval when he wrote Sterling's life, Carlyle had been growling in print and talk over all manner of men and things. The revolutions of 1848 had aggravated his natural tendencies. He had thought ill enough before of the modern methods of acting and thinking, and had foreseen that no good would come of them. The universal crash of European society had confirmed his convictions. He saw England hurrying on to a similar catastrophe. He had lifted up his voice in warning, and no one would listen to him, and he was irritated, disappointed, and perhaps surprised at the impotence of his own admonitions. To go on with them, to continue railing like Timon, was waste of time and breath; and time and breath had been given to him to use and not to waste. His best resource, he knew, was to engage with some subject large enough and difficult enough to take up all his attention, and he had fixed at last on Frederick of Prussia. He had discerned for one thing that Prussia, in those days of tottering thrones, was, or would be, the centre of European stability, and that it was Frederick who had made Prussia what she was. It was an enormous undertaking; nothing less than the entire history, secular and spiritual, of the eighteenth century. He was not one of those easy writers who take without inquiry the accredited histories, and let their own work consist in hashing and seasoning and flavouring. He never stated a fact without having himself gone to the original authority for it, knowing what facts suffer in the cooking process. For Carlyle to write a book on Frederick would involve the reading of a mountain of books, memoirs, journals, letters, state papers. The work with Cromwell would be child's play to it. He would have to travel over a large part of Germany, to see Berlin and Potsdam, to examine battlefields and the plans of campaigns. He would have to make a special study, entirely new to him, of military science and the art of war; all this he would have to do, and do it thoroughly, for he never went into any work by halves. He was now fifty-six years old, and might well pause before such a plunge. Frederick himself, too, was not a man after Carlyle's heart. He had "no piety" like Cromwell, no fiery convictions, no zeal for any "cause of God," real or imagined. He lived in an age when sincere spiritual belief had become difficult, if not impossible. But he had one supreme merit, that he was not a hypocrite: what he did not feel he did not pretend to feel. Of cant— either conscious cant, or the "sincere cant" which Carlyle found to be so loathsome in England—there was in Frederick absolutely none. He was a man of supreme intellectual ability. One belief he had, and it was the explanation of his strength—a belief in *facts*. To know the fact always ex-

508

actly as it was, and to make his actions conform to it, was the first condition with him; never to allow facts to be concealed from himself, or distorted, or pleasantly flavoured with words or spurious sentiments; and therefore Frederick, if not a religious man, was a true man, the nearest approach to a religious man that Carlyle believed perhaps to be in these days possible. He might not be true in the sense that he never deceived others. Politicians, with a large stake upon the board, do not play with their cards on the table. But he never, if he could help it, deceived himself; never hid his own heart from himself by specious phrases, or allowed voluntary hallucinations to blind his eyes, and thus he stood out an exceptional figure in the modern world. Whether at his age he could go through with such an enterprise was still uncertain to him; but he resolved to try, and on coming back from Paris sat down to read whatever would come first to hand.

Six months now followed of steady reading and excerpting. He went out little, except to ride in the afternoons, or walk at midnight when the day's work was over. A few friends were admitted occasionally to tea. If any called before, he left them to his wife and refused to be disturbed. I was then living in Wales, and saw and heard nothing of him except in some rare note.

He had decided on going to Germany in August. With the exception of the yacht trip to Ostend, he had never been beyond Paris. Mrs. Carlyle had never been on the Continent at all; and the plan was for them to go both together. Repairs were needed in the house again. He was anxious to complete a portion of his reading before setting out, and fancied that this time he could stay and live through the noise; but the workmen when they came in were too much for him. She undertook to remain and superintend as usual. He had to fly if he would not be driven mad—fly to Scotland, taking his books with him; perhaps to his friend Mr. Erskine.[17]

Erskine, who loved Carlyle and delighted in his company, responded with a hearty invitation, and on July 21, the weather still flaming hot, Carlyle dropped down the river in a boat from Chelsea to the Dundee steamer, which was lying in the Pool, his wife and Nero accompanying to see him off. She was delighted that he should go, for her own sake as well

JANE WELSH CARLYLE, 1852. (Portrait in oil by Samuel Laurence, courtesy of the National Portrait Gallery, London.)

as for his. When he was clear off, she could go about her work with a lighter heart.

The German problem seemed frightful as the time drew on. "Travelling, of all kinds, grows more and more horrible to me; nor do I yet quite see that there lies in *Frederick* alone sufficient motive to lead me into such a set of sufferings and expenses."[18] Linlathen itself became tedious: he admitted that all the circumstances were favourable—the kindest of hosts, the best of lodging; but "the *wearisome* is in permanence here, I think."[19] They would make him talk, that was the offence; yet it was his own fault. His talk was so intensely interesting, so intensely entertaining. No one who heard him flowing on could have guessed at the sadness which weighed upon him when alone. Those bursts of humour, flashing out amidst his wild flights of rhetoric, spoke of anything but sadness; even the servants at places where he dined had to run out of the room, choking down their laughter. The comic and the tragic lie close together, inseparable like light and shadow, as Socrates long ago forced Aristophanes himself to acknowledge.[20] He escaped to Scotsbrig after a fortnight with the Erskines, and there he hoped his wife would join him. But the work at Cheyne Row lingered on, and was far from completion. He felt that he ought to go to Germany; yet he was unwilling to leave her behind him. She had looked forward with some eagerness to seeing a foreign country, and Carlyle knew it. "You surely deserve this one little pleasure," he said; "there are so few you can get from me in this world!" To himself it would be no pleasure at all. "Curtainless beds, noisy sleepless nights" were frightful to contemplate. He, individually, was "disheartened, dyspeptical; and in fine contemptible . . . in some degree!"[21] Still, for her sake, and for the little bit of duty he could get done, he was ready to encounter the thing. Especially he wished her to come to him at Scotsbrig. She had held aloof of late years, since things had gone awry. "My poor old Mother," he wrote, "comes in with her anxious sincere old face: 'Send my love to Jane, and tell her' (this with a *wae*ish tone) 'I wad like richt weel to have a crack wi' her,'—'ance mair.' "[22]

He concluded that he must go to Germany. She, if things were well, might come out afterwards, and join him in Silesia. He found that he did not "care much" for *Frederick* after all; but it would be "disgraceful to be driven away" by mere travelling annoyances.[23] Letter followed letter, in the same strain. It was not jest, it was not earnest; it was a mere wilfulness of humour. He told her not to mind what he said; "it is merely the grumbling incidental to dyspepsia and the load of life; it is on the whole the nature of the beast, and must be put up with as the wind and the rain."[24] She had to decide, perhaps prudently, that she could not go, either with him or after him.

All was settled at last—resolution, passport, and everything else that was required; and on Sunday, August 29, Carlyle found himself "on board this greasy little wretch of a Leith Steamer (laden to the waters-edge with pig iron and herrings),"[25] bound for the country whose writers had been the guides of his mind, and whose military hero was to be the subject of his own greatest work. He reached Rotterdam at noon on September 1. He was not to encounter the journey alone. Mr. Neuberg was to join him there, a German admirer, a gentleman of good private fortune, resident in London, who had volunteered his services to conduct Carlyle over the Fatherland, and afterwards to be his faithful assistant in the *Frederick* biography. In both capacities Neuberg was invaluable, and Carlyle never forgot his obligation to him. His letters are the diary of his adventures. He went first to Bonn, to study a few books before going farther.

Bonn, Sunday, 6 September, 1852—

Yesterday, as my first day's *work*, I went to the University Library here; found very many good books, unknown to me hitherto, on Vater Fritz; took down the titles of what, on inspection, promised to be useful; brought some 20 away with me,—and the plan at present is that Neuberg and I shall go with them to a rural place in the Siebengebirge, called Roland's Eck for one week, where sleep is much more possible, and there examine my 20 Books before going farther, and consider what *is* the best to be done farther.[26]

[Unable to work or sleep at Roland's Eck, Carlyle decided to push on, via Frankfurt, to Homburg, Neuberg's home.]

Homburg (vor der Höhn) 15 September, 1852—

Of the Rhine you shall hear enough by and by: it is verily a "noble river"; much broader than the Thames at full tide, and rolling along many feet in depth, with banks quite trim, at a rate of 4 or 5 miles an hour, *without* voice, but full of boiling eddies; the most magnificent image of silent power I have ever seen; and in fact one's *first* idea of a world-*river*. This broad swift sheet, rolling strong and calm (in *silent* rage) for 3 or 4 hundred miles is itself far the grandest thing I have seen here, or shall likely see.[27]

[Carlyle and Neuberg made an excursion to Bad Ems before proceeding up the Rhine.]

Next morning we left Ems; joined our Steamboat at Coblenz, and away again to the *sublime* portions of the Rhine country: very sublime indeed,—really worth a sight; say a 100 miles of a Loch Lomond (or *half* Loch Lomond) all rushing on at 5 miles an hour, and with queer old towers and ruined castles on the banks: a grand silence too; and *gray* day, adding to one's *sadness* of mood; for "a fine sorrow" (not coarse) is the utmost I can bring it too [*sic*] in this world usually![28]

[Carlyle journeyed down the Rhine to Mainz, where he took the train to Frankfurt, spending the night there.]

In shaving next morning, with my face to the Square, which was very lively and had trees in the middle, I caught with the corner of my eye sight of a *face* which was evidently Goethe's: *ach Gott*, merely in *stone*, in the middle of the Platz among the trees;—I had so longed to see that face alive, and here it was given to me at last, as if with huge world-irony, in stone! An emblem of so much that happens: this also gave me a moment's *genial* sorrow, or something of the sort. . . .

At Frankfurt yesterday, after breakfast and your Letter, we saw (weariedly I) all manner of things: Goethe's House (were in Goethe's *room*, a little garret, not much bigger than my dressing-room), and wrote our names "in silence"; the Judengasse, grimmest section of the Middle-Ages and their Pariar-hood I ever saw; the Römer, where old Kaisers all were elected;—on the whole, a stirring strange old-Teutonic Town, all bright with *paint* and busy trade. . . . I calculate there will but little good come to me from this journey: *reading* of Books I find to be impossible;—the thing that I *can* do is to see certain places, and to try if I can gather certain books. Wise people also to talk with, or inquire of, I as good as despair of seeing. *All* Germans, one becomes convinced, are not wise!— On the whole, however, one cannot but like this honest-hearted hardy population: very coarse of feature, for most part, yet seldom radically *hässlich* [ugly]; a *sonsy* [cheerful] look rather, and very frugal, goodhumouredly poor, in their way of life.[29]

The next letter is to his mother dated from Weimar, September 19. She, he well knew, if she cared for nothing else, would care to hear about the Luther localities. She had a picture of Luther in her room at Scotsbrig. He was her chief Saint in the Christian calendar.

The next morning brought us from Cassel to *Eisenach* with its *Wartburg*, where Luther lay concealed translating the Bible; and there I spent one of the most interesting forenoons I ever got by travelling. . . . On the top of this Hill stands the old *Wartburg*, which it takes over 3/4 of an hour to reach. . . . an old Castle ("Watch-Castle" is the name of it) near 800 years old. . . . I heeded little of all else they had to shew except *Junker Georg's*

(Martin Luther's) Chamber, which is in the *nearest* of the "Peat-stacks," the one nearest Eisenach, and close by the Gate when you enter, on your right hand. A short stair of old-worn stone conducts you up; they open the door; you enter a little apartment, *less* than your best room at Scotsbrig, I almost think less than your smallest; a very poor low room, with one old *leaded* lattice-window: to me the most venerable of all rooms I ever entered. Luther's old oak-table is there (about 3 feet square), and a huge fossil-bone (*vertebra* of a mammoth) which served him for footstool: nothing *else* now in the room did certainly belong to him, but these did. I kissed his old oak-table; looked out of his window (making them open it for me) down the sheer Castle-wall into deep chasms, over the great ranges of silent woody mountains, and thought to myself, Here once lived for a time one of God's soldiers, be honour given him![30]

So far about Luther. [On to Gotha and Erfurt traveled Carlyle and his companion and finally reached Weimar.]

Weimar; a little bright enough place, smaller than Dumfries, with three steeples, and totally without smoke; standing amid dull undu-lating country, flat mostly, and tending towards ugliness, except for trees. . . .

Goethe's house (which was opened by *favour*) kept us occupied in a strange mood for 2 hours or more; Schiller's for one ditto: everybody knows the Goethe'sche &c Haus, and poor Schiller and Goethe here are dandled about and multiplied in miserable little bustkins and other dilettantisms, till one is sick and sad! Goethe's house is quite like the *Picture*, but 1/3 *smaller*: on the whole his effective *lodging*, I found, was small, low-roofed, and almost mean to what I had conceived,—hardly equal (nay not at all equal had my little *Architect* once done her work) to my own at Chelsea. On the Book shelves I found the last Book I ever sent Goethe (*Taylor's Survey of German Poetry*), and a crum of Paper, torn from some scroll of my own (*Johnson,* as I conjectured) still sticking in it after 20 years! Schiller's House was still more affecting: the room where he wrote, his old table (exactly like the *model*), the bed where he died (and a portrait of his dead face in it): a poor man's house and a brave, who had fallen at his post there. *Eheu, Eheu,* what a world![31]

[A few days later he addressed his wife:]

Nieder-Rathen . . . near Dresden,
25 September . . . 1852—

I wrote to you from Weimar, some five days ago; and therefore there is nothing pressing me at present to write: but having a quiet hour here by the side of the Elbe river, at the foot of wild rock mountains in the queerest region you ever saw, I throw you another word, not knowing when I may have another chance as good. . . . I am on the second floor in a little German Country inn, literally *washed* by the Elbe, which is lying in the moonshine as clear as a mirror and as silent: right above us is a high Peak called the *Bastei* (Bastion) a Kind of thing you are obliged to *do* (by Tourist law); this we have *done*, & are to go tomorrow towards Frederick's first battle field in the 7-Years' war; after which the second day (if all go well) will bring us into Berlin. We came by an Elbe steamer; go on tomorrow at nine . . . by another steamer, then by railway,— and hope to *see*, tho' alas in quiet confused circumstances and to little advantage, some of the actual footsteps of Father Fritz, for here too amid these rocks, as well as farther on at Lobositz, he did feats.[32]

Mrs. Carlyle was still in Chelsea with her workmen all this time. It had been a trying summer to her. But she had the comfort of knowing that her husband was achieving the part of the business which had fallen to his share, better than might have been looked for.

[From Bad Töplitz Carlyle wrote to Jane two days later.]

We have actually *seen* Lobositz, the first Battlefield of Fritz in the 7-Years War; and walked over it all, this morning before break-fast under the guidance of a Christian native, checked by my best memory of reading and maps; and found it do very tolerably well.[33]

[By 1 October he was in Berlin.]

Here you see we are; at the *summit* of these wanderings; from which, I hope, there is for me a swift *perpendicular* return before long, not a slow parabolic one as the ascent has been. We came four-and-twenty hours ago, latish last night, from Frankfurt on the Oder, from the field of Cunersdorf (a dreadful scraggy village, where Fritz received his worst defeat). . . .

Berlin is *loud* almost as London, but in no other way great [or] among the greatest. I should guess it about the size of Liverpool, and more like Glasgow in the straight openness of its streets. Many grand public edifices about this eastern end of the Town; but on the whole it looks in many quarters almost shabby, in spite of its noise and paint, so *low* are the houses for a Capital city; more like ware-houses, or malt kilns with the very chimneys wanting (for within is nothing but stoves). This *Unter den Linden* (under the lime-trees) is the *one* good street of the place; as if another Princes-street at 300 yards distance and with tree-rows between them ran parallel to the Princes Street we know.[34]

[A week later he again wrote to Jane:]

We do leave Berlin tomorrow (Saturday the 9th); go by Bruns-wick, by Hanover, Cologne . . . and from thence on *Tuesday eve-ning* at Ostend I find a steamer direct for London. . . .

I have had a terrible tumbling week in Berlin,—O what a month in general I have had; month of the profoundest, ghastliest *solitude*, in the middle of incessant talk and locomotion!—but here, after all, I have got my things not so intolerably *done*; and have accomplished what was reasonably possible. . . . Yesterday I saw old Tieck: beautiful old man; so serene, so calm, so sad. . . . You will see me (*Deo volente*) on *Wednesday* but not till *noon* or later.[35]

So was this terrible journey got done with, which to anyone but Carlyle would have been a mere pleasure trip; to him terrible in prospect, terrible in the execution, terrible in the retrospect. His wife said he could not conceal that he was pretty well, and had nothing really to complain of.

chapter twenty-six

1852–1858

The Cock Torment. Death of Carlyle's
Mother. Jane Carlyle's Domestic
Budget. Death of Lady Ashburton.
Carlyle as Historian

The painters had not completed their work, and the smell was insupportable when Carlyle got home in the middle of October. He was in no condition to face any more annoyances, and he and his wife took refuge for three weeks at the Grange with the ever hospitable Ashburtons. There, too, the sulphurous mood was still predominant, and things did not go well with him. It was not till November that he was fairly re-established in his own quarters, and in a condition to so much as think of seriously beginning his work. A preliminary skirmish became necessary, to put to silence his neighbour's cocks. Mr. Remington, who then lived near him, and was the owner of the offenders, has kindly sent me the correspondence which passed on the occasion; very gracious and humble on Carlyle's part, requesting only that the cocks in question should be made inaudible from midnight till breakfast time;[1] Mr. Remington, though they were favourites which he had brought from Northumberland, instantly consenting to suppress them altogether. This accomplished, Carlyle proceeded as it were to clear the stage by recovering his own mental condition, and took himself severely to task for what he found amiss. Much that he says will seem exaggerated, but it will be remembered that he was not speaking to the world but to himself. It is idle to judge him by common rules. His nerves were abnormally sensitive. He lived habitually, unless he violently struggled against it, in what he had described as "an element of black streaked with lightning."

To begin *Frederick* then! It was easier to propose than to do. When a writer sets to work again after a long pause, his faculties have, as it were, to be caught in the field and brought in and harnessed. There was anxiety about his wife too, who was worn out by her summer discipline, and was never "thinner these seven years."[2]

He would have got underway in some shape, but, before starting, any distraction is enough to check the first step, and there were distractions in plenty; among the rest the Duke of Wellington's funeral. The Duke had died in September. He was now to be laid in his tomb in the midst of a mourning nation; and Carlyle did not like the display. The body lay in state at Chelsea, "all the empty fools of creation" running to look at it. One day two women were trampled to death in the throng at the hospital close by; and the whole thing, except for that dreadful accident, was, in his eyes, "a big bag of wind and nothingness." "It is indeed," he said,

> a sad and solemn fact for England, that such a man has been called away: the *last* perfectly honest and perfectly brave Public Man they had; and they ought, in reverence, to reflect on that, and sincerely testify that (if they could), while they commit him to his resting place. But alas for the "sincerity!" It is even professedly all hypocrisy, noise, and expensive upholstery; from which a serious mind turns away with sorrow and abhorrence.[3]

[Early in 1853] he began at last to write something—but it was wrongly pitched. It would not do, and he threw it aside. In March he was off to the Grange again—off there always when the Ashburtons invited him—but always, or almost so, to no purpose. "Worse than useless to me," he said when the visit was over. The party at the Grange was in itself brilliant enough. Venables was there, whom he liked better than most men; and Azeglio and other notabilities.[4] But even Venables, on this occasion, he found "full of dogmatic convictions," and to Azeglio he was rude. Azeglio had been talking contemptuously of Mazzini. " 'Monsieur,' " said Carlyle to him, " 'vous ne le connaissez pas du tout, du tout,' and turned abruptly away, and sat down to a Newspaper." I "cannot *ever* get a word of sense talked to me except by accident."[5] A week at the Grange was as much as he could bear, and it did not seem to have done very much for him.

To try to work Carlyle was determined enough. He went

nowhere in the summer, but remained at Chelsea chained to *Frederick*, and, moving ahead at last, leaving his wife to take a holiday. His brother John, who was now married, had taken a house at Moffat, and Mrs. Carlyle, needing change, went off to stay with him there. Paint was wanted in Cheyne Row again, and Carlyle was exquisitely sensitive to the smell of it. Other cocks—not, it is to be hoped, Mr. Remington's—set up their pipes in the summer mornings. A "vile yellow Italian" came grinding under his windows.[6] He had a terrible time of it; but he set his teeth and determined to bear his fate.

"Greater than man, less than woman," as Essex said of Queen Elizabeth.[7] The cocks were locked up next door, and the fireworks at Cremorne were silent, and the rain fell and cooled the July air; and Carlyle slept, and the universe became once more tolerable.

A real calamity, sad but inevitable and long foreseen, was now approaching. Signs began to show that his old mother at Scotsbrig was drawing near the end of her pilgrimage. She was reported to be ill, and even dangerously ill. Mrs. Carlyle hurried over from Moffat to assist in nursing her, meeting, when she arrived there, the never-forgotten but humbly offered birthday present of July 14 from her poor husband. Her mother-in-law, while she was there, sank into the long, death-like trance which she so vividly describes.[8] Contrary to all expectations, the strong resolute woman rallied from it, and Carlyle, always hopeful, persuaded himself that for the time the stroke had passed over.

The alarm at Scotsbrig having passed off, minor evils became again important. The great cock question revived in formidable proportions. Mrs. Carlyle had gone to her cousin's at Liverpool, but her presence was needed urgently in Cheyne Row to deal with it. A room was to be constructed at the top of the house, where neither cockcrows nor other sound could penetrate; but until it was completed the *"unprotected Male,"* as Carlyle called himself,[9] was suffering dismally. Morning after morning the horrid clarions blew. "Those Cocks must either withdraw or die," he cried. "That is a fixed point;—and I must do it myself if no one will help."[10] For some cause there was a respite for a night or two, but now the owner of the cocks, one Ronca, was heard

THE SOUNDPROOF ROOM. Built on to the Chelsea home in 1853 at considerable cost. Carlyle describes it as "a dreadful enterprise, that proved, the *chaotic* element throughout:—a true *Satan's Invisible World Displayed*." And Jane Carlyle: "Alas! and the silent apartment has turned out the noisiest apartment in the house." Here Carlyle labored for many years over his six-volume *History of Friedrich II. of Prussia, called Frederick the Great.* After the work's completion in 1865, he rarely used the upstairs study. (A Gordon Fraser card, published for the National Trust.)

coughing at half-past eight in the morning, and this—but this could hardly be made a crime. "Poor Devil," he said to himself, with a tinge of remorse, "a bad cough indeed, as I said to myself; and I am to be annoyed at the mere *noise* of it! Selfish mortal indeed!"[11] Lady Ashburton, hearing of his forlorn condition, made over the now vacant Addiscombe to him. His wife came back. The cocks were for a time disposed of, and the new room was set about. The new room was the final hope. Till it was finished there could be no surety of peace. "Ach Gott!" he said, "I am wretched, and (in silence) nearly mad!"[12]

To *great* evils one must oppose great virtues;—and also to *small*; which is the harder task of the two. Masons (who have already *killed* a year of my life, in a too sad manner), are again upon the roof of the house,—after a dreadful bout of resolution on my part,—building me a SOUNDLESS ROOM! "The world, which can do me no good, shall at least not torment me with its street and backyard *noises*." . . . Alas, alas, my dear old Mother seems to be fading fast away from me: my thoughts are dark and sad continually with that idea, *inexorabile fatum*; the great the eternal is there; and also the paltriest and smallest, to load me down. I seem to be sinking inextricably into Chaos.[13]

Of the two extreme trials of which Carlyle spoke, the greatest, the one which really and truly was to shake his whole nature, was approaching its culmination. Although his mother had rallied remarkably from her attack in the summer, and was able to read and converse as usual, there had been no essential recovery; there was to be and there could be none. His mother, whom he had regarded with an affection "passing the love of sons," with whom, in spite of, or perhaps in consequence of, her profound Christian piety, he had found more in common, as he often said, than with any other mortal—was now evidently about to be taken away from him. A feeling peculiarly tender had united these two. . . . Carlyle, as his letters show, had been haunted from his earliest days by the terror that he must one day lose her. She had watched over the workings of his mind with passionate solicitude: proud of his genius, and alternately alarmed for his soul. In the long evenings when they had sate together over the fire with their pipes at Mainhill, he had half-satisfied her that he and she were one in heart and in essentials. His first earnings, when a school usher, were spent in con-

521

tributing to her comforts. When money came from Boston for *The French Revolution,* the "Kitlin" instantly sent "the auld cat" an "American mouse."[14] If she gloried in his fame and greatness, he gloried more in being the son of the humble Margaret Carlyle—and while she lived, she, and only she, stood between him and the loneliness of which he so often and so passionately complained. No one else, perhaps, ever completely understood his character; and of all his letters none are more tenderly beautiful than those which he sent to Scotsbrig.

It could not have been with any pleasure that, at a moment when his mother was so manifestly sinking, Carlyle felt himself called on to go again to the Grange. He had been at home only a month since he last left. But there was to be a grand gathering of great London people there. The Ashburtons were pressing, and he was under too many obligations to refuse. They went, both of them, into the midst of London intellect and social magnificence. Mrs. Carlyle was able to stay a few days only, for the cock problem had reached a crisis. In his despair, Carlyle had thought of actually buying the lease of the house where the dreadful creatures were nourished, turning the people out and leaving it empty. The "Demon Fowls" were a standing joke at the witty Grange. Either he or his wife was required upon the spot to make an arrangement. He says that she proposed to go; she indicates that the pressure was on his side, and that she thought it a "wildgoose enterprize."[15] At any rate, the visit which was to have improved her health was cut short on this account, and she was packed off to Chelsea. He continued on in the shining circle till, on December 20, news came from Scotsbrig that his mother was distinctly worse and could not long survive. It was not quite clear that the danger was immediate. He tried to hope, but to no purpose. He felt that he ought to go down to her, at any rate that he ought not to continue where he was. His hostess consented to his going; he writes as if he had been obliged to apply for permission. Lady Ashburton, he says in one place, gave him leave.[16] He hurried to Scotsbrig, stopping only a night in London, and was in time to see his mother once more alive. He has left several accounts of the end of this admirable woman. That in his Journal is the most concise.

The stroke has fallen; my dear old Mother is gone from me; and in the winter of the year, confusedly under darkness of weather and of mind, the stern final epoch, *epoch of old age,* is beginning to unfold itself for me. . . . It is matter of perennial thankfulness to me, and beyond my *desert* in that matter by far, that I found my dear old Mother still alive, able to recognise me with a faint joy, her former *self* still strangely visible there in all its lineaments, tho' worn to the uttermost thread. The brave old Mother, and the good,— whom to lose had been my fear ever since intelligence awoke in me in this world;—arrived now at the final bourne. . . . I came into the room where John was now watching: "Here is Tom come to bid you goodnight, Mother," said he; she smiled assent, took leave of me as usual (tho' I kissed her lips, which was not usual): as I turned to go, she said . . . "I'm muckle obleeged t' ye." Those were her last voluntary words in this world. . . . After that she spoke no more; slept ever deeper. Her sleep lasted almost 16 hours; she lay on her back, stirred no muscle; the face was as that of a statue, with slight changes of expression ("infinite astonishment" was what one might have fancied to read on it at one time); the breathing not very hard nor quick, yet evidently difficult, and not changing sensibly in character,—till 4 p.m. when it suddenly fell lower; paused, again paused, perhaps still again,—and our good and dear old Mother was gone from her sorrows and from us. I did not weep much, or at all except for moments; but the sight, too, and the look backwards and forwards was one that a far harder heart might have melted under. Farewell, farewell.— She was about 84 years of age; and could not with advantage to any side, remain with us longer. Surely it was a good Power that gave us such a Mother; and good tho' stern, that took her away, from amid such "grief and labour," by a death beautiful to our thoughts. "All the days of my appointed time will I wait, till my change come," this they often heard her muttering, amid many other less-frequent pious texts and passages. Amen, Amen— Sunday, 25 december. It was on Christmas day, 1853; a day henceforth memorable to me.[17]

In London, when settled there again, he lived for many weeks in strictest seclusion, working at his task or trying to work, but his mind dwelling too constantly on his irreparable loss to allow him to make progress. His Journal shows a gradual but slow, very slow recovery out of his long prostration.

The year 1854 was spent almost entirely in London. Neither Carlyle nor his wife was absent for more than a day or two; she in indifferent health, to which she was stoically resigning herself; he "in dismal continual wrestle" with *Frederick,* "the inexecutable book," and rather "in bilious condition," which meant what we know. The work which he

JANE WELSH CARLYLE. On this photograph Carlyle has written: "28*th* July 1854 (by Tait): some considerable likeness." (Courtesy of the Columbia University Libraries.)

had undertaken was immense; desperate as that of the girl in the fairy tale with the pile of tangled silks before her; and no beneficent godmother to help him through with it; and the *gea* [wane] of life, the spring and fire of earlier years, gone out of him. He allowed what was going on in the world to distract him as little as possible; but the sounds of such things broke in upon him, and were as unwelcome as the cocks had been. The Crimean war was in prospect, and the newspapers were crowing as loud as the Demon Fowls.

The French alliance, into which we were drawn by the Crimean affair, was not, in Carlyle's opinion, a compensating circumstance—very much the reverse. The Revolution of 1848, a weak repetition of 1793, had been followed by a corresponding Napoleonic Empire, a parody on the first. Carlyle had known Louis Napoleon in England. He had watched him stepping to the throne through perjury and massacre, and had been indignant and ashamed for the nation who could choose or tolerate at its head an adventurer unrecommended by a single virtue. From the first, he was certain that for such a man no good end was to be looked for. It was with a feeling of disgust that he found the English newspapers now hailing the "scandalous Copper Captain,"[18] as he called him, as the saviour of European order, and a fit ally for England. It was with something more than disgust that he heard of this person paying a visit to the Queen of England, and being welcomed by her as a friend and brother sovereign. The war and its consequences and circumstances he thrust out of his mind, to the utmost possible distance, and thought of other things.

At Cheyne Row the great feature was the completion of the "sound-proof" room, into which he was "whirled by angry elements."[19] It was built above the highest story, the roof being, as it were, lifted over it, and was equal in size to the whole area on which the house stood. A second wall was constructed inside the outer one, with a space between to deaden external noise. There were doors in the inner wall, and windows in the outer, which could be opened for ventilation, but the room itself was lighted from above. It had no outlook except to the sky. Here Carlyle spent his working hours, cut off from everyone—"whirled" aloft, as he said; angry at the fate which had driven him into such a refuge, and finding in it, when finished, the faults inseparable from all human contrivances. But he did admit that the "light" was "perfectly superb," and all "*softer*" sounds were "all killed in their road" to him, and that of "sharp sound" scarce "the 20*th* or 30*th* part" could penetrate.[20] The cocks had been finally abolished, *purchased* out of existence by

CARLYLE IN 1854. Photograph almost in profile by Robert Tait taken 31 July
1854, a few days before Carlyle ceased shaving as a result of a wager with Lord
Ashburton. With the return of the army from the Crimean War, beards came
into fashion. Every subsequent photograph or painting of Carlyle shows him with
a beard. "Carlyle in 1869 described this as the best likeness known to him, and,
discounting something immobile in the expression and set in the pose, as if he were
holding himself in position, it seems a very true record of his features if not a very
profound index of his mind" (James L. Caw, "A Commentary on Carlyle's
Portraits"). (Courtesy of the Scottish National Portrait Gallery.)

a £5 note and Mrs. Carlyle's diplomacy. Thus they "were quiet as mice," he working with all his might, dining out nowhere, save once with the Procters, to meet Dickens, and finding it "the most *hideous* evening I have had for years."[21] Under these conditions, *Frederick* ought to have made progress, if it could progress at all. But it seemed as if it could not.

Advancing years have one inseparable accompaniment, painful if we like to make it so, or soft and sad, as an ordinance of nature—a thing which has to be, and must be so accepted. Each season takes away with it more and more of the friends whom we have known and loved, cutting one by one the strings which attach us to our present lives, and lightening the reluctance with which we recognise our own time approaching. Anyone at all that we have personally known has a friendly aspect when we hear that he is dead. Even if he has done us an ill turn, he cannot do it again. We forget the injuries we have received, because, after all, they did not seriously hurt us; we remember the injuries which we have done, because they are past remedy. With the dead, whatever they were, we only desire to be at peace. Between John Wilson and Carlyle there had never been any cordial relation. They had met in Edinburgh in the old days; on Carlyle's part there had been no backwardness, and Wilson was not unconscious of Carlyle's extraordinary powers. But he had been shy of Carlyle, and Carlyle had resented it, and now this April the news came that Wilson was gone, and Carlyle had to write his epitaph.

> John Wilson dead at Edinburgh about 10 days ago: apoplexy had gradually cut him out of the lists of the active, years ago, and for 6 months had quite broken his memory, &c., and rendered recovery hopeless. I knew his figure well; remember well first seeing him on Princes Street, on a bright April afternoon probably 1814 (exactly forty years ago!). . . . The broad shouldered stately bulk of the man struck me; his flashing eyes, copious dishevelled head of hair, and rapid unconcerned progress (like that of a plough thro' stubble): I really liked him, but only from the distance, and thought no more of him. It must have been 14 years later before I once saw his figure again, and began to have some distant straggling acquaintance of a personal kind with him. Glad could I have been to be better and more familiarly acquainted; but tho' I liked much in him, and he somewhat in me, it would not do. He was always very kind to me; but seemed to have a feeling I should (could) not be-

come wholly *his* (in which he was right), and that on other terms he could not have me. So we let it so remain; and for many years (indeed, ever after quitting Edinburgh), I had no acquaintance with him,—occasionally got symptoms of his ill-humour with me (ink-spurts in *Blackwood*, read or heard of), which I in a surly silent manner strove to consider *flattering* rather. . . . In London, indeed, I seldom or never heard any talk of him; I never read his blustering, drunken *Noctes* (after Gordon in Edinburgh ceased to *bring* them to me): we lived *apart*, as if in different centuries,—tho', to say the truth, I always *loved* Wilson (really rather loved him), and could have fancied a most strict and very profitable *friendship* between us in different, happier circumstances. But it was not to be. . . . Wilson seemed to me always by far the most *gifted* of all our literary men, either then or still; and yet intrinsically he has written nothing that can endure: the central gift was wanting! Adieu, adieu! o, noble, ill-starred brother. . . . I know not if among all his "friends" he has left one who feels more recognisingly what he was, and how tragical his life when seemingly most successful, than I now. Adieu to him, good grand ruined soul, that never could be great, or indeed *be* anything.[22]

Carlyle's own special work at this time was confined almost to reading books. The little that he composed was unsatisfactory, and the entries in his Journal, which were unusually numerous in the period of forced inactivity, were at once an occupation and a relief. When once he was launched upon his enterprise, he had little leisure for self-reflection.

Miss Jewsbury says that no one who visited the Carlyles could tell whether they were poor or rich.[23] There were no signs of extravagance, but also none of poverty. The drawing-room arrangements were exceptionally elegant. The furniture was simple, but solid and handsome; everything was scrupulously clean; everything good of its kind; and there was an air of ease, as of a household living within its means. Mrs. Carlyle was well dressed always. Her admirable taste would make the most of inexpensive materials; but the materials themselves were of the very best. Carlyle himself generally kept a horse. They travelled, they visited, they were always generous and open-handed. They had their house on easy terms. The rent, which when they came first was £30 a year,[24] I think was never raised—out of respect for Carlyle's character; but it had many rooms in it, which, because they could not bear to have them otherwise, were maintained in the best condition. There was much

THE DRAWING ROOM. On the first floor front, this room was Carlyle's study in which he wrote *The French Revolution*. After 1843 it was used as a drawing room; in it the Carlyles entertained their many distinguished guests. Mrs. Carlyle, whose portrait by Gambardella is on the right, followed a Victorian fashion in covering the screen with prints. The armchair, with its swing reading desk, was given to Carlyle on his eightieth birthday by his friend John Forster. The fine three-quarter figure portrait by Robert Tait (1855) hangs above the mantle. (A Gordon Fraser card, published for the National Trust.)

curiosity among their friends to know how their establishment was supported. Mrs. Carlyle had £150 a year from
Craigenputtoch. He himself, in a late calculation, had set
down his average income from his books at another £150.
For several years before the time at which we have now
arrived he had published little which materially added to
this. There was a fixed annual demand for his works, but
not a large one. The *Cromwell* was a large book, and had
gone through three editions. I do not know precisely how
much he had received from it; perhaps £1,500. The *Latter-
Day Pamphlets* had produced little beyond paying their
expenses. The *Life of Sterling* was popular, but that too only
in a limited circle. Carlyle was thrifty, but never penurious;
he gave away profusely in his own family, and was liberal
beyond his means elsewhere. He had saved, I think, about
£2,000 in all, which was lying at interest in Dumfries bank,
and this was all. Thus his entire income at this time could
not have exceeded £400, if it was as much. His German tour
had been expensive. The new room had cost £170. The cost
of living was increasing through the rise in prices, which no
economy could guard against, and though they had but one
servant the household books mounted disagreeably. Mrs.
Carlyle, not wishing to add to her husband's troubles, had
as far as possible kept her anxieties to herself. Indeed, Carlyle was like most husbands in this matter, and was inclined
to be irritable when spoken to about it. But an explanation at
last became necessary, and the humorous acidity of tone
with which she entered on it shows that she had borne much
before she presented her statement. It is dated 12 February,
1855, and is endorsed by Carlyle "Jane's Missive on the
Budget," with a note appended.

> The inclosed was read with great laughter (had been found lying
> on my table, as I returned out of the frosty garden from smok-
> ing);—"debt" is already paid off; quarterly income to be £55 [?—MS
> torn] henceforth; and all is settled to poor Goody's heart's content.
> The Piece is so clever, that I cannot just yet, find in my heart to
> burn it, as perhaps I ought to do.— T.C.
>
> Chelsea . . . 17 february 1855—[25]

[Entitling her statement "Budget of a Femme Incom-
prise," Jane listed in detail and with much irony the rising
costs that necessitated a raise in her household allow-

ance.][26] Mrs. Carlyle, it must be admitted, knew how to administer a "shrewing." Her poor husband, it must be admitted, also knew how to bear one. He, perhaps, bore it too well, for there were parts of what she said which he might with advantage have laid to heart seriously. At any rate, he recognized instantly and without the least resentment the truth of a statement to which he had been too impatient to listen. The cleverness of it delighted him, in spite of the mockery of himself and his utterances.

No man ever behaved better under such a chastisement. Not a trace is visible of resentment or impatience, though also less regret than a perfect husband ought to have felt that he had to a certain extent deserved it. Unfortunately, knowing that he had meant no harm and had done all that he was asked to do the instant that the facts were before him, he never could take a lesson of this kind properly to heart, and could be just as inconsiderate and just as provoking on the next occasion that arose. Poor Carlyle! Well he might complain of his loneliness! though he was himself in part the cause of it. Both he and she were noble and generous, but his was the soft heart, and hers the stern one.

Frederick meanwhile, in spite of lamentations over failure, was at last moving. Carlyle had stood steadily to it for eighteen months, and when August came he required rest and change. Many friends were eager for the honour of entertaining him. There was no longer any mother to call him down to Scotsbrig. He selected among them Mr. Edward Fitzgerald, who had been useful to him in the *Cromwell* days, investigating Naseby field, and whose fine gifts of intellect and character he heartily loved and admired.[27] Mr. Fitzgerald lived at Woodbridge, near Farlingay, in Suffolk, an old-fashioned mansion-house of his own, in which he occupied a few rooms, the rest being a farm-house. The scene was new to him. A Suffolk farmer, "with a dialect almost equal to that of Nithsdale,"[28] was a fresh experience. The farm cookery was simple and wholesome, the air perfect, the sea, with a beach where he could bathe, at no great distance; his host ready to be the pleasantest of companions if his society was wished for, and as willing "to efface himself" when not wanted. Under these conditions, a "retreat" for a few days to Woodbridge was altogether agreeable. The love which all persons who really knew him felt for Carlyle made it a delight to minister to his comfort. His humours were part of himself. They took him as he was, knowing well how amply his conversation would pay for his entertainment. He, for his part, enjoyed himself exceptionally; he complained of nothing. Place, lodging, company were equally to his mind. "Fitz has been the best of Landlords, and has discharged the sacred rites really with a kind of Irish zeal and piety. A man not to be forgotten. . . . Fitz has done everything, *except* 'leave me well alone':—that he has not quite done; and to say truth, I shall not care to be off, and lie down in my own corner again, even with the sputter of Cremorne in the distance."[29]

Restless spirit! for "in his own corner," when "he did lie down in it," he grew "sleepless, disconsolate & good for little or nothing:"[30] The Ashburtons, knowing his condition, offered him Addiscombe again for the short remains of the summer, and there he and Mrs. Carlyle tried to make a brief holiday together. It did not answer. She preferred Chelsea and solitude, and left him to wander about the Surrey lanes alone.

I had not yet settled in London; but I came up occasionally to read books in the Museum, etc. I called as often as I ventured in Cheyne Row, and was always made welcome there. But I was a mere outward acquaintance, and had no right to expect such a man as Carlyle to exert himself for me. I had, however, from the time when I became acquainted with his writings, looked on him as my own guide and master—so absolutely that I could have said: "*errare malo cum Platone . . . quam cum istis vera sentire*" [I would rather be wrong with Plato than right with such men as these];[31] or, in Goethe's words, which I often indeed did repeat to myself: "*Mit deinem Meister zu irren ist dein Gewinn*" [To err with your Master is your reward].[32] The practice of submission to the authority of one whom one recognises as greater than one's self outweighs the chance of occasional mistake. If I wrote anything, I fancied myself writing it to him, reflecting at each word on what he would think of it, as a check on affectations. I was busy then on the first volume of my *History of England*. I had set the first two chapters in print that I might take counsel with friends upon them. I sent a copy to Carlyle, which must have reached him about the time of this Addiscombe sojourn, and it came back to me with pencil criticisms which, though not wanting in severity, consoled me for the censures which fell so heavily on those chapters when the book was published.[33]

Autumn passed on, and winter and spring, and Carlyle was still at his desk. At Christmas [1855] there was another visit to the Grange. "Company at first aristocratic and select (Lord Lansdowne and Robert Lowe); then miscellaneous, shifting, chiefly of the scientific kind,"[34] and moderately interesting. But his stay was short, and he was absorbed again at his work in the garret room. With Mrs. Carlyle, unfortunately, it was a period of ill-health, loneliness, and dispiritment. At the end of 1855 she had commenced the diary, from which her husband first learnt, after her death, how miserable she had been, and learnt also that he himself had been in part the cause.[35] It was continued on into the next spring and summer, in the same sad, stoically indignant tone; the consummation of ten years of resentment at an intimacy which, under happier circumstances, should have been equally a delight to herself, yet was ill-managed by all parties concerned, and steeped in gall and bitterness her own married life. It is impossible to suppose that Lady Ashburton was not aware of Mrs. Carlyle's feelings towards her. She had a right perhaps to think them ridiculous, but for Carlyle's own sake she ought to have been careful how she behaved to her. If nine-tenths of Mrs. Carlyle's injuries were imaginary, if her proud and sensitive disposition saw affronts where there had been only a great lady's negligence, there was a real something of which she had a right to complain; only her husband's want of perception in such matters could have prevented him from seeing how unfit it was that she should have to go and come at Lady Ashburton's bidding, under fear of her husband's displeasure.

A small incident in the summer of 1856, though a mere trifle in itself, may serve as an illustration of what she had to undergo. The Carlyles were going for a holiday to Scotland. Lady Ashburton was going also. She had engaged a palatial carriage, which had been made for the Queen and her suite, and she proposed to take the Carlyles down with her. The carriage consisted of a spacious saloon, to which, communi-

cating with it, an ordinary compartment with the usual six
seats in it was attached. Lady Ashburton occupied the saloon alone. Mrs. Carlyle, though in bad health and needing
rest as much as Lady Ashburton, was placed in the compartment with her husband, the family doctor, and Lady Ashburton's maid, a position perfectly proper for her if she was
a dependent, but in which no lady could have been placed
whom Lady Ashburton regarded as her own equal in rank.[36]
It may be that Mrs. Carlyle chose to have it so herself.
But Lady Ashburton ought not to have allowed it, and Carlyle ought not to have allowed it, for it was a thing wrong in
itself. One is not surprised to find that when Lady Ashburton offered to take her home in the same way she refused to
go.[37] "If there were any *companionship* in the matter,"
she said bitterly, when Carlyle communicated Lady Ashburton's proposal, "it would be different; and if *you* go back
with the Ashburtons it would be different, as then I should
be going merely as part of your luggage—without self responsibility."[38] Carlyle regarded the Ashburtons as "great people," to whom he was under obligations: who had been very
good to him: and of whose train he in a sense formed a
part. Mrs. Carlyle, with her proud, independent, Scotch republican spirit, imperfectly recognised these social distinctions. This it may be said was a trifle, and ought not to have
been made much of. But there is no sign that Mrs. Carlyle
did make much of what was but a small instance of her general lot. It happens to stand out by being mentioned inciden-
tally. That is all. But enough has been said of this sad matter,
which was now drawing near its end.

On reaching Scotland the party separated. Lady Ashburton went to the Highlands, where Carlyle was to follow in
September. Mrs. Carlyle went to her cousins in Fife and he
to Scotsbrig, which he had left last after his mother's funeral. All his family were delighted to see him once more
amongst them. His brother James was waiting for him at the
station. His sister-in-law had provided a long new pipe of
the right Glasgow manufacture: he would smoke nothing
else. His mother—she, alas! was not there: only the chair in
which she had sate, now vacant.

He had not come to Scotsbrig to be idle; he had his work
with him, at which he toiled on steadily. He had expected his

wife to join him there, but she showed no intention that way. He wrote to her regularly with his usual quiet affection. Her answers he found "sombre and distrustful perhaps beyond need," but "kind and good"; he begged her to "know, if you can, that in my own way none loves you so well, nor feels that he has better cause to do so."[39] From Scotsbrig he moved to his sister's at the Gill, by Annan—happy among his own kindred, longing to be "out of London, never to return," and to spend the rest of his days in a scene where health of mind and body would not be impossible.

There is one remedy for all evils. The occasion of the "rifts" in Carlyle's life was to be removed for ever in the ensuing spring.

> Monday, 4*th* May, 4 1/2 p.m., at Paris, died Lady Ashburton: a great and irreparable sorrow to me; yet with some beautiful consolations in it too. A thing that fills all my mind, since yesterday afternoon that Milnes came to me with the sad news,—which I had never once anticipated, tho' warned sometimes vaguely to do so. "God sanctify my sorrow," as the old pious phrase went! To her I believe it is a great gain, and the exit has in it much of noble beauty as well as pure sadness,—worthy of such a woman. Adieu, . . . adieu! Her work, call it her grand and noble Endurance of want of work—is all done![40]

He was present at the funeral, at Lord Ashburton's particular entreaty. It seemed like taking leave of the most precious possession which had belonged to him in the world. A few days after, the 22nd of May, he writes to his brother John: "I have indeed lost such a friend as I never had, nor am again in the least likelihood to have, in this *stranger* world: a magnanimous and beautiful soul, which had *furnished* the English Earth and made it homelike to me in many ways, is not now here. . . . Not since our Mother's [death] has there been to me anything resembling it."[41]

After this the days went on with sombre uniformity, Mrs. Carlyle still feeble and growing indeed yearly weaker, Carlyle toiling on in his "mud element," driving his way through it, hardly seeing anyone, and riding for three hours every afternoon. He had called his horse Fritz. "He was a very clever fellow," he said of him to me, "was much attached to me, and understood my ways. He caught sight in Palace Yard of King Richard's horse, clearly perceived that it was a horse, and was greatly interested in it. "Ah, Fritz," he once

535

apostrophised him, "you don't know all your good fortune. You were well brought up to know and do your duty. Nobody ever told you any lies about some one else that had done it for you."

The *Frederick* work did not grow more easy. The story, as it expanded, became the history of contemporary Europe, and even of the world, while Carlyle, like a genuine craftsman as he was, never shirked a difficulty, never threw a false skin over hollow places, or wrote a sentence the truth of which he had not sifted. One day he described himself as "busy drawing water for many hours; & from the deep Brandenburg Well, comes nothing but a coil of *wet rope*."[42] Still progress was made in July of this year 1857. The opening chapters were getting into print. He did not himself stir from London. The weather indoors had grown calmer after the occasion of difference was gone, and the gentle companionship of early days, never voluntarily impaired on his part, had partially returned. But change was necessary for her health. Her friends at Sunny Bank [Haddington] were really eager to have her, and he was glad to send her off.

The news of the Sepoy rebellion coming in this summer of course affected Carlyle, more, however, with sorrow than surprise. "Tongue cannot speak," he wrote, "the horrors that were done on the English by those mutinous hyaenas. Allow hyaenas to mutiny and strange things will follow." But he had long thought that "many British interests besides India were on a baddish road." The best that *he* could do was to get on with his own work, and not permit his attention to be drawn from it. Mrs. Carlyle greatly approved of the opening of *Frederick*. She recognised at once the superiority of it to any other work that he had done, and she told him so. He was greatly delighted; he called her remarks "the only bit of human criticism" which he had heard from anyone.[43]

> It would be worth while to write Books if mankind would read them as you do. . . . From the first discovery of me you have predicted good in a confident manner: all the *same* whether the world were singing chorus, or no part of the world dreaming of such a thing, but of much the reverse.[44]

He was essentially peaceable the whole time of her absence; a flash might come now and then, but of summer sheet-lightning, which meant no harm. Even distant cocks and wandering organ-grinders got nothing but a passing anathema.

[Early in September] she came home to him, and there was "joy in Nero and the Canaries, and in creatures more important here."[45] Work went on without interruption. Fritz gave increasing satisfaction, taking better care of his rider than his rider could have taken of himself, and showing fresh signs of the excellence of his education. Not only was the moral part of him what it should be, but he had escaped the special snare of London life. "He had not been brought up to think that the first duty of a horse was to say something witty." The riding was late in the afternoon, and lasted long after dusk, along the suburban roads, amidst the glare of the red and green railway lamps at the bridges, and the shrieks and roars of the passing trains; Fritz never stumbling or starting, or showing the least sign of alarm.

The Scotch do not observe times and seasons, and Christmas in London to so true a Scot as Carlyle was a periodic nuisance. The printers suspended work, and proof-sheets hung fire. English holidays might have been beautiful things in old days, in country manors and farms; but in modern Chelsea they meant husbands staggering about the streets, and their miserable wives trying to drag them home before the last of the wages was spent on beer and gin.

Indoors, happily, the old affectionate days had come back —the old tone, the old confidences. It had really been as he had said in the summer: "*Then*, for the rest of our life, we will be *more* to another than we ever were,—if it please Heaven!"[46] But Mrs. Carlyle suffered more than she had yet done from the winter cold, and a shadow of another kind now darkened the prospect.

> She has a particular *pain*, about a handbreadth below the heart, rather sore to the touch (or the pressure), not sore at all if not stirred; nor seemingly connected with *coughing* otherwise than by the mere *stir* produced: this is now some 3 weeks old, and vexes her somewhat;—Tait yesterday (judicious kind man!) assured her *he* knew that; and it was an "inflammation of the pleura" just getting under way!— If you can form any guess about it by this description, you may tell *me*."[47]

House worries, with servants, etc., did not improve Mrs. Carlyle. Fritz had been left at the Grange. Carlyle, driven to

"A CHELSEA INTERIOR" (1857) BY ROBERT TAIT. Carlyle, in a long figured dressing gown, stands at the mantelpiece filling his clay pipe (called a "churchwarden"); Mrs. Carlyle sits in the armchair. The view is of the dining or sitting room, looking toward the breakfast room, seen through the open folding doors. Mrs. Carlyle wrote in a letter of "that weary artist who took the bright idea last spring that he would make a picture of our Sitting Room to be 'amazingly interesting to posterity a hundred years hence.'" This Victorian ensemble conveys an atmosphere of domesticity quite convincing in its way. The painting was done for Lord Ashburton. (Postcard photograph, courtesy of the National Trust.)

his feet again, had lost his own chief comfort, and *Frederick* had to be continued in more indifferent spirits.

In spite of anxieties and "sordid miseries," the two volumes of *Frederick* meanwhile drew to completion. Carlyle (for him) was amazingly patient, evidently for his wife's sake having laid strong constraint on himself. His complaints, when he did complain, were of a human reasonable kind. Neuberg was most assiduous, and another young intelligent admirer—Mr. Larkin, who lived next door to him—had volunteered his services, which were most gratefully recognised.[48]

By the first of May the printers had their last "copy." By the end of May all was in type. In the second week in June the first instalment of the work on which he had been so busy toiling was complete and off his hands, waiting to be published in the autumn. For six years he had been labouring over it. In 1851 he had begun seriously to think about the subject. In 1852 he made his tour to Berlin and the battlefields. Ever since he had lain as in eclipse, withdrawn from all society save that of his most intimate friends. The effort had been enormous. He was sixty-three years old, and the furnace could be no longer heated to its old temperature. Yet he had thrown into the task all the strength he had left; and now, although the final verdict has long been pronounced on this book, in Germany especially, where the merits of it can be best appreciated, I must say a very few words myself about it, and on Carlyle's historical method generally.

History is the account of the actions of men; and in "actions" are comprehended the thoughts, opinions, motives, impulses of the actors and of the circumstances in which their work was executed. The actions without the motives are nothing, for they may be interpreted in many ways, and can only be understood in their causes. If *Hamlet* or *Lear* was exact to outward fact—were they and their fellow-actors on the stage exactly such as Shakespeare describes them, and if they did the acts which he assigns to them, that was perfect history; and what we call history is only valuable as it approaches to that pattern. To say that the characters of men cannot be thus completely known, that their inner nature is beyond our reach, that the dramatic portraiture of things is only possible to poetry, is to say that history ought not to be written, for the inner nature of the persons of whom it speaks is the essential thing about them; and, in fact, the historian assumes that he does know it, for his work without it is pointless and colourless. And yet to penetrate really into the hearts and souls of men, to give each his due, to represent him as he appeared at his best, to himself and not to his enemies, to sympathize in the collision of principles with each party in turn; to feel as they felt, to think as they thought, and to reproduce the various beliefs, the acquirements, the intellectual atmosphere of another age, is a task which requires gifts as great or greater than those of the greatest dramatists; for all is required which is required of the dramatist, with the obligation to truth of ascertained fact besides. It is for this reason that historical works of the highest order are so scanty. The faculty itself, the imaginative and reproductive insight, is among the rarest of human qualities. The moral determination to use it for purposes of truth only is rarer still—nay, it is but in particular ages of the world that such work can be produced at all. The historians of genius themselves, too, are creatures of their own time, and it is only at periods when men of intellect have "swallowed formulas," when conventional and established ways of thinking have ceased to satisfy, that, if they are serious and conscientious, they are able "to sympathize with opposite sides."

It is said that history is not of individuals; that the proper concern of it is with broad masses of facts, with tendencies which can be analysed into laws, with the evolution of humanity in general. Be it so—but a science can make progress only when the facts are completely ascertained; and before any facts of human life are available for philosophy we must have those facts exactly as they were. You must have Hamlet before you can have a theory of Hamlet, and it is to be observed that the more completely we know the truth of any incident, or group of incidents, the less it lends itself to theory. We have our religious historians, our constitutional historians, our philosophical historians; and they tell their stories each in their own way, to point conclusions which they have begun by assuming—but the conclusion seems plausible only because they know their case imperfectly, or because they state their case imperfectly. The writers of books are Protestant or Catholic, religious or atheistic, despotic or Liberal; but nature is neither one nor the other, but all in turn. Nature is not a partisan, but out of her ample treasure-house she produces children in infinite variety, of which she is equally the mother, and disowns none of them; and when, as in Shakespeare, nature is represented truly, the impressions left upon the mind do not adjust themselves to any philosophical system. The story of Hamlet in Saxo-Grammaticus might suggest excellent commonplace lessons on the danger of superstition, or the evils of uncertainty in the law of succession to the crown, or the absurdity of monarchical government when the crown can be the prize of murder. But reflections of this kind would suggest themselves only where the story was told imperfectly, and because it was told imperfectly. If Shakespeare's *Hamlet* be the true version of that Denmark catastrophe, the mind passes from commonplace moralising to the tragedy of humanity itself. And it is certain that if the thing did not occur as it stands in the play, yet it did occur in some similar way, and that the truth, if we knew it, would be equally affecting—equally unwilling to submit to any representation except the undoctrinal and dramatic.

What I mean is this, that whether the history of humanity can be treated philosophically or not, whether any evolutionary law of progress can be traced in it or not, the facts must be delineated first with the clearness and fulness which we demand in an epic poem or a tragedy. We must have the real thing before we can have a science of a thing. When that is given, those who like it may have their philosophy of history, though probably they will care less about it; just as wise men do not ask for theories of Hamlet, but are satisfied with Hamlet himself. But until the real thing *is* given, philosophical history is but an idle plaything to entertain grown children with.

And this was Carlyle's special gift—to bring dead things and dead people actually back to life; to make the past once more the present, and to show us men and women playing their parts on the mortal stage as real flesh-and-blood human creatures, with every feature which he ascribes to them authenticated, not the most trifling incident invented, and yet as a result with figures as completely alive as Shake-

541

speare's own.[49] Very few writers have possessed this double gift of accuracy and representative power. I could mention only two, Thucydides and Tacitus; and Carlyle's power as an artist is greater than either of theirs. Lockhart said, when he read *Past and Present,* that, except Scott, in this particular function no one equalled Carlyle.[50] I would go farther, and say that no writer in any age had equalled him. Dramatists, novelists have drawn characters with similar vividness, but it is the inimitable distinction of Carlyle to have painted actual persons with as much life in them as novelists have given to their own inventions, to which they might ascribe what traits they pleased. He worked in fetters—in the fetters of fact; yet, in this life of Frederick, the king himself, his father, his sister, his generals, his friends, Voltaire, and a hundred others, all the chief figures, large and small, of the eighteenth century, pass upon the stage once more, as breathing and moving men and women, and yet fixed and made visible eternally by the genius which has summoned them from their graves. A fine critic once said to me that Carlyle's Friedrich Wilhelm was as peculiar and original as Sterne's Walter Shandy; certainly as distinct a personality as exists in English fiction. It was no less an exact copy of the original Friedrich Wilhelm—his real self, discerned and reproduced by the insight of a nature which had much in common with him.

chapter twenty-seven

1858–1862

Second Tour of Germany. Publication of
First Two Volumes of *Frederick*.
Carlyle's Character. Jane Carlyle's
Declining Health. Friendship with
Ruskin. *Frederick* Marches On

No further progress could be made with *Frederick* till there
had been a second tour in Germany, which was to be
effected, if possible, in the summer or autumn of this year,
1858. The immediate necessity, after the completion of the
present volumes, was for rest. When the strain was taken
off, Carlyle fell into a collapsed condition. Notwithstanding
his good resolutions, he became slightly fretful and troublesome, having nothing immediate to do. He was somewhat
out of health, and fancied himself worse than he was. Mrs.
Carlyle had grown better with the warmer weather; he could
venture to leave her, and he went off in the middle of June to
his sister in Annandale.

He bethought himself that before he left London he had
been more cross than he ought to have been, indeed both
cross and perverse. It was "the nature of the beast," as he
often said, and had to be put up with, like the wind and the
rain. Gloom, as usual, clung to him like a shadow.

> I go on well; am very sad and solitary; ill in want of a horse. . . .
> The evening walks in the grey howl of the winds, by the loneliest
> places I can find, are like walks in Hades; yet there is something
> wholesome in them, something stern & grand: as if one had the
> Eternities for company in defect of suitabler.[1]

The Eternities, however fond he was of their company, left
him time to think of other things. His wife's cousin, John
Welsh, was ill. He at once insisted that the boy should go to
Madeira, and should go at his own and his wife's expense.
If thoughtful charity recommends men to the Higher Pow-

ers, none ever better deserved of them than Carlyle. But he thought nothing of such things.

One of Mrs. Carlyle's letters had been delayed in the post. It arrived a day later. He writes:

> All yesterday, I remarked in speaking to [his sister] Jean, if any tragic topic came in sight, I had a difficulty to keep from breaking down in my speech, and becoming *in*articulate with emotion over it! It is as if the scales were falling from my eyes; and I were beginning to *see*, in this my solitude, things that touch me into the very quick. Oh my little woman, what a suffering thou hast had; and how nobly borne,—with a simplicity, a silence, courage and patient *heroism* which are now only too evident to me! Three *waer* [sadder] days I can hardly remember in my life;—but they were not without worth either; very blessed some of the feelings, tho' many so sore and miserable. It is very good to be *left alone* with the truth sometimes; to hear with all its sternness what *it* will say to one.[2]

All this was extremely morbid; but it was not an unnatural consequence of habitual want of self-restraint, coupled with tenderness of conscience when conscience was awake and could speak. It was likely enough that in those night-watches, *when the scales fell off,* accusing remembrances must have risen before him which were not agreeable to look into. With all his splendid gifts, moral and intellectual alike, Carlyle was like a wayward child—a child in wilfulness, a child in the intensity of remorse.

His brother James provided him with a horse—a "dromedary," he called it, "a loyal horse too, but an extremely stupid"[3]—to ride or drive about among the scenes of his early years. One day he went past Hoddam Hill, Repentance Tower, Ecclefechan churchyard, etc., beautiful, quiet, all of it, in the soft summer air, and yet he said, "the Valley of Jehoshaphat could not have been more stern and terribly impressive to me. I shall never forget that afternoon and evening. The poor old Churchyard tree at Ecclefechan, . . . *the* white Headstone, of which I caught one steady look: . . . the deepest *De Profundis* is poor to the feeling one's poor heart has."[4] The thought of his wife, ill and solitary in London, tortured him. Would she come to the Gill to be nursed? No one in the world loved her more dearly than his sister Mary. The daughters would wait on her, and be her servants. He would himself go away, that he might be no trouble to her. Amidst his sorrows the ridiculous lay close at hand. If he was to go to Germany, his clothes had to be seen to. An entire new wardrobe was provided, dressing-gown, coats, trousers lying "like a considerable Hay-Coil round me"; rather well-made too, after all, though "this whole clothes operation has been scandalous and disgusting to me in some measure,—owing to the anarchy of things and shopkeepers in these parts." He had been recommended to wear a leather belt for the future when he rode.[5] His sisters did their best, but "the problem has become abstruse,—to me inexpressively wearisome"; a saddler had to be called in from Dumfries, and there was adjusting and readjusting. Carlyle, "sad and mournful," impatient, irritated, declared himself disgusted with the "problem," and more disgusted with himself, when he witnessed his sister's "industrious helpfulness, and my own unhelpable nature."[6]

A visit to Craigenputtoch had become necessary. There was business to be attended to, the tenant to be seen and spoken with, etc. He rather dreaded this adventure, but it was not to be avoided.[7]

Germany was to come next, and to come immediately, before the days drew in. He shuddered at the recollection of the *zwei rühige Zimmer* [two quiet rooms], etc., in which he had suffered so much torture. But he felt that he must go, cost what it might. Some friend had proposed to take him in a yacht to the Mediterranean and land him at Trieste. Lord Ashburton more reasonably had offered him a cast in another yacht to the Baltic. But Carlyle chose to stand by the ordinary modes of conveyance. He sent for his passport, nailed a map of Germany to his wall, daily perused it, and sketched an outline of his route. Mr. Neuberg, who was at Leipzig, was written to, but it was doubtful whether he was attainable. A Mr. Foxton, a slight acquaintance, offered his companionship, and was conditionally accepted; and after one or two "preliminary shivers" and "shuddering recoils," Carlyle screwed his courage to the sticking-point and, in spite of nerves and the rest of it, got through with the operation. The plan was to go by steam to Hamburg; whither next was not quite decided when an invitation came from Baron von Usedom and his English wife to visit them in the Isle of Rügen. It was out of the way; but Stralsund, Rügen, the

Baltic, were themselves interesting. The Usedoms' letter was most warm, and Carlyle, who rather doubted Mr. Foxton's capabilities as courier, thought that this excursion might "put him on his trial." He could be dismissed afterwards if found unsuitable. Much anxiety was given to poor Mr. Foxton. Neuberg held out hopes of joining, and Foxton in that case would not be wanted. But John Carlyle suggested that Neuberg and he would perhaps neutralize each other, like alkali and acid. On August 21 Carlyle went off to Edinburgh, whither poor Mr. Foxton had come, at great inconvenience to himself. He found his friend "very talky, scratch'-o-plastery somewhat, but serviceable, assiduous, and good compared with *nothing*."[8] The evening of the same day they sailed from Leith.

[Carlyle narrates his journey through his letters to Jane Carlyle.]

> Hamburg . . .
> 24 August 1858

Dearest,—

Here I am safe enough since 8 hours, after such a voyage for tumult and discomfort (now forgotten) as I have seldom made. The Leith people, innocent but ineffectual souls, forgot every promise they had made,—except that of sailing 5 hours after their time, and landing us at last, 15 hours after ditto. . . . Neuberg had a man *in wait* (poor good soul, after all!) to say that *he* was ready at any hour &c.[9]

> Carzitz,
> Insel Rügen, bei Stralsund
> 27th August, 1858

Yesterday about 11 a.m. after two rather sleepless and miserable nights on land, which with the 3 preceding at sea, had reduced me to a bad pitch,—I had, with poor helpless but assiduous Foxton, stepped out of the railway train at Rostock (biggish Sea Capital of Mecklenburg); and was hurrying along to get a place in the Stralsund *Diligence*, with no prospect but eight hours of suffocation and a night to follow without sleep, when a jolly plump Lady attended by her maid addressed me with sunny voice and look, "Was not I Mr. Carlyle?" "I am the Frau von Usedom," rejoined she on my answer; "*here* to seek you" (64 miles from home!) "and you must go with me henceforth!" Hardly in my life had such a manus e nubibus [hand from heaven] been extended to me. I need not say how thrice gladly I accepted;—I had in fact done with all my labour then; and was carried on thenceforth like a mere child in arms, nothing to do or care for, but all conceivable accommodations gracefully provided me up hither to this pleasant Isle of the Sea, where I now am, a considerably rested man! . . . Oh my poor little Jeannie, if I knew you were but *well*, I think I could be almost happy here today, in the silent sunshine, on these remote Scandinavian shores. . . . The wind is singing and the sun sporting in the Lindens, and I hear *doves* cooing: windows up—two rooms all to myself—"Coo, coo!"[10]

> Berlin,
> 5 September (Sunday) 1858—

The Herr von Usedom is a fine fat substantial intelligent and good man; we really had a great deal of nice speech together, and did beautifully together; only that I was so weak and sickly, and except keeping me to the picturesque, he would not take almost any wise charge of my ulterior affairs. *At length*, Friday afternoon last [3 September], he did set out with me towards Berlin and practicalities: "To stay overnight at Putbus the Richmond of Rügen, and then catch the Steamer for Stettin (& thence rail to Berlin) next day." . . .

Berlin is loud under my windows, a grey, close, hottish sunday; but I will take care not to concern myself with it beyond the needful: tomorrow we [Carlyle, Neuberg, and Foxton] are off,—Liegnitz, Breslau, Prag, then *Dresden*; . . . after which, only *two* Battlefields remain; and London is within a week. Neuberg is also going straight to London: you may compute that all the travelling *details*, washtubs, railways, money-settlements &c are fairly off my hands from this point. I have strength *enough* in me, too; with the snatches of sleep fairly expectable, I conclude myself roadworthy for 14 days. Then adieu, *Keil-kissen* [wedge-shaped pillows of German beds], sloppy greasy victual (all *cold* too, including especially the coffee and the tea); adieu Teutschland; adieu travelling altogether, and I will never leave my Goody any more.[11]

> Brieg (Lower Silesia)
> 10 September (friday) 1858

We quitted Berlin, under fair auspices, Monday morning last; fortified with a general letter from "the Prince's Aide-de-camp" to all Prussian Officers whatsoever: but hitherto, owing to an immense *review* which occupies everybody, it has done us less good than was expected. At Cüstrin, that first Monday night, a benevolent Major did attend us to the Field of Zorndorf, & shewed us everything: but in other places hitherto the "review at Liegnitz" has been fatal to help from such quarter. We have done pretty well without;—have seen 3 other fields, and had adventures, of a confused, not wholly unpleasant, character. . . . Our second place was Liegnitz itself (full of soldiers, oak-garlands, coloured lamplets, and expectation of "the Prince"): we were *on* the Battlefield, and could use our natural eyes; but for the rest had no other guidance worth other than contempt. Did well enough, nevertheless, and got fairly *out* of Liegnitz, to Breslau, Wednesday Evening, which has been headquarters ever since (a dreadfully noisy place at night), out of which were excursions—yesterday to Leuthen (the grandest of all the Battles); today hither, about 50 miles away, to Molwitz the *first* of Fritz's Fights; from which we have just now returned. . . . Leuthen yesterday & Molwitz today, with their respective steeples and adventures, I shall never forget.[12]

Breslau
11 September (10 a.m.) 1858

This is as queer an old City as you ever heard of. High, as Edinburgh or more so; streets very strait and winding: roofs 30 feet or so in height, and of proportionate steepness, ending in chimney-heads like the *half* of a Butter firkin set on its side. The people are not beautiful; but they seem innocent and obliging: brown-skinned scrubby bodies a good many of them, of Polack or Slavic breed. . . . Neuberg is a perfect Issachar for taking labour on him;— needs to be led with a strongish curb. Scratchy Foxton & he are much more tolerable *together*:—grease *plus* vinegar; *that is the rule.*[13]

Prag (Hotel zum Englischen Hof)
14 September (Tuesday Evening) 1858—

From Breslau, where I wrote, our adventures have been miscellaneous, our course painful but successful. At Landshut (edge of the Riesengebirge) where we arrived near eleven the first night, in a crazy vehicle of one horse,—you never saw such a scene of squalid desolation. . . . The gents, that night led us to a place called *Pardubitz* (terribly familiar to me from those dull Friedrich Books); where one of the detestablest nights of all this Expedition was provided me. Big noisy inn, full of evil smells; contemptible little wicked village; where a *worse* than Jerry[gin]-shop close over the way raged like Bedlam or Erebus,—to cheer one in a "bed" (*i.e. trough*) 18 inches too short, and a mattress *forced* into it, which cocked up at both ends, as if you had been lying in the trough of a saddle: *Ach Himmel!* We left it at 4 a.m. to do the hardest day of any: Chotusitz, Kolin; such a day: in a wicked vehicle, with a spavined horse, amid clouds of dust under a blazing sun. . . .

There are now but 3 Battlefields to do: one double, day after to-morrow by a "return-ticket" to be had in Dresden; the two next (Torgau, Rossbach) in two days following.[14]

Dresden (*zum Stadt Wien*),
15th September, 1858 (7 p.m.)

Our journey from Prag has excelled in confusion all I ever witnessed in this world; the beautifullest country ever seen too, and the beautifullest weather; but—Ach Gott! However, we are now

548

FREDERICK THE GREAT. Attached to this engraving is a sprig of pink, under which Carlyle has written, "wild pink, plucked from the Battlefield of Prag (e. of the Ziscaberg half a mile or more) Sep*tr* 1858.—" Frederick's wide-eyed, no-nonsense stare seems to have intrigued Carlyle, for this engraving is similar to several others that hung in his soundproof room. (An engraving of the portrait by Anton Graff, courtesy of the Manuscript Division, Duke University Library.)

near the end of it. . . . I am not hurt, I really do not think myself
much hurt: but Oh what a need of sleep, of silence, of a right good
washing with soap and water all over![15]

On September 22 he was safe at home again at Chelsea—
having finished his work in exactly a month. Nero was
there to express "a decent joy"[16] at seeing him again—
Nero, but not his mistress. She was away in Scotland with
her friends, Dr. and Mrs. Russell. He had charged her not
to return on his account as long as she was getting good
from the change of air and scene.

Such was Carlyle's second tour in Germany, as sketched
in these letters by himself. One misses something of the
liveliness of the experiences of the first, when everything
was new, and was seized upon by his insatiable curiosity.[17]
It was a journey of business, and was executed with a vigour
and rapidity remarkable in so old a man. There were fewer
complaints about sleep—fewer complaints of any kind. How
well his surveying work was done, the history of Frederick's
campaigns, when he came to write them, were ample evidence. He speaks lightly of having seen Kolin, Torgau, etc.,
etc. No one would guess from reading these short notices
that he had mastered the details of every field which he
visited; not a turn of the ground, not a brook, not a wood, or
spot where wood had been, had escaped him. Each picture
was complete in itself, unconfused with any other; and, besides the picture, there was the character of the soil, the extent of cultivation—every particle of information which
would help to elucidate the story.

There are no mistakes.[18] Military students in Germany
are set to learn Frederick's battles in Carlyle's account of
them—altogether an extraordinary feat on Carlyle's part, to
have been accomplished in so short a time. His friends had
helped him no doubt; but the eye that saw and the mind
that comprehended were his own.

Very soon after his return the already finished volumes
of *Frederick* were given to the world. No work of his had as
yet obtained so instant and wide a welcome. The literary success was immediate and exceptionally great. Two thousand
copies had been printed—they were sold at the first issue.
A second two thousand were disposed of almost as rapidly,
and by December there was a demand for more. He had

himself been singularly indifferent on this part of the business. In his summer correspondence there is not a single word of expectation or anxiety. As little was there sign of exultation when the world's verdict was pronounced. The child that is born with greatest difficulty is generally a favourite, but it was not so in this instance. In his Journal he speaks of the book as "by far the most heartrending enterprise he had ever had" as "worth nothing," though "faithfully done on his part." In Scotland he describes himself as having been "perfectly dormant," "in a sluggish, sad way, till the end of August." In Germany he had seen the battlefields—"a quite frightful month of physical discomfort," with no result that he could be sure of, "except a great mischief to health." He had returned, he said, "utterly broken and degraded." This state of feeling, exaggerated as it was, survived the appearance of the two volumes. He had complained little while the journey was in progress—when he was at home again there was little else but sadness and dispiritment.

A few words which I will quote tell of something which proved of immeasurable consequence, both to Carlyle and to his wife.

> Lord Ashburton has wedded again, a Miss Stuart-Mackenzie; and they are off to Egypt about a fortnight ago: "The changes of this age," (as minstrel Burns has it), "which fleeting Time procureth,"—ah me, ah me![19]

Carlyle sighed; but the second Lady Ashburton became the guardian genius of the Cheyne Row household;[20] to Mrs. Carlyle the tenderest of sisters, to Carlyle, especially after his own bereavement, sister, daughter, mother, all that can be conveyed in the names of the warmest human ties. But the acquaintance had yet to begin. Miss Stuart-Mackenzie had hitherto been seen by neither of them.

No one who has read the letters of Carlyle can entertain a doubt of the tenderness of his heart, or of his real gratitude to those relations and friends who were exerting themselves to be of use to him. As little can anyone have failed to notice the waywardness of his humour, the gusts of "unjust impatience" and "sulky despair" with which he received sometimes their best endeavours to serve him, or, again, the remorse with which he afterwards reflected on his unreasonable outbursts. "The nature of the beast" was the main explanation. His temperament was so constituted. It could not be altered, and had to be put up with, like changes of weather. But nature and circumstances worked together; and Lord Jeffrey had judged rightly when he said that literature was not the employment best suited to a person of Carlyle's disposition.[21] In active life a man works at the side of others. He has to consider them as well as himself. He has to check his impatience, he has to listen to objections even when he knows that he is right. He must be content to give and take, to be indifferent to trifles, to know and feel at all times that he is but one among many, who have all their humours. Every day, every hour teaches him the necessity of self-restraint. The man of letters has no such wholesome check upon himself. He lives alone, thinks alone, works alone. He must listen to his own mind; for no other mind can help him. He requires correction as others do; but he must be his own school-master. His peculiarities are part of his originality, and may not be eradicated. The friends among whom he lives are not the partners of his employment; they share in it, if they share at all, only as instruments or dependents. Thus he is an autocrat in his own circle, and exposed to all the temptations which beset autocracy. He is subject to no will, no law, no authority outside himself; and the finest natures suffer something from such unbounded independence. Carlyle had been made by nature sufficiently despotic, and needed no impulse in that direction from the character of his occupations,—while his very virtues helped to blind him when it would have been better if he could have been more on his guard. He knew that his general aim in life was pure and unselfish, and that in the use of his time and talents he had nothing to fear from the sternest examination of his stewardship. His conscience was clear. His life from his earliest years had been pure and simple, without taint of selfish ambition. He had stood upright always in many trials. He had become at last an undisputed intellectual sovereign over a large section of his contemporaries, who looked to him as disciples to a master whose word was a law to their belief. And thus habit, temperament, success itself had combined to deprive him of

552

the salutary admonitions with which the wisest and best of mortals cannot entirely dispense. From first to last he was surrounded by people who allowed him his own way, because they felt his superiority—who found it a privilege to minister to him as they became more and more conscious of his greatness—who, when their eyes were open to his defects, were content to put up with them, as the mere accidents of a nervously sensitive organization.

This was enough for friends who could be amused by peculiarities from which they did not personally suffer. But for those who actually lived with him—for his wife especially, on whom the fire-sparks fell first and always, and who could not escape from them—the trial was hard. The central grievance was gone, but was not entirely forgotten. His letters had failed to assure her of his affection, for she thought at times that they must be written for his biographer. She could not doubt his sincerity when, now after his circumstances became more easy, he gave her free command of money; when, as she could no longer walk, he insisted that she should have a brougham twice a week to drive in, and afterwards gave her a carriage of her own. But affection did not prevent outbursts of bilious humour, under which, for a whole fortnight, she felt as if she was "keeper in a madhouse."[22] When he was at a distance from her he was passionately anxious about her health. When he was at home, his own discomforts, real or imaginary, left no room for thought of others. "If Carlyle wakes once in a night," she said to me, "he will complain of it for a week. I wake thirty times every night, but that is nothing." Notwithstanding all his resolutions, notwithstanding the fall of "the scales . . . from my eyes"[23] and the intended amendment for the future, things relapsed in Cheyne Row after Carlyle returned from Germany, and settled again to his work, much into their old condition. Generally the life was smooth and uneventful, but the atmosphere was always dubious, and a disturbed sleep or an indigestion would bring on a thunderstorm. Mrs. Carlyle grew continually more feeble, continual nervous anxiety allowing her no chance to rally; but her indomitable spirit held her up; she went out little in the evenings, but she had her own small tea parties, and the talk was as brilliant as ever. Carlyle worked all day, rode late in the afternoon, came home, slept a little, then dined and went out afterwards to walk in the dark. If any of us were to spend the evening there, we generally found her alone; then he would come in, take possession of the conversation and deliver himself in a stream of splendid monologue, wise, tender, scornful, humorous, as the inclination took him—but never bitter, never malignant, always genial, the fiercest denunciations ending in a burst of laughter at his own exaggerations. Though I knew things were not altogether well, and her drawn, suffering face haunted me afterwards like a sort of ghost, I felt for myself that in him there could be nothing really wrong, and that he was as good as he was great.

So passed the next two or three years; he toiled on unweariedly, dining nowhere, and refusing to be disturbed.

In June [1859] after months of uselessness and wretchedness, he was "tumbled" into what he called "active chaos,"[24] i.e. he took a house for the summer at Humbie, near Aberdour in Fife. The change was not very successful. He had his horse with him, and "rode fiercely about, haunted by the ghosts of the past." Mrs. Carlyle followed him down. John Carlyle was charged to meet her at Edinburgh, and see her safe for the rest of her journey. "Be good and soft with her," he said; "you have no notion what ill any flurry or fuss does her,—and I know always how kind your thoughts are (and also *hers*, in spite of any flaws that may arise!)."[25] Was it that he could not "reck his own rede!" or was Mrs. Carlyle herself exaggerating, when she described the next fortnight with him at Humbie, as like being "keeper in a madhouse"? They went afterwards to the cousins at Auchtertool, and from Auchtertool she wrote the sad letter to a young friend in London who had asked to be congratulated on her marriage.[26]

There was a short visit to the Grange in January (1860), another in April to Lord Sandwich at Hinchinbrook—from which he was frightened away prematurely by the arrival of Hepworth Dixon. He had evidently been troublesome at home, for from Hinchinbrook he wrote to his wife begging her to "be patient with me; I am the unhappy animal, but don't *mean* ill!"[27] With these exceptions, and a week at Brighton in July, he stayed fixed at his desk, and in August, leaving his wife in London, where nervousness had reduced her to the brink of a bilious fever, he went off, taking his work with him, to stay at Thurso Castle with Sir George Sinclair. There he remained several weeks in seclusion as complete as he could wish.

He had wished his wife to have a taste of Scotch air too before the winter, and had arranged that she should go to his sister at the Gill. She had started, and was staying on the way with her friends the Stanleys at Alderley, when her husband discovered that he could do no more at Thurso, and must get home again. The period of his visit had been indefinite. She had supposed that he would remain longer than he proposed to do. The delay of posts and a misconstruction of meanings led Mrs. Carlyle to suppose that he was about to return to Chelsea immediately, and that her own presence there would be indispensable; and, with a resentment, which she did not care to conceal, at his imagined want of consideration for her, she gave up her expedition and went back. It was a mistake throughout, for he had intended himself to take Annandale on his way home from Thurso; but he had not been explicit enough, and she did not spare him. He was very miserable and very humble.[28] He promised faithfully that when at home again he would worry her no more till she was strong enough to be " 'kept un[e]asy.' "[29]

> I will be quiet as a Dream . . . surely I ought to be rather a protection to your poor sick fancy than a new disturbance. Be still, be quiet, poor Goody of my heart; I swear to do thee no mischief at all![30]

Alas! he might swear; but with the excellentest intentions, he was an awkward companion for a nervous, suffering woman. He had *meant* no mischief. It was impossible that he could have meant it. His misfortune was that he had no perception.[31] He never understood that a delicate lady was not like his own robuster kindred, and might be shivered into fiddlestrings while they would only have laughed.

This was his last visit to Scotland before the completion of *Frederick*. In his wife's weakened condition he thought it no longer right that she should be left to struggle on with a single maid-of-all-work. He had insisted that she should have a superior class of woman as cook and housekeeper, with a girl to assist. He himself was fixed to his garret room again, rarely stirring out except to ride, and dining nowhere save now and then with Forster, to meet only Dickens, who loved him with all his heart.

The new year brought the Grange again, where Mrs. Carlyle was now as glad to go as before she had been reluctant. "Everybody, especially the Lady, is as kind as possible: our party too is small & insignificant; nobody but ourselves, and Venables (an honest old dish) and Kingsley (a *new*, of higher pretensions but inferior flavour)."[32]

In this year he lost a friend whom he valued beyond any one of the younger men whom he had learnt to know. Arthur Clough died at Florence, leaving behind him, of work accomplished, a translation of Plutarch, a volume of poems (which by-and-by, when the sincere writing of this ambitious age of ours is sifted from the insincere, may survive as an evidence of what he might have been had fulness of years been granted to him), and, besides these, a beautiful memory in the minds of those who had known him. "A man more vivid, ingenious, veracious, mildly radiant, I have seldom met with" [wrote Carlyle to Froude], "and in a character so honest, modest, kindly. I expected very considerable things of him."[33]

Every available moment was guaranteed to *Frederick.* Clough was gone; but another friendship had been formed which was even more precious to Carlyle. He had long been acquainted with Ruskin, but hitherto there had been no close intimacy between them, *art* not being a subject especially interesting to him. But Ruskin was now writing his "Letters on Political Economy" in the *Cornhill Magazine.*[34] The world's scornful anger witnessed to the effect of his strokes, and Carlyle was delighted. Political Economy had been a creed while it pretended to be a science. Science rests on reason and experiment, and can meet an opponent with calmness. A creed is always sensitive. To express a doubt of it shakes its authority, and is therefore treated as a moral offence. One looks back with amused interest on that indignant outcry now, when the pretentious science has ceased to answer a political purpose and has been banished by its chief professor to the exterior planets.

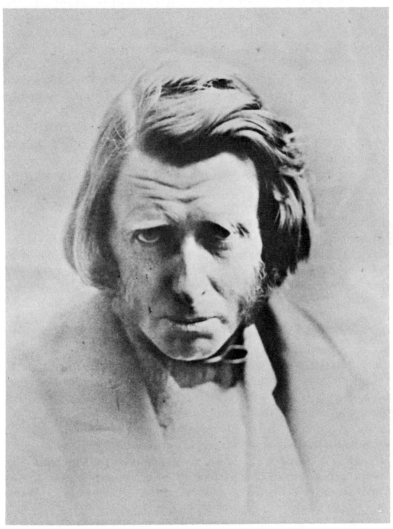

JOHN RUSKIN. The personal agony of Ruskin's life finds reflection in the brood-
ing, contemplative, worried face of this photograph, probably taken in the 1860s
when Carlyle's influence upon him was strongest. The large number of photographs of Ruskin in the Carlyle family albums indicates the esteem in which
Carlyle held him. (Photograph by Elliott & Fry, courtesy of the Columbia University Libraries.)

But Carlyle had hitherto been preaching alone in the wilderness, and rejoiced in this new ally. He examined Ruskin more carefully. He saw, as who that looked could help seeing, that here was a true "man of genius," peculiar, uneven, passionate, but wielding in his hand real levin bolts, not mere flashes of light merely—but fiery arrows which pierced, where they struck, to the quick. He was tempted one night to go to hear Ruskin lecture, not on the "Dismal Science," but on some natural phenomena, which Ruskin, while the minutest observer, could convert into a poem. "*Sermons* in Stones" had been already Carlyle's name for *The Stones of Venice*.[35] Such a preacher he was willing to listen to on any subject.

This was a mere episode, however, in a life which was as it were chained down to "an undoable task." Months went by; at last the matter became so complicated, and the notes and corrections so many, that the printers were called in to help. The rough fragments of manuscript were set in type that he might see his way through them.

No leisure—leisure even for thought—could be spared to other subjects. Even the great phenomenon of the century, the civil war in America, passed by him at its opening without commanding his serious attention. To him that tremendous struggle for the salvation of the American nationality was merely the efflorescence of the "Nigger Emancipation" agitation, which he had always despised. "No war ever raging in my time," he said, when the first news of the fighting came over, "was to me more profoundly foolish-looking. Neutral I am to a degree: I for one." He spoke of it scornfully as "a smoky chimney which had taken fire." When provoked to say something about it publicly, it was to write his brief *Ilias Americana in Nuce* [*American Iliad in a Nutshell*].

> Peter of the North (to Paul of the South): Paul, you unaccountable scoundrel, I find you hire your servants for life, not by the month or year as I do. You are going straight to Hell, you

> Paul: Good words, Peter. The risk is my own. I am willing to take the risk. Hire you your servants by the month or the day, and get straight to Heaven; leave me to my own method.

> Peter: No, I won't. I will beat your brains out first! [And is trying dreadfully ever since, but cannot yet manage it.]

T. C.[36]

CARLYLE ON FRITZ. Photograph taken on 2 August 1861 in Hyde Park. To escape after his daily labor on *Frederick*, Carlyle took afternoon rides. He later wrote that he "rode some 35,000 miles,—more disgusting to me at last than walking in the Tread-wheel would have been,—during those 10 years of *Friedrich*." (Courtesy of the Carlyle House, Chelsea.)

At the Grange where he had gone in January 1862, the subject was of course much talked of. The Argyles were there, the Sartoris's, the Kingsleys, the Bishop of Oxford, Milnes, Venables, and others. The Duke and Duchess were strong for the North, and there was much arguing, not to Carlyle's satisfaction. The Bishop and he were always pleased to meet each other, but he was not equally tolerant of the Bishop's friends. Of one of these there is a curious mention in a letter written from the Grange during this visit. Intellect was to him a quality which only showed itself in the discovery of truth. In science no man is allowed to be a man of intellect who uses his faculties to go ingeniously wrong. Still less could Carlyle acknowledge the presence of such high quality in those who went wrong in more important subjects. Cardinal Newman, he once said to me, had not the intellect of a moderate-sized rabbit.[37] He was yet more uncomplimentary to another famous person whom the English Church has canonized. "We are a brisk party here, full of locomotion, speculation; and really are in some sort agreeable to one another. . . . The Bear, the Duke, with the woman-kind wholly are off some 20 miles,— mostly in an open carriage. . . . The Bishop of Oxford is here (gone with these women, to see some little Ape called Keble, of *The 'Christian Year'*)."[38]

Frederick, meanwhile, was making progress, though but slowly. The German authorities he found to be raw metallic matter, unwrought, unorganised, the ore nowhere smelted out of it. It is curious that on the human side of things the German genius should be so deficient, but so it is. We go to them for poetry, philosophy, criticism, theology. They have to come to us for a biography of their greatest poet and the history of their greatest king. The standard *Life of Goethe* in Germany is Lewes's; the standard *History of Frederick* is Carlyle's. But the labour was desperate, and told heavily both on him and on his wife. When the summer came she went for change to Folkestone. He in her absence was like a forsaken child.

"A spectre moving in a world of spectres"—"one mass of burning sulphur"—these were images in which he now and then described his condition. At such times, if his little finger ached he imagined that no mortal had ever suffered

560

so before. If his liver was amiss he was a chained Prometheus with the vulture at his breast, and earth, ether, sea, and sky were invoked to witness his injuries. When the fit was on him he could not, would not, restrain himself, and now when Mrs. Carlyle's condition was so delicate, her friends, medical and others, had to insist that they must be kept apart as much as possible. He himself, lost as he was without her, felt the necessity, and when she returned from Folkestone he sent her off to her friend Mrs. Russell in Nithsdale.

The third volume of *Frederick* was finished and published this summer. The fourth volume was getting into type, and the fifth and last was partly written.[39] The difficulties did not diminish; "one only consolation there was in it, that *Frederick* was better worth doing than other foul tasks he had had."

He had one other great pleasure this summer. Ruskin's *Unto This Last*, a volume of essays on political economy, was now collected and re-published. Carlyle sent a copy to Mr. Erskine, with the following letter:

Two years ago, when the Essays came out in the fashionable magazines, there rose a shriek of anathema from all newspaper and publishing persons. But I am happy to say that the subject is to be taken up again and heartily gone into by the valiant Ruskin, who, I hope, will reduce it to a *dog's likeness*—its real physiognomy for a long time past to the unenchanted eye, and peremptorily bid it prepare to quit this afflicted earth, as R. has done to several things before now. He seems to me to have the best talent for *preaching* of all men now alive. . . . I have read nothing that pleased me better for many a year than these new *Ruskiniana*.[40]

chapter twenty-eight

1862–1865

Froude's Impressions of Carlyle. Serious
Accident to Jane Carlyle. Death of
Lord Ashburton. Jane Carlyle's
Illness and Apparent Recovery.
Completion of *Frederick*

So far my account of Carlyle has been taken from written
memorials, letters, diaries, and autobiographic fragments.
For the future the story will form itself round my own personal intercourse with him. Up to 1860 I had lived in the
country. I had paid frequent visits to London, and while
there had seen as much of Cheyne Row and its inhabitants
as Mrs. Carlyle would encourage. I had exchanged letters
occasionally with her and her husband, but purely on external subjects, and close personal intimacy between us there
had as yet been none. In the autumn of that year, however,
London became my home. Late one afternoon, in the middle
of the winter, Carlyle called on me, and said that he wished
to see more of me—wished me in fact to be his companion,
so far as I could, in his daily rides or walks. Ride with him I
could not, having no horse; but the walks were most welcome—and from that date, for twenty years, up to his own
death, except when either or both of us were out of town, I
never ceased to see him twice or three times á week, and to
have two or three hours of conversation with him. The first
of these walks I well remember, from an incident which happened in the course of it. If was after nightfall. At Hyde
Park Corner, we found a blind beggar anxious to cross over
from Knightsbridge to Piccadilly, but afraid to trust his dog
to lead him through the carts and carriages. Carlyle took the
beggar's arm, led him gently over, and offered to help him
further on his way. He declined gratefully; we gave him
some trifle, and followed him to see what he would do. His

dog led him straight to a public-house in Park Lane. We both laughed, and I suppose I made some ill-natured remark. "Poor fellow," was all that Carlyle said; "he perhaps needs warmth and shelter."

This was the first instance that I observed of what I found to be a universal habit with him. Though still far from rich, he never met any poor creature, whose distress was evident, without speaking kindly to him and helping him more or less in one way or another. Archbishop Whately said that to relieve street beggars was a public crime. Carlyle thought only of their misery. "Modern life," he said, "doing its charity by institutions," is a sad hardener of our hearts. "We should give for our own sakes. It is very low water with the wretched beings, one can easily see that."

Even the imps of the gutters he would not treat as reprobates. He would drop a lesson in their way, sometimes with a sixpence to recommend it. A small vagabond was at some indecency. Carlyle touched him gently on the back with his stick. "Do you not know that you are a little man," he said, "and not a whelp, that you behave in this way?" There was no sixpence this time. Afterwards a lad of fourteen or so stopped us and begged. Carlyle lectured him for beginning so early at such a trade, told him how, if he worked, he might have a worthy and respectable life before him, and gave him sixpence. The boy shot off down the next alley. "There is a sermon fallen on stony ground," Carlyle said, "but we must do what we can." The crowds of children growing up in London affected him with real pain; these small plants, each with its head just out of the ground, with a whole life ahead, and such a training! I noticed another trait too—Scotch thrift showing itself in hatred of waste. If he saw a crust of bread on the roadway he would stop to pick it up and put it on a step or a railing. Some poor devil might be glad of it, or at worst a dog or a sparrow. To destroy wholesome food was a sin. He was very tender about animals, especially dogs, who, like horses, if well treated, were types of loyalty and fidelity. I horrified him with a story of my Oxford days. The hounds had met at Woodstock. They had drawn the covers without finding a fox, and, not caring to have a blank day, one of the whips had caught a passing sheep dog, rubbed its feet with aniseed, and set it to run. It made for Oxford in its terror, the hounds in full cry behind. They caught the wretched creature in a field outside the town, and tore it to pieces. I never saw Carlyle more affected. He said it was like a human soul flying for salvation before a legion of fiends.

Occupied as he had always seemed to be with high-soaring speculations, scornful as he had appeared, in the *Latter-Day Pamphlets*, of benevolence, philanthropy, and small palliations of enormous evils, I had not expected so much detailed compassion in little things. I found that personal sympathy with suffering lay at the root of all his thoughts;[1] and that attention to little things was as characteristic of his conduct as it was of his intellect.

His conversation when we were alone together was even more surprising to me. I had been accustomed to hear him impatient of contradiction, extravagantly exaggerative, overbearing opposition with bursts of scornful humour. In private I found him impatient of nothing but of being bored; gentle, quiet, tolerant; *sadly*-humoured, but never *ill*-humoured; ironical, but without the savageness, and when speaking of persons always scrupulously just. He saw through the "clothes" of a man into what he actually was. But the sharpest censure was always qualified. He would say, "If we knew how he came to be what he is, poor fellow, we should not be hard with him."

But he talked more of things than of persons, and on every variety of subject. He had read more miscellaneously than any man I have ever known. His memory was extraordinary, and a universal curiosity had led him to inform himself minutely about matters which I might have supposed that he had never heard of. With English literature he was as familiar as Macaulay was. French and German and Italian he knew infinitely better than Macaulay, and there was this peculiarity about him, that if he read a book which struck him he never rested till he had learnt all that could be ascertained about the writer of it. Thus his knowledge was not in points or lines, but complete and solid.

Even in his laughter he was always serious. I never heard a trivial word from him, nor one which he had better have left unuttered. He cared nothing for money, nothing for promotion in the world. If his friends gained a step anywhere

JAMES ANTHONY FROUDE. "His presence was striking and impressive," John Skelton wrote of Froude a year after his death in 1894, "—coal-black eyes, wonderfully lustrous and luminous . . . ; coal-black hair, only latterly streaked with grey; massive features strongly lined,—massive yet mobile, and capable of the subtlest play of expression. For myself I can say without any reserve that he was, upon the whole, the most interesting man I have ever known" (*The Table-Talk of Shirley*). This photograph is one of the best of Froude in later years. (Reproduced from the frontispiece to George Haven Putnam, comp., *Prose Masterpieces from Modern Essayists* [London: Bickers & Son, 1896].)

he was pleased with it—but only as worldly advancement might give them a chance of wider usefulness. Men should think of their duty, he said;—let them do that, and the rest, as much as was essential, "would be added to them." I was with him one beautiful spring day under the trees in Hyde Park, the grass recovering its green, the elm buds swelling, the scattered crocuses and snowdrops shining in the sun. The spring, the annual resurrection from death to life, was especially affecting to him. "Behold the lilies of the field!" he said to me; "they toil not, neither do they spin. Yet Solomon, in all his glory, was not arrayed like one of these.[2] What a word was that? and the application was quite true too. Take no thought for the morrow—care only for what you know to be right. That is the rule."

He had a poor opinion of what is called science; of political economy; of utility as the basis of morals; and such-like, when they dealt with human life. He stood on Kant's Categorical Imperative. Right was right, and wrong was wrong, because God had so ordered; and duty and conduct could be brought under analysis only when men had disowned their nobler nature, and were governed by self-interest. Interested motives might be computed, and a science might grow out of a calculation of their forces. But love of Truth, love of Righteousness—these were not calculable, neither these nor the actions proceeding out of them.

Sciences of natural things he always respected. *Facts* of all kinds were sacred to him. A fact, whatever it might be, was part of the constitution of the universe, and so was related to the Author of it. Of all men that have ever lived he honoured few more than Kepler. Kepler's *"laws"* he looked on as the grandest physical discovery ever made by man; and as long as philosophers were content, like Kepler, to find out facts without building theories on them to dispense with God, he had only good to say of them. Science, however, in these latter days, was stepping beyond its proper province, like the young Titans trying to take heaven by storm. He liked *ill* men like Humboldt, Laplace, or the author of the *Vestiges*.[3] He refused Darwin's transmutation of species as unproved; he fought against it, though I could see he dreaded that it might turn out true. If man, as explained by Science, was no more than a developed animal, and conscience and

intellect but developments of the functions of animals, then
God and religion were no more than inferences, and inferences which might be lawfully disputed. That the grandest
achievements of human nature had sprung out of beliefs
which might be mere illusions, Carlyle could not admit.
That intellect and moral sense should have been put into
him by a Being which had none of its own was distinctly
not conceivable to him. It might perhaps be that these high
gifts lay somewhere in the original germ, out of which
organic life had been developed; that they had been intentionally and consciously placed there by the Author of nature, whom religious instincts had been dimly able to discern. It might so turn out, but for the present the tendency
of science was not in any such direction. The tendency of
science was to Lucretian Atheism; to a belief that no "intention" or intending mind was discoverable in the universe
at all. If the life of man was no more than the life of an animal—if he had no relation, or none which he could discern
with any being higher than himself, God would become an
unmeaning word to him. Carlyle often spoke of this, and
with evident uneasiness. Earlier in his life, while he was
young and confident, and the effects of his religious training were fresh in him, he could fling off the whispers of
the scientific spirit with angry disdain; the existence, the
omnipresence, the omnipotence of God, were then the
strongest of his convictions. The faith remained unshaken in
him to the end; he never himself doubted; yet he was perplexed by the indifference with which the Supreme Power
was allowing its existence to be obscured. I once said to
him, not long before his death, that I could only believe in a
God which *did* something. With a cry of pain, which I shall
never forget, he said, "He does nothing." For himself, however, his faith stood firm. He did not believe in historical
Christianity. He did not believe that the facts alleged in the
Apostles' creed had ever really happened. The resurrection
of Christ was to him only a symbol of a spiritual truth. As
Christ rose from the dead so were we to rise from the death
of sin to the life of righteousness. Not that Christ had actually died and had risen again. He was only *believed* to have
died and *believed* to have risen in an age when legend was
history, when stories were accepted as true from their

beauty or their significance. As long as it was supposed that the earth was the centre of the universe, that the sky moved round it, and that sun and moon and stars had been set there for man's convenience, when it was the creed of all nations that gods came down to the earth, and men were taken into heaven, and that between the two regions there was incessant intercourse, it could be believed easily that the Son of God had lived as a man among men, had descended like Hercules into Hades, and had returned again from it. Such a story then presented no internal difficulty at all. It was not so now. The soul of it was eternally true, but it had been bound up in a mortal body. The body of the belief was now perishing, and the soul of it being discredited by its connection with discovered error, was suspected not to be a soul at all; half mankind, betrayed and deserted, were rushing off into materialism. Nor was materialism the worst. Shivering at so blank a prospect, entangled in the institutions which remained standing when the life had gone out of them, the other half were "reconciling faith with reason," pretending to believe, or believing that they believed, becoming hypocrites, conscious or unconscious, the last the worst of the two, not daring to look the facts in the face, so that the very sense of truth was withered in them. It was to make love to delusion, to take falsehood deliberately into their hearts. For such souls there was no hope at all. Centuries of spiritual anarchy lay before the world before sincere belief could again be generally possible among men of knowledge and insight. With the half-educated and ignorant it was otherwise. To them the existing religion might still represent some real truth. There alone was any open teaching of God's existence, and the divine sanction of morality. Each year, each day, as knowledge spread, the power of the established religion was growing less; but it was not yet entirely gone, and it was the only hold that was left on the most vital of all truths. Thus the rapid growth of materialism had in some degree modified the views which Carlyle had held in early and middle life. Then the "Exodus from Houndsditch" had seemed as if it might lead immediately into a brighter region. He had come to see that it would be but an entry into a wilderness, the promised land lying still far away. His own opinions seemed to be taking no hold. He had cast his bread upon the waters and it was not returning to him, and the exodus appeared less entirely desirable. Sometimes the old fierce note revived. Sometimes, and more often as he grew older, he wished the old shelter to be left standing as long as a roof remained over it—as long as any of us could profess the old faith with complete sincerity. Sincerity, however, was indispensable. For men who said one thing and meant another, who entered the Church as a profession, and throve in the world by it, while they emasculated the creeds, and watered away the histories—for them Carlyle had no toleration. Religion, if not honest, was a horror to him. Those alone he thought had any right to teach Christianity who had no doubts about its truth. Those who were uncertain ought to choose some other profession, and if compelled to speak should show their colours faithfully. Thirlwall, who discharged his functions as a Macready, he never blamed to me; but he would have liked him better could he have seen him at some other employment. The Essayists and Reviewers, the *Septem contra Christum,* were in people's mouths when my intimacy with Carlyle began. They did not please him. He considered that in continuing to be clergymen they were playing tricks with their consciences. The Dean of Westminster he liked personally, almost loved him indeed, yet he could have wished him anywhere but where he was.[4]

"There goes Stanley," he said one day as we passed the Dean in the park, "boring holes in the bottom of the Church of England!" Colenso's book came out soon after. I knew Colenso; we met him in one of our walks. He joined us, and talked of what he had done with some slight elation. "Poor fellow!" said Carlyle, as he went away; "he mistakes it for fame. He does not see that it is only an extended pillory that he is standing on." I thought and think this judgement a harsh one. No one had been once more anxious than Carlyle for the "Exodus." No one had done more to bring it about than Colenso, or more bravely faced the storm which he had raised, or I may add, more nobly vindicated, in later life, his general courage and honesty when he stood out to defend the Zulus in South Africa. Stanley spoke more truly, or more to his own and Colenso's honour, when he told the infuriated Convocation to its face, that the

Bishop of Natal was the only English prelate whose name would be remembered in the next century.

Literature was another subject on which Carlyle often talked with me. In his Craigenputtoch Essays he had spoken of literature as the highest of human occupations, as the modern priesthood, etc., and so to the last he thought of it when it was the employment of men whom nature had furnished gloriously for that special task, like Goethe and Schiller. But for the writing function in the existing generation of Englishmen he had nothing but contempt. A "man of letters," a man who had taken to literature as a means of living, was generally some one who had gone into it because he was unfit for better work, because he was too vain or too self-willed to travel along the beaten highways, and his writings, unless he was one of a million, began and ended in nothing. Life was action, not talk. The speech, the book, the review or newspaper article was so much force expended—force lost to practical usefulness. When a man had uttered his thoughts, still more when he was always uttering them, he no longer even attempted to translate them into act. He said once to me that England had produced her greatest men before she began to have a literature at all. Those Barons who signed their charter by dipping the points of their steel gauntlets in the ink, had more virtue, manhood, practical force and wisdom than any of their successors, and when the present disintegration had done its work, and healthy organic tissue began to form again, tongues would not clatter as they did now. Those only would speak who had call to speak. Even the Sunday sermons would cease to be necessary. A man was never made wiser or better by talking or being talked to. He was made better by being trained in habits of industry, by being enabled to *do* good useful work and earn an honest living by it. His excuse for his own life was that there had been no alternative. Sometimes he spoke of his writings as having a certain value; generally, however, as if they had little, and now and then as if they had none. "If there be one thing," he said, "for which I have no special talent, it is literature. If I had been taught to *do* the simplest useful thing, I should have been a better and happier man. All that I can say for myself is, that I have done my best." A strange judgement to come from a man who has exerted so vast an influence by writing alone. Yet in a sense it was true. If literature means the expression by thought or emotion, or the representation of facts in completely beautiful form, Carlyle was inadequately gifted for it. But his function was not to please, but to instruct. Of all human writings, those which perhaps have produced the deepest effect on the history of the world have been St. Paul's Epistles. What Carlyle had he had in common with St. Paul: extraordinary intellectual insight, extraordinary sincerity, extraordinary resolution to speak out the truth as he perceived it, as if driven on by some impelling internal necessity. He and St. Paul—I know not of whom else the same thing could be said—wrote as if they were pregnant with some world-important idea, of which they were labouring to be delivered, and the effect is the more striking from the abruptness and want of artifice in the utterance. Whether Carlyle would have been happier, more useful, had he been otherwise occupied, I cannot say. He had a fine aptitude for all kinds of business. In any practical problem, whether of politics or private life, he had his finger always, as if by instinct, on the point upon which the issue would turn. Arbitrary as his temperament was, he could, if occasion rose, be prudent, forbearing, dexterous, adroit. He would have risen to greatness in any profession which he had chosen, but in such a world as ours he must have submitted, in rising, to the *"half-sincerities,"* which are the condition of success. We should have lost the Carlyle that we know. It is not certain that we should have gained an equivalent of him.

This is the sort of thing which I used daily to hear from Carlyle. His talk was not always, of course, on such grave matters. He was full of stories, anecdotes of his early life, or of people that he had known.

For more than four years after our walks began, he was still engaged with *Frederick*. He spoke freely of what was uppermost in his mind, and many scenes in the history were rehearsed to me before they appeared, Voltaire, Maupertuis, Chatham, Wolfe being brought up as living figures. He never helped himself with gestures, but his voice was as flexible as if he had been trained for the stage. He was never tedious, but dropped out picture after picture in inimitable finished sentences. He was so quiet, so unexagerative, so well-humoured in these private conversations, that I could scarcely believe he was the same person whom I used to hear declaim in the *Pamphlet* time. Now and then, if he met an acquaintance who might say a foolish thing, there would come an angry sputter or two; but he was generally so patient, so forbearing, that I thought age had softened him, and I said so one day to Mrs. Carlyle. She laughed and told him of it. "I wish," she said, "Froude had seen you an hour or two after you seemed to him so lamblike."[5] But I was relating what he was as I knew him, and as I always found him from first to last.

Through the winter of 1862–1863 Mrs. Carlyle seemed tolerably well. The weather was warm. She had no serious cold. She was very feeble, and lay chiefly on the sofa, but she contrived to prevent Carlyle from being anxious about her. He worked without respite, rode, except on walking days, chiefly late in the afternoon, in the dark in the winter months, about the environs of London; and the roaring of the suburban trains and the gleam of the green and crimson signal lamps were wildly impressive to him. On his return he would lie down in his dressing gown by the drawing-room fire, smoking up the chimney, while she would amuse him with accounts of her daily visitors. She was a perfect artist, and could carve a literary vignette out of the commonest materials. These were his happiest hours, and his only mental refreshment.

Age so far was dealing kindly with him. There was no falling off in bodily strength. His eyes were failing slightly, but they lasted out his life. His right hand had begun to shake a little, and this unfortunately was to develop till he was eventually disabled from writing; but as yet about himself there was nothing to give him serious uneasiness. A misfortune, however, was hanging over him of another kind, which threatened to upset the habits of his life. All his days he had been a fearless rider. He had a loose seat and a careless hand, but he had come to no misfortune, owing, he thought, to the good sense of his horse, which was much superior to that of most of his biped acquaintances. Fritz, even Fritz, was now to misbehave and was

OLD CHEYNE WALK. The Thames embankment was not built until the 1870s, and such a sight as this would have been familiar to Carlyle in his daily walk or ride. (Drawn and etched by Arthur Severn; from an engraving in the editor's possession.)

sold for nine pounds.[6] What became of him further I never heard. Lady Ashburton supplied his place with another, equally good and almost with Fritz's intellect. Life went on as before after this interruption, and leaves little to record. On April 29 he writes:

> I had to go yesterday to Dicken's Reading: "8 p.m. Hanover Rooms";—to the complete oversetting of my evening habitudes, and spiritual composure. Dickens does do it capitally (such as *it* is); *acts* better than any Macready in the world; a whole tragic-comic-farcic *theatre* visible performing under one *hat*; and keeping us laughing (in a sorry way, some of us thought) the whole night. He is a good creature too;—and makes 50 or £60 by each of these readings.[7]

From dinner parties he had almost wholly withdrawn, but in the same letter he mentions one to which he had been tempted by a new acquaintance, who grew afterwards into a dear and justly valued friend, Miss Davenport Bromley. He admired Miss Bromley from the first, for her light, airy ways, and compared her to a "flight of larks."

Summer came, and hot weather; he descended from his garret to the awning in the garden again. By August he was tired, *Frederick* spinning out beyond expectation, and he and Mrs. Carlyle went for a fortnight to the Grange. Lord Ashburton seemed to have recovered [from a severe illness he had had in Paris late in 1862] but was very delicate. There was no party, only Venables, the guest of all others whom Carlyle best liked to meet. The visit was a happy one, a gleam of pure sunshine before the terrible calamity which was now impending.

One evening, after their return, Mrs. Carlyle had gone to call on a cousin at the post office in St. Martin's Lane. She had come away, and was trying to reach an omnibus, when she was thrown by a cab on the kerbstone. Her right arm being disabled by neuralgia, she was unable to break her fall. The sinews of one thigh were sprained and lacerated, and she was brought home in a fly in dreadful pain. She knew that Carlyle would be expecting her. Her chief anxiety, she told me, was to get into the house without his knowledge, to spare him agitation. For herself, she could not move. She stopped at the door of Mr. Larkin, who lived in the adjoining house in Cheyne Row, and asked him to help her. The sound of the wheels and the noise of voices reached Carlyle in the drawing-room. He rushed down, and he and Mr. Larkin together bore her up the stairs, and laid her on the bed. There she remained, in an agony which, experienced in pain as she was, exceeded the worst that she had known. Carlyle was not allowed to know how seriously she had been injured. The doctor and she both agreed to conceal it from him, and during those first days a small incident happened, which she herself described to me, showing the distracting want of perception which sometimes characterised him—a want of perception, not a want of feeling, for no one could have felt more tenderly. The nerves and muscles were completely disabled on the side on which she had fallen, and one effect was that the under jaw had dropped, and that she could not close it. Carlyle always disliked an open mouth; he thought it a sign of foolishness. One morning, when the pain was at its worst, he came into her room, and stood looking at her, leaning on the mantelpiece. "Jane," he said presently, "ye had better shut your mouth." She tried to tell him that she could not. "Jane," he began again, "ye'll find yourself in a more compact and pious frame of mind, if ye shut your mouth."[8] In old-fashioned and, in him, perfectly sincere phraseology he told her that she ought to be thankful that the accident was no worse. Mrs. Carlyle hated cant as heartily as he, and to her, in her sore state of mind and body, such words had a flavour of cant in them. True herself as steel,[9] she would not bear it. "Thankful!" she said to him; "thankful for what? for having been thrown down in the street when I had gone on an errand of charity? for being disabled, crushed, made to suffer in this way? I am not thankful, and I will not say that I am." He left her, saying he was sorry to see her so rebellious. We can hardly wonder after this that he had to report sadly to his brother: "She speaks little to me, and does not accept me as a sick nurse, which, truly, I had never any talent to be."[10]

Of course he did not know at first her real condition. She had such indomitable courage that she persuaded him that she was actually better off since she had become helpless than "when she was forcing herself out every day: 'returned so utterly done out; joints like to fall in pieces.' "[11]

For a month she could not move—at the end of it she was able to struggle to her feet and crawl occasionally into the adjoining room. Carlyle was blind. Seven weeks after the accident he could write: "she actually sleeps better, eats better, & is cheerfuller than formerly. For perhaps 3 weeks past she has been hitching about; . . . she can walk too, but slowly, without stick: in short, she is doing well enough. As indeed am I;—and have need to be."[12]

He had need to be, for he had just discovered that he could not end with *Frederick* like a rocket-stick,[13] but that there must be a new volume; and for his sake, and knowing how the truth, if he was aware of it, would agitate him, with splendid heroism she had forced herself prematurely to her feet again, the mental resolution conquering the weakness of the body. She even received visitors again, and in the middle of November, I and my own wife once more spent an evening there.[14] But it was the last exertion which she was able to make. The same night there came on neuralgic pain—rather torture than pain—of which the doctor could give no explanation. "A mere cold," he said, "no cause for alarm"; but the weeks went on and there was no abatement, still pain in every muscle, misery in every nerve, no sleep, no rest from suffering night or day—save in faint misleading intervals—and Carlyle knew at last how it was with her, and had to go on with his work as he could. "We are in great trouble, anxiety, confusion," he wrote on the 29th of December to John, in one of those intervals: "poor Jane's state such as to fill one with the saddest thoughts. She does not gather strength: how can she? . . . Her state is one of weakness, utter restlessness, depression and misery: such a scene as I never was in before."[15]

Other remedies failing, the last chance was in change and sea air. Dr. Blakiston, an accomplished physician at St. Leonards, whose wife was an old friend of Mrs. Carlyle, offered to receive her as a guest.[16] She was taken thither in a "sick carriage," in construction and appearance something like a hearse, in the beginning of March. Carlyle attended her down, left her, with her cousin Maggie Welsh, in the Blakistons' affectionate hands, and himself returned to his solitary home and task. There, in Hades as he called it, he sate toiling on, watching for the daily bulletins, now worse, now a little better, his own letters full of passionate grief and impatience with intruders, who came with the kindest purpose to enquire, but just then could better have been spared.

Sorrows did not come single. [On March 25] came news that Lord Ashburton was dead, the dearest friend that had been left to him. As an evidence of regard Lord Ashburton had left him £2,000, or rather had not left it, but had desired that it should be given to him, that there might be no deduction for legacy duty. It was a small matter at such a moment that there appeared in the *Saturday Review* "an extremely contemptible *review* . . . (hostile if the dirty puppy durst[)]," on the last published volumes of *Frederick*. This did not even vex him, was "not worth a snuff of tobacco";[17] only he thought it was a pity that Venables just then should have allowed the book to fall into unworthy hands. He wrote to his wife daily—a few words to satisfy her that he was well. At length the absence from her became unbearable. He took a house at St. Leonards, to which she could be removed; and, leaving Cheyne Row to the care of Mr. Larkin, he went down, with his work, to join her.[18] Most things in this world have their sunny side—the planet itself first, and then the fortunes of its occupants. His grief and anxiety had convinced Mrs. Carlyle of her husband's real love for her, which she had long doubted. But that was all, for her sufferings were of a kind which few human frames could bear without sinking under them. Carlyle was patient and tender; all was done for her which care and love could provide; she had not wholly lost her strength or energy; but the pain and sleeplessness continued week after week without sign of abating. They remained at St. Leonards till the middle of July, when desperate, after twelve nights absolutely without sleep of any kind, she rallied her force, rose, and went off, under John Carlyle's charge, through London to Annandale, there to shake off the horrible enchantment or else to die.

It was on the eve of her birthday that she made her flight. The journey did not hurt her. She recovered sleep a little, strength a little. Slowly, very slowly and with many relapses, she rallied into a more natural state, first at the Gill and afterwards with the Russells in Nithsdale.[19] Carlyle could not follow except with his heart, but the thoughts which he could spare from his work were given to what he would do for her if she was ever restored to him alive.

There was to be no more hiring of carriages, no more omnibuses. She was henceforth to have a brougham of her own. Her room in Cheyne Row in which she had so suffered, was re-papered, re-arranged with the kind help of Miss Bromley, that she might be surrounded with objects unassociated with the past.

I was absent from London during the summer. I had heard that the Carlyles had left St. Leonards and that she was in Scotland, and I wrote to him under the impression that she must be recovering. He answered that I had been *far* too hopeful.

> The accounts have mostly been bad; but, for two days past, seem (to myself) to indicate something of real improvement. I am always very sanguine, in the matter;—but get the saddest rebukes, as you see. . . . I have no company here but my Horse; indeed I have mainly consorted with my Horse for 8 years back;—and he, the staff of my life otherwise, is better company than any I could get at present in these latitudes: an honest creature that is always candid with me, and actually useful in a small way, which so few are![20]

To her his letters continued constant, his spirits varying with her accounts of herself, but, as he had said to me, always trying to be sanguine.

Mrs. Carlyle came back to Cheyne Row [in October], from which she had been carried six months before as in a hearse, expecting to see it no more. She reappeared in her old circle, weak, shattered, her body worn to a shadow, but with her spirit bright as ever—brighter perhaps; for Carlyle's tenderness in her illness had convinced her that he really cared for her, and the sunset of her married life recovered something of the colours of its morning. He, too sanguine always, persuaded himself that her disorder was now worn out, and that she was on the way to a perfect restoration. She, I think, was under no such illusion. There was a gentle smile in her face, if one ever spoke of it, which showed her incredulity. But from London she took no hurt. She seemed rather to gain strength than to lose it. To her friends she was as risen from the dead, and it was a pleasure to her to see how dear she was to them and with what eagerness they pressed forward to be of use. No one could care *a little* for Mrs. Carlyle, and the singular nature of her illness added to the interest which was felt for her. She required new milk in the morning. A supply was sent in daily, fresh from the Rector's cow. The brougham was bought, and she had a childlike pride in it, as her husband's present. "Strange and precious to look back upon," he says, "those last eighteen months, as of a second youth (almost a second childhood with the wisdom and graces of old age), which by Heaven's great mercy were conceded her and me."[21]

Frederick was finished in January, the last of Carlyle's great works, the last and grandest of them. "That dreary task of *Friedrich*," he says in his Journal, "and the sorrows & obstructions attending it; which are a magazine of despair, 'impossibilities,' and ghastly difficulties, miseries and spasmodic struggles, never to be known except to myself, and by myself never to be forgotten," all was over, locked away and "the key on them for all time. They have nearly killed me, they, & the sore additaments,—my poor Jane's dreadful illness (now happily *over* again) &c. No sympathy could be found on Earth for those horrid struggles of 12 years;—nor happily is any needed. On Sunday evening (I now forget which) in the end of January last (1865), I walked out, with the multiple feeling (*joy* not very prominent in it, but a kind of solemn thankfulness traceable) that I had *written* the last sentence of that unutterable Book; and, contrary to many forebodings in bad hours, had actually got done with it for ever!"[22]

Frederick was translated instantly into German, and in Germany, where the conditions were better known in which Carlyle had found his materials, there was the warmest appreciation of what he had done.[23] The sharpest scrutiny only served to show how accurate was the workmanship. Few people anywhere in Europe dreamt twenty years ago of the position which Germany, and Prussia at the head of it, were so soon to occupy. Yet Carlyle's book seemed to have been composed in conscious anticipation of what was coming. He had given a voice to the national feeling. He had brought up as it were from the dead the creator of the

Prussian monarchy, and had replaced him among his people as a living and breathing man. He had cleared the air for the impending revolution, and Europe, when it came, could see how the seed had grown which had expanded into the German Empire.

In England it was at once admitted that a splendid addition had been made to the national literature. The book contained, if nothing else, a gallery of historical figures executed with a skill which placed Carlyle at the head of literary portrait painters. The English mind remains insular and is hard to interest supremely in any history but its own. The tone of *Frederick* nowhere harmonized with popular sentiment among us, and every page contained something to offend. Yet even in England it was better received on its first appearance than any of Carlyle's other works had been, and it gave solidity and massiveness to his already brilliant fame. No critic, after the completion of *Frederick*, challenged Carlyle's right to a place beside the greatest of English authors, past or present.

He had sorely tried America; but America forgave his sarcasms—forgot the "smoky chimney," forgot the "Iliad in a Nutshell,"[24] and was cordially and enthusiastically admiring. Emerson sent out a paragraph, which went the round of the Union, that *Frederick* was "infinitely the wittiest book that ever was written; a book that, one would think, the English people would rise up in a mass to thank him for, by cordial acclamation, and signify, by crowning him with chaplet of oak-leaves, their joy that such a head existed among them, and sympathizing and much-reading America would make a new treaty or send a minister extraordinary to offer congratulations of honoring delight to England in acknowledgment of such a donation."[25] A rather sanguine expectation on Emerson's part! England has ceased to stone or burn her prophets, but she does not yet make them the subject of international treaties. She crowns with oak leaves her actors and her prima-donnas, her politicians, who are to-day her idols, and to-morrow will find none so poor to do them reverence; to wise men she is contented to pay more moderate homage, and leaves the final decorating work to time and future generations.

chapter twenty-nine

1865–1866

Summer in Annandale. Installation as
Rector of Edinburgh University.
Inaugural Speech and Public Acclaim.
Death of Jane Carlyle

The last proofs of *Frederick* being corrected and dismissed,
the Carlyles went down, in the spring of 1865, to stay with
Lady Ashburton at a seaside cottage at Seaton, in Devon-
shire. They spent a few quiet weeks there, and then went
home again—Carlyle, so he says, "sank and sank into ever
new depths of stupefaction and dark misery of body and
mind."[1] He was a restless spirit. When busy, he complained that his work was killing him; when he was idle,
his mind preyed upon itself. Perhaps, as was generally the
case, he exaggerated his own discomforts. Long before he
had told his family, when he had terrified them with his
accounts of himself, that they ought to know that when he
cried Murder he was not always being killed.[2] When his
soul seemed all black, the darkness only broken by light-
nings, he was aware that sometimes it was only a want of
potatoes. Still in the exhaustion which followed on long
exertion he was always wildly humoured. About May he
found that he wanted fresh change. Something was amiss
with Mrs. Carlyle's right arm, so that she had lost the use
of it for writing. She seemed well otherwise, however;
she had no objection to being left alone, and he set off for
Annandale, where he had not been for three years. Mrs.
Carlyle made shift to write to him with the hand which
was left to her; lively as ever, careful, for his sake, to take
her misfortunes lightly.

[In Scotland] he had his horse with him—Fritz's successor, Lady Ashburton's present, whom he called Noggs.

581

On Noggs's back he wandered round the old neighbourhood, which he had first known as a schoolboy and then
as usher.[3] So went Carlyle's summer at the Gill. She
meanwhile, dispirited by her lamed hand, and doubtful of
the future, resolved that she, too, would see Scotland once
more before she died.

Mrs. Carlyle was proud of her husband; she honoured his
character, she gloried in his fame, and she was sure of his
affection. But in her sick state she needed rest, and rest,
when the dark spirit was on him, she could not find at his
side. He had his sister with him; he had his brother James
close at hand. To these kind kindred she might safely leave
him; and she went on past Annan to the good Russells in
Nithsdale, who had nursed her in the past year. Carlyle
wished her only to do what would give her most pleasure.
He went to see her at Thornhill, met her at Dumfries, was
satisfied to know that she was in safe hands, and was blind
to the rest.

To Mrs. Carlyle Nithsdale this time had been a failure.
The sleeplessness came on again, and she fled back to
Cheyne Row. "My poor witch-hunted Goody," he said; "oh
what a chace of the fiends."[4] Miss Bromley took charge of
her at Folkestone, from which she was able to send a brighter
account of herself. He, meanwhile, lingered on at his
brother's at Scotsbrig.

The peaceable torpor did not last long. He was roused
first into a burst of indignation by reading an "insolent
and vulgar" review upon Ruskin's *Sesame and Lilies*. It
was written by a man who professed attachment to Mrs.
Carlyle. I need not name him; he is dead now, and cannot
be hurt by reading Carlyle's description of him to her:

> A dirtyish little pug, . . . irredeemably imbedded in common-
> place, and grown fat upon it, & prosperous to an unwholesome
> degree. Don't *you* return his love; nasty gritty creature, with no
> eye for "the Beautiful the" &c,—and awfully "interesting to him-
> self, he too."[5]

In August Carlyle started on a round of visits—to Mr.
Erskine at Linlathen, to Sir William Stirling at Keir, to
Edinburgh, to Lord and Lady Lothian at Newbattle, and
then again to Scotsbrig.

The summer ended, as summers do and summers will,

and autumn saw the Carlyles together once more in their Chelsea home, which one of them was not again to leave alive. The great outward event of Carlyle's own life, Scotland's public recognition of him, was now lying close ahead. This his wife was to live to witness as her final happiness in this world. She seemed stronger, slept tolerably, drove about daily in her brougham; occasionally even dined out. Once I remember meeting her and Carlyle this autumn at the Dean of Westminster's, and walking home with him. Once they dined with me to meet Mr. Spedding of Mirehouse, Ruskin, and Dean Milman. Ruskin, I recollect, that night was particularly brilliant, and with her was a special favourite. She was recovering slightly the use of her right hand; she could again write with it; and nothing visible on the surface indicated that danger was near.

I had been at Edinburgh, and had heard Gladstone make his great oration on Homer there, on retiring from office as Rector. It was a grand display. I never recognised before what oratory could do; the audience being kept for three hours in a state of electric tension, bursting every moment into applause. Nothing was said which seemed of moment when read deliberately afterwards; but the voice was like enchantment, and the street, when we left the building, was ringing with a prolongation of the cheers. Perhaps in all Britain there was not a man whose views on all subjects, in heaven and earth, less resembled Gladstone's than those of the man whom this same applauding multitude elected to take his place. The students too, perhaps, were ignorant how wide the contradiction was; but if they had been aware of it they need not have acted differently. Carlyle had been one of themselves. He had risen from among them—not by birth or favour, not on the ladder of any established profession, but only by the internal force that was in him—to the highest place as a modern man of letters. In *Frederick* he had given the finish to his reputation; he stood now at the summit of his fame; and the Edinburgh students desired to mark their admiration in some signal way. He had been mentioned before, but he had declined to be nominated, for a party only were then in his favour.

On this occasion the students were unanimous, or nearly so. His own consent was all that was wanting, and the question lay before him whether, hating as he did all public displays, he would accept a quasi-coronation from them.

On November 7, 1865, he wrote to his brother:

> My Rectorate, it seems, is a thing "settled"; which by no means oversets my composure with joy! A young Edinburgh man came here two weeks ago to remind [me] that, last time, in flatly refusing, I had partly promised for *this,* if my work were done; I objected to the *Speech* &c, he declared that to be a thing they would dispense with: "Well, if *so*—!" I concluded; but do not yet entirely see my way through that latter clause, which is the sore one. Indeed I have yet heard *nothing* of official upon it; and did not even see the Newspaper Paragraphs till yesterday. *Hat gar wenig zu bedeuten* [of very little importance], one way or the other.[6]

Hat wenig zu bedeuten. So Carlyle might say—but it was *bedeutend* [important] to him nevertheless, and still more so to his wife. It seemed strange to me, so strange as to be almost incredible, that the Rectorship of a Scotch University could be supposed to add anything to the position which Carlyle had made for himself. But there were peculiar circumstances which gave to this one special form of recognition an exceptional attractiveness. Carlyle's reputation was English, German, American—Scotch also—but Scotch only to a certain degree. There had always in Scotland been an opposition party; and if the prophet had some honour in his own country, it was less than in other places. At least some feeling of this kind existed in Cheyne Row, though it may have been partly fancy, and due to earlier associations. Carlyle's Edinburgh memories were almost all painful. His University days had been without distinction. They had been followed by dreary schoolmastering days at Kirkcaldy, and the scarcely less dreary years of private tutoring in Edinburgh again. When Miss Welsh, of Haddington, announced that she was to be married to him, the unheard of *mésalliance* had been the scoff of Edinburgh society and of her father's and mother's connections there.[7] It had been hoped after the marriage that some situation might have been found for him, and they had settled in Comely Bank with a view to it. All efforts failed, however, and nothing could be done. At Craigenputtoch he laid the foundation of his reputation—but his applications for employment in Scotland had been still refused invariably, and sometimes contumeliously. London treated him, in 1831, as a person of importance; when he spent the winter following in Edinburgh he was coldly received there—received with a dislike which was only not contempt because it was qualified with fear. This was all past and gone, but he had always a feeling that Edinburgh had not treated him well. The Rectorship would be a public acknowledgment that his countrymen had been mistaken about him, and he had an innocent satisfaction in the thought of it. She, too, had a similar feeling. Among old friends of his family, who knew little about literature, there was still an impression that "Jeannie Welsh had thrown herself away." They would be forced to say now that "Jeannie was right after all." She laughed when she talked about it, and I could hardly believe that she was serious. But evidently both in him and her some consciousness of the kind was really working, and this perhaps more than anything else determined him to go through with a business which, in detail, was sure to be distressing to him.

Thus it was all settled. Carlyle was chosen Rector of Edinburgh University, and was to be installed in the ensuing spring. The congratulations which poured in all the winter—especially from Mrs. C.'s Scotch kinsfolk—"amused" them. Even a speech had been promised, and so long as it was at a distance seemed not inexecutable.

During the winter I saw much of him. He was, for him, in good spirits, lighter-hearted than I had ever known him. He would even admit occasionally that he was moderately well in health. Even on the public side of things he fancied that there were symptoms of a possibility of a better day coming.

The time approached for the installation and the delivery of the speech in Edinburgh. Through the winter Carlyle had dismissed it from his mind as the drop of bitter in his cup; but it had now to be seriously faced. To read would have been handiest to him, but he determined to speak. A speech was not an essay. A speech written and delivered, or even written and learnt by heart was to him an imposture, or, at best, an insincerity. He did not seem to be anxious, but anxious he was, and painfully so. He had never spoken

585

in public since the lecture days. He had experienced then
that he could do it, and could do it eminently well if he had
practised the art—but he had not practised. In private talk
he had no living equal; words flowed like Niagara. But a
private room among friends, and a hall crowded with
strangers where he was to stand up alone under two thousand pairs of eyes, were things entirely different; and Carlyle, with all his imperiousness and high scornful tones, was
essentially shy—one of the shyest of men. He resolved, however, as his father used to say, to "gar [make] himself to go
through with the thing," or at least to try. If he broke down,
as he thought that he probably would, he was old and weak,
and it could signify little. Still, he says that he "was very
miserable (angry with himself for getting into such a coil
of vanity . . .),"[8] provoked that a performance which, to a
vulgar orator would be a pride and delight, should to him appear so dreadful. Mrs. Carlyle kept up his spirits, made fun
of his fears, bantered him, encouraged him, herself at heart
as much alarmed as he was, but conscious, too, of the ridiculous side of it. She had thought of going with him, as she
had gone with him to his lectures, but her courage misgave
her. Among the freaks of her imagination she fancied that
he might fall into a fit, or drop down dead in the excitement. She had herself been conscious lately of curious sensations and sharp twinges, which might mean worse than
she knew. A sudden shock might make an end of her also,
"and then there would be a scene."[9] There would be plenty
of friends about him. Huxley was going down, and Tyndall,
who, wide as his occupations and line of thought lay from
Carlyle's, yet esteemed, honoured, loved him as much as
any man living did. Tyndall made himself responsible to
Mrs. Carlyle that her husband should be duly attended to
on the road and at the scene of action; and to Tyndall's care
she was content to leave him. The journey was to be broken at Fryston, where he would be received by Milnes, now
Lord Houghton. There he was to stay two nights, and then
go on to Scotland.

Accordingly, on Thursday, the 29th of March, at nine
a.m., Tyndall appeared with a cab in Cheyne Row, he himself radiant—confident—or if he felt misgivings (I believe he
felt none), resolute not to show them. Carlyle submitted

JOHN TYNDALL. An important Victorian scientist, Tyndall was one of Carlyle's closest associates in later years. He accompanied Carlyle to Edinburgh in 1866 upon the occasion of Carlyle's inaugural address as Rector of the University, and later that same year he took a disconsolate Carlyle, mourning the death of his wife, to pass the winter in the south of France as guest of the second Lady Ashburton. (Photograph by Elliott & Fry, courtesy of the Columbia University Libraries.)

passively to his directions, and did not seem outwardly disturbed, "in the saddest sickly mood, full of gloom and misery, but striving to hide it."[10] She, it was observed, looked pale and ill, but in those days she seldom looked otherwise. She had been busy providing little comforts for his journey. Remembering the lecture days she gave him her own small travelling flask, with a single glass of brandy in it, that he might mix and drink it in the Hall, and think of her and be inspired.

"The last I saw of her," he says, "was as she stood with her back to the Parlour-door to bid me her good-bye. She kissed me twice (she me once, I her a second time)."[11] The cab drove away. They were never to meet again in this world. "Tyndall," he says in the *Reminiscences*, "was kind, cheery, inventive, helpful; the loyalest *Son* could not have more faithfully striven to support his father, under every difficulty that rose. And they were many."[12] In a letter he says, "Tyndall's conduct to me has been loyalty's own self; no adoring son could have more faithfully watched a decrepit Father."[13] Fryston was reached without misadventure. "Lord Houghton's and Lady's, kindness to me was unbounded."[14] Tyndall wrote to Mrs. Carlyle daily reporting everything on its brightest side, though the omens did not open propitiously. "My first night here," he wrote himself, "owing to railway and other *noises* all thro', not to speak of excitations, talkings, dinnering &c, was *totally* sleepless;—a night of wandering, starting to (vain) tobacco, and utter misery," thought of flying off next morning to Auchtertool for quiet.[15] Morning light and reflection restored some degree of composure. He was allowed to breakfast alone— Tyndall took him out for a long, brisk ride. He dined again alone, threw himself on a sofa, "and, by Heaven's blessing, had for the first time an hour & half of real *sleep*." In his bed he slept again for seven or eight hours, and on the Saturday on which he was to proceed found himself "a new man."[16]

Huxley had joined the party at Fryston. Lord Houghton went with them as far as York. The travelling was disagreeable. Carlyle reached Edinburgh in the evening, "the forlornest of all physical wretches."[17] There too the first night was "totally hideous," with dreadful feelings "that speaking would be impossible; that I should utterly break down,—

to which, indeed, I had in my mind said, 'Well then,' and was preparing to treat it with the best *contempt* I could."[18] On Sunday, however, he found himself surrounded with friendly faces. Mr. Erskine had come from Linlathen. His two brothers were there from Scotsbrig; all Edinburgh was combining to do him honour, and was hearty and warm and enthusiastic. His dispiritment was not proof against a good-will which could not but be agreeable. He collected himself, slept well the Sunday night (as felons sleep, he would himself probably have said, the night before execution), and on the Monday was ready for action.

The installation of a Rector is a ceremonious affair. Ponderous robes have to be laid on, and there is a marching in procession of officials and dignitaries in crimson and ermine through the centre of the crowded Hall. The Rector is led to a conspicuous chair; an oath is administered to him, and the business begins.

When Carlyle rose in his seat he was received with an enthusiasm at least as loud as had been shown for Mr. Gladstone—and perhaps the feeling of the students, as he had been one of themselves—was more completely genuine. I believe—for I was not present—that he threw off the heavy academical gown. He had not been accustomed to robes of honour. He had been only a man all his life; he chose to be a man still; about to address a younger generation who had come together to hear something that might be of use to them. He says of himself, "My Speech was delivered as in a mood of defiant despair, and under the pressure of nightmares. Some feeling that I was *not* speaking lies, alone sustained me. The applause etc., I took for empty noise, which it really was not altogether."[19] This is merely his own way of expressing that he was doing what he did not like; that, having undertaken it, he became interested in what he was about, grew possessed with his subject, and fell into the automatic state in which alone either speaking or any other valuable work can be done as it ought to be. His voice was weak. There were no more volleys of the old Annandale grape-shot; otherwise he was easy, fluent, and like himself in his calmest mood.

He began with a pretty allusion to the time when he had first come up (fifty-six years before) to Edinburgh to at-

589

tend the University classes. Two entire generations had passed away since that time. A third, in choosing him as Rector, was expressing its opinion of the use which he had made of his life, and was declaring that "you are not altogether an unworthy labourer in the vineyard."[20] At his age, and residing as he did, far away in London, he could be of little service to the University, but he might say a few words to the students which might perhaps be of some value to them. In soft, earnest language, with the plainest commonsense, made picturesque by the form in which it was expressed, he proceeded to impress on them the elementary duties of diligence, fidelity, and honest exertion, in their present work, as a preparation for their coming life. Their line of study was, in the main, marked out for them. So far as they could choose (after a half-reverent, half-humorous allusion to theology, exactly in the right tone for a modern audience) he advised them to read history—especially Greek and Roman history—and to observe especially how, among these nations, piety and awe of the gods lay at the bottom of their greatness; that without such qualities no man or nation ever came to good. Thence he passed to British history, to Oliver Cromwell, to their own Knox (one of the select of the earth), to the Covenanters, to the resolute and noble effort of the Scotch people to make Christ's gospel the rule of their daily lives. Religion was the thing essential. Theology was not so essential. He was giving in brief a popular epitome of his own opinions and the growth of them.

In early life he had himself been a Radical. He was a Radical still in substance, though no longer after the popular type. He was addressing students who were as ardent in that matter as he had himself once been, and he was going on dangerous ground as he advanced. But he chose to speak as he felt. He touched upon democracy. He showed how democracies, from the nature of things, never had been, and never could be of long continuance; how essential it was, in such a world as ours, that the noblest and wisest should lead and that the rest should obey and follow. It was thus that England and Scotland had grown to be what they were. It was thus only that they could keep the place which they had won. We were apt to think that through the spread of reading and knowledge the conditions of human nature were changed, and that inequalities no longer existed. He thought slightly of the spread of knowledge as it was called, "Maid-servants . . . getting instructed in the 'ologies,' and are apparently becoming more and more ignorant of brewing, boiling, and baking; and above all, are not taught what is necessary to be known, from the highest of us to the lowest,—faithful obedience, modesty, humility, and correct moral conduct."[21] Knowledge, wisdom, true superiority was as hard to come at now as ever, and there were just as few that arrived at it. He then touched on another branch of the same subject, one on which he was often thinking, the belief in oratory and orators which was now so widely prevailing. Demosthenes might be the greatest of orators, but Phocion proved right in the facts. And then after a word from Goethe on education, he came to speak of this present age, in which our own lot was cast. He spoke of it then as he always did—as an era of anarchy and disintegration, in which all things, not made of asbestos, were on the way to being consumed. He did not complain of this. He only bade his hearers observe it and make the best of it. He told them to be true and faithful in their own lives; to endeavour to do right, not caring whether they succeeded, as it was called, in life; to play their own parts as quietly and simply as they could, and to leave the rest to Providence. "Don't suppose," he said, "that people are hostile to you or have you at ill-will, in the world. . . . You may feel often as if the whole world were obstructing you, setting itself against you: but you will find that to mean only, that the world is travelling in a different way from you, and, rushing on in its own path, heedlessly treads on you. That is mostly all: to you no specific ill-will."[22] He bade them walk straight forward; not expecting that life would be strewed with roses; and knowing that they must meet their share of evil as well as good. But he told them, too, that they would find friends if they deserved them, and in fact would meet the degree of success which they had on the whole deserved. He wound up with Goethe's hymn, which he had called, to Sterling, the "marching-music of the great brave Teutonic Kindred"; and he finished with the words which to the end were so often upon his own lips:

Wir heissen euch hoffen. (We bid you be of hope.)[23]

591

He was long puzzled at the effect upon the world's estimate of him which this speech produced. There was not a word in it which he had not already said, and said far more forcibly a hundred times. But suddenly and thenceforward, till his death set them off again, hostile tongues ceased to speak against him, and hostile pens to write. The speech was printed in full in half the newspapers in the island. It was received with universal acclamation. A low price edition of his works became in demand, and they flew into a strange temporary popularity with the reading multitude. *Sartor*, "poor beast," had struggled into life with difficulty, and its readers since had been few, if select. Twenty thousand copies of the shilling edition of it were now sold instantly on its publication. It was now admitted universally that Carlyle was a "great man." Yet he saw no inclination, not the slightest, to attend to his teaching. He himself could not make it out, but the explanation is not far to seek. The Edinburgh address contained his doctrines with the fire which had provoked the animosity taken out of them. They were reduced to the level of church sermons; thrown into general propositions which it is pretty and right and becoming to confess with our lips, while no one is supposed to act on them. We admire and praise the beautiful language, and we reward the performance with a bishopric, if the speaker be a clergyman. Carlyle, people felt with a sense of relief, meant only what the preachers meant, and was a fine fellow after all.

The address had been listened to with delight by the students, and had ended amidst rounds of applause. Tyndall telegraphed to Mrs. Carlyle his brief but sufficient message, " '*A perfect triumph.*' "[24] The maids in Cheyne Row clapped their hands when it arrived. Maggie Welsh danced for delight. Mrs. Carlyle drove off to Forster's, where she was to dine. Dickens and Wilkie Collins were there, and they drank Carlyle's health, and it was, as she said, " 'a good joy.' "[25] He meanwhile had escaped at his best speed from the scene of his exploit; making for his brother's lodgings in George Street, where he could smoke a pipe and collect himself. Hundreds of lads followed him, crowding and hurrahing. "I waved my hand prohibitively at the door," he wrote, "perhaps lifted my hat; and they gave but one cheer more,—something in the tone of *it*, which did for the first time go into my heart. 'Poor young men; so well affected to the poor old brother or grandfather here; and in such a black whirlpool of a world, all of us!' "[26]

Anxiety about the speech and its concomitants had, as Mrs. Carlyle expressed it, "tattered [her] to fiddle-strings."[27] The sudden relief, when it was over, was scarcely less trying. She had visitors to see, who came with their congratulations. She had endless letters to receive and answer. To escape from part of this she had gone to Windsor, to spend two days with her friend Mrs. Oliphant, and had greatly enjoyed her visit. On coming back she had dined with Lady William Russell, in Audley Square, and had there a smart passage of words with Mr. Hayward, on the Jamaica disturbances, the news of which, and of Governor Eyre's action, had just arrived.[28] The chief subject of conversation everywhere was her husband's address, and of this there was nothing said but good. Tyndall came back. She saw him, heard all particulars from him, and was made perfectly happy about it. Carlyle himself would be home in a day or two. For Saturday the 21st, purposely that it might be got over before his arrival, she had invited a small party to tea.

Principal Tulloch and his wife were in London; they wished to meet me or else I to meet them. I forget which it was. I hope the desire was mutual. I, the Tullochs, Mr. and Mrs. Spottiswoode, and Mrs. Oliphant were to be Mrs. Carlyle's guests in Cheyne Row that evening. Geraldine Jewsbury, who was then living in Markham Square, was to assist in entertaining us. That morning Mrs. Carlyle wrote her daily letter to Carlyle, and took it herself to the post. In the afternoon she went out in her brougham for the usual drive round Hyde Park, taking her little dog with her. Nero lay under a stone in the garden in Cheyne Row, but she loved all kinds of animals, dogs especially, and had found another to succeed him. Near Victoria Gate she had put the dog out to run. A passing carriage went over its foot, and, more frightened than hurt, it lay on the road on its back crying. She sprang out, caught the dog in her arms, took it with her into the brougham, and was

593

never more seen alive. The coachman went twice round the drive, by Marble Arch down to Stanhope Gate, along the Serpentine and round again. Coming a second time near to the Achilles statue, and surprised to receive no directions, he turned round, saw indistinctly that something was wrong, and asked a gentleman near to look into the carriage. The gentleman told him briefly to take the lady to St. George's Hospital, which was not two hundred yards distant. She was sitting with her hands folded on her lap dead.

I had stayed at home that day, busy with something, before going out in the evening. A servant came to the door, sent by the housekeeper at Cheyne Row, to say that something had happened to Mrs. Carlyle, and to beg me to go at once to St. George's. Instinct told me what it must be. I went on the way to Geraldine; she was getting ready for the party, and supposed that I had called to take her there. I told her the message which I had received. She flung a cloak about her, and we drove to the hospital together. There, on a bed in a small room, we found Mrs. Carlyle, beautifully dressed, dressed as she always was, in quietly perfect taste. Nothing had been touched. Her bonnet had not been taken off. It was as if she had sate upon the bed after leaving the brougham, and had fallen back upon it asleep. But there was an expression on her face which was not sleep, and which, long as I had known her, resembled nothing which I had ever seen there. The forehead, which had been contracted in life by continued pain, had spread out to its natural breadth, and I saw for the first time how magnificent it was. The brilliant mockery, the sad softness with which the mockery alternated, both were alike gone. The features lay composed in a stern majestic calm. I have seen many faces beautiful in death, but never any so grand as hers. I can write no more of it. I did not then know all her history. I knew only how she had suffered, and how heroically she had borne it. Geraldine knew everything.[29] Mrs. Carlyle, in her own journal, calls Geraldine her Consuelo, her chosen comforter.[30] She could not speak. I took her home. I hurried down to Cheyne Row, where I found Forster half-distracted, yet, with his vigorous sense, alive to what must immediately be done. Mr. Blunt, the Rector of Chelsea, was also there; he, too, dreadfully shaken, but collected and considerate. Two points had immediately to be considered: how to communicate the news to Carlyle; and how to prevent an inquest and an examination of the body, which Forster said would kill him. Forster undertook the last. He was a lunacy commissioner, and had weight with official persons. Dr. Quain had attended Mrs. Carlyle in her illness, and from him I believe Forster obtained a certificate of the probable cause of the death, which was received as sufficient. As to Carlyle, we did not know precisely where he was, whether at Dumfries or Scotsbrig. In the uncertainty a telegram was sent to John Carlyle at Edinburgh, another to Dr. John Brown, should John Carlyle be absent. By them the news was forwarded the same night to Dumfries, to his brother-in-law, Mr. Aitken, with whom he was staying, to be communicated according to Mr. Aitken's discretion.

And now I go on with Carlyle's own narrative written a fortnight after.

> Saturday night about half-past nine, I was sitting in Sister Jean's at Dumfries; thinking of my Railway to Chelsea on Monday, and perhaps of a sprained ankle I had got at Scotsbrig two weeks or so before,—when the fatal telegram (two of them in succession) came; it had a kind of *stunning* effect upon me; not for above two days could I estimate the immeasurable depth of it, or the infinite sorrow which had peeled my life all bare, and, in one moment, shattered my poor world to universal ruin. They took me out next day, to wander (as was medically needful) in the green sunny Sabbath fields; and ever and anon there rose from my sick heart the ejaculation "My poor little Woman!"—but no full gust of tears came to my relief, nor has yet come. . . .
>
> Monday morning, John set off with me for London;—never, for a thousand years, should I forget that arrival here of ours,—my first *un*welcomed by her; *she* lay in her coffin, lovely in death . . . pale Death and things not mine or *ours* had possession of our poor dwelling. Next day wander over the fatal localities in Hyde Park; Forster and Brother John settling, apart from me, every thing for the morrow. Morrow, Wednesday morning, we were under way with our sacred burden; John and Forster kindly did not speak to me (good Twistleton too was in the train without consulting me): I looked out upon the Spring fields, the everlasting Skies, in silence; and had for most part a more endurable day,—till Haddington where Dods etc. were waiting with hospitalities, with etc. etc. which almost drove me openly wild. I went out to walk in the moonlit silent streets; *not* suffered to go alone: I looked up at the windows of the old Room where I had first

GRAVE OF JANE WELSH CARLYLE. Jane Carlyle, who died unexpectedly on 21 April 1866 while Carlyle was away in Scotland, lies buried according to her wish with her father in the ruined chancel of Haddington Parish Church. (Photograph by the editor.)

seen her,—1821 on a Summer evening after Sunset,—five and forty years ago. Edward Irving had brought me out, walking to Haddington; *she* the first thing I had to see there. The beautifullest young creature I had ever beheld; sparkling with grace and talent, though sunk in sorrow (for loss of her Father), and speaking little. I noticed her once looking at me,—Oh Heaven, to think of that now! . . .

Thursday (26th April 1866), wandered out into the Churchyard etc.: at one P.M. came the Funeral; silent, small (only twelve old friends, and two *volunteer*, besides us three), very beautiful and noble to me: and I laid her head in the grave of her Father (according to covenant of forty years back); and all was ended. In the nave of the old Abbey Kirk, long a ruin, now being saved from further decay, with the skies looking down on her, there sleeps my little Jeannie, and the light of her face will never shine on me more.[31]

In these days, with mournful pleasure, Carlyle composed the beautiful epitaph which is printed in the *Letters and Memorials*, "a word," he said, "all true at least, and coming from my heart, which feels a momentary solace from it."[32]

chapter thirty

1866–1872

Carlyle's Remorse. Governor Eyre Affair.
Menton. Disraeli and the Tories.
"Shooting Niagara." Franco-Prussian
War of 1870. *Letters and Memorials of
Jane Welsh Carlyle*

The installation at Edinburgh had drawn the world's eyes on
Carlyle. His address had been in everyone's hands, had been
admired by the wise, and had been the fashion of the moment with the multitude. The death of his wife following
immediately, in so sudden and startling a manner, had given
him the genuine sympathy of the entire nation. His enemies,
if enemies remained, had been respectfully silent. The
Queen represented her whole subjects and the whole
English-speaking race when she conveyed to Cheyne Row,
through Lady Augusta Stanley, a message delicate, grace-
full, and even affectionate.

Personally Carlyle was unknown to the Queen. He had
never been presented, had never sought admission within
the charmed circle which surrounds the constitutional crown.
Perhaps, in reading Lady Augusta's words, he thought more
of the sympathy of the "bereaved widow" than of the notice
of his sovereign.[1]

What he was to do next, how he was to live for the future,
who was to live with him and take care of him, were questions which his friends were anxiously asking among themselves. Somewhere about in the first week in May, Carlyle,
who had hitherto desired to be left alone, sent me a message
that he would like to see me. He came down to me into
the library in his dressing gown, haggard and as if turned
to stone. He had scarcely slept, he said, since the funeral.
He could not "cry." He was stunned and stupefied. He
had never realised the possibility of losing her. He had

settled that he would die first, and now she was gone. From this time and onwards, as long as he was in town, I saw him almost daily. He was looking through her papers, her notebooks and journals; and old scenes came mercilessly back to him in vistas of mournful memory. In his long sleepless nights, he recognised too late what she had felt and suffered under his childish irritabilities. His faults rose up in remorseless judgement, and as he had thought too little of them before, so now he exaggerated them to himself in his helpless repentance. For such faults an atonement was due, and to her no atonement could now be made. He remembered, however, Johnson's penance at Uttoxeter;[2] not once, but many times, he told me that something like that was required from him, if he could see his way to it. "Oh!" he cried, again and again, "if I could but see her once more, were it but for five minutes, to let her know that I always loved her through all that! She never did know it, never." "If he could but see her again!"[3] His heart seemed breaking as he said it, and through these weeks and months he was often mournfully reverting to the subject, and speculating whether such future meeting might be looked for or not. He would not let himself be deluded by emotion. His intellect was vigorous as ever, as much as ever on its guard against superstition. The truth about the matter was, he admitted, absolutely hidden from us; we could not know, we were not meant to know. It would be as God willed. "In my Father's house are many mansions."[4] "Yes," he said, "if you are God, you may have a right to say so; if you are man, what do you know more than I or any of us?" Yet then and afterwards when he grew calm, and was in full possession of himself, he spoke always of a life to come, and the meeting of friends in it as a thing not impossible. In spite of science he had a clear conviction that everything in this universe, to the smallest detail, was ordered with a conscious purpose. Nothing happened to any man which was not ordained to happen. No accident, no bullet on battlefield, or sickness at home, could kill a man till the work for which he was appointed was done, and if this was so, we were free to hope that there was a purpose in our individual existence which was not exhausted in our earthly condition. The spirit, the soul of man, was not an accident or mere result of the organisation of protoplasm.

Intellect and moral sense were not put into man by a being which had none of its own. At no time of Carlyle's life had such a conclusion as this been credible to him. Again it was unlike nature so to waste its energies as to spend seventy years in training and disciplining a character, and to fling it away when complete, as a child flings away a plaything. It is possible that his present and anguished longing lent more weight to these arguments than he would otherwise have been able to allow them. At any rate it was round this hope and round his own recollections and remorse that our conversations chiefly turned when we took up our walks again; the walks themselves tending usually to the spot where Mrs. Carlyle was last seen alive; where, in rain or sunshine, he reverently bared his head.

By degrees he roused himself to think of trying some work again. He could still do something. Politics, philosophy, literature, were rushing on faster than ever in the direction which he most disliked. He sketched a scheme for a journal in which there was to be a running fire of opposition to all that. I and Ruskin were to contribute, and it might have come to something if all three of us had been willing, which it appears we were not.

John Carlyle stayed on in Cheyne Row, with no fixed arrangement, but as an experiment to see how it would answer. We all hoped it might continue; but struck down as Carlyle had been he was still himself, and his self-knowledge made him amusingly cautious. John, good-natured though he might be, had his own ways and humours, and his own plainness of speech; and to live easily with Carlyle required that one must be prepared to take stormy weather when it came in silence. He would be penitent afterwards; he knew his brother's merits and his own faults. "Your readiness," he said, "and eagerness at all times to be of help to me,—this, you may depend on it, is a thing I am always well aware of, at the bottom of all my impatiences and discontents."[5] But the impatiences and discontents were there, and had to be calculated upon. John was willing to go on, and Carlyle did not absolutely refuse, but both, after some months' trial, doubted if the plan would answer.

The wish to live together was evidently more on John's part than on Carlyle's. Carlyle was perhaps right. The two *"beasts"*[6] were both too old to change their natures, and they would agree best if they did not see each other too often. John went back to Scotland; Carlyle was left alone: and other friends now claimed the privilege of being of use to him, especially Miss Davenport Bromley, the "flight of skylarks," and Lady Ashburton. They had been both *her* friends also, and were, therefore, in his present mood, especially dear to him.

The affair of Governor Eyre had blown into white heat. In submission to general clamour Eyre had been recalled in disgrace. He had applied for other employment and had been refused. He had several children, and was irretrievably ruined. It was, Carlyle said to me, as if a ship had been on fire; the captain, by immediate and bold exertion, had put the fire out, and had been called to account for having flung a bucket or two of water into the hold beyond what was necessary. He had damaged some of the cargo, perhaps, but he had saved the ship. The action of the Government, in Carlyle's opinion, was base and ungenerous, and when the recall was not sufficient, but Eyre was threatened with prosecution, beaten as he himself was to the ground, he took weapon in hand again, and stood forward, with such feeble support as he could find for an unpopular cause, in defence of a grossly injured man. "Yesterday, in spite of the rain," he wrote to Miss Davenport Bromley,

> I got up to the Eyre Committee, and even let myself be voted into the chair, such being the post of danger on the occasion, and truly something of a forlorn hope, and place for *enfans perdus*. . . . Poor Eyre! I am heartily sorry for him, and for the English nation, which makes such a dismal fool of itself. Eyre, it seems, has fallen suddenly from £6,000 a year into almost zero, and has a large family and needy kindred dependent on him. Such his reward for saving the West Indies, and hanging one incendiary mulatto, well worth the gallows, if I can judge.[7]

I was myself one of the cowards. I pleaded that I did not understand the matter, that I was editor of *Fraser*, and should disturb the proprietors; mere paltry excuses to escape doing what I knew to be right. Ruskin was braver far, and spoke out like a man. "While all the world stands tremulous, shilly-shallying from the gutter," Carlyle wrote Miss Bromley, "impetuous Ruskin plunges his rapier up to

601

the very hilt in the abominable belly of the vast blockhead-
ism, and leaves it staring very considerably."[8]

The monster, alas! was an enchanted monster, and, "as
the air, invulnerable."[9] Its hour had not come, and has not
yet, in spite of Ruskin's rapier. Carlyle gave his money and
his name, but he was in no condition for rough struggling
with the "blatant beast." He soon saw that he could make
no impression upon the Government, and that Eyre was in
no personal danger from the prosecution. He wrote a few
words to one of the newspapers, expressing briefly his own
feeling about the matter, and so left it.

> Country very base and mad, so far as I survey its proceedings;
> Bright Beales, Gladstone, Mill, & Co. busy on the "Suffrage
> Question" (kindling up the slow *canaille* what they can): this and
> "Oh, make the Nigger happy!" seem to be the two things needful
> with these sad people. Sometimes [I] think the tug of revolution-
> struggle may be even *near* for poor England, much nearer than I
> once judged? Very questionable to *me* whether England won't go
> quite to *smash* under it, perhaps better than it *do*, having reached
> such a pitch of spiritual *beggary*.[10]

The world was going *its* way, and not Carlyle's. He was
finding a more congenial occupation for himself, in reviving
the history of his own young days, of the life at Ecclefechan
and Mainhill, with the old scenes and the old companions.
He had begun "languidly," as he said, to write the "Reminiscences of Edward Irving," which were more about
himself than his friend; and to recall and write down fragments of his mother's talk.

He allowed me to see as much of him as I liked. He did
not tell me what he was doing, but talked much on the subject of it. He often said—the wish no doubt suggesting the
expectation—that he thought his own end was near. He was
endeavouring to preserve the most precious parts of his recollections, before they and he should pass away together.
The Irving memories were dear to him, but there was
something else that was still dearer. Putting these aside for
the time, he set himself to write a memoir of the beautiful
existence which had gone at the side of his own, a record of
what his wife had been to him, and a testimony of his own
appreciation. At their first acquantance, it was she who
was to make a name in literature, and he was to have supported and stood by her. It was a consolation to him to de-

scribe the nature and the capabilities which had been sacrificed to himself, that the portrait of her might still survive. He was not writing it for the world. He finished it just before he went abroad, when he was expecting that in all probability he would never see England again. He left it sealed up, with directions to those into whose hands it might fall, that it was not to be published, no one being capable of properly editing it after he should be gone.

He had decided that he would try Menton. Lady Ashburton had entreated. His friends believed that change would be good for him. He himself, languid, indifferent, but having nothing of special consequence to retain him in England, had agreed to go. He was not equal to the journey alone. The same friend who had taken charge of him to Edinburgh undertook to place him safely under Lady Ashburton's roof, an act of respectful attention which Carlyle never forgot, "so chivalrous it was."[11] For Tyndall was not an idle gentleman, with time on his hands. He had his own hard work to attend to in London, and would be obliged to return on the instant. But he was accustomed to travelling. He was as good a courier as Neuberg, and to sacrifice a few days to Carlyle was an honour and a pleasure. They started on the 22nd of December, and in two days were transported from the London fogs to the sunny shores of the Mediterranean.

Carlyle was left in a new environment; nothing save the face of his hostess not utterly strange to him, among olive groves and palms and oranges, the mountains rising behind into the eternal snow, and the sea before his windows— Homer's violet sea at last under his eyes. Here he got his papers about him. Lady Ashburton left him to himself. He went on with his "Reminiscences," and in the intervals wandered as he pleased. Everyone feels well on first reaching the Riviera. Carlyle slept soundly, discovered "real improvement" in himself, and was almost sorry to discover it.

Distinguished visitors called in passing on their way to or from Italy; among others, Mr. Gladstone, "on return from Rome & the Man of Sin,"[12] "intending for Paris, and an interview with M. Fould."

Gladstone, en route homewards, had called on Monday; and sat a long time, talking,—principally *waiting* for Madame Bunsen his old friend, whom it was his one chance of seeing, as he had to leave for Paris next day—talk copious, ingenious, but of no worth or sincerity (pictures, literature, finance—prosperities, greatness of outlook for Italy, for &c.) a man ponderous, copious, of evident faculty, but all gone irrevocably into House of Commons shape; man once of some wisdom (or possibility of it), but now all as if possessed by the Prince or many Princes of the Power of the *Air*![13]

His chief pleasure at Menton was in long walks about the neighbourhood. He was the best of literary landscape painters, and his Journal, with his letters to myself and others, are full of exquisite little sketches, like the pictures of the old masters, where you have not merely a natural scene before you, but the soul of the man who looks upon it. Shadows of the great sorrow, however, clung to him.

The party at Menton broke up in the second week in March. Lady Ashburton went to Rome and Naples, having tried in vain to induce Carlyle to accompany her. He prepared for home again, and, shrinking from the solitude waiting him in Cheyne Row, he wrote, before leaving, to ask his brother to meet him there, with some consciousness that he had not received, as graciously as he might have done, his brother's attempts to live with him.

Tyndall's escort was not needed a second time. He found his way back to Chelsea without misadventure. John Carlyle was waiting as he desired, and he settled in with more composure than he had felt since his bereavement. The "intrusions" had to be dealt with, but were not easily disposed of. Mrs. Carlyle once said she had the faculty of attracting all miserable people that wanted consolation. Carlyle seemed to attract everyone who wanted help for body or soul, or advice on the conduct of life. The number of people who worried him on such matters, most of them without a form of introduction, is hardly to be believed. Each post brought its pile of letters. One admirer wanted a situation under Government, another sent a manuscript to be read and recommended to a publisher, another complained that Nature had given him a hideous face; he had cursed his life, and cursed his mother for bearing him; what was he to do? All asked for interviews. Let them but see him, and they would convince him of their deserts. He was marvellously patient. He answered most of the letters, he saw most of the applicants.

He gave advice. He gave money, infinitely too much. Sometimes, when it was beyond endurance, he would order the servant to admit no strange face at all. In such cases men would watch in the street, and pounce upon him when he came out for his walk. I have been with him on such occasions, and have been astonished at the efforts which he would make to be kind. Once I recollect a girl, an entire stranger, wrote to him to say that in order to get books she had pawned some plate of her grandmother's. She was in danger of discovery and ruin. Would Carlyle help her to redeem it? He consulted me. A relation of mine, who lived in the neighbourhood, made inquiry, saw the girl, and found that the story was true. He replied to her letter as the kindest of fathers might have done, paid the money, and saved her from shame. Sometimes the homage was more disinterested. I had just left his door one day, when a bright eager lass of seventeen or eighteen stopped me in the Row, and asked me if Thomas Carlyle lived there. I showed her the house, and her large eyes glowed as if she was looking upon a saint's shrine. This pleased him when I mentioned it. The feeling was good and honest and deserved recognition. But altogether he was terribly worried. Intruders worried him. Public affairs worried him. Disraeli was bringing in his scandalous Reform Bill "to dish the Whigs." Worse than all, there was no work cut out for him, and he could make none for himself.

In this tragic state Carlyle found one little thing to do which gave him a certain consolation. By his wife's death he had become the absolute owner of the old estate of the Welshes at Craigenputtoch. An unrelenting fatality had carried off one by one all her relations on the father's side, and there was not a single person left of the old line to whom it could be bequeathed. He thought that it ought not to lapse to his own family; and he determined to leave it to his country, not in his own name, but as far as possible in hers. With this intention he had a deed drawn, by which Craigenputtoch, after his death, was to become the property of the University of Edinburgh, the rents of it to be laid out in supporting poor and meritorious students there, under the title of "the John Welsh Bursaries." Her name he could not give, because she had taken his own. Therefore he gave her father's.[14]

He remembered his wife's pensioners: but he had as long or a longer list of his own. No donation of his ever appeared in printed lists; what he gave he gave in secret, anonymously as here, or else with his own hand as one human being to another; and of him it may be truly said that the left hand did not know what the right was doing. The undeserving were seldom wholly refused. The deserving were never forgotten. I recollect an old man, past eighty, in Chelsea, who had refused parish help, and as long as he could move earned his living by wheeling cheap crockery about the streets. Carlyle had a genuine respect for him, and never missed a chance of showing it. Money was plentiful enough now, as he would mournfully observe. Edition followed edition of the completed works. He had more thousands now than he had hundreds when he published *Cromwell*—but he never altered his thrifty habits, never, even in extreme age, allowed himself any fresh indulgence. His one expensive luxury was charity.

The shadow of his lost wife seemed to rise between him and every other object on which he tried to fix his thoughts. If anything like duty called to him, however, he could still respond—and the political state of England did at this time demand a few words from him. Throughout his life he had been studying the social and political problems of modern Europe. For all disorders modern Europe had but one remedy, to abolish the subordination of man to man, to set every individual free, and give him a voice in the government, that he might look after his own interests. This once secured, with free room and no favour, all would compete on equal terms, and might be expected to fall into the places which naturally belonged to them. None at any rate could then complain of injustice; and peace, prosperity, and universal content would follow. Such was and is the theory; and if the human race, or the English race, were all wise and all good, and had unbounded territorial room over which to spread, something might be said for it. As the European world actually was, in the actual moral and material condition of European mankind, with no spiritual convictions, no sincere care for anything save money and what money could buy, this notion of universal liberty in Carlyle's opinion could end in nothing save universal wreck. If the English nation had needed governing when they had a real religious belief, now, when their belief had become conventional, they needed it, he thought, infinitely more. They could bear the degree of freedom which they had already, only in virtue of ancient habits, contracted under wiser arrangements. They would need the very best men they had among them if they were to escape the cataracts of which he heard the approaching thunder. Yet it was quite certain to him that, with each extension of the franchise, those whom they would elect as their rulers would not be fitter men, but steadily inferior and more unfit. Under any conceivable franchise the persons chosen would represent the level of character and intelligence in those who chose them, neither more nor less, and therefore the lower the general average the worse the government would be. It had long been evident to him how things were going; but every descent has a bottom, and he had hoped up to this time that the lowest point had been reached. He knew how many fine qualities the English still possessed. He did not believe that the majority were bent of themselves on these destructive courses. If the wisest and ablest would come forward with a clear and honourable profession of their true convictions, he had considered it at least possible that the best part of the nation would respond before it was too late. The Tories had just come into office. He had small confidence in them, but they at least repudiated the new creed, and represented the old national traditions. They had an opportunity, if they would use it, of insisting that the poor should no longer be robbed by false weights and measures and adulterated goods, that the eternal war should cease between employers and employed, and the profits of labour should be apportioned by some rule of equity; that the splendid colonial inheritance which their forefathers had won should be opened to the millions who were suffocating in the fetid alleys of our towns; that these poor people should be enabled to go where they could lead human lives again. Here, and not by ballot-boxes and anarchic liberty, lay the road to salvation. Statesmen who dared to try it would have Nature and her laws fighting for them. They might be thrown out, but they would come back again—come in stronger and stronger, for the good sense of England would be on their side.

With a languid contempt, for he half-felt that he had been indulging in a dream, Carlyle in this year found the Tories preparing to outbid their rivals, in their own arts or their own folly, courting the votes of the mob by the longest plunge yet ventured into the democratic whirlpool; and in the midst of his own grief he was sorry for his country.

Disraeli had given the word, and his party had submitted to be educated. Political emancipation was to be the road for them—not practical administration and war against lies and roguery. Carlyle saw that we were in the rapids, and could not any more get out of them; but he wished to relieve his own soul, and he put together the pamphlet which he called "Shooting Niagara: and After?" When Frederick Maurice published his heresies about Tartarus, intimating that it was not a place, but a condition, and that the wicked are in Tartarus already, James Spedding observed to me that "one was relieved to know that it was no worse." Carlyle's Niagara, now that we are in the middle of it, seems to us for the present nothing very dreadful, and we are preparing with much equanimity, at this moment, to go down the second cataract. The broken water, so far, lies on the other side of St. George's Channel.[15] The first and immediate effect of the Reform Bill of 1867 was the overthrow of Protestant ascendency in Ireland. After five centuries of failure in that country, the English Protestants succeeded in planting an adequate number of loyal colonists in the midst of an incurably hostile population, and thus did contrive to exercise some peaceful influence there, and make constitutional government in that island not wholly impossible. The English Democracy, as soon as they were in possession of power, destroyed that influence. The result we have partly seen, and we shall see more fully hereafter. Carlyle, however, did not anticipate, as the consequence of the Niagara shooting, any immediate catastrophe; not even this in Ireland. He meant by it merely the complete development of the present tendency to regard money-making as the business of life, and the more rapid degradation of the popular moral character—at the end of which perhaps, but still a long way off, would be found some "scandalous Copper Captaincy." The believers in progress on these lines, therefore, may breathe freely, and, like Spedding, be "glad that it is no worse."

"Shooting Niagara" appeared first in *Macmillan's Magazine* for August 1867. It was corrected and republished as a pamphlet in September, and was Carlyle's last public utterance on English politics.[16] He thought but little of it, and was aware how useless it would prove.

A stereotyped edition of the "Collected Works" was now to be issued, and, conscientious as ever, Carlyle set himself to revise and correct the whole series.[17] He worked hard on the "revising" business, but felt no enthusiasm about the interest which "his works" were exciting; "nothing but languor, contempt, and indifference for said works—or at least for their readers *and* them." "The works had indeed cost him his life, and were in some measure from the heart, and all he could do. But the *readers* of them were and had been—what should he say?" and in fact "no man's work in this world could demand for itself the smallest doit of wages, or were intrinsically better than zero. That was the fact, when one had arrived where he had arrived." The money which was now coming in was actually painful.

The persecution of General Eyre had been protracted with singular virulence. He had been recalled from Jamaica. His pension was withheld, and he was financially a ruined man. The Eyre Committee continued, doing what it could for him. Carlyle was anxious as ever. I never knew him more anxious about anything. It had been resolved to present a petition in Eyre's behalf to the Government. Carlyle drew a sketch of one "tolerably to his own mind," and sent it to the Committee. It appeared, however, not to be to *their* minds. They thanked him, found what he said "fine and true"; but, in short, they did not like it, and he acquiesced.[18]

Proof-sheets of the new edition of his works were waiting for him [in the spring of 1868]. He found himself "willing to *read* those Books &c, and follow the Printer thro' them,— as almost the one thing I am good for, in those final down-pressed empty & desolate years." The demand for them was "mainly indifferent" to him. "What are my bits of 'Works,' what are anybody's 'Works'? Those whom I wish to please are sunk into the *grave*: the work & its praises & 'successes' are to me, more and more, a reminiscence merely." On the other hand, "the thought of a selection from HER Letters &c (could I but execute it well, and leave it legible behind me, 'to be printed after 20 years'?) has not yet quitted me;—nor should."[19] The selection and the copying was taken in hand.

Meantime his life fell back into something like its old routine. While his strength lasted he went annually to Scotland; never so happy as among his own kindred. Yet even among them he was less happy than sadly peaceful.

An incident befell him in the beginning of 1869 of a pleasing kind. He received an intimation from Dean Stanley that her Majesty would like to become personally acquainted with a man of whom she had heard so much, and in whose late sorrows she had been so interested. He was not a courtier; no one could suspect him of seeking the favour of the great of this world, royal or noble. But for the Queen throughout his life he had entertained always a loyal respect and pity, wishing only that she could be less enslaved by "the talking apparatus" at Westminster. He had felt for her in her bereavement, as she had remembered him in his own.

The meeting was at the Westminster Deanery:

> The Queen was really very gracious and pretty in her demeanour thro'out; *rose* gently in my esteem, by everything that happened, did not fall in any point incorrect &, tho' well-meaning, worthless. — The "Interview" was quietly very mournful to me; the one point of real interest, a sombre thought, "Alas, how would it have cheered *Her* bright soul (for my sake), had she been here!"[20]

The "Letters," however, and his own occupation with them, were the absorbing interest, although to me at this time he never mentioned the subject. Though I was aware that he was engaged in some way with his autobiography, I had no conjecture as to what it was. Finished in a sort the collection was, but it needed close revision, and there was an introductory narrative still to be written. Carlyle, however, could then touch it no further, nor did a time ever come when he felt himself equal to taking it up again. It was tied together and laid aside for the present, and no

MARY AITKEN CARLYLE. The daughter of Carlyle's sister Jean, Mary Aitken Carlyle came to Cheyne Row to take care of her uncle in 1868 and stayed with him until his death. In 1879 she married her first cousin A. Carlyle. After Carlyle's death she became involved in an acrimonious quarrel with Froude over the disposition of Carlyle's papers. (Courtesy of the Columbia University Libraries.)

resolution was then formed as to what was to be done with it.

This subject being off his mind, he was able to think more calmly of ordinary things. Ruskin was becoming more and more interesting to him. Ruskin seemed to be catching the fiery cross from his hand, as his own strength was failing. Writing this autumn to myself, he said, "One day, by express desire on both sides, I had Ruskin for some hours. Really interesting & entertaining. . . . He is full of projects, of generous prospective activities, some of which, I opined to him, would prove chimerical. There is (in singular environment) a ray of real Heaven in poor Ruskin;—passages of that last book (*Queen of the Air*) went into my heart like arrows."[21]

Among the infirmities of age, a tremulous motion began to show itself in his right hand, which made writing difficult and threatened to make it impossible. It was a twitching of the muscles, an involuntary lateral jerk of the arm when he tried to use it. And no misfortune more serious could have befallen him, for "it came," he said, "as a sentence not to do any more work while thou livest"—a very hard one, for he had felt a return of his energy. "In brighter hours he saw many things which he might write, were the mechanical means still there." He could expand the thoughts which lay scattered in his Journal. He could occupy himself at any rate, in itself so necessary to so restless a spirit. He tried "dictation," but it resulted only in "diluted moonshine."[22] Letters he could dictate, but nothing else, and the case was cruel.

The finer forces of nature were not sleeping everywhere, and Europe witnessed this summer [1870], in the French and German war, an exhibition of Divine judgement which was after Carlyle's own heart. So suddenly too it came; the whole sky growing black with storm, and the air ablaze with lightning, "in an hour when no man looked for it." France he had long known was travelling on a bad road, as bad as England's, or worse. The literature there was "a *new* astonishing Phallus-Worship," "with Balzac, Sue and Company for Evangelists, and Madame Sand for Virgin."[23] The Church getting on its feet again, with its Pope's infallibility, etc., was the re-establishment of exploded lies. As the people were, such was their government. The "Copper Captain," in his eyes, was the abomination of desolation, a mean and perjured adventurer. He had known him personally in his old London days, and had measured his nature. Prince Napoleon had once spent an evening in Cheyne Row. Carlyle had spoken his mind freely, as he always did, and the Prince had gone away inquiring "if that man was mad."[24] Carlyle's madness was clearer-sighted than Imperial cunning. He regarded the Emperor's presence on a throne which he had won by so evil means as a moral indignity, and had never doubted that in the end Providence would in some way set its mark upon him. When war was declared, he felt that the end was coming. He had prophesied, in the *Life of Frederick*, that Prussia would become the leading State of Germany, perhaps of Europe. Half that prophecy had been fulfilled already through the war of 1866. The issue of the war with France was never for a moment doubtful to him, though neither he nor any one could foresee how complete the German victory would be.

France had so clearly been the aggressor in the war with Germany that the feeling in England at the outset had been on the German side. The general belief, too, had been that France would win. Sympathy, however, grew with her defeats. The English are always restive when other nations are fighting, and fancy that they ought to have a voice in the settlement of every quarrel. There is a generous disposition in us, too, to take the weaker side; to assume that the stronger party is in the wrong, especially if he takes advantage of his superiority. When Germany began to formulate her terms of peace, when it became clear that she meant, as Carlyle foretold, to take back Alsace and Lorraine, there was a cry of spoliation, sanctioned unfortunately in high Liberal quarters where the truth ought to have been better known. A sore feeling began to show itself, aggravated perhaps by the Russian business,[25] which, if it did not threaten to take active form, encouraged France to prolong its resistance. The past history of the relations between France and Germany was little understood in England. Carlyle perhaps alone among us knew completely how France had come by those essentially German provinces, or how the bill was now

613

being presented for payment which had been running for
centuries. To allay the outcry which was rising he reluctantly
buckled on his armour again. With his niece's help he dictated a long letter to the *Times*, telling his story simply and
clearly, without a trace of mannerism or exaggeration.[26]
It appeared in the middle of November, and at once cooled
the water which might otherwise have boiled over. We think
little of dangers escaped; but wise men everywhere felt that
in writing it he had rendered a service of the highest kind to
European order and justice. His own allusions to what he
had done are slight and brief. As usual he thought but little
of his own performance.

Carlyle's letter most effectually answered its purpose.
There was no more talk of English interposition. M. Thiers
came over to beg for help; if not material, at least moral. We
had to decline to interfere, and France was left to its fate—a
fate terrible beyond Carlyle's expectation, for Paris, after
being taken by the Germans, had to be recovered again out
of the hands of the French Commune amidst the ashes of the
Tuileries, and a second "September" massacre, to be
avenged by a massacre in turn.

It was Carlyle's deliberate conviction that a fate like that
of Paris, and far worse than had yet befallen Paris, lay
directly ahead of all great modern cities, if their affairs were
allowed to drift on under *laissez-faire* and so-called Liberty.

But the world and its concerns, even Franco-German wars
and Paris revolutions, could not abstract his mind, except
fitfully, from the central thoughts which occupied his heart.
His interest had essentially gone from the Present to the
Past and Future, the Past so painfully beautiful, the Future
with the veil over it which no hand had lifted or could lift.
Could he but hope to see *her* once more, if only for five
minutes? By the side of this the rest was nothing.

In the following spring there are the saddest notices of the
failure of his hand, as if he was still eager to write something,
but could not:

> Loss of my own right hand for writing with a terrible loss; never
> shall I learn to "write by dictation," I perceive. Alas, alas! for I
> might still work a little if I had my hand. And the *Night* cometh
> wherein no man can work![27]

Carlyle's impatience with his inability to write perhaps
arose from an eagerness to leave complete, with a fitting

introduction, the letters and memorials of his wife, before making a final disposition of the manuscript. He could not do it. He was conscious that he would never be able to do it, and that he must decide on some other course. I was still his constant companion, but up to this time he had never mentioned these memoirs to me. Of her he spoke continually, always in the same remorseful tone, always with bitter self-reproach; but of the monument which he had raised to her memory he had never spoken at all. One day—the middle or end of June, 1871—he brought, himself, to my house a large parcel of papers. He put it in my hands. He told me to take it simply and absolutely as my own, without reference to any other person or persons, and to do with it as I pleased after he was gone. He explained, when he saw me surprised, that it was an account of his wife's history, that it was incomplete, that he could himself form no opinion whether it ought to be published or not, that he could do no more to it, and must pass it over to me. He wished never to hear of it again. I must judge. I must publish it, the whole, or part—or else destroy it all, if I thought that this would be the wiser thing to do. He said nothing of any limit of time. I was to wait only till he was dead, and he was then in constant expectation of his end. Of himself he desired that no biography should be written, and that this Memoir, if any, should be the authorised record of him. So extraordinary a mark of confidence touched me deeply, but the responsibility was not to be hastily accepted. I was then going into the country for the summer. I said that I would take the manuscript with me, and would either write to him or would give him an answer when we met in the autumn.

On examining the present which had been thus singularly made to me I found that it consisted of a transcript of the "Reminiscence" of Mrs. Carlyle, which he had written immediately after her death, with a copy of the old direction of 1866, that it was not to be published; two other fragmentary accounts of her family and herself; and an attempt at a preface, which had been abandoned. The rest was the collection of her own letters, etc.—almost twice as voluminous as that which has been since printed—with notes, commentaries, and introductory explanations of his own. The perusal was infinitely affecting. I saw at once the meaning of his passionate expressions of remorse, of his allusions to Johnson's penance, and of his repeated declaration that something like it was due from himself. He had never properly understood till her death how much she had suffered, and how much he had himself to answer for. She, it appeared, in her young days had aspired after literary distinction. He had here built together, at once a memorial of the genius which had been sacrificed to himself, and of those faults in himself which, though they were faults merely of an irritable temperament, and though he extravagantly exaggerated them, had saddened her married life. Something of this I had observed, but I had not known the extent of it; and this action of Carlyle's struck me as something so beautiful, so unexampled in the whole history of literature, that I could but admire it with all my heart. Faults there had been; yes, faults no doubt, but such faults as most married men commit daily and hourly, and never think them faults at all: yet to him his conduct seemed so heinous that he could intend deliberately that this record should be the only history that was to survive of himself. In his most heroic life there was nothing more heroic, more characteristic of him, more indicative at once of his humility and his intense truthfulness. He regarded it evidently as an expiation of his own conduct, all that he had now to offer, and something which removed the shadow between himself and her memory. The question before me was whether I was to say that the atonement ought not to be completed, and that the bravest action which I had ever heard of should be left unexecuted, or whether I was to bear the reproach, if the letters were given to the world, of having uncovered the errors of the best friend that I had ever had. Carlyle himself could not direct the publication, from a feeling, I suppose, of delicacy, and dread of ostentation. I could not tell him that there was nothing in his conduct to be repented of, for there was much, and more than I had guessed; and I had again to reflect that, if I burnt the manuscript, Mrs. Carlyle had been a voluminous letter-writer, and had never been reticent about her grievances. Other letters of hers would infallibly in time come to light, telling the same story. I should then have done Carlyle's memory irreparable wrong. He had himself been ready with a frank and noble confession, and the world, after its first astonishment, would have felt increased admiration for the man who had the courage to make it. I should have stepped between him and the completion of a purpose which would have washed his reputation clear of the only reproach which could be brought against it. Had Carlyle been an ordinary man, his private life would have concerned no one but himself, and no one would have cared to inquire into it. But he belonged to the exceptional few of whom it was certain that everything that could be known would eventually be sifted out. Sooner or later the whole truth would be revealed. Should it be told voluntarily by himself, or maliciously by others hereafter? That was the question.

When I saw him again after the summer we talked the subject over with the fullest confidence. He was nervously anxious to know my resolution. I told him that, so far as I could then form an opinion, I thought that the letters *might* be published, provided the prohibition was withdrawn against publishing his own Memoir of Mrs. Carlyle. That would show what his feeling had really been, and what she had really been, which also might perhaps be misconstrued. It would have been hard on both of them if the sharp censures of Mrs. Carlyle's pen had been left unrelieved. To this Carlyle instantly assented. The copy of the Memoir had indeed been given to me among the other papers, that I might make use of it if I liked, and he had perhaps forgotten that any prohibition had been attached, but I required, and I received, a direct permission to print it. The next question was about the time of publication. On the last page of the manuscript was attached a pencil note naming, first, twenty years after his death. The "after my death" had been erased, but the twenty years remained. Though I was considerably younger than he was, I could not calculate on living twenty years, and the letters, if published at all, were to be published by me. When he had given them to me in June he had told me only that I was to wait till he was gone. He said now that ten years would be enough—ten years from that time. There were many allusions in the letters to people and things, anecdotes, criticisms, observations, written in the confidence of private correspondence, which ought not to be printed within so short a time. I mentioned some of these, which he directed me to omit.

On these conditions I accepted the charge, but still only

617

hypothetically. It had been entrusted to me alone, and I wished for further advice. He said that if I was in a difficulty I might consult John Forster, and he added afterwards his brother John. John Carlyle I had never an opportunity of consulting. I presumed that John Carlyle was acquainted with his brother's intentions, and would communicate with me on the subject if he wished to do so; but I sent the manuscript to Forster, that I might learn generally his opinion about it. Forster had been one of Mrs. Carlyle's dearest friends, much more intimate with her than I had been. He, if any one, could say whether so open a revelation of the life at Cheyne Row was one which ought to be made. Forster read the letters. I suppose that he felt as uncertain as I had done, the reasons against the publication being so obvious and so weighty. But he admired equally the integrity which had led Carlyle to lay bare his inner history. He felt as I did, that Carlyle was an exceptional person, whose character the world had a right to know, and he found it difficult to come to a conclusion. To me at any rate he gave no opinion at all. He merely said that he would talk to Carlyle himself, and would tell him that he must make my position perfectly clear in his will, or trouble would certainly arise about it. Nothing more passed between Forster and myself upon the subject. Carlyle, however, in the will which he made two years later bequeathed the manuscript to me specifically in terms of the tenderest confidence. He desired that I should consult Forster and his brother when the occasion came for a final resolution; but especially he gave the trust to me, charging me to do my best and wisest with it. He mentioned seven years or ten from that date (1873)[28] as a term at which the manuscript might be published; but, that no possible question might be raised hereafter on that part of the matter, he left the determination of the time to myself, and requested others to accept my judgement as his own.

Under these conditions the *Letters and Memorials* remained in my hands. At the date of his will of 1873 he adhered to his old resolution, that of himself there should be no biography, and that these letters and these letters alone should be the future record of him. Within a few weeks or months, however, he discovered that various persons who had been admitted to partial intimacy with him were busy upon his history. If he was to figure before the world at all after his death he preferred that there should be an authentic portrait of him; and therefore at the close of this same year (1873) again, without note or warning, he sent me his own and his wife's private papers, journals, correspondence, "reminiscences," and other fragments, a collection overwhelming from its abundance, for of his letters from the earliest period of his life his family and friends had preserved every one that he had written, while he in turn seemed to have destroyed none of theirs. "Take them," he said to me, "and do what you can with them. All I can say to you is, Burn freely. If you have any affection for me, the more you burn the better."[29]

I burnt nothing, and it was well that I did not, for a year before his death he desired me, when I had done with these manuscripts to give them to his niece. But indeed everything of his own which I found in these papers tended only to raise his character. They showed him, in all his outward conduct, the same noble, single-minded, simple-hearted, affectionate man which I myself had always known him to be; while his inner nature, with this fresh insight into it, seemed ever grander and more imposing.

The new task which had been laid upon me complicated the problem of the *Letters and Memorials*. My first hope was, that, in the absence of further definite instructions from himself, I might interweave parts of Mrs. Carlyle's letters with his own correspondence in an ordinary narrative, passing lightly over the rest, and touching the dangerous places only so far as was unavoidable. In this view I wrote at leisure the greatest part of "the first forty years" of his life. The evasion of the difficulty was perhaps cowardly, but it was not unnatural. I was forced back, however, into the straighter and better course.

chapter thirty-one

1872–1881

The Early Kings of Norway. Death of Mill.
Acceptance of Prussian Order of Merit.
Refusal of Grand Cross of Bath.
Russo-Turkish War of 1877. Froude's
Recollections of Carlyle's Character.
Death of John Carlyle. Death and
Burial of Carlyle

Carlyle lived on after this more easy in his mind, but other-wise weary and "heavy laden"; for life, after he had lost the power of working, was become a mere burden to him. Often and often he spoke enviously of the Roman method of taking leave of it. He had read of a senator in Trajan's time who, slipping upon the pavement from infirmity, kissed the ground, exclaiming "Proserpine, I come!" put his house in order, and ended. Greatly Carlyle approved of such a termination, and regretted that it was no longer per-mitted. He did not conceive, he said, that his Maker would resent the voluntary appearance before Him of a poor crea-ture who had laboured faithfully at his task till he could labour no more. He made one more effort to produce some-thing. He had all along admired the old Norsemen, hard of hand and true of speech, as the root of all that was noblest in the English nation. Even the Scandinavian gods were nearer to him than the Hebrew. With someone to write for him, he put together a sketch of the Norse kings. The stories, as he told them to me, set off by his voice and manner, were vigorous and beautiful; the end of Olaf Trygveson, for instance, who went down in battle into the fiord in his gilded armour.[1] But the greater part of them were weakened by the process of dictation. The thing, when finished, seemed di-luted moonshine, and did not please him.

He wrote also a criticism on the portraits of John Knox, in which he succeeded in demolishing the authority of the accepted likenesses, without, however, completely establishing that of another which he desired to substitute for them. He had great insight into the human face, and into the character which lay behind it. *"Aut Knox aut Diabolus* [Either Knox or the Devil]," he said, in showing me the new picture; "if not Knox who can it be? A man with that face left his mark behind him."[2] But physiognomy may be relied upon too far, and the outward evidence was so weak that in his stronger days he would not have felt so confident.

This, with an appendix to his *Life of Schiller*, was the last of his literary labours. He never tried any thing again. The pencil entries in the Journal grew scantier, more illegible, and at last ceased altogether. The will was resolute as ever, but the hand was powerless to obey.

The end of the summer of 1872 was spent at Seaton with Lady Ashburton, whose affectionate care was unwearied. In a life now falling stagnant it is unnecessary to follow closely henceforth the occupation of times and seasons. The chief points only need be now noted. The rocket was burnt out and the stick falling. In November of that year Emerson came again to England, and remained here and on the Continent till the May following. He had brought his daughter with him, and from both of them Carlyle received a faint pleasure. But even a friend so valued could do little for him. His contemporaries were dropping all round; John Mill died; Bishop Wilberforce died; everyone seemed to die except himself.

His remarks on Mill and Mill's autobiography are curious.

Yesterday I got a great shock when Norton told me when we were stepping out into the street that John Mill was dead! I had heard no whisper of such a thing before; & a great black sheet of mournful more or less tragic memories, not about Mill alone, rushed down upon me: Poor Mill, he too has worked out his Life Drama in sight of me; & that scene too has closed before my old eyes, though he was so much my junior![3]

You have lost nothing by missing of the Autobiography of Mill. I have never read a more uninteresting book; nor I should say a sillier, by a man of sense, integrity and seriousness of mind. The penny-a-liners were very busy with it, I believe, for a week or two; but were evidently pausing in doubt and difficulty by the time the *2nd* edition came out. . . . It is wholly the life of a logic-chopping engine, little more of human in it than if it had been done by a thing of mechanized iron: "Autobiography of a Steam Engine"

621

perhaps you may sometime read it as a mournful psychical curiosity, but in no other point of view can it interest anybody— I suppose it will deliver us henceforth from the *cocka leerie crow* about "Great Thinker of the Age"; which will be a kind of deliverance, welcome, though inconsiderable. The thought of poor Mill altogether, and of his life and history in this poor muddy world, gives me real pain and sorrow.[4]

Such a sentence, so expressed, is a melancholy ending to the affectionate intimacy which had once existed between Mill and Carlyle. At heart, perhaps, they remained agreed— at least as much agreed as Carlyle and Bishop Wilberforce could have been; both believed that the existing social arrangements in this country were incurably bad, that in the conditions under which the great mass of human beings in all civilised countries now lived, moved, and had their being, there was at present such deep injustice that the system which permitted such things could not be of long endurance. Carlyle felt this to his latest hours. Without justice society is sick, and will continue sick till it dies. The modern world, incapable of looking duty in the face, attempts to silence complaint with issuing flash-notes on the Bank of Liberty, and will leave all men free to scramble for as much as they can secure of the swine's trough. This is the notion which it forms to itself of justice, and of the natural aid which human beings are bound to give to one another. Of the graces of mutual kindliness, of the dignity and beauty which rise out of organically-formed human society, it politically knows nothing, and chooses to know nothing. The battle is no longer, even to the strong, who have, at least, the one virtue of courage; the battle is to the cunning, in whom is no virtue at all. In Carlyle's opinion no remedy lay in political liberty. Anarchy only lay there, and wretchedness, and ruin. Mill had struck into that road for himself. Carlyle had gone into the other. They had drifted far apart, and were now separated for ever. Time will decide between them. Mill's theory of things is still in the ascendant. England is moving more eagerly than ever in the direction of enfranchisement, believing that there lies the Land of Promise. The orators echo Mill's doctrines: the millions listen and believe. The outward aspect of things seems to say that Mill did, and that Carlyle did not, understand the conditions of the age. But the way is long, the expected victories are still to be won—are

622

postponed till the day when "England, the mother of free nations, herself is free." There are rapids yet to be stemmed, or cataracts to descend, and it remains uncertain whether on arriving (if we do arrive) at a finished democracy, it will be a land flowing with milk and honey, or be a waste heaving ocean strewed with the wrecks of dead virtues and ruined institutions.

Carlyle was often taunted—once, I think, by Mr. Lecky—with believing in nothing but the divine right of strength. To me, as I read him, he seems to say, on the contrary, that, as this universe is constructed, it is "right" only that is strong.[5]

Old and weary as he was, the persistent belief of people in the blessings of democracy, and the confidence which they gave to leaders who were either playing on their credulity or were themselves the dupes of their own phrases, distressed and provoked Carlyle. He was aware that he could do nothing, that self-government by count of heads would be tried out to the end before it would be abandoned; but in his conversation and letters he spoke his opinions freely.

Of [Sir James] Stephen, Ruskin, and one or two others, Carlyle could still think with a degree of comfort. He would gladly have struck one more blow against "things not true"; for his intellect was strong as ever and his sight as piercing; but he sadly found that it was not to be. On December 6 he made the last pencil entry, or the last that is legible,[6] in his Journal. From this time his hand failed him entirely, and the private window that opened into his heart was closed up—no dictation being there admissible.[7]

He seemed to be drifting calmly towards the end, as if of outward incidents or outward activities there would be nothing more to record. But there was still something wanting, and he was not to leave the world without an open recognition of his services to mankind. In January 1874, there came a rumour from Berlin that Prussia proposed to reward the author of the *History of Frederick the Great*, by conferring on him the Order of Merit, which Frederick himself had founded. Possibly the good turn which he had done to Germany by his letter during the siege of Paris, might have contributed to draw the Emperor's attention to him. But his great history, translated and universally accepted by Frederick's countrymen as the worthiest account of their national hero, was itself claim sufficient without additional motive. Carlyle had never been ambitious of public honours. He had never even thought of such things, and the news, when it first reached Cheyne Row, was received without particular flutter of heart. "Were it never so well-meant," he said, "it can be of no value to me whatever. *Dy the naither ill na' gude.*"[8] The Order of Merit was the most flattering distinction which could have been offered him, for it really means "merit," and must be earned, even by the Princes of the Blood. Of course he could not refuse it, and, at the bottom, I am sure that he was pleased. Yet it seemed as if he would not let himself enjoy anything which *she* was no longer alive to enjoy with him.

To his friends this act of the German Government was a high gratification, if to himself it was a slight one. The pleasure which men receive from such marks of respect is in most cases "satisfied vanity"; and Carlyle never thought of his own performances, except as "duty" indifferently done.

We, however, were all glad of it, the more so because I then believed that when I wrote his life I should have to say that although for so many · years he had filled so great a place amongst us, and his character was as noble as his intellect, the Government, or Governments, of his own country—Tory, Liberal, or whatever they might be—had passed him over without notice. The reproach, however—for reproach it would have been—was happily removed while there was yet time.

It is rather for their own sakes, than for the recipients of their favours, that Governments ought to recognise illustrious services. The persons whom they select for distinction are a test of their own worth.

Benjamin Disraeli could not have been unaware of the unfavourable light in which he was regarded by Carlyle, but he by no means reciprocated the feeling. He was essentially goodnatured, as indeed Carlyle always acknowledged, and took any blow that might be aimed at him with undisturbed composure. He had been a man of letters before he was a politician. He was proud of his profession and of the distinction which he had himself conquered as a novelist. He was personally unacquainted with Carlyle; they had moved in different circles, and I believe had never met. But in early life he had been struck with *The French Revolution*; he had imitated the style of it, and distinctly regarded the author of that book as the most important of living writers. Perhaps he had heard of the bestowal of the Order of Merit, and had felt that a scandal would rest on England if a man whom Germany could single out for honour was left unnoticed in his own land. Perhaps the consideration might have been forced upon him from some private source. At any rate, he forgot, if he had ever resented, Carlyle's assaults upon him, and determined to use his own elevation as Premier to confer some high mark of distinction on a person who was so universally loved and admired. It was indeed time, for Carlyle hitherto had been unnoticed entirely, and had been left without even the common marks of confidence and recognition which far inferior men are seldom without an opportunity of receiving. He would not have accepted a pension even when in extremity of poverty. But a pension had never been offered. Eminent men of letters were generally appointed trustees of the British Museum; Carlyle's name had not been found among them. The post of Historiographer Royal for Scotland had been lately vacant. This, at least, his friends expected for him; but he had been intentionally passed over. The neglect was now atoned for.

> When I consider the literary world [Disraeli wrote to Carlyle], I see only two living names, which, I would fain believe, will be remembered; & they stand out in uncontested superiority. One is that of a poet; if not a great poet, a real one; & the other is your own.
>
> I have advised the Queen to offer to confer a Baronetcy on Mr Tennyson, & the same distinction sho*d* be at your command, if you liked it.
>
> But I have remembered that, like myself, you are childless, & may not care for hereditary honors. I have, therefore, made up my mind, if agreeable to yourself, to recommend Her Majesty to confer on you the highest distinction for merit at Her command, & which, I believe has never yet been conferred by Her except for direct services to the State. And that is the Grand Cross of the Bath.
>
> I will speak with frankness on another point. It is not well, that, in the sunset of life, you should be disturbed by common cares. I see no reason, why a great author should not receive from the nation a pension as well as a lawyer & a statesman. . . .[9]

To which Carlyle replied:

> Your splendid & generous proposals for my practical behoof

FROUDE'S LIFE OF CARLYLE

must not any of them take effect; that titles of honour are in all degrees of them out of keeping with the tenor of my poor existence
hitherto in this epoch of the world, and would be an encumbrance
not a furtherance to me; that as to money, it has after long years of
rigorous and frugal, but also (thank God, & those that are gone
before me) not degrading, poverty, become in this later time amply
abundant, even superabundant. . . .[10]

The Government was unwilling to accept the refusal, and
great private efforts were tried to induce him to reconsider
his resolution. It was intimated to him that Her Majesty herself would regret to be deprived of an opportunity of showing
the estimation which she felt for him. But the utter unsuitableness of a "title of honour" to a person of his habits and
nature, was more and more obvious to him. "The Grand
Cross," he said to me, "would be like a cap and bells to
him." And there lay below a yet prouder objection. "You
accepted the Order of Merit?" I said. "Yes," he answered,
"but that is a reality, never given save for merit only; while
this ———." The Prussian Order besides did not require
him to change his style. It would leave him, as it found him,
plain Thomas Carlyle.

So this small circumstance ended. The endeavour to mark
his sense of Carlyle's high deserts, which no other Premier
had thought of noticing, will be remembered hereafter to
Lord Beaconsfield's credit, when "peace with honour" is
laughed at or forgotten. The story was a nine days' wonder,
with the usual conflict of opinion. The final judgement was
perhaps most completely expressed to me by the conductor
of an omnibus: "Fine old gentleman that, who got in along
with you," said he to me, as Carlyle went inside and I
mounted to the roof; "we thinks a deal on him down in Chelsea, we does." "Yes," I said, "and the Queen thinks a deal
on him too, for she has just offered to make him a Grand
Cross." "Very proper of she to think of it," my conductor
answered, "and more proper of he to have nothing to do
with it. 'Tisn't that as can do honour to the likes of he."

More agreeable to Carlyle were the tributes of respect
which poured in upon Cheyne Row when the coming December brought his 80th birthday. From Scotland came a
gold medal; from Berlin two remarkable letters. One was
from a great person whom I do not know; the other was from

Prince Bismarck, written in his own large clear hand, which Carlyle showed me.

The Scotch medal too was an agreeable tribute, due, he believed, to the kind exertions of Professor Masson. But he was naturally shy, and disliked display when he was himself the object of it. The excitement worried him. He described it as "the birthday of a skinless old man; a day of the most miserable agitation he could recollect in his life." "The noble & most unexpected note from Bismarck," he said, "was the only real glad event of the day; the crowd of others, including even that of the Edinburgh Medal, was mere fret & fuss to me intrinsically of no value at all,—at least till one had time to recognise from the distance that kindness and goodwill had lain at the heart of every part of it."[11]

"Kindness and goodwill," yet not in the form which he could best have welcomed. The respect of the nineteenth century, genuine though it be, takes the colours of the age, and shows itself in testimonials, addresses, compliments. "They say I am a great man now," he observed to me, "but not one of them believes my report; not one of them will do what I have bidden them do."

His time was chiefly passed in reading and in dictating letters. He was still ready with his advice to all who asked for it, and with help when help was needed. He walked in the mornings on the Chelsea Embankment. "A real improvement that," as he reluctantly admitted. In the afternoon he walked in the park with me or some other friend; ending generally in an omnibus, for his strength was visibly failing.

Thus calmly and usefully Carlyle's later years went by. There was nothing more to disturb him. His health (though he would seldom allow it) was good. He complained of little, scarcely of want of sleep, and suffered less in all ways than when his temperament was more impetuously sensitive. One form of sorrow—inevitable when life is far prolonged, that of seeing those whom he had known and loved pass away—this he could not escape. In February, 1876, John Forster died, the dearest friend that he had left. I was with him at Forster's funeral in Kensal Green; and a month later at the funeral of Lady Augusta Stanley at the Abbey. In April his brother Alick went, far off in Canada.

627

CARLYLE IN 1876. (From a photograph in the Carlyle House, Chelsea.)

Though he felt his life to be fast ebbing, he still watched the course of things outside him. He had, as has been seen, been touched by Mr. Disraeli's action towards him, but it had not altered in the least his distrust of Disraeli's character; and it was thus with indignation, but without surprise, that he found him snatch the opportunity of the Russian-Turkish War [of 1877] to prepare to play a great part in European politics. The levity with which Parliament, press, and platform were lending themselves to the Premier's ambition, was but an illustration of what Carlyle had always said about the practical value of English institutions; but he was disgusted that the leaders in the present insanity should be those from whom alone resistance could be hoped for against the incoming of democracy. It was something worse than even their Reform Bill ten years before. He saw that it could lead to nothing but the discredit, perhaps the final ruin of the Conservative party, and the return of Mr. Gladstone, to work fresh mischief in Ireland. He foresaw all that has happened as accurately as if he had been a mechanically inspired prophet; and there was something of the old fire of the *Latter-Day Pamphlets* in the tone in which he talked of what was coming.

Events move fast in these days, and one nail drives out another; but we all remember the winter campaign which brought the Russians to Constantinople and the English fleet to the Dardanelles. Opinion in England was all but prepared to allow the Government to throw itself into the fray— all but—but not entirely. If initiative could be forced upon the Russians, those who wished for a fresh struggle could have it. A scheme was said to have been formed either to seize Gallipoli or to take some similar step, under pretence of protecting English interests, which would have driven Russia, however reluctant she might be, into a declaration of war. The plan, whatever it may have been, was kept a secret; but there is reason to believe that preparations were actually made, that commanders were chosen, and instructions were almost on their way, which would have committed the country beyond recall. Carlyle heard of this, not as he said from idle rumour, but from some authentic source; and he heard too that there was not a moment to lose. On the 5th of May he writes to his brother: "After much urgency and with a dead-lift effort against my burden & incumbrances I have this day got issued through the Times a small indes- pensible [*sic*] deliverance on the Turk & Dizzy question."[12]

The letter to the *Times* was brief, not more than three or four lines; but it was emphatic in its tone, and was positive about the correctness of the information.[13] Whether he was right, or whether some one had misled him, there is no evi- dence before the public to show. But the secret, if secret there was, had thus been disclosed prematurely. The letter commanded attention as coming from a man who was un- likely to have spoken without grounds, and any unexpected shock, slight though it may be, will disturb a critical opera- tion. This was Carlyle's last public act in this world; and if he contributed ever so little to preventing England from com- mitting herself to a policy of which the mischief would have been immeasurable, counterbalanced by nothing, save a brief popularity to the Tory party, it was perhaps also the most useful act in his whole life.

My tale draws to an end. In representing Carlyle's thoughts on men and things, I have confined myself as much as possible to his own words in his journals and letters. To report correctly the language of conversations, especially when extended over a wide period, is almost an impossi- bility. The listener, in spite of himself, adds something of his own in colour, form, or substance.

I knew Carlyle, however, so long and so intimately, that I heard many things from him which are not to be found under his hand; many things more fully dilated on, which are there only hinted at, and slight incidents about himself for which I could make no place in my narrative. I have already noticed the general character of his talk with me. I add here some few memorabilia, taken either from notes hastily written down, or from my own recollection, which I believe in the main to be correct.

When the shock of his grief had worn off, and he had com- pleted his expiatory memoir, he became more composed, and could discourse with his old fulness, and more calmly than in earlier times. A few hours alone with him furnished then the most delightful entertainment. We walked five or six miles a day in Hyde Park or Battersea, or in the environs of Kensington. As his strength declined, we used the help of an omnibus, and extended our excursions farther. In his last years he drove daily in a fly, out Harrow way, or to Richmond or Sydenham, or wherever it might be. Occasionally, in the warm days of early summer, he would go with me to Kew Gardens to see the flowers or hear the cuckoo and the nightingales. He was impervious to weather—never carried an umbrella, but, with a mackintosh and his broad-brimmed hat, let the rain do its worst upon him. The driving days were the least interesting to me, for his voice grew weak, and, my own hearing being imperfect, I lost much of what he said; but we often got out to walk, and then he was as audible as ever.

He was extremely sensitive, and would become uneasy and even violent—often without explaining himself—for the most unexpected reasons. It will be remembered that he had once stayed at Malvern with Dr. Gully, and on the whole had liked Gully, or had at least been grateful to him. Many years after Dr. Gully's name had come before the world again, in connection with the Balham mystery, and Carlyle had been shocked and distressed about it. We had been out at Sydenham. He wished to be at home at a particular hour. The time was short, and I told the coachman to go back quickly the nearest way. He became suddenly agitated, insisted that the man was going wrong, and at last peremptorily ordered him to take another road. I said that it would be a long round, and that we should be late, but to no purpose, and we gave him his way. By-and-by, when he grew cool, he said, "We should have gone through Balham. I cannot bear to pass that house."[14]

In an omnibus his arbitrary ways were very amusing. He always craved for fresh air, took his seat by the door when he could get it, and sat obliquely in the corner to avoid being squeezed. The conductors knew him, and his appearance was so marked that the passengers generally knew him also, and treated him with high respect. A stranger on the box one day, seeing Carlyle get in, observed that the "old fellow 'ad a queer 'at." "Queer 'at!" answered the driver; "ay, he may wear a queer 'at, but what would you give for the 'edpiece that's inside of it?"

He went often by omnibus to the Regent Circus, walked

631

from thence up Regent Street and Portland Place into the Park, and returned the same way. Portland Place, being airy and uncrowded, pleased him particularly. We were strolling along it during the Russo-Turkish crisis, one afternoon, when we met a Foreign Office official, who was in the Cabinet secrets. Knowing me, he turned to walk with us, and I introduced him to Carlyle, saying who he was. Carlyle took the opportunity of delivering himself in the old eruptive style; the Geyser throwing up whole volumes of steam and stones. It was very fine, and was the last occasion on which I ever heard him break out in this way. Mr.——— wrote to me afterwards to tell me how much interested he had been, adding, however, that he was still in the dark as to whether it was his eyes or the Turks' that had been damned at such a rate. I suppose I might have answered both.

He spoke much on politics and on the character of public men. From the British Parliament he was profoundly convinced that no more good was to be looked for. A democratic Parliament, from the nature of it, would place persons at the head of affairs increasingly unfit to deal with them. Bad would be followed by worse, and worse by worst, till the very fools would see that the system must end. Lord Wolseley, then Sir Garnet, went with me once to call in Cheyne Row, Carlyle having expressed a wish to see him. He was much struck with Sir Garnet, and talked freely with him on many subjects. He described the House of Commons as "six hundred talking asses, set to make the laws and administer the concerns of the greatest empire the world had ever seen"; with other uncomplimentary phrases. When he rose to go, he said, "Well, Sir, I am glad to have made your acquaintance, and I wish you well. There is one duty which I hope may yet be laid upon you before you leave this world—to lock the door of yonder place, and turn them all out about their business."

Of the two Parliamentary chiefs then alternately ruling, he preferred Mr. Disraeli, and continued to prefer him, even after his wild effort to make himself arbiter of Europe. Disraeli, he thought, was under no illusions about himself. To him the world was a mere stage, and he a mere actor playing a part upon it. He had no serious beliefs, and made no pretences. He understood, as well as Carlyle himself, whither England was going, with its fine talk of progress; but it would last his time; he could make a figure in conducting its destinies, or at least amuse himself scientifically, like Mephistopheles. He was not an Englishman, and had no true care for England. The Conservatives, in choosing him for their leader, had sealed their own fate. He had made his fame by assailing Peel, the last of the great order of English ministers. He was dexterous in Parliamentary maneuvers, but looked only to winning in divisions, and securing his party their turn of power. If with his talents he had possessed the instincts of a statesman, there was anarchic Ireland to be brought to order; there were the Colonies to be united with the Empire; there was the huge, hungry, half-human population of our enormous towns to be drafted out over the infinite territories of Canada, Australia, and New Zealand, where, with land to cultivate and pure air to breathe, they might recover sanity of soul and limb.

He used to speak with real anger of the argument that such poor wretches were wanted at home in their squalid alleys, that labour might continue cheap. It was an argument worthy only of Carib cannibals. This was the work cut out for English Conservatives, and they were shutting their eyes to it because it was difficult, and were rushing off, led by Dizzy, into Russian wars.

Mr. Disraeli, however, had, he admitted, some good qualities. He could see *facts,* a supreme merit in Carlyle's eyes. He was good-natured. He bore no malice. If he was without any lofty virtues, he affected no virtuous airs. Mr. Gladstone Carlyle considered to be equally incapable of high or sincere purpose, but with this difference, that he supposed himself to have what he had not. He did not look on Mr. Gladstone merely as an orator, who, knowing nothing as it ought to be known, had flung his force into words and specious sentiments; but as the representative of the multitudinous cants of the age—religious, moral, political, literary; differing in this point from other leading men, that the cant seemed actually true to him; that he believed it all and was prepared to act on it. He, in fact, believed Mr. Gladstone to be one of those fatal figures, created by England's evil genius, to work irreparable mischief, which no one but he could have executed.

London housebuilding was a favourite text for a sermon from him. He would point to rows of houses so slightly put together that they stood only by the support they gave to one another, intended only to last out a brief lease, with no purpose of continuance, either to themselves or their owners. "Human life," he said, was not possible in such houses. All real worth in man came of stability. Character grew from roots like a tree. In healthy times the family home was constructed to last for ages; sons to follow their fathers, working at the same business, with established methods of thought and action. Modern houses were symbols of the universal appetite for change. They were not houses at all. They were tents of nomads. The modern artisan had no home, and did not know what home meant. Everything was now a makeshift. Men lived for the present. They had no future to look forward to, for none could say what the future was to be. The London streets and squares were an unconscious confession of it.

For the same reason he respected such old institutions as were still standing among us—not excepting even the Church of England. He called it the most respectable teaching body at present in existence; and he thought it might stand for a while yet if its friends would let it alone. "Your rusty kettle," he said, "will continue to boil your water for you if you don't try to mend it. Begin tinkering, and there is an end of your kettle." It could not last for ever, for what it had to say was not wholly true. Puritanism was a noble thing while it was sincere, but that was not true either. All doctrines had to go, after the truth of them came to be suspected. But as long as men could be found to work the Church of England who believed the Prayer-book sincerely, he had not the least wish to see the fall of it precipitated. He disliked the liberal school of clergy. Let it once be supposed that the clergy generally were teaching what they did not believe themselves, and the whole thing would become a hideous hypocrisy.

He himself had for many years attended no place of worship. Nowhere could he hear anything which he regarded as true, and to be insincere in word or act was not possible to him. But liturgies and such-like had a mournful interest for him, as fossils of belief which once had been genuine. A lady—Lady Ashburton, I think—induced him once, late in his life, to go with her to St. Paul's. He had never before heard the English Cathedral Service, and far away in the nave, in the dim light, where the words were indistinct, or were disguised in music, he had been more impressed than he expected to be. In the prayers he recognised "a true piety," which had once come straight out of the heart. The distant "Amen" of the choristers and the roll of the great organ brought tears into his eyes. He spoke so feelingly of this that I tempted him to try again at Westminster Abbey. I told him that Dean Stanley, for whom he had a strong regard, would preach, and this was perhaps another inducement. The experiment proved dangerous. We were in the Dean's seat. A minor canon was intoning close to Carlyle's ear. The chorister boys were but three yards off, and the charm of distance was exchanged for contact which was less enchanting. The lines of worshippers in front of him, sitting while pretending to kneel, making their responses, bowing in the creed by habit, and mechanically repeating the phrases of it, when their faces showed that it was habit only without genuine conviction; this and the rest brought back the feeling that it was but play-acting after all. I could see the cloud gathering in his features, and I was alarmed for what I had done before the service was half over. Worst of all, through some mistake, the Dean did not preach, and in the place of him was a popular orator, who gave us three quarters of an hour of sugary eloquence. For a while Carlyle bore it like a hero. But by-and-by I heard the point of his stick rattle audibly on the floor. He crushed his hat angrily at each specially emphatic period, and groans followed, so loud that some of the congregation sitting near, who appeared to know him, began to look round. Mrs. D———, the Dean's cousin, who was in the seat with us, exchanged frightened glances with me. I was the most uneasy of all, for I could see into his mind; and at the too florid peroration I feared that he would rise and insist on going out, or even, like Oliver, exclaim, "Leave your fooling, sir, and come down!"[15] Happily the end arrived before a crisis, and we escaped a catastrophe which would have set London ringing.

The loss of the use of his right hand was more than a common misfortune. It was the loss of everything. The power of writing, even with pencil, went finally seven years before his death. His mind was vigorous and restless as ever. Reading without an object was weariness. Idleness was misery; and I never knew him so depressed as when the fatal certainty was brought home to him. To this, as to other immediate things, time partly reconciled him; but at first he found life intolerable under such conditions. Increasing weakeness only partially tamed him into patience, or reconciled him to an existence which, even at its best, he had more despised than valued.

To Carlyle, as to Hamlet, the modern world was but a "pestilent congregation of vapours."[16] Often and often I have heard him repeat Macbeth's lines:

> To-morrow, and to-morrow, and to-morrow
> Creeps in this petty pace from day to day
> To the last syllable of recorded time;
> And all our yesterdays have lighted fools
> The way to dusty death. Out, out, brief candle!
> Life's but a walking shadow, a poor player
> That struts and frets his hour upon the stage
> And then is heard no more. It is a tale
> Told by an idiot, full of sound and fury,
> Signifying nothing.[17]

He was especially irritated when he heard the ordinary cant about progress, unexampled prosperity, etc. Progress whither? he would ask, and prosperity in what? People talked as if each step which they took was in the nature of things a step upward; as if each generation was necessarily wiser and better than the one before; as if there was no such thing as progressing down to hell; as if human history was anything else but a history of birth and death, advance and decline, of rise and fall, in all that men have ever made or done. The only progress to which Carlyle would allow the name was moral progress; the only prosperity the growth of better and nobler men and women; and as humanity could only expand into high dimensions in an organic society when the wise ruled and the ignorant obeyed, the progress which consisted in destroying authority, and leaving everyone to follow his own will and pleasure, was progress down to the devil and his angels. That, in his opinion, was the evident goal of the course in which we were all hurrying on in such high spirits. Of the theory of equality of voting, the good and the bad on the same level, Judas Iscariot and Paul of Tarsus counting equal at the polling booth, the annals of human infatuation, he used to say, did not contain the equal.

Sometimes he thought that we were given over and lost without remedy; that we should rot away through inglorious centuries, sinking ever deeper into anarchy, protected by our strip of sea from a violent end till the earth was weary of us. At other times the inherent manliness of the English race, inherited from nobler ages, and not yet rinsed out of them, gave him hopes that we might yet be delivered.

I reminded him of the comment of Dion Cassius on the change in Rome from a commonwealth to an empire. In a democracy, Cassius says, a country cannot be well administered, even by accident, for it is ruled by the majority, and the majority are always fools. An emperor is but a single man, and may, if the gods please, be a wise one. But this did not please Carlyle either. The emperors that Rome got, and that we should be likely to get, were of the Copper Captain type, and worse than democracy itself. The hope, if there was hope, lay in a change of heart in the English people, and the reawakening of the nobler element in them; and this meant a recovered sense of "religion." They would rise out of their delusions when they recognised once more the sacred meaning of *duty*. Yet *what religion?* He did not think it possible that educated honest men could even profess much longer to believe in historical Christianity. He had been reading the Bible. Half of it seemed to be inspired truth, half of it human illusion. "The prophet says, 'Thus saith the Lord.' Yes, sir, but how if it be not the Lord, but only you who take your own fancies for the word of the Lord?" I spoke to him of what he had done himself. Then as always he thought little of it, but he said, "They must come to something *like* that if any more good is to grow out of them." Scientific accountings for the moral sense were all moonshine. Right and wrong in all things, great and small, had been ruled eternally by the Power which made us. A friend was arguing on the people's right to decide this or that, and, when Carlyle dissented, asked who was to be the judge. Carlyle fiercely answered, "Hell fire will be the judge. God Almighty will be the judge, now and always."

The history of mankind is the history of creeds growing

one out of the other. I said it was possible that if Protestant Christianity ceased to be credible, some fresh superstition might take its place, or even that Popery might come back for a time, developed into new conditions. If the Olympian gods could survive Aristophanes 800 years; if a Julian could still hope to maintain Paganism as the religion of the empire, I did not see why the Pope might not survive Luther for at least as long. Carlyle would not hear of this; but he did admit that the Mass was the most genuine relic of religious belief now left to us. He was not always consistent in what he said of Christianity. He would often speak of it with Goethe "as a height from which, when once achieved, mankind could never descend." He did not himself believe in the Resurrection as a historical fact, yet he was angry and scornful at Strauss's language about it. "Did not our heart burn within us?" he quoted, insisting on the honest conviction of the apostles.[18]

The associations of the old creed which he had learnt from his mother and in the Ecclefechan kirk hung about him to the last. I was walking with him one Sunday afternoon in Battersea Park. In the open circle among the trees were a blind man and his daughter, she singing hymns, he accompanying her on some instrument. We stood listening. She sang Faber's "Pilgrims of the Night." The words were trivial, but the air, though simple, had something weird and unearthly about it. "Take me away!" he said after a few minutes, "I shall cry if I stay longer."

He was not what is commonly called an amiable man. Amiability runs readily into insincerity. He spoke his mind freely, careless to whom he gave offence: but as no man ever delighted more to hear of any brave or good action, so there was none more tender-hearted or compassionate of suffering. Stern and disdainful to wrongdoers, especially if they happened to be in high places, he was ever pitiful to the children of misfortune. Whether they were saints or sinners made no difference. If they were miserable his heart was open to them. He was like Goethe's elves:

> ob er heilig, ob er böse,
> jammert sie der Unglücksmann.
> (be he holy, be he evil,
> they grieve for the man of ill-fortune.)[19]

638

His memory was extremely tenacious, as is always the case with men of genius. He would relate anecdotes for hours together of Scotch peasant life, of old Edinburgh students, old Ecclefechan villagers, wandering from one thing to another, but always dwelling on the simple and pious side of things, never on the scandalous or wicked. Burns's songs were constantly on his lips. He knew them so well that they seemed part of his soul. Never can I forget the tone in which he would repeat to me, revealing unconsciously where his own thoughts were wandering, the beautiful lines:

> Had we never loved sae kindly,
> Had we never loved sae blindly,
> Never met—or never parted,
> We had ne'er been broken-hearted.[20]

Not once but many times the words would burst from him, rather as the overflow from his own heart than as addressed to me.

In his last years he grew weak, glad to rest upon a seat when he could find one, glad of an arm to lean on when on his feet. He knew that his end must be near, and it was seldom long out of his mind. But he was not conscious of a failure of intellectual power, nor do I think that to the last there was any essential failure. He forgot names and places, as old men always do, but he recollected everything that was worth remembering. He caught the point of every new problem with the old rapidity. He was eager as ever for new information. In his intellect nothing pointed to an end; and the experience that the mind did not necessarily decay with the body confirmed his conviction that it was not a function of the body, that it had another origin and might have another destination. When he spoke of the future and its uncertainties he fell back invariably on the last words of his favourite hymn:

> *Wir heissen euch hoffen.* (We bid you be of hope.)

Meanwhile his business with the world was over, his connection with it was closing in, and he had only to bid it Farewell.

> Fear no more the heat o' the sun,
> Nor the furious winter's rages;
> Thou thy worldly task hast done,
> Home art gone and ta'en thy wages.

Golden lads and girls all must,
As chimney-sweepers, come to dust.[21]

Often these words were on his lips. Home, too, he felt that he was going; home to those "dear" ones who had gone before him. His wages he has not taken with him. His wages will be the love and honour of the whole English race who read his books and know his history. If his writings are forgotten, he has left in his life a model of simplicity and uprightness which few will ever equal and none will excel. For he had not been sustained in his way through this world by an inherited creed which could give him hope and confidence. The inherited creed had crumbled down, and he had to form a belief for himself by lonely meditation. Nature had not bestowed on him the robust mental constitution which passes by the petty trials of life without heeding them, or the stubborn stoicism which endures in silence. Nature had made him weak, passionate, complaining, dyspeptic in body and sensitive in spirit, lonely, irritable, and morbid. He became what he was by his moral rectitude of principle, by a conscientious resolution to do right, which never failed him in serious things from his earliest years, and, though it could not change his temperament, was the inflexible guide of his conduct. Neither self-indulgence, nor ambition, nor any meaner motive, ever led him astray from the straight road of duty, and he left the world at last, having never spoken, never written a sentence which he did not believe with his whole heart, never stained his conscience by a single deliberate act which he could regret to remember.

All things and all men come to their end. This biography ends. The biographer himself will soon end, and will go where he will have to answer for the manner in which he has discharged his trust, happy so far that he has been allowed to live to complete an arduous and anxious undertaking. In the summer of 1877 Carlyle, at my urgent entreaty, sat for his picture to Mr. Millais. Mr. Boehm had made a seated statue of him, as satisfactory a likeness in face and figure as could be rendered in sculpture; and the warm regard which had grown up between the artist and himself had enabled Mr. Boehm to catch with more than common success the shifting changes of his expression. But there was still something wanting. A portrait of Carlyle completely satisfactory did not yet exist, and if executed at all could be executed only by the most accomplished painter of his age. Millais, I believe, had never attempted a more difficult subject. In the second sitting I observed what seemed a miracle. The passionate vehement face of middle life had long disappeared. Something of the Annandale peasant had stolen back over the proud air of conscious intellectual power. The scorn, the fierceness was gone, and tenderness and mild sorrow had passed into its place. And yet under Millais's hands the old Carlyle stood again upon the canvas as I had not seen him for thirty years. The inner secret of the features had been evidently caught. There was a likeness which no sculptor, no photographer, had yet equalled or approached. Afterwards, I knew not how, it seemed to fade away. Millais grew dissatisfied with his work and, I believe, never completed it. Carlyle's own verdict was modestly uncertain. "The picture I think does not please Mary, nor in fact myself altogether; but it is surely strikingly like in every feature & the fundamental condition was that Millais should paint what he himself was able to see there."[22]

His correspondence with his brother John, never intermitted while they both lived, was concerned chiefly with the books with which he was occupying himself. He read Shakespeare again. He read Goethe again, and then went completely through the *Decline and Fall*. "I have finished Gibbon," he wrote.

> with a great deduction from the high esteem I have had of him ever since old Kirkcaldy days when I first read the twelve volumes of poor Irving's copy in twelve successive days,—a man of endless reading & research, but of a most disagreeable style and a great want of the highest faculties which indeed are very rare of what we could call a classical historian. Compared with Herodotus for instance and his grand simplicity and his perfect clearness in every part. . . .[23]

He continued to read the Bible, "the significance of which" he found "deep & wonderful almost as much as it ever used to be to me."[24] Bold and honest to the last, he would not pretend to believe what his intellect rejected, and even in Job, his old favourite, he found more wonder than satisfaction. But the Bible itself, the Bible and Shakespeare, remained "the best books" to him that were ever written.

641

As long as John Carlyle survived, he had still the associate of his early years, on whose affection he could rely, and John, as the younger of the two, might be expected to outlive him. But this last consolation he was to see pass from him. John Carlyle, too, was sinking under the weight of years. Illness bore heavily on him, and his periodic visits to Chelsea had ceased to be manageable. His home was at Dumfries, and the accounts of him which reached Cheyne Row all through that winter were less and less hopeful. It was a winter memorable for its long, stern, implacable frost, which bore hard on the aged and the failing.

As his condition grew hopeless, Carlyle was afraid every day that the end had come, and that the news had been kept back from him. "Is my brother John dead?" he asked me one day as I joined him in his carriage. He was not actually dead then, but he suffered only for a few more days.[25] John Carlyle would have been remembered as a distinguished man if he had not been overshadowed by his greater brother. After his early struggles he worked in his profession for many careful years, and saved a considerable fortune. Then, in somewhat desultory fashion, he took to literature. He wanted brilliancy, and still more he wanted energy, but he had the virtue of his family—veracity. Whatever he undertook he did faithfully, with all his ability, and his translation of Dante is the best that exists. He needed the spur, however, before he would exert himself, and I believe he attempted nothing serious afterwards. In disposition he was frank, kind-hearted, generous; entirely free from all selfishness or ambition; simple as his brother in his personal habits; and ready always with money, time, or professional assistance, wherever his help was needed. When Carlyle bequeathed Craigenputtoch to the University of Edinburgh, John too settled a handsome sum for medical bursaries there, to encourage poor students. These two brothers, born in a peasant's home in Annandale, owing little themselves to an Alma Mater which had missed discovering their merits, were doing for Scotland's chief University what Scotland's peers and merchants, with their palaces and deer forests and social splendour, had, for some cause, too imperfectly supplied.

James Carlyle and three sisters still remained, and Carlyle was tenderly attached to them. But John had been his early friend, the brother of his heart, and his death was a sore blow. He bore his loss manfully, submitting to the inevitable as to the will of his Father and Master. He was very feeble, but the months went by without producing much visible change, save that latterly in his drives he had to take a supply of liquid food with him. He was still fairly cheerful, and tried, though with diminished eagerness, to take an interest in public affairs. He even thought for a moment of taking a personal part in the preparation of his Memoirs. Among his papers I had found the "Reminiscences" of his father, of Irving, of Jeffrey, of Southey and Wordsworth. I had to ask myself whether these characteristic, and as I thought, and continue to think, extremely beautiful autobiographical fragments, should be broken up and absorbed in his biography, or whether they ought not to be published as they stood, in a separate volume. I consulted him about it. He had almost forgotten what he had written; but as soon as he had recalled it to his recollection he approved of the separate publication, and added that they had better be brought out immediately on his death.[26] The world would then be talking about him, and would have something authentic to go upon. It was suggested that he might revise the sheets personally, and that the book might appear in his lifetime as edited by himself. He turned the proposal over in his mind, and considered that perhaps he might try. On reflection, however, he found the effort would be too much for him. He gave it up, and left everything as before to me, to do what I thought proper.

At this time there had been no mention and no purpose of including in the intended volume the Memoir of Mrs. Carlyle. This was part of his separate bequest to me, and I was then engaged, as I have already said, in incorporating both memoir and letters in the history of his early life. I think a year must have elapsed after this before the subject was mentioned between us again. At length, however, one day about three months before his death, he asked me very solemnly, and in a tone of the saddest anxiety, what I proposed to do about "the Letters and Memorials." I was sorry—for a fresh evidence at so late a date of his wish that the Letters should be published as he had left them would take away my discretion, and I could no longer treat them as I had begun to do. But he was so sorrowful and earnest— though still giving no positive order—that I could make no objection. I promised him that the Letters should appear with such reservations as might be indispensable. The Letters implied the Memoir, for it had been agreed upon from the first between us that, if Mrs. Carlyle's Letters were published, his Memoir of her must be published also. I decided, therefore, that the Memoir should be added to the volume of Reminiscences; the Letters to follow at an early date. I briefly told him this. He was entirely satisfied, and never spoke about it again.[27]

I have said enough already of Carlyle's reason for preparing these papers, of his bequest of them to me, and of the embarrassment into which I was thrown by it. The arguments on either side were weighty, and ten years of consideration had not made it more easy to choose between them. My final conclusion may have been right or wrong, but the influence which turned the balance was Carlyle's persevering wish, and my own conviction that it was a wish supremely honourable to him.

This was in the autumn of 1880, a little before his 85th birthday. He was growing so visibly infirm, that neither he himself nor any of us expected him to survive the winter. He was scarcely able even to wish it.

He was entirely occupied with his approaching change, and with the world and its concerns we could see that he had done for ever. In January he was visibly sinking. His political anticipations had been exactly fulfilled. Mr. Gladstone had come back to power. Fresh jars of paraffin had been poured on the fire in Ireland, and anarchy and murder were the order of the day. I mentioned something of it to him one day. He listened indifferently. "These things do not interest you?" I said. "Not the least," he answered, and turned languidly away. He became worse a day or two after that. I went down to see him. His bed had been moved into the drawing-room, which still bore the stamp of his wife's hand upon it. Her workbox and other ladies' trifles lay about in their old places. He had forbidden them to be removed, and they stood within reach of his dying hand.

He was wandering when I came to his side. He recognised

me. "I am very ill," he said. "Is it not strange that those people should have chosen the very oldest man in all Britain to make suffer in this way?"

I answered, "We do not exactly know why those people act as they do. They may have reasons that we cannot guess at." "Yes," he said, with a flash of the old intellect, "it would be rash to say that they have no reasons."

When I saw him next his speech was gone. His eyes were as if they did not see, or were fixed on something far away. I cannot say whether he heard me when I spoke to him, but I said, "Ours has been a long friendship; I will try to do what you wish."

This was on the 4th of February, 1881. The morning following he died. He had been gone an hour when I reached the house. He lay calm and still, an expression of exquisite tenderness subduing his rugged features into feminine beauty. I have seen something like it in Catholic pictures of dead saints, but never, before or since, on any human countenance.

So closed a long life of eighty-five years—a life in which extraordinary talents had been devoted, with an equally extraordinary purity of purpose, to his Maker's service, so far as he could see and understand that Maker's will—a life of single-minded effort to do right and only that; of constant truthfulness in word and deed. Of Carlyle, if of anyone, it may be said that "he was a man indeed in whom was no guile." No insincerity ever passed his lips; no dishonest or impure thought ever stole into his heart. In all those long years the most malicious scrutiny will search in vain for a single serious blemish. If he had frailties and impatiences, if he made mistakes and suffered for them, happy those whose conscience has nothing worse to charge them with. Happy those who, if their infirmities have caused pain to others who were dear to them, have, like Carlyle, made the fault into a virtue by the simplicity and completeness of their repentance.

He had told me when Mrs. Carlyle died, that he hoped to be buried beside her at Haddington. It was ordered otherwise, either by himself on reconsideration, or for some other cause. He had foreseen that an attempt might be made to give him a more distinguished resting-place in Westminster

645

Abbey. For many reasons he had decided that it was not to be. He objected to parts of the English burial service, and, veracious in everything, did not choose that words should be read over him which he regarded as untrue. "The grain of corn," he said, "does not die; or if it dies, does not rise again." Something, too, there was of the same proud feeling which had led him to decline a title. Funerals in the Abbey were not confined to the deserving. When ———— was buried there he observed to me, "There will be a general gaol delivery in that place one of these days." His own direction was that he was to lie with his father and mother at the spot where in life he had made so often a pious pilgrimage, the old kirkyard at Ecclefechan.

Dean Stanley wrote to me, after he was gone, to offer the Abbey, in the warmest and most admiring terms. He had applied to me as one of the executors, and I had to tell him that it had been otherwise arranged. He asked that the body might rest there for a night on the way to Scotland. This also we were obliged to decline. Deeply affected as he was, he preached on the Sunday following on Carlyle's work and character, introducing into his sermon a beautiful passage which I had given to him out of the last journal.

The organ played afterwards the Dead March in *Saul*— grand, majestic—as England's voice of farewell to one whose work for England had closed, and yet had not closed. It is still, perhaps, rather in its infancy; for he, being dead, yet speaks to us as no other man in this century has spoken or is likely to speak.

He was taken down in the night by the railway. I, Lecky, and Tyndall, alone of his London friends, were able to follow. We travelled by the mail train. We arrived at Ecclefechan on a cold dreary February morning; such a morning as he himself describes when he laid his mother in the same grave where he was now to rest. Snow had fallen, and road and field were wrapped in a white winding-sheet. The hearse, with the coffin, stood solitary in the station yard, as some waggon might stand, waiting to be unloaded. They do not study form in Scotland, and the absence of respect had nothing unusual about it. But the look of that black, snow-sprinkled object, standing there so desolate, was painful; and, to lose sight of it in the three hours which we had to wait, we walked up to Mainhill, the small farmouse, two miles distant, where he had spent his boyhood and his university vacations. I had seen Mainhill before, my companions had not. The house had been enlarged since my previous visit, but the old part of it, the kitchen and the two bedrooms, of which it had consisted when the Carlyles lived there, remained as they had been, with the old alcoves, in which the beds were still standing. To complete the resemblance, another family of the same station in life now occupied it—a shrewd industrious farmer, whose wife was making cheeses in the dairy. Again there were eight children, the elder sons at school in the village, the little ones running about barefoot as Carlyle had done, the girls with their brooms and dusters, and one little fellow not strong enough for farm work, but believed to have gifts, and designed, by-and-by, for college. It was the old scene over again, the same stage, the same play, with new players. We stayed looking about us till it was time to go, and then waded back through the half-melted snow to the station. A few strangers had arrived from Edinburgh and elsewhere, but not many; for the family, simple in their habits, avoided display, and the day, and even the place, of the funeral, had not been made public. Two or three carriages were waiting, belonging to gentlemen in the neighbourhood. Mr. James Carlyle and his sisters were there, with their children, in carriages also, and there was a carriage for us. The hearse was set in movement, and we followed slowly down the half-mile of road which divides the station from the village. A crowd had gathered at the churchyard, not disorderly, but seemingly with no feeling but curiosity. There were boys and girls bright with ribands and coloured dresses, climbing upon the kirkyard walls. There was no minister—or at least no ceremony which implied the presence of a minister. I could not but contrast, in my own thoughts, that poor and almost ragged scene, with the trampled sleet and dirt, and *un*ordered if not *dis*ordered assemblage, with the sad ranks of mourners who would have attended in thousands had Dean Stanley's offer been accepted. I half-regretted the resolution which had made the Abbey impossible. Melancholy, indeed, was the impression left upon me by that final leave-taking of my honoured master. The kirkyard was peopled with ghosts. All round me were headstones, with the names of the good old villagers of whom I had heard so many stories from him: the schoolmaster from whom he had learnt his first Latin, the blacksmith with whom his father had argued on the resurrection of the body, his father, mother, sister, woven into the life which was now over, and which it was to fall to myself to describe. But the graves were soiled with half-thawed sleet, the newspaper correspondents were busy with their pencils, the people were pressing and pushing as the coffin was lowered down. Not in this way, I thought for a moment, ought Scotland to have laid her best and greatest in his solemn sleeping-place. But it was for a moment only. It was as he had himself desired. They whom he had loved best had been buried so—all so—and with no other forms. The funeral prayers in Scotland are not offered at the grave, but in private houses, before or after. There was nothing really unsuitable in what habit had made natural and fit. It was over, and we left him to his rest.

In future years, in future centuries, strangers will come from distant lands—from America, from Australia, from New Zealand, from every isle or continent where the English language is spoken—to see the house where Carlyle was born, to see the green turf under which his dust is lying. Scotland will have raised a monument over his grave; but no monument is needed for one who has made an eternal memorial for himself in the hearts of all to whom truth is the dearest of possessions.

> For, giving his soul to the common cause, he has won for himself a wreath which will not fade and a tomb the most honourable, not where his dust is decaying, but where his glory lives in everlasting remembrance. For of illustrious men all the earth is the sepulchre, and it is not the inscribed column in their own land which is the record of their virtues, but the unwritten memory of them in the hearts and minds of all mankind.[28]

Notes to the Life

FROUDE'S PREFACE

1. For the Journal passages, see p. 321 below.

2. In 1871. The "Introduction" became the reminiscence of Jane Welsh Carlyle, first published in Froude's edition of the *Reminiscences* (1881).

3. All but three were published by Froude and in Norton's edition of the *Reminiscences* (1887); the reminiscences of John Wilson and Sir William Hamilton are available in the Everyman edition, ed. Ian Campbell (1972); that of Adam and Archibald Skirving, as well as Carlyle's notes to the biography of him by Friedrich Althaus, in Clubbe, *Two Reminiscences.*

4. "Sir Walter Scott" (1838), a review of John Gibson Lockhart's biography of Scott, *Works*, 29:29–32, passim.

5. Compare a similar statement in a letter to William Allingham (Clubbe, *Carlyle and His Contemporaries*, p. 321).

6. An unpublished manuscript by Froude, probably designed as part of this preface but not used, casts light on his course of action:

> In the discharge of the first part of my duty [publication of the *Reminiscences*] I have laid myself open to misconstruction. I ought perhaps to have realised more clearly how impossible it was for the world to comprehend, or make allowance for so singular a commission.
>
> The English people who owe so much to Carlyle will not fail to judge him generously. My claim for indulgence is nothing. They will be sorry for much which they have read—and "the first bringer of unwelcome news hath but a losing office.["] Yet I too feel sure that I shall not ask in vain for a fair construction of my execution of a service itself so sad—a service perhaps the most unwelcome which ever was required in the name of friendship.
>
> In this as in all things he desired to be true. He would never

flatter—and his most intimate friends least of all and those whom he made smart had generally to acknowledge if they were honest that his words had hit the mark. (MS: Beinecke Library, Yale)

The document is in Margaret Froude's hand, and she has entitled it "MS (preface probably) not used." The remainder, discussing the various changes in Carlyle's timetable for the publication of the *LMJWC*, duplicates material in chap. 30.

7. Froude changed his mind. The last two volumes are more substantial than the first two.

8. Compare a letter of 1886 to Ruskin, in Viljoen, p. 46.

9. Pindar *Olympians* 1. 33–34. Froude gives the Greek.

CHAPTER ONE

1. Mary Aitken Carlyle: "Not entailed & were left to Elizabeth Carlyle who married a Douglas." In a related passage later in the life (p. 406 below), Froude again discusses the possibility of the Carlyles' having noble blood. A. Carlyle, denying this, wrote opposite this passage "None! His Father was not the eldest son."

2. See *Reminiscences*, 1:27. Opposite "it is certain that James Carlyle's grandmother," Mary Aitken Carlyle has written, "It does not appear"; she queries, "Was she of the second generation?"; and crosses out "the early part of the last century," substituting "1759." In the sentence following, after "for some time" she inserts "perhaps."

3. Ibid., p. 24. Froude's account of the Carlyle family is based not only on the *Reminiscences* but on Frederick Martin, "Thomas Carlyle: A Biography with Autobiographical Notes," *Biographical Magazine* 1 (1877): 1–22. Though attributed to Martin, this biography is probably by John T. Wells of Ecclefechan.

4. *Reminiscences*, 1:28.

5. See ibid., pp. 28–29.

6. Ibid., p. 29.

7. August 1758.

8. Mary Aitken Carlyle adds: "It might have been in."

9. *Reminiscences*, 1:34.

10. Ibid., p. 39.

11. Ibid., p. 40.

12. Ibid., p. 42. They were married on 5 March 1795.

13. Ibid.

14. For both the tombstone in Ecclefechan Kirkyard records "Jannet." The daughter died 27 January 1801, aged seventeen months.

15. *Reminiscences*, 1:45.

16. Ibid., p. 33. Mary Aitken Carlyle notes that John died in 1801, grandfather Thomas in 1806.

17. Ibid., p. 26.

18. Ibid., p. 44.

19. Clubbe, *Two Reminiscences*, p. 27.

20. *Reminiscences*, 1:46.

21. Harrold, *Sartor*, pp. 103-4. After Entepfuhl Froude inserts in parentheses "Ecclefechan."

22. Clubbe, *Two Reminiscences*, p. 32.

23. Ibid. Brasidas (d. 422 B.C.), the Spartan general mentioned in the previous sentence, spared the mouse that bit its finger for its show of fight. Plutarch recounts the story several times in the *Moralia*.

24. Ibid., pp. 29-30, 31-32.

25. Mary Aitken Carlyle: "New Year's day. No Xmas observed in Scotland."

26. *Reminiscences*, 2:17.

27. Ibid.

28. Ibid., 1:15-16, 8.

29. Ibid., p. 5.

30. About seventy.

31. See *Reminiscences*, 2:222-24.

32. Ibid., p. 26.

33. Clubbe, *Two Reminiscences*, p. 33.

34. Ibid., pp. 34, 36.

35. A. Carlyle: "Not true. He won the prize (College, I suppose) in the First Class in Mathematics. See his old teacher Mr. Morley's Letter of 4 July 1812 [NLS, 1764.2]."

36. Harrold, *Sartor*, p. 113.

37. See *CL*, 1:166-67.

38. Clubbe, *Two Reminiscences*, p. 39.

CHAPTER TWO

1. £70. See *CL*, 1:26. TC to Robert Mitchell, 18 October 1814. The position was, as Mary Aitken Carlyle notes, a mastership, not a tutorship.

2. Mary Aitken Carlyle: "He was a tutor too,—to General Dirom's sons." See references in *CL*, vol. 1.

3. See also pp. 111, 123, 145, 159, 170-71, 203, 306, and 383 below for instances in which Froude insists upon the closeness of Carlyle's tie with his mother. I have discussed elsewhere his treatment of this relationship within the context of what we now call the Oedipus complex (*Carlyle and His Contemporaries*, pp. 344-46, upon which the following paragraphs draw). I bring up the subject at this time so that the reader may be aware of the implications that this relationship had for Carlyle, in particular for his marriage, as developed by Froude within the perspective of the above-cited passages.

Froude believed that Carlyle would have been happier living with his mother, with whom he had a lifelong rapport, than with the woman he eventually married. Carlyle's regard for his mother was not only abnormally strong, in Froude's view, but a major reason why he should never have married Jane Welsh. Carlyle admired his father greatly, yet his relationship with him contains elements of ambiguity (as his dreams indicate, e.g., *Reminiscences*, 1:196); that with his mother, as many letters testify, was extremely close. Obviously Carlyle, unlike Oedipus, did not murder his father and marry his mother. But perhaps subconsciously he would have liked to do so—or so, at least, the dreams he records suggest.

Froude, in his understanding of human relationships, reveals himself to be uncannily prophetic of insights Freud had twenty years later. Although he does not anticipate Freud in full and conscious understanding of the nature of the Oedipus complex, he views Carlyle in a perspective similar to that which led Freud to formulate his famous theory. Freud, of course, achieved a fundamental insight into human nature; Froude anticipates Freud in divining it in a basic way, yet does not express it theoretically, probably because he does not fully understand it, but perhaps also because he may have found the insight so overwhelming that he could express it only partially and by allusion. He thus reaches the brink of Freudian discovery—only to stop. Inevitably, the strength or reality of the Oedipal drive, wrapped for Carlyle himself in a cloud of unknowing, emerges only with difficulty for those who look at it from the outside. In the biography Froude wavers between forthrightness and recoil. It may have been a failure of nerve, for although he pushes his intuitive understanding of Carlyle's relationship with his mother as far as he dares, he stops short of a comprehensive statement. In part, his ambiguous vocabulary—e.g., "lovers" (see p. 383 below)—causes difficulty, for words that in his day may have had similar denotations have now different emotional resonance. So pervasive is irony of language in the biography that we cannot always decide what Froude wishes to imply.

In my view Froude inferred too much, perhaps more than he realized, in depicting Carlyle's relationship with his mother. Nothing I have found in Carlyle's letters will warrant a future biographer's inferring more than he did. Still, one should not delude oneself into thinking one can foreclose upon the insights of future investigators. As with other matters in this intricate and teasing book, the last word on Carlyle's "Oedipus complex" remains to be written and may never be.

4. 1815. J. M. Sloane, in *The Carlyle Country* (London: Chapman & Hall, 1904), pp. 90–92, qualifies Froude's grim description of the Mainhill farm.

5. Mary Aitken Carlyle correctly notes that Carlyle tutored the children of the Reverend Henry Duncan at Ruthwell Manse.

6. Robert Mitchell to TC, 2 November 1814 (NLS, 1764.31).

7. Thomas Murray to TC, 27 July 1814 (NLS, 1764.23). Published in part in *CL*, 1:19–20.

8. *CL*, 1:20–21. TC to Thomas Murray, 24 August 1814.

9. *Reminiscences*, 2:20. The Latin title was *"Num detur religio naturalis."* Carlyle gave his "discourse" in December 1815.

10. Ibid., pp. 24–25. Cf. Clubbe, *Two Reminiscences*, pp. 37–38. See M. O. W. Oliphant, *The Life of Edward Irving*, 2 vols. (London: Hurst & Blackett, 1862), and A. L. Drummond, *Edward Irving and His Circle* (London: James Clarke, [1937]).

11. *Reminiscences*, 2:24–59.

12. Ibid., pp. 57–59.

13. Disputed by later scholars, e.g., Harrold, *Sartor*, p. 137 n, who find traces of Catherine Aurora ("Kitty") Kirkpatrick and Jane Welsh Carlyle as well as literary sources.

14. On Margaret Gordon, see R. C. Archibald, *Carlyle's First Love: Margaret Gordon Lady Bannerman* (London: John Lane, The Bodley Head, 1910); and, for a résumé, A. Carlyle, *LL*, 2:387–400, where the two letters were first published. A more recent study is Murdoch MacKinnon, "Carlyle's Imperious Queen of Hearts," *Queens Quarterly* 38 (1961): 52–62.

CHAPTER THREE

1. Clubbe, *Two Reminiscences*, p. 35.

2. Ibid., p. 50; also *Reminiscences*, 2:232.

3. Clubbe, *Two Reminiscences*, pp. 51–52; and Harrold, *Sartor*, p. 129.

4. During 1818–19, his first year in Edinburgh on his own, Carlyle attended Professor Robert Jameson's lectures on mineralogy. The next year he attended lectures on Scots law given by David Hume, nephew of the philosopher and historian, but gradually lost interest and abandoned the subject by spring 1820.

5. Clubbe, *Two Reminiscences*, p. 48; and cf. ibid., p. 51.

6. *CL*, 1:213. TC to MAC, 15 December 1819.

7. " 'Thou's gey' (pretty, pronounced *gyei*) 'ill to deal wi'—mother's allocution to me once, in some unreasonable moment of mine" (TC's note, in Froude, *LMJWC*, 1:49). Froude cited the phrase often and, as his detractors never tired of pointing out, incorrectly as "gey ill to live wi'." See Norton, *L26–36*, p. 33 n; Moncure Daniel Conway, *Autobiography*, 2 vols. (Boston and New York: Houghton, Mifflin & Co., 1904), 2:215–16; and Dunn, *F and C*, pp. 184–91. In *LMJWC* Froude printed the phrase correctly, and he also changed it in the biography's 1890 edition, which is followed here.

8. Froude places in 1820 Carlyle's report of his February 1821 illness. See *CL*, 1:324–30.

9. *Reminiscences*, 2:73.

10. Ibid., pp. 89–90.

11. For Carlyle's interest in German, which he began to study seriously in 1819 (not 1820, as Froude implies), see Clubbe, *Two Reminiscences*, pp. 12–14, 42–47.

12. Seventeen of Carlyle's twenty articles for David Brewster's *Edinburgh Encyclopaedia* were reprinted in *Montaigne and Other Essays*, ed. S. R. Crockett (London: James Gowans, 1897); A. Carlyle noted an eighteenth in *LL*, 1:268; and G. B. Tennyson published the

final two in "Unnoted Encyclopaedia Articles by Carlyle," *English Language Notes* 1 (December 1963): 108–12. The articles were written between 1820 and 1823.

13. The proposal came from Matthew Allen, for whom see *CL*, 1:250.

14. Carlyle's complete translation of Schiller was projected in 1824–25, a little later than implied by Froude, but Froude may have had in mind Carlyle's hope to translate Schiller's *History of the Thirty Years War* (see *CL* 1:299). The "specimen" Carlyle translated, never published, is now in the Beinecke Library, Yale.

15. Clubbe, *Two Reminiscences*, pp. 51, 49. A. Carlyle convincingly places Carlyle's conversion, set by Froude in June 1821, in July or early August 1821 or, more likely, in 1822 (see *LL*, 2:380–82). This latter date, which Carlyle's commentary in *Two Reminiscences* confirms, is accepted today. The improvement in Carlyle's mental state came about through a number of causes. These include his first meeting with Jane Baillie Welsh late in May 1821 and the generally favorable progress of his largely epistolary courtship of her; his first thorough reading sometime in 1821 of *Wilhelm Meisters Lehrjahre*, which proved a revelation; his engagement as tutor for Charles and Arthur Buller in January 1822, which provided a measure of financial stability; his growing realization that literature was to be his life's work; and, of course, his gradually improving health. Froude, by placing the conversion in 1821, implies, though never specifically states, that Jane Welsh had more to do with it than she actually did. That it was not as abrupt as in *Sartor* and that his recovery extended over many years is the argument of two important articles by Carlisle Moore, "*Sartor Resartus* and the Problem of Carlyle's 'Conversion,' " *PMLA* 70 (September 1955): 662–81, and "The Persistence of Carlyle's 'Everlasting Yea,' " *Modern Philology* 54 (February 1957): 187–96.

16. Harrold, *Sartor*, pp. 163–68 passim.

CHAPTER FOUR

1. " 'Craigen*puttock*,' or the stone-mountain, 'Craig' of the 'Puttock,'—puttock being a sort of *Hawk*, both in Galloway Speech, and in Shakespeare's Old English" (*Reminiscences*, 1:87). Cf. Clubbe, *Two Reminiscences*, p. 67.

2. Probably legend. See A. Carlyle, *LL*, 2:196 n and *CL*, 3:420; and cf. *Reminiscences*, 1:133–35.

3. *Reminiscences*, 1:136.

4. Ibid., p. 78.

5. Ibid., p. 55.

6. Mary Aitken Carlyle: "not so[:] all taught together in the Scotch parish schools."

7. A. Carlyle: "Heaven help us! She confesses that she never could say the multiplication table,—for a whole day together."

8. *The Rival Brothers*, first published in *CL*, 7:361–68.

9. *Reminiscences*, 1:71–72.

10. A. Carlyle comments that the engagement was "fully-formed." See *CL*, 2:413–14.

11. Ibid., 3:357. JBW to TC, [24 July 1825].

12. In "The Everlasting No." See also Clubbe, *Two Reminiscences*, p. 51.

13. Actually late May.

14. *CL*, 3:376–77. TC's note, JBW to TC, [2 September 1825]. On Carlyle's first meeting with Jane, see also *CL*, 1:363; and *Reminiscences*, 2:85–87, 1:146–48. All did not go smoothly at first. Writing to Jane almost immediately (4 June 1821), Carlyle rhapsodized over "those few Elysian hours we spent together lately" and closed with *"Addio, Donna mia cara"* (*CL*, 1:360, 361). Jane's angry rebuke for such over-familiarity has not survived, but something of its sting is suggested in the contrite beginning of TC to JBW, 16 July 1821 (ibid., p. 368). See p. 140.

15. Carlyle's knowledge of Italian was slight at this time; Spanish he only took up with Jane in the autumn of 1828.

16. "Apostles of freedom" from Goethe, *Venezianische Epigramme* (1790), no. 20. Goethe found the apostles distasteful because they were self-serving. Carlyle quoted his quatrain as motto to volume 3 of *The French Revolution*.

17. "Goethe's Works" (1832), *Works*, 27:438. See also *Reminiscences*, 2:115, and Clubbe, *Two Reminiscences*, p. 45.

CHAPTER FIVE

1. Edward Irving to TC, 30 December 1821 (NLS, 1764.211).

2. Carlyle assumed the position of tutor to Charles (1806–48) and Arthur Buller (1808–69) in January 1822 and resigned it in July 1824. For the Bullers see the *Dictionary of National Biography* (*DNB*) and *CL*, 2:4–5.

3. First published in *New Edinburgh Review* 2 (April 1822): 316–34; republished in *Collectanea: Thomas Carlyle, 1821–1825*, ed. S. A. Jones (Canton, Pa.: Kirgate Press, 1902), pp. 59–92. "Legendre" refers to *Elements of Geometry and Trigonometry* (Edinburgh: Oliver & Boyd, 1824), Carlyle's translation (with help from his brother John) of the eleventh edition of A. M. Legendre's *Eléments de Géométrie*, first published in 1794.

4. Edward Irving to TC, 29 April 1822 (NLS, 1764.227).

5. Although Froude's detractors have attacked his interpretation of both Carlyle's courtship of Miss Welsh and her relationship with Edward Irving, publication of the complete correspondence in the *CL* generally supports his interpretation of the events and his understanding of the psychology of those involved. Whether or not one agrees with Froude's belief that the Carlyles would have been better off not married to each other, it is hard to deny the acuity of his insight into their motivations. See also chap. 8, n. 24.

6. A. Carlyle: "So Miss Jewsbury." Cf. Wilson, *Carlyle*, 1:300.

7. *CL*, 2:151. TC to JAC, 25 July 1822.

8. Froude wrote "his exercises," but "her exercises" seems more likely.

9. Next youngest. Janet, born in 1813, followed Jean (Jane), born in 1810.

10. Published in A. Carlyle, *LL*, 2:352–53.

11. *CL*, 2:309. TC to MAC, 22 March 1823.

12. Ibid.

13. Ibid., p. 261. TC to MAC, 4 January 1823.

14. Ibid., 3:51–52. TC to JBW, 22 March 1824.

15. Ibid., 2:415. JBW to TC, 19 August [1823]. The house was Templand, home of her maternal grandfather, Walter Welsh.

16. Ibid., pp. 427–28. JBW to TC, 16 September [1823].

17. Ibid., p. 433. TC to JBW, 18 September 1823.

18. A. Carlyle: *"Ball* & Socket, you born ass!"

19. See *CL*, 2:305; 3:352–54; 4:144. In the sentence following, by "the whole of her property" we should understand "Craigenputtoch."

20. Ibid., 2:383. TC to JAC, 24 June 1823.

21. Published in Norton, *Two Note Books*. Carlyle's "Schiller's Life and Writings" was first published in the *London Magazine* (October 1823; January, July, August, and September 1824) and republished, in expanded form, by Taylor & Hessey in 1825 as the *Life of Friedrich Schiller*.

22. George Bell (1777–1832), celebrated Edinburgh surgeon. The "cure," which Carlyle followed for several months, proved unsuccessful.

23. *CL*, 2:466. TC to JAC, 11 November 1823.

24. Carlyle's term for the maidservants.

25. *CL*, 3:46. JBW to TC, [14 March 1824].

26. Ibid., p. 53. TC to JBW, [22 March 1824].

27. Ibid., p. 43. TC to JBW, 7 March 1824.

28. Ibid., pp. 69–70. JBW to TC, 20 May 1824.

29. Ibid., p. 68. TC to JBW, 19 May 1824. "We shall go . . .": 2 Sam. 12:23. See Charles Richard Sanders, "The Byron Closed in *Sartor Resartus*," *Studies in Romanticism* 3 (Winter 1964): 77–108, for a study of Carlyle's changing attitude toward Byron. A. Carlyle notes that Thomas's and Jane's letters crossed.

Carlyle's impetuousness continued to threaten the delicate equilibrium of his relationship with Jane. Shortly after this exchange, he and Jane met again at Haddington. A few days later [5 June 1824] he waxed ecstatic, calling her his *"Herzens Liebling"* (heart's darling), his "love," and closing: "Adieu! I press you to my bosom, and pray that God may keep for me, what is more to me than all things else. Farewell my Dearest! I am ever your own . . ." (*CL*, 3:75, 76). A startled Jane responded in dismay: "Rash, headstrong Man! . . . For mercy's sake keep in mind that my peace of mind, my credit with my Mother, the continuance of our correspondence everything depends upon your appearing as my friend and not my Lover" (ibid., p. 79 [10 June 1824]). Her mother at this time usually read her letters from Carlyle, and only through a subterfuge did Jane prevent her from seeing this one.

CHAPTER SIX

1. *Reminiscences*, 2:116–77.

2. *CL*, 3:84. TC to JBW, 23 June 1824. The "orator" was a nickname used by Carlyle and Jane Welsh for Irving.

3. *Works*, 11:52–62.

4. *CL*, 3:90–91. "Skluiffing" means "trailing the feet along the ground in walking." See also ibid., pp. 139, 261, 351–52. Charles Richard Sanders expands his earlier treatment of the Coleridge-Carlyle relationship (in *Coleridge and the Broad Church Movement* [see chap. 25, n. 9]) in "The Background of Carlyle's Portrait of Coleridge in *The Life of John Sterling*," *Bulletin of the John Rylands University Library of Manchester* 55 (Spring 1973): 434–58.

5. *CL*, 3:103–5. TC to MAC, 6 July 1824.

6. Ibid., pp. 120–21. TC to JAC, 10 August 1824. For Carlyle's later account, see *Reminiscences*, 2:145–55. He gives a still more graphic description of the Birmingham coal- and ironworks in a letter to Alexander Carlyle of 11 August 1824:

> I was one day thro the iron and coal works of this neighbourhood—a half-frightful scene! A space perhaps 30 square miles to the north of us, covered over with furnaces, rolling-mills, steam-engines and sooty men. A dense cloud of pestilential smoke hangs over it forever, blackening even the grain that grows upon it; and at night the whole region burns like a volcano spitting fire from a thousand tubes of brick. But oh the wretched hundred and fifty thousand mortals that grind out their destiny there! In the coal-mines they were literally naked, many of them, all but trowsers; black as ravens; plashing about among dripping caverns, or scrambling amid heaps of broken mineral; and thirsting unquenchably for beer. In the iron-mills it was little better: blast-furnaces were roaring like the voice of many whirlwinds all around; the fiery metal was hissing thro' its moulds, or sparkling and spitting under hammers of a monstrous size, which fell like so many little earthquakes. Here they were wheeling charred coals, breaking their iron-stone, and tumbling all into their fiery pit; there they were turning and boring cannon with a hideous shrieking noise such as the earth could hardly parallel; and thro' the whole, half-naked demons pouring with sweat and besmeared with soot were hurrying to and fro in their red night-caps and sheet-iron breeches rolling or hammering or squeezing their glowing metal as if it had been wax or dough. They also had a thirst for ale. Yet on the whole I am told they are very

happy: they make forty shillings or more per week, and few of them will work on Mondays. It is in a spot like this that one sees the sources of British power. The skill of man combining these coals and that iron-ore (till forty years ago—iron was smelted with charcoal only) has gathered three or four hundred thousand human beings round this spot, who send the products of their industry to all the ends of the Earth. (*CL,* 3:125-26).

7. *CL,* 3:142. TC to MAC, 29 August 1824.

8. *Reminiscences,* 2:155-66, and *CL,* 3:165-89.

9. *Reminiscences,* 2:158.

10. *CL,* 3:186-87. TC to JAC, 7 November 1824. Cf. Carlyle's impressions of Paris in 1824 with those recorded in "Excursion (Futile Enough) to Paris; Autumn 1851 . . . ," published in *The Last Words of Thomas Carlyle* (New York: D. Appleton, 1892), pp. 207-66.

11. Paraphrased from Johann Peter Eckermann's *Conversations with Goethe,* trans. John Oxenford (London: George Bell, 1874), pp. 276-77. Conversation of 25 July 1827.

12. *CL,* 3:233-34. TC to JBW, 20 December 1824. Froude deleted the names of Hook, William Maginn, and George Darley.

13. Ibid., pp. 235-36.

14. Ibid., pp. 250-51. JBW to TC, 13 January [1825]. The Bass Rock is a large barren rock off the coast of East Lothian, now a bird sanctuary.

15. A. Carlyle: "The function of *this* biographer seems to have been to howl like a dog to the music he could not appreciate or understand."

16. *Hamlet* 1. 2. 141-42. Hamlet recalls his father's conduct to his mother.

17. *CL,* 3:258. TC to JBW, 20 January 1825.

18. Ibid., pp. 266-67. JBW to TC, [29 January 1825].

19. Mary Aitken Carlyle: "where, to whom, to J. A. F. or Geraldine or to herself?" Said presumably in conversation, perhaps to others as well as to Froude. Wilson, *Carlyle,* 1:300 speaks of "sundry persons," but adds that A. Carlyle did not share this view.

CHAPTER SEVEN

1. *Reminiscences,* 2:177.

2. Ibid., pp. 177-79. The passage is further evidence that the Leith Walk experience of 1822 (described in "The Everlasting No" of *Sartor*) was not unique, but that Carlyle's spiritual regeneration extended over several years.

3. "I have alluded to the subject only because Mrs. Carlyle said afterwards that but for the unconscious action of a comparative stranger her engagement with Carlyle would probably never have been carried out" (Froude's note). Anna Montagu, the "comparative stranger," is not named in Froude's first volume (except once, presumably inadver-

tently). Her letters to the Carlyles are in the NLS. Selections have been published in A. Carlyle, *LL*, and in *CL*.

4. *CL*, 3:356–57, JBW to TC, [24 July 1825]. Carlyle wrote on this letter "don't Copy." Froude, uneasy about quoting from it directly, paraphrases it closely. I have quoted the letter.

5. Ibid., p. 359. TC to JBW, 29 July 1825.

6. Ibid., p. 375. JBW to TC, [2 September 1825].

7. Ibid., pp. 378, 379. TC's note, JBW to TC, [2 September 1825]. Jane Welsh stayed at Hoddam Hill 2–19 September.

8. *Terar dum prosim:* Let it be consumed, provided I be of use. See *CL*, 3:398, 404, 408; and (for discussion of the motto's significance) Tennyson, *Sartor*, pp. 89–90.

CHAPTER EIGHT

1. *CL*, 4:142, 143, 144. TC's note, JBW to Mrs. George Welsh, 1 October [1826]. Froude includes Carlyle's note to the words "my life black and bitter": "First battle won in the Rue de l'Enfer—Leith Walk—four years before. Campaign not ended till now." Froude notes that Comely Bank was "a row of houses to the north of Edinburgh, then among open fields between the city and the sea."

2. Various compilations exist under this title, including Andrew Knapp and William Baldwin, *The Newgate Calendar; comprising interesting memoirs of the most notorious characters who have been convicted of outrages on the laws of England since the commencement of the eighteenth century* . . . , 4 vols. (1824–28). I have not found Carlyle's reference, but compare his observation to Leigh Hunt, "There are hardly any readable Lives in our language except those of Players. One may see the reason too" (*CL*, 7:31, 29 October 1833).

3. *Hamlet* 5. 1. 298–302.

4. *CL*, 4:19. TC to JBW, [17 January 1826].

5. Ibid., p. 35. TC to JBW, [5 February 1826].

6. Ibid., pp. 38–39. JBW to TC, [21 February 1826].

7. Ibid., p. 42. TC to JBW, 26 February 1826.

8. Ibid., p. 43.

9. Ibid.

10. Ibid., p. 53. TC to JBW, 7 March 1826.

11. Ibid.

12. Ibid., pp. 59–60. JBW to TC, [16 March 1826].

13. Ibid., p. 69. TC to JBW, 2 April 1826.

14. Ibid., p. 53. TC to JBW, 7 March 1826.

15. Ibid., p. 89. TC to JBW, 13 May 1826.

16. Ibid., p. 77. TC to JBW, 22 April 1826.

17. Cf. *Hamlet* 1. 1. 143–44. Marcellus speaks of the Ghost.

18. *CL*, 4:125. TC to JBW, [12 August 1826].

19. Ibid., p. 132. TC to JBW, 19 September 1826.

20. Ibid., p. 137. TC to JBW, [27 September 1826]. Carlyle apparently never finished reading the *Critique of Pure Reason*.

21. Ibid., p. 150. TC to JBW, [9 October 1826]. It is Carlyle who heads his reply with these words.

22. Ibid., pp. 150, 151.

23. Actually, the Carlyles were married in Mrs. Welsh's home at Templand.

24. Froude was told by Geraldine Jewsbury that "the morning after his wedding-day he tore to pieces the flower-garden at Comeley [*sic*] Bank in a fit of ungovernable fury" (Froude, *My Relations with Carlyle*, p. 23).

The degree of intimacy within the Carlyles' marriage has intrigued all subsequent biographers. Few deny the sincerity behind the frequent expressions of tenderness in letters on both sides, but most have doubted that they corresponded to actual physical harmony. The clear implication that Froude leaves in *My Relations with Carlyle* (which he did not intend for publication) is that Carlyle was impotent. Underlying his narrative in the biography is his opinion that the marriage was not consummated, although he could do no more than imply this, chiefly through his portrayal of Jane Carlyle as a modern Iphigenia. For a number of reasons, Froude's opinion seems untenable to me. The chief of these is that the frequent expressions of strong emotion in Carlyle's letters to his wife and in hers to him are hard to reconcile with a platonic relationship. It is inconceivable that either partner, detesting cant and believing in honesty of self-expression, would have engaged in an elaborate hypocrisy in correspondence that neither one had cause to believe would ever be published. "The truth must remain a matter of opinion," note Lawrence and Elisabeth Hanson, Mrs. Carlyle's latest biographers, in a sensitive discussion based on much study of her correspondence that they append to their *Necessary Evil: The Life of Jane Welsh Carlyle* (New York: Macmillan Co., 1952). "We feel that the truth is most probably to be found in the simple fact that the parties were sexually ill-matched. We think it likely, in view of the evidence in the letters, that there were sexual relations of a kind at least until the move to London, but we think it unlikely that they were continued long, or at all, after the move" (p. 550).

My own view, also based on extensive reading of available evidence, is that the Carlyles, probably after an initial period of adjustment, did have a satisfactory physical relationship in the early years of their marriage. No other explanation accounts for the intensity of feeling in their correspondence with each other during these years. Surviving letters written when they were apart (and almost all have survived) reveal desperate longing for each other in language explicitly suggesting physical intimacy and equally desperate eagerness to be reunited. The interested reader should consult especially their correspondence in August and September 1831 and again in May 1834 (the only times they were separated for more than a few days). It may be argued that evidence in letters may lead others to interpretations different from mine and that, after all, intimacy of tone, even a kind of sexual feverishness, is not incompatible with hysterical (e.g., psychological) impotence. I admit that the intangibles of a relationship are always difficult, sometimes virtually impossible, to recapture from documents. But marriages are based on many things besides sex. We should note that in most fundamental matters Jane and Thomas Carlyle were in accord—in the priorities of Carlyle's career, in value judgments about people, in disposition of money, in what we may loosely call style of life, and perhaps even in their attitude toward sex. In a letter of 1833, Jane observes to her close friend from childhood Eliza Stodart that "almost the only, discrepancy in our habits" is that she is invariably a little early, he invariably a little late (*CL*, 6:393; 24 May). And Carlyle took immense pride in his wife. To his mother he wrote from London the next year that she had, "as poor Irving said, 'always a little bower of elegance round her be where she will': in truth, a shifty [resourceful], true, gleg [quickly perceptive] little creature, worth any twenty Cockney wives that I have yet met with" (ibid., 7:322; 25 [October] 1834).

There is no reason to suppose that they did not, at least for a time, continue to share the same bed after their move to Chelsea in 1834. Yet Mrs. Carlyle's insomnia made sleeping together increasingly difficult. "Jane was a bad sleeper," writes Thea Holme in her informative *The Carlyles at Home* (London: Oxford University Press, 1965). "At Cheyne Row she moved from bed to bed, from room to room, in search of sleep." Not until about 1842 did the arrangement of sleeping in separate beds become a permanent one. Even then it was adopted more because of their extreme sensitivity to noise and disturbance of any kind than because of diminution of affection, and, too, because of Mrs. Carlyle's gradually declining health. Both Carlyles were sickly people, Jane being far more often in ill-health than Carlyle (though Carlyle complained more). Their illnesses, Mrs. Carlyle's nervous tension especially, would have further impeded maintaining a healthy sexual relationship. Neither sensitivity to noise nor insomnia nor ill-health necessarily implies impotence, partial or total, on Carlyle's part, and to make such an assumption seems to me unwarranted. Their later letters, if less impassioned than the earlier, continue tender, affectionate, loving to the end. Although the belief that Carlyle was impotent will probably die a hard death (it is still current in academic circles today), we should recognize that the surest evidence against it lies in the letters of the Carlyles.

25. For Froude's conception of Jane Welsh as an Iphigenia figure, see my Introduction.

26. An overstatement. See chap. 11, n. 1.

CHAPTER NINE

1. *Reminiscences*, 1:62, 63.

2. The incomplete *Wotton Reinfred: A Romance*, begun in January 1827 and put aside in June. Although Carlyle believed he had consigned it to the flames (*CL*, 4:191), the manuscript was stolen in 1856 by his amanuensis Frederick Martin and eventually published in *The Last*

Words of Thomas Carlyle. I have brought together Froude's discussion of the novel from several pages of the biography. *Sartor Resartus* duplicates, to a greater or lesser degree, a number of passages from *Wotton Reinfred.* For an even earlier attempt at fiction, see Marjorie P. King, " 'Illudo Chartis': An Initial Study in Carlyle's Mode of Composition," *Modern Language Review* 49 (April 1954): 164–75.

3. The Edinburgh-Craigenputtoch contrast is a frequent one in Carlyle's letters of this time, e.g., *CL*, 4:337–38.

4. See *CL*, 1:216, 223; *Reminiscences*, 2:235–37.

5. *CL*, 4:245. Jeffrey to TC, [undated, ca. July–August 1827].

6. *Reminiscences*, 2:252, 255. " 'You are so dreadfully in earnest!' said he to me, once or oftener." Carlyle often used Jeffrey's expression in letters and published writings.

7. Clubbe, *Two Reminiscences*, p. 59.

8. *CL*, 4:236. TC to JAC, [July? 1827]. Froude's text.

9. See ibid., 3:86–87, 226; 4:209–12, 229, 246–49. At the time that he wrote his biography, Froude had access to only a few of Goethe's letters to Carlyle; he would also have seen several of Carlyle's incomplete transcriptions in letters to other correspondents. Carlyle's admiration for the German poet, which began in 1820 with his reading of *Faust,* cannot be exaggerated. To Goethe he wrote on 20 August 1827: "As it is, your works have been a mirror to me; unasked and unhoped for, your wisdom has counselled me; and so peace and health of soul have visited me from afar" (ibid., 4:248). For the letters between the two men (including the German originals of Goethe's letters and much miscellaneous information), see Norton, *GC.*

10. Compare similar passages in *Reminiscences*, 2:236–38, and Clubbe, *Two Reminiscences*, p. 53.

11. *CL*, 4:337. Goethe to TC, 1 January 1828. In TC to Goethe, 17 April 1828 (ibid., p. 364), Carlyle identified himself as the author of "State of German Literature."

12. Jeffrey to TC, [postmarked 18 October 1827] (NLS, 787.9). See *CL*, 4:262 ff.

13. See my "John Carlyle in Germany and the Genesis of *Sartor Resartus*," in *Romantic and Victorian: Studies in Memory of William H. Marshall,* ed. W. Paul Elledge and Richard L. Hoffman (Rutherford, N.J.: Fairleigh Dickinson University Press, 1971), pp. 264–89.

14. *CL*, 4:298. TC to James Carlyle, the elder, 21 December 1827. The professorship was in Moral Philosophy.

15. Ibid., p. 337. TC to JAC, 7 March 1828. The "suspense" lasted a few months, not, as Froude states, "weeks." The "someone else" appointed was an "old stager," George Cook (1772–1845).

16. Ibid., p. 329. TC's note, Jean Carlyle, JWC, and TC to MAC, [19 February 1828]. On this occasion Carlyle visited Craigenputtoch alone.

17. *Works*, 26:1–257.

18. *CL*, 4:325. For the German and English texts of the testimonial, see Norton, *GC*, pp. 71–80.

19. Actually six years.

20. See *CL*, 4:242, 375, 382–83, and p. 230 of this volume. Scott acknowledged the medals to Jeffrey but not to Carlyle. Here ends vol. 1 of Froude's biography.

CHAPTER TEN

1. See pp. 164, 217–18 above.

2. I include only one representative passage from this essay, published in part by Froude under the title "Spiritual Optics." For a transcript of the complete essay (with discussion of Froude's interpretation and editorial methods), see Murray Baumgarten, "Carlyle's Manuscript on Optics," *Victorian Studies* 9 (June 1968): 503–22, where it is entitled "Manuscript on Creeds." The passage retained is on pp. 513–14. Froude valued Carlyle's intensity of vision: "His eye was a perfect optical Instrument which saw things & people as they *were* & not as they are supposed to be" (Froude to Ruskin, [1884?], in Viljoen, p. 31).

3. Froude's text.

4. *CL*, 4:142. TC's note, JBW to Mrs. George Welsh, 1 October [1826].

5. Cf. *Heroes and Hero-Worship, Works*, 5:201.

CHAPTER ELEVEN

1. Much ink has been spilled over Froude's description of Craigenputtoch and his interpretation of the period from 1828 to 1834. Only a few years after he visited Craigenputtoch in September 1879, he described the site in his biography "as the dreariest spot in all the British dominions." At the time of his visit he had written to Carlyle that "the place in externals must be very much in the state in which you left it. . . . The weather was characteristic and at any rate suited the scene—high wind with driving showers and brilliant gleams of sunshine on the heather now in its fullest bloom. The general aspect . . . not unkindly, and suited to the work which was done there" (7 September [1879] [NLS, 666.132]). Others have differed in their impressions. Not always does it seem the bleak and windy moorland farm that Froude describes. Yet even today it is a solitary spot, and in winter (the present owners inform me) the isolation can become almost unbearable.

Froude drew a picture of the Craigenputtoch years largely based on evidence that he found in the correspondence and in other papers of the Carlyles. On the whole, their references to Craigenputtoch are more unfavorable than favorable. In 1825 Jane Welsh had said that she "would not spend a month on it with an Angel" (*CL*, 3:250); later the same year she spoke of it as "the dreariest spot of the whole world" (ibid., p. 384)— almost exactly the same words for which critics have so berated Froude. Once living at Craigenputtoch the Carlyles valued the solitary beauty of the spot but regretted the loneliness of their existence. "At Craigenputtoch we have always had a secret suspicion," Jane Carlyle wrote to her husband on 11 September 1831, halfway through their stay, "that we were quite wrong—removed out the the sphere of human activity fully as much thro' cowardice as superior wisdom." She wrote this letter to Carlyle in London, where she soon joined him for the winter. During their six months in London they met many notables, found stimulation in the currents of ideas flowing around them, and began to conceive an alternative to life at Craigenputtoch. Upon their return both Carlyles increasingly felt the isolation to which the "Dunscore Tartarus" doomed them. Thus overpowering solitude, not the rigorous climate or the difficulty in getting servants, was the chief reason they decided to leave their moorland home. Carlyle incessantly lamented the impossibility of finding good talk. By 1834 getting out had become, for both, a necessity.

Froude's interpretation of the Craigenputtoch years is biased not so much in its overall picture as it is through his conception of Jane Carlyle as a tragic heroine. He presents her as forced to do menial tasks: some she did indeed do, such as make bread and care for poultry (e.g., ibid., 4:417), but she had nothing to do with cattle. Alexander Carlyle, not Thomas and Jane, actually farmed Craigenputtoch. Geraldine Jewsbury was the source for many of the "myths" that Froude related concerning Jane Carlyle's life at the "whinstone castle." Although a core of truth often exists in what Froude says, his emphasis is distorted, and we may dismiss as misleading his depiction of Jane Carlyle toiling away as servant-of-all-tasks "while Carlyle looked on encouragingly with his pipe" (p. 235 below). Sir James Crichton-Browne attacks Froude's interpretation of the Craigenputtoch period in his introduction to A. Carlyle, *NLMJWC*, 1:xl–xliii; Dunn defends it in *F and C*, chap. 16.

Despite Froude's implication that Jane Carlyle suffered more in health from the climate and the solitude than her husband, Carlyle was the more dissatisfied and initiated the move to London in 1834. Even his family recognized the need for a change. "Has not Craigenputtoch been the Haven of Despair all along?" his brother John wrote him on 19 April of that year. "Is there any worse place for you in your present state anywhere with[in] the compass of the British Isles?" In later years the Carlyles occasionally talked about returning to Craigenputtoch but, like the idea of emigrating to America, they never entertained it seriously as a practical possibility. They recognized as wise the decision to move to London. A retreat from London would have been, as Carlyle realized in a letter to his brother John of 12 April 1838, "at bottom I admit . . . perhaps not good for me." He knew that although a part of his nature demanded solitude, an even more vital part demanded the company of men and women who stimulated him intellectually. Only London provided this environment.

2. *CL*, 4:383. TC to JAC, 10 June 1828. In the previous sentence "cosmic" expresses the emergence of order from confusion, as "chaos" becomes "cosmos." Cf., e.g., *Latter-Day Pamphlets*, *Works*, 20:7, 60, 77.

3. Norton, *Two Note Books*, p. 129.

4. See *CL*, 4:375. Jeffrey to TC, 16 July 1828 (NLS, 787.24).

5. The NLS holds Jeffrey's extensive correspondence with both Carlyles; selections from it are quoted in the *CL*. Only one letter from Carlyle to Jeffrey has survived. After Carlyle's death, Jeffrey's daughter, Mrs. Empson—dismayed at the tone of Carlyle's remarks in the *Reminiscences* on Jeffrey, her husband, and herself—asked for the return of the letters of the Carlyles to Jeffrey and probably destroyed them. See *CL*, 4:259.

6. Jeffrey to TC, 23 September 1828 (NLS, 787.28).

7. Froude takes his analogy from a tale in the *Arabian Nights* and uses it elsewhere to describe his perseverance in continuing the biography (see Clubbe, *Carlyle and His Contemporaries*, p. 322).

8. Jeffrey to TC, 3 October [1828] (NLS, 787.30).

9. *Reminiscences*, 2:245-46. The Jeffreys stayed 8-10 October 1828.

10. Jeffrey to TC, [postmarked 13 October 1828] (NLS, 787.32).

11. *CL*, 4:413. TC to JAC, 10[?] October 1828.

12. Jeffrey to TC, 11 November 1828 (NLS, 787.36).

13. *CL*, 4:421-22. TC to JAC, 26 November 1828.

14. Ibid., 5:6. TC to JAC, 13 January 1829.

15. Ibid., p. 11. TC to JAC, 5 March 1829.

16. *Reminiscences*, 2:254.

17. Boswell, *Life of Johnson*, pp. 55-56; and cf. *Works*, 28:94; 5:179. The story is also in Hawkins's biography of Johnson.

18. Never completed and not published until 1951 as *Carlyle's Unfinished History of German Literature*, ed. Hill Shine (Lexington: University of Kentucky Press, 1951).

19. *Teufelsdreck* (or *Dreck*)—"devil's dung"—was Carlyle's name for *Sartor* until February 1833, when he not only changed the title but also emended "Teufelsdreck" to "Teufelsdröckh."

20. *CL*, 5:91. TC to JAC, 10 April 1830. William Fraser, editor of the *Foreign Review*, had offered to bring out the projected study of Luther. It was never written.

21. *Reminiscences*, 2:193-95. Although Froude believed that Margaret died of consumption, her disease appears to have been cancer.

22. Edwin W. Marrs, Jr., ed., *The Letters of Thomas Carlyle to His Brother Alexander, With Related Family Letters* (Cambridge: Harvard University Press, 1968), p. 788.

23. See p. 210 above. "Sosii," mentioned above, were Roman booksellers in Horace's time.

CHAPTER TWELVE

1. *CL*, 5:202. TC to JAC, 19 December 1830.

2. Ibid., p. 175. TC to JAC, 19 October 1830.

3. See Harrold, *Sartor*, p. 130.

4. Ibid. Count Zaehdarm "during his sublunary existence"—so the epitaph runs—"shot five thousand partridges." The epitaph satirizes the "Corn-law, game-preserving Aristocracy."

5. Froude's translation. Norton, *GC*, p. 225. Goethe to TC, 17 October 1830.

6. In *A Modest Proposal* (1729): that surplus children be sold and eaten as food. Cf. Harrold, *Sartor*, pp. 229-31. The comparison between Carlyle's "Occasional Discourse on the Negro Question" and *Sartor*, which follows in the next paragraph, is strained.

7. The new tenant paid £170, £30 less than Alexander Carlyle had been paying. See Marrs, *Letters of Thomas Carlyle to His Brother Alexander*, p. 274; and Clubbe, *Two Reminiscences*, p. 66.

8. *CL*, 5:242-43. TC to JAC, 4 March 1831.

9. Ibid., p. 243. Cf. Harrold, *Sartor*, p. 20.

10. *CL*, 5:271. TC to JAC, 8 May 1831.

11. Actually, as A. Carlyle points out, from a horse epidemic. See A. Carlyle, *NLMJWC*, 1:33.

12. *CL*, 5:283. TC to JAC, 6 June 1831.

13. Ibid., p. 303. Carlyle paraphrases his (lost) letter to Jeffrey in TC to JAC, 12 July 1831.

14. Ibid. See also ibid., 2:412, and Harrold, *Sartor*, p. 140.

15. *CL*, 5:305. TC to JAC, 17 July 1831.

CHAPTER THIRTEEN

1. *CL*, 5:354. TC to JWC, 22 August 1831. Froude lets Carlyle himself recount his journey to London and his experiences there through extracts from his Journal (published accurately and completely in Norton, *Two Note Books*) and through his detailed letters back to Scotland. I base this summary paragraph on them.

2. *CL*, 5:399. TC to JWC, 4 September 1831.

3. Ibid. Jeffrey to TC, 3 September 1831 (NLS, 787.62).

4. Ibid., p. 441. Murray to TC, 17 September 1831.

5. Harrold, *Sartor*, p. 320. Carlyle always believed Murray's reader to have been John Gibson Lockhart, though it may have been someone else. See Tennyson, *Sartor*, p. 148. Froude, writing to John Murray III, noted that "the *third* [letter] from your father is the original of the communication from 'the Bookseller' which is printed in the Appendix to Sartor Resartus. I (as I believe the world generally) have hitherto regarded it as 'a work of imagination' " (3 June [1881?]. MS: John Murray). Although Froude spoke of *Sartor* in the biography as "beautiful and brilliant," he found it "the least readable . . . of all Carlyles writings" and could not understand why it "should have had the largest sale of them in the popular Edition" (5 June [1881?]. MS: John Murray). He told Murray that "the reception which Sartor actually met with— universal condemnation for three or four years—completely justified

your father from a business point of view, and if publishers do not wish to find their way into the Gazette they are bound to consider whether a book is likely to sell.— This is what I mean to say about the matter" (22 November [1881?]. MS: John Murray).

6. Napier to TC, 9 September 1831 (NLS, 665.32). In his letter to Napier of 5 September, Carlyle had said " 'Long enough,' the Public hereby exclaims, 'have ye fed me on froth.' " Napier picked up the expression in his reply. The article on Luther mentioned in the next paragraph was never written. In 1883 Froude himself published a short study of Luther.

7. Norton *Two Note Books*, pp. 217-19.

8. *CL*, 5:448. TC's note, JWC to TC, [27 September 1831]. For other pen portraits of Lamb, see *Reminiscences*, 1:94; and *CL*, 1:xxxvi-xxxviii; 3:39; 5:375; and 6:50-51. Carlyle occasionally had second thoughts about his severe judgments of Lamb, as A. Carlyle indicated in a letter to Charles Eliot Norton: "I remember my Wife telling me that she once read to her Uncle, as they lingered over dinner, Lamb's 'Old Familiar Faces.' He listened attentively, and when she had finished he asked, 'Who wrote *that* Mary?' She told him, and he replied, 'I should not have believed Lamb could ever have written any thing so touching & pretty.' The truth is that Lamb disgusted him at that interview at Enfield and he disregarded both Lamb & his writings ever afterwards" (8 July 1898. MS: Houghton Library, Harvard). Reading B. W. Procter's biography of Lamb (*Charles Lamb: A Memoir*, 1866) in the summer of 1866, Carlyle wrote to the author to tell him that he found "in your work something so touching, brave, serene, and pious, that I cannot but write you one brief word of recognition" (17 August 1866. Typescript: Free Library of Philadelphia).

9. *CL*, 6:24-25. TC to MAC, 20 October 1831.

10. See *Reminiscences*, 2:204-8, and *CL*, 6:33 (to JAC) and 41 (to MAC).

11. *Hamlet* 1. 2. 101-6. Froude reduces and paraphrases the lines. I include the full quotation.

12. *Reminiscences*, 1:1-52.

13. *CL*, 6:124. TC to JAC, 16 February 1832.

14. Ibid., pp. 126-27. "Magazine Fraser" was James Fraser (d. 1841), publisher of *Fraser's Magazine*. Froude omits, in Carlyle's reference to Jeffrey, the words "to see hopping round one." Jeffrey may have provided the model for Hofrath Heuschrecke (Councillor Grasshopper) in *Sartor*.

CHAPTER FOURTEEN

1. Carlyle's letters to Mill, unavailable to Froude, have survived. A. Carlyle published those in the NLS in *CMSB*. For Mill's letters to Carlyle, see the six-volume *Letters* (Toronto: University of Toronto Press; London: Routledge & Kegan Paul), edited by Francis E. Mineka (*The*

Earlier Letters of John Stuart Mill, 1812–1848, 2 vols., 1963) and by Mineka and Dwight Lindley (*The Later Letters of John Stuart Mill, 1849–1873*, 4 vols., 1972). Carlyle first described Mill in a letter to his wife of 29 August 1831: "Of young Mill (the *Spirit of the Age* man) he [William Empson] speaks very highly, as of a converted Utilitarian, who is studying German" (*CL*, 5:379). And on 4 September he wrote to her: "This young Mill I fancy and hope is 'a baying [being] you can love.' A slender rather tall and elegant youth, with small clear roman-nosed face, two small earnestly-smiling eyes: modest, remarkably gifted with precision of utterance; enthusiastic, yet lucid, calm; not a great, yet distinctly a gifted and amiable youth. We had almost four hours of the best talk I have mingled in for long. The youth walked home with me almost to the door; seemed to profess almost as plainly as modesty would allow that he had been converted by the Head of the Mystic School, to whom personally he testified very hearty-looking regard" (ibid., p. 398). Even before he met Carlyle, Mill had submitted to his intellectual influence in the manner described in his *Autobiography*. Their friendship was strengthened when Carlyle moved to London in 1834, remained firm for several years, but gradually waned as the two men came to realize that their views were irreconcilable.

2. A. Carlyle: "He was no 'Cousin': it is doubtful if any relative in even the remotest degree short of being one of Adam's posterity." Whether or not Jeffrey was related by blood to Mrs. Carlyle remains uncertain, but it is in any case secondary to the fact that his belief that he was made their friendship closer. See, for example, *Reminiscences*, 2:239.

3. *CL*, 6:193. TC to JAC, 31 July 1832.

4. Ibid., p. 205. TC to MAC, 21 August 1832. I have omitted the sentence in Froude that precedes the quotation: "Her place could not be immediately filled, and all the work fell on Mrs. Carlyle." Actually the Carlyle household had a new maid the next day. Here, as elsewhere, Froude overstresses the impact that the solitude of Craigenputtoch had on Mrs. Carlyle's health and loneliness.

5. Ibid., p. 214. TC to MAC, 28 August 1832. The bracketed words are Froude's.

6. Journal, 29 October 1832. This is the first of a number of passages in Froude that I identify as being quoted from the Journal.

7. *CL*, 6:253. TC to JWC, 12 November 1832.

8. Ibid., p. 296. TC to MAC, 12 January 1833.

9. Ibid., p. 307. TC to Alexander Carlyle, 27 January 1833.

10. Ibid., p. 308. The Glasgow professorship—in astronomy—did not fall vacant until 1836. Nothing came of Carlyle's half-hearted try for it.

11. Ibid., pp. 322–23. JWC's postscript, TC to JAC, 10 February 1833.

12. Ibid., pp. 344–45. TC to MAC, 16 March 1833.

13. Ibid., p. 323. TC to MAC, 13 February 1833.

14. Ibid., p. 387. TC to JAC, 17 May 1833.

15. Ibid., p. 388.

16. Actually, eight guineas a sheet. Carlyle made £82 1s on *Sartor*. See Tennyson, *Sartor*, p. 154.

17. Journal, 7 July 1833.

18. Ralph Waldo Emerson, *English Traits*, ed. Howard Mumford Jones (1856; rpt. Cambridge: Harvard University Press, 1966), pp. 8–11. The man of letters to whom Emerson refers is Mill. The Latin phrase is from Suetonius *Lives of the Caesars* 6. 49. As Froude points out in an omitted footnote, the letter that Emerson brought from Rome was from Gustave d'Eichthal. "Emerson does not mention the note from Mill," Froude states. "Perhaps their mutual impressions were not dissimilar." Mill had said of Emerson in his letter to Carlyle of 2 August 1833, "I do not think him a very hopeful subject." Emerson stayed the night of 25 August.

19. *CL*, 6:430. TC to MAC, 27 August 1833. See also TC to JAC, 27 August 1833, ibid., pp. 425–26. Carlyle's friendship with Emerson, despite increasingly divergent views, lasted until his death in 1881. See the introduction to Slater, *CEC*, for a full study.

20. *CL*, 6:124. TC to JAC, 16 February 1832 (see p. 273 above).

21. Ibid., 7:38. TC to JAC, 18 November 1833.

22. Ibid., pp. 37–38. Janet, not Jean, was the youngest child. For Carlyle's account of Jean as a child, see ibid., 3:414–15.

23. Ibid., 7:38. TC to JAC, 18 November 1833.

24. Ibid., p. 15. TC to James Carlyle, 8 October 1833.

CHAPTER FIFTEEN

1. Journal, 6 February 1834.

2. See p. 210 above.

3. Jeffrey to TC, 14 January 1834 (NLS, 787.64). Carlyle referred to Jeffrey's letter as "a kind of polite Fishwoman-shriek!" (*CL*, 7:79. TC to JAC, 21 January 1834).

4. Edinburgh. It went eventually to George Moir.

5. Froude may refer to Jeffrey's observation near the end of his letter to Carlyle of 14 January 1834: "I am glad that my fair cousin is better— tho' I cannot approve of her taking to nurse lunatics—and shall not feel quite easy till I hear she is out of that [perilous?] occupation." Froude perhaps assumes that Carlyle took "lunatics" to refer to himself, but Carlyle would surely have understood that Jeffrey meant William Glen, a young man of unstable mind who was living near Craigenputtoch and whom Carlyle was caring for. D. A. Wilson purposely misses the point in his *Carlyle*, 2:355.

6. *CL*, 4:53. TC to JBW, 7 March 1826. But Carlyle refers, not to "the principle on which he guided his earlier life," but to his oncoming marriage.

7. Journal, 21 February 1834. See also *Reminiscences*, 2:210–11.

8. Loosely recalled from Jane's gay exclamation "Burn our ships!" (*Reminiscences*, 1:97), repeated in TC to JAC, 25 February 1834 (*CL*, 7:104).

9. A. Carlyle: "So, too, had M*rs* C. under difficulties of a weak constitution." On balance, Mrs. Carlyle emerged from the Craigenputtoch years stronger in health, but Froude, ever the dramatic historian, not only exaggerates the differing response of both Carlyles to Craigenputtoch, but also in this paragraph accentuates the differences between Craigenputtoch and London.

10. *Reminiscences*, 1:63-67, but Carlyle qualified her anecdotes as having only "a certain mythical truth" (p. 69).

11. *CL*, 7:171. TC to JWC, 21 May 1834.

12. Ibid., pp. 172-74.

13. Ibid., pp. 207-8. TC to MAC, 12 June 1834.

14. The *London Review*, whose first number dates from April 1835. The following year it bought out the *Westminster Review* and became the *London and Westminster Review*.

15. *CL*, 7:270. TC to JAC, 15 August 1834.

16. Ibid., p. 289. TC's note, JWC to MAC, [1 September 1834].

17. Ibid., p. 319. TC to Alexander Carlyle, 24 October 1834.

18. Ibid.

19. Ibid., pp. 340-41. TC's note, JWC to MAC, 21 November 1834. Carlyle slightly misdates Irving's visit (which probably took place in late August) both here and in *Reminiscences*, 2:215-16. See *CL*, 7:282.

20. *CL*, 7:354-55. TC to MAC, 24 December 1834.

21. "Death of the Rev. Edward Irving," *Works*, 28:319-23; first published in *Fraser's Magazine*, January 1835.

22. Journal, 1 January 1835.

23. For Froude's change of plan for his biography, see Introduction (p. 22) and p. 325 below.

24. Harrold, *Sartor*, p. 196.

25. See *Reminiscences*, 1:108, and Clubbe, *Two Reminiscences*, p. 86.

26. *Reminiscences*, 1:106-7. See the description of this incident below, pp. 334-36.

27. See *Reminiscences*, 1:108-9.

28. See p. 164 above. Here ends Froude's *Thomas Carlyle: A History of the First Forty Years of His Life, 1795-1835*.

CHAPTER SIXTEEN

1. Froude writes in *My Relations with Carlyle* that Carlyle "had said in his Journal that there was a secret connected with him unknown to his closest friends, that no one knew and no one would know it, and that without a knowledge of it no true biography of him was possible. He never told me in words what this secret was, but I suppose he felt that I should have it from his papers" (p. 17). The passage in Carlyle's

Journal to which Froude refers can only be this entry of 29 December 1849 (or the previous one, of 10 October 1843). Froude does not comment on either passage, but he understood them, as *My Relations with Carlyle* makes clear, in the light of his conversations with Geraldine Jewsbury, a close friend of Mrs. Carlyle's. "Geraldine when she heard that I was to undertake the Biography," Froude told Ruskin in 1886, "came to me & said that I ought to know that Carlyle 'was one of those persons who ought never to have married,' and that this was at the bottom of all the trouble" (Viljoen, pp. 64–65). Nothing in the Journal passages, however, implies that Carlyle's "secret" was sexual in nature. Carlyle speaks only of "elements in my little destiny" that "have all along lain deep below view or surmise." What he says of himself there would hold true for most human beings. "What are faults, what are the outward details of a life," he asks in *Heroes*, "if the inner secret of it, the remorse, temptations, true, often-baffled, never-ended struggle of it, be forgotten?" (*Works*, 5:46). Every human being has mysteries that no biographer will fathom. They need not be sexual.

Froude himself came to have doubts about the correctness of his supposition that the Journal passages refer to sexual impotence. "I am not sure that I know now what he meant," he admits in *My Relations with Carlyle* (p. 20). His admission in no way denies the value of his hypotheses concerning the Carlyles' relationship, but suggests instead that, like a good historian, he continued to weigh the evidence and to consider the different interpretations it allowed. It also suggests that if in his biography he was to indicate something of the nature of their relationship (as he understood it), he would have to do so indirectly.

2. Matt. 7:29.

3. A. Carlyle puts a question mark in the margin opposite this sentence.

4. Froude elaborates on this aspect of Carlyle's character in a note (preserved in Margaret Froude's hand) now in the Beinecke Library, Yale:

Fault in Carlyle that he attended too much to his own humours & fancies—made them an object to his thoughts instead of throwing such things by, or taking them as they came. he reflected upon his glooms, upon his tenderness, or upon his imagination, as if they were something in themselves remarkable—which marked him like Owen Glendower as not upon the roll of common men[.] He was perhaps irritated when others about him treated such things less respectfully—knowing that very often "it was only potatoes." Things could have gone more smoothly with him if he had himself remembered more continuously that it might be only Potatoes.

St Teresa & her visions—she set little by them, knowing that some at least were only indigestion—& the others might be.

Carlyles imagination was feverishly active. He could not keep— he need not have tried to keep strange images, strange feelings, coming upon him— such things belonged to him, as to all men of genius— they were the outcome of the poetry of his nature, & might each take any form it pleased[.]

671

But habitually to make the general character of such things a fresh subject of meditation &consideration was but another form of the disease of self consciousness, so common among young men, but recognised by the wise among them as morbid & unwholesome. It continued with Carlyle to the end of his life[.]

CHAPTER SEVENTEEN

1. *Reminiscences*, 2:24.

2. The phrase, not traced to Milton, was used by Carlyle in his biography of John Sterling. See *Works*, 11:97.

3. Journal, 1 January 1835.

4. "The '*First Book*' was the original first *volume*. The arrangement was afterwards altered" (Froude's note).

5. Norton, *L26–36*, p. 498. TC to JAC, 23 March 1835. The book on "The Feast of Pikes" begins vol. 2.

6. Froude's reference to "a thing which they had long feared" is clarified by an unpublished passage in TC to JAC, 23 March 1835, in which the "some one" in the carriage is identified as Mrs. Harriet Taylor, "(his Platonic inamorata); with whom Jane fancied he must have at length *run off*, and so was come, before setting out for the Devil, to take solemn leave of us" (MS: Huntington Library).

7. Ibid., and TC to James Fraser, 7 March 1835 (MS: Mrs. Jane S. Napier). The volume was burned accidentally by Mill's housemaid, who thought the manuscript sheets were waste paper.

8. Journal, 7 March 1835. Froude's account of this incident, placing the blame on Mill rather than on Mrs. Taylor, is more accurate than that in Wilson, *Carlyle*, 2:379–80.

9. Norton, *L26–36*, p. 504, TC to JAC, 23 March 1835.

10. Ibid., pp. 505–6. Burns may be the "great man" Carlyle has in mind.

11. JWC's postscript, TC to JAC, 30 April 1835 (NLS, 523.29).

12. Journal, 9 and 11 May 1835.

13. Ibid., 26 May 1836. "A mixture of good and evil" was one of John Carlyle's favorite expressions (see *CL*, 3:412).

14. Journal, 26 May 1836.

15. A. Carlyle, *CMSB*, pp. 191–92. TC to John Sterling, 4 June 1835. Sterling's extended critique of *Sartor*, to which Carlyle answers in the above letter, was first published by Carlyle in his life of Sterling and is reprinted, along with the greater part of Carlyle's reply, in Harrold, *Sartor*, pp. 307–18.

16. A. Carlyle, *CMSB*, p. 203. TC to John Sterling, 9 June 1837.

17. Journal, 1 June 1835.

18. A. Carlyle, *CMSB*, pp. 192–93. TC to John Sterling, 4 June 1835. Among those who "responded" favorably were Emerson and Father

O'Shea of Cork. See Clubbe, *Two Reminiscences*, pp. 74-75, and TC to JWC, 21 May 1834 (*CL*, 7:175).

19. Carlyle's phrase. See TC to JAC, 12 April 1838 (NLS, 523.57) and cf. *Reminiscences*, 1:109.

20. TC to JAC, 2 July 1835 (NLS, 523.31).

21. Journal, 15 July 1835.

22. Ibid.

23. An incomplete and unpublished manuscript entitled "National Education" that Carlyle wrote at this time has been preserved in the NLS (1798.xiii). It will be published in *CL*, vol. 8.

24. Froude mentions Mrs. Montagu by name in the third volume of his biography as he had not, except perhaps accidentally, in the first. His account of the slow cooling of the Carlyles' regard for her is substantially correct.

25. TC to JAC, 26 January 1836 (NLS, 520.50).

26. Froude was never more Carlyle's disciple than in his admiration for Germany.

27. In Sterling's sentimental *roman à clef*, published in *Blackwood's* in November and December 1838 and January 1839, Carlyle appears as the hermit Collins and Goethe as the rake Walsingham. Carlyle thought the novel poor. See Anne Kimball Tuell, "Carlyle's Marginalia in Sterling's *Essays and Tales*," *PMLA* 54 (September 1939): 815-24; and William Blackburn, "Carlyle and the Composition of *The Life of John Sterling*," *Studies in Philology* 44 (October 1947): 672-87.

28. Journal, 1 June 1836.

29. For Mill's *London and Westminster Review*, Carlyle wrote "Memoirs of Mirabeau" and "Parliamentary History of the French Revolution," published in the January and April 1837 numbers.

30. A. Carlyle, *NLMJWC*, 1:54. JWC to TC, 19 July 1836.

31. A. Carlyle: "Has it? Knave!"

32. Froude, *LMJWC*, 1:62. JWC to Mrs. John Welsh, 4 September 1836.

33. "So Carlyle said later; but in the letter to Sterling he says ten o'clock at night. Perhaps he added a word or two" (Froude's note).

34. Froude, *LMJWC*, 1:70. TC's note, JWC to John Welsh, 4 March 1837. Froude's text.

35. The literal translation of the last line of Goethe's poem "Symbolum" ("Des Maurers Wandeln"), often repeated with reverence by Carlyle throughout his life.

36. A. Carlyle, *NL*, 1:50-52. TC to John Sterling, 17 January 1837. I have taken the text of the poem (slightly modified) from *Past and Present, Works*, 10: 237-38. In his letter Carlyle omits stanzas one and four. He usually entitles the poem "Mason-Lodge." The German phrases in the letter are from the poem's third and fourth stanzas.

CHAPTER EIGHTEEN

1. By John Stuart Mill, in the *London and Westminster Review* 27 (July 1837): 17.

2. TC to JWC, 2 November 1835 (NLS, 610.28).

3. A. Carlyle, *NL*, 1:50. TC to John Sterling, 17 January 1837.

4. Carlyle wrote in *The French Revolution*: "These are the Phenomena, or visual Appearances, of this wide-working terrestrial world: which truly is phenomenal, what they call spectral; and never rests at any moment; one never at any moment can know why" (*Works*, 3:159). See also p. 343 of this volume.

5. Alexander Pope, *An Essay on Man*, 3:303-4.

6. See *Reminiscences*, 1:176-80.

7. From the syllabus in the Carlyle House, Chelsea.

8. Froude, *LMJWC*, 1:75. TC's note, JWC to MAC, 22 September 1837.

9. TC to JAC, 30 May 1837 (NLS, 523.49). The lectures on German literature were never published. See Archibald MacMechan's account of this lecture series in his edition of Carlyle's *On Heroes, Hero-Worship, and the Heroic in History* (Boston: Ginn, 1901), pp. xv-xx.

10. TC to JAC, 30 May 1837 (NLS, 523.49).

11. Ibid. It was Jeffrey who predicted that Carlyle "will be called affect[e]d." Jeffrey to TC, 18 May 1837 (NLS, 787.72).

12. TC to JAC, 30 May 1837. Jeffrey, in his letter to TC of 18 May 1837, had spoken of *The French Revolution* as written "by a man of Genius and originality. . . . It is no doubt a very strange piece of work, and is really, as Coleridge I think said of something else, like reading a story by flashes of lightning!" Jeffrey remembered Coleridge's remark in *Table Talk* on Edmund Kean's acting of Shakespeare.

13. Froude, *LMJWC*, 1:76. TC's note, JWC to MAC, 22 September 1837.

14. TC to JAC, 7 July 1837 (NLS, 523.50).

15. *The Faerie Queene*, 1. 11. 48, quoted from *Edmund Spenser's Poetry*, ed. Hugh Maclean, Norton Critical Edition (New York: W. W. Norton, 1968), pp. 136-37.

16. A. Carlyle, *NL*, 1:87. TC to JAC, 21 September 1837.

17. Ibid.

18. Ibid., pp. 90-91. TC to MAC, 22 September 1837.

19. Cf. TC to MAC, 7 December 1837 (NLS, 520.63): "I felt disgusted with the task, but in some measure bound to it."

20. Journal, 7 December 1837.

21. Ibid., 14 February 1838.

22. TC to MAC, 7 December 1837 (NLS, 520.63). James Munro of Boston published the *Critical and Miscellaneous Essays* in four vol-

umes in 1838; the next year they came out in England under the imprint of James Fraser. See Dyer, pp. 187–88.

23. TC to MAC, 7 December 1837 (NLS, 520.63).

24. Journal, 14 February 1838. Orson, carried off by a bear as a child and suckled with its cubs, grew up an uncouth, rough man and was called "The Wild Man of the Forest." He became the hero of the fifteenth-century French romance *Valentine and Orson,* retold in English by Henry Watson about 1550.

25. Journal, 14 February 1838.

26. Cf. *CL,* 4:173. TC to Anna D. B. Montagu, 25 December 1826.

27. Literally: he carries hay on his horns. Horace *Satires* 1. 4. 34. Froude might have seen the phrase in Boswell's *Life of Johnson,* p. 408.

28. Journal, 19 February 1838.

29. *Odyssey* 11. 489–91. I omit Froude's Greek. A related earlier passage in the life sheds light on Froude's attitude toward literature, his approach to Carlyle's own works, and his biographical method:

> The outward life of a man of letters is in his works. But in his works he shows only so much of himself as he considers that the world will be benefited or interested by seeing; or rather, if he is true artist he does not show his own self at all. The more excellent the thing produced, the more it resembles a work of nature in which the creation is alone perceived, while the creating hand is hidden in mystery. Homer and Shakespeare are the greatest of poets, but of the men Homer and Shakespeare we know next to nothing. "The blind old bard of Chio's rocky isle" has been even criticised out of existence, and ingenious inquirers have been found to maintain that the Stratford player furnished but a convenient name, and that the true authors of *Henry IV* or *Hamlet* were Queen Elizabeth's courtiers and statesmen.
>
> Men of genius do not care to hang their hearts upon their sleeve for daws to peck at; yet if they have left anywhere their written conversations with themselves, if they have opened a door into the laboratory where the creative force can be seen in its operation, and the man himself can be made known to us as he appeared in undress and in his own eyes, the public who are interested in his writings may count it as a piece of rare good fortune. No man who has any vital force in him ever lies to himself. He may assume a disguise to others; but the first condition of success is that he be true to his own soul and has looked his own capacities and his own faults fairly in the face. (2:71–72)

30. Loosely paraphrased by Froude from Jeffrey to TC, 12 December 1837 (NLS, 1766.54).

31. A. Carlyle underscores this sentence and comments (in purple pencil), "Whow!!"

32. TC to JAC, 12 April 1838 (NLS, 523.57).

33. The lectures "On the History of Literature" were published in

1892 in two editions based on shorthand notes taken by Thomas Chisholm Anstey (1816–73): *Carlyle's Unpublished Lectures: Lectures on the History of Literature or the Successive Periods of European Culture* . . . , ed. R. P. Karkaria, and *Lectures on the History of Literature* . . . , ed. J. Reay Greene. Because of illness Anstey missed the ninth lecture, on Voltaire, of which there is no detailed record.

34. *Reminiscences*, 1:115. See also Froude, *LMJWC*, 1:115, TC's note, JWC to MAC, 20 May 1839.

35. Journal, 20 and 31 May 1838.

36. TC to JAC, 14 July 1838 (NLS, 523.58). Carlyle netted £264 from this lecture series but had "about £300 to front the coming year with" (ibid.).

37. JWC to TC, [ca. 18 September 1838] (NLS, 601.51).

CHAPTER NINETEEN

1. In Oliver Goldsmith's *Vicar of Wakefield* (1766), the chief adventures of the Reverend Charles Primrose and his wife, when in their prosperity, "were by the fire-side, and all his migrations from the blue bed to the brown" (chap. 1, par. 2).

2. A. Carlyle, *NL*, 1:143. TC to JWC, [6 September 1838].

3. Actually, the beginning of the Journal (published in Norton, *Two Note Books*, pp. 1–31) has many references to a projected "Essay on the Civil Wars" that Carlyle had seriously meditated writing in 1821–22. For references in letters, see the index to *CL*, vols. 1–4. Because of Carlyle's other commitments and his lack of readiness for the project, it came to nothing. Froude had spoken of Carlyle's early interest in Cromwell (see p. 140 above) but apparently had forgotten that he had done so.

4. John Robertson did write an essay on Cromwell.

5. A. Carlyle, *NL*, 1:147. TC to MAC, 13 January 1839. It was Douglas Heath, acting for others and described as "a promising young Barrister" (ibid., p. 149), who sent Carlyle books from Cambridge.

6. See *Carlyle and the London Library*, ed. Frederick Harrison (London: Chapman & Hall, 1907); and Simon Nowell-Smith, "Carlyle and the London Library," in *English Libraries, 1800–1850: Three Lectures Delivered at University College* (London: E. K. Lewis, 1958).

7. A. Carlyle, *NL*, 1:149. TC to JAC, 5 February 1839.

8. TC to Jean Carlyle Aitken, 13 February 1839 (NLS, 1763.185).

9. A. Carlyle, *NL*, 1:148–49. TC to JAC, 5 February 1839.

10. See C. O. Parsons, "Carlyle's Gropings about Montrose," *Englische Studien* 71 (1937): 360–71.

11. Journal, 22 February 1839.

12. A. Carlyle: "What evil?" For a discussion of the Carlyles and the Ashburtons (and of Lady Harriet as "Gloriana"), see Clubbe, *Carlyle and His Contemporaries*, pp. 324–31.

13. A. Carlyle, *NL*, 1:155. TC to MAC, 8 March 1839.

14. TC to JAC, 11 March 1839 (NLS, 522.62).

15. A. Carlyle, *NL*, 1:161. TC to JAC, 26 May 1839. After the word "Harrow," Froude interpolates "like a Faust's flight thro' an ocean of green," which as A. Carlyle notes, "is transferred from C's *Journal* of 9th Oct 1839."

16. TC to JAC, 26 May 1839 (NLS, 523.64).

17. A. Carlyle, *NL*, 1:161–62. TC to JAC, 26 May 1839.

18. A. Carlyle, *CMSB*, p. 220. TC to John Sterling, 19 June 1839.

19. Ibid., pp. 220–21.

20. Recorded in TC to MAC, 19 June 1839 (NLS, 520.81).

21. See TC to JAC, 2 August 1839: "I am always moderately well in solitude, utterly alone; and oftenest contrive to be that way" (NLS, 523.68).

22. TC to JAC, 13 September 1839 (NLS, 523.70).

23. *London and Westminster Review* 33 (October 1839): 1–68. Reprinted in John Sterling, *Essays and Tales*, ed. J. C. Hare, 2 vols. (London: John W. Parker, 1848), 1:252–381.

24. A. Carlyle, *NL*, 1:176. TC to MAC, 5 December 1839.

25. Ibid.

26. Ibid.

27. TC to MAC, [January 1840] (NLS, 520.88).

28. Ibid.

29. A. Carlyle, *NL*, 1:185. TC to MAC, 11 February 1840.

30. Froude expresses his disbelief in the idea of progress (and in Buckle's theories) in "The Science of History," *Short Studies*, vol. 1.

31. A. Carlyle, *NL*, 1:188. TC to JAC, 27 February 1840.

32. The incident of the Irish corporal is also in one of Byron's letters (to Francis Hodgson, 4 December 1811), *Byron's Letters and Journals*, ed. Leslie A. Marchand (London: John Murray, 1973–), 2:136.

33. TC to JAC, 17 March 1840 (NLS, 523.78). The "Queen of Beauty" was Lady Seymour, granddaughter of R. B. Sheridan. On Dickens and Carlyle, see William Oddie, *Dickens and Carlyle: The Question of Influence* (London: Centenary Press, 1972); Michael Goldberg, *Carlyle and Dickens* (Athens: University of Georgia Press, 1972); and K. J. Fielding's perceptive review of both in the *Dickensian* 69 (May 1973): 111–18.

34. Arthur Penrhyn Stanley, *The Life and Correspondence of Thomas Arnold, D.D.*, 5th ed., 2 vols. (London: B. Fellowes, 1845), 2:189. Arnold's letter is dated "Rugby, January, 1840."

35. Neither a letter to Carlyle from William Bowie, the "poor Paisley weaver," nor a reply from Carlyle has been found. On Bowie, see Andrew James Symington, *Some Personal Reminiscences of Carlyle* (Paisley and London: Alex. Gardner, 1886), pp. 41–49.

36. TC to JAC, 30 March 1840 (NLS, 523.80).

37. Froude's memory makes a minor slip here. It was not "with the

Bullers at Kinnaird" (1823-24) but in 1821 that Carlyle had "terrified" his family with reports of ill-health. See p. 120 above, and *CL*, 1:324-30.

38. A. Carlyle: "Doubtless a most sweet morsel to *you!*"

39. TC to MAC, 9 May 1840 (typescript: NLS, 520.92).

40. Not found, but see the account in the *Examiner*, 28 June 1840, p. 408.

41. A. Carlyle, *CMSB*, p. 235. TC to John Sterling, 3 July 1840. "Die in my hole like a poisoned rat" is loosely recalled from Swift's letter to Bolingbroke from Ireland, 21 March 1730 (*The Correspondence of Jonathan Swift*, ed. Harold Williams, 5 vols. [Oxford: Clarendon, 1963], 3:383).

42. See Froude, *LMJWC*, 1:118.

43. TC to JAC, 1 July 1840 (NLS, 523.89).

44. TC to JAC, 5 September 1840 (NLS, 523.95). See Charles Richard Sanders, "Carlyle and Tennyson," *PMLA* 76 (March 1961): 82-97, and Tennyson's poem "The Dead Prophet."

45. TC to JAC, 24 July 1840 (NLS, 511.67). Merivale's article on Carlyle's *French Revolution* appeared in the *Edinburgh Review* 71 (July 1840): 411-45.

46. TC to JAC, 23 August 1840 (NLS, 523.94).

47. *Quarterly Review* 66 (September 1840): 446-503. In a letter to John Murray III, publisher of the *Quarterly*, Sir John Barrow referred to "your late abominable article on such a person as Carlyle, which every one condemns" (Samuel Smiles, *A Publisher and His Friends: Memoir and Correspondence of the Late John Murray*, 2 vols. [London: John Murray, 1891], 2:455). In 1849 Sewell burned Froude's *Nemesis of Faith* in the hall of Exeter College, Oxford.

48. Jane Frances Tuckerman.

49. Dr. Syntax was an eccentric clergyman whose adventures were told by William Coombe (1742-1823) in three octosyllabic *Tours*, published 1812-21; his horse Grizzle was all skin and bones.

50. TC to JAC, 23 August 1840 (NLS, 523.94). In his text Froude changed "whores" to "improper females."

51. A. Carlyle, *NL*, 1:220-21. TC to JAC, 29 October 1840.

CHAPTER TWENTY

1. Froude, *LMJWC*, 1:126. JWC to MAC, [27 October 1840].

2. See p. 364 above and Froude, *LMJWC*, 1:76.

3. TC to MAC, 18 February 1841 (NLS, 520.104). The lectures were published in 1841 as *On Heroes, Hero-Worship, and the Heroic in History*.

4. TC to JAC, 3 March 1841 (NLS, 524.16). Froude omitted "a most heroic-looking damsel."

5. Journal, 4 June 1841. Elsewhere, Carlyle notes that "Literature of Desperation" (*Literatur der Verzweiflung*) "was Goethe's definition of

Victor Hugo and Co.'s new gospel" (Froude, *LMJWC*, 1:172). He was apparently introduced to the phrase in a letter from Mill of 2 August 1833. See also *On Heroes and Hero-Worship, Works*, 5:187.

6. "Model Prisons," *Latter-Day Pamphlets, Works*, 20:81, 80.

7. A. Carlyle: "Bah!" On Geraldine Jewsbury, see Susanne Howe's biography, *Geraldine Jewsbury: Her Life and Errors* (London: George Allen & Unwin, 1935); and Susanne H. Nobbe, "Four Unpublished Letters of Thomas Carlyle," *PMLA* 70 (September 1955): 876-84. In the three letters of 1840, Carlyle gives counsel to Miss Jewsbury in her spiritual struggles.

8. TC to JWC, [12 April 1841] (NLS, 610.45). For the Carlyles' relationship with the Marshall family, see *Reminiscences*, 1:181-84.

9. TC to JAC, 3 May 1841 (NLS, 524.19).

10. Journal, 4 June 1841.

11. A. Carlyle, *NL*, 1:236. TC to John Sterling, 14 July 1841.

12. A. Carlyle crosses out "usher" and substitutes "teacher": this is technically correct, though Carlyle's post was a lowly one. See p. 105 above.

13. Journal, 3 October 1841.

14. A. Carlyle: "I never heard of one." There was none.

15. Bliss, *TC*, p. 109. TC to JWC, 2 November 1835.

16. A. Carlyle: "About £150 net." The income from Craigenputtoch varied from £170 in the early 1830s to £250 in the mid-1860s.

17. See TC to JWC, 22 July 1841 (NLS, 610.51).

18. Stanley, *Life of Arnold*, 2:317, 326.

19. See A. Carlyle, ed., "Notes on a Three Days' Tour to the Netherlands: August, 1842.—T. Carlyle," *Cornhill Magazine*, n.s. 53 (October–November 1922): 493–512, 626–40. Carlyle visited Ostend, Bruges, and Ghent.

20. Froude, *LMJWC*, 1:152–82.

21. A. Carlyle, *NL*, 1:268–69. TC to John Sterling, 6 September 1842. See also *Reminiscences*, 1:187, and, for Cromwell's words, *Works*, 6:179.

CHAPTER TWENTY-ONE

1. TC to John Sterling, 21 December 1842 (NLS, 531.59).

2. See *Works*, 29:353–54: "the Social Science,—not a 'gay science,' but a rueful,—which finds the secret of this Universe in 'supply and demand.' . . . what we might call, by way of eminence, the *dismal science*."

3. Actually the writing of *Past and Present* took "a good five months" and was not accomplished with "singular ease." See Grace J. Calder, *The Writing of "Past and Present": A Study of Carlyle's Manuscripts* (New Haven: Yale University Press, 1949); and Edwin W. Marrs, Jr., "Dating the Writing of 'Past and Present,'" *Notes and Queries*, n.s. 14 (October 1967): 370–71.

4. Andrew Lang, *The Life and Letters of John Gibson Lockhart* . . . (New York: Charles Scribner's, 1897), 2:238–39. Lockhart to TC, 27 April 1843. Lockhart echoes Carlyle's "Thou art wrong; thou art like to be damned" (*Past and Present, Works*, 10:117). In the last half of the paragraph, Froude apparently paraphrases a part of Lockhart's letter not given in Lang's biography.

5. I have not traced the phrase, but it embodies the gist of Emerson's perspective on Carlyle. See his review of *Past and Present* in the *Dial* for July 1843, reprinted in *The Complete Works of Ralph Waldo Emerson*, ed. E. W. Emerson, 12 vols. (Boston and New York: Houghton Mifflin Co., 1904; rpt. 1921), 12:379–91.

6. Eccles. 2:16. I have substituted the King James translation for Froude's Greek.

7. Froude alludes thus to Knox's voice in his *History of England from the Fall of Wolsey to the Defeat of the Spanish Armada*, 12 vols. (London: Longmans, Green & Co., 1856–70), 10:443, but changed his own copy of the biography (now in the Beinecke Library, Yale) to say: "Elizabeth's ambassador Randolph said that John Knox's voice was like the sound of 'five hundred trumpets.' "

8. Cf. Matt. 7:29.

9. A. Carlyle: "Pity but you had been saved from *lying* too!"

10. Cf. TC to JAC, 17 March 1840: "a brown-skinned, silent, sad-concentrated, proud old dame."

11. Not always. See Mabel Davidson, "The Record of a Broken Friendship," *South Atlantic Quarterly* 24 (July 1925): 278–92. The friendship was John's with Mrs. Carlyle. Despite A. Carlyle's arguments (*NLMJWC*, 1:240), Froude bent over backward to be fair to John, indeed glossed over his boorishness and occasional insensitivity to Mrs. Carlyle.

12. Bliss, *TC*, p. 164. TC to JWC, 8 July 1843.

13. Ibid., p. 165. TC to JWC, 9 July 1843.

14. Ibid., p. 170. TC to JWC, 18 July 1843.

15. Ibid., p. 172. TC to JWC, 19 July 1843.

16. Ibid., p. 175. TC to JWC, 23 July 1843.

17. A. Carlyle: "How clever!"

18. TC to JWC, 27 July 1843 (NLS, 611.139).

19. TC to JWC, 5 August 1843 (NLS, 611.144).

20. TC to JWC, 2 September 1843 (NLS, 611.160).

21. Bliss, *TC*, p. 191. TC to JWC, 4 September 1843.

22. A. Carlyle: "where *yours* now is, I hope."

23. Bliss, *TC*, p. 192. TC to JWC, 4 September 1843.

24. Ibid., pp. 194–95. TC to JWC, 12 September 1843.

CHAPTER TWENTY-TWO

1. Froude, *LMJWC*, 1:264. JWC to Jean Carlyle Aitken, [early October 1843].

2. Ibid., p. 267. JWC to Susan Hunter Stirling, [October 1843]. Froude's text. Although A. Carlyle comments, "O what a lie, or concatenation of lies!", Froude bases every statement concerning this incident on Jane Carlyle's letters.

3. A. Carlyle: "No! 2:30 is not the middle of the day."

4. Journal, 23 October 1843.

5. Froude, *LMJWC*, 1:276. JWC to John Welsh (her maternal uncle), 28 November 1843.

6. TC to MAC, 31 December 1843 (NLS, 521.23).

7. Froude, *LMJWC*, 1:278-90; see also A. Carlyle, *NLMJWC*, 1: 136-55, and Trudy Bliss, ed., *Jane Welsh Carlyle: A New Selection of Her Letters* (New York: Macmillan, 1950), pp. 148-53.

8. A. Carlyle: "*Your* Gloriana was Geraldine Jewsbury!" "Mr. Baring" was William Bingham Baring (1799-1864), who became second Lord Ashburton upon the death of his father, Alexander Baring (1774-1848). Froude, in passages on pp. 365 and 406 above, has earlier prepared his readers for this characterization of Carlyle as a "rustic Red Cross Knight." See also, for a brief comment on the analogies with *The Faerie Queene*, Introduction, n. 19.

9. TC to JWC, 12 September 1844 (NLS, 611.184).

10. *Life of John Sterling*, *Works*, 11:260-61. John Sterling to TC, 10 August 1844.

11. A. Carlyle: "No! 'Bobus' was his name, except for the first week or so."

12. The name by which Carlyle "often laughingly designated his wife" (Froude's note). See TC to JWC, 12 September 1844 (NLS, 611.84) and A. Carlyle, *NLMJWC*, 1:149.

13. Bliss, *TC*, pp. 210-11. TC to JWC, 26 August 1845.

14. Subsequent historians—among them C. H. Firth, in the introduction to his edition of Carlyle's *Letters and Speeches of Oliver Cromwell* (3 vols. [London: Methuen, 1904])—have concurred with Froude's judgment that Carlyle's history revolutionized the study of Cromwell and the Commonwealth.

15. For Carlyle's clarifying explanation of the "right vs. might" concept, frequently misunderstood by later writers, see Clubbe, *Two Reminiscences*, pp. 98-99.

16. A. Carlyle: "a 'week' Mrs C. says."

17. Bliss, *TC*, p. 217. TC to JWC, 26 September 1845.

18. Ibid., pp. 217-18.

19. Ibid., p. 218. See Froude, *LMJWC*, 1:339-40, for JWC's mention of Mrs. Paulet's letter (JWC to TC, 23 September 1845).

20. TC to JWC, 27 September 1845 (NLS, 612.215).

21. Froude, *LMJWC*, 1:365. TC's note, JWC to Mrs. Russell, 2 July 1846. Some of the additional letters—including the Squire papers—turned out to be forgeries.

22. JWC to Jean Carlyle Aitken, [ca. April 1846] (NLS, 603.217).

23. Ibid.

24. A. Carlyle: "No. She only promised to 'announce her arrival,' which she did in good time." See A. Carlyle, *NLMJWC*, 1:191 n.

25. Bliss, *TC*, p. 224. TC to JWC, 13 July 1846.

26. Froude, *LMJWC*, 1:367–69. JWC to TC, 14 July 1846.

27. Ibid., p. 367.

28. TC to JWC, 22 July 1846 (NLS, 612.244).

29. TC to JWC, 20 August 1846 (NLS, 612.251).

30. Ibid.

31. Ibid.

32. A. Carlyle: "Some of her letters of July & August '46 were never seen by Froude,—Carlyle himself considered them too private. They are very self-accusing."

CHAPTER TWENTY-THREE

1. TC to JWC, 8 September 1846 (NLS, 612.259). For Carlyle's first Irish tour, see Froude, *LMJWC*, 1:371–74; and Sir Charles Gavan Duffy, *Conversations with Carlyle* (New York: Charles Scribner's Sons, 1892), pp. 15–23.

2. Froude, *LMJWC*, 1:374–86. Opposite this paragraph A. Carlyle writes: "They had the servant (Helen) for 11 years." On Helen, see Froude, *LMJWC*, 1:121–22, 378.

3. TC to JAC, 8 October 1846 (NLS, 524.69).

4. Possibly Bronson Alcott.

5. *Memoirs of Margaret Fuller Ossoli*, 2 vols. (Boston: Phillips, Sampson, 1852), 2:184–88 passim. See also her account in *At Home and Abroad* (Boston: Crosby, Nichols, 1856), pp. 183–85. Together, these narratives form one of the most successful of the many attempts to capture the brilliance of Carlyle's conversation and its effect upon others. Her letter to Emerson on Carlyle is reprinted in Ray Cecil Carter, "Margaret Fuller and the Two Sages," *Colby Library Quarterly* 6 (March 1963): 198–201. Emerson observed that Carlyle's conversational powers were such that fashionable Londoners "keep Carlyle as a sort of portable cathedral-bell, which they like to produce in companies where he is unknown, and set a-swinging" (*Lectures and Biographical Sketches* [Boston: Houghton Mifflin, 1883], p. 456). And David Masson described the effect of Carlyle's conversation on John Robertson, by no means an unqualified admirer of Carlylean doctrines: "It was a testimony to the extraordinary depth of the impression which Carlyle had by that time [1841] made on all who were within his circle, that there had been formed in Robertson, even then, that habit of always speaking of Carlyle, always recurring to Carlyle after any range of the conversation among other things, which I was to observe for the next forty years in every person, without exception, that had come within Carlyle's influence, whether personally or through his books" (*Memories of*

London in the 'Forties [Edinburgh and London: William Blackwood, 1908], p. 9). For another perspective on Carlyle's conversation, see William Baker, "Herbert Spencer's Unpublished Reminiscences of Thomas Carlyle . . . ," *Neophilologus* 60 (January 1976): 145–52.

6. TC to JAC, 2 December 1846 (NLS, 524.72).

7. TC to JAC, 17 January 1847 (NLS, 524.74).

8. TC to MAC, 15 February 1847 (NLS, 521.46).

9. I have restored Carlyle's words (paraphrased by Froude) in TC to MAC, 8 March 1847 (NLS, 521.47). See Duffy, *Conversations with Carlyle*, pp. 24–28.

10. See TC to MAC, 29 August 1847 (NLS, 512.70), and T. Wemyss Reid, *Life of the Right Honourable William Edward Forster* (London: Chapman & Hall, 1889), pp. 115–21.

11. Bliss, *TC*, pp. 235–36. TC to JWC, 13 September 1847. Mrs. Carlyle had seen "Sharp's cyclopean Smithy" in a previous year. See also Froude, *LMJWC*, 2:16; and Francis Espinasse, *Literary Recollections and Sketches* (London: Hodder & Stoughton, 1893), pp. 149–53, which corrects Froude on a few points.

12. TC to JWC, 17 September 1847 (NLS, 612.264).

13. Daniel O'Connell.

14. TC to JWC, 23 September 1847 (NLS, 612.267).

15. Bliss, *TC*, pp. 239–40. TC to JWC, 3 October 1847.

16. TC to JWC, 7 October 1847 (NLS, 612.275).

17. TC to JWC, 10 October 1847 (NLS, 612.276). Carlyle writes from "Greta Bank, Keswick," having left Scotsbrig.

18. TC to MAC, 8 November 1847 (NLS, 521.61).

19. TC to MAC, 13 December 1847 (NLS, 521.63).

20. TC to JWC, 13 January 1848 (NLS, 521.64).

21. TC to JWC, 23 January 1848 (NLS, 612.285).

22. See A. Carlyle, *NLMJWC*, 1:247; and JWC to TC, 2 April 1866: "Why on Earth did you ever get into this galley" (NLS, 609.767).

23. Journal, 9 February 1848. Carlisle Moore has described the "Exodus from Houndsditch" as "a work whose message should succeed, where that of the Everlasting Yea had not, in effecting the deliverance of England from her commercial cheapness, her atheism, and her political chaos. With complete confidence in his own faith, he felt the need of a newer truth which should be more pertinent to the newer age" ("The Persistence of Carlyle's 'Everlasting Yea,'" *Modern Philology* 54 [February 1957]: 195–96). Conceived at least as early as 1848, this projected work was still in mind while Carlyle was writing "Jesuitism," the last of the *Latter-Day Pamphlets*. See *Works*, 20:329–30.

24. Cf., e.g., *Works*, 20:330, and Harrold, *Sartor*, p. 76.

25. A. Carlyle, ed., "Notes on a Three Days' Tour to the Netherlands, p. 510.

26. Journal, 7 March 1848.

27. Arthur S. Way's translation (in the Loeb Classical Library edition) of the original Greek (given by Froude) of Euripides *Medea* 410.

28. Journal, 14 March 1848. See R. C. Beatty, "Macaulay and Carlyle," *Philological Quarterly* 18 (October 1939): 25-33; and A. J. P. Taylor, "Macaulay and Carlyle," in *Englishmen and Others* (London: Hamish Hamilton, 1956).

29. Journal, 27 March 1848. After Peel's death Carlyle wrote in his Journal for 24 July 1850: "I had an authentic regard for this man; and a wish to know more of him. Nearly the one man alive of whom I could say so much."

30. Journal, 27 March 1848.

31. Newman entered the Roman Catholic Church in 1845.

32. Cf. " 'unintelligible moonshine' " in Slater, *CEC*, pp. 416-17. TC to Emerson, 2 March 1847.

33. For Emerson's account of this visit, see *English Traits*, chap. 16.

34. TC to MAC, 31 August 1848 (NLS, 521.70). Froude's paraphrase omits mention of "Marquises of Landsdown [Lansdowne]."

35. 2 December 1848. Reprinted in *Rescued Essays*, ed. Percy Newberry (London: Leadenhall Press, 1892), pp. 117-25. See also Froude, *LMJWC*, 1:152-54.

36. A. Carlyle: "No!" Arthur and Reginald Buller, Charles's two younger brothers, survived him.

37. TC to MAC, 10 February 1849 (NLS, 521.77).

38. Journal, 17 May 1849.

39. *The Nemesis of Faith* (1849).

40. A Carlyle: "Mine Gott!" An independent observer confirms Froude here. H. Weigall, who had done a bust of Carlyle in 1837, wrote to a Mr. Leutzner on about 15 February 1882: "His Eyes were the most beautiful I think I ever saw in a man[.] At that time they were of a deep violet blue color & sorrowful observant reflective far seeing yet introspective in their expression" (MS: Beinecke Library, Yale).

41. Here ends vol. 3 of Froude's biography.

CHAPTER TWENTY-FOUR

1. "Now" is the early 1880s, when the Liberals, under Gladstone, again attempted to restore order in Ireland by passing a second land act (1881). Froude, who wrote much on Ireland, argued that a policy of conciliation was useless.

2. First in the *Century Magazine*, then as *Reminiscences of My Irish Journey in 1849* (London: Sampson, Low, 1882), with a preface by Froude. Carlyle had given the manuscript (now in the Huntington Library) to Joseph Neuberg, who in turn gave it to Thomas Ballantyne.

3. *Reminiscences of My Irish Journey in 1849*, pp. 116-17. See also Clubbe, *Two Reminiscences* pp. 74-75.

4. Froude omits the name of Sir William Beecher. See *Reminiscences of My Irish Journey in 1849*, pp. 126, 154–63; and C. R. Sanders, "Retracing Carlyle's Irish Journey (1849)," *Studies: An Irish Quarterly Review* 50 (Spring 1961): 44.

5. *Reminiscences of My Irish Journey in 1849*, p. 201.

6. Forster, the chief secretary for Ireland, had been instrumental in pushing through in February 1881 a coercion bill involving the suspension of *habeas corpus*. It did little to quiet Ireland.

7. Journal, 17 May 1849. See p. 473 above.

8. "Much Ado About Nothing," in Froude, *LMJWC*, 2:52–75 (MS: Bodleian).

9. Froude, *LMJWC*, 2:75–76. TC's note, JWC to TC, 5 September 1849. Froude's text.

10. TC to JWC, 2 September 1849 (NLS, 612.301). "Gunner bodies" designates the members of the shooting party.

11. TC to JWC, 7 September 1849 (NLS, 613.303).

12. Adalbert von Chamisso's *Peter Schlemihls wundersame Geschichte* (1814).

13. See p. 459 above.

14. Juvenal *Satires* 1. 1. 79: "If nature refuses, indignation makes the verse."

15. *Works*, 29:348–83. First published in *Fraser's Magazine* 40 (December 1849): 670–79. "Occasional Discourse on the Negro Question" is not formally one of the *Latter-Day Pamphlets* but a "Precursor" (*Works*, 29:348). In 1853 he published the essay independently as "Occasional Discourse on the Nigger Question."

16. *Works*, 29:354. The two terms are yoked elsewhere in Carlyle's essay.

17. John Stuart Mill, "The Negro Question," *Fraser's Magazine* 41 (January 1850): 25–31. See also Froude, *LMJWC*, 2:99.

18. "The Present Time," *Works*, 20:12.

19. Ibid., p. 16. I retain Froude's italics for the clause "*since . . . laws.*" Carlyle's parable of the ship of democracy may derive from Plato *Republic* 6. 488A–489A.

20. "Model Prisons," *Works*, 20:50. On p. 51 Carlyle refers to " 'universal sluggard-and-scoundrel protection-societies.' "

21. Ibid., pp. 52, 53, 55, 56, 58. The prison Carlyle visited was Tothill Fields, not Millbank Penitentiary, and the "literary Chartist rebel" was Ernest Jones. See Jules Seigel, "Carlyle's Model Prisons and Prisoners Identified," *Victorian Periodicals Newsletter* 9 (September 1976): 81–83.

22. Aristotle *Politics* 3. 6–18.

23. See Harrold, *Sartor*, p. 130, for Zaehdarm's epitaph. For "Pig Philosophy," the passage referred to in "Jesuitism," see *Works*, 20: 315–18.

24. "Punch's Police. A Very Melancholy Case," *Punch* 18 (January–

June 1850): 107. In "Carlyle Made Easy" (ibid., p. 110), *Punch* "translates" into English a short passage of "Carlylese" from "The Present Time." Both parodies are reprinted in *Thomas Carlyle: The Critical Heritage*, ed. Jules Paul Seigel (London: Routledge & Kegan Paul, 1971).

25. Cf. Slater, *CEC*, pp. 461–63 (Emerson to TC, 5 August 1850). I have not found evidence linking Thackeray to either of the parodies in *Punch*.

26. Froude paraphrases from "Pig Philosophy" in "Jesuitism" (*Works*, 20:316).

27. Journal, 27 May 1850.

28. Ibid., 25 June 1850. See also *Reminiscences*, 1:129–31.

29. Journal, 24 July 1850.

30. William Cobbett, *Rural Rides*, 2 vols. (London: Reeves & Turner, 1885), 1:32. Cf. *CL*, 3:219.

31. Bliss, *TC*, p. 261. TC to JWC, 2 August 1850.

32. Ibid., p. 266. TC to JWC, 28 August 1850.

33. Ibid., p. 267.

34. Ibid. I have slightly rearranged Froude's quotations in order to follow the sequence of events narrated by Carlyle.

35. TC to JWC, 22 September 1850 (NLS 613.334).

36. Froude, *LMJWC*, 2:133–36. JWC to TC, 23 September 1850.

37. TC to JWC, 24 September 1850 (NLS, 613.335).

38. A. Carlyle: "No! only 'after dark!' " TC to JWC, 29 September 1850: "in the evening a dark walk to Ecclefechan" (NLS, 613.337).

39. Bliss, *TC*, p. 270. TC to JWC, 1 October 1850.

40. Ibid., pp. 270–71. TC to JWC, 3 October 1850.

41. Ibid., p. 272.

42. Ibid., p. 273. TC to JWC, 4 October 1850.

43. A. Carlyle: "Carlyle came home alone and writes to his Wife *still at the Grange* on 21 October." This is correct.

CHAPTER TWENTY-FIVE

1. Journal, 30 October 1850.

2. TC to MAC, 26 October 1850 (NLS, 521.94).

3. David Masson, "Latter-Day Pamphlets," *North British Review* 14 (November 1851): 1–40. The Wellesley Index attributes "Carlyle's Works," in the *Dublin Review* 29 (September 1850): 169–206, to John O'Hagan. Even before Masson, O'Hagan clearly perceived the sudden waning of Carlyle's reputation and his total break with orthodox Christianity.

4. Eccles. 2:14.

5. Journal 8, November 1850.

6. Ibid., 10 December 1850. The "fat Pedant" is Antonio Panizzi (1797–1879), Keeper of Printed Books in the British Museum and Car-

lyle's longtime antagonist. See Espinasse, *Literary Recollections and Sketches*, pp. 189–92, and Edward Miller, *Prince of Librarians: The Life and Times of Antonio Panizzi of the British Museum* (Athens: Ohio University Press, 1967), pp. 213–14.

7. TC to JWC, 31 January 1851 (NLS, 613.344). Thirlwall was "the Bishop."

8. See Euripides *Medea* 410 and p. 460 above.

9. For Carlyle's relationship to the Broad Church movement, see Charles Richard Sanders, *Coleridge and the Broad Church Movement* (Durham, N.C.: Duke University Press, 1942), chap. 6.

10. TC to MAC, 5 April 1851 (NLS, 521.96).

11. See chap. 10 of this edition, esp. n. 2.

12. "In 1876 Gully's name was frequently mentioned at the sensational inquiry into the death of a barrister named Charles Bravo, who, it was suspected, had been poisoned by his wife. Disclosures as to Gully's intimacy with Mrs. Bravo greatly damaged his reputation" (*DNB*). See also Froude, *LMJWC*, 2:149–50, and p. 631 below.

13. Mentioned in TC to JWC, 7 September 1851 (NLS, 613.347).

14. Bliss, *TC*, p. 276. TC to JWC, 28 September 1851.

15. Ibid., pp. 277–78. TC to JWC, 1 October 1851.

16. Carlyle wrote up his trip as "Excursion (Futile Enough) to Paris; Autumn 1851," published in *The Last Words of Thomas Carlyle*.

17. Thomas Erskine (1788–1870), Scottish religious writer much esteemed by Carlyle, who occasionally called him "Evidence Erskine" after his most popular work, *Remarks on the Internal Evidence for the Truth of Revealed Religion* (1820). To Jane Carlyle he was "Saint Thomas." He lived at Linlathen.

18. TC to JWC, 30 July 1852 (NLS, 613.361).

19. Ibid.

20. At the end of the *Symposium*.

21. TC to JWC, 9 August 1852 (NLS, 613.364).

22. Bliss, *TC*, p. 279. TC to JWC, 9 August 1852.

23. Ibid., p. 280. TC to JWC, 13 August 1852. Froude's "mere travelling annoyances" Carlyle specifies in this letter as "beds without curtains, and the freaks of a diseased fancy and exasperated nerves."

24. TC to JWC, 23 August 1852 (NLS, 613.370).

25. Bliss, *TC*, p. 284. TC to JWC, 1 September 1852.

26. Ibid., p. 287. TC to JWC, 6 September 1852.

27. Ibid., p. 290. TC to JWC, 15 September 1852.

28. Ibid., p. 291.

29. Ibid., pp. 292–93.

30. TC to MAC, 19 September 1852 (NLS, 521.98).

31. Bliss, *TC*, pp. 295–96. TC to JWC, 20 September 1852.

32. Ibid., p. 296. TC to JWC, 25 September 1852.

33. Ibid., p. 298. TC to JWC, 27 September 1852.

34. Ibid., pp. 299-300. TC to JWC, 1 October 1852.

35. Ibid., pp. 301-2. TC to JWC, 8 October 1852. On Carlyle and Tieck, see E. H. Zeydel, *Tieck and England* (Princeton: Princeton University Press), pp. 122-28.

CHAPTER TWENTY-SIX

1. A. Carlyle, *NL*, 2:139-40. TC to G. Remington, 12 November 1852.

2. TC to MAC, 15 October 1852 (NLS, 521.99).

3. TC to MAC, 15 November 1852 (NLS, 521.101).

4. TC to JWC, 28 March 1853 (NLS, 614.384). G. S. Venables (1810-88), barrister and writer, noted for the extraordinary force and charm of his character. He recorded his impressions of the Carlyles in two articles for the *Fortnightly Review* in 1883 and 1884.

5. TC to JWC, 31 March 1853 (NLS, 614.385). Massimo Taparelli, Marchese d'Azeglio (1798-1866), was an Italian statesman and author, Manzoni's son-in-law, and a leader in the risorgimento who helped foment revolution in 1848.

6. TC to JWC, 8 July 1853 (NLS, 614.389). Organ-grinders never ceased to plague Carlyle. "I have seen him rush out of his house in his morning wrap, sending a torrent of words, not descriptive of the state of the blest, over two Italians who were playing an orchestration opposite. The poor men gave way at once to the general imprecations, asked his pardon, and departed; and I thought they were a shilling the better for the transaction. He really suffered from street-noises" (*Threescore Years and Ten: Reminiscences of the late Sophie Elizabeth De Morgan*, ed. May A. De Morgan [London: Richard Bentley, 1895], p. 231). This passage describes an episode after 1873, the year Mrs. De Morgan moved to Cheyne Row, three doors down from Carlyle.

7. Froude elaborated on this analogy in a letter to Lord Lytton of 4 December [1881?]: "Carlyle was like Q*n* Elizabeth 'more than man and less than woman.' He had no vices, nor the least tendency to vices—but he had *humours* infinite which he let grow as they pleased and never weeded his garden. He had the grandest intellect and the grandest conscience—but his conscience though it governed absolutely the main direction of his life, yet otherwise was active only in his work and left the every day details of common duty to go as they liked. He was treated by others as an exceptional person and this was all right because it was true. But he came to think himself as an exceptional person, and that is not good for any of us. Even the most gifted.— No painter ever' succeeded with his pen.— He wants a genius like his own to make an adequate biography of him" (MS: Hon. David Lytton Cobbold and Hertfordshire County Council).

8. Froude, *LMJWC*, 2:221-26. JWC to TC, 20 July 1853.

9. TC to JWC, 28 July 1853 (NLS, 614.398).

10. TC to JWC, 29 July 1853 (NLS, 614.399).

11. TC to JWC, 30 July 1853 (NLS, 614.400). Cf. Froude, *LMJWC*, 2:230.

12. Journal, ca. 17 August 1853.

13. Ibid.

14. A. Carlyle, *NL*, 1:145. TC to MAC, 29 December 1838.

15. Froude, *LMJWC*, 2:236 (TC's note, JWC to TC, 19 December 1853); ibid., p. 239 (JWC to TC, 31 December 1853). See also *Reminiscences*, 1:194–95.

16. Froude, *LMJWC*, 2:242. TC's note, JWC to TC, 27 December 1853.

17. Journal, 8 January 1854. Froude omitted after "took leave of me as usual" the words "(tho' I kissed her lips, which was not usual)." Other omissions are not indicated. See also Froude, *LMJWC*, 2:221.

18. After John Fletcher's *Rule a Wife and Have a Wife* (1624), in which Michael Perez, a penniless but pretentious captain, seeks to market his person and commission by marrying an heiress. Elsewhere Carlyle calls Louis Napoleon "this poor Opera-King." For other expressions of Carlyle's opinion of the French emperor, see *William Allingham: A Diary*, ed. H. Allingham and D. Radford (London: Macmillan, 1907), p. 261; and *Letters of Charles Eliot Norton*, ed. Sara Norton and M. A. DeWolfe Howe, 2 vols. (Boston and New York: Houghton Mifflin, 1913), 1:452–53.

19. TC to JAC, 16 May 1854 (NLS, 524.104).

20. Ibid. See also Froude, *LMJWC*, 2:230, 235–36; *Reminiscences*, 1:198–200; and Clubbe, *Two Reminiscences*, p. 113.

21. TC to JAC, 9 May 1854 (NLS, 524.103).

22. Journal, 29 April 1854. Carlyle later wrote a reminiscence of Wilson ("Christopher North"), first published by A. Carlyle in *The Nineteenth Century and After* (1920) and reprinted in the Everyman edition of the *Reminiscences*, ed. Walter Murdoch (1932) and Ian Campbell (1972). The greater part is also available in *CL*, 4:236–43. TC to Jean Carlyle Aitken, 19 April 1854 (NLS, 515.71) contains a graphic sketch of Wilson.

23. *Reminiscences*, 1:62.

24. £35 was, as A. Carlyle notes, the rent for 5 Cheyne Row.

25. MS: Bodleian.

26. Jane Carlyle's "Budget," an eleven-page folio manuscript, is also in the Bodleian. Published in Froude, *Carlyle*, 4:162–70.

27. See T. A. Kirby, "Carlyle, Fitzgerald, and the Naseby Project," *Modern Language Quarterly* 8 (September 1947): 364–66.

28. TC to JWC, 9 August 1855 (NLS, 614.412).

29. TC to JWC, 17 August 1855 (NLS, 614.416). "The sputter of Cremorne" refers to sounds from Cremorne Gardens above Battersea Bridge, a place of public entertainment.

30. TC to JAC, 28 August 1855 (NLS, 525.8).

31. Cicero *Tusculan Disputations* 1. 17. 39. See Introduction, n. 74. Cf. Boswell, *Life of Johnson*, p. 693.

32. "Willst du dir aber das Beste tun, / So bleib nicht auf dir selber ruhn, / Sondern folg eines Meisters Sinn; / Mit ihm zu irren ist dir Gewinn" (Goethe's "Sprichtwörtlich," ca. 1810-12).

33. Froude's twelve-volume *History of England from the Fall of Wolsey to the Defeat of the Spanish Armada* appeared between 1856 and 1870. Vol. 1 was subtitled "Henry the Eighth"; its first two chapters were "Social Condition of England in the Sixteenth Century" and "The Last Years of the Administration of Wolsey." Carlyle's comments on Froude's *History* have been published in Dunn, *Froude*, 1:208-9, 245-51. Espinasse wrote in his *Literary Recollections:* "Carlyle's oral criticism on the earliest volumes of Mr. Froude's history was brief and abrupt: 'Meritorious but too much raw material' " (p. 218).

34. Froude, *LMJWC*, 2:278. TC's note, JWC to TC, 29 July 1856. See TC to JAC, 30 December 1855 (NLS, 525.13) for Carlyle's immediate impression.

35. A. Carlyle writes: "Mrs. Carlyle's Journal was written in two little Notebooks, labelled 'No. 1' and 'No. 2' respectively; the first of these begins on the 21st of October, 1855, and ends with the entry for the 14th of April, 1856; and the second extends from April 15th to the 5th of July, 1856. Only the latter of these Note-books had been discovered when Carlyle was writing (in July, 1866) that part of the *Reminiscences* called 'Jane Welsh Carlyle' " (*NLMJWC*, 2:87). Froude published part of the first notebook in *LMJWC*, 2:254-75; A. Carlyle published the second (*NLMJWC*, 2:87-109) and part of another (ibid., pp. 109-15). The manuscript of the second notebook is NLS, 533. On Mrs. Carlyle's sensitivity regarding her notebooks, see John Tyndall, *New Fragments* (New York: D. Appleton, 1897), p. 370 n. See also Froude's commentary in *LMJWC*, 2:254-57.

36. See *Reminiscences*, 1:204-6, and A. Carlyle, *NLMJWC*, 2:115-17.

37. See A. Carlyle, *NLMJWC*, 2:118.

38. Froude, *LMJWC*, 2:301. JWC to TC, 18 September 1856.

39. TC to JWC, 1 August 1856 (NLS, 614.423).

40. Journal 6 May 1857. Cf. Froude, *LMJWC*, 2:310.

41. TC to JAC, 23 May 1857 (NLS, 525.26).

42. TC to JWC, 24 May 1857 (NLS, 614.440).

43. Froude, *LMJWC*, 2:334, 332. TC's note, JWC to TC, 24 August 1857. Carlyle excepts "a small patch of writing by Emerson," for which see p. 580 below.

44. Bliss, *TC*, p. 327. TC to JWC, 25 August 1857.

45. TC to JWC, 7 September 1857 (NLS, 614.464).

46. Bliss, *TC*, p. 321. TC to JWC, 9 July 1857.

47. TC to JAC, 22 January 1858 (NLS, 525.34).

48. See Froude, *LMJWC,* 2:363. Indispensable to Carlyle in the menial work necessary for *Frederick,* Larkin published after Carlyle's death *Carlyle and the Open Secret of His Life* (1886). David Alec Wilson describes him accurately as "a neighbour and a friend and one of his most efficient helpers, as sort of volunteer secretary for press work with a genius for index-making" (*Carlyle,* 4:331).

49. The reader should compare Froude's estimate of Carlyle's power as a historian with twentieth-century assessments: e.g., G. P. Gooch, "Carlyle and Froude," chap. 16 of *History and Historians in the Nineteenth Century* (London: Longmans, 1913; rev. ed., 1952), pp. 301–16; Lytton Strachey, "Carlyle," in *Portraits in Miniature and Other Essays* (New York: Harcourt, Brace & Co., 1931), pp. 178–90; Charles Frederick Harrold, "Carlyle's General Method in *The French Revolution,*" *PMLA* 43 (1928): 1150–69; Louise Merwin Young, *Carlyle and the Art of History* (Philadelphia: University of Pennsylvania Press, 1939); Carlisle Moore, "Carlyle's 'Diamond Necklace' and Poetic History," *PMLA* 58 (1943): 537–57; Pieter Geyl, "Carlyle: His Significance and Reputation," *Debates with Historians* (Groningen: J. B. Wolters; The Hague: Martinus Nijhoff, 1955), pp. 35–55; Roger Sharrock, "Carlyle and the Sense of History," in *Essays and Studies,* ed. R. M. Wilson (for the English Association) (London: John Murray, 1966), pp. 74–91; and Hedva Ben-Israel, *English Historians on the French Revolution* (Cambridge: At the University Press, 1968), pp. 127–47.

50. See p. 416 above.

CHAPTER TWENTY-SEVEN

1. TC to JWC, 30 June 1858 (NLS, 615.472).

2. TC to JWC, 11 July 1858 (NLS, 615.478).

3. TC to JWC, 20 July 1858 (NLS, 615.484). A. Carlyle: "No, you ass, it was Dr. C." This is correct.

4. TC to JWC, 12 July 1858 (NLS, 615.479). The "Headstone" is his mother's tomb.

5. TC to JWC, 19 July 1858 (NLS, 615.483); TC to JWC, 21 July 1858 (NLS, 615.485). A. Carlyle: "!!Idiot! It was a *Truss* for hernia or rupture."

6. TC to JWC, 23 July 1858 (NLS, 615.486).

7. See Bliss, *TC,* pp. 333–35.

8. TC to JWC, 21 August 1858 (NLS, 615.503).

9. Bliss, *TC,* pp. 336–37. TC to JWC, 24 August 1858.

10. Ibid., pp. 337–39. TC to JWC, 27 August 1858.

11. Ibid., pp. 340–41. TC to JWC, 5 September 1858.

12. Ibid., pp. 341–42. TC to JWC, 10 September 1858.

13. Ibid., pp. 342–43. TC to JWC, 11 September 1858.

14. Ibid., pp. 343–45. TC to JWC, 14 September 1858.

15. Ibid., p. 345. TC to JWC, 15 September 1858.

16. TC to JWC, 22 September 1858 (NLS, 1774.139).

17. R. A. E. Brooks, the editor of *Thomas Carlyle: Journal to Germany, Autumn 1858* (New Haven: Yale University Press, 1940), affirms that the *Journal* "completely disproves Froude's statement, which is a perfectly just inference from the letters Carlyle wrote to his wife on this trip . . . but it amply corroborates his next sentence" (pp. xx–xxi). It is unlikely that Froude saw Carlyle's journal of this trip.

18. Carlyle indeed made a few mistakes. See the one-volume abridgments of *Frederick* by A. M. D. Hughes (*Carlyle's Frederick the Great* [Oxford: Clarendon, 1916]) and John Clive (*History of Friedrich II of Prussia Called Frederick the Great,* Classic European Historians Series [Chicago and London: University of Chicago Press, 1969]). The introduction to the latter offers a cogent reassessment of *Frederick's* present value as history.

19. Journal, 28 December 1858.

20. A Carlyle: "*Bah!* This is arrant nonsense, put here by Froude to flatter the second Lady Ashburton." Froude's estimate is essentially correct.

21. See p. 369 above and Jeffrey to TC, 12 December 1837 (NLS, 1766.54).

22. Froude, *LMJWC,* 3:4. JWC to George Cooke, 9 September 1859. See also ibid., p. 140.

23. TC to JWC, 11 July 1858 (NLS, 615.478). See also Froude, *LMJWC,* 3:86.

24. TC to JAC, 21 June 1859 (NLS, 525.50).

25. TC to JAC, 27 June 1859 (NLS, 525.51). For "reck his own rede" in the next sentence, see *Hamlet* 1. 3. 51.

26. Froude, *LMJWC,* 3:1–3. JWC to Isabella Emily Barnes, 24 August 1859. The curious may read Jane Carlyle's narrative, "The Simple Story of My Own First-Love," in A. Carlyle, *NLMJWC,* 2:47–57.

27. TC to JWC, 27 April 1860 (NLS, 615.523).

28. See Froude, *LMJWC,* 3:47–52 (JWC to TC, 2 September 1860); and TC to JWC, 5 September 1860 (NLS, 615.534).

29. TC to JWC, 18 September 1860 (NLS, 615.540).

30. TC to JWC, 21 September 1860 (NLS, 615.543).

31. A. Carlyle: "What a fine perception is *yours,* coquin!"

32. TC to JAC, 16 January 1861 (NLS, 525.72).

33. Carlyle's letter to Froude has not been found, but Froude speaks of it in a letter to Mrs. Clough of 27 January 1862: "I enclose you a note which I had a few days ago from Carlyle. I saw him yesterday—and he speaks as if he had lost a dear son or brother.— He has felt so acutely about it, that I think he may bye & bye be disposed to write something—if he is not pressed now. The weight of his present work makes it seem an impossibility—but when the time comes for it to be done it may appear more possible[.] I wish you had heard what he said.— A H C. had been to him like a beautiful piece of music or a picture of Raphael[']s"

(MS: Bodleian Eng. lett. d. 178, fol. 28). Carlyle did not write on Clough. Elsewhere Froude wrote to Mrs. Clough: "Carlyle has many times told me he thought more highly of him than of any [other?—MS torn] one of our generation—and he will grieve for him as a father for his son" (undated, but late 1861 or early 1862. MS: Bodleian Eng. lett. d. 178, fol. 10).

34. W. M. Thackeray edited the *Cornhill* at this time; in 1862 Ruskin published the essays under the title of *Unto This Last*.

35. TC to John Ruskin, 9 March 1851, in W. G. Collingwood, *The Life and Work of John Ruskin*, 2 vols. (Boston and New York: Houghton Mifflin, 1898), 1:175. For *"Sermons* in Stones," see *As You Like It* 2. 1. 17.

36. *"Macmillan's Magazine*, August 1863.—Carlyle admitted to me after the war ended that perhaps he had not seen into the bottom of the matter" (Froude's note). Other contemporaries—Moncure D. Conway, for one—noted Carlyle's change of attitude. See his *Thomas Carlyle* (New York: Harper & Bros., 1881), pp. 93–100; and also Henry J. Nicoll, *Thomas Carlyle* (Edinburgh: Macniven & Wallace, 1881), pp. 198–99.

37. Froude clarified Carlyle's statement in a letter to Ruskin of about 1884: "When he said that Newman had not the intellect of a rabbit, he meant that no intellect was worth the name which could look for truth in these days on the road back to Popery" (Viljoen, p. 31).

38. TC to JWC, 29 January 1862 (NLS, 615.550). "The Bear" is Edward Ellice (1781–1863), Whig politician, a hospitable, disinterested, and esteemed figure, universally known by this nickname because of his connection with the Northwest fur trade (see *Reminiscences*, 1:206). "The Duke" is the Duke of Argyle. Samuel Wilberforce (1805–73), at that time in the thick of the controversy over *Essays and Reviews* (written by seven concerned Anglicans in 1860), was Bishop of Oxford. The author of the immensely popular *Christian Year* (1827) was John Keble (1792–1866), Anglican divine and initiator of the Oxford Movement. Froude wrote to Ruskin (in the letter cited in the previous note): "Those words about Newman—and 'some little ape called Keble' have given fearful offense" (Viljoen, p. 31).

39. Froude's slip is unintentional: he discusses in due course *Frederick's* sixth volume.

40. TC to Erskine, 4 August 1862. Froude's text.

CHAPTER TWENTY-EIGHT

1. A. Carlyle underlines this sentence and marks it in the margin.

2. See Matt. 6:28–29. I have left the quotation as Froude gives it.

3. Alexander von Humboldt (1769–1859) was a famous naturalist and explorer. Pierre Simon, Marquis de Laplace (1749–1827), was a French mathematician and astronomer and the author of *Mécanique céleste*, 5 vols. (1799–1825), mentioned by Carlyle in early letters and in *Sartor Resartus*. Robert Chambers published *Vestiges of the Natural History of Creation* anonymously in 1844. A controversial precursor of Darwin's

693

attempt to explain the evolution of man from simpler forms of life, the book caused a great outcry.

4. For a discussion of *Essays and Reviews* and the theological views of the "seven against Christ," see Basil Willey, *More Nineteenth Century Studies: A Group of Honest Doubters* (New York: Columbia University Press, 1956), chap. 4. Connop Thirlwall (1797–1875), Bishop of Saint David's, joined in censuring *Essays and Reviews*, but was one of the four bishops who refused to inhibit from preaching John William Colenso (1814–83), Bishop of Natal, whose book—mentioned in the next paragraph—was *The Pentateuch and the Book of Joshua Critically Examined*, 7 parts (1862–79). It brought down upon him an avalanche of criticism and was condemned in both Houses of Convocation. Froude praised Colenso's courageous behavior in Natal in *Two Lectures on South Africa* (1880; rpt. London: Longmans, Green, 1900), pp. 43–45. William Charles Macready (1793–1873) was a famous early Victorian tragic actor. Arthur Penrhyn Stanley (1815–1881) was dean of Westminster from 1863 to 1881.

5. See Froude, *LMJWC*, 3:256.

6. TC to JAC, 13 February 1863 (NLS, 526.3). Cf. Froude, *LMJWC*, 3:171–72.

7. TC to JAC, 29 April 1863 (NLS, 526.5).

8. A. Carlyle: "not so at all!" Opposite the next sentence he writes: "Clash [gossip]!"

9. Phrase based on TC to JWC, 18 July 1864 (NLS, 616.630).

10. David Masson provides an important corrective to Froude's narrative here:

> This story Mr. Froude received, he tells us, from Mrs. Carlyle herself; and there is no doubt as to its authenticity. What I am sure of is that Mr. Froude treats it too gravely, or might lead his readers to treat it too gravely, by missing that sense of the pure fun of the thing which was present in Mrs. Carlyle's mind when she remembered it afterwards, however provoking it may have been at the moment. She used to tell the story, I believe, to others, generally with the explanation that Carlyle had been reading Catlin's book on the North American Indians, and had been struck with Catlin's observation that the good health of the red men was owing in great measure to their rule of keeping their mouths always closely shut and breathing only through their nostrils. Indeed, it was one of Mrs. Carlyle's habits, just because of her boundless respect and affection for her husband, to play in imagination with his little eccentricities, and amuse her friends and bewilder his worshippers with satirical anecdotes at his expense. (*Carlyle Personally and in His Writings* [London: Macmillan, 1885], pp. 20–21).

See also Moncure D. Conway, *Autobiography*, 2 vols. (Boston and New York: Houghton, Mifflin & Co., 1904), 2:214–15.

11. TC to JAC, 13 November 1863 (NLS, 526.490).

12. Ibid.

13. Phrase based on TC to JAC, 28 December 1862 (NLS, 525.100).

14. Froude, *LMJWC*, 3:178. TC's note, JWC to Grace Welsh, 20 October 1863.

15. TC to JAC, 29 December 1863 (NLS, 526.13A).

16. A. Carlyle crosses out "friend" and writes opposite "servant." Mrs. Blakiston was the former Bessy Barnett and had indeed been Mrs. Carlyle's servant in 1834. Froude, in the third volume of *LMJWC*, regularly deletes Mrs. Blakiston's name (which he spells "Blakeston" in the biography). See *Reminiscences*, 2:145-47.

17. TC to JWC, 4 April 1864 (NLS, 616.595). The review, which appeared in *Saturday Review* 17 (2 April 1864): 414-15, discussed only vol. 4. Merle M. Bevington (in *The Saturday Review 1855-1868* [New York: Columbia University Press, 1941], p. 385) conjectures that "internal evidence suggests the hand of Fitzjames Stephen" as reviewer of vols. 5 and 6 the next year. Perhaps Stephen also reviewed the fourth volume, for it is unlikely that G. S. Venables, the reviewer of the first three and a friend of Carlyle, would have called forth Carlyle's "dirty puppy."

18. *Reminiscences*, 1:224-33.

19. Froude, *LMJWC*, 3:204-18. The Gill was the home of Carlyle's sister Mary.

20. Waldo H. Dunn, "Carlyle's Last Letters to Froude," *Twentieth Century* 159 (January 1956): 46. TC to Froude, 6 August 1864.

21. Froude, *LMJWC*, 3:215. TC's note, JWC to TC, 28 September 1864.

22. Journal, 1 October 1865.

23. *Frederick* appeared in German translation over the years 1858-69, not quite, as Froude claims and A. Carlyle corrects, "instantly."

24. See p. 558 above.

25. "Art and Criticism," in *Natural History of Intellect and Other Papers*, vol. 12 of *The Complete Works of Ralph Waldo Emerson*, ed. E. W. Emerson, 12 vols. (Boston and New York: Houghton Mifflin, 1904), p. 12. Emerson's comments, made in the spring of 1859, refer to the first two volumes of *Frederick*.

CHAPTER TWENTY-NINE

1. Froude, *LMJWC*, 3:243. TC's note, JWC to Mrs. Mary Carlyle Austin, February 1865. Froude's text.

2. In February 1821. See p. 120 above and *CL*, 1:324-30.

3. A. Carlyle: "Never 'usher,' " See p. 105 above.

4. TC to JWC, 23 July 1865 (NLS, 617.715).

5. Bliss, *TC*, p. 381. TC to JWC, 27 July 1865, Froude omitted "that Trollope," which follows "dirtyish little pug." The review (signed) appeared in the *Fortnightly Review* 1 (1865): 633-35; in it Trollope chided Ruskin for his "Carlylesque denunciations" on social issues and expressed hope that he would return to art criticism. Trollope died in 1882.

6. TC to JAC, 7 November 1865 (NLS, 526.33).

7. See p. 196 above. Froude exaggerates slightly, presumably for dramatic effect, the reaction to "the unheard of *mésalliance*." Yet both Carlyles believed theirs was a marriage between social unequals. See *CL*, 4:140–41, 143–44; and 7:289, where Carlyle writes: "From birth upwards she had lived in opulence; and now for my sake had become poor,—so nobly poor" (TC's note, JWC to MAC, [1 September 1834]).

8. *Reminiscences*, 1:245. See also Froude, *LMJWC*, 3:312.

9. Cf. Froude, *LMJWC*, 3:312–13.

10. *Reminiscences*, 1:246. John Tyndall (1820–93), professor of natural philosophy at the Royal Institution, recorded his impressions of his trip with Carlyle to Edinburgh in "Personal Recollections of Thomas Carlyle," *New Fragments*, pp. 357–64.

11. *Reminiscences*, 1:246.

12. Ibid.

13. TC to JWC, 30 March 1866 (NLS, 617.753).

14. *Reminiscences*, 1:247.

15. TC to JWC, 30 March 1866 (NLS, 617.753).

16. Ibid.

17. *Reminiscences*, 1:247.

18. Ibid., pp. 246–47.

19. Ibid., p. 247.

20. *Works*, 29:449. In these paragraphs Froude paraphrases Carlyle's "Inaugural Address," published in ibid., pp. 449–82.

21. Ibid., p. 470. I have restored several lines of Carlyle's address omitted by Froude.

22. Ibid., pp. 480–81.

23. Ibid., p. 482. See also pp. 352–53 above and the accompanying notes. For a somewhat more cheerful account of the days in Edinburgh and the address, see David Masson, *Carlyle Personally and in His Writings*, pp. 25–30.

24. Froude, *LMJWC*, 3:318. JWC to TC, dated "Tuesday" (4 April) but postmarked 3 April 1866.

25. Ibid., p. 320. JWC to TC, dated "Wednesday" (5 April) but postmarked 4 April 1866. "A good joy" is coterie speech deriving from "one of Leigh Hunt's children, on the sight of flowers" (ibid., 1:104).

26. *Reminiscences*, 1:248.

27. Froude, *LMJWC*, 3:327. JWC to Susan Hunter Stirling, 11 April 1866.

28. The news of the Jamaica disturbances reached England in November 1865. See p. 601 below.

29. A. Carlyle: "and more!" Geraldine Jewsbury burned the letters Mrs. Carlyle addressed to her, but many of hers to Mrs. Carlyle were published in *Selections from the Letters of Geraldine Endsor Jewsbury to Jane Welsh Carlyle*, ed. Mrs. Alexander Ireland (1892).

30. Consuelo is the heroine of a novel by George Sand, a novelist admired by both Miss Jewsbury and Mrs. Carlyle, though not (as we have seen) by Carlyle.

31. *Reminiscences*, 1:252-54.

32. Journal, 15 May 1866. John Welsh's inscription reads "Sacred to the Memory of John Welsh of Craigenputtoch Surgeon in Haddington who Died the 19th of September 1819. Aged Forty-four years." Underneath Thomas Carlyle wrote the epitaph for his wife: "Here likewise now rests JANE WELSH CARLYLE, Spouse of Thomas Carlyle, Chelsea, London. She was born at Haddington, 14th July 1801; only child of the above John Welsh, and of Grace Welsh, Caplegill, Dumfriesshire, his wife. In her bright existence she had more sorrows than are common; but also a soft invincibility, a clearness of discernment, and a noble loyalty of heart, which are rare. For forty years she was the true and everloving helpmate of her husband; and, by act and word, unweariedly forwarded him, as none else could, in all of worthy that he did or attempted. She died at London, 21st April, 1866; suddenly snatched away from him, and the light of his life as if gone out."

CHAPTER THIRTY

1. Victoria had lost Albert in 1861.

2. Boswell, *Life of Johnson*, p. 1357. See Carlyle's discussion of the passage in *Works*, 28:129; and also Froude, *LMJWC*, 3:243.

3. See Froude, *LMJWC*, 3:257; and also *Reminiscences*, 1:236, 2:168-69. Part of this paragraph is based on Carlyle's Journal, 11 May 1866. See also A. Carlyle, *NLMJWC*, 1:xxxi-xxxii.

4. John 14:2.

5. TC to JAC, 22 August 1866 (NLS, 526.44).

6. Carlyle's expression in TC to JAC, 5 July 1867 (NLS, 526.63).

7. TC to Miss Davenport Bromley, 30 August 1866. Froude's text. The Eyre Defence Committee was formed in August 1866 in response to the Jamaica Committee, organized in July with Mill as chairman. It provided funds for the defence of Edward John Eyre, Governor of Jamaica. Carlyle attended the first meeting of the committee on 29 August and several subsequent meetings. Throughout he gave strong support to Eyre, who was eventually acquitted and pensioned. Geoffrey Dutton, *The Hero as Murderer: The Life of Edward John Eyre, Australian Explorer and Governor of Jamaica, 1815-1901* (London: Collins, 1967) examines the evidence thoroughly and comes up with a verdict on the whole favorable to Eyre. He discusses Carlyle's involvement in chaps. 19 and 20. See also Gillian Workman, "Thomas Carlyle and the Governor Eyre Controversy: An Account with Some New Material," *Victorian Studies* 18 (September 1974): 77-102, which corrects Froude in a few details. The Eyre case was a Victorian *cause célèbre*.

8. TC to Miss Davenport Bromley, 15 September 1866. Froude's text.

9. *Hamlet* 1. 1. 145.

10. Journal, 26 September 1866.

11. See Tyndall's account in *New Fragments*, pp. 371-76.

12. Journal, 20 January 1867.

13. Ibid., 23 January 1867.

14. See *Reminiscences*, 1:261-77, for the text of Carlyle's bequest. Craigenputtoch, later sold by the University, is again in private hands.

15. I.e., in Ireland. The Reform Bill of 1884, passed in the time of a Gladstone ministry, added about two million electors; a redistribution act of 1885 made representation nearly proportional to population.

16. *Works*, 30:1-48. Froude forgets that Carlyle's letters of 1870 and 1877 to the *Times* were also "public utterances."

17. The "Library Edition," 30 vols., 1869-71.

18. Gillian Workman argues that the petition was used ("Thomas Carlyle and the Governor Eyre Controversy," pp. 98, 102).

19. Journal, 27 April 1868. Froude states in a footnote: "In his will of 1873 Carlyle says ten or seven years, and finally leaves the time of publication to me." See pp. 618-19 below.

20. Journal, 4 March 1869.

21. Waldo H. Dunn, "Carlyle's Last Letters to Froude," p. 51. TC to Froude, 14 September 1869. *The Queen of the Air* (1869), ostensibly about the Greek myths, revealed much about Ruskin himself.

22. Journal, 10 September 1870 (and elsewhere).

23. *Works*, 20:81, 80. See also pp. 396-97 above.

24. See p. 525 above and the accompanying note.

25. Froude wrote (in a passage that I have omitted): "It will be remembered that Russia took advantage of the state of Europe and tore the article in the Treaty of Paris [1856] which limited her Black Sea fleet. When the article was drawn, the essentially temporary character of it was well understood; but England bristled up when the trophies of her Crimean glories were shattered and flung in her face so cavalierly; for a week or two there was talk of war again between us and Russia" (4:401-2).

26. *Times*, 18 November 1870 (letter dated 11 November). The niece was Mary Carlyle Aitken (ca. 1848-95), who married Alexander Carlyle (1843-1931) a few years later.

27. Journal, 3 June 1871.

28. A. Carlyle: "No. After his own departure."

29. A. Carlyle: "O! what a fib!"

CHAPTER THIRTY-ONE

1. *Works*, 30:247.

2. Carlyle's "The Portraits of John Knox" is in *Works*, 30:313-67; opposite p. 313 is a reproduction of the Somerville portrait, for whose authenticity Carlyle argues. *"Aut Knox aut Diabolus"* plays on *"Aut Caesar, aut nihil,"* the motto of Cesare Borgia (1476-1507).

698

3. TC to JAC, 10 May 1873 (NLS, 527.94).

4. TC to JAC, 5 November 1873 (NLS, 527.99). Mill's *Autobiography* was first published in 1873 and first edited "without alterations or omissions from the original manuscript" by John Jacob Coss in 1924.

5. Carlyle clarifies this point in Clubbe, *Two Reminiscences,* pp. 98–99.

6. A. Carlyle: "to you! No!" Froude's statement is true.

7. A. Carlyle: "A good many of the entries in the Journal were dictated & stand in his Niece's hand!"

8. TC to JAC, 2 January 1874 (NLS, 528.2).

9. Disraeli to TC, 27 December 1874. MS: Carlyle House, Chelsea.

10. TC to Disraeli, 29 December 1874. MS: Carlyle House, Chelsea.

11. TC to JAC, 15 December 1875 (NLS, 528.46).

12. TC to JAC, 5 May 1877 (NLS, 528.67).

13. *Times,* 5 May 1877 (letter dated 4 May). Carlyle's letter is in three paragraphs.

14. For Dr. Gully, see p. 506 above and the accompanying note.

15. See p. 409 above.

16. *Hamlet* 2. 2. 314.

17. *Macbeth* 5. 5. 19–28.

18. Luke 24:32.

19. *Faust* 2. 4619–20. The "man of ill-fortune" is Faust, who under the ministrations of the elves begins to recover from his collapse after Gretchen's death.

20. Robert Burns, "Ae Fond Kiss," stanza 2.

21. *Cymbeline,* 4. 2. 258–63. Froude's text has "lasses" for "girls."

22. TC to JAC, 16 June 1877 (NLS, 528.72). For "Mary" Froude has "many."

23. TC to JAC, 2 July 1877 (NLS, 528.75).

24. TC to JAC, 2 November 1878 (NLS, 528.91). In this letter Carlyle writes, not that he is reading the Bible (as Froude states), but that he is thinking of "going into" it again.

25. John Carlyle died 15 September 1879.

26. A. Carlyle: "that's not true."

27. Opposite the last sentences of this paragraph A. Carlyle wrote: "These are all afterthoughts of Froude's invention—not a word of truth in them." I have found no reason to question Froude's account.

28. From the Funeral Oration given by Pericles, in Thucydides *History of the Peloponnesian War* 2. 43. Froude's translation.

Index

Abbeville, 160

Aberdeenshire Gordons, 114

Aberdour, 554

Achilles, 369

Acta Sanctorum, 475

Addiscombe Farm (Ashburton residence), 446, 447, 457, 458, 461, 521, 532

Aeschylus, 119, 354, 370

Africa, 390, 442. *See also* South Africa

Agamemnon, 17, 19, 54

Agnosticism, 268

Airy, Sir George Biddell, 296, 299

Aitken, James (husband of TC's sister Jean), 292, 595

Aitken, Jean (Jane) (Carlyle) (1810–88, TC's sister), 3, 51, 144–45, 174, 175, 206, 217, 279, 292–93, 442, 543, 544, 555, 595, 611, 642, 647, 656, 669, 680, 681

Alaric, 255

Albert (prince consort), 506, 697

Alcott, Bronson, 682

Allen, Matthew, 654

Allingham, William, 649, 689

Alsace, 613

Althaus, Friedrich, 649

America, 254–55, 285, 288, 295, 302, 319, 340–42, 345, 359, 363, 371, 372–73, 375, 382, 390, 393, 402, 435, 444, 455, 462, 471, 483, 485, 522, 580, 584, 648, 664. *See also* Boston

American Civil War. *See* Civil War (American)

Anglican Church. *See* Church of England

Animal imagery, TC's use of, 60

Annan (river), 85

Annan (town), 85, 86, 95–100, 105, 106, 108, 109, 274, 285, 308, 317, 350, 364, 399, 400, 405, 427, 442, 496, 497, 535

Annan Academy, 95–100, 105, 109, 110, 521, 582, 679, 695

Annandale, 85, 86, 90, 103, 106, 109, 110, 111, 145, 216, 244, 270, 279, 283, 331, 339, 343, 344, 362, 363, 389, 443, 459, 462, 498, 555, 581, 589, 641, 642

Annan woods, Mount, 122

Annual Register, 501

Anson, George: *Voyages*, 89, 93

Anstey, Thomas Chisholm, 676

Anthony, Saint, 11

Apostles of freedom. *See Freiheits Apostel*

Arabian Nights, 89, 93, 232, 506, 665

Arched House, Ecclefechan (TC's birthplace), 86, 87, 91

Archibald, R. C., 653

Argyle, Duke and Duchess of, 560, 693

Aristophanes, 511, 638

Aristotle, 297; *Poetics*, 5, 16, 53; *Politics*, 488–89, 685

Arithmetic: JWC's interest in, 129; TC's interest in, 93, 95, 98, 113. *See also* Mathematics; Geometry, TC's interest in

Armytage, J. C., 373

701

Galloway, 108, 126, 654

Galt, John, 273

Galway, 480

Gambardella, Spiridione, 529

Garnett, Richard, 3

Gellert, Christian Fürchtegott, 360

Geography, 98

Geometry, TC's interest in, 98, 103, 113, 303, 415

German language, literature, and civilization, 21–22, 30, 54, 106, 122, 134–36, 148, 153, 158, 166, 173, 174, 230, 231–32, 242–43, 257, 275, 287, 337, 340, 353, 356, 359–63, 368, 369, 370, 513, 539, 564, 579, 584, 591, 653, 668, 673. *See also* individual authors

"German Literature." *See* "History of German Literature"

German literature: TC's lectures on, 359–63, 368, 369, 674

German Romance, 174, 177, 185, 186, 188, 198, 207, 211, 243

Germany, 35, 134, 190, 214, 242, 390, 508, 509–16, 530, 543, 545–50, 551, 553, 579–80, 613, 623–24, 625, 673

Gessner, Salomon, 360

"Gey ill to deal wi' " (coterie speech), 72, 120, 194, 195, 202, 236, 653

Geyl, Pieter, 691

Ghent, 409, 679

Gibbon, Edward, 32, 265, 287, 641; *Decline and Fall of the Roman Empire*, 115, 265, 641

Gigmanity, 259

Gill, the, 695

Gladstone, William Ewart, 35, 390, 583, 589, 602, 603–4, 629, 632–33, 644, 684, 698

Glasgow, 98, 100, 120, 121–22, 123, 133, 138, 153, 165, 282, 287, 312, 313, 380, 515, 534, 668

Gleim, J. W. L., 360

Glen, William, 303, 669

Glendower, Owen, 11–12, 47, 671

"Gloriana." *See* Ashburton, Harriet, 1st Lady

Gloucester, 425, 426

Godwin, William, 263

"Goethe," 217, 232

Goethe, Johann Wolfgang von, 12, 21, 29, 30, 78, 119, 134, 135–36, 144, 148, 151, 154, 163–64, 165–67, 174, 211, 213, 214–15, 217, 218, 219, 230, 231, 232, 242, 243, 244, 254, 263, 269, 275, 276, 278, 285, 301, 318, 320, 325, 331, 360, 365, 369, 370, 507, 513, 514, 532, 560, 570, 591, 638, 641, 655, 658, 662, 673, 678; *Dichtung und Wahrheit*, 154; *Elective Affinities*, 21, 54; *Faust*, 11, 32, 106, 124, 125, 136, 217, 360, 384, 633, 638, 662, 677, 699; *Götz von Berlichingen*, 360; *Iphigenie auf Tauris*, 21–22, 54; *Das Mährchen*, 275; "Mason-Lodge," 352–53, 591, 673; "Prometheus," 136; *Sorrows of Young Werther*, 136, 293, 348, 360, 370; "Sprichwörtlich," 29, 56–57, 532, 639, 690; "Symbolum" ("Des Maurers Wandeln") (*see* Goethe, Johann Wolfgang von, "Mason-Lodge"); *Venezianische Epigramme*, 655; *Wilhelm Meister*, 136, 151, 166, 174, 368, 502, 591, 654 (*see also Wilhelm Meister*, TC's translation of)

"Goethe's *Helena*," 217

"Goethe's Works," 275, 278, 291, 655

Goldberg, Michael, 677

Goldsmith, Oliver: *Vicar of Wakefield*, 372, 676

Gooch, G. P., 691

Gordon (aunt of Margaret Gordon). *See* Usher, Elizabeth (Gordon)

Gordon, John, 528

Gordon, Margaret, 114, 119, 372, 653

Gotha, 514

Grace (servant), 236

Graff, Anton, 549

Grand Cross of the Bath (TC refuses), 625–26

Grange, the (Ashburton home in Hampshire), 435, 436, 457, 472, 499, 502, 517, 518, 522, 533, 537, 554, 556, 560, 574, 686

Grattan, Henry, 481

Graves, Charles, 53

Great Exhibition of 1851, 506

Greek chorus, Froude's use of, 9–11, 24, 47, 52, 170, 195

Greek language, literature, and civilization, 15, 31, 98, 134, 222, 303, 369–70,

Ostend, 408, 509, 515, 679

Ouvry, Frederic, 51

Oxford, 367, 493, 563–64, 693

Oxford movement, 338, 393, 417–18, 421, 693

Oxford University, 28, 33, 36, 38, 41–42, 338, 374–75, 417, 423, 462, 473, 475; All Souls' College, 374–75; Exeter College, 678; Oriel College, 41; Pembroke College, 241

Page, Mrs., 156

Paisley, 388

Panizzi, Antonio, 502, 686–87

Paoli, General Pasquale de, 29, 30

Pardubitz, 548

Paris, 32, 159, 160–62, 343, 467, 468, 470, 507, 509, 574, 603–4, 614, 623, 658

Parliament: TC asked to stand for, 408, 485, 497; Houses of, 312, 407–8, 417, 438, 439, 440, 446, 469, 472, 479, 488–89, 491, 494, 495, 610, 629, 632 (*see also* Commons, House of)

Parliamentary Radicalism. *See* Philosophic Radicals

Parsons, C. O., 676

Past and Present, 411, 414–17, 423, 431, 446, 492, 542, 673, 679, 680

Paston, George, 53

Patrick, Saint, 475

Patrick, John (of Kirkcaldy), 87–88, 96, 107, 175, 178, 187, 228, 250, 289

Pattison, Mark, 36

Paul, Saint, 11, 60, 170, 244, 295, 486, 571, 637

Paul, Herbert, 41, 67

Paulet, Mr., 426–27, 434, 442, 447

Paulet, Elizabeth, 426–27, 434, 442, 447, 681

Peebles, 90

Peel, Sir Robert, 446, 468–69, 472, 493, 494–95, 633, 684

Peloponnesian War, 20

Penfillan, 127

Pentonville (London), 154, 157

Pericles, 699

Petrie, George, 479

Philanthropists (Philanthropic Liberalism), 484, 485, 487, 564

Philistines, 317, 356

Philosophic Radicals, 268, 310, 311, 326, 358, 381–82, 401. *See also* Radicals and Radicalism

Phocion, 591

Pickford's (moving company), 308

Pindar, 83, 650

Pisa, 165

Plato, 29, 56, 287, 532, 672; *Republic*, 685; *Symposium*, 687

Plutarch, 32, 57, 556, 651; *Moralia*, 651

Plymouth, 479

Poet, TC as, 163, 244, 284, 292, 318, 356

"Polar Bear," 47–48, 347

Political Economy, 380, 381, 401, 413, 415, 421, 489–90, 556, 561, 566

Poor Law Bill, 312

Pope, Alexander, 78, 357, 331; *Essay on Man*, 357, 674

Pope-Hennessy, James, 58

"Portraits of John Knox, The," 620–21, 698

Portsmouth, 463

Positivism, 421

Post-Waterloo depression in Britain, 108, 117–18, 330–31, 380

Potsdam, 508

Powles, Cowley, 51

Prague, 547, 548, 549

Pre-Raphaelite movement, 476

Preston, 384, 444

Preuss, Johann David Erdmann, 444

Procter, Anne (Skepper), 527

Procter, B. W. ("Barry Cornwall"), 155, 165, 273, 527, 667

Progress, Gospel of, 329, 380, 456, 466, 484, 491, 506, 609, 633, 636, 677

Prometheus, 11, 355, 561

Prophet, TC as, 82, 318, 418–19, 561, 584, 629. *See also* individual prophets

Prussia, 347, 508, 547, 579–80, 613, 623

Ptolemaic universe, 225

Punch, 490, 685–86

Puritans and Puritanism, 210, 329, 412, 426, 634